W9-CJX-301

05/24
STAND PRICE
$ 5.00

THE MODERN ENCYCLOPEDIA OF BASKETBALL

THE MODERN ENCYCLOPEDIA OF BASKETBALL

Edited by Zander Hollander

An Associated Features Book

FOUR WINDS PRESS • NEW YORK

Published by Four Winds Press
A Division of Scholastic Magazines, Inc., New York, N. Y.
By arrangement with Associated Features, Inc.

Printed in the United States of America.

Library of Congress Catalogue Card Number: 70-81705

To those for whom basketball has meant a way out

FOREWORD

At last basketball has a definitive work covering the broad spectrum of one of the world's most popular sports. THE MODERN ENCYCLOPEDIA OF BASKETBALL is exactly what it says it is. Although concentrating on the modern era which began in the mid-1930s with the game's expansion on every level—from college and professional to scholastic and playground—the encyclopedia extends back to the time of Dr. James A. Naismith, founding father of the sport in 1891.

The editor, Zander Hollander, has combined the human story of the game—its players, its teams, its coaches—with an awesome array of vital statistics and dramatic, historic photographs.

Mr. Hollander and his able corps of contributors have produced a unique book that is invaluable to fans and scholars alike. It fills a void that we have long been conscious of in basketball.

Walter Kennedy
Commissioner
National Basketball Association

CONTENTS

INTRODUCTION xvii

THE EARLY YEARS

1. THE INVENTION 3
Dr. James Naismith • Original 13 Rules

2. THE ROAD TO POINT-A-MINUTE 6
Naming the Game • The First Team • YMCA • The Colleges Begin • The Wonder Five • Racehorse Basketball

THE COLLEGES

3. THE MODERNS 13
Ned Irish and Intersectional Play • Yearly Roundups with AP and UPI Top Ten Teams, Conference Champions, Leading Scorers, All-Americans, National Invitation Tournament and NCAA Tournament Results and Box Scores • All-Time Records • The Scandals

4. THE GREATEST COLLEGIANS 102
Lew Alcindor • Vince Boryla • Harry Boykoff • Bill Bradley • Bob Davies • Tom Gola • Dick Groat • K.C. Jones • Wallace "Wah Wah" Jones • Bob Kurland • Clyde Lovellette • Jerry Lucas • Hank Luisetti • Andy Phillip • Oscar Robertson • Guy Rodgers • Cazzie Russell • Maurice Stokes • Ernie Vandeweghe • Jimmy Walker

5. THE COACHES 137
Phog Allen • Clair Bee • John Bunn • Doc Carlson • Ed Diddle • Tony Hinkle • Nat Holman • Hank Iba • George Keogan • Piggy Lambert • Joe Lapchick • Branch McCracken • John McLendon • Adolph Rupp • John Wooden • Phil Woolpert

6. THE MAJOR COLLEGES 146
Season Records and Coaches

7. THE SMALL COLLEGES 201
NCAA College Division Champions and All-Time Records • NAIA Champions and All-Time Records

THE PROFESSIONALS

8. THE PIVOTAL ERA 211
First Pro Game • Early Leagues • Original Celtics • American Basketball League • Renaissance Big Five • National Basketball League

9. BIG LEAGUE 220
Birth of the Basketball Association of America • War Between Leagues • Creation of the National Basketball Association • Yearly Roundups, with Standings, Playoff Results, Individual Leaders • All-Time Records • All-NBA Teams • Most Valuable Players • Rookies of the Year

10. THE GREATEST PROS 283
Paul Arizin • Rick Barry • Elgin Baylor • Carl Braun • Wilt Chamberlain • Bob Cousy • Joe Fulks • Neil Johnston • Ed Macauley • George Mikan • Vern Mikkelsen • Bob Pettit • Jim Pollard • Frank Ramsey • Oscar Robertson • Bill Russell • Dolph Schayes • Bill Sharman • Jack Twyman • Jerry West

11. THE TEAMS 315
Yearly Directory of NBA Teams • Coaches' Records • All-Rookie Teams

12. ALL-TIME NBA REGISTER 320
Season and Career Records of Every Player in NBA History

13. THE OTHER PROS 377
American Basketball Association • American Basketball League • Eastern League • The Writers

14. THE GLOBETROTTERS 381
Basketball's Funniest Show • Abe Saperstein • Goose Tatum • Marques Haynes • Meadowlark Lemon

15. THE HIGH SCHOOLS 385
National Federation of State High School Athletic Associations • State High School Champions • Scholastic Coach All-Americans

16. THE AMATEURS 407
Olympics • AAU Men's and Women's Champions • Biddy Basketball

17. THE OFFICIALS 416
Making the Grade • Differences in Interpretation • International Association of Approved Basketball Officials • George Hepbron • Pat Kennedy • Chuck Solodare • John Nucatola • Mendy Rudolph • Sid Borgia

18. THE HALL OF FAME 421
History • Elections • Members and their Achievements

APPENDICES

APPENDIX A THE RULES 435
Complete National Basketball Committee Rules

APPENDIX B FURTHER READING 449
Books on Basketball Currently in Print

INDEX 453

THE
MODERN ENCYCLOPEDIA
OF BASKETBALL

INTRODUCTION

Landmarks in basketball, as in anything, often depend on one's point of view. When a New York sports writer, Ned Irish, ripped his pants climbing through the window of a crowded college gym in the early 1930s, it meant more than just another mending job for Ned's tailor. Irish figured if basketball was so popular that even a working reporter had to worm his way into a game, it deserved a bigger, more glamorous setting. The torn trousers led to Irish's hiring of a hall, Madison Square Garden, and thus inspired the modern era of college basketball.

When World War II ended in 1945, many basketball players—their best years behind them—embarked on new careers. The younger stars were more fortunate. Opportunity beckoned in the form of what was to become the major league in professional basketball—the National Basketball Association.

When City College of New York achieved an unprecedented grand slam of the National Invitation Tournament and the National Collegiate championship in 1950, this was a basketball landmark, indeed. But when players from CCNY's Cinderella team and a number of other colleges were found guilty of "shaving points," the resulting scandal established another type of landmark: the end of the age of innocence.

The modern era of basketball has witnessed such milestones as the signing of the first Negro head coach in any major league, Boston's Bill Russell in the NBA; a 100-point game by Wilt Chamberlain, and an estimated $1.4 million contract for Lew Alcindor, the UCLA star who signed to play professionally with the Milwaukee Bucks.

Call them landmarks, milestones, turning points or simply evolution. They constitute an integral part of the history that Dr. James A. Naismith began with a peach basket and a soccer ball in 1891.

The early years of the game have been covered in an assortment of books. But it has been in the last 35 years—starting with the introduction of intersectional collegiate play at New York's Madison Square Garden and on into the television age—that basketball has experienced its greatest growth.

Fans, players, sports writers and coaches have expressed the need for a single book that would accent the moderns, yet tell it all from the beginning: A book that would not depend alone on statistics. A book that would have feature stories on the stars, the teams, the coaches, the scandal, the referees. A book that would carry year-by-year roundups of the major colleges and the pros, and all-time records. A book that would also cover the high schools, the Olympics, the AAU, and Biddy Basketball.

A book that would contain a unique section—an all-time NBA Register, comprising the season and career records of every player (more than 900) in NBA history.

To attain these objectives, I enlisted the aid of a number of sports writers as contributors, and the research took me to such diverse settings as the Basketball Hall of Fame in Springfield, Mass.; the Yonkers, N. Y., attic of Original Celtic and Hall of Fame member Joe Lapchick, and to Trenton, N. J., where a police magistrate testified that his uncle played in the first professional game.

More than any other figure in the sport, Joe Lapchick provided me with the opinion and guidance that can only come from one who has devoted more than a half-century to basketball as player and coach.

My own personal landmarks in basketball are not likely to be found anywhere but here. As a boy in the early 1930s in Edgemere, N. Y., I used to set local backyard records for consecutive layups on a shaky home-made basket. I earned my high school letter as the center (6-1) at Far Rockaway High and a varsity "Q" at Queens College in Flushing, New York. As a sports writer for the late *New York World-Telegram*, I broke in by covering high school quintuple-headers at the 50th St. Madison Square Garden. I was there on assignment during basketball's blackest days in the early '50s. The sport came back. I never left it.

As it happened, this was all part of my preparation for THE MODERN ENCYCLOPEDIA OF BASKETBALL.

Zander Hollander
Baldwin, New York

ACKNOWLEDGMENTS

Doc Naismith first envisioned basketball as a game in which any number could play. The editor of THE MODERN ENCYCLOPEDIA OF BASKETBALL proceeded along the same lines, although all was not play; many would participate in the challenging task of researching, assembling, writing, rewriting and copyreading the various sections of the manuscript.

The editor wishes to thank sports columnist Sandy Padwe of the *Philadelphia Inquirer* for starting the ball rolling. He suggested the encyclopedia in the first place.

Also a salute of the highest order to the three young men—knowledgeable about basketball far beyond their years—who were indispensable to the project: Bruce Weber of Scholastic Magazines, David Rosen of the Columbia *Daily Spectator* and Associated Features, and Dave Schulz, Editor of *The Villager.*

Also to Original Celtics Joe Lapchick and Dutch Dehnert, and Mrs. Everett B. Morris, widow of the *New York Herald Tribune* basketball and yachting expert, for making available their scrapbooks and libraries.

Also to contributing writers Sandy Padwe (The Greatest Pros); Steve Jacobson of Long Island's *Newsday* (The Scandal); Ira Berkow of Newspaper Enterprise Association (The Officials); Phil Pepe of the New York *Daily News* (The Coaches), and Maury Allen of the *New York Post.*

An encyclopedia must depend in part on what has been written before—in newspapers, magazines, books. Among the helpful books were The Cavalcade of Basketball by Alexander M. Weyand, the Converse Basketball Yearbooks, the NCAA's Official Basketball Guides, the official NBA Guides and Ronald's Encyclopedia of Basketball by William G. Mokray.

For their cooperation, the editor also thanks Walter Kennedy, the commissioner of the National Basketball Association, Lee Williams of the Basketball Hall of Fame, Larry Klein and Jack Waters of National Collegiate Sports Services, Mike Kleinman of the National Association of Intercollegiate Athletics, Cliff Fagan and Richard Schafer of the National Federation of State High School Athletic Associations, Gus Steiger of the Amateur Athletic Union, Bob Paul of the United States Olympic Committee, Ed Snyder of Chicago's *American* and the U. S. Basketball Writers Association, George Durham of Phillips Petroleum Co., Wallace Lord of the Converse Rubber Co., Eddie Gottlieb, Philadelphia's basketball pioneer, Jay Archer of Biddy Basketball, and Haskell Cohen, former NBA publicist.

Also Joe Val of the Madison Square Garden Hall of Fame, John Nucatola of the Eastern Collegiate Athletic Conference, Stuart Paxton of the International Association of Approved Basketball Officials, Herman L. Masin of *Scholastic Coach,* Leonard Koppett of *The New York Times*, Bus Saidt of the *Trenton Times*, Ray Saul of the *Hazelton Standard-Speaker*, Harry Rudolph of the Eastern League, Frank Blauschild and Jim Wergeles of Madison Square Garden, Bill Esposito of St. John's University, Jay Simon of the University of Kansas and all of the other college sports information directors who supplied and confirmed so much of the material in the encyclopedia.

It is impossible to credit everyone who contributed a fact or a suggestion, but three others who cannot be anonymous are Connie Maroselli of the NBA, for help in the bureau of missing persons and missing statistics; Annette Katz Weber, for peerless and tireless typing, and Phyllis Hollander of Associated Features, for faith and all-around performance.

PHOTO CREDITS

Hall of Fame	2, 7, 8, 210, 219, 422
Barton Silverman	273
UPI	8, 9, 12, 16, 17, 19, 20, 24, 28, 29, 30, 32, 33, 34, 35, 37, 38, 39, 41, 43, 44, 46, 48, 49, 54, 56, 59, 62, 64, 67, 69, 72, 77, 82, 100, 105, 113, 117, 120, 123, 125, 128, 134, 137, 140, 221, 222, 224, 225, 227, 229, 230, 232, 234, 236, 238, 240, 242, 245, 247, 249, 252, 257, 269, 284, 291, 292, 293, 295, 297, 298, 300, 303, 304, 309, 376, 380, 383, 408, 419
George Kalinsky	270, 307
Madison Square Garden Hall of Fame	14–15, 18
National Basketball Association	261
From Joe Lapchick	212, 214, 215, 215, 216
From Dutch Dehnert	214, 218
From Allie Schuckman	10
UCLA	22, 87
Ohio U.	25
From Stan Stutz	27
Holy Cross	40
West Virginia	74
Cincinnati	75, 127
St. John's	107
Princeton	89
Seton Hall	111
Malcolm W. Emmons	80, 84, 92, 93, 95, 98, 103, 109, 122, 130, 135, 143, 144, 254, 256, 262, 266, 267, 271, 274, 275, 285, 287, 289, 301, 305
Duke	114
San Francisco	116, 144
Oklahoma A&M	119, 140
St. Francis	132
Kansas	138
LIU	138
Colorado State College	139
Pittsburgh	139
Western Kentucky	139
Butler	140
Notre Dame	141
Purdue	141
Indiana	142
Kentucky State	143
New York Knickerbockers	142, 203, 276, 288, 312
Atlanta Hawks	203
Philadelphia 76ers	203, 261
Rio Grande	204
From Eddie Gottlieb	243
Cincinnati Royals	251
Los Angeles Lakers	259, 314
Detroit Pistons	264
Boston Celtics	311
Power Memorial H.S.	384
Griggs	411
From Jay Archer	415

THE MODERN ENCYCLOPEDIA OF BASKETBALL

THE EARLY YEARS

The inventor, Dr. James Naismith, in the early 1890s.

1: THE INVENTION

The origins of most sports are lost in time. Either they evolved from some everyday activity like running or jumping and needed only to have the rules formalized, or they traced their beginnings to some earlier, less organized game. But not basketball. The birth of this game can be pinpointed with total accuracy.

The time was autumn, 1891, the place was Springfield, Massachusetts, and the inventor was Dr. James Naismith. At the time he was 30 years old. He had been born in Almonte, Ontario, and had attended McGill University in Canada and then spent three years studying for the ministry before deciding that his real interests were in physical education.

He enrolled in the International Young Men's Christian Association Training School (today Springfield College) in Springfield. The school trained general secretaries and physical education instructors for YMCAs throughout the country. Naismith soon joined the faculty as a physical education instructor.

Springfield's physical education program included an hour of daily activity. In the fall the students played football outdoors. And in the spring they went outdoors again to play baseball. But for their exercise between seasons they had to move indoors.

The indoor program for the potential YMCA general secretaries included marching and calisthenics, and the students could see no particular value in those exercises. They protested and were assigned a new instructor, who substituted apparatus work for the calisthenics and marching. But the class grew even more hostile toward physical activity, and this instructor gave up too.

Finally Dr. Luther S. Gulick, the head of the physical education department, assigned Naismith the job of doing something about the incorrigible class.

His first move was to abandon all the exercises and calisthenics and to concentrate on games. But both he and the class found all the popular indoor games both boring and tiring. So Naismith set out to develop some new indoor game. He first thought of adapting one of the popular outdoor games to indoor play.

He tried rugby, but the rough tackling made the game impractical on a hard gym floor. Then he tried soccer, but in the confined area available, many players were bruised and many windows broken by hard shots. Lacrosse also failed as the players frequently beat each other with their sticks.

Naismith soon realized that no existing game was suitable for his purposes and that he would have to invent some sort of new game.

He decided to employ a ball, and settled on a large ball because no intermediate equipment like a bat, stick or racket was necessary to manipulate it. He realized that if the players couldn't run with the ball, there would be no need for rough tackling.

He concluded that by using an elevated goal, he would force the players to shoot on an arc, making accuracy more important than brute strength and eliminating many of the bruises resulting from hard shots.

Then he sat down and wrote out the first set of rules for the new game. He had his secretary type the "Thirteen Rules" and posted them on the bulletin board in the gymnasium.

Because the janitor in the gym did not have the boxes that Naismith envisioned as goals, he was forced to substitute a pair of peach baskets. The height of ten feet for the baskets was established because that was the height of a balcony at each end of the gym to which the baskets were attached.

Naismith announced to the class that if this game was a failure, he was finished with his experiments. But from its first moments of existence, basketball was a success.

Naismith envisioned the new sport as a mass game, in which any number of players could participate. The class had eighteen members, so the first game, played in mid-December, 1891, had nine men on a side. They used an "Association football" (soccer ball).

Over the Christmas vacation of that year, several members of the class introduced the game in their home towns. But none of them had copies of the rules and each played the game as he rather imperfectly remembered it. Not until January, 1892, when the students returned from their vacations, did the school paper publish the rules of the new game.

These were Naismith's original 13 rules:

1. The ball may be thrown in any direction with one or both hands.

2. The ball may be batted in any direction with one or both hands (never with the fist).

3. A player cannot run with the ball. The player must throw it from the spot on which he catches it; allowance to be made for a man who catches the ball when running at a good speed.

4. The ball must be held in or between the hands; the arms or body must not be used for holding it.

5. No shouldering, holding, pushing, tripping or striking, in any way the person of an opponent shall be allowed; the first infringement of this rule by any person shall count as a foul, the second shall disqualify him until the next goal is made; or, if there was evident intent to injure the person for the whole of the game, no substitute shall be allowed.

6. A foul is striking at the ball with the fist, violation of Rules 3, 4, and such as described in Rule 5.

7. If either side makes three consecutive fouls, it shall count a goal for the opponents. (Consecutive means without the opponents in the meantime making a foul.)

8. A goal shall be made when the ball is thrown or batted from the ground into the basket and stays there, providing those defending the goal do not touch or disturb the goal. If the ball rests on the edge and the opponent moves the basket, it shall count as a goal.

9. When the ball goes out of bounds, it shall be thrown into the field and played by the person first touching it. In case of a dispute, the umpire shall throw it straight into the field. The thrower-in is allowed five seconds. If he holds it longer, it shall go to the opponent. If any side persists in delaying the

game, the umpire shall call a foul on them.

10. The umpire shall be judge of the men and shall note the fouls and notify the referee when three consecutive fouls have been made. He shall have power to disqualify men according to Rule 5.

11. The referee shall be judge of the ball and shall decide when the ball is in play, in bounds, to which side it belongs, and shall keep the time. He shall decide when a goal has been made, and keep account of the goals, with any other duties that are usually performed by a referee.

12. The time shall be two fifteen minute halves, with five minutes rest between.

13. The side making the most goals in that time shall be declared the winners. In case of a draw, the game may, by agreement of the captains, be continued until another goal is made.

2: THE ROAD TO POINT-A-MINUTE

The game had its rules, but it had no name. One of Dr. Naismith's students suggested it be called Naismith Ball. The modest inventor vetoed the suggestion and settled on Basketball.

The name and the game caught on immediately. In 1892 Naismith organized the first basketball team with nine members from the International Young Men's Christian Association Training School. The first team went on exhibition tour and performed in Albany, Troy and Schenectady, New York, and Providence and Newport, Rhode Island.

The first game between teams from two different organizations took place in Springfield, Massachusetts, in February, 1892. The teams represented the Central and Armory Hill branches of the YMCA and battled to a 2-2 tie. A month later the two teams met again and the Armory Hill team scored a one goal to zero victory.

Girls got involved in basketball almost at the game's beginning. In March, 1892, a match pitted a team of local Springfield girls against a squad of women teachers. Naismith apparently liked what he saw at the game because he married one of the players, Maude Sherman. Vassar and Smith, both women's colleges, added basketball to their activities in 1892.

In the same year, Amos Alonzo Stagg, who had been a contemporary of Naismith on the faculty at Springfield, introduced the new game at the University of Chicago. The first college to field a men's team was Vanderbilt University, which defeated the Nashville, Tennessee, YMCA in March 1893. That same month Hamline College in Minneapolis lost to the Minneapolis YMCA, 13-12.

By 1893 YMCA teams had become widespread enough to be organized into leagues, and various sectional champions emerged. Among the early powerhouse teams were the Brooklyn Central YMCA, which was New York champion in 1893, 1894 and 1895, and Trenton, New Jersey. The Chicago West Side team boasted a 6-4 center, the first of basketball's big men. Trenton's stars, Fred Cooper and Albert Bratton, introduced the use of the short pass to get the ball close to the basket.

A YMCA tournament for the "Championship of America" was staged in Brooklyn on April 24, 1896. All but two of the entrants were from New York. In the final, East District defeated Brooklyn Central, 4-0.

But the spread of basketball among the colleges lagged behind the YMCAs. The first game between two colleges took place on February 9, 1895, when the Minnesota State School of

One of the strongest of the college teams in the late 1920s—at least in the East—was St. John's. Coached by James "Buck" Freeman and known as the "Wonder Five," the team compiled a record of 86 victories and eight defeats over a four-year period. Half the losses came in 1927, the first year they played together, so over the next three years the Wonder Five turned in a record of 70-4. Matty Begovich, a 6-5 center, Mac Kinsbrunner and Max Posnack, forwards, and Rip Gerson and Allie Schuckman, the guards, made up the team. The Wonder Five prided itself on its defensive abilities, and in its senior year the only team which managed to score as many as 30 points against it was the St. John's alumni.

The five players stayed together after college and played as a touring team for two seasons before moving as a unit into the professional ranks. As the Brooklyn Jewels and later the New York Jewels, the team played for many years in the professional American Basketball League.

(The St. John's quintet was not the only so-called Wonder Five of this era. The Passaic, N.J., High School "Wonder Teams" of 1919–1925 won 159 consecutive games.)

Other great teams of the 1920s and early '30s included Kansas, coached by Phog Allen, and California, which won four straight Pacific Coast Conference titles between 1924 and 1927.

The 1930s also marked the introduction of a new style of play. Frank Keaney, coach of Rhode Island State College, developed a system characterized by fast-breaking, long passes upcourt, and plenty of shooting. His Rhode Islanders became known as "point-a-minute" teams. As other schools adopted this style, the move toward higher-scoring, free-wheeling basketball got underway.

But despite some increase in intersectional play, most teams still played the majority of their games against teams from their own region of the country. Experts found it difficult to compare the merits of the outstanding teams from one section with those of another.

The Jewels, made up mostly of the St. John's Wonder Five: (l. to r.) Allie Schuckman, Mac Kinsbrunner, Rip Gerson, George Slott, Max Posnack, Jack Poliskin, Honey Russell and Matty Begovich.

The Passaic (N.J.) High School "Wonder Fives" won 159 consecutive games.

Wabash College of Indiana claimed the world championship. Over a four-year stretch, Wabash won 66 games and lost only three.

During these years the game, although conceived by Dr. Naismith as a non-contact sport, became so rough that efforts were made to legislate against the violence. In 1915, representatives of the Amateur Athletic Union, the International YMCA, and the National Collegiate Athletic Association attempted to formulate a single uniform code of basketball rules.

Whatever the problems of standardization, basketball continued to grow as an attraction. A game between New York University and City College of New York in 1920 drew a crowd of 10,000 to the 22nd Regiment Armory in New York. This was, at the time, the largest crowd ever to see a basketball game. By then basketball had become firmly established in all sections of the country, and each area had its dominant teams. But except for occasional tours by one of the eastern colleges, there was little intersectional play. All debates about the merits of teams from the various sections and possible national championships had to remain unresolved.

One of the greatest problems the game faced in the 1920s was a reduction in the number of personal fouls. A steady parade of players to the free-throw line interfered severely with the flow of the game. The rules committee in 1923 changed such things as running with the ball or double-dribbling from the designation of fouls, which required free throws, to the category of violations, which merely resulted in loss of possession of the ball.

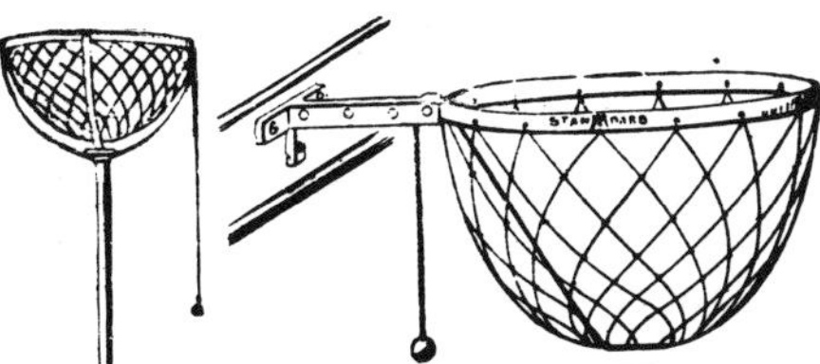

INDOOR BASKET.

The baskets are strong iron hoops, with braided cord netting, arranged to be secured to a gymnasium gallery or wall for indoor use, or on an upright pipe the bottom of which is spiked to be driven into the ground for outdoor use. By means of a cord the ball is easily discharged after a goal is made.

Indoor Goals, per pair,	$15.00
Outdoor Goals, per pair,	30.00
No. 10 Association Foot Ball, each,	3.25
American Rubber Foot Ball,	1.25

Prices for Special Portable Baskets for Exhibitions in Halls or low priced outfits given on application

The basket as it appeared in the Rules Book of 1893.

Maude Sherman, first of the ladies to play the game, became Mrs. James Naismith.

Agriculture crushed Hamline College, 9-3. The winners immediately claimed the Minnesota championship. The first eastern intercollegiate game matched Haverford and Temple, with Haverford winning, 6-4, on March 23, 1895.

Interest in basketball began to pick up among the colleges. Yale and Minnesota began playing against club teams. Yale faced the University of Pennsylvania on March 20, 1897, in what is regarded as the first modern intercollegiate game played with five men on a team. The Elis won, 32-10.

Yale, probably the nation's strongest team, went on a western tour in 1900, marking the introduction of intersectional play. Columbia, Cornell, Harvard, Princeton and Yale organized the Eastern League in 1901 and Yale won the first championship. In the same year, Dartmouth, Holy Cross, Williams, Amherst, and Trinity formed the New England League.

By 1908 the focus of basketball power had shifted from the East to the Midwest and little

The game as played in 1892 (from lecture material of Amos Alonzo Stagg).

2: THE ROAD TO POINT-A-MINUTE

The game had its rules, but it had no name. One of Dr. Naismith's students suggested it be called Naismith Ball. The modest inventor vetoed the suggestion and settled on Basketball.

The name and the game caught on immediately. In 1892 Naismith organized the first basketball team with nine members from the International Young Men's Christian Association Training School. The first team went on exhibition tour and performed in Albany, Troy and Schenectady, New York, and Providence and Newport, Rhode Island.

The first game between teams from two different organizations took place in Springfield, Massachusetts, in February, 1892. The teams represented the Central and Armory Hill branches of the YMCA and battled to a 2-2 tie. A month later the two teams met again and the Armory Hill team scored a one goal to zero victory.

Girls got involved in basketball almost at the game's beginning. In March, 1892, a match pitted a team of local Springfield girls against a squad of women teachers. Naismith apparently liked what he saw at the game because he married one of the players, Maude Sherman. Vassar and Smith, both women's colleges, added basketball to their activities in 1892.

In the same year, Amos Alonzo Stagg, who had been a contemporary of Naismith on the faculty at Springfield, introduced the new game at the University of Chicago. The first college to field a men's team was Vanderbilt University, which defeated the Nashville, Tennessee, YMCA in March 1893. That same month Hamline College in Minneapolis lost to the Minneapolis YMCA, 13-12.

By 1893 YMCA teams had become widespread enough to be organized into leagues, and various sectional champions emerged. Among the early powerhouse teams were the Brooklyn Central YMCA, which was New York champion in 1893, 1894 and 1895, and Trenton, New Jersey. The Chicago West Side team boasted a 6-4 center, the first of basketball's big men. Trenton's stars, Fred Cooper and Albert Bratton, introduced the use of the short pass to get the ball close to the basket.

A YMCA tournament for the "Championship of America" was staged in Brooklyn on April 24, 1896. All but two of the entrants were from New York. In the final, East District defeated Brooklyn Central, 4-0.

But the spread of basketball among the colleges lagged behind the YMCAs. The first game between two colleges took place on February 9, 1895, when the Minnesota State School of game, the umpire shall call a foul on them.

10. The umpire shall be judge of the men and shall note the fouls and notify the referee when three consecutive fouls have been made. He shall have power to disqualify men according to Rule 5.

11. The referee shall be judge of the ball and shall decide when the ball is in play, in bounds, to which side it belongs, and shall keep the time. He shall decide when a goal has been made, and keep account of the goals, with any other duties that are usually performed by a referee.

12. The time shall be two fifteen minute halves, with five minutes rest between.

13. The side making the most goals in that time shall be declared the winners. In case of a draw, the game may, by agreement of the captains, be continued until another goal is made.

THE COLLEGES

Ned Irish, the "boy promoter" responsible for big-time basketball.

3: THE MODERNS

College basketball entered the modern era on December 29, 1934. That night 16,188 fans watched NYU defeat Notre Dame, 25-18, and Westminster beat St. John's, 37-33, in the first regularly scheduled doubleheader in New York's Madison Square Garden.

From that night on, the Garden became the showplace of college basketball. Spectators in unprecedented numbers came to watch New York's strongest teams take on the best from around the nation.

"Garden basketball" was the brainchild of Ned Irish, a 29-year-old "boy promoter." Irish was a sports writer on the *New York World-Telegram.* At that time, Columbia and Fordham were the only local schools with gyms that could hold more than 1,200 people. With limited seating capacity, few schools could make basketball pay.

The story, never denied by Irish, or his tailor, was that Ned had a personal reason for moving college basketball into bigger quarters. One night Irish was assigned to cover a basketball game in Manhattan College's tiny gym. Fighting his way into the cramped arena through a window, Irish tore his pants. This convinced him that basketball should be made more accessible to the public.

Irish's theory gained support during the winter of 1931. James J. Walker, the Mayor of New York, had asked a group of sports writers, including Irish, to arrange a college basketball program to raise money for the relief of the unemployed. On December 31, a capacity crowd watched a tripleheader at the Garden involving six New York City colleges. Similar shows in the next two winters did just as well.

Impressed by the drawing power of college basketball, Irish tried to match NYU and CCNY, both unbeaten, in the Garden in March, 1934. NYU had been playing to standing-room-only audiences at almost every game, yet had been losing money (about $3,000) on the season. The Garden couldn't come up with a suitable night for the NYU-CCNY battle. Next, Irish proposed a post-season charity game between NYU and Notre Dame, but the Violets turned it down.

Undaunted, Irish, the following season, worked out a rental arrangement with the Garden, scheduling his first doubleheader for December 29; as an indication of its success he quit his newspaper job and moved full-time into basketball promotion. In his first season, eight Garden doubleheaders (two more than originally planned) drew 99,528 enthusiasts. Its intro-

NYU vs. Notre Dame in first regular doubleheader at Madison Square Garden December 29, 1934

N Y U
NOTRE DAME
CHICAGO
TORONTO
BOSTON
MONTREAL
DETROIT
ST-LOUIS

duction at the Garden put the game on a sound financial footing, made it available to a wider audience, and generated a tremendous upsurge in intersectional play.

The large audiences enabled Irish to bring in the best teams in the country. Previously, prohibitive transportation costs had precluded visits from schools in the hinterlands. All this was changed as New York became the basketball capital of the nation. Playing in the Garden became the dream of every college basketball player.

One of the greatest of the early intersectional games in the Garden occurred in December, 1936. Stanford, led by Hank Luisetti, defeated Long Island University, 45-31, ending the Blackbirds' 43-game winning streak. Luisetti's stunning one-handed shots, new to the East, not only proved too much for LIU but also revolutionized shooting.

With the increase in intersectional play, the fans began to follow the national basketball picture. The idea of a college tournament among the best teams was a natural evolvement. A group of New York sports writers set it up, and the first National Invitation Tournament was played at Madison Square Garden at the end of the regular 1937–38 season.

NYU's Rubinstein (4) vies with Notre Dame's Jordan at the Garden.

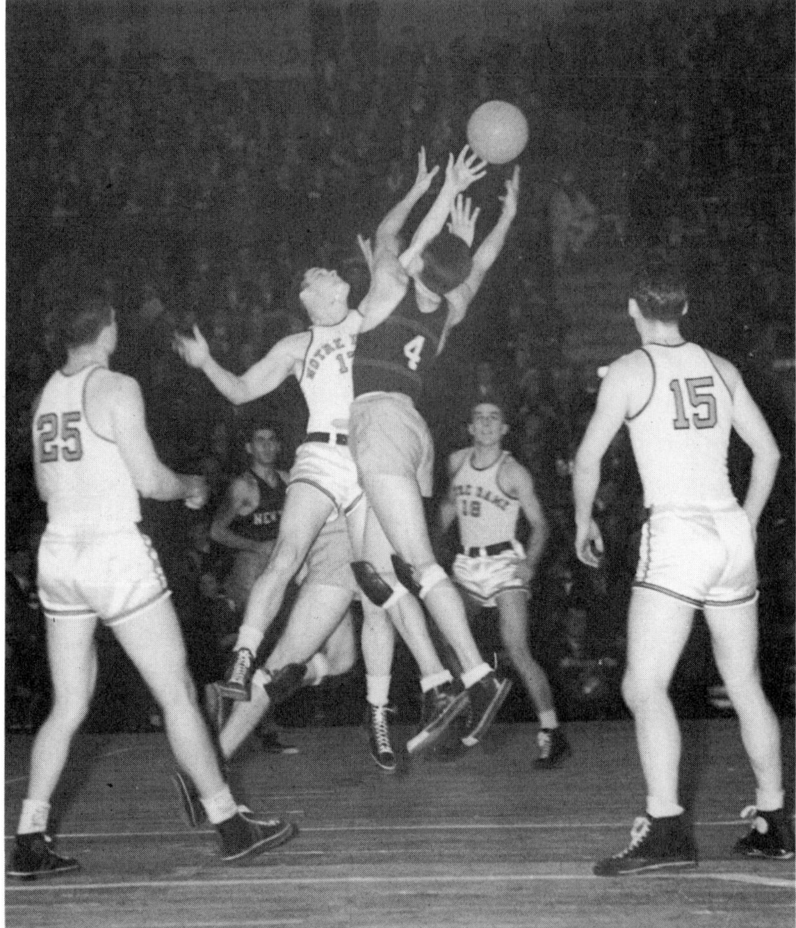

YEARLY ROUNDUPS

1937–38

A revolutionary change—the elimination of the center jump after each score—resulted in more playing time, higher scores, and patterned offenses and defenses.

Another trend-setting change was the one-handed "Wild West" style of shooting as practiced by Stanford's Hank Luisetti as he led the Indians past Oregon State in the best-of-three playoff series for the Pacific Coast Conference championship. Luisetti finished a four-year career at Stanford in which he scored 1,596 points, a national collegiate record.

The first big national post-season tournament made its debut in Madison Square Garden as the National Invitation Tournament was started by the Metropolitan Basketball Writers Association in New York. Six teams competed, with Bradley meeting Temple and LIU playing NYU in first round games. Oklahoma A&M and Colorado were given byes.

Temple, which had finished the season with a 23-2 record, was the Eastern Intercollegiate Conference champion. The Owls won the first NIT by downing Colorado, 60-36, as Ed

Colorado's Whizzer White (later Supreme Court Justice White) is at far left in NIT game against Temple.

Boyle of Temple led all scorers with 39 points in three games. Another Owl, Don Shields, was named MVP.

All-America football player Byron "Whizzer" White, a Rhodes scholar who nearly two decades later would be named to the Supreme Court of the United States, led Colorado to a tie with Utah for the first championship in the newly formed Big Seven Conference.

Oklahoma A&M took the Missouri Valley Conference crown with a 13-1 record in league play and 25-3 overall. Purdue won the Big Ten title while Arkansas raced to the Southwest Conference championship. Kentucky captured the regular season title in the Southeastern Conference, but Georgia Tech won the league's post-season tournament.

Kansas, led by Fred Pralle, took the Big Six championship, while Dartmouth won in the Ivy League. Strong independents included Notre Dame, with John Moir and Paul Nowak, and Loyola (Ill.) with Mike Novak.

Marquette was another strong team in the Midwest; Rhode Island, with a 19-2 mark, was acclaimed No. 1 in New England. Lou Boudreau, a future major league baseball player and manager, was playing for Illinois, and Matt Goukas was leading St. Joseph's to a good season.

Stars included Jewell Young, Purdue; Meyer Bloom, Temple; John Townsend, Michigan; Chuck Chuckovitz, Toledo; Ernie Andres, Indiana; Robert Johnson, Georgia Tech; Jack Robbins, Arkansas; Bonnie Graham, Mississippi; Hubert Kirkpatrick, Baylor; Nat Volpe, Manhattan; John O'Brien, Columbia; Martin Rolek, Minnesota, and Bernard Fliegel, CCNY.

Stanford's Hank Luisetti

NIT Championship Game

At New York

Temple (60)	FG	FT	Pts.	Colorado (36)	FG	FT	Pts.
Shields	8	0	16	Schwartz	1	5	7
Usilton	1	0	2	Grove	0	0	0
Alfano	0	0	0	Hendrick	2	1	5
Black	7	0	14	Sidwell	0	0	0
Freiberg	1	0	2	Thurman	0	0	0
Bloom	2	2	6	Harvey	3	5	11
McDermott	1	0	2	Willcoxen	1	1	3
Nicol	1	1	3	White	5	0	10
Henderson	0	1	1				
Boyle	7	0	14				
Busha	0	0	0				
Totals	28	4	60		12	12	36

NIT Scores

Quarterfinals: Temple 53, Bradley 40; NYU 39, LIU 37

Semifinals: Temple 54, Oklahoma A&M 44; Colorado 48, NYU 47

Championship: Temple 60, Colorado 36

Consolation: Oklahoma A&M 37, NYU 24

1938-39

College basketball's growing popularity was evidenced by the start of the NCAA post-season championship tournament. Oregon met Ohio State in the final at Patten Gymnasium on the campus of Northwestern University in Evanston, Ill., with Oregon winning, 46-43.

The Webfoots of Oregon, with Laddie Gale, Urgel "Slim" Wintermute, Bob Anet, John Dick, and Wally Johansen, won the Pacific Coast Conference championship by downing California in the traditional North-South playoff. Ohio State, led by James Hull, qualified for

Oregon's Bob Anet is in the middle against Ohio State in NCAA final.

the NCAA tourney by winning the Big Ten title, finishing a game ahead of Indiana, led by Ernie Andres.

In the second year of the National Invitation Tournament in New York, undefeated Loyola (Ill.) met unbeaten LIU for the championship. LIU, with Irving Torgoff, extended its winning streak to 26 by beating Loyola, 44-32. The losers were paced by Mike Novak and Wilbert Kautz.

Bill Lloyd of St. John's, who scored 31 points against Roanoke and led the NIT in scoring with 50 points in three games, was named MVP although his Redmen lost two of their three games. St. John's had averaged better than 50 points a game during the season.

Marquette, with Irwin "Ike" Graf and Dave Quabius, was strong, as were DePaul, with Bob Neu; Temple, with Howie Black; NYU, with Bob Lewis; Bradley; Villanova; Duquesne, and Notre Dame.

The Midlands teams were evenly matched as Oklahoma, sparked by James McNatt, and Missouri, paced by John Lobsinger, tied for the Big Six Conference title. Drake and Oklahoma A&M shared the Missouri Valley Conference crown.

Colorado took the Big Seven title while New Mexico A&M won its third straight Border Conference championship. Bobby Moers led Texas to the top of the Southwest Conference, and Dartmouth, powered by sophomore guard Gus Broberg, won in the Ivy League.

Alabama finished first in the regular season race in the Southeastern Conference, but Kentucky, with Bernie Opper, won the league's post-season tourney. Banks McFadden led Clemson, eighth-place finisher in the season standings, to the championship in the post-season tournament of the Southern Conference. Carnegie Tech and Georgetown shared the crown in the last season of play in the Eastern Intercollegiate Conference.

Chet Jaworski led Rhode Island State, the highest scoring team in the country with its 70-point-per-game average, to the New England Conference title. Other strong teams included Illinois, with Lew Dehner; George Washington, with Bob Faris; and little Roanoke College, which earned an NIT bid on the strength of a 20-game winning streak.

St. John's Bill Lloyd (left), who became the MVP of the NIT, accepts congratulations of Roanoke's Gene Studebaker after scoring 31 points in quarterfinal.

NCAA Championship Game

At Evanston, Ill.

Oregon (46)	FG	FT	Pts.	Ohio St. (33)	FG	FT	Pts.
Gale	2	4	8	Maag	0	0	0
Dick	5	5	15	Scott	0	1	1
Wintermute	2	0	4	Hull	5	2	12
Anet	4	2	10	Baker	0	0	0
Johansen	4	1	9	Schick	1	0	2
Mullen	0	0	0	Lynch	3	1	7
Pavalunas	0	0	0	Boughner	1	0	2
				Dawson	1	0	2
				Sattler	3	1	7
				Mickelson	0	0	0
				Stafford	0	0	0
Totals	17	12	46		14	5	33

NIT Championship Game

At New York

LIU (44)	FG	FT	Pts.	Loyola (Ill.) (32)	FG	FT	Pts.
Torgoff	5	2	12	Hogan	2	0	4
King	0	0	0	Schell	1	0	2
Kaplowitz	4	1	9	O'Brien	4	1	9
Schwartz	0	2	2	Graham	1	0	2
Scharf	0	0	0	Novak	0	1	1
Sewitch	0	1	1	Kautz	3	0	6
Lobello	0	0	0	Driscoll	0	0	0
Newman	1	1	3	Wenskus	4	0	8
Shelly	1	0	2				
Bromberg	2	1	5				
Shechtman	4	1	9				
Zeitlin	0	1	1				
Totals	17	10	44		15	2	32

NCAA Scores

REGIONALS

East

Semifinals: Villanova 43, Brown 30; Ohio State 64, Wake Forest 52

Championship: Ohio State 53, Villanova 36

West

Semifinals: Oklahoma 50, Utah State 39; Oregon 56, Texas 41

Championship: Oregon 55, Oklahoma 37

FINALS

Championship: Oregon 46, Ohio State 33

NIT Scores

Quarterfinals: LIU 52, New Mexico A&M 45; St. John's 71, Roanoke 47

Semifinals: LIU 36, Bradley 32; Loyola (Ill.) 51, St. John's 46

Championship: LIU 44, Loyola (Ill.) 32

Consolation: Bradley 40, St. John's 35

1939–40

Two events marked the widespread changes in the development of basketball during this year. Dr. James Naismith, founder of the game nearly 50 years before, died on November 28, 1939. Exactly three months later, Feb. 28, 1940, experimental station W2XBS, forerunner of WNBC in New York, televised college basketball for the first time when it carried the Pitt-Fordham and NYU-Georgetown doubleheader from Madison Square Garden.

Indiana, although finishing second in the Big Ten behind Purdue, won the NCAA tournament by beating Kansas, 60-42. The Hoosiers had a well-balanced team, with any man capable of scoring in double figures, and were selected for NCAA play because they dealt Purdue both of its league losses. Indiana center Marv Huffman was named MVP in the tourney.

Kansas gained its berth in the NCAA tourney after finishing in a three-way tie with Missouri and Oklahoma in the Big Six Conference race. One of the teams the Jayhawks beat enroute to the championship was Southern California, considered by many to be the best team in the country. The Trojans, led by Ralph Vaughn, were the Pacific Coast Conference champions and during the season snapped LIU's 34-game winning streak. Jackie Robinson, who would later become the first Negro to play major league baseball, led the Pacific Coast Conference in scoring at UCLA with 148 points in 12 games.

Big Seven Conference champion Colorado, led by Jack Harvey and Bob Doll, won the NIT by beating DePaul and then Duquesne, 51-40, in the championship game. Doll was named MVP, but scoring honors went to Paul Widowitz of Duquesne.

Rhode Island State and sophomore Stanley "Stutz" Modzelewski set scoring records all over as Modzelewski averaged more than 23 points a game and led the Rams to the New England Conference championship. North Carolina, with George Glamack, took the Southern Conference title by downing Duke in the post-season tournament play, and Alabama finished first in the Southeastern Conference race only to yield to Kentucky in the post-season tournament play.

Oklahoma A&M, with Jesse Renick, won the Missouri Valley Conference championship while other conference champions were Dartmouth, Ivy League; Rice, Southwest; and New Mexico A&M and Arizona, tied, Border.

UCLA's Jackie Robinson was Pacific Coast scoring champ.

Among the strong independents were Villanova, 20-2, and NYU, which won its first 18 games only to lose its finale to CCNY. Also strong were DePaul, with Lou Possner and Stan Szukala; LIU; Duquesne; St. John's; and little Springfield (Mass.).

Outstanding players included Bill Hapac, Illinois; Fred Beretta, Purdue; Ed Riska, Notre Dame; Larry Kenny, St. Joseph's; Chet Aubucher, Michigan State; Ralph Giannini, Santa Clara; and Carlisle Towery, Western Kentucky.

NCAA Championship

At Kansas City

Indiana (60)	FG	FT	Pts.	Kansas (42)	FG	FT	Pts.
Schafer	4	1	9	Ebling	1	2	4
McCreary	6	0	12	Hunter	0	1	1
Armstrong	4	2	10	Engleman	5	2	12
Gridley	0	0	0	Hogben	2	0	4
Bill Menke	2	1	5	Allen	5	3	13
Bob Menke	0	0	0	Kline	0	0	0
Huffman	5	2	12	Miller	0	2	2
Zimmer	2	1	5	Voran	0	1	1
Dro	3	1	7	Harp	2	1	5
Francis	0	0	0	Sands	0	0	0
				Johnson	0	0	0
Totals	26	8	60		15	12	42

NIT Championship

At New York

Colorado (51)	FG	FT	Pts.	Duquesne (40)	FG	FT	Pts.
Hendricks	3	0	6	Kasperik	3	0	6
Doll	6	3	15	Becker	3	2	8
Harvey	4	6	14	Milkovich	0	2	2
McCloud	1	0	2	Reiber	1	0	2
Hamburg	1	2	4	Lacey	2	3	7
Thurman	4	2	10	Widowitz	7	0	14
				Debnar	0	1	1
Totals	19	13	51		16	8	40

NCAA Scores

REGIONALS

East

Semifinals: Duquesne 40, Western Kentucky 29; Indiana 48, Springfield 24

Championship: Indiana 39, Duquesne 30

West

Semifinals: Kansas 50, Rice 44; Southern California 38, Colorado 32

Championship: Kansas 43, Southern California 42

FINALS

Championship: Indiana 60, Kansas 42

NIT Scores

Quarterfinals: DePaul 45, LIU 38; Duquesne 38, St. John's 31

Semifinals: Colorado 52, DePaul 37; Duquesne 34, Oklahoma A&M 30

Championship: Colorado 51, Duquesne 40

Consolation: Oklahoma A&M 23, DePaul 22

1940–41

It was 50 years ago this season that the first soccer ball was thrown into a peach basket in that YMCA in Springfield, Mass. The development of the sport had been surprising, and one of the surprises this season was Wisconsin's Badgers.

Wisconsin, ninth-place finisher in the Big Ten in 1939–40, edged defending NCAA champion Indiana for the conference title. The Badgers, led by jumping-jack center Gene Englund and high-scoring sophomore Johnny Kotz, won their last 15 games in a row, including a 39-34 decision over Washington State for the NCAA crown. Kotz was named MVP, although Washington State's Kirk Gebert scored 21 points in the NCAA final.

The NIT field was expanded to eight teams, with independents Duquesne and Ohio U. rated as co-favorites. Also entered were high-scoring Rhode Island, averaging better than 73 points a game; Seton Hall, paced by Bob Davies and winner of 42 straight games; Westminster, with a 20-1 record; LIU; Virginia; and CCNY.

13
31

LIU, with Oscar Schectman, snapped Seton Hall's victory skein and then downed Ohio U., 56-42, for the championship to become the first team to win the NIT twice. Ohio U.'s Frank Baumholtz, a future major league baseball star, was MVP and tournament high scorer with 53 points in three games.

Washington State, led by Paul Lindeman, had won the Pacific Coast Conference championship by beating Stanford in the North-South playoff, and Arkansas, with Johnny Adams, won the Southwest Conference crown. Gus Broberg, the Ivy League MVP, led Dartmouth to its fourth straight title, while Stanley "Stutz" Modzelewski and Fred Conley sparked Rhode Island State to a tie with Connecticut in the New England Conference race.

George Glamack did most of the scoring as North Carolina produced the best record in the Southern Conference. Glamack scored 45 points in one game, only five shy of the national record held by Stanford's Hank Luisetti.

Other conference champions: Creighton, Missouri Valley; Iowa State and Kansas, tied, Big Six; Wyoming, Big Seven; and Kentucky, Southeastern, although Tennessee beat the Wildcats, 36-33 in the post-season conference tournament.

Toledo, with Bob Gerber; Duquesne, with Moe Becker; and Notre Dame, with George Sobek, were strong independents, as were DePaul, with Elmer Gainer; Pitt, Marquette, Bradley, and CCNY.

Among the stars were Bob Kinney, Rice; Howard Engleman, Kansas; Bruce Hale, Santa Clara; Vic Townsend, Oregon; John Barr, Penn State; and Jackie Robinson, UCLA.

Ohio University's Frankie Baumholtz was MVP and high scorer in the NIT.

LIU's Hank Beenders (30) is about to recover rebound against Seton Hall in NIT semifinal which saw the Blackbirds end Seton Hall's winning streak.

NCAA Championship

At Kansas City

Wisconsin (39)	FG	FT	Pts.	Washington State (34)	FG	FT	Pts.
Epperson	2	0	4	Gentry	0	1	1
Schrage	0	0	0	Gilberg	1	0	2
Kotz	5	2	12	Butts	1	1	3
Englund	5	3	13	Lindeman	0	3	3
Timmerman	1	0	2	Zimmerman	0	0	0
Rehm	2	0	4	Gebert	10	1	21
Strain	0	2	2	Hunt	0	0	0
Alwin	1	0	2	Sundquist	2	0	4
				Hooper	0	0	0
Totals	16	7	39		14	6	34

NIT Championship

At New York

LIU (56)	FG	FT	Pts.	Ohio University (42)	FG	FT	Pts.
Lobello	5	1	11	Baumholtz	8	3	19
Cohen	1	1	3	Snyder	2	0	4
Schneider	0	1	1	Deinzer	0	0	0
Beenders	2	4	8	Bl'k'sd'rf'r	0	0	0
Holub	1	0	2	Lalich	1	2	4
Shechtman	5	2	12	Miller	1	0	2
Schwartz	7	5	19	McSherry	2	2	6
				Wren	0	0	0
				Ott	2	3	7
Totals	21	14	56		16	10	42

NCAA Scores

REGIONALS

East

Semifinals: Wisconsin 51, Dartmouth 50; Pittsburgh 26, North Carolina 20

Championship: Wisconsin 36, Pittsburgh 30

West

Semifinals: Washington State 48, Creighton 39; Arkansas 52, Wyoming 40

Championship: Washington State 64, Arkansas 53

FINALS

Championship: Wisconsin 39, Washington State 34

NIT Scores

Quarterfinals: CCNY 64, Virginia 35; Ohio U. 55, Duquesne 40; Seton Hall 70, Rhode Island 54; LIU 48, Westminster 36

Semifinals: LIU 49, Seton Hall 26; Ohio U. 45, CCNY 43

Championship: LIU 56, Ohio U. 42

Consolation: CCNY 47, Seton Hall 27

1941–42

The season had just begun when the Japanese attacked Pearl Harbor, and the nation entered World War II. Athletes were soon enlisting in the Armed Forces, some doing so during the season. But play continued, although in some cases on a reduced basis.

Pacific Coast Conference champion Stanford swept to the NCAA title despite the loss of its star, Jim Pollard, who was benched with influenza during the championship game. West Virginia, rated last in the eight-team field, surprised everyone by winning the NIT.

Ivy League kingpin Dartmouth, which had to win its title in a playoff with Princeton, advanced all the way to the NCAA finale before bowing to Stanford, 53-38. Stanford's Pollard had scored 43 points in his first two tournament games, but Don Burness, Ed Voss, Jack Dana and sophomore Howard Dallmar filled in for him in the championship game. Dallmar outplayed Dartmouth's George Munroe, scoring 15 points to earn MVP honors.

West Virginia, compiling a 19-4 record as an independent, started its NIT bid by upsetting top-seeded LIU in overtime. The Mountaineers then leveled Toledo as Rudy Baric held Toledo's Bob Gerber, the tourney's leading scorer, to 14 points. West Virginia won the championship by beating Western Kentucky, 47-45, on free throws in the last 20 seconds by Roger Hicks and Scotty Hamilton. WVU's Baric was named MVP.

Paced by sophomore Andy Phillip, Illinois took the Big Ten title, while Rice, with center Bob Kinney, shared the Southwest Conference crown with Arkansas. Colorado, with its one-two punch of Leason McCloud and Bob Doll, won the Big Seven competition, and West Texas State, billed as "the world's tallest team" because of its height average of 6-6½ per man, took Border Conference honors.

Stan "Stutz" Modzelewski of Rhode Island State set all sorts of scoring marks.

Other conference champions: Creighton and Oklahoma A&M, tied, Missouri Valley; Kansas and Oklahoma, tied, Big Six; Duke, Southern, and Rhode Island, New England Conference. Tennessee, with Bernie and Dick Mehen, took regular season play in the Southeastern Conference, only to yield to Kentucky in the post-season tournament.

Bob Davies was the workhorse of a strong Seton Hall team. Notre Dame, with Bob Faught, was strong in the Midwest. Other outstanding independents were CCNY, with Bill Holzman; LIU; St. John's; Penn State; Duquesne, and Syracuse.

Several scoring records were set, including the four-year career mark by Stanley "Stutz" Modzelewski of Rhode Island. His 1,730 points surpassed the 1,596 accumulated by Hank Luisetti six years earlier at Stanford. West Texas State's Price Brookfield set a single-season mark with 520 points.

Among the outstanding players were Johnny Kotz, Wisconsin; John Mandic, Oregon State; Forest Sprowl, Purdue, and Andy Zimmer, Indiana.

NCAA Championship

At Kansas City

Stanford (53)	FG	FT	Pts.	Dartmouth (38)	FG	FT	Pts.
Dana	7	0	14	Meyers	4	0	8
Eikelman	0	0	0	Parmer	1	0	2
Burness	0	0	0	Munroe	5	2	12
Linari	3	0	6	Shaw	0	0	0
Voss	6	1	13	Olsen	4	0	8
Madden	0	0	0	Pogue	0	0	0
Cowden	2	1	5	Pearson	2	2	6
McCaffery	0	0	0	McKernan	0	0	0
Dallmar	6	3	15	Skaug	1	0	2
Oliver	0	0	0	Briggs	0	0	0
Totals	24	5	53		17	4	38

NIT Championship

At New York

West Virginia (47)	FG	FT	Pts.	Western Kentucky (45)	FG	FT	Pts.
Hicks	3	3	9	Day	0	0	0
Hamilton	2	1	5	Blevins	4	1	9
Rollins	0	0	0	Shelton	2	1	5
Raese	0	0	0	D. Downing	0	0	0
Kesling	5	4	14	McKinney	4	1	9
Baric	7	3	17	Ray	2	0	4
Kalmar	1	0	2	H. Downing	4	1	9
				Sydnor	4	1	9
Totals	18	11	47		20	5	45

NCAA Scores
REGIONALS
East

Semifinals: Dartmouth 44, Penn State 39; Kentucky 46, Illinois 44

Championship: Dartmouth 47, Kentucky 28

West

Semifinals: Stanford 53, Rice 47; Colorado 46, Kansas 44

Championship: Stanford 46, Colorado 35

FINALS

Championship: Stanford 53, Dartmouth 38

NIT Scores

Quarterfinals: West Virginia 58, LIU 49; Creighton 59, West Texas State 58; Western Kentucky 49, CCNY 46; Toledo 82, Rhode Island 71

Semifinals: West Virginia 51, Toledo 39; Western Kentucky 49, Creighton 36.

Championship: West Virginia 47, Western Kentucky 45

Consolation: Creighton 48, Toledo 46

1942-43

Because of the war many colleges dropped athletics while other schools made freshmen eligible for varsity competition in order to maintain their squads. Players were being drafted in the middle of the season, and in some cases schedules had to be cancelled for want of a team.

Wyoming and St. John's won the two big post-season tournaments and then met in a Red Cross benefit game with Wyoming winning, 52-47. The Cowboys from Laramie won the NCAA title with a string of come-from-behind victories over Oklahoma, led by Gerry Tucker, and Texas, with John Hargis, in the Western Regionals. Wyoming then came from behind to beat Georgetown, 46-34, in the championship game. Georgetown was led by John Mahnken, but it was Kenny Sailors of Wyoming who won the MVP award. Wyoming's Milo Komenich

Illinois' Whiz Kids: Jack Smiley, Art Mathisen, Ken Menke, Gene Vance and Andy Phillip.

Wyoming's Ken Sailors scoops ball from St. John's Al Moschetti in Red Cross benefit.

was tourney high-scorer with 48 points in three games.

Harry Boykoff, a 6-9 sophomore, and Andrew "Fuzzy" Levane, the Player of the Year in the New York metropolitan area, teamed to lead St. John's to a 48-27 victory over Toledo, led by Davage Minor, in the NIT final. Boykoff scored 56 points in three games, highest in the tourney, and was named MVP.

Illinois, led by Big Ten MVP Andy Phillip, won all 12 conference games as the team, dubbed the "Whiz Kids," passed up post-season competition in the NCAA and NIT. With Phillip were Art Mathisen, Jack Smiley, Gene Vance and Ken Menke.

Creighton, with Ed Beisser, won 19 straight games, including all 10 of its Missouri Valley Conference encounters before being beaten in the opening round of the NIT. Rhode Island, scoring a record 80.7 points a game, won in the New England Conference and Dartmouth, sparked by Stan Skaug, wrapped up its sixth straight Ivy League title.

George Washington, in its second year in the Southern Conference, won the league's post-season tourney after finishing second to Duke in the regular season standings. In the Southeastern Conference, Kentucky finished just ahead of Louisiana State in the regular season race, only to lose to Tennessee in the league's post-season tournament.

West Texas State and Arizona tied for the Border Conference crown after a round-robin league tourney. Rice, with Bill Closs, tied Texas for the Southwest Conference championship; and Kansas, sparked by C.B. Black, won the Big Six title undefeated. William Morris led Washington over Southern California in the North-South playoff for Pacific Coast Conference honors.

Though noted as a football player, Northwestern's Otto Graham also was a star in basketball.

Among the leading independents were St. Joseph's with high-scoring George Senesky; NYU, with Jerry Fleishman; Fordham, with Robert Mullen; Manhattan; Villanova; Notre Dame; Marquette; Bowling Green; and DePaul, with a freshman named George Mikan.

Outstanding players included: Gale Bishop, Washington State; Ray Evans, Kansas; Johnny Kotz, Wisconsin; Don Durden, Oregon State; Hal Gensich, Western Michigan; Joe Walthall, West Virginia; Milton Ticco, Kentucky; Clayton Wynne, Arkansas; and footballer Otto Graham, Northwestern.

NCAA Championship

At New York

Wyoming (46)	FG	FT	Pts.	Georgetown (34)	FG	FT	Pts.
Sailors	6	4	16	Reilly	1	0	2
Collins	4	0	8	Potolicchio	1	2	4
Weir	2	1	5	Gabbianelli	1	2	4
Waite	0	0	0	Hyde	0	0	0
Komenich	4	1	9	Mahnken	2	2	6
Volker	2	1	5	Hassett	3	0	6
Roney	0	1	1	Kraus	2	0	4
Reese	1	0	2	Finnerty	0	0	0
				Feeney	4	0	8
				Duffey	0	0	0
Totals	19	8	46		14	6	34

NIT Championship

At New York

St. John's (48)	FG	FT	Pts.	Toledo (27)	FG	FT	Pts.
Levane	3	0	6	Bolyard	2	1	5
Baxter	3	2	8	Tunnell	0	0	0
Boykoff	5	3	13	Minor	0	0	0
Moschetti	6	1	13	Edwards	0	0	0
Plantamura	1	1	3	Glass	1	0	2
Gotkin	2	1	5	Heiny	0	0	0
				Harmon	2	2	6
				Zuber	3	3	9
				Grove	2	1	5
				Kucer	0	0	0
Totals	20	8	48		10	7	27

NCAA Scores

REGIONALS

East

Semifinals: DePaul 45, Dartmouth 35; Georgetown 55, NYU 36

Championship: Georgetown 53, DePaul 49

West

Semifinals: Texas 59, Washington 55; Wyoming 53, Oklahoma 50

FINALS

Championship: Wyoming 46, Georgetown 34

NIT Scores

Quarterfinals: St. John's 51, Rice 49; Fordham 60, Western Kentucky 58; Toledo 54, Manhattan 47; Washington & Jefferson 43, Creighton 42

Semifinals: Toledo 46, Washington & Jefferson 39; St. John's 69, Fordham 43

Championship: St. John's 48, Toledo 27

Consolation: Washington & Jefferson 39, Fordham 34

1943–44

Freshmen and the military had a big effect on teams, with teenagers like Arnie Ferrin at Utah, Bob Brannum at Kentucky, and Dick McGuire and Bill Kotsores at St. John's moving their teams into the national spotlight.

The military effect was a two-edged sword, cutting away varsity players and coaches at some schools via the draft, while adding experienced personnel to teams at schools where special Armed Forces training programs were established. McGuire is a case in point. He was named the outstanding player in the New York area while playing at St. John's, but before the season was over he was a military trainee playing in the NCAA tourney for Dartmouth.

The team of the year was Utah, with its "Cinderella Kids" averaging 18½ years of age. Utah was eliminated in the first round of the NIT, but was extended an NCAA bid after Southwest Conference co-champions Arkansas and Rice had to decline invitations.

Utah edged Dartmouth, 42-40, for the NCAA title on a basket by Herb Wilkinson with three seconds left in overtime. Freshman Ferrin was named MVP. The Utes then gained a measure of revenge by beating NIT champion St. John's, 43-36, in a Red Cross fund-raising game.

St. John's won the NIT by beating Bowling Green, Kentucky, and DePaul, 47-39, to become the first team ever to win two consecutive NIT titles. Freshman Kotsores was MVP for the Redmen as DePaul's 6-9 George Mikan led the scoring with 49 points in three games.

Washington and California won the Northern and Southern divisions respectively of the Pacific Coast Conference, but travel restrictions again forced cancellation of the playoff. Ohio State, with Don Grate and Arnie Risen, won in the Big Ten, while Iowa State and Oklahoma, led by Alva Paine, shared the Big Six championship.

Kentucky defeated Tulane, 62-46, for the championship in the six-team Southeastern Conference tournament. Duke bested North Carolina in the Southern Conference tourney. Yale and Harvard didn't compete, but Dartmouth, led by Aud Brindley, still kept winning in the Ivy League, taking a seventh straight title. Army rolled to a 15-0 record, but didn't participate in the post-season tournaments.

The Big Seven, Border, and New England conferences were among the many which held no regular competition. Missouri Valley Conference coaches voted Oklahoma A&M the title at the end of a 27-6 season.

Freshman Arnie Ferrin (22) led Utah to victory over St. John's NIT champions.

Bill Kotsores, a freshman, poses with his MVP trophy and teammate Hy Gotkin after NIT triumph.

Other strong teams included Bowling Green, with 6-11 Don Otten; Loyola (La.); Catholic University; and Missouri. Ernie Calverley of Rhode Island led the nation in scoring with a 26.7-point-per-game average as he scored a record 534 points. Rhode Island was the best scoring team in the country, averaging 78.8 points a game while Oklahoma A&M yielded 28.8 points a game.

NCAA Championship

At New York

Utah (42)	FG	FT	Pts.	Dartmouth (40)	FG	FT	Pts.
Ferrin	8	6	22	Gale	5	0	10
Smuin	0	0	0	Mercer	0	1	1
Sheffield	1	0	2	Leggat	4	0	8
Misaka	2	0	4	Nordstrom	0	0	0
Wilkinson	3	1	7	Brindley	5	1	11
Lewis	2	3	7	McGuire	3	0	6
				Murphy	0	0	0
				Vancisin	2	0	4
				Goering	0	0	0
Totals	16	10	42		19	2	40

NIT Championship

At New York

St. John's (47)	FG	FT	Pts.	DePaul (39)	FG	FT	Pts.
Kotsores	3	4	10	Dean	4	0	8
Larkin	0	0	0	Allen	1	0	2
Wertis	6	0	12	Kachan	1	0	2
Summer	4	1	9	DiBenedetto	0	0	0
Wehr	1	1	3	Mikan	4	5	13
Gotkin	2	0	4	Phelan	0	0	0
Duym	3	3	9	Triptow	4	2	10
				Condon	0	0	0
				Stump	1	0	2
				Comerford	1	0	2
				Riordan	0	0	0
Totals	19	9	47		16	7	39

NCAA Scores

REGIONALS

East

Semifinals: Dartmouth 63, Catholic U. 38; Ohio State 57, Temple 47

Championship: Dartmouth 60, Ohio State 53

West

Semifinals: Utah 45, Missouri 35; Iowa State 44, Pepperdine 39

Championship: Utah 40, Iowa State 31

FINALS

Championship: Utah 42, Dartmouth 40

NIT Scores

Quarterfinals: Oklahoma A&M 43, Canisius 29; Kentucky 46, Utah 38; St. John's 44, Bowling Green 40; DePaul 68, Muhlenberg 45

Semifinals: St. John's 48, Kentucky 45; DePaul 41, Oklahoma A&M 38

Championship: St. John's 47, DePaul 39

Consolation: Kentucky 45, Oklahoma A&M 29

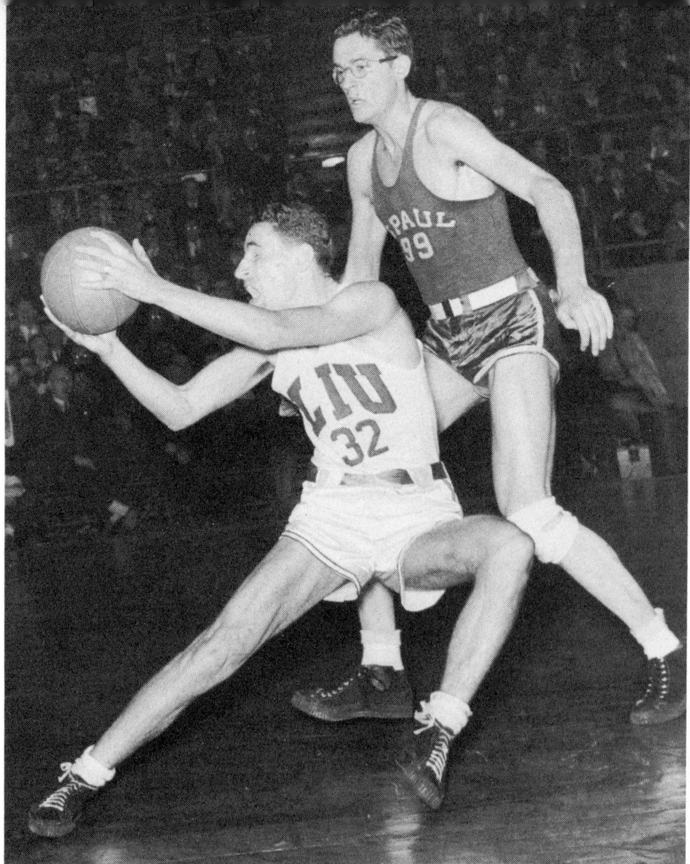

Little Lou Goldstein of LIU scurries against 6-9 George Mikan of DePaul.

1944–45

In an attempt to take away some of the advantage of extremely tall players like DePaul's 6-9 George Mikan and Oklahoma A&M's 7-foot Bob Kurland, the goal-tending rule was introduced this season. This regulation made it illegal for a player to knock away a shot after the ball had begun its downward flight to the basket.

The new rule, though, didn't stop Oklahoma A&M from winning the NCAA tournament or DePaul from capturing the NIT title. Big Ten champion Iowa, led by Dick Ives and former Utah star Dave Wilkinson, was another contender for national honors, but the Hawkeyes didn't compete in either post-season tournament. Iowa lost only one game all year, and that by a single point to Illinois.

Once again, a mixture of freshmen, army rejects, and military trainees formed the backbone of many teams. Oklahoma A&M used the scoring of Cecil Hankin and the 7-foot Kurland to down NYU, 49-45, in the NCAA title game. A&M's tight defense bottled up the Violets' fast break attack and Sid Tannenbaum, who was held to four points. Kurland was named MVP.

DePaul made a shambles of the NIT record book as the Demons set 10 team records and Mikan accounted for 10 individual marks, including a 53-point performance against Rhode Island. Mikan, the tourney MVP, scored a record 120 points in three games. DePaul held Bowling Green's Wyndol Gray to nine points in beating the Falcons, 71-54, in the championship game.

Oklahoma A&M beat DePaul, 52-44, when they met in the annual Red Cross benefit game at the end of the season. The giant battle between Kurland and Mikan failed to

Oklahoma A&M's 7-foot Bob Kurland demonstrates against Temple.

AGGIE
90
17
3
17

materialize, however, as Mikan fouled out after 14 minutes of play. He had nine points at the time. Kurland finished with 14 points.

Defending NCAA champion Utah won the Big Seven title, but lost Arnie Ferrin and Fred Sheffield to the military just before tournament time. Rice, sparked by pivotman Bill Henry, won the Southwest Conference and lost only one game all season—that to Oklahoma A&M.

Former Stanford ace Howard Dallmar, a Navy trainee at Penn, led the Quakers to the Ivy League crown, ending Dartmouth's seven-year reign. Penn also handed Army its only defeat of the season, ending the Cadets' three-year winning streak at 27. Another Navy trainee, Jim Jordan, led North Carolina to the Southern Conference championship.

Tennessee, the best defensive team in the country, won the regular season competition in the Southeastern Conference, but Kentucky took the league's post-season tourney.

UCLA took the Southern Division and Oregon, playing a 47-game schedule, won the Northern Division in the Pacific Coast Conference. No playoff was held. New Mexico was undefeated in the Border Conference; Iowa State won the Big Six, and Oklahoma A&M was voted the Missouri Valley Conference crown. No championships were decided in the other conferences.

St. John's, with Hy Gotkin and Bill Kotsores, and Notre Dame, with Bill Hassett, were strong independents, as was West Virginia, which brought an all-freshman team to the NIT. Other strong squads included Rhode Island, which scored a record 81.7 points a game; Rensselaer, which won all 13 regular season games before losing in the NIT; Valparaiso; Louisville; Loyola (La.); Tufts; Muhlenberg; and Army.

NCAA Championship

At New York

Oklahoma A&M (49)	FG	FT	Pts.	NYU (45)	FG	FT	Pts.
Hankins	6	3	15	Grenert	5	2	12
Parks	0	0	0	Forman	5	1	11
Kern	3	0	6	Goldstein	0	2	2
Wylie	0	0	0	Schayes	2	2	6
Kurland	10	2	22	Walsh	0	0	0
Parrack	2	0	4	Tannenbaum	2	0	4
Williams	1	0	2	Mangiapane	2	2	6
				Most	1	2	4
Totals	22	5	49		17	11	45

NIT Championship

At New York

DePaul (71)	FG	FT	Pts.	Bowling Green (54)	FG	FT	Pts.
Stump	6	3	15	Gray	4	1	9
Phelan	0	0	0	Whitehead	7	3	17
DiBenedetto	1	2	4	Inman	0	1	1
Comerford	0	0	0	Otten	3	1	7
G. Mikan	15	4	34	Rosedale	0	0	0
E. Mikan	0	0	0	Knierim	1	0	2
Allen	2	1	5	Kubiak	1	2	4
LaRochelle	0	0	0	Piel	1	0	2
Furman	0	0	0	Payak	5	2	12
Kachan	6	1	13	Gantt	0	0	0
Niemiera	0	0	0				
Halloran	0	0	0				
Totals	30	11	71		22	10	54

NCAA Scores

REGIONALS

East

Semifinals: NYU 59, Tufts 44; Ohio State 45, Kentucky 37

Championship: NYU 70, Ohio State 65

West

Semifinals: Oklahoma A&M 62, Utah 37; Arkansas 79, Oregon 76

Championship: Oklahoma A&M 49, NYU 45

NIT Scores

Quarterfinals: Rhode Island 51, Tennessee 44; Bowling Green 60, Rensselaer Poly 45; DePaul 76 West Virginia 52; St. John's 34, Muhlenberg 33

Semifinals: DePaul 97, Rhode Island 53; Bowling Green 57, St. John's 44

Championship: DePaul 71, Bowling Green 54

Consolation: St. John's 64, Rhode Island 57

1945-46

With World War II over, the veterans returned to find college basketball dominated by 7-foot Bob Kurland and his teammates at Oklahoma A&M. The Aggies became the first team ever to win two NCAA titles, consecutively or otherwise, as they rolled to a 31-2 record.

A&M, the Missouri Valley Conference champion, defeated Baylor and California before beating North Carolina, 43-40, to retain the NCAA crown. The red-headed Kurland, nicknamed "Foothills" because of his height, scored 71 points in three games as he won MVP honors for the second straight year. Kurland, who scored 58 points against St. Louis in the last home game of his collegiate career, finished the season with a record 643 points.

Kentucky, with Jack Parkinson, finished second to Louisiana State, led by Robert Lowther, in the Southeastern Conference. But the Wildcats went on to win the NIT with a 46-45 victory over Rhode Island in the championship game. Freshman Ralph Beard hit a free throw in the final seconds to give Kentucky the victory.

Ernie Calverley, high-scorer and MVP in the NIT, had propelled Rhode Island into the finale when, in an opening-round game against Bowling Green, he hit on a 55-foot shot in the closing seconds of play to send the game into overtime.

New York University, with Sid Tannenbaum, and St. John's battled for supremacy in the New York City area, while West Virginia, using three sophomores and two freshmen, rolled to its best record ever, 24-3, as an independent. Other strong independents included DePaul, with 6-9 George Mikan; Bowling Green, with Don Otten; Syracuse, with Bill Gabor; Navy and Notre Dame, led by Leo Klier and Bill Hassett.

Duke, led by Ed Koffenberger, won the Southern Conference crown with a 13-1 record, but runner-up North Carolina, paced by Jim Jordan and John Dillon, finished with a 12-1 record and received an NCAA bid. Harvard, with former Bowling Green star Wyndol Gray, and Yale, with Tony Lavelli, played as independents, while Dartmouth won the Ivy League competition.

Arizona, with Stewart Udall, who was later to become Secretary of the Interior, won the Border Conference crown. Other conference champions: Ohio State, Big Ten; Kansas, Big Six; Baylor, Southwest; Lafayette, Middle Atlantic; and Wyoming, Big Seven. Idaho won its

Henry Iba, Oklahoma A&M coach, congratulates Bob Kurland after Aggies win second NCAA crown in a row.

3
4

first Pacific Coast Conference title in 23 years by downing California in the North-South playoff, but California was selected for the NCAA tournament.

One of the largest crowds ever, 28,822, jammed Chicago Stadium to see Ohio State, with Paul Huston, beat Northwestern, led by Max Morris, and DePaul defeat Notre Dame.

Ernie Vandeweghe, a 17-year-old freshman at Colgate, was named MVP in the first Fresh Air Fund East-West All-Star game in New York. Among the outstanding players this season were C.B. Black, Kansas; Jack Robinson, Baylor; Herb Wilkinson, Iowa; Jack Goldsmith, LIU; George Kok, Arkansas; Tony Jaros, Minnesota; Paul Hoffman, Purdue; Fred Quinn, Idaho; Andy Wolfe, California; and Kenny Sailors, Wyoming.

NCAA Championship

At New York

Oklahoma A&M (43)	FG	FT	Pts.	North Carolina (40)	FG	FT	Pts.
Aubray	0	1	1	Dillon	5	6	16
Bennett	3	0	6	Anderson	3	2	8
Kern	3	1	7	Paxton	2	0	4
Bradley	1	1	3	McKinney	2	1	5
Kurland	9	5	23	White	0	1	1
Halbert	0	0	0	Thorne	1	0	2
Williams	0	2	2	Jordan	0	4	4
Bell	0	1	1				
Parks	0	0	0				
Totals	16	11	43		13	14	40

NIT Championship

At New York

Kentucky (46)	FG	FT	Pts.	Rhode Island (45)	FG	FT	Pts.
Tingle	2	1	5	Hole	5	2	12
Holland	1	0	2	Nichols	5	1	11
Schu	3	3	9	Palmieri	0	0	0
Jones	3	4	10	Calverley	2	4	8
Campbell	0	2	2	Shea	1	2	4
Parkinson	1	0	2	Allen	3	4	10
Beard	5	3	13	Sclafani	0	0	0
Parker	1	1	3				
Totals	16	14	46		16	13	45

NCAA Scores

REGIONALS

East

Semifinals: Ohio State 46, Harvard 38; North Carolina 57, NYU 49

Championship: North Carolina 60, Ohio State 57

West

Semifinals: Oklahoma A&M 44, Baylor 29; Cal fornia 50, Colorado 44

Championship: Oklahoma A&M 52, California 35

FINALS

Championship: Oklahoma A&M 43, North Carolina 40

Consolation: Ohio State 63, California 45

NIT Scores

Quarterfinals: Rhode Island 82, Bowling Green 79; West Virginia 70, St. John's 58; Kentucky 77, Arizona 53; Muhlenberg 47, Syracuse 41

Semifinals: Rhode Island 59, Muhlenberg 49; Kentucky 59, West Virginia 51

Championship: Kentucky 46, Rhode Island 45

Consolation: West Virginia 65, Muhlenberg 40

Rhode Island's Ernie Calverley lofts one against Bowling Green.

Stewart Udall, a future Secretary of the Interior, led his Arizona team to the NIT.

1946–47

Fifty years ago this season, on March 20, 1897, Penn visited Yale to play the first intercollegiate game between five-man basketball teams. This season New England again made news as Holy Cross became the first team from that section to win an NCAA championship.

Holy Cross had no gymnasium at its Worcester, Mass., campus and had to play all its games on the road. The Crusaders won 27 of 30, including the last 23 in a row enroute to the title. Big Six champion Oklahoma, led by center Gerry Tucker, earned one- and two-point victories in regional games before bowing to Holy Cross, 58-47, in the NCAA finale. Holy Cross' George Kaftan was named MVP for his 18 points and strong rebounding.

Alex Groza was back at Kentucky and Arnie Ferrin returned to Utah after military service. The two teams met for the NIT championship and Utah's deliberate style calmed Kentucky's whirlwind attack, 49-45. Utah's little Wat Misaka bottled up Kentucky's high-scoring Ralph Beard, but it was Ute center Vern Gardner, with 51 points in three games, who won MVP honors.

Texas lost only two games, each by one point, as John Hargis led the Longhorns to the Southwest Conference title. Bob Cook sparked Wisconsin to the top of the Big Ten. St. Louis, with Ed Macauley, won the Missouri Valley Conference crown.

The trio of Lou Beck, Cliff Crandall, and Ephraim "Red" Rocha led Oregon State to the Pacific Coast Conference championship after State downed UCLA, with Don Barksdale and Dave Minor, in the North-South playoff.

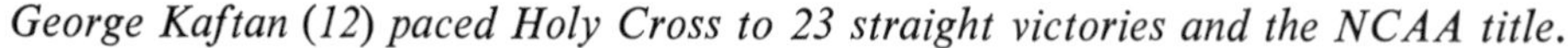

George Kaftan (12) paced Holy Cross to 23 straight victories and the NCAA title.

LSU's Joe Adcock tugs with St. Francis of Brooklyn's Joe Dolan.

L. S. U
12
7

Other conference champions: Wyoming, Big Seven; Columbia, Ivy League; Arizona, Border; North Carolina State, Southern; Kentucky, Southeastern; and Montana State, Rocky Mountain. Butler and Cincinnati shared the first title in the Mid-American Conference while the newly formed Yankee Conference produced strong teams in Rhode Island, Connecticut, and Vermont.

West Virginia, paced by Leland Byrd; Notre Dame, with Kevin O'Shea and Johnny Brennan; and St. John's, whose Harry Boykoff scored 54 points in a game against St. Francis, were strong independents. Also powerful were Loyola (Ill.) with Jack Kerris; Navy, with Ken Shugart; LIU; Duquesne; LaSalle; Western Michigan; Georgetown; Santa Clara; and Gonzaga.

Conference also-rans compiling good over-all records included Louisiana State, with future major league baseball player and manager Joe Adcock; Duke; North Carolina; George Washington; Oklahoma A&M; Washington State; and California.

Rhode Island upped the scoring record again, averaging 82.5 points a game while Oklahoma A&M retained its defensive title, yielding 34.8 points per game. Dallas Zuber of Toledo led major college scorers with 441 points.

Some of the better players were Walt Budko, Columbia; James Homer, Alabama; Sid Tannenbaum, NYU; Ralph Hamilton, Indiana; Joe Lord, Villanova; and Jack Smiley and Andy Phillip, both of Illinois.

NCAA Championship
At New York

Holy Cross (58)	FG	FT	Pts.	Oklahoma (47)	FG	FT	Pts.
Kaftan	7	4	18	Reich	3	2	8
Laska	0	0	0	Waters	0	0	0
O'Connell	7	2	16	Day	0	0	0
Curran	0	0	0	Courty	3	2	8
Reilly	0	0	0	Pryor	0	1	1
Oftring	6	2	14	Tucker	6	10	22
Mullaney	0	0	0	Paine	2	2	6
Haggerty	0	0	0	Landon	1	0	2
McMullin	2	4	8	Merchant	0	0	0
Cousy	0	2	2				
Bollinger	0	0	0				
Graver	0	0	0				
Totals	22	14	58		15	17	47

NIT Championship
At New York

Utah (49)	FG	FT	Pts.	Kentucky (45)	FG	FT	Pts.
Watson	3	7	13	Holland	1	0	2
Misaka	0	2	2	Jones	2	4	8
Gardner	5	5	15	Groza	5	2	12
Ferrin	6	3	15	Tingle	0	0	0
Weidner	1	2	4	Barker	0	0	0
Clark	0	0	0	Rollins	3	0	6
				Line	6	0	12
				Beard	0	1	1
				Jordan	1	2	4
Totals	15	19	49		18	9	45

NCAA Scores
REGIONALS

East

Semifinals: Holy Cross 55, Navy 47; CCNY 70, Wisconsin 56

Championship: Holy Cross 60, CCNY 45

West

Semifinals: Texas 42, Wyoming 40; Oklahoma 56, Oregon State 54

Championship: Oklahoma 55, Texas 54

FINALS

Championship: Holy Cross 58, Oklahoma 47

Consolation: Texas 54, CCNY 50

NIT Scores

Quarterfinals: Utah 45, Duquesne 44; Kentucky 66, LIU 62; North Carolina State 61, St. John's 55; West Virginia 69, Bradley 60

Semifinals: Utah 64, West Virginia 62; Kentucky 60, North Carolina State 42

Championship: Utah 49, Kentucky 45

Consolation: North Carolina State 64, West Virginia 52

1947–48

Kentucky's three-pronged attack of Alex Groza, Ralph Beard, and Wallace "Wah Wah" Jones brought the Wildcats their first NCAA title in a season that saw them win their fifth consecutive Southeastern Conference championship, lose only two games to collegiate opponents, and finish with a 36-3 record.

Groza, a 6-7 center, was named MVP in the NCAA tourney after the speed, height, and savvy of the Wildcats proved too much for Southwest Conference champion Baylor in a 58-42 rout. The Bears were led by Don Heathington and Jack Robinson.

Another big center, "Easy Ed" Macauley of St. Louis, led the Billikens to the NIT championship as he scored 24 points and outplayed NYU's Dolph Schayes in a 65-52 triumph in the title game. NYU had won 19 straight games before succumbing. The Violets were hampered by the loss of Don Forman who was out with a back injury. Macauley was voted MVP honors ahead of his teammate, D. C. Wilcutt, while scoring honors went to DePaul's Ed Mikan, brother of George, with 64 points in three games.

Holy Cross, with George Kaftan and Bob Cousy, won 18 straight games in an effort to retain its NCAA crown, but the Crusaders were beaten by Kentucky in the NCAA Eastern regional tourney. West Virginia was hurt early in the season when Freddie Schaus sustained a broken ankle, but the Mountaineers finished strong. Larry Foust, at 6-9, led LaSalle; sophomore Paul Unruh sparked Bradley; and 6-10 Charlie Share paced Bowling Green to NIT bids.

Notre Dame, with Kevin O'Shea; Loyola, with Jack Kerris; and Colgate, with Ernie Vandeweghe, were strong independents, as were LIU, CCNY, Xavier (O.), Gonzaga, Montana, and Seton Hall.

Washington, led by hook-shot artist Jack Nichols, defeated Oregon State for the Pacific Coast Conference's Northern Division title before beating Southern Division winner California, with Andy Wolfe and Chuck Hangar, for the league championship.

North Carolina State, sparked by Dick Dickey, retained its Southern Conference crown; Michigan, with Pete Elliott and Bob Harrison, won its first Big Ten title since 1927; and Kansas State jumped from last to first in one season to win the title in the Big Seven (the Big Six before the addition of Colorado).

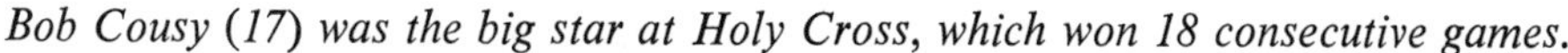

Bob Cousy (17) was the big star at Holy Cross, which won 18 consecutive games.

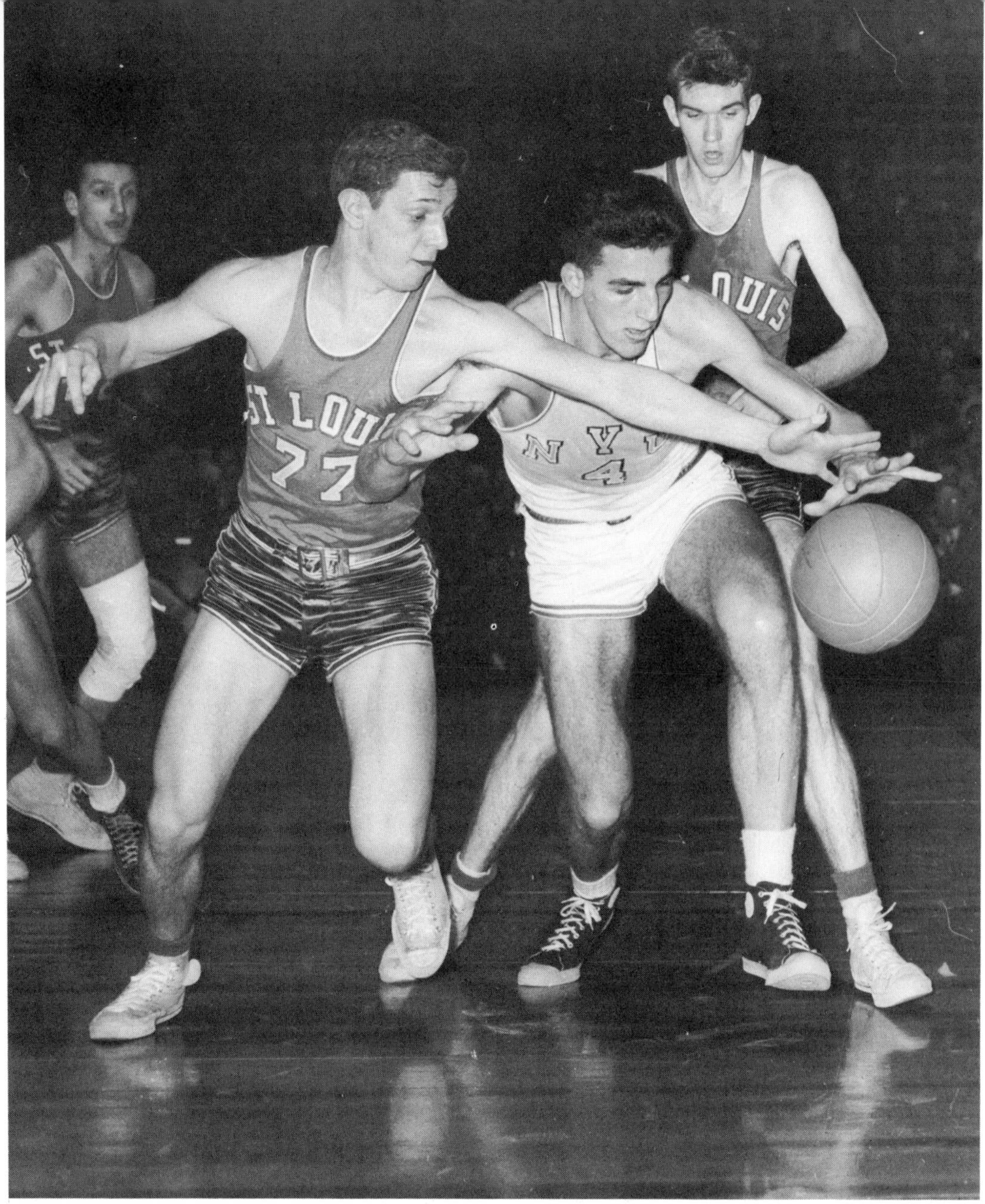

NIT: Dolph Schayes (4) and St. Louis' Lou Lehman (77) and Ed Macauley.

Other conference champions: Columbia, Ivy League; Connecticut, Yankee; Cincinnati, Mid-American; Oklahoma A&M, Missouri Valley; Arizona, Border; Brigham Young, Skyline Six; Colorado State, Rocky Mountain; and San Jose State, California Collegiate Athletic Association.

Rhode Island, North Carolina State, and Bowling Green averaged more than 70 points a game, led by Rhode Island's 76.3 points a game. Oklahoma A&M and Alabama held opponents to less than 40 points a game. Norm Hankins of Lawrence Tech led scorers with his 22.5 point average.

Among the outstanding players were Murray Weir, Iowa; Tony Lavelli, Yale; George Kok, Arkansas; Leon Watson, Utah; Bob Cook, Wisconsin; Gene Berce, Marquette; and Alex Hannum, Southern California.

NCAA Championship
At New York

Kentucky (58)	FG	FT	Pts.	Baylor (42)	FG	FT	Pts.
Jones	4	1	9	Owen	2	1	5
Line	3	1	7	Pulley	0	1	1
Barker	2	1	5	DeWitt	3	2	8
Groza	6	2	14	Hickman	1	0	2
Holland	1	0	2	Heathington	3	2	8
Beard	4	4	12	Preston	0	0	0
Rollins	3	3	9	Johnson	3	4	10
Barnstable	0	0	0	Srack	0	0	0
				Robinson	3	2	8
Totals	23	12	58		15	12	42

NIT Championship
At New York

St. Louis (65)	FG	FT	Pts.	NYU (52)	FG	FT	Pts.
Wilcutt	7	2	16	Kelly	0	1	1
Ossola	1	3	5	Kaufman	6	2	14
Cordia	1	0	2	Lumpp	5	4	14
Schatzmann	1	1	3	Barry	1	1	3
Wrape	0	0	0	Schayes	4	0	8
J. Schmidt	1	1	3	Dolhon	3	1	7
Macauley	11	2	24	DeBonis	1	0	2
B. Schmidt	1	4	6	Benanti	1	0	2
Lehman	0	2	2	Derderian	0	0	0
Cary	0	0	0	Kor	0	0	0
Miller	2	0	4	Quilty	0	1	1
Raymonds	0	0	0				
Totals	25	15	65		21	10	52

NCAA Scores
REGIONALS

East

Semifinals: Kentucky 76, Columbia 53; Holy Cross 63, Michigan 45

Championship: Kentucky 60, Holy Cross 52

West

Semifinals: Washington 57, Wyoming 47; Baylor 60, Kansas State 52

Championship: Baylor 64, Washington 62

FINALS

Championship: Kentucky 58, Baylor 42

Consolation: Holy Cross 60, Washington 54

NIT Scores

Quarterfinals: Western Kentucky 68, LaSalle 61; St. Louis 69, Bowling Green 53; NYU 45, Texas 43; DePaul 75, North Carolina State 64

Semifinals: NYU 72, DePaul 59; St. Louis 60, Western Kentucky 53

Championship: St. Louis 65, NYU 52

Consolation: Western Kentucky 61, DePaul 59

All-Americans
AP

Murray Weir, Iowa
Jim McIntyre, Minnesota
Ed Macauley, St. Louis
Ralph Beard, Kentucky
Kevin O'Shea, Notre Dame

1948–49

Kentucky, with the returning trio of Alex Groza, Ralph Beard, and "Wah Wah" Jones, set 22 NCAA team and individual records in repeating as national champion. The Wildcats raced through 13 Southeastern Conference games unbeaten before downing Villanova, Illinois, and Oklahoma A&M to win the NCAA crown. This was the year that a new rule allowing coaches to talk to their teams during a time-out went into effect. But it was Kentucky's Adolph Rupp who obviously knew what to say.

The 6-7 Groza scored a record 82 points in three games and was again named MVP. One of the few jarring notes in the 36-2 season for the Wildcats was a loss to Loyola (Ill.) in the first round of the NIT. Kentucky was rated No. 1 in the country in the Associated Press nationwide poll, taken for the first time this season.

Kentucky, St. Louis, Western Kentucky, and Utah were the top four seeded teams in the NIT and all lost opening round games. St. John's, NYU, CCNY, and Manhattan also lost their opening round NIT games, all on the same day, in what was called the "Manhattan Massacre." San Francisco, with Don Lofgran, Joe McNamee, and Rene Herrerias, defeated Loyola, 48-47, for the championship. Lofgran, who scored 20 points for the Dons and accidentally tapped in a basket for Loyola, was named MVP. Bradley's Paul Unruh was high scorer with 80 points in four games.

Ralph Beard (12) vs. Illinois as Wah Wah Jones (27) and Alex Groza (15) look on.

Nine major individual scoring records were set, including a single season total of 740 points by William and Mary's Chet Giermak. His 673 field goal attempts and 301 field goals were also records. Paul Arizin of Villanova scored more points, 85, and more field goals, 35, in one game than any other player.

Other records included a career high of 2,199 points by Jim Lacy of Loyola (Md.) while Cornell's Hillary Chollet made a record 19 free throws in one game. Yale's stellar accordion player and scorer, Tony Lavelli, attempted 261 free throws and made 215, both records.

Lavelli led Yale to its first Ivy League championship in 16 years while North Carolina State, with Dick Dickey, Sam Ranzino and Vic Bubas, won its third straight Southern Conference title. Illinois, led by Bill Erickson and Dwight Eddleman, took the Big Ten crown, and Bob Harris powered Oklahoma A&M to the Missouri Valley Conference championship. A&M was pushed by Bradley and St. Louis, with Ed Macauley who made 52.4 per cent of his shots, best in the nation. All three teams were ranked in the top ten.

Other conference champions: Oregon State, Pacific Coast; Wyoming and Utah, tied, Skyline Six; Nebraska and Oklahoma, tied Big Seven; Arkansas, Baylor and Rice, tied, Southwest; Western Kentucky, Ohio Valley; Cincinnati, Mid-American; Connecticut, Yankee; Arizona, Border; Colorado State, Rocky Mountain; and San Jose, California Collegiate Athletic Association.

Holy Cross, with Bob Cousy; Colgate, with Ernie Vandeweghe; Bowling Green; Duquesne; Siena; LaSalle; West Virginia; Niagara; Miami (Fla.); and Notre Dame were the best of the non-tournament independents.

Teams that lost conference races but were still noteworthy were Texas, with Slater Martin; Minnesota, led by Meyer "Whitey" Skoog; and Denver, with Vince Boryla. Despite Denver's 18-15 record, the 6-5 Boryla broke virtually every individual shooting record in the Skyline Conference.

NCAA Championship

At Seattle

Kentucky (46)	FG	FT	Pts.	Oklahoma A&M (36)	FG	FT	Pts.
Jones	1	1	3	Yates	1	0	2
Line	2	1	5	Shelton	3	6	12
Groza	9	7	25	Harris	3	1	7
Beard	1	1	3	Bradley	0	3	3
Barker	1	3	5	Parks	2	3	7
Barnstable	1	1	3	Jaquet	0	1	1
Hirsch	1	0	2	McArthur	0	2	2
				Pilgrim	0	2	2
				Smith	0	0	0
Totals	16	14	46		9	18	36

NIT Championship

At New York

San Francisco (48)	FG	FT	Pts.	Loyola (Ill.) (47)	FG	FT	Pts.
Benington	2	1	5	Earle	3	4	10
Hanley	0	0	0	O'Grady	1	0	2
Lofgran	9	2	20	Klaerich	4	2	10
McNamee	1	3	5	Bluitt	4	1	9
Geisen	1	0	2	Kerris	3	1	7
Kuzara	3	1	7	Dawson	1	0	2
Guidice	1	3	5	Nicholl	0	1	1
Herrerias	0	4	4	Hildebrand	1	2	4
				Nagel	0	0	0
Totals	17	14	48		17*	11	45*

*Lofgran scored one goal for Loyola

NCAA Scores

REGIONALS

East

Semifinals: Kentucky 85, Illinois 71; Villanova 72, Yale 67

Championship: Kentucky 76, Illinois 47

West

Semifinals: Oklahoma A&M 40, Wyoming 39; Oregon State 56, Arkansas 38

Championship: Oklahoma A&M 55, Oregon State 30

FINALS

Championship: Kentucky 46, Oklahoma A&M 36

Consolation: Illinois 57, Oregon State 53

NIT Scores

First Round: Bowling Green 77, St. John's 64; San Francisco 68, Manhattan 43; Bradley 89, NYU 67; Loyola 62, CCNY 47

Quarterfinals: Loyola 61, Kentucky 56; Bradley 95, Western Kentucky 86; San Francisco 64, Utah 63; Bowling Green 80, St. Louis 74

Semifinals: San Francisco 49, Bowling Green 39; Loyola 55, Bradley 50

Championship: San Francisco 48, Loyola 47

Consolation: Bowling Green 82, Bradley 77

Top Ten

AP

Kentucky	Minnesota
Oklahoma A&M	Bradley
St. Louis	San Francisco
Illinois	Tulane
Western Kentucky	Bowling Green

All-Americans

AP	UP
Tony Lavelli, Yale	Tony Lavelli, Yale
Vince Boryla, Denver	Ed Macauley, St. Louis
Alex Groza, Kentucky	Wallace Jones, Kentucky
Ed Macauley, St. Louis	Alex Groza, Kentucky
Ralph Beard, Kentucky	Ralph Beard, Kentucky

Villanova's Paul Arizin scores in the East-West game.

1949–50

City College of New York became the first team ever to win both the NCAA and NIT championships in the same year. More important, however, was the subsequent revelation that CCNY was among the teams involved in a point-rigging scandal that shocked the nation.

Starting the season with only one veteran, 6-4 Irwin Dambrot, CCNY had a respectable, but not outstanding, 17-5 record. The Beavers were unranked nationally and were overlooked in the All-America selections.

The first surprise came in the NIT when CCNY upset Bradley, 69-61, in the championship game. Later, in the NCAA title game, CCNY again beat Bradley, 71-68. CCNY's Ed Warner was the NIT's leading scorer with 87 points in four games and was named MVP. Dambrot won MVP honors in the NCAA tourney.

Bradley, paced by Paul Unruh and Gene "Squeaky" Melchiorre, won the Missouri Valley Conference, while North Carolina State, with Dick Dickey and Sam Ranzino, won its fourth straight Southern Conference crown. Dick Schnittker led Ohio State to the Big Ten title, while 6-9 Clyde Lovellette, a sophomore, lifted Kansas into a three-way tie with Nebraska and Kansas State for the Big Seven championship.

Western Kentucky, with Bob Lavoy, went through the Ohio Valley Conference unbeaten, but was upended by Eastern Kentucky in the league's post-season tournament.

UCLA's Ralph Joeckel hit on a shot from more than 50 feet with three seconds remaining to give the Bruins a 60-58 victory over Washington State in the North-South playoff for the Pacific Coast Conference crown. Other conference winners: Kentucky, Southeastern; Cincinnati, Mid-American; Princeton, Ivy; Rhode Island, Yankee; Montana State, Rocky Mountain; Brigham Young, Skyline Six; Muhlenberg, Middle Atlantic; Baylor and Arizona, tied, Southwest; and Arizona, for the fifth year in a row in the Border Conference.

Among the independents, Bob Cousy led Holy Cross while the nation's leading scorer, Paul Arizin, was averaging 25.3 points a game for Villanova. Arizin's 735 points were only five shy of the single-season mark held by William and Mary's Chet Giermak. Other strong independents included Notre Dame, with Kevin O'Shea; LIU, with Sherm White; Duquesne, with Charlie Cooper; Niagara; Syracuse; LaSalle; Toledo; San Francisco; and St. John's, whose Robert "Zeke" Zawoluk scored 65 points in one game.

Led by Arizin, Villanova was the top-scoring team in the country, averaging 72.8 points a game and Oklahoma A&M, as usual, led the defensive rankings, yielding 39.2 points per game.

Coach Nat Holman celebrates CCNY's championship in NCAA tourney.

Among the outstanding players were Bill Sharman, Southern California; Don Rehfeldt, Wisconsin; John Pilch, Wyoming; George Stannich, UCLA; Richard Harmon, Kansas State; Ed Gayda, Washington State; Bob MacKinnon, Canisius; George Yardley, Stanford; and Lou Watson, Indiana.

CCNY's post-season tournament record included victories over defending NIT champion San Francisco and defending NCAA champion Kentucky in the first two rounds of the NIT. In order to win both the NIT and NCAA tourney, CCNY had to beat the 12th, 6th, 5th, 3rd and 2nd ranked teams in the country. In each championship game CCNY beat Bradley, rated No. 1 in the nation.

But the triumphs were to be proven hollow as an extensive investigation turned up evidence of the scandal that took the glitter off basketball's shining stars and shook the game to its very foundations.

NCAA Championship

At New York

CCNY (71)	FG	FT	Pts.	Bradley (68)	FG	FT	Pts.
Dambrot	7	1	15	Grover	0	2	2
Roman	6	0	12	Schlictman	0	0	0
Warner	4	6	14	Unruh	4	0	8
Roth	2	1	5	Behnke	3	3	9
Mager	4	6	14	Kelly	0	0	0
Galiber	0	0	0	Mann	2	5	9
Layne	3	5	11	Preece	6	0	12
Nadell	0	0	0	D. M'lch'rre	0	0	0
				G. M'lch'rre	7	2	16
				Chianakas	5	1	11
				Stowell	0	1	1
Totals	26	19	71		27	14	68

NIT Championship

At New York

CCNY (69)	FG	FT	Pts.	Bradley (61)	FG	FT	Pts.
Dambrot	10	3	23	Grover	3	0	6
Warner	6	4	16	Preece	2	0	4
Roman	9	1	19	Unruh	7	1	15
Galiber	0	1	1	Schlictman	1	0	2
Roth	0	0	0	Chianakas	0	0	0
Cohen	0	0	0	Behnke	6	3	15
Mager	2	0	4	Kelly	0	2	2
Layne	2	2	6	Mann	4	0	8
				G. M'lch'rre	2	5	9
Totals	29	11	69		25	11	61

NCAA Scores

REGIONALS

East

Semifinals: CCNY 56, Ohio State 55; North Carolina State 87, Holy Cross 74

Championship: CCNY 78, North Carolina State 73

West

Semifinals: Baylor 56, Brigham Young 55; Bradley 73, UCLA 59

Championship: Bradley 68, Baylor 66

FINALS

Championship: CCNY 71, Bradley 68

Consolation: North Carolina State 53, Baylor 41

NIT Scores

First Round: Western Kentucky 79, Niagara 72; CCNY 65, San Francisco 46; Syracuse 80, LIU 52; LaSalle 72, Arizona 66

Quarterfinals: St. John's 69, Western Kentucky 60; Bradley 78, Syracuse 66; Duquesne 49, LaSalle 47; CCNY 89, Kentucky 50

Semifinals: CCNY 62, Duquesne 52; Bradley 83, St. John's 72

Championship: CCNY 69, Bradley 61

Consolation: St. John's 69, Duquesne 67

Top Ten

AP

Bradley
Ohio State
Kentucky
Holy Cross
North Carolina State
Duquesne
UCLA
Western Kentucky
St. John's
LaSalle

All-Americans

AP

Bob Cousy, Holy Cross
Dick Schnittker, Ohio State
Paul Arizin, Villanova
Paul Unruh, Bradley
Kevin O'Shea, Notre Dame

UP

Dick Schnittker, Ohio State
Paul Unruh, Bradley
Paul Arizin, Villanova
Bob Cousy, Holy Cross
Kevin O'Shea, Notre Dame

THE SCANDALS

A part of basketball will always turn away its face in shame. A marvelous game played honestly by so many young men will always have, dark in its history, the record of those who played the game not always to win. The fear is never far away that those tragedies may leave their mark again.

The name for basketball's tragedy varies, but each is pronounced with the bite of bitterness and contempt: "Scandal," "Fix," "Dump." There's no trace of dignity to any of them.

The basketball team of City College of New York was returning home by train from Philadelphia on February 19, 1951. CCNY had just scored an impressive victory over Temple, and people were talking about CCNY as the greatest college team of all time. It had won both the National Invitation Tournament and the National Collegiate Athletic Association tournament in 1949–50 with a team composed mostly of sophomores. They and 20,000 undergraduates had made a cheer called "Allagaroo" ring throughout the land. No other team had ever won the NIT and NCAA in the same season, and these young men were still growing, still improving.

"The kids were all gay, having a good time celebrating their big victory. They were terrific against Temple," observed the coach, Nat Holman, who was then known as Mr. Basketball. He was one of the early greats of the game, a player with the Original Celtics, a pioneer, an innovator as coach for generations at CCNY.

"As we neared New Brunswick (N. J.) a gentleman approached me, apologized and said, 'I have some bad news for you, Nat. I've got orders to pick up some of your boys. But I don't want to make a scene.' " The gentleman was from the office of the District Attorney of New York.

"I took the boys aside one at a time and told them I wanted to speak to them when we got to Pennsylvania Station," Holman said. "When we arrived I told them individually, 'When they speak to you, boys, tell them the truth. If your conscience is clear, you have nothing to fear.' "

Tragically, there was so much to fear.

There had been hints of the boil that was building under the skin. In 1945, five Brooklyn College players admitted they had accepted bribes to throw their game with Akron, which was never played. Rumors flowed after that.

In 1949, a George Washington University player reported that he had been approached by gamblers asking that he "do business" with them. There were other signs for everybody to read. They were there in the arenas in the lust of the crowd as it screamed in the last moments of a game. It wasn't only the enthusiastic rooting of the fans for their team to win; some of the fervor was from those to whom the final margin of victory meant winning or losing a bet.

The point spread, as established by bookmakers, is a device to equalize two teams for betting purposes. If one team is considered by the bookmakers to be five points better than the other, then the spread is five points. If a bettor puts his money on the favorite and the team wins by more than the spread, he collects. If the team wins by less than the spread or loses—that difference is inconsequential in gambling terms—the bettor loses. Thus, the margin of victory is actually more important than the outcome of the game. Even if a team is so far behind in the last few minutes of a game that it has no chance of winning, the bettors still can hope that it will manage to beat the spread.

Early in 1951 the rumors of wrongdoing turned into fact. Junius Kellogg, a 6-8 star at Manhattan College, reported that he had been offered $1,000 to control the point spread of a game. Two of his teammates and three gamblers were arrested. Kellogg was far from the best player in the country, but none could have been more honest. The arrests to which Kellogg's testimony led were just a prelude.

The investigation of the 1951 basketball scandal showed that between 1947 and 1950, 86 games had been fixed in 23 cities in 17 states by 32 players from seven colleges: CCNY, LIU, NYU, Manhattan, Kentucky, Bradley, and Toledo. And hardly anybody was certain that all the guilty parties had been caught.

The collusion did not stop there, however. The lesson was not learned. In 1961 another scandal involved 37 players from 22 colleges. New York District Attorney Frank Hogan was now almost as well known a basketball figure as Dr. Naismith.

Still there was more. In 1965 two Seattle University players were arrested. Each time the sports world hoped it would be the last time.

No sport has ever been so damaged as college basketball. Baseball had a scandal in 1919 that gave the tag "Black Sox" to every dishonest athlete since. But that incident involved only one team and there has been no hint of anything shady since. Professional football has had one significant incident of two players being suspended for a year for betting on games, but there has been no evidence of point fixing. College football has had only a few minor incidents.

Basketball stands apart, perhaps because of the nature of the game. It is a fluid game with both teams scoring repeatedly. It is played with only five on a side, and if one star or two stars on an outstanding team could be controlled, then the margin of victory or even the winning or losing could be altered. One missed layup and two properly-directed bad passes could turn an 11-point margin into a five-point spread. Or the star of the underdog team could make sure that his team lost by more than the bookmakers expected.

The 1951 scandal took a terrible toll of the stars of the game. Most of them have paid for their parts. Professional careers that might have been worth fortunes were wiped out, others never began. Those players who destroyed so much of their lives hardly had a chance to spend the money.

"Tell any others who are tempted to do what I did to look at me," one of the players lamented. "I'm a fine example. I did it because I wanted to be grown up. Sounds funny, doesn't it? I mean I was sick and tired of asking my father for money all the time."

Some of the explanation was simply need. Some of the players were married and had children. Basketball and school didn't leave much time for a man to earn what it took to feed a family. For some others it was easy to blame New York and the environment of Madison Square Garden. In Lexington, University of Kentucky coach Adolph Rupp pontificated that the gamblers couldn't touch his boys "with a 10-foot pole."

Bradley, the team CCNY had beaten in the finals of both tournaments, was implicated. Three of its players were arrested. Then came Kentucky, with the stars of Rupp's two-time NCAA champions.

It was easy for the public, which didn't know the machinery of recruiting and producing big-time basketball, to blame the players. Only days before Kentucky was implicated, Rupp had spoken out for public leniency toward the other players involved. "The Chicago Black Sox threw games," Rupp said, "but these kids shaved only points."

However, among the games the Kentucky players tried to shave was the Loyola of Chicago game in the 1949 NIT. Mighty Kentucky ended up losing, 67-56.

In Madison Square Garden, college basketball doubleheaders had filled the 18,000 seats to the limit of the fire laws. That's where LIU first made itself known to basketball fans in California, Florida, and Illinois.

In 1952 heartbroken Clair Bee, coach of LIU, wrote in the *Saturday Evening Post:*

> " 'I'm bringing in all these people and playing my heart out for them,' the boys must have said to themselves. 'Clair Bee is getting all the credit and Ned Irish [Madison Square Garden president] and the college are getting all the gravy. Where do I come in?'
>
> " . . . The point system enabled fixers to approach players with propositions that seemed to take the curse off dishonesty. 'What's the difference, kid, if you win by eight points instead of 10?' they said. 'You're not letting down the school or the team. We're not asking you to lose the game. Just ease up a little. Everybody's making a good thing out of basketball. Don't be a sucker. There's a thousand bucks in it for you.'
>
> "Boys who fell for that spiel were tragically wrong on two counts. There is no degree of honesty, of course. Shaving points was just as much a criminal offense, morally and legally, as throwing games. That, too, came inevitably when fixers forced players to go all the way by threatening them with exposure."

Judge Saul B. Streit, who presided at the players' trial, had still stronger evidence to uncover in the courtroom. A judge with a famous reputation for austerity, he pointed to the education the basketball players were receiving on their scholarships. Two CCNY players had been admitted through forged entrance papers. The school later admitted that four other players had matriculated the same way.

Judge Streit said that two players were attending college and remaining eligible with IQs in the 80s. In his senior year the academic load of one of the players consisted of public speaking, oil painting, rhythm and dance, and a music seminar.

Still, 10 years later, college basketball had to learn the same lesson again. The names could go on another list, and then another list. The crimes were still the same, just other names at other schools, and sometimes the same schools.

When Joe Lapchick returned from the professional Knickerbockers to coach at St. John's University he had assembled a scrapbook to show his players. Before each season they looked at the black pages with their clippings of the scandals, the pictures with the tortured young faces of basketball heroes staring at courtroom floors, surrounded by detectives and unshaven racketeer types. When Lapchick retired, he passed his scrapbook on to his successor, Lou Carnesecca. Pages have been added to keep up with the news: St. Joseph's, Connecticut, Seattle, Seton Hall . . .

How thick the book grows depends on overzealous alumni, unscrupulous coaches, and indifferent college presidents as much as on the players themselves.

1950–51

Revelations of the scandal still had not reached their full extent when the season began. Kentucky, after a year's absence from the throne, was again crowned NCAA champion and became the first team to win the title three times.

Kentucky was fortunate to make it into the NCAA tourney since one of its two losses of the season came in the championship game of the Southeastern Conference tournament when Vanderbilt beat the Wildcats, 61-57. But in a rule change implemented this season, the NCAA berth went to the team with the best regular-season record and not the conference tournament winner, as in the past.

Cliff Hagan (6) leads Kentucky against St. John's in NCAA semifinal.

The NCAA field was expanded to 16 teams, but it made little difference to Kentucky, led by 7-foot Bill Spivey, Frank Ramsey, and sophomore substitute Cliff Hagan. By a 68-58 margin, the Wildcats beat Big Seven champion Kansas State, with Ernie Barrett and Lew Hitch, in the championship game. Spivey grabbed 55 rebounds and earned the MVP award, although Don Sunderlage of Big Ten champion Illinois, which took third place in the tourney, set four individual records.

Roland "The Cat" Minson and Mel Hutchins paced Brigham Young, Skyline Conference champion, to the NIT crown with a 62-43 victory over Dayton in the final game. Minson was voted MVP while Dayton's Don Meineke, who led the nation with a 51.2 field goal accuracy percentage, scored 85 points in four games for scoring honors.

Duke's Dick Groat, a future major league baseball star, scored 831 points, attempted 338 free throws and made 261 of them, all single season records. Bill Mlkvy of Temple had the highest single season average ever, 29.2 points a game, while taking a record 964 shots.

Lou Rossini was a last minute replacement as coach at Columbia and the Lions, led by John Azary, responded by winning all 22 regular season games and the Ivy League championship. Sam Ranzino, Paul Horvath, and Vic Bubas led North Carolina State to still another

Southern Conference title, although the Wolfpack was pushed by West Virginia, with scoring hotshot Mark Workman. Oklahoma A&M, behind Gale McArthur, edged Bradley and St. Louis for the Missouri Valley Conference title. Walter Davis, the 1952 Olympic high jump champion, led Texas A&M to a tie with Texas and Texas Christian in the Southwest Conference.

St. John's, sparked by Bob "Zeke" Zawoluk and Al McGuire, was the leading independent, while Seton Hall, with 6-10 Walter Dukes, was also strong. Larry Hennessey led Villanova and Seattle featured the "Mighty Mites," twins Johnny and Eddie O'Brien, among other independents. Also strong were LaSalle, Holy Cross, Louisville, Toledo, Portland, St. Bonaventure, San Jose, and Lawrence Tech.

Conference champions were Washington, Pacific Coast; Arizona, Border; Texas Christian, Texas and Texas A&M, tied, Southwest; Montana State, Rocky Mountain; Connecticut, Yankee; Murray State, Ohio Valley; and Pepperdine, California Collegiate Athletic Association. Cincinnati lost its first league game in three years but retained the Mid-American Conference title.

NCAA Championship

At Minneapolis

Kentucky (68)	FG	FT	Pts.	Kansas State (58)	FG	FT	Pts.
Whitaker	4	1	9	Head	3	2	8
Linville	2	4	8	Stone	3	6	12
Spivey	9	4	22	Hitch	6	1	13
Ramsey	4	1	9	Barrett	2	0	4
Watson	3	2	8	Iverson	3	1	7
Hagan	5	0	10	Rousey	2	0	4
Ts'r'p'lous	1	0	2	Gibson	0	1	1
Newton	0	0	0	Upson	0	0	0
				Knostman	1	1	3
				Peck	2	0	4
				Schuyler	1	0	2
Totals	28	12	68		23	12	58

NIT Championship

At New York

Brigham Young (62)	FG	FT	Pts.	Dayton (43)	FG	FT	Pts.
Richey	2	1	5	Boyle	2	1	5
Hillman	3	2	8	Oberst	0	0	0
Craig	0	1	1	Hickey	1	0	2
Minson	11	4	26	Grigsby	0	1	1
Thorne	0	0	0	Joseph	2	0	4
Hutchins	3	0	6	Meineke	1	5	7
Jarman	0	0	0	Taylor	0	0	0
Christensen	4	1	9	Campbell	1	1	3
Heaps	0	0	0	Stein	0	0	0
Jones	0	0	0	Norris	7	6	20
Romney	2	3	7	Flynn	0	1	1
Olson	0	0	0	Hough	0	0	0
Totals	25	12	62		14	15	43

NCAA Scores

REGIONALS

East

First Round: St. John's 63, Connecticut 52; Kentucky 79, Louisville 68; North Carolina State 67, Villanova 62; Illinois 79, Columbia 71

Semifinals: Kentucky 59, St. John's 43; Illinois 84, North Carolina State 70

Championship: Kentucky 76, Illinois 74

West

First Round: Washington 62, Texas A&M 40; Oklahoma A&M 50, Montana State 46; Brigham Young 68, San Jose 61; Kansas State 61, Arizona 59

Semifinals: Oklahoma A&M 61, Washington 57; Kansas State 64, Brigham Young 54

Championship: Kansas State 68, Oklahoma A&M 44

FINALS

Championship: Kentucky 68, Kansas State 58

Consolation: Illinois 61, Oklahoma A&M 46

NIT Scores

First Round: Dayton 77, Lawrence Tech 71; Seton Hall 71, Beloit 57; St. Louis 73, LaSalle 61; St. Bonaventure 70, Cincinnati 67

Quarterfinals: St. John's 60, St. Bonaventure 58; Brigham Young 75, St. Louis 58; Dayton 74, Arizona 68; Seton Hall 71, North Carolina State 59

Semifinals: Dayton 69, St. John's 62; Brigham Young 69, Seton Hall 59

Championship: Brigham Young 62, Dayton 43

Consolation: St. John's 70, Seton Hall 68

Top Ten

AP	UP
Kentucky	Kentucky
Oklahoma A&M	Oklahoma A&M
Columbia	Kansas State
Kansas State	Illinois
Illinois	Columbia
Bradley	Bradley
Indiana	North Carolina State
North Carolina State	Indiana
St. John's	St. John's
St. Louis	Brigham Young

All-Americans

AP	UP
Bill Mlkvy, Temple	Bill Mlkvy, Temple
Sam Ranzino, N. C. State	Sam Ranzino, N. C. State
Bill Spivey, Kentucky	Bill Spivey, Kentucky
Gene Melchiorre, Bradley	Gene Melchiorre, Bradley
Clyde Lovellette, Kansas	Clyde Lovellette, Kansas

1951–52

With the U.S. involvement in the Korean War, a number of teams faced manpower shortages. As a result, many conferences made freshmen eligible for varsity competition. The freshmen who played didn't have the same effect as freshmen did during World War II, but they did add unpredictability.

St. John's surprised the No. 1 and No. 2 rated teams in the country, Kentucky and Illinois, to gain a berth in the NCAA finale against Kansas. The Jayhawks whipped St. John's 80-63, as "Man Mountain" Clyde Lovellette, at 6-9, scored 33 points and won MVP honors for Kansas. Kansas earned the championship berth by downing upstart Santa Clara, led by

Seattle's Johnny O'Brien set an individual scoring record with this free throw.

Kenny Sears, which had previously upset UCLA and Wyoming.

Lovellette ended his career with a national record of 1,888 points, breaking the old record of 1,886 set two days earlier by Dick Groat of Duke. Lovellette also led the nation in scoring, with a 28.4-point-per-game average, while Groat, who averaged 26.0 points, led the country in assists. Bob Pettit of Louisiana State and Chuck Darling of Iowa each averaged 25.5 points.

Tom Gola, a freshman, and Norm Grekin shared the MVP award as they led LaSalle to a 75-64 victory over Dayton before 18,845 fans to win the NIT championship. Dayton, which finished second for the second consecutive year, was led by Don Meineke, who repeated as top scorer with 84 points in four games.

West Virginia, with 6-9 Mark Workman, had the best regular-season record in the Southern Conference, but lost the post-season tournament to North Carolina State, paced by Lee Terrell. Kentucky's one-two punch of Cliff Hagan and Frank Ramsey enabled the Wildcats to easily outdistance the rest of the teams in the Southeastern Conference.

The balanced play of Rod Fletcher, Irv Bemoras, Clive Follmer, and sophomore Johnny Kerr put Illinois at the top of the Big Ten. Wyoming won the Skyline Conference title in the expanded league, now eight teams with the inclusion of Montana and New Mexico. UCLA, with Don Johnson, beat Washington, despite the hook-shot artistry of Bob Houbregs, for the Pacific Coast Conference crown. Western Kentucky's 6-9 Art Spoelstra led the Hilltoppers to the Ohio Valley Conference championship.

Other conference champions: Princeton, Ivy League; Connecticut, Yankee; Texas Christian, Southwest; Colorado State and Montana State, tied, Rocky Mountain; Miami (O.) and Western Michigan, tied, Mid-American; New Mexico A&M and West Texas State, tied, Border; and Pepperdine, California Collegiate Athletic Association.

"Zeke" Zawoluk, Ron MacGilvary, and Jack McMahon led St. John's to pre-eminence among independents, while other powers included Seton Hall, Holy Cross, DePaul, Oklahoma City, Penn State, and Boston College. Seattle, with 5-9 Johnny O'Brien becoming the first player to score more than 1,000 points (1,051) in one season, ran up a 29-8 record, including an 84-81 triumph over the Harlem Globetrotters. Other strong teams were Louisville, Mississippi Southern, Memphis State, Duke, Indiana, and Marquette.

Among the better players were Bill Stauffer, Missouri; Ab Nicholas, Wisconsin; Ernie Beck, Pennsylvania; Glenn Smith, Utah; Dickie Hemric, Wake Forest; and future professional football star Rick Casares, Florida.

NCAA Championship

At Seattle

Kansas (80)	FG	FT	Pts.	St. John's (63)	FG	FT	Pts.
Kenney	4	4	12	McMahon	6	1	13
Davenport	0	0	0	Davis	1	2	4
Keller	1	0	2	Walsh	3	0	6
Hoag	2	5	9	Zawoluk	7	6	20
Lovellette	12	9	33	Peterson	0	0	0
Born	0	0	0	MacGilvray	3	2	8
D. Kelley	2	3	7	Giancontieri	0	0	0
Smith	0	0	0	Duckett	2	2	6
Lienhard	5	2	12	Walker	0	0	0
Hougland	2	1	5	McMorrow	1	0	2
Heitholt	0	0	0	Sagona	2	0	4
A. Kelley	0	0	0				
Totals	28	24	80		25	13	63

NIT Championship

At New York

LaSalle (75)	FG	FT	Pts.	Dayton (64)	FG	FT	Pts.
Grekin	5	5	15	Grigsby	8	2	18
Iehle	8	2	18	Meineke	4	5	13
Jones	0	1	1	Paxson	5	5	15
Gilson	0	0	0	Taylor	0	0	0
O'Hara	0	0	0	Donoher	0	0	0
Gola	9	4	22	Horan	3	0	6
Moore	3	2	8	Norris	3	1	7
Donnelly	5	1	11	Boyle	0	0	0
French	0	0	0	Sallee	1	1	3
Altieri	0	0	0	Harris	0	0	0
				Joseph	1	0	2
				Weywood	0	0	0
Totals	30	15	75		25	14	64

NCAA Scores

REGIONALS

East

Semifinals: Kentucky 82, Penn State 54; St. John's 60, North Carolina State 49

Championship: St. John's 64, Kentucky 57

Mideast

Semifinals: Illinois 80, Dayton 61; Duquesne 60, Princeton 49

Championship: Illinois 74, Duquesne 68

Midwest

Semifinals: Kansas 68, Texas Christian 64; St. Louis 62, New Mexico A&M 53

Championship: Kansas 74, St. Louis 55

Far West

Semifinals: Santa Clara 68, UCLA 59; Wyoming 54, Oklahoma City 48

Championship: Santa Clara 56, Wyoming 53

FINALS

Semifinals: Kansas 74, Santa Clara 55; St. John's 61, Illinois 59

Championship: Kansas 80, St. John's 63

Consolation: Illinois 67, Santa Clara 64

NIT Scores

First Round: Dayton 81, NYU 66; Western Kentucky 62, Louisville 59; LaSalle 80, Seton Hall 76; Holy Cross 77, Seattle 72

Quarterfinals: St. Bonaventure 70, Western Kentucky 69; LaSalle 51, St. John's 45; Duquesne 78, Holy Cross 68; Dayton 68, St. Louis 58

Semifinals: LaSalle 59, Duquesne 46; Dayton 69, St. Bonaventure 62

Championship: LaSalle 75, Dayton 64

Consolation: St. Bonaventure 48, Duquesne 34

Top Ten

AP	UP
Kentucky	Kentucky
Illinois	Illinois
Kansas State	Kansas
Duquesne	Duquesne
St. Louis	Washington
Washington	Kansas State
Iowa	St. Louis
Kansas	Iowa
West Virginia	St. John's
St. John's	Wyoming

All-Americans

AP	UP
Chuck Darling, Iowa	Chuck Darling, Iowa
Mark Workman, West Virginia	Mark Workman, West Virginia
Clyde Lovellette, Kansas	Clyde Lovellette, Kansas
Dick Groat, Duke	Dick Groat, Duke
Cliff Hagan, Kentucky	Cliff Hagan, Kentucky

1952–53

Indiana and Seton Hall, each with a 6-10 center, were rated one-two in the wire service polls, and went on to win the NCAA and NIT championships, respectively.

Indiana counted on 6-3 Bob Leonard and lanky sophomore pivotman Don Schlundt to win its first Big Ten title ever. The Hoosiers and Kansas' surprising Jayhawks then waded through an expanded 22-team field before meeting for the NCAA crown. Indiana won, 69-68, on a free throw by Leonard with 27 seconds remaining. Kansas' southpaw center, Bertram H. Born, who scored 26 points, was named MVP. This was the first time a player on a non-champion team received the NCAA's MVP award.

Seton Hall used the inside strength of big Walter Dukes and the steady outside play of Richie Regan to cop the NIT. The Pirates downed St. John's, 58-46, as Dukes won MVP honors. He scored 70 points in three games.

Kentucky was barred from Southeastern Conference competition for recruiting violations. In the Wildcats' absence, the Tigers of Louisiana State, led by sophomore Bob Pettit, won the crown. In the Southern Conference tournament, Dickie Hemric led Wake Forest to a 71-70 triumph over regular-season champion North Carolina State. Bob Houbregs led Washington to the Pacific Coast Conference championship.

Other conference champions: Miami (O.), Mid-American; Oklahoma A&M, Missouri Valley; Eastern Kentucky, Ohio Valley; Texas Christian, Southwest; Hardin-Simmons and

Niagara's Larry Costello (69) watches as Seton Hall's Walter Dukes (20) scores.

NIAGAR
69
TON HALL
20
AGARA
15

Arizona, tied, Border; Connecticut, Yankee; Wyoming, Skyline; Idaho State, Rocky Mountain; and Santa Clara and San Francisco shared the crown in the new California Basketball Association.

Among the outstanding independents were LaSalle, with Tom Gola; Duquesne, paced by Dick Ricketts and Jim Tucker; Fordham, with the nation's leading rebounder in Ed Conlin; Notre Dame; DePaul; Louisville; Mississippi Southern; East Tennessee; and Manhattan. Highly regarded Niagara, with set-shot artist Larry Costello, had to go into six overtimes to beat Siena, 88-81.

The one-and-one free throw rule, awarding a bonus shot, sent scoring averages soaring. Furman scored more points, 90.2 per game, and connected on more shots, 44.4 per cent, than any team had before. Leading Furman was Frank Selvy, whose 29.5-point-per-game average was tops in the nation. Villanova's Larry Hennessey was a shade behind, averaging 29.2. Oklahoma A&M, with Bob Mattick at center, won its 14th defensive title in 19 years, allowing a record high 53.8 points per game.

Some of the outstanding players were Togo Palazzi, Holy Cross; Arnie Short, Oklahoma City; Al Bianchi, Bowling Green; Al Ferrari, Michigan State; Gene Shue, Maryland; Dick Knostman, Kansas State; and rebounder Charlie Slack and shooter Walt Walowac at Marshall.

Johnny O'Brien completed three years at Seattle in which he played 99 games, scored 2,537 points on 838 field goals and 861 free throws, all national records.

NCAA Championship

At Kansas City

Indiana (69)	FG	FT	Pts.	Kansas (68)	FG	FT	Pts.
Kraak	5	7	17	Patterson	1	7	9
DeaKyne	0	0	0	A. Kelley	7	6	20
Farley	1	0	2	Davenport	0	0	0
Schlundt	11	8	30	Born	8	10	26
White	1	0	2	Smith	0	1	1
Leonard	5	2	12	Alberts	0	0	0
Poff	0	0	0	D. Kelley	3	2	8
Scott	2	2	6	Reich	2	0	4
Byers	0	0	0				
Totals	25	19	69		21	26	68

NIT Championship

At New York

Seton Hall (58)	FG	FT	Pts.	St. John's (46)	FG	FT	Pts.
Nathanic	1	2	4	Cunningham	2	0	4
Hannon	1	0	2	Walker	2	0	4
Ring	3	1	7	McMorrow	1	0	2
Dukes	5	11	21	Satalino	3	1	7
Regan	5	3	13	Sagona	0	0	0
Brooks	4	3	11	Davis	5	1	11
O'Hara	0	0	0	Peterson	0	0	0
				Duckett	7	2	16
				Walsh	1	0	2
				Romano	0	0	0
				Nolan	0	0	0
				Giancontieri	0	0	0
Totals	19	20	58		21	4	46

NCAA Scores

REGIONALS

East

First Round: Lebanon Valley 80, Fordham 67; Holy Cross 87, Navy 74

Semifinals: Louisiana State 89, Lebanon Valley 76; Holy Cross 79, Wake Forest 71

Championship: Louisiana State 81, Holy Cross 73

Mideast

First Round: Notre Dame 72, Eastern Kentucky 57; DePaul 74, Miami (O.) 72

Semifinals: Notre Dame 69, Pennsylvania 57; Indiana 82, DePaul 80

Championship: Indiana 79, Notre Dame 66

NIT Scores

First Round: Duquesne 88, Tulsa 69; Louisville 92, Georgetown 79; St. John's 81, St. Louis 66; Niagara 82, Brigham Young 76

Quarterfinals: St. John's 75, LaSalle 74; Manhattan 79, Louisville 66; Seton Hall 79, Niagara 74; Duquesne 69, Western Kentucky 61

Semifinals: Seton Hall 74, Manhattan 56; St. John's 64, Duquesne 55

Championship: Seton Hall 58, St. John's 46

Consolation: Duquesne 81, Manhattan 67

NCAA Scores (cont.)

Midwest

Semifinals: Oklahoma A&M 71, Texas Christian 54; Kansas 73, Oklahoma City 65

Championship: Kansas 61, Oklahoma A&M 55

Far West

First Round: Seattle 88, Idaho State 77; Santa Clara 81, Hardin-Simmons 56

Semifinals: Washington 92, Seattle 70; Santa Clara 67, Wyoming 52

Championship: Washington 74, Santa Clara 62

FINALS

Semifinals: Indiana 80, Louisiana State 67; Kansas 79, Washington 53

Championship: Indiana 69, Kansas 68

Consolation: Washington 88, Louisiana State 69

Top Ten

AP	UP
Indiana	Indiana
Seton Hall	Washington
Kansas	LaSalle
Washington	Seton Hall
Louisiana State	Kansas
LaSalle	Louisiana State
St. John's	Oklahoma A&M
Oklahoma A&M	North Carolina State
Duquesne	Kansas State
Notre Dame	Illinois

All-Americans

AP	UP
Walter Dukes, Seton Hall	Walter Dukes, Seton Hall
John O'Brien, Seattle	John O'Brien, Seattle
Bob Houbregs, Washington	Bob Houbregs, Washington
Tom Gola, LaSalle	Tom Gola, LaSalle
Ernie Beck, Pennsylvania	Ernie Beck, Pennsylvania

1953–54

Scoring reached new peaks as Furman's Frank Selvy scored 100 points in a single game and broke virtually every major college scoring record on the books. Selvy finished with a 41.7 average for the season. His 100 points came against Newberry. Selvy scored 50 or more points in eight games. Among his career marks were most field goals (922), most points (2,538) and best average (32.5 points a game).

Eastern independents cornered the market on team laurels as LaSalle downed Bradley, 92-76, for the NCAA title, and Holy Cross beat Duquesne, 71-62, for the NIT championship.

Versatile Tom Gola led LaSalle past a first-round scare from Fordham and Eddie Conlin, to sweep past North Carolina State, Navy, Penn State, and Bradley for the NCAA crown in an expanded 24-team field. Gola was MVP and high scorer with 114 points.

Holy Cross, with Togo Palazzi and Tom Heinsohn, beat top-seeded Duquesne, despite the presence of Dick Ricketts, Jim Tucker, and sophomore Sihugo Green. Palazzi was MVP while scoring honors went to Tom Marshall of Western Kentucky's Ohio Valley Conference champions with 82 points.

Kentucky, led by Cliff Hagan, Frank Ramsey and Lou Tsiropoulos, finished in a 14-0 tie with Bob Pettit-led Louisiana State in the Southeastern Conference. But the Wildcats, with a 25-0 overall record, declined post-season tournament competition when their three graduate student stars were declared ineligible for tournament play.

Led by Selvy, Furman set team marks for highest average, 91.7 points a game, and accuracy, 45.6 percent from the field. Other new team highs included most free throws attempted, 1,263, and most free throws made, 865, both by Bradley.

Don Schlundt, Bob Leonard, and Dick Farley led Indiana to the Big Ten crown while Bob Mattick paced Oklahoma A&M to the Missouri Valley title. B. H. Born was back to take Kansas to a Big Seven Conference tie with Oklahoma. Southern California, with Roy Irvin, won the Pacific Coast Conference championship in a playoff with Oregon State, featuring 7-3 Wade Halbrook.

Other conference champions: Colorado A&M, Skyline; Cornell, Ivy League; Santa Clara, California Basketball Association; Texas and Rice, tied, Southwest; Texas Tech, Border; and

Toledo, Mid-American. North Carolina State won the Southern Conference tournament after George Washington had finished atop the regular season standings.

Among the independents, Notre Dame, with Dick Rosenthal, and Penn State, with Jesse Arnelle, were highly rated. Also strong were Oklahoma City, with Arnie Short; Niagara, with Larry Costello; Navy, with John Clune; and Seattle, which had its 26-game winning streak snapped in the NCAA tourney by Rocky Mountain Conference champion Idaho State.

Other strong teams were Illinois, with Johnny Kerr; Iowa, led by Carl Cain; Maryland, with Gene Shue; Ohio State, with Paul Ebert; Marshall, with Walt Walowac; Wichita, with Cleo Littleton; and St. Francis of Loretto, Pa., with Maurice Stokes.

Furman's Frank Selvy set major college scoring records with a 100-point game.

NCAA Championship

At Kansas City

LaSalle (92)	FG	FT	Pts.	Bradley (76)	FG	FT	Pts.
Singley	8	7	23	Petersen	4	2	10
Greenberg	2	1	5	Babetch	0	0	0
Maples	2	0	4	King	3	6	12
Blatcher	11	1	23	Gower	0	1	1
Gola	7	5	19	Estergard	3	11	17
O'Malley	5	1	11	Carney	3	11	17
Yodsnukis	0	0	0	Utt	0	0	0
O'Hara	2	3	7	Kent	8	0	16
				Riley	1	1	3
Totals	37	18	92		22	32	76

NIT Championship

At New York

Holy Cross (71)	FG	FT	Pts.	Duquesne (62)	FG	FT	Pts.
Palazzi	6	8	20	Ricketts	6	1	13
Liebler	4	2	10	Green	6	4	16
Heinsohn	6	8	20	Fallon	0	0	0
Kasprazk	3	0	6	Iezza	0	0	0
Perry	2	3	7	Tucker	4	3	11
Prothovich	1	3	5	Johnson	0	2	2
Supronowicz	1	0	2	Winograd	4	7	15
Early	0	1	1	Dambrot	2	1	5
Totals	23	25	71		22	18	62

NCAA Scores

REGIONALS

East

First Round: LaSalle 76, Fordham 74; North Carolina State 75, George Washington 73; Navy 85, Connecticut 80

Semifinals: LaSalle 88, North Carolina State 81; Navy 69, Cornell 67

Championship: LaSalle 64, Navy 48

Mideast

First Round: Penn State 62, Toledo 50; Notre Dame 80, Loyola (La.) 70

Semifinals: Penn State 78, Louisiana State 70; Notre Dame 65, Indiana 64

Championship: Penn State 71, Notre Dame 63

Midwest

First Round: Bradley 61, Oklahoma City 55

Semifinals: Bradley 76, Colorado 64; Oklahoma A&M 51, Rice 45

Championship: Bradley 71, Oklahoma A&M 57

Far West

First Round: Idaho State 77, Seattle 75; Santa Clara 73, Texas Tech 64

Semifinals: Southern California 73, Idaho State 59; Santa Clara 73, Colorado A&M 50

Championship: Southern California 66, Santa Clara 65

FINALS

Semifinals: LaSalle 69, Penn State 54; Bradley 74, Southern California 72

Championship: LaSalle 92, Bradley 76

Consolation: Penn State 70, Southern California 61

NIT Scores

First Round: St. Francis (N. Y.) 60, Louisville 55; Dayton 90, Manhattan 79; Bowling Green 88, Wichita 84; St. Francis (Pa.) 81, Brigham Young 68

Quarterfinals: Western Kentucky 95, Bowling Green 81; Niagara 77, Dayton 74; Duquesne 69, St. Francis (Pa.) 63; Holy Cross 93, St. Francis (N. Y.) 69

Semifinals: Duquesne 66, Niagara 51; Holy Cross 75, Western Kentucky 69

Championship: Holy Cross 71, Duquesne 62

Consolation: Niagara 71, Western Kentucky 65

Top Ten

AP	UP
Kentucky	Indiana
LaSalle	Kentucky
Holy Cross	Duquesne
Indiana	Oklahoma A&M
Duquesne	Notre Dame
Notre Dame	Western Kentucky
Bradley	Kansas
Western Kentucky	Louisiana State
Penn State	Holy Cross
Oklahoma A&M	Iowa

All-Americans

AP	UP
Frank Selvy, Furman	Frank Selvy, Furman
Don Schlundt, Indiana	Don Schlundt, Indiana
Tom Gola, LaSalle	Tom Gola, LaSalle
Cliff Hagan, Kentucky	Cliff Hagan, Kentucky
Bob Pettit, Louisiana State	Bob Pettit, Louisiana State

1954–55

A lone defeat by UCLA early in the season prevented San Francisco from becoming the first unbeaten team to win an NCAA championship. The Dons, who led the nation in defense by allowing only 52.1 points a game, finished the year by winning 26 straight games, for a 28-1 record.

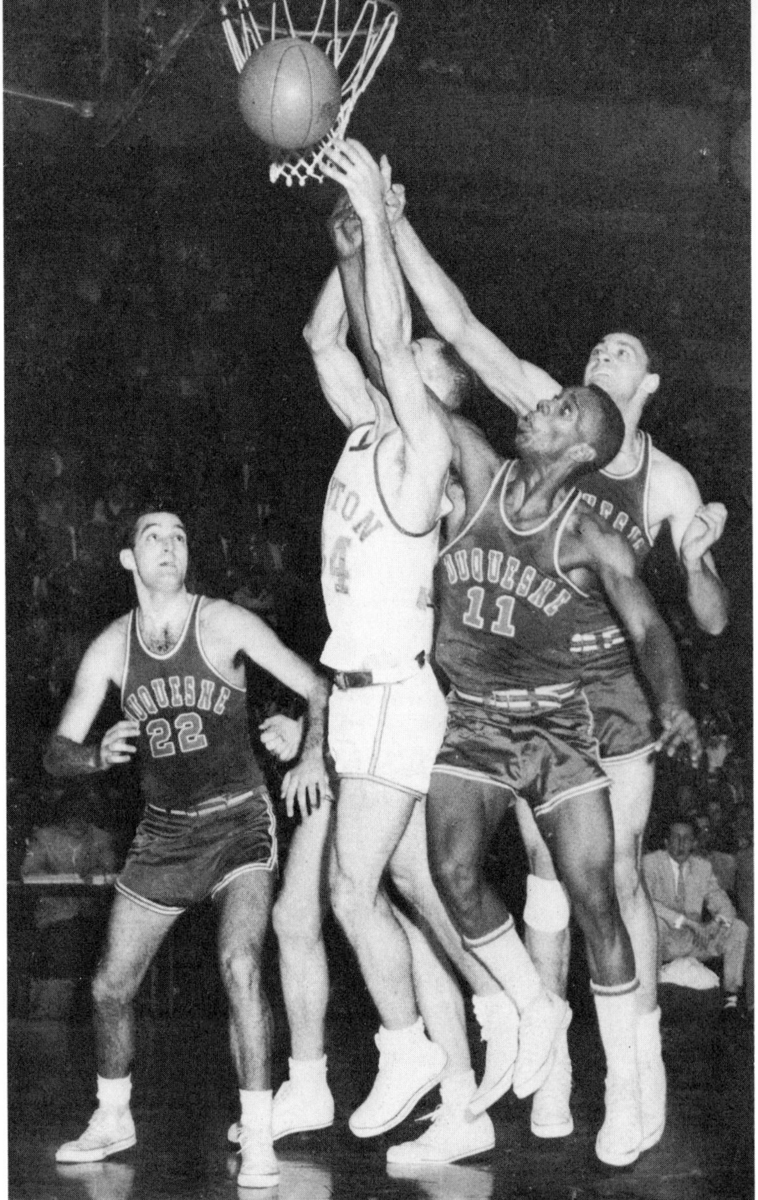

Duquesne's Si Green (11) scored 33 in NIT finale.

The NCAA title came on a 77-63 victory over defending champion LaSalle, with Tom Gola. San Francisco center Bill Russell was MVP and tournament high scorer with 118 points in five games. Prior to the finale, the closest call for the Dons, the California Basketball Association champions, was a one-point victory over Pacific Coast Conference champion Oregon State, led by 7-3 Wade Halbrook, in the NCAA quarterfinals.

Si Green and Dick Ricketts combined for 56 of Duquesne's 70 points as the Iron Dukes downed Dayton, 70-58, for the NIT crown. MVP honors went to Maurice Stokes of fourth-place St. Francis of Loretto, Pa. Stokes scored a record 124 points in four games, including 43 against Dayton.

A crowd of 20,176 saw Minnesota, with Chuck Mencel and Dick Garmaker, clinch the Big Ten championship against Iowa, led by Deacon Davis. Kentucky won the Southeastern Conference title even though its 129-game home court winning streak was snapped by lowly Georgia Tech. Princeton beat Columbia and Penn in a playoff for the Ivy League crown, and

Jim Krebs led Southern Methodist to Southwest Conference honors. Bob Patterson sparked Tulsa to the top of the Missouri Valley Conference.

Other conference champions: North Carolina, in the newly formed Atlantic Coast; West Texas State and Texas Tech, tied, Border; Connecticut, Yankee; Idaho State, Rocky Mountain; Miami (O.), Mid-American; and Colorado, Big Seven. Western Kentucky won the regular season title in the Ohio Valley Conference, but yielded to Eastern Kentucky in the league's post-season tourney, and Art Bunte led Utah to the Skyline Conference crown.

West Virginia, with sophomore Rod "Hot Rod" Hundley, had the best record in the Southern Conference, but George Washington, with Corky Devlin, won the post-season conference tournament. Other strong teams included UCLA, with Willie Naulls; Santa Clara, with Kenny Sears; Texas Christian, with Richard O'Neal; St. Louis, with Dick Boushka; and Duke and Maryland.

Marquette, led by Terry Rand, won 22 straight games, and Manhattan, whose Ed O'Conner made a record 60.5 percent of his field goal attempts, were strong independents, as were Cincinnati, with Jack Twyman; Notre Dame, with Jack Stephens; Fordham, with Ed Conlin; Holy Cross, with Tommy Heinsohn; and Canisius, with John McCarthy. Other outstanding teams were Villanova, Penn State, Memphis State, Oklahoma City, Bradley, Seattle, Louisville, Niagara, and Seton Hall.

Marshall's Charlie Slack averaged a record 25.6 rebounds a game, while Darrell Floyd of Furman led all scorers with 35.9 points a game, just ahead of Virginia's Richard "Buzz" Wilkinson, who averaged 32.1. Floyd led Furman to its third straight scoring title, as the Paladins averaged a record 95.3 points a game. Wake Forest's Dickie Hemric finished with a career record of 2,587 total points.

NCAA Championship

At Kansas City

San Francisco (77)	FG	FT	Pts.	LaSalle (63)	FG	FT	Pts.
Mullen	4	2	10	O'Malley	4	2	10
Buchanan	3	2	8	Singley	8	4	20
Russell	9	5	23	Gola	6	4	16
Jones	10	4	24	Lewis	1	4	6
Perry	1	2	4	Greenberg	1	1	3
Wiebusch	2	0	4	Blatcher	4	0	8
Zannini	1	0	2	Maples	0	0	0
Lawless	1	0	2	Fredericks	0	0	0
Kirby	0	0	0				
Totals	31	15	77		24	15	63

NCAA Scores

REGIONALS

East

First Round: LaSalle 95, West Virginia 61; Canisius 73, Williams 60; Villanova 74, Duke 73

Semifinals: LaSalle 73, Princeton 46; Canisius 73, Villanova 71

Championship: LaSalle 99, Canisius 64

Mideast

First Round: Marquette 90, Miami (O.) 79; Penn State 59, Memphis State 55

Semifinals: Marquette 79, Kentucky 71; Iowa 82 Penn State 53

Championship: Iowa 86, Marquette 81

NIT Championship

At New York

Duquesne (70)	FG	FT	Pts.	Dayton (58)	FG	FT	Pts.
Green	13	7	33	Horan	6	8	20
Dave Ricketts	0	0	0	Almashy	0	0	0
				Parin	0	0	0
Severine	1	2	4	Walsh	0	1	1
Dick Ricketts	7	9	23	Uhl	10	5	25
				Riazzi	0	0	0
Winograd	2	2	6	Sicking	0	0	0
Fallon	1	2	4	Harris	1	2	4
				Sallee	1	0	2
				Jacoby	0	0	0
				Dieringer	0	2	2
				Fiely	2	0	4
Totals	24	22	70		20	18	58

NIT Scores

First Round: Louisville 91, Manhattan 86; Niagara 83, Lafayette 70; St. Francis (Pa.) 89, Seton Hall 78; St. Louis 110, Connecticut 103

Quarterfinals: Duquesne 74, Louisville 66; Cincinnati 85, Niagara 83; St. Francis (Pa.) 68, Holy Cross 64; Dayton 97, St. Louis 81

Semifinals: Dayton 79, St.Francis (Pa.) 73; Duquesne 65, Cincinnati 51

Championship: Duquesne 70, Dayton 58

Consolation: Cincinnati 96, St. Francis (Pa.) 91

NCAA Scores (cont.)

Midwest

First Round: Bradley 69, Oklahoma City 65

Semifinals: Bradley 81, Southern Methodist 79; Colorado 69, Tulsa 59

Championship: Colorado 93, Bradley 81

Far West

First Round: Seattle 80, Idaho State 63; San Francisco 89, West Texas State 66

Semifinals: Oregon State 83, Seattle 71; San Francisco 78; Utah 59

Championship: San Francisco 57, Oregon State 56

FINAL

Semifinals: LaSalle 76, Iowa 73; San Francisco 62, Colorado 50

Championship: San Francisco 77, LaSalle 63

Consolation: Colorado 75, Iowa 54

Top Ten

AP	UP
San Francisco	San Francisco
Kentucky	Kentucky
LaSalle	LaSalle
North Carolina State	Utah
Iowa	Iowa
Duquesne	North Carolina State
Utah	Duquesne
Marquette	Oregon State
Dayton	Marquette
Oregon State	Dayton

All-Americans

AP	UP
Tom Gola, LaSalle	Tom Gola, LaSalle
Robin Freeman, Ohio State	Bill Russell, San Francisco
Bill Russell, San Francisco	Dick Garmaker, Minnesota
Dick Ricketts, Duquesne	Si Green, Duquesne
Darrell Floyd, Furman	Dick Ricketts, Duquesne

1955–56

San Francisco, paced by 6-10 Bill Russell, won 29 straight games—stretching its unbeaten string to a record 55 games over two seasons—and successfully defended its NCAA crown.

The Dons were ranked No. 1 by everyone as they swept to the California Basketball Association title and used the best defense in the country to limit opponents to 52.2 points a game. All season long the emphasis lay on the Dons' teamwork, despite the awesome presence of Russell. In the tournament, K. C. Jones was declared ineligible, and reserve Gene Brown filled in to keep the team winning.

The spectre of unbeaten San Francisco probably frightened the two best independents, Louisville and Dayton, into the NIT. In the NCAA tourney, the Dons rolled past UCLA, Utah, and Southern Methodist before beating Big Ten champion Iowa, with Carl Cain and Bill Logan, 83-71, for the NCAA crown. So balanced was San Francisco's team play that MVP honors went to Temple's Hal Lear, who scored a record 160 points in five games in leading the Owls to a third-place finish.

Generally regarded as the No. 2 team in the country was Atlantic Coast Conference champion North Carolina State, led by Ronnie Shavlik and Vic Molodet. The Wolfpack never got a chance to test San Francisco, however, as Canisius, with John McCarthy, scored a first-round upset victory in four overtimes to oust N.C. State from NCAA play.

The NIT finale saw Louisville defeat Dayton, 93-80, for the third time in the season. Charlie Tyra, tournament high scorer and MVP, paced the Cardinals as he outplayed Dayton's 7-foot Bill Uhl. St. Joseph's hit on 31 free throws to take third place from St. Francis (N.Y.).

The free throw lane was expanded this season from six to twelve feet in an effort to neutralize a tall man's height advantage by increasing the three-second area.

Conference champions: Alabama, Southeastern; West Virginia, Southern; Southern Methodist, Southwest; Dartmouth, Ivy League; Marshall, Mid-American; Houston, Missouri Valley; Utah, Skyline; Kansas State, Big Seven; Texas Tech, Border; and Morehead State, Ohio Valley.

Darrell Floyd of Furman and Robin Freeman of Ohio State staged a two-man battle for

San Francisco's Bill Russell after deflecting shot in NCAA final against Iowa.

individual scoring honors, averaging 33.8 and 32.9 points per game, respectively. George Washington's Joe Holup was the top rebounder, grabbing 23 per game, and was the most accurate shooter, making 64.7 per cent of his field goal attempts.

Among the independents, Holy Cross, with Tommy Heinsohn, was tough, as were Duquesne, with Si Green; Notre Dame, with Lloyd Aubrey; Detroit, with Bill Ebben; DePaul, with Ron Sobieszczyk; Oklahoma City; and Seattle.

Stars included Willie Naulls, UCLA; Bob Burrow, Kentucky; Lennie Rosenbluth, North Carolina; Rod Hundley, West Virginia; Norm Stewart, Missouri; Julius McCoy, Michigan State; Jerry Harper, Alabama; Art Bunte, Utah; Paul Judson and Bill Ridley, both Illinois; Joe Capua, Wyoming; James Ray, Toledo; and Temple Tucker, Rice.

NCAA Championship

At Evanston, Ill.

San Francisco (83)	FG	FT	Pts.	Iowa (71)	FG	FT	Pts.
Boldt	7	2	16	Cain	7	3	17
Farmer	0	0	0	Schoof	5	4	14
Preaseau	3	1	7	Logan	5	2	12
Russell	11	4	26	George	0	0	0
Nelson	0	0	0	Scheuerman	4	3	11
Perry	6	2	14	Seaberg	5	7	17
Brown	6	4	16	Martel	0	0	0
Baxter	2	0	4	McConnell	0	0	0
Totals	35	13	83		26	19	71

NIT Championship

At New York

Louisville (93)	FG	FT	Pts.	Dayton (80)	FG	FT	Pts.
Darragh	4	3	11	Paxson	4	2	10
Harrah	6	0	12	McCarthy	0	0	0
Moreman	0	10	10	Lane	0	2	2
Keffer	0	0	0	Palmer	9	3	21
Tyra	11	5	27	Uhl	6	7	19
Dupont	1	0	2	Sicking	3	2	8
Rollins	6	5	17	Dieringer	2	0	4
Morgan	3	8	14	Riazzi	2	0	4
				Bockhorn	6	0	12
				Almashy	0	0	0
				Bogenrife	0	0	0
Totals	31	31	93		32	16	80

NCAA Scores

REGIONAL

East

First Round: Connecticut 84, Manhattan 75; Temple 74, Holy Cross 72; Dartmouth 61, West Virginia 59; Canisius 79, North Carolina State 78

Semifinals: Temple 65, Connecticut 59; Canisius 66, Dartmouth 58

Championship: Temple 60, Canisius 58

Mideast

First Round: Morehead State 107, Marshall 92; Wayne 72, DePaul 63

Semifinals: Kentucky 84, Wayne 64; Iowa 97 Morehead State 83

Championship: Iowa 89, Kentucky 77

Midwest

First Round: Southern Methodist 68, Texas Tech 67; Oklahoma City 91, Memphis State 81

Semifinals: Southern Methodist 89, Houston 74; Oklahoma City 97, Kansas State 93

Championship: Southern Methodist 84, Oklahoma City 63

Far West

First Round: Seattle 68, Idaho State 66

Semifinals: Utah 81, Seattle 72; San Francisco 72, UCLA 61

Championship: San Francisco 92, Utah 77

FINAL

Semifinals: San Francisco 86, Southern Methodist 68; Iowa 83, Temple 76

Championship: San Francisco 83, Iowa 71

Consolation: Temple 90, Southern Methodist 81

NIT Scores

First Round: St. Francis (N. Y.) 85, Lafayette 74; Duquesne 69; Oklahoma A&M 61; Seton Hall 96, Marquette 78; Xavier (O.) 84, St. Louis 80

Quarterfinals: Louisville 84, Duquesne 72; St. Francis (N. Y.) 74 Niagara 72; St. Joseph's 74, Seton Hall 65; Dayton 72, Xavier (O.) 68

Semifinals: Dayton 89, St. Francis (N. Y.) 58; Louisville 89, St. Joseph's 79

Championship: Louisville 93, Dayton 80

Consolation: St. Joseph's 93, St. Francis (N. Y.) 82

Top Ten

AP	UP
San Francisco	San Francisco
North Carolina State	North Carolina State
Dayton	Dayton
Iowa	Iowa
Alabama	Alabama
Louisville	Southern Methodist
Southern Methodist	Louisville
UCLA	Illinois
Kentucky	UCLA
Illinois	Vanderbilt

All-American

AP	UP
Bill Russell, San Francisco	Bill Russell, San Francisco
Robin Freeman, Ohio State	Si Green, Duquesne
Si Green, Duquesne	Robin Freeman, Ohio State
Darrell Floyd, Furman	Darrell Floyd, Furman
Tom Heinsohn, Holy Cross	K. C. Jones, San Francisco

1956–57

North Carolina withstood successive triple-overtime challenges from Michigan State and Kansas to capture the NCAA championship at the end of a 32-0 season, best record ever for a tourney winner.

The championship game was set up after Big Ten ruler Michigan State, led by Johnny Green and Jack Quiggle, pushed North Carolina into three extra periods before succumbing in a semifinal. Kansas breezed through the Western regionals into the final. The Jayhawks were led by a highly publicized sophomore, 7-foot Wilt Chamberlain, who forced the opposition to devise special defenses for him.

Atlantic Coast Conference champion North Carolina, with Lennie Rosenbluth countering Chamberlain, was pushed into three overtimes again in the championship game before downing Kansas, 54-53. Chamberlain outpolled Rosenbluth for MVP, 17-15, as he averaged 30.3 points in four games. Rosenbluth was high scorer, however, with 140 points in five games.

Kansas' Wilt Chamberlain has it as North Carolina's Len Rosenbluth reaches in NCAA final.

13

Bradley's one-two punch of Barney Cable and Shelly McMillon led the Braves to an 84-83 victory over Memphis State for the NIT championship. Win Wilfong of the losers was high scorer with 89 points in four games and took MVP honors.

Chamberlain, and Seattle's 6-5 Elgin Baylor, also a sophomore, were involved in a hot five-man battle for individual scoring honors, eventually won by South Carolina's Grady Wallace (31.2 points a game.) Mississippi's Joe Gibbon, a future major league baseball pitcher, was second with 30.0 points a game, followed by Baylor, Chamberlain, and Columbia's Chet Forte.

Rod "Hot Rod" Hundley, with his Harlem Globetrotter-like antics, ended his collegiate career by leading West Virginia to the Southern Conference crown, while Jim Krebs sparked Southern Methodist to the title in the Southwest Conference. San Francisco, featuring Gene Brown and Mike Farmer, had its three-season winning streak snapped at 60 games, but easily won the California Basketball Association championship.

Morehead, led by another future big league baseball pitcher, Steve Hamilton, was the best rebounding team in the country as it won the Ohio Valley Conference race, and Miami (O.), powered by Wayne Embry, was the Mid-American Conference titlist. Other conference champions were: Yale, Ivy League; California, Pacific Coast; Kentucky, Southeastern; Brigham Young, Skyline; St. Louis, Missouri Valley; Texas Western, Border; Idaho State, Rocky Mountain; and Connecticut, Yankee.

Strong independents included Louisville, with Charlie Tyra; Oklahoma City, with Hub Reed; Niagara, with Alex "Boo" Ellis; Temple, with Guy Rodgers; and St. Bonaventure, led by Brendan McCann. Other prominent teams were Manhattan, which made a record 45.6 percent of its shots from the floor; Mississippi State, with Bailey Howell; Kansas State, with Jack Parr; Syracuse, with Vince Cohen; Illinois, led by George Bonsalle; and Iowa State, with Gary Thompson.

Several quintets featured players who achieved fame in other sports. They included Ron Kramer (football and track) at Michigan; Frank Howard (football and baseball) at Ohio State; Rafer Johnson (decathlon) at UCLA; Bob Gibson (baseball) at Creighton; and Jimmy Brown (football and lacrosse) at Syracuse.

NCAA Championship

At Kansas City

North Carolina (54)	FG	FT	Pts.	Kansas (53)	FG	FT	Pts.
Rosenbluth	8	4	20	Elstun	4	3	11
Lotz	0	0	0	Loneski	0	2	2
Brennan	4	3	11	L. Johnson	0	2	2
Young	1	0	2	Chamberlain	6	11	23
Quigg	4	2	10	King	3	5	11
Cunningham	0	0	0	Parker	2	0	4
Kearns	4	3	11	Billings	0	0	0
Totals	21	12	54		15	23	53

NCAA Scores

REGIONALS

East

First Round: Syracuse 82, Connecticut 76; Canisius 64, West Virginia 56; North Carolina 90, Yale 74

Semifinals: Syracuse 75, Lafayette 71; North Carolina 87, Canisius 75

Championship: North Carolina 67, Syracuse 58

NIT Championship

At New York

Bradley (84)	FG	FT	Pts.	Memphis State (83)	FG	FT	Pts.
Cable	8	1	17	Wilfong	10	11	31
McDade	1	3	5	Ragan	3	4	10
B. Mason	5	12	22	Hockaday	0	2	2
Johnson	0	0	0	Arnold	5	4	14
McMillon	8	2	18	Butcher	7	7	21
Emerson	0	1	1	Swander	2	1	5
Sedgewick	0	0	0	Hays	0	0	0
Myers	1	2	4				
Morse	4	1	9				
Dhabalt	3	2	8				
Totals	30	24	84		27	29	83

NIT Scores

First Round: Memphis State 77, Utah 75; Xavier (O.) 85, Seton Hall 79; Dayton 79, St. Peter's (N. J.) 71; St. Bonaventure 90, Cincinnati 72

Quarterfinals: Memphis State 80, Manhattan 73; St. Bonaventure 85, Seattle 68; Bradley 116, Xavier (O.) 81; Temple 77, Dayton 66

NCAA Scores (cont.)

Mideast

First Round: Pittsburgh 86, Morehead State 85; Notre Dame 89, Miami (O.) 77

Semifinals: Kentucky 98, Pittsburgh 92; Michigan State 85, Notre Dame 83

Championship: Michigan State 80, Kentucky 68

Midwest

First Round: Oklahoma City 76, Loyola (La.) 55

Semifinals: Oklahoma City 75, St. Louis 66; Kansas 73, Southern Methodist 65

Championship: Kansas 81, Oklahoma City 61

Far West

First Round: Idaho State 68, Harden-Simmons 57

Semifinals: California 86, Brigham Young 59; San Francisco 50, California 46

FINALS

Semifinals: North Carolina 74, Michigan State 70; Kansas 80, San Francisco 56

Championship: North Carolina 54, Kansas 53

Consolation: San Francisco 67, Michigan State 60

NIT Scores (cont.)

Semifinals: Memphis State 80, St. Bonaventure 78; Bradley 94, Temple 66

Championship: Bradley 84, Memphis State 83

Consolation: Temple 67, St. Bonaventure 50

Top Ten

AP	UPI
North Carolina	North Carolina
Kansas	Kansas
Kentucky	Kentucky
Southern Methodist	Southern Methodist
Seattle	Seattle
Louisville	California
West Virginia	Michigan State
Vanderbilt	Louisville
Oklahoma City	UCLA
St. Louis	St. Louis

All-Americans

AP	UPI
Wilt Chamberlain, Kansas	Wilt Chamberlain, Kansas
Lennie Rosenbluth, North Carolina	Chet Forte, Columbia
Rod Hundley, West Virginia	Lennie Rosenbluth, North Carolina
Gary Thompson, Iowa State	Grady Wallace, South Carolina
Chet Forte, Columbia	Rod Hundley, West Virginia

1957–58

Oscar Robertson became the first sophomore ever to win a national scoring title as he averaged 35.1 points and teamed with 6-9 Connie Dierking to lead Cincinnati to a 25-3 record and the Missouri Valley Conference title.

A change in the free throw bonus rule, awarding the extra shot only after six team fouls in each half, generally lowered scoring averages. Robertson, Seattle's Elgin Baylor, and Kansas' Wilt Chamberlain were the only players to average more than 30 points a game. Marshall, with Leo Byrd averaging 25.0 points and Hal Greer 23.6 points, led in team scoring with an 88.0 average.

Lightly regarded Kentucky accomplished the unprecedented feat of winning a fourth NCAA championship. The Wildcats, led by Vern Hatton and Adrian Smith, beat Seattle, 84-72, for the NCAA title. Seattle's Baylor won the MVP award as he scored 135 points in tourney play. Southeastern Conference champion Kentucky had the dubious honor of owning the worst record ever for an NCAA champion, 23 victories and six losses.

Another unheralded team, Xavier (O.), took the NIT crown by beating second-seeded Dayton, 78-74, in overtime. Xavier had to overcome a 41-point performance by Niagara's Alex "Boo" Ellis in an early round game in order to advance. Hank Stein of Xavier, with 90 points in four games, won scoring honors and the MVP trophy.

West Virginia, powered by 6-10 Lloyd Sharrar and 6-3 Jerry West, was generally regarded as the top team in the country after winning the Southern Conference title, but the Mountaineers couldn't overcome their NCAA tournament jinx and again lost in the first round. Temple, with Guy Rodgers and Jay Norman, had its 25-game winning streak snapped in the NCAA tourney by Kentucky.

The best defensive team in the country, San Francisco, led by Mike Farmer, won the West Coast Athletic Conference (formerly California Basketball Association) race and Kansas State, paced by Bob Boozer, beat out Chamberlain and Kansas for the Big Eight (formerly Big Seven) title. Rudy LaRusso led Dartmouth to the Ivy League title and Miami (O.), once again powered by Wayne Embry, repeated in the Mid-American Conference. Notre Dame, with Tom Hawkins, was one of the outstanding teams in the Midwest, as was Big Ten champion Indiana, with Archie Dees.

Conference champions: Arkansas and Southern Methodist, tied, Southwest; Tennessee Tech, Ohio Valley; Duke, Atlantic Coast; Connecticut, Yankee; Arizona State, Border; and Idaho State, Rocky Mountain.

Strong teams included Pitt, with little Don Hennon; St. John's with Al Seiden; St. Bonaventure, with Tom Stith; North Carolina, with Pete Brennan; Mississippi State, with Bailey Howell; Washington & Lee, with Dom Flora; Illinois, with Don Ohl; Drake, with Phil Murrell; and Oregon State, with Dave Gambee.

Future major league pitcher Sonny Siebert was the leading scorer for Missouri and Jerry Adair, another big league baseball player, played basketball for Oklahoma State (formerly Oklahoma A&M).

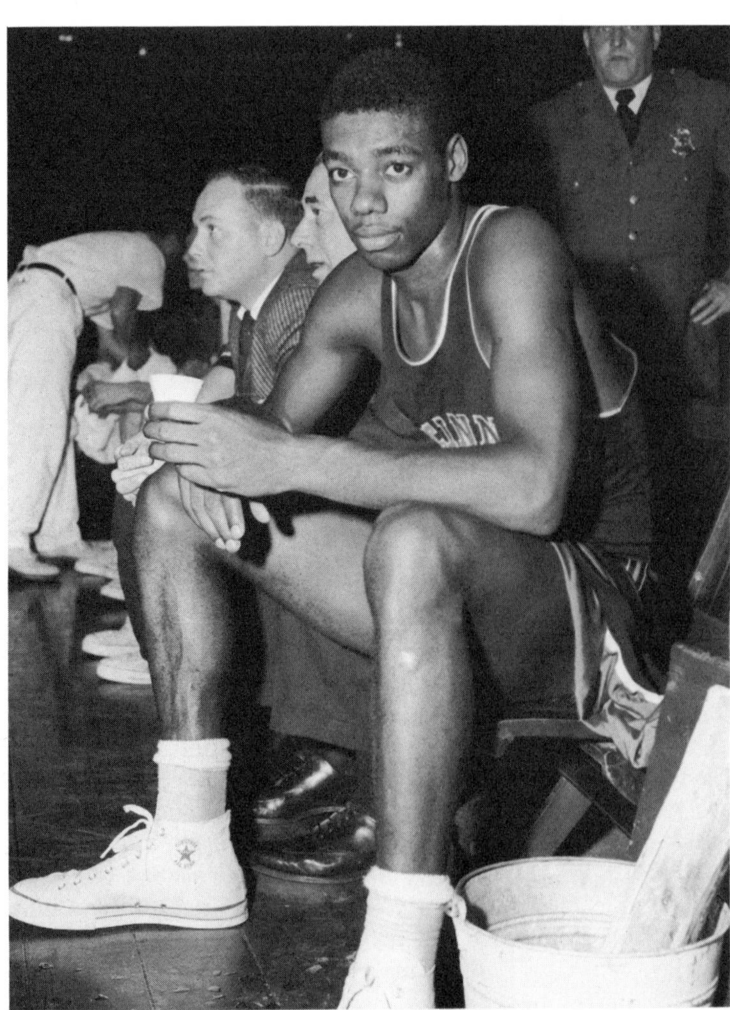

Only a sophomore, Oscar Robertson of Cincinnati won national scoring honors with a 35.1 average.

NCAA Championship
At Louisville

Kentucky (84)	FG	FT	Pts.	Seattle (72)	FG	FT	Pts.
Cox	10	4	24	Frizzell	4	8	16
Crigler	5	4	14	Ogorek	4	2	10
Beck	0	0	0	Baylor	9	7	25
Mills	4	1	9	Harney	2	0	4
Hatton	9	12	30	Brown	6	5	17
Smith	2	3	7	Saunders	0	0	0
				Piasecki	0	0	0
Totals	30	24	84		25	22	72

NCAA Scores
REGIONALS
East

First Round: Maryland 86, Boston College 63; Manhattan 89, West Virginia 84; Dartmouth 75, Connecticut 64

Semifinals: Temple 71, Maryland 67; Dartmouth 79, Manhattan 62

Championship: Temple 69, Dartmouth 50

Mideast

First Round: Miami (O.) 82, Pittsburgh 77; Notre Dame 94, Tennessee Tech 61

Semifinals: Kentucky 94, Miami (O.) 70; Notre Dame 94, Indiana 87

Championship: Kentucky 89, Notre Dame 56

Midwest

First Round: Oklahoma State 59, Loyola (La.) 52

Semifinals: Oklahoma State 65, Arkansas 40; Kansas State 83, Cincinnati 80

Championship: Kansas State 69, Oklahoma State 57

Far West

First Round: Seattle 88, Wyoming 51; Idaho State 72, Arizona State 68

Semifinals: Seattle 69, San Francisco 67; California 54, Idaho State 43

Championship: Seattle 66, California 62

FINALS

Semifinals: Kentucky 61, Temple 60; Seattle 73, Kansas State 51

Championship: Kentucky 84, Seattle 72

Consolation: Temple 67, Kansas State 57

NIT Championship
At New York

Xavier (O.) (78)	FG	FT	Pts.	Dayton (74)	FG	FT	Pts.
Viviano	5	0	10	A. Bockhorn	5	0	10
Olberding	2	2	6	Case	10	1	21
Tartaron	6	2	14	McCarthy	9	3	21
Stein	9	5	23	Lane	6	4	16
Castelle	8	3	19	T. Bockhorn	1	4	6
Piontek	3	0	6	H. Bockhorn	0	0	0
				Josefczyk	0	0	0
				Bogenrife	0	0	0
Totals	33	12	78		31	12	74

NIT Scores

First Round: St. John's 76, Butler 69; St. Joseph's 83, St. Peter's (N. J.) 76; Xavier (O.) 95, Niagara 86; Fordham 83, St. Francis (Pa.) 59

Quarterfinals: St. John's 71, Utah 70; St. Bonaventure 79, St. Joseph's 75; Xavier (O.) 72, Bradley 62; Dayton 74, Fordham 70

Semifinals: Dayton 80, St. John's 56; Xavier (O.) 72, St. Bonaventure 53

Championship: Xavier (O.) 78, Dayton 74

Consolation: St. Bonaventure 84, St. John's 69

Top Ten

AP	UPI
West Viginia	West Virginia
Cincinnati	Cincinnati
Kansas State	San Francisco
San Francisco	Kansas State
Temple	Temple
Maryland	Maryland
Kansas	Notre Dame
Notre Dame	Kansas
Kentucky	Dayton
Duke	Indiana

All-Americans

AP	UPI
Wilt Chamberlain, Kansas	Wilt Chamberlain, Kansas
Oscar Robertson, Cincinnati	Oscar Robertson, Cincinnati
Elgin Baylor, Seattle	Elgin Baylor, Seattle
Guy Rogers, Temple	Guy Rodgers, Temple
Don Hennon, Pittsburgh	Don Hennon, Pittsburgh

1958–59

Defense, as executed by its foremost practitioner, California, reigned supreme as the Golden Bears won their last 16 games in a row, including a 71-70 triumph over West Virginia, to gain the NCAA championship.

California, Pacific Coast Conference champion, allowed an average of 51 points a game in compiling a 25-4 record. Leading the Bears were 6-10 Darrall Imhoff and 6-5 defensive specialist Bill McClintock. West Virginia finally made it past the first round of an NCAA tourney as the Mountaineers qualified by winning their fifth consecutive Southern Conference crown. Jerry West and Willie Akers were the mainstays of the West Virginia attack.

St. John's led a New York area resurgence as the Redmen won the NIT, beating Bradley, 76-71, in the championship game. This was the third NIT title for St. John's, the only team to accomplish this feat. Al Seiden of the Redmen set a pair of free throw records and his teammate, Tony Jackson, won MVP honors. Cal Ramsey of third-place NYU was high scorer with 82 points in four games.

The tournament play revealed that ratings meant little, as Kansas State and Kentucky, generally rated one-two in the country, were eliminated in early play. Kansas State, led by Bob Boozer, was the Big Eight champion while Kentucky, with Johnny Cox, played in the NCAA tourney after Southeastern Conference champion Mississippi State withdrew because of the presence of Negro players in the tournament.

Oscar Robertson retained his individual scoring title, averaging 32.6 points a game, as he took Cincinnati to the Missouri Valley Conference title ahead of strong teams at Bradley, with Bobby Joe Mason, and St. Louis, led by Bob Ferry.

Several conference races ended in ties, including the Ivy League where Dartmouth, with Rudy LaRusso, defeated Princeton in a playoff, and the Atlantic Coast Conference, where North Carolina and North Carolina State were knotted. Bowling Green and Miami (O.) shared the Mid-American Conference honors, and New Mexico State, Arizona State, and Texas Western all tied in the Border Conference.

Tom Meschery led St. Mary's to the West Coast Athletic Conference crown, while other conference champions included Michigan State, Big Ten; Texas Christian, Southwest; St. Joseph's, Middle Atlantic; Idaho State, Rocky Mountain; Eastern Kentucky, Ohio Valley; and Connecticut, Yankee.

Jerry West made the headlines as West Virginia won the Southern Conference championship.

Cincinnati's Oscar Robertson straddled the world as he took his second scoring title.

Marquette, with Don Kojis and Mike Moran, was strong in the Midwest while Miami (Fla.), with Dick Hickox, was the nation's top scoring team, averaging 87.6 points a game. Other strong teams: Auburn, with Rex Frederick; Denver, with Tim Peay; Marshall, with Leo Byrd; UCLA, with Walt Torrence; Washington, with Doug Smart; Louisville, with Don Goldstein; Tennessee, with Gene Tormohlen; Seattle, with Charlie "Sweet Charlie" Brown; Air Force, with Bob Beckel; Wyoming, with Tony Windis; and Northwestern, with Joe Ruklick.

NCAA Championship

At Louisville

California (71)	FG	FT	Pts.
Dalton	6	3	15
McClintock	4	0	8
Imhoff	4	2	10
Buch	0	2	2
Fitzpatrick	8	4	20
Grout	4	2	10
Simpson	0	0	0
Doughty	3	0	6
Totals	29	13	71

West Virginia (70)	FG	FT	Pts.
West	10	8	28
Clousson	4	2	10
Akers	5	0	10
Bolyard	1	4	6
Smith	2	1	5
Retton	0	2	2
Ritchie	1	2	4
Patrone	2	1	5
	25	20	70

NIT Championship

At New York

St. John's (76)	FG	FT	Pts.
Engert	2	0	4
Jackson	9	3	21
Roethel	5	2	12
Seiden	7	8	22
Alfieri	5	5	15
Pedone	0	0	0
Ryan	1	0	2
Totals	29	18	76

Bradley (71)	FG	FT	Pts.
Smith	4	0	8
Morse	6	4	16
McDade	6	4	16
Mason	7	4	18
Owens	4	2	10
Saunders	1	1	3
Hewitt	0	0	0
Voegele	0	0	0
	28	15	71

NCAA Scores

REGIONALS

East

First Round: West Virginia 82, Dartmouth 68; Boston U. 60, Connecticut 58; Navy 76, North Carolina 63

Semifinals: West Virginia 95, St. Joseph's 92; Boston U. 62, Navy 55

Championship: West Virginia 86, Boston U. 82

Mideast

First Round: Louisville 77, Eastern Kentucky 63; Marquette 89, Bowling Green 79

Semifinals: Louisville 76, Kentucky 61; Michigan State 74, Marquette 69

Championship: Louisville 88, Michigan State 81

Midwest

First Round: DePaul 57, Portland 56

Semifinals: Kansas State 102, DePaul 70; Cincinnati 77, Texas Christian 73

Championship: Cincinnati 85, Kansas State 75

Far West

First Round: Idaho State 62, New Mexico State 61

Semifinals: St. Mary's 80, Idaho State 71; California 71, Utah 53

Championship: California 66, St. Mary's 46

FINALS

Semifinals: West Virginia 94, Louisville 79; California 64, Cincinnati 58

Championship: California 71, West Virginia 70

Consolation: Cincinnati 98, Louisville 85

NIT Scores

First Round: Butler 94, Fordham 80; NYU 90, Denver 81; Providence 68, Manhattan 66; St. John's 75, Villanova 67

Quarterfinals: Bradley 83, Butler 77; NYU 63, Oklahoma City 48; Providence 75, St Louis 72; St. John's 82, St Bonaventure 74

Semifinals: Bradley 59, NYU 57; St. John's 76, Providence 55

Championship: St. John's 76, Bradley 71

Consolation: NYU 71, Providence 57

Top Ten

AP	UPI
Kansas State	Kansas State
Kentucky	Kentucky
Mississippi State	Michigan State
Bradley	Cincinnati
Cincinnati	North Carolina State
North Carolina State	Tie { North Carolina
Michigan State	{ Mississippi State
Auburn	Bradley
North Carolina	California
West Virginia	Auburn

All-Americans

AP	UPI
Oscar Robertson, Cincinnati	Oscar Robertson, Cincinnati
Jerry West, West Virginia	Bailey Howell, Mississippi State
Bob Boozer, Kansas State	Bob Boozer, Kansas State
Bailey Howell, Mississippi State	Jerry West, West Virginia
Johnny Cox, Kentucky	Don Hennon, Pittsburgh

1959-60

The Big "O", Oscar Robertson, finished a career at Cincinnati that brought innumerable scoring records, including the national scoring title three consecutive years. He led his team to 79 victories in 88 games and three straight Missouri Valley Conference championships. About the only thing that eluded him and his teammates was an NCAA championship.

The NCAA title game this year was a battle between offense and defense, with Pacific Coast Conference champion California yielding 49.5 points a game and Big Ten titlist Ohio State scoring 90.5 points a game. Each team led the nation in its specialty.

California had Darrall Imhoff, Bill McClintock, and Earl Shultz, but Ohio State shot a dazzling 68.4 percent from the field as 6-8 sophomore Jerry Lucas, John Havlicek, Larry Siegfried, Joe Roberts, and Mel Nowell blended to rout the Golden Bears, 75-55, in the championship game. Lucas was named MVP while Robertson, leading Cincinnati to the consolation title, was the leading scorer with 122 points.

The NIT saw Bradley, runner-up to Cincinnati in the Missouri Valley race, outscore Providence 38-10 in the final ten minutes of the championship game to gain an 88-72 victory. Bradley was led by Chet Walker and Bobby Joe Mason, but it was Providence's Lenny Wilkens who received the MVP award. Tom Stith of St. Bonaventure was the leading scorer with 114 points as the Bonnies scored a record 354 points in their four tourney games.

MVP of the NCAA tourney: Ohio State sophomore Jerry Lucas.

11
31

Billy "The Hill" McGill, a 6-9 sophomore, led Utah to the Skyline Conference title ahead of Utah State, featuring future professional football star Cornell Green. Indiana, with 6-11 Walt Bellamy, was runner-up to Ohio State in the Big Ten, while Wally Frank took Kansas State to a tie in the Big Eight with Kansas, featuring Bill Bridges and Wayne Hightower.

Auburn gained the Southeastern Conference championship ahead of Georgia Tech, with little Roger Kaiser, and Kentucky. West Virginia had its 56-game Southern Conference winning streak snapped as the Mountaineers, led by Jerry West, finished second to Virginia Tech in the regular season standings but won the league's post-season tourney.

Duke emerged as Atlantic Coast Conference titlist after winning the conference post-season tournament, although Wake Forest, with Dave Budd and Len Chappell, and North Carolina, with Lee Shaffer, Doug Moe and York Larese, had better regular season records. Jay Arnett led Texas to the Southwest Conference crown while other conference champions were Ohio U., Mid-American; St. Joseph's, Middle Atlantic; Santa Clara and Loyola (Calif.), tied, West Coast Athletic Conference; Idaho State, Rocky Mountain; Princeton, Ivy League; Connecticut, Yankee; Western Kentucky, Ohio Valley; and New Mexico State, Border.

NYU, with Tom Sanders, was a surprising semifinalist in the NCAA tourney as the Violets vied for independent honors with St. John's, led by Tony Jackson; Holy Cross, with sharp-shooting sophomore Jack "The Shot" Foley, and Detroit, with Dave DeBusschere. Other strong teams were Niagara, with Al Butler; Purdue, with Terry Dischinger; Bowling Green, with Jim Darrow; Villanova; Memphis State; Notre Dame; and DePaul.

NCAA Championship

At San Francisco

Ohio State (75)	FG.	FT	Pts.	California (55)	FG	FT	Pts.
Havlicek	4	4	12	McClintock	4	2	10
Roberts	5	0	10	Gillis	4	0	8
Lucas	7	2	16	Imhoff	3	2	8
Nowell	6	3	15	Wendell	0	4	4
Siegfried	5	3	13	Shultz	2	2	6
Gearhart	0	0	0	Mann	3	1	7
Cedargren	0	1	1	Doughty	4	3	11
Furry	2	0	4	Stafford	0	1	1
Hoyt	0	0	0	Morrison	0	0	0
Barker	0	0	0	Averbuck	0	0	0
Knight	0	0	0	Pearson	0	0	0
Nourse	2	0	4	Alexander	0	0	0
Totals	31	13	75		20	15	55

NIT Championship

At New York

Bradley (88)	FG.	FT	Pts.	Providence (72)	FG	FT	Pts.
Smith	6	3	15	Whelan	3	0	6
Herndon	11	4	26	Leonard	3	1	7
Walker	4	1	9	Hadnot	5	0	10
Saunders	1	9	11	Egan	5	10	20
Owens	5	3	13	Wilkins	10	5	25
Wodka	3	1	7	Moynahan	2	0	4
Tiemann	1	0	2	Gulmares	0	0	0
Edwards	1	1	3	Folliard	0	0	0
Roecker	1	0	2	Gibson	0	0	0
Granby	0	0	0				
Kissock	0	0	0				
Sash	0	0	0				
Totals	33	22	88		28	16	72

NCAA Scores

REGIONALS

East

First Round: Duke 84, Princeton 60 West Virginia 94, Navy 86; NYU 78, Connecticut 59

Semifinals: Duke 58, St. Joseph's 56; NYU 82, West Virginia 81

Championship: NYU 74, Duke 59

Mideast

First Round: Ohio U. 74, Notre Dame 66; Western Kentucky 107, Miami (Fla.) 84

Semifinals: Georgia Tech 57, Ohio U. 54; Ohio State 98, Western Kentucky 79

Championship: Ohio State 86, Georgia Tech 69

NIT Scores

First Round: Villanova 88, Detroit 86; Providence 71, Memphis State 70; St. Bonaventure 94, Holy Cross 81; Dayton 72, Temple 51

Quarterfinals: Utah State 73, Villanova 72; Providence 64, St. Louis 53; Bradley 78, Dayton 64; St. Bonaventure 106, St. John's 71

Semifinals: Bradley 82, St. Bonaventure 71; Providence 68, Utah State 62

Championship: Bradley 88, Providence 72

Consolation: Utah State 99, St. Bonaventure 83

NCAA Scores (cont.)

Midwest

First Round: DePaul 69, Air Force 63

Semifinals: Cincinnati 99, DePaul 59; Kansas 90, Texas 81

Championship: Cincinnati 82, Kansas 71

Far West

First Round: California 71, Idaho State 44; Oregon 68, New Mexico State 60; Utah 80, Southern California 73

Semifinals: California 69, Santa Clara 49; Oregon 65, Utah 54

Championship: California 70, Oregon 49

FINALS

Semifinals: Ohio State 76, NYU 54; California 77, Cincinnati 69

Championship: Ohio State 75, California 55

Consolation: Cincinnati 95, NYU 71

Top Ten

AP	UPI
Cincinnati	California
California	Cincinnati
Ohio State	Ohio State
Bradley	Bradley
West Virginia	Utah
Utah	West Virginia
Indiana	Utah State
Utah State	Georgia Tech
St. Bonaventure	Villanova
Miami (Fla.)	Indiana

All-Americans

AP	UPI
Jerry West, West Virginia	Jerry West, West Virginia
Oscar Robertson, Cincinnati	Oscar Robertson, Cincinnati
Jerry Lucas, Ohio State	Jerry Lucas, Ohio State
Darrall Imhoff, California	Darrall Imhoff, California
Tony Jackson, St. John's	Tom Stith, St. Bonaventure

1960–61

The gamblers and point shavers were once again exposed on college campuses, but the improprieties did not involve as many teams, nor was it as far reaching as the 1951 scandal. Schools acted quickly and decisively, in some cases dismissing freshmen who had never played a game but nevertheless had taken money from gamblers.

On the court, Cincinnati, with Bob Wiesenhahn and Paul Hogue, snapped defending champion Ohio State's 32-game winning streak with a 70-65 overtime victory in the NCAA championship game. Big Ten champion Ohio State was led by Larry Siegfried, John Havlicek and Jerry Lucas, who repeated as MVP. Billy McGill of Utah's Skyline Conference co-champions (with Colorado State) was tournament high scorer with 117 points, including 32 in the consolation playoff with Middle Atlantic Conference champion St. Joseph's. Utah won, 127-120.

St. Bonaventure's 99-game home court winning skein was snapped, but Tom Stith took the Bonnies to the NIT for the third straight year. St. Bonaventure, the highest-scoring team in the nation with an 88.5-point-per-game average, was eliminated early, however, as Providence and St. Louis battled into the championship game. Providence was led by 6-10 Jim Hadnot and 6-0 Johnny Egan, but it was little (5-8) Vinnie Ernst who won MVP honors as the Friars beat St. Louis, 62-59. Jack "The Shot" Foley of Holy Cross was high scorer with 120 points in four games.

North Carolina won the regular season race in the Atlantic Coast Conference, but Wake Forest, with Len Chappell, took the post-season conference tournament.

Mississippi State refused to play in the racially integrated NCAA tourney after winning the Southeastern Conference title and was again replaced by Kentucky, while Southern California, paced by John Rudometkin, won the title in the AAWU (successor to the Pacific Coast Conference). West Virginia, with Lee Patrone and Rod Thorn, finished first in the regular season standings in the Southern Conference, but George Washington, with a 3-9 league record, captured the league's post-season tourney.

Texas Tech, with Del Ray Mounts, swept the Southwest Conference, while other league

Cincinnati's Paul Hogue helped snap Ohio State's winning streak despite Jerry Lucas and John Havlicek (5).

champions were Kansas State, Big Eight; Loyola (Calif.), West Coast Athletic; Arizona State and New Mexico State, tied, Border; Ohio U., Mid-American; Princeton, Ivy; Rhode Island, Yankee; and Morehead, Eastern Kentucky, and Western Kentucky, tied, Ohio Valley. Missouri Valley Conference teams turned in outstanding records, with NCAA champion Cincinnati; NIT finalist St. Louis; Bradley, with Chet Walker; Wichita and Drake all winning more than 70 percent of their non-conference games.

St. John's, with Tony Jackson, was the leading independent in the New York area, while, Dayton, with Gary Roggenburk; Seattle, with Eddie Miles; Detroit, with Dave DeBusschere; Marquette, with Don Kojis; and Louisville, with John Turner, were also strong.

Some of the season's better players: Tom Meschery, St. Mary's (Calif.); Terry Dischinger, Purdue; Walt Bellamy, Indiana; Don Nelson, Iowa; Roger Kaiser, Georgia Tech; Gary Phillips, Houston; Bill Bridges and Wayne Hightower, Kansas; Jeff Cohen, William and Mary; Carroll Broussard, Texas A&M; and Howie Carl, DePaul.

NCAA Championship
At Kansas City

Cincinnati (70)	FG	FT	Pts.	Ohio State (65)	FG	FT	Pts.
Wiesenhahn	8	1	17	Havlicek	1	2	4
Thacker	7	1	15	Hoyt	3	1	7
Hogue	3	3	9	Lucas	10	7	27
Yates	4	5	13	Nowell	3	3	9
Bouldin	7	2	16	Siegfried	6	2	14
Sizer	0	0	0	Knight	1	0	2
Heidotting	0	0	0	Gearhart	1	0	2
Totals	29	12	70		25	15	65

NCAA Scores
REGIONALS
East

First Round: Princeton 84, George Washington 67; St. Bonaventure 86, Rhode Island 76; Wake Forest 97, St. John's 74

Semifinals: St. Joseph's 72, Princeton 67; Wake Forest 78, St. Bonaventure 73

Championship: St. Joseph's 96, Wake Forest 86

Mideast

First Round: Louisville 76, Ohio U. 70; Morehead State 71, Xavier (O.) 66

Semifinals: Ohio State 56, Louisville 55; Kentucky 71, Morehead State 64

Championship: Ohio State 87, Kentucky 74

Midwest

First Round: Houston 77, Marquette 61

Semifinals: Kansas State 75, Houston 64; Cincinnati 78, Texas Tech 55

Championship: Cincinnati 69, Kansas State 64

Far West

First Round: Arizona State 72, Seattle 70; Southern California 81, Oregon 79

Semifinals: Arizona State 86, Southern California 71, Utah 91, Loyola (Cal.) 75

Championship: Utah 88, Arizona State 80

FINALS

Semifinals: Ohio State 95, St. Joseph's 69; Cincinnati 82, Utah 67

Championship: Cincinnati 70, Ohio State 65

Consolation: St. Joseph's 127, Utah 120

NIT Championship
At New York

Providence (62)	FG	FT	Pts.	St. Louis (59)	FG	FT	Pts.
Zalucki	7	3	17	Reid	3	2	8
Moynahan	3	0	6	Harris	0	0	0
Flynn	3	2	8	Hartwager	0	0	0
Hadnot	6	6	18	Book	2	1	5
Ernst	2	0	4	Nordmann	5	6	16
Egan	4	1	9	Luechtfield	0	0	0
				Kieffer	9	0	18
				Latinovich	0	0	0
				Mankowsky	6	0	12
Totals	25	12	62		25	9	59

NIT Scores

First Round: St. Louis 58, Miami (Fla.) 56; Holy Cross 86, Detroit 82; Temple 79, Army 66; Providence 73, DePaul 67

Quarterfinals: St. Louis 59, Colorado State 53; Holy Cross 81, Memphis State 69; Dayton 62, Temple 60; Providence 71, Niagara 68

Semifinals: St. Louis 67, Dayton 60; Providence 90, Holy Cross 83

Championship: Providence 62, St. Louis 59

Consolation: Holy Cross 85, Dayton 67

Top Ten

AP	UPI
Ohio State	Ohio State
Cincinnati	Cincinnati
St. Bonaventure	St. Bonaventure
Kansas State	Kansas State
North Carolina	Southern California
Bradley	North Carolina
Southern California	Bradley
Iowa	St. John's
West Virginia	Duke
Duke	Wake Forest

All-Americans

AP	UPI
Jerry Lucas, Ohio State	Jerry Lucas, Ohio State
Tom Stith, St. Bonaventure	Tom Stith, St. Bonaventure
Terry Dischinger, Purdue	Terry Dischinger, Purdue
Roger Kaiser, Georgia Tech	Roger Kaiser, Georgia Tech
Chet Walker, Bradley	Chet Walker, Bradley

1961–62

Cincinnati and Ohio State, the only teams from the same state ever to meet in the NCAA championship game, became the only teams ever to play for the championship two years in a row.

Cincinnati barely made it into the finals after being tied by Bradley, with Chet Walker, in the Missouri Valley Conference race. The Bearcats won the playoff and then had to survive an upset bid by UCLA, led by Johnny Green, in a semifinal game.

Ohio State breezed through the Big Ten and the Eastern Regionals, but Jerry Lucas, John Havlicek, Mel Nowell and Co. could not offset the inspired play of the Bearcats, led by Paul Hogue. Cincinnati won, 71-59, with Hogue taking the MVP trophy.

Dayton, after finishing second five times, finally won an NIT crown as the Flyers beat St. John's, 73-67. The title game pitted 6-9 Leroy Ellis of St. John's against 6-10 Bill Chmielewski of Dayton and the big Flyer got the better of it as he won MVP honors and the individual scoring title. It was Bill Green of Colorado State who turned in the outstanding shooting performance, however, as he hit on 14 of 14 shots from the floor in a losing game against Holy Cross.

Billy McGill scored 60 points in one game and topped the nation in scoring with a 38.8 average as he led Utah to the Skyline Conference crown. The Utes were denied an NCAA tourney berth, however, because of a rule infraction. Nate Thurmond and Howie Komives powered Bowling Green to the Mid-American Conference title while Mississippi State, with W. D. Stroud, and Kentucky, led by Cotton Nash, tied in the Southeastern Conference.

Jerry Lucas, with his 20-10 vision, led the nation for the third year in field goal accuracy and for the second time in rebounding. He was one of several Big Ten standouts, which included Purdue's Terry Dischinger; Iowa's Don Nelson; Indiana's Jimmy Rayl; and future professional football flanker Pete Gent of Michigan State.

Loyola (Ill.) was one of the top independents as the Ramblers, sparked by Jerry Harkness, had the highest scoring average in the nation, 90.2 points a game. Sophomores Barry Kramer and Harold "Happy" Hairston led NYU while little Willie Somerset powered Duquesne. Also strong were Creighton, with rebounder Paul Silas; Seattle with John Tresvant and Eddie Miles; Villanova, with Hubie White; Holy Cross; Providence; Memphis State; and Air Force.

Lenny Chappell once again sparked Wake Forest to the Atlantic Coast Conference title after being pushed by Duke, with Art Heyman. Bobby Rascoe and Darel Carrier led Western Kentucky to the Ohio Valley Conference crown while Texas Tech, with Harold Hudgens, defeated Southern Methodist, led by Jan Loudermilk, for Southwest Conference honors. Other champions: Colorado, Big Eight; West Virginia, Southern; Arizona State, Border; St. Joseph's, Middle Atlantic; Massachusetts, Yankee; Yale, Ivy; and Pepperdine, West Coast Athletic Conference.

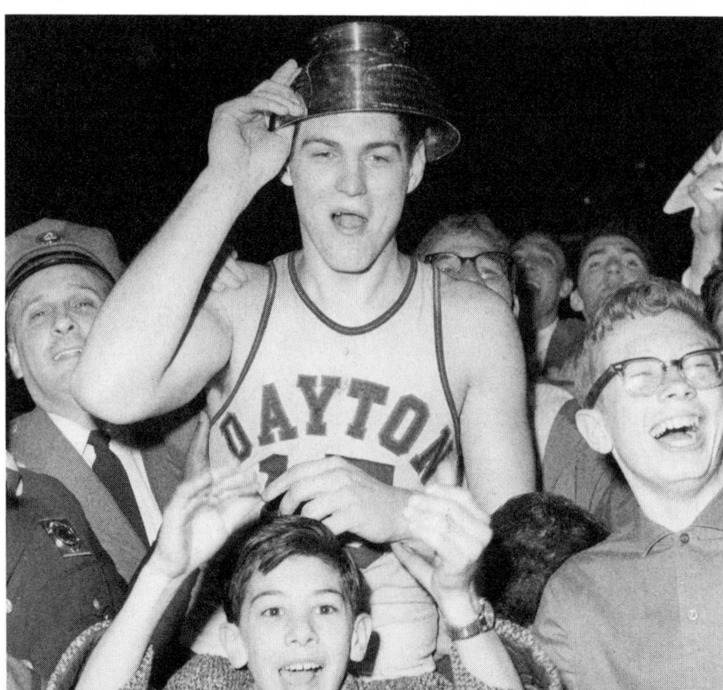

Dayton's Bill Chmielewski was NIT MVP.

NCAA Championship

At Louisville

Cincinnati (71)	FG	FT	Pts.	Ohio State (59)	FG	FT	Pts.
Bonham	3	4	10	Havlicek	5	1	11
Wilson	1	4	6	McDonald	0	3	3
Hogue	11	0	22	Lucas	5	1	11
Thacker	6	9	21	Reasebeck	4	0	8
Yates	4	4	12	Nowell	4	1	9
Sizer	0	0	0	Doughty	0	0	0
				Gearhart	1	0	2
				Bradds	5	5	15
Totals	25	21	71		24	11	59

NIT Championship

At New York

Dayton (73)	FG	FT	Pts.	St. John's (67)	FG	FT	Pts.
Roggenburk	3	2	8	Hall	2	0	4
Schoen	5	2	12	Loughery	10	6	26
Greenberg	0	0	0	Ellis	5	12	22
Chmielewski	11	2	24	Kovac	2	1	5
G. Hatton	6	6	18	Burks	3	2	8
T. Hatton	4	3	11	O'Hara	0	0	0
				O'Sullivan	1	0	2
Totals	29	15	73		23	21	67

NCAA Scores

REGIONALS

East

First Round: Wake Forest 92, Yale 82; NYU 70, Massachusetts 50; Villanova 90, West Virginia 75

Semifinals: Wake Forest 96, St. Joseph's 85, Villanova 79, NYU 76

Championship: Wake Forest 79, Villanova 69

Mideast

First Round: Butler 56, Bowling Green 55; Western Kentucky 90, Detroit 81

Semifinals: Kentucky 81, Butler 60; Ohio State 93, Western Kentucky 73

Championship: Ohio State 74, Kentucky 64

Midwest

First Round: Texas Tech 68, Air Force 66; Creighton 87, Memphis State 83

Semifinals: Colorado 67, Texas Tech 60, Cincinnati 66, Creighton 46

Championship: Cincinnati 73, Colorado 46

Far West

First Round: Oregon State 69, Seattle 65; Utah State 78, Arizona State 73

Semifinals: Oregon State 69, Pepperdine 67; UCLA 73, Utah State 62

Championship: UCLA 88, Oregon State 69

FINALS

Semifinals: Ohio State 84, Wake Forest 68; Cincinnati 72, UCLA 70

Championship: Cincinnati 71, Ohio State 59

Consolation: Wake Forest 82, UCLA 80

NIT Scores

First Round: Dayton 79, Wichita 71; Temple 80, Providence 78; Holy Cross 72, Colorado State 71; Duquesne 70, Navy 58

Quarterfinals: Dayton 94, Houston 77; Loyola (Ill.) 75, Temple 64; Duquesne 88, Bradley 85; St. John's 80, Holy Cross 74

Semifinals: Dayton 98, Loyola (Ill.) 82; St. John's 75, Duquesne 65

Championship: Dayton 73, St. John's 67

Consolation: Loyola (Ill.) 95, Duquesne 84

Top Ten

AP	UP
Ohio State	Ohio State
Cincinnati	Cincinnati
Kentucky	Kentucky
Mississippi State	Mississippi State
Bradley	Kansas State
Kansas State	Bradley
Utah	Wake Forest
Bowling Green	Colorado
Colorado	Bowling Green
Duke	Utah

All-Americans

AP	UP
Jerry Lucas, Ohio State	Jerry Lucas, Ohio State
Terry Dischinger, Purdue	Terry Dischinger, Purdue
Billy McGill, Utah	Billy McGill, Utah
Chet Walker, Bradley	Chet Walker, Bradley
Len Chappell, Wake Forest	John Havlicek, Ohio State

1962-63

Loyola (Ill.), the nation's highest scoring team with a 91.8 average, weathered a case of championship jitters to end Cincinnati's bid for a third straight NCAA title.

Loyola, with Jerry Harkness, Les Hunter, Ron Miller, Vic Rouse, and John Egan, opened its NCAA bid by routing Ohio Valley Conference representative Tennessee Tech by 69 points. The Ramblers won the next three games by 10, 15 and 19 points before meeting Missouri

Enroute to NCAA crown, Loyola's Les Hunter scores on Cincinnati's George Wilson.

Valley Conference champion Cincinnati, the best defensive team in the nation. The Bearcats had yielded 52.9 points a game.

A record crowd of 19,153 in Louisville's Freedom Hall saw Cincinnati dominate the game for 30 minutes before Ron Bonham, Tom Thacker, George Wilson, and Tony Yates got into foul trouble. Loyola then roused itself to earn a 60-58 victory in overtime.

The tourney MVP was Art Heyman of Duke's Atlantic Coast Conference champions, who defeated Oregon State in the consolation game. Oregon State, an independent like Loyola, was led by 7-foot Mel Counts and football Heisman Trophy winner Terry Baker.

Providence, with Ray Flynn, Vinnie Ernst and 6-10 John Thompson, waltzed to the NIT championship with an 81-66 triumph over Canisius, led by Bill O'Connor. Flynn took MVP honors and was high scorer with 83 points in three games.

Juniors Nick Werkman of Seton Hall and Barry Kramer of NYU staged the closest battle ever for the individual scoring crown. Werkman's 29.5-point average was .2 of a point better than Kramer's. Creighton's Paul Silas, also a junior, edged Gus Johnson of Idaho for the rebounding title, 20.6 rebounds per game to 20.3.

Arizona State, with Art Becker and Joe Caldwell, won the first title in the newly formed Western Athletic Conference as the Border and Skyline leagues disbanded. Ohio State, with Gary Bradds, tied Illinois, led by Dave Downey, in the Big Ten; while UCLA, sparked by Walt Hazzard, was knotted with Tom Dose-led Stanford in the AAWU. Sharing the Big Eight title were Colorado, with Ken Charlton, and Kansas State, led by Willie Murrell.

NYU, with Kramer teaming with Harold "Happy" Hairston, was strong among the independents, as were Marquette, with Ron Glaser, Bob Hornack and Dick Nixon; Miami (Fla.) with 7-foot Mike McCoy and Rick Barry, and Seattle, once again powered by Eddie Miles.

Sophomore Bill Bradley made his debut in leading Princeton to the Ivy League title. Other conference champions were San Francisco, West Coast Athletic; Texas, Southwest; Bowling Green, Mid-American; West Virginia, Southern; Mississippi State, Southeastern; St. Joseph's, Middle Atlantic; and Connecticut, Yankee.

Among the stars: Rod Thorn, West Virginia; Fred Hetzel, Davidson; Bud Koper, Oklahoma City; Jeff Mullins, Duke; Ollie Johnson, San Francisco; Billy Cunningham, North Carolina; Bill Buntin, Michigan; Fred Crawford, St. Bonaventure; Nate Thurmond, Bowling Green; Dave Stallworth, Wichita; Cotton Nash, Kentucky; W.D. Stroud, Mississippi State; Wayne Estes, Utah State; and Jimmy Rayl, Indiana.

NCAA Championship

At Louisville

Loyola (Ill.) (60)	FG	FT	Pts.	Cincinnati (58)	FG	FT	Pts.
Harkness	5	4	14	Bonham	8	6	22
Rouse	6	3	15	Thacker	5	3	13
Hunter	6	4	16	Wilson	4	2	10
Egan	3	3	9	Yates	4	1	9
Miller	3	0	6	Shingleton	1	2	4
				Heidotting	0	0	0
Totals	23	14	60		22	14	58

NIT Championship

At New York

Providence (81)	FG	FT	Pts.	Canisius (66)	FG	FT	Pts.
Kovalski	4	2	10	McClory	0	0	0
Stone	7	9	23	Chester	10	1	21
Thompson	6	3	15	O'Connor	7	8	22
Flynn	9	2	20	Gennari	7	0	14
Ernst	2	5	9	Turtle	0	0	0
Simoni	0	0	0	Swiatek	0	0	0
Spencer	1	2	4	O'Mara	3	1	7
Stein	0	0	0	Kemmer	0	0	0
Nyire	0	0	0	Bossert	0	0	0
Dutton	0	0	0	Harrigan	0	0	0
				Oberding	0	2	2
				Brennan	0	0	0
Totals	29	23	81		27	12	66

NCAA Scores

REGIONALS

East

First Round: NYU 93, Pittsburgh 83; West Virginia 77, Connecticut 71; St. Joseph's 82, Princeton 81

Semifinals: Duke 81, NYU 76; St. Joseph's 97, West Virginia 88

Championship: Duke 73, St. Joseph's 59

NIT Scores

First Round: Villanova 63, DePaul 51; St. Louis 63, LaSalle 61; Memphis State 70, Fordham 49; Miami (Fla.) 71, St. Francis (N.Y.) 70

Quarterfinals: Villanova 54, Wichita 53; Canisius 76, Memphis State 67; Marquette 84, St. Louis 49; Providence 106, Miami (Fla.) 96

Semifinals: Providence 70, Marquette 64; Canisius 61, Villanova 46

Championship: Providence 81, Canisius 66

Consolation: Marquette 66, Villanova 58

NCAA Scores (cont.)

Mideast

First Round: Bowling Green 77, Notre Dame 72; Loyola (Ill.) 111, Tennessee Tech 42

Semifinals: Illinois 70, Bowling Green 67; Loyola (Ill.) 61, Mississippi State 51

Championship: Loyola (Ill.) 79, Illinois 64

Midwest

First Round: Oklahoma City 70, Colorado State 67; Texas 67, Texas Western 47

Semifinals: Colorado 78, Oklahoma City 72; Cincinnati 73, Texas 68

Championship: Cincinnati 67, Colorado 60

Far West

First Round: Arizona State 79, Utah State 75; Oregon State 70, Seattle 66

Semifinals: Arizona State 93, UCLA 79; Oregon State 65, San Francisco 61

Championship: Oregon State 83, Arizona State 65

FINALS

Semifinals: Loyola (Ill.) 94, Duke 75; Cincinnati 80, Oregon State 46

Championship: Loyola (Ill.) 60, Cincinnati 58

Consolation: Duke 85, Oregon State 63

Top Ten

AP	UPI
Cincinnati	Cincinnati
Duke	Duke
Loyola (Ill.)	Arizona State
Arizona State	Loyola (Ill.)
Wichita	Illinois
Mississippi State	Wichita
Ohio State	Mississippi State
Illinois	Ohio State
NYU	Colorado
Colorado	Stanford

All-Americans

AP	UPI
Art Heyman, Duke	Art Heyman, Duke
Ron Bonham, Cincinnati	Ron Bonham, Cincinnati
Jerry Harkness, Loyola (Ill.)	Jerry Harkness, Loyola (Ill.)
Gary Bradds, Ohio State	Gary Bradds, Ohio State
Barry Kramer, NYU	Tom Thacker, Cincinnati

1963–64

A methodic, balanced UCLA, averaging only 6-5 per man and led by guards Walt Hazzard and Gail Goodrich and forward Kenny Washington, managed to win 30 straight games, including the NCAA championship match against Duke, 98-83.

Although generally rated No. 1 in the country, UCLA was not spectacular as it won the AAWU title and then plodded through three NCAA games, winning none by more than six points, before meeting Duke. The Blue Devils, champions of the Atlantic Coast Conference, featured Jay Buckley and Hack Tison, both 6-10, and flashy Jeff Mullins, but it was the steady play of Hazzard that spelled the difference and won MVP honors for the 6-3 Bruin.

Bradley's Braves hit on 62 percent of their shots to overwhelm New Mexico, 86-54, and win the NIT. Bradley was powered by MVP Levern Tart and Joe Strawder, while New Mexico, Western Athletic Conference co-champion with Arizona State, countered with Ira "Large" Harge. NYU's Harold "Happy" Hairston was tournament high scorer with 91 points.

Bowling Green's Howie Komives won the individual scoring race with a 36.7 average as he was one of seven players to average better than 30 points, the most ever to average that many points in one season. The others were Nick Werkman, Seton Hall; Manny Newsome, Western Michigan; Bill Bradley, Princeton; Rick Barry, Miami (Fla.); Gary Bradds, Ohio State; and Steve Thomas, Xavier (O.). Another Xavier player, Bob Pelkington, edged Creighton's Paul Silas for the rebounding crown, averaging 21.80 rebounds a game to Silas' 21.75.

Michigan, with Bill Buntin and sophomore Cazzie Russell, tied Ohio State for the Big Ten title, while Wichita State, led by Dave Stallworth, and Drake, featuring McCoy McLemore, shared the Missouri Valley Conference crown. Perennial power Cincinnati, with Ron Bonham, finished fourth.

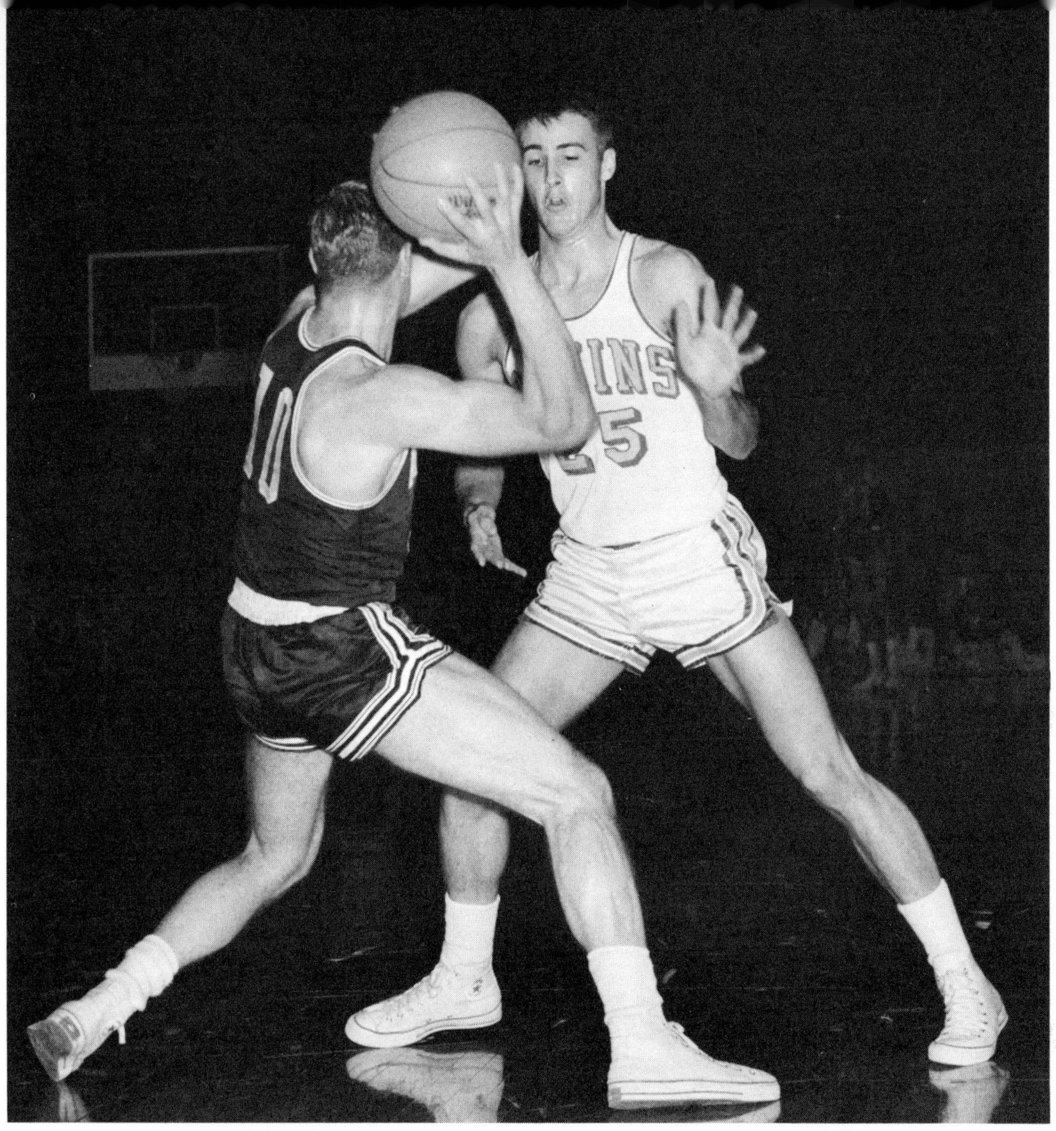

Gail Goodrich (25) was one of the mainstays of UCLA's 30-0 NCAA champions.

Davidson, sparked by Fred Hetzel, made a record 54.4 per cent of its field goal attempts in winning the Southern Conference crown, although yielding to Virginia Military in the league's post-season tournament. Ollie Johnson and Erwin Mueller led San Francisco to the West Coast Athletic Conference crown as John Beasley took Texas A&M to the top of the Southwest Conference and Cotton Nash sparked Kentucky to the Southeastern Conference title.

Other champions: Kansas State, Big Eight; Ohio U., Mid-American; Temple, Middle Atlantic; Murray State, Ohio Valley; Princeton, Ivy League; Connecticut and Rhode Island, tied, Yankee; and Montana State in the newly formed Big Sky.

Oregon State, with 7-foot Mel Counts, was strong among the independents, as were Texas Western, with Jim "Bad News" Barnes; Villanova, sparked by little Wally Jones; and Syracuse, with Dave Bing. Also formidable were defending NCAA champion Loyola (Ill.); Army, with Mike Silliman; Providence, with John Thompson; and St. Bonaventure, with Fred Crawford.

Some of the other stars: Billy Cunningham, North Carolina; Wayne Estes, Utah State; Bud Koper, Oklahoma City; Barry Kramer, NYU; Willie Murrell, Kansas State; Dan Schultz, Tennessee; Steve Courtin, St. Joseph's; Mel Northway, Minnesota; and John Tresvant, Seattle.

NCAA Championship
At Kansas City

UCLA (98)	FG	FT	Pts.	Duke (83)	FG	FT	Pts.
Goodrich	9	9	27	Ferguson	2	0	4
Hazzard	4	3	11	Buckley	5	8	18
Hirsch	5	3	13	Tison	3	1	7
Erickson	2	4	8	Harrison	1	0	2
McIntosh	4	0	8	Mullins	9	4	22
Washington	11	4	26	Marin	8	0	16
Darrow	0	3	3	Vacendak	2	3	7
Hoffman	1	0	2	Mann	0	3	3
				Herbster	1	0	2
				Kitching	1	0	2
Totals	36	26	98		32	19	83

NIT Championship
At New York

Bradley (86)	FG	FT	Pts.	New Mexico (54)	FG	FT	Pts.
R. Patterson	0	0	0	C. Williams	3	1	7
Jackson	7	0	14	Lucero	1	1	3
Strawder	9	3	21	Harge	2	4	8
West	5	2	12	Ellis	7	4	18
Tart	4	5	13	Kruzich	3	1	7
Hall	0	0	0	Zarr	3	0	6
R. Williams	0	1	1	Howard	0	0	0
Thompson	5	1	11	J. Patterson	0	3	3
Martin	3	0	6	Wasson	1	0	2
Frederick	1	2	4	Jordan	0	0	0
Day	2	0	4	Johnstone	0	0	0
Hutchinson	0	0	0	Edsen	0	0	0
Totals	36	14	86		20	14	54

NCAA Scores
REGIONALS
East

First Round: Villanova 77, Providence 66; Connecticut 53, Temple 48; Princeton 86, Virginia Military 60

Semifinals: Duke 87, Villanova 73; Connecticut 52, Princeton 50

Championship: Duke 101, Connecticut 54

Mideast

First Round: Ohio U. 71, Louisville 69; Loyola (Ill.) 101, Murray State 91

Semifinals: Ohio U. 85, Kentucky 69; Michigan 84, Loyola (Ill.) 80

Championship: Michigan 69, Ohio U. 57

Midwest

First Round: Creighton 89, Oklahoma City 78; Texas Western 68, Texas A&M 62

Semifinals: Wichita 84, Creighton 68; Kansas State 64, Texas Western 60

Championship: Kanas State 94, Wichita 86

Far West

First Round: Seattle 61, Oregon 57; Utah State 92, Arizona State 90

Semifinals: UCLA 95, Seattle 90; San Francisco 64, Utah State 58

Championship: UCLA 76, San Francisco 72

FINALS

Semifinals: Duke 91, Michigan 80; UCLA 90, Kansas State 84

Championship: UCLA 98, Duke 83

Consolation: Michigan 100, Kansas State 90

NIT Scores

First Round: St. Joseph's 86, Miami (Fla.) 76; NYU 77, Syracuse 68; Army 64, St. Bonaventure 62; Drake 87, Pittsburgh 82

Quarterfinals: Bradley 83, St. Joseph's 81; NYU 79, DePaul 66; New Mexico 65, Drake 60; Army 67, Duquesne 65

Semifinals: New Mexico 72, NYU 65; Bradley 67, Army 52

Championship: Bradley 86, New Mexico 54

Consolation: Army 60, NYU 59

Top Ten

AP	UPI
UCLA	UCLA
Michigan	Michigan
Duke	Kentucky
Kentucky	Duke
Wichita	Oregon State
Oregon State	Wichita
Villanova	Villanova
Loyola (Ill.)	Loyola (Ill.)
DePaul	Texas Western
Davidson	Davidson

All-Americans

AP	UPI
Gary Bradds, Ohio State	Gary Bradds, Ohio State
Cotton Nash, Kentucky	Walt Hazzard, UCLA
Walt Hazzard, UCLA	Cotton Nash, Kentucky
Bill Bradley, Princeton	Bill Bradley, Princeton
Dave Stallworth, Wichita	Dave Stallworth, Wichita

1964–65

Joe Lapchick, as a coach, and Bill Bradley, as a player, ended their collegiate careers in spectacular fashion as Lapchick's St. John's team won an unprecedented fourth NIT championship and Bradley, the Player of the Year, led Princeton to the consolation title in the NCAA tournament.

St. John's upset top-seeded Villanova, 55-51, for the NIT title to give Lapchick a victory and NIT crown in his final game as a coach. Villanova was led by Jim Washington, but it was Ken McIntyre of St. John's, scoring 101 points including 16 straight free throws without a miss in one game, who won MVP honors. With an expanded field of 14 teams, a record 114,714 people attended the seven NIT sessions at Madison Square Garden.

Bradley, who refused immediate offers to play professional basketball in order to accept a Rhodes scholarship to study at Oxford, scored a record 58 points in leading Ivy League champion Princeton to a third-place victory over Wichita State, 118-82, in the NCAA tourney. Bradley, who had turned down scholarship offers from schools throughout the country to pay his own way at Princeton, scored a record 177 points during the tourney to win the MVP trophy.

UCLA won its second straight NCAA title with a 91-80 triumph over Big Ten champion Michigan, with Cazzie Russell and Bill Buntin. UCLA was led by Gail Goodrich, who scored 42 points in the championship game, and Keith Erickson.

Rick Barry was the nation's top scorer with a 37.4 average as he led Miami (Fla.) to a record scoring average of 98.4 points a game. Miami made 79.6 percent of its free throw attempts, also a record high. Runnerup to Barry was Utah State's Wayne Estes, who was accidentally electrocuted midway through the season when his head brushed a live electric power line following a traffic accident.

Princeton's Bill Bradley was Player of the Year.

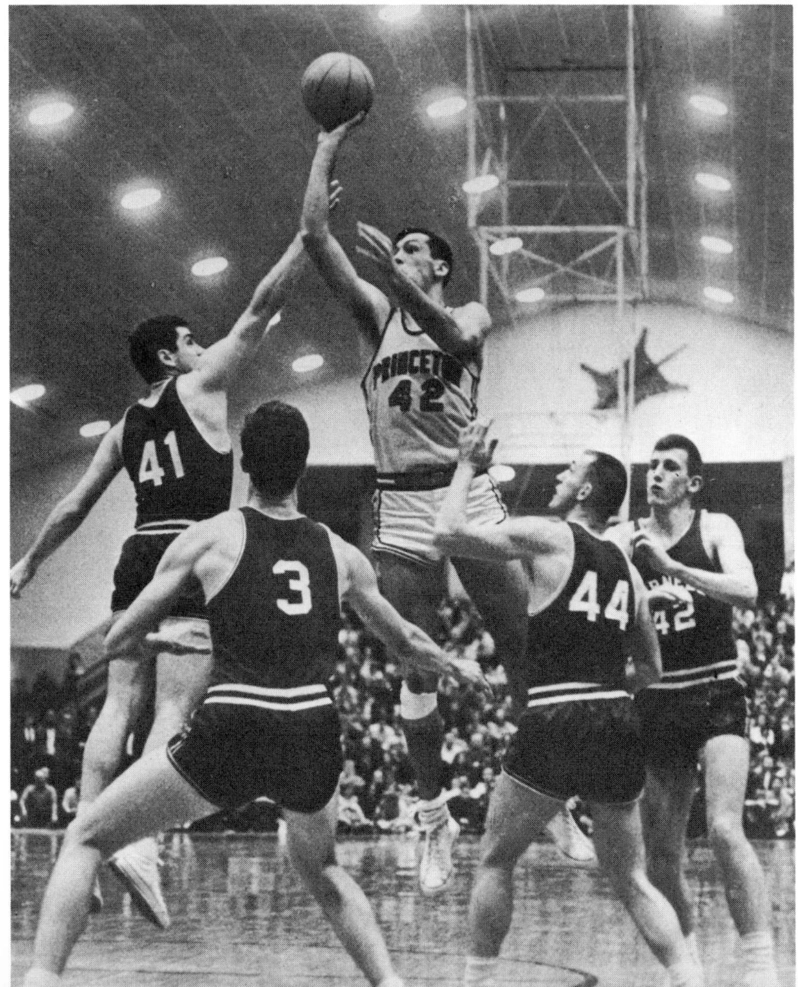

Fred Hetzel and Dick Snyder combined to lead Davidson to the Southern Conference title while 6-9 Clyde Lee took Vanderbilt to Southeastern Conference honors. Connecticut won the Yankee Conference race behind Toby Kimball, the nation's leading rebounder. Duke, with Bobby Verga and Jack Marin, won the Atlantic Coast Conference title. Wichita State won the Missouri Valley Conference crown on the strength of Kelly Pete and mid-year graduate Dave Stallworth.

St. Joseph's, with Matt Goukas, whose father led the same team 25 years earlier, won the Middle Atlantic Conference crown; and Brigham Young, with John Fairchild, won the Western Athletic Conference race. Other champions: San Francisco, West Coast Athletic; Eastern Kentucky, Ohio Valley; Oklahoma State, Big Eight; Miami (O.), and Ohio U., tied, Mid-American; and Weber State, Big Sky. Texas and Southern Methodist were declared Southwest Conference co-champions after Texas Tech used an ineligible player.

Providence, with sophomore Jimmy Walker, was strong among independents, as were Boston College, with John Austin; Detroit, with Dorrie Murray; Dayton, with Henry Finkel; Duquesne, with Willie Somerset; and Colorado State, with Lonnie Wright. Other quality teams were Minnesota, with Lou Hudson, Archie Clark and Don Yates; New Mexico, with Dick Ellis and Mel Daniels; Kansas, with Walt Wesley; and Oregon State, with Jim Jarvis.

Among the stars: Billy Cunningham, North Carolina; Dave Bing, Syracuse; Tal Brody and Skip Thoren, both Illinois; A.W. Davis, Tennessee; Flynn Robinson, Wyoming; Gary Keller, Florida; Dave Schellhase, Purdue; Dick and Tom Van Arsdale, Indiana; Jim King, Oklahoma State; and Warren Isaac, Iona.

NCAA Championship

At Portland, Oregon

UCLA (91)	FG	FT	Pts.	Michigan (80)	FG	FT	Pts.
Erickson	1	1	3	Darden	8	1	17
Lacey	5	1	11	Pomey	2	0	4
McIntosh	1	1	3	Buntin	6	2	14
Goodrich	12	18	42	Russell	10	8	28
Goss	4	0	8	Tregoning	2	1	5
Washington	7	3	17	Myers	0	0	0
Lynn	2	1	5	Ludwig	1	0	2
Lyons	0	0	0	Clawson	3	0	6
Galbraith	0	0	0	Dill	1	2	4
Hoffman	1	0	2	Brown	0	0	0
Levin	0	0	0	Thompson	0	0	0
Chambers	0	0	0	Bankey	0	0	0
Totals	33	25	91		33	14	80

NIT Championship

At New York

St. John's (55)	FG	FT	Pts.	Villanova (51)	FG	FT	Pts.
B. McIntyre	6	4	16	Soens	2	0	4
Duerr	1	0	2	Erickson	3	0	6
Dove	7	0	14	Washington	6	6	18
Houston	1	3	5	Leftwich	7	1	15
K. McIntyre	8	2	18	Melchionni	2	0	4
Wirell	0	0	0	Schaeffer	2	0	4
Swartz	0	0	0	Kenny	0	0	0
Totals	23	9	55		22	7	51

NCAA Scores

REGIONALS

East

First Round: Princeton 60, Penn State 58; St. Joseph's 67, Connecticut 61; Providence 91, West Virginia 67

Semifinals: Princeton 66, North Carolina State 48; Providence 81, St. Joseph's 73

Championship: Princeton 109, Providence 69

NIT Scores

First Round: St. John's 114, Boston College 92; Manhattan 71, Texas Western 53; Western Kentucky 57, Fordham 53; Army 70, St. Louis 66; NYU 71, Bradley 70; Detroit 93, LaSalle 86

Quarterfinals: St. John's 61, New Mexico 54; Villanova 73, Manhattan 71; NYU 87, Detroit 76; Army 58, Western Kentucky 54

Semifinals: Villanova 91, NYU 69; St. John's 67, Army 60

Championship: St. John's 55, Villanova 51

Consolation: Army 75, NYU 74

NCAA Scores (cont.)

Mideast

First Round: Dayton 66, Ohio U. 65; DePaul 99, Eastern Kentucky 52

Semifinals: Michigan 98, Dayton 71; Vanderbilt 83, DePaul 79

Championship: Michigan 87, Vanderbilt 85

Midwest

First Round: Houston 99, Notre Dame 98

Semifinals: Oklahoma State 75, Houston 60; Wichita State 86, Southern Methodist 81

Championship: Wichita State 54, Oklahoma State 46

Far West

First Round: Oklahoma City 70, Colorado State 68

Semifinals: San Francisco 91 Oklahoma City 67; UCLA 100, Brigham Young 76

Championship: UCLA 101, San Francisco 93

FINALS

Semifinals: Michigan 93, Princeton 76; UCLA 108 Wichita State 89

Championship: UCLA 91, Michigan 80

Consolation: Princeton 118, Wichita State 82

Top Ten

AP	UPI
Michigan	Michigan
UCLA	UCLA
St. Joseph's	St. Joseph's
Providence	Providence
Vanderbilt	Vanderbilt
Davidson	Brigham Young
Minnesota	Davidson
Villanova	Minnesota
Brigham Young	Duke
Duke	San Francisco

All-Americans

AP	UPI
Bill Bradley, Princeton	Bill Bradley, Princeton
Cazzie Russell, Michigan	Cazzie Russell, Michigan
Rick Barry, Miami (Fla.)	Gail Goodrich, UCLA
Gail Goodrich, UCLA	Fred Hetzel, Davidson
Fred Hetzel, Davidson	Rick Barry, Miami (Fla.)
Wayne Estes, Utah State (posthumously)	

1965–66

Duke's Atlantic Coast Conference champions, with Bobby Verga, Jack Marin and Steve Vacendak, and Southeastern Conference titlist Kentucky, with Louis Dampier, Pat Riley and Larry Conley, were considered the teams to beat.

But unheralded Texas Western came from out of nowhere to capture the NCAA tournament as the Miners upset Kentucky, 72-65, in the championship game. Texas Western, featuring Bobby Joe Hill, Dave Lattin, Willie Cager, Orsten Artis, Neville Shed and Willie Worsley, had lost only one game all season. Duke meanwhile took consolation honors, while the MVP trophy went to Jerry Chambers of Western Athletic Conference champion Utah.

Tall and powerful Brigham Young, with 6-10 Craig Raymond and Steve Kramer leading the way after Dick Nemelka got into foul trouble, defeated small but game NYU, 97-84, for the NIT title. NYU was led by 6-1 Mal Graham, 6-4 Stan MacKenzie, 6-3 Rich Dyer and 6-4 Bruce Kaplan. Villanova's Bill Melchionni was named MVP as he led all scorers with 109 points in four games.

Contrasts were recorded in the scores of Houston, led by Joe Hamood and sophomore Elvin Hayes, which beat Texas Wesleyan, 154-67, and Duke, which barely beat North Carolina, 21-20. Syracuse, behind the shooting of Dave Bing, rang up a record 99.0 points a game while making 40.4 field goals per game, also a record. Individual honors went to Purdue's Dave Schellhase, who averaged 32.54 points a game to edge Idaho's Dave Wagnon, averaging 32.50 points.

Rice ended a 27-game losing streak by beating Baylor and Texas A&M used Olympic shotputter Randy Matson, but Southwest conference honors went to Southern Methodist.

The trio of Cliff Anderson, Matt Goukas, and Billy Oakes took St. Joseph's to the top of the Middle Atlantic conference, while the efforts of Cazzie Russell and Oliver Darden retained the Big Ten title for Michigan. Clem Haskins led Western Kentucky to the Ohio Valley

OHIO
MICHIGAN
33

Conference crown, and Walt Wesley teamed with sophomore Jo Jo White to win the Big Eight crown at Kansas.

The University of the Pacific, with Keith Swagerty, won the West Coast Athletic Conference race. Dick Snyder sparked Davidson to the Southern Conference crown, and Oregon State, with Loy Peterson, won the AAWU championship. Other champions: Cincinnati, Missouri Valley; Miami (O.), Mid-American; Manhattan, Metropolitan; Penn, Ivy League; Weber State and Gonzaga, tied, Big Sky; and Rhode Island and Connecticut, tied, Yankee.

Jimmy Walker teamed with Dexter Westbrook to make Providence a strong independent, while Loyola (Ill.) with Corky Bell and Jim Coleman, was also powerful. Other independents of note were Boston College, with John Austin; St. John's, with Sonny Dove; DePaul, with Dave Mills; Dayton, with Henry Finkel; and Army, with Mike Silliman.

Among stars of the season: Clyde Lee, Vanderbilt; Don Freeman, Illinois; Lou Hudson, Minnesota; Westley Unseld, Louisville; Bob Lloyd, Rutgers; John Wetzel, Virginia Tech; Dorrie Murray, Detroit; Stan Washington, Michigan State; Joe Allen, Bradley; Warren Armstrong, Wichita State; Clarence McHenry, Hardin-Simmons; George Peeples, Iowa; Jon Block, Southern California; and Jim Barnett and Nick Jones, both Oregon.

Willie Cager controls ball as Texas Western beats Kentucky for NCAA crown.

Cazzie Russell led Michigan to the Big Ten title.

NCAA Championship

At College Park, Maryland

Texas Western (72)	FG	FT	Pts.	Kentucky (65)	FG	FT	Pts.
Hill	7	6	20	Dampier	7	5	19
Artis	5	5	15	Kron	3	0	6
Shed	1	1	3	Conley	4	2	10
Lattin	5	6	16	Riley	8	3	19
Cager	1	6	8	Jaracz	3	1	7
Flournoy	1	0	2	Berger	2	0	4
Worsley	2	4	8	Gamble	0	0	0
				LeMaster	0	0	0
				Tallent	0	0	0
Totals	22	28	72		27	11	65

NIT Championship

At New York

Brigham Young (97)	FG	FT	Pts.	NYU (84)	FG	FT	Pts.
Kramer	9	2	20				
Hill	9	3	21	MacKenzie	10	7	27
Raymond	10	1	21	Kaplan	9	0	18
Nemelka	5	5	15	Silen	3	3	9
Congdon	5	1	11	Graham	8	2	18
Jimas	2	1	5	Dyer	5	2	12
Ruffner	1	0	2	Witrock	0	0	0
Schouten	1	0	2				
Eakins	0	0	0				
James	0	0	0				
Fisher	0	0	0				
Totals	42	13	97		35	14	84

NCAA Scores

REGIONALS

East

First Round: St. Joseph's 65, Providence 48; Davidson 95, Rhode Island 65

Semifinals: Syracuse 94, Davidson 79; Duke 76, St. Joseph's 74

Championship: Duke 91, Syracuse 81

Mideast

First Round: Dayton 58, Miami (O.) 51; Western Kentucky 105, Loyola (Ill.) 86

Semifinals: Kentucky 86, Dayton 79; Michigan 80, Western Kentucky 79

Championship: Kentucky 84, Michigan 77

Midwest

First Round: Texas Western 89, Oklahoma City 74

Semifinals: Texas Western 78, Cincinnati 76; Kansas 76, Southern Methodist 70

Championship: Texas Western 81, Kansas 80

Far West

First Round: Houston 82, Colorado State 79

Semifinals: Oregon State 63, Houston 60; Utah 83, University of the Pacific 74

Championship: Utah 70, Oregon State 64

FINALS

Semifinals: Kentucky 83, Duke 79; Texas Western 85, Utah 78

Championship: Texas Western 72, Kentucky 65

Consolation: Duke 79, Utah 77

NIT Scores

First Round: Temple 88, Virginia Tech 73; NYU 68, DePaul 65; San Francisco 89, Penn State 77; Villanova 63, St. John's 61; Army 71, Manhattan 66; Boston College 96, Louisville 90

Quarterfinals: Brigham Young 90, Temple 78; NYU 90, Wichita State 84; Army 80, San Francisco 63; Villanova 86, Boston College 85

Semifinals: Brigham Young 66, Army 60; NYU 69, Villanova 63

Championship: Brigham Young 97, NYU 84

Consolation: Villanova 76, Army 65

Top Ten

AP	UPI
Kentucky	Kentucky
Duke	Duke
Texas Western	Texas Western
Kansas	Kansas
St. Joseph's	Loyola (Ill.)
Loyola (Ill.)	St. Joseph's
Cincinnati	Michigan
Vanderbilt	Vanderbilt
Michigan	Cincinnati
Western Kentucky	Providence

All-Americans

AP	UPI
Cazzie Russell, Michigan	Cazzie Russell, Michigan
Clyde Lee, Vanderbilt	Clyde Lee, Vanderbilt
Dave Schellhase, Purdue	Jimmy Walker, Providence
Louis Dampier, Kentucky	Dave Schellhase, Purdue
Dave Bing, Syracuse	Dave Bing, Syracuse

1966–67

To the surprise of almost no one, UCLA swept past 30 opponents to capture its third NCAA title in four seasons. Led by 7-foot sophomore Lew Alcindor, a unanimous All-America choice, the Bruins had only one close call all season, a 40-35 overtime victory over arch-rival Southern California.

UCLA became only the second team ever to win three NCAA titles in four years. Kentucky turned the trick in 1948, 1949, and 1951. UCLA, dominating the all-tournament team with MVP Alcindor and guards Lucius Allen and Mike Warren, beat the tourney's Cinderella team, Dayton, 79-64, in the final.

The last NIT in the 49th street Madison Square Garden saw the nation's No.1 small college team, Southern Illinois, surprise St. Peter's of Jersey City, Duke, and Rutgers before downing Marquette, led by Bob Wolfe and George Thompson, 71-56, in the title game. SIU's backcourt whiz Walt Frazier was named MVP while Bob Lloyd of Rutgers tallied 129 points in four games. George Stone collected 46 points as Marshall scored a record total of points in beating Nebraska, 119-88.

North Carolina, with Larry Miller and Bob Lewis, swept to the Atlantic Coast Conference,

Lew Alcindor's sophomore season at UCLA was capped with an NCAA championship.

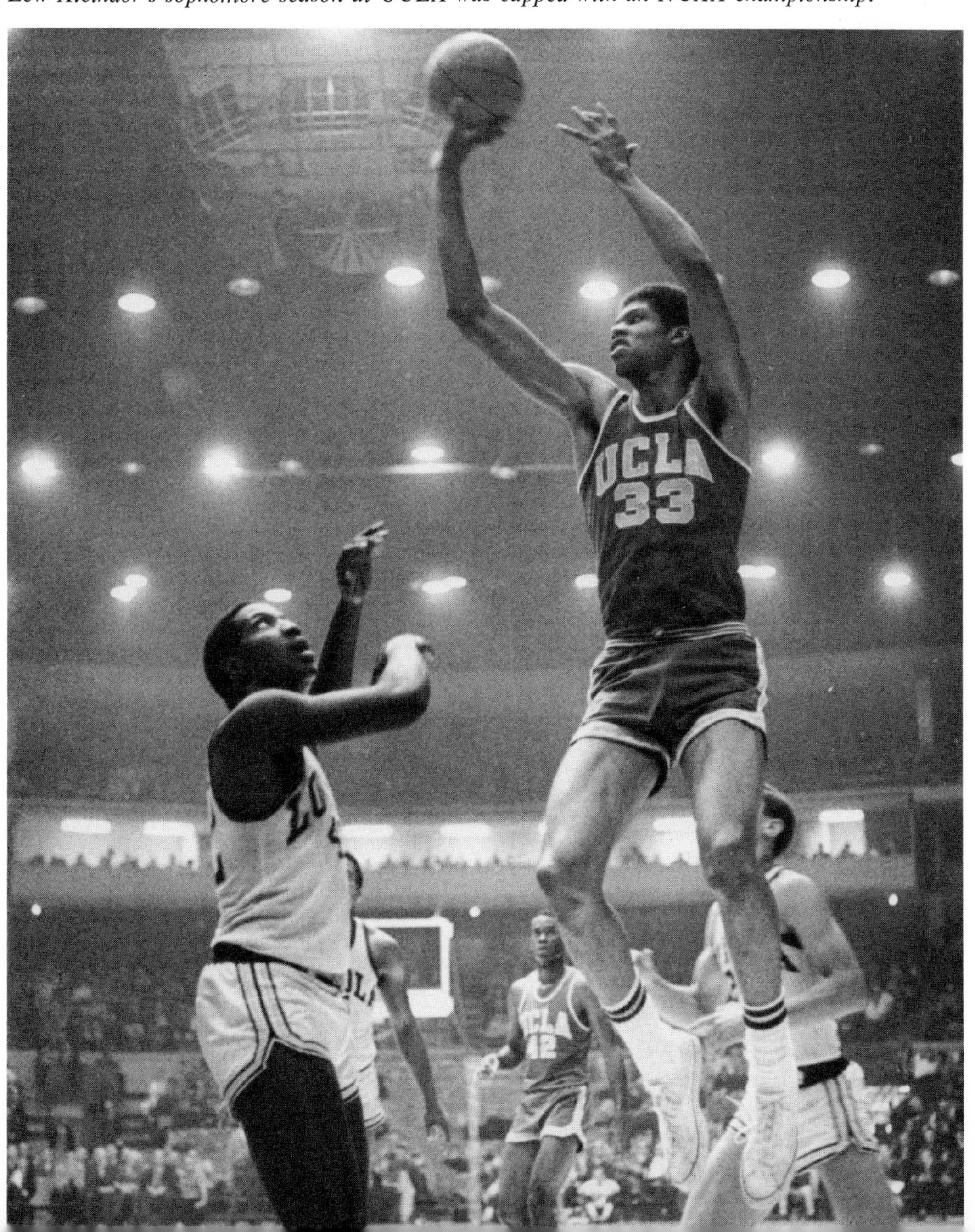

while three-sport star Ron Widby sparked Tennessee past Florida and Vanderbilt in the Southeastern Conference. Indiana and Michigan State tied for the championship in one of the closest Big Ten races in years. Peck Hickman closed out a 23-year coaching career at Louisville as the Cardinals, powered by 6-8 Westley Unseld and 6-4 Butch Beard, reigned in the Missouri Valley Conference.

West Virginia, with Ron Williams, Carl Head, and Dave Reaser each averaging 20 points a game, captured both the regular season title and the Southern Conference tournament crown. Other champions: Kansas, Big Eight; Princeton, Ivy League; Temple, Middle Atlantic; Connecticut, Yankee; Western Kentucky, Ohio Valley; Toledo, Mid-American; Southern Methodist, Southwest; University of the Pacific, West Coast Athletic; and Wyoming and Brigham Young, tied, Western Athletic.

UCLA's Alcindor made a record 66.7 percent of his shots for a 29.0-point-per-game average, second only to the 30.4-point average of Providence's Jimmy Walker. Mal Graham of NYU was third with a 28.7-point-per-game average.

Elvin Hayes led Houston to the top spot among independents, while Dayton, with Don May, was the surprise team in the Midwest. Other strong independents were Boston College, with Terry Driscoll; St. John's, with Sonny Dove; Virginia Tech, with Glen Combs; Oklahoma City, the top-scoring team in the country with a 96.0-point average; Marquette; Providence; Texas Western; New Mexico State, and Seattle.

Some of the outstanding players: Clem Haskins, Western Kentucky; Bob Verga, Duke; Bob Lloyd, Rutgers; Mel Daniels, New Mexico; Chris Thomforde, Princeton; Walt Piatkowski, Bowling Green; Russ Critchfield, California; Tom Kondla, Minnesota; Art Stephenson, Rhode Island; and Dave Lattin, Texas Western.

NCAA Championship

At Louisville

UCLA (79)	FG	FT	Pts.	Dayton (64)	FG	FT	Pts.
Heitz	2	0	4	May	9	3	21
Shackleford	5	0	10	Sadlier	2	1	5
Alcindor	8	4	20	Obrovac	0	0	0
Allen	7	5	19	Klaus	4	0	8
Warren	8	1	17	Hooper	2	2	6
Nielsen	0	0	0	Torain	3	0	6
Sweek	1	0	2	Waterman	4	2	10
Saffer	2	0	4	Sharpenter	2	4	8
Saner	1	0	2	Samanich	0	0	0
Chrisman	0	1	1	Beckman	0	0	0
Sutherland	0	0	0	Inderrieden	0	0	0
Lynn	0	0	0	Wannemacher	0	0	0
Totals	34	11	79		26	12	64

NIT Championship

At New York

Southern Illinois (71)	FG	FT	Pts.	Marquette (56)	FG	FT	Pts.
Garrett	5	2	12	Thompson	4	4	12
C. Smith	3	7	13	Brunkhorst	2	1	5
Johnson	3	1	7	P. Smith	1	2	4
Frazier	8	5	21	Burke	6	3	15
Zastrow	2	0	4	Wolf	7	3	17
Bechtold	3	4	10	Anderson	1	0	2
Griffin	0	0	0	Simmons	0	0	0
Westcott	0	0	0	Luchini	0	1	1
Whitaker	0	0	0	Curran	0	0	0
Taylor	0	0	0	Langenkamp	0	0	0
Benson	2	0	4				
Totals	26	19	71		21	14	56

NCAA Scores

REGIONALS

East

First Round: Princeton 68, West Virginia 57; St. John's 57, Temple 53

Semifinals: North Carolina 78, Princeton 70; Boston College 63, St. John's 62

Championship: North Carolina 96, Boston College 80

NIT Scores

First Round: Marshall 70, Villanova 68; Southern Illinois 103, St. Peter's (N. J.) 58; Providence 77, Memphis State 68; New Mexico 66, Syracuse 64; Marquette 64, Tulsa 60; Rutgers 78, Utah State 76

Quarterfinals: Southern Illinois 72, Duke 63; Marshall 119, Nebraska 88; Rutgers 65, New Mexico 60; Marquette 81, Providence 80

NCAA Scores (cont.)

Mideast

First Round: Dayton 69, Western Kentucky 67; Virginia Tech 82, Toledo 76

Semifinals: Dayton 53, Tennessee 52; Virginia Tech 79, Indiana 70

Championship: Dayton 71, Virginia Tech 66

Midwest

First Round: Houston 59, New Mexico State 58

Semifinals: Houston 66, Kansas 53; Southern Methodist 83, Louisville 81

Championship: Houston 83, Southern Methodist 75

Far West

First Round: Texas Western 62, Seattle 54

Semifinals: Pacific 72, Texas Western 63; UCLA 109, Wyoming 60

Championship: UCLA 80, Pacific 64

FINALS

Semifinals: Dayton 76, North Carolina 62; UCLA 73, Houston 58

Championship: UCLA 79, Dayton 64

Consolation: Houston 84, North Carolina 62

NIT Scores (cont.)

Semifinals: Marquette 83, Marshall 78; Southern Illinois 79, Rutgers 70

Championship: Southern Illinois 71, Marquette 56

Consolation: Rutgers 93, Marshall 76

Top Ten

AP	UPI
UCLA	UCLA
Louisville	Louisville
Kansas	North Carolina
North Carolina	Kansas
Princeton	Princeton
Western Kentucky	Houston
Houston	Western Kentucky
Tennessee	Texas Western
Boston College	Tennessee
Texas Western	Boston College

All-Americans

AP	UPI
Lew Alcindor, UCLA	Lew Alcindor, UCLA
Jimmy Walker, Providence	Jimmy Walker, Providence
Westley Unseld, Louisville	Westley Unseld, Louisville
Elvin Hayes, Houston	Elvin Hayes, Houston
Clem Haskins, Western Kentucky	Bob Lloyd, Rutgers

1967–68

UCLA, with Big A, and Houston, with Big E, were in competition all season for headlines, ratings, and finally, the national championship. Houston's Big E was 6-9 Elvin Hayes, who led the Cougars to a 71-69 victory over UCLA, featuring 7-1 Lew "Big A" Alcindor, before 52,693 people in Houston's Astrodome. The victory, witnessed by the largest crowd ever to watch a basketball game in the United States, snapped UCLA's 47-game winning streak in a season which brought the no-dunk rule aimed at big men like Alcindor and Hayes.

The Bruins, after winning the Pacific Eight title, took revenge against Houston, highest scoring team in the country with its 97.8-point-per-game average, in the semifinal game of the NCAA tournament. Hayes was held to 10 points, the lowest of his varsity career, as UCLA won, 101-69. The Bruins went on to beat Atlantic Coast Conference champion North Carolina, with Larry Miller and Charlie Scott, to retain the NCAA crown. So overwhelming was UCLA's triumph, 78-55 (the widest spread ever in a championship game), that four Bruins were named to the all-tournament team: MVP Alcindor, Mike Warren, Lucius Allen and Lynn Shackleford, along with North Carolina's Larry Miller.

Dayton used height and strength to overpower Kansas, with Jo Jo White and Roger Bohnenstiehl, 61-48, to win the first NIT in the new Madison Square Garden atop Penn Station in New York. Dayton's Don May was voted MVP after scoring 106 points in the tourney, although Elnardo Webster of St. Peter's scored 51 points against Marshall.

Sophomores Pete Maravich of Louisiana State and Calvin Murphy of Niagara finished one-two in the individual scoring race. Maravich joined Oscar Robertson as the only sophomores ever to lead the nation in scoring as he averaged a record 43.8 points, compared to Murphy's

Elvin Hayes, the Big E, led Houston to national acclaim.

38.2. Florida's Neal Walk led in rebounding with an average of 19.8.

Army, with Bill Schutsky, was the leading defensive team in the country, yielding 57.9 points a game, and was a strong independent, as were St. Bonaventure, with Bob Lanier and Bill Butler; Marquette, with George "Brute Force" Thompson; Oklahoma City, with Rich Travis; Boston College, with Terry Driscoll; and Notre Dame, with Bob Arnzen and Bob Whitemore.

Louisville, led by Westley Unseld, won the Missouri Valley Conference, while Columbia, powered by 7-foot Dave Newmark and sophomore Jim McMillian, beat Princeton in a playoff for the Ivy League title. New Mexico, led by Ron Nelson, won the Western Athletic Conference honors, and Davidson, featuring Mike Maloy, took the Southern Conference crown. Other champions: Bowling Green, Mid-American; Kansas State, Big Eight; Rhode Island and Massachusetts, tied, Yankee; Texas Christian, Southwest; Kentucky, Southeastern; Santa Clara, West Coast Athletic; and Murray State and East Tennessee, tied, Ohio Valley. Ohio State defeated Iowa for the Big Ten berth in the NCAA tourney.

Among the better teams were Duke, with Mike Lewis; Georgia, with Bob Leinhard; Marshall, with George Stone and Danny D'Antoni; Tennessee, with 7-foot Tom Boerwinkle; and Purdue, with sophomore Rick Mount. There were such outstanding players as: Warren Armstrong, Wichita State; Merv Jackson, Utah; Ron Williams, West Virginia; Joe Franklin,

Wisconsin; Shaler Halimon, Utah State; Fred Foster, Miami (O); Joe Allen, Bradley; Harry Hollines, Denver; and Manny Leaks, Niagara.

NCAA Championship

At Los Angeles

UCLA (78)	FG	FT	Pts.
Shackleford	3	0	6
Lynn	1	5	7
Alcindor	15	4	34
Warren	3	1	7
Allen	3	5	11
Nielson	1	0	2
Heitz	3	1	7
Sutherland	1	0	2
Sweek	0	0	0
Saner	1	0	2
Totals	31	16	78

North Carolina (55)	FG	FT	Pts.
Miller	5	4	14
Bunting	1	1	3
Clark	4	1	9
Scott	6	0	12
Grubar	2	1	5
Fogler	1	2	4
Brown	2	2	6
Tuttle	0	0	0
Frye	1	0	2
Whitehead	0	0	0
Delany	0	0	0
Fletcher	0	0	0
Totals	22	11	55

NCAA Scores

REGIONALS

East

First Round: Columbia 83, LaSalle 69; Davidson 79, St. John's 70; St. Bonaventure 102, Boston College 93

Semifinals: Davidson 61, Columbia 59; North Carolina 91, St. Bonaventure 72

Championship: North Carolina 70, Davidson 66

Mideast

First Round: Marquette 72, Bowling Green 71; East Tennessee State 79, Florida State 69

Semifinals: Kentucky 107, Marquette 89; Ohio State 79, East Tennessee State 72

Championship: Ohio State 82, Kentucky 81

Midwest

First Round: Houston 94, Loyola (Ill.) 76

Semifinals: Houston 91, Louisville 75; Texas Christian 77, Kansas State 72

Championship: Houston 103, Texas Christian 68

Far West

First Round: New Mexico State 68, Weber State 57

Semifinals: Santa Clara 86, New Mexico 73; UCLA 58, New Mexico State 49

Championship: UCLA 87, Santa Clara 66

FINALS

Semifinals: North Carolina 80, Ohio State 66; UCLA 101, Houston 69

Championship: UCLA 78, North Carolina 55

Consolation: Ohio State 89, Houston 85

NIT Championship

At New York

Dayton (61)	FG	FT	Pts.
May	8	6	22
Sadlier	4	1	9
Obrovac	0	4	4
Jim G'ttsch'll	1	6	8
Hooper	5	6	16
Leffel	0	0	0
Wannemacher	0	0	0
Janky	0	0	0
Jer. G'ttsch'll	0	2	2
Torain	0	0	0
Totals	18	25	61

Kansas (48)	FG	FT	Pts.
Bohnenstiel	6	0	12
Douglas	3	0	6
Nash	4	2	10
Harmon	1	0	2
White	5	0	10
Bradshaw	1	0	2
Sloan	3	0	6
Totals	23	2	48

NIT Scores

First Round: Duke 97, Oklahoma City 81; St. Peter's (N. J.) 102, Marshall 93; Kansas 82, Temple 76; Villanova 77, Wyoming 66; Dayton 87, West Virginia 68; Fordham 69, Duquesne 60; LIU 80, Bradley 77; Notre Dame 62, Army 58

Quarterfinals: St. Peter's (N. J.) 100, Duke 71; Kansas 55, Villanova 49; Dayton 61, Fordham 60; Notre Dame 62, LIU 60

Semifinals: Kansas 58, St. Peter's (N. J.) 46; Dayton 76, Notre Dame 74

Championship: Dayton 61, Kansas 48

Consolation: Notre Dame 81, St. Peter's (N. J.) 78

Top Ten

AP	UPI
Houston	Houston
UCLA	UCLA
St. Bonaventure	St. Bonaventure
North Carolina	North Carolina
Kentucky	Kentucky
New Mexico	Columbia
Columbia	New Mexico
Davidson	Louisville
Louisville	Davidson
Duke	Marquette

All-Americans

AP	UPI
Elvin Hayes, Houston	Elvin Hayes, Houston
Westley Unseld, Louisville	Lew Alcindor, UCLA
Lew Alcindor, UCLA	Pete Maravich, Louisiana State
Pete Maravich, Louisiana State	Westley Unseld, Louisville
Calvin Murphy, Niagara	Larry Miller, North Carolina

14
35

ALL-TIME MAJOR COLLEGE RECORDS

(Based on statistics from National Collegiate Sports Services)

INDIVIDUAL

Single Game

Most Points	100	Frank Selvy, Furman, vs Newberry, 1954

Season

Most Points	1,214	Elvin Hayes, Houston, 1968
Highest Scoring Avg.	43.8	Pete Maravich, Louisiana State, 1968
Most F.G. Attempted	1,022	Pete Maravich, Louisiana State, 1968
Most F.G. Made	519	Elvin Hayes, Houston, 1968
Highest F.G. Percentage	.667	Lew Alcindor, UCLA, 1967
Most F.T. Attempted	444	Frank Selvy, Furman, 1954
Most F.T. Made	355	Frank Selvy, Furman, 1954
Highest F.T. Percentage	.933	Tom Boyer, Arkansas, 1962
Most Rebounds	734	Walter Dukes, Seton Hall, 1953
Highest Rebounding Avg.	25.6	Charlie Slack, Marshall, 1955

Career

Most Points	2,973	Oscar Robertson, Cincinnati, 1957-60
Highest Scoring Avg.	33.8	Oscar Robertson, Cincinnati, 1957-60
Most Field Goals	1,215	Elvin Hayes, Houston, 1965-68
Most Free Throws	*905	Dickie Hemric, Wake Forest, 1951-55

*Four-year total

TEAM

Single Game

Most Points, one team	158	Houston vs Valparaiso (81), Feb. 24, 1968
Most Points, two teams	260	Houston 152, Texas Wesleyan 108, Feb. 25, 1966

Season

Most Consecutive Victories	60	San Francisco, 1954-55 to 1956-57
Most Victories in Perfect Season	32	North Carolina, 1957
Most Points	3,226	Houston, 1968
Highest Scoring Avg.	99.0	Syracuse, 1966
Highest F.G. Percentage	.544	Davidson, 1964
Highest F.T. Percentage	.796	Miami (Florida), 1965
Highest Rebound Percentage	.644	Fordham, 1953
Most Personal Fouls per game	29.3	Indiana, 1952

UCLA's Lew Alcindor (left) and Houston's Elvin Hayes reach for the sky at the Astrodome.

4: THE GREATEST COLLEGIANS

Joe Lapchick has been connected with the game of basketball for more than 50 years. As a player with the original Celtics and many other early teams, as a professional coach with the New York Knickerbockers and a college coach at St. John's University, Lapchick was such a distinguished figure that he inevitably was elected to the Basketball Hall of Fame.

His career stretches from the early days of the game to the modern era. Lapchick has seen virtually every outstanding player and all the great teams. Naturally, choosing the top players must be a subjective process. One can not measure greatness on statistics alone. Many intangibles—ranging from desire to often unsung skills such as defense and playmaking—serve as a truer yardstick than scoring average.

Lapchick took all this into account when he chose the following as the 20 greatest college basketball players of the modern era.

LEW ALCINDOR

Not since the Oscar Robertson regime at Cincinnati in 1956–60 did one player dominate the college game the way Lew Alcindor did at UCLA. In three varsity seasons, 7-1⅜ Ferdinand Lewis Alcindor led the Bruins to three consecutive NCAA titles losing only two games in the process.

Lew could do everything. He moved with surprising grace for a man of his size, picking off rebounds, blocking shots, triggering the fast break with bullet passes, and scoring on short jump shots, hooks, and tip-ins. After his first season, the NCAA rules committee outlawed his favorite, the dunk shot, but it didn't stop Lew. He could score, it seemed, almost anytime he wanted to.

Alcindor scored 30 points in his first frosh scrimmage against the UCLA varsity despite a three-man platoon guarding him, and he scored 56 points in his first varsity game. But no one could ever call him a gunner. "I don't care about points," Alcindor said. "I care about winning. Frank Selvy once scored 100 points in a college game. It's been done before. I don't want them to remember me for scoring records. Bob Cousy doesn't own any scoring records, but I don't think anybody will forget him."

Nobody is likely to forget Alcindor. After one varsity season at UCLA, he was already being compared to the all-time greats.

Alcindor was born large. He was 22½ inches long at birth, weighing 12 pounds, 11 ounces. He was the only child of a 6-2 New York subway policeman and a 6-foot housewife. When he entered St. Jude's school in Manhattan at the age of six, he already towered more than a foot above his classmates.

On the first day of school his teacher spotted the long, lanky figure in the back of the room and yelled, "You, there, please sit down."

Said Alcindor in a soft voice, "But I am sitting down."

Alcindor was a six-footer by the time he was 10 years old. The coach at St. Jude's, Farrell Hopkins, automatically put him on the basketball team. A program of weightlifting, rope-jumping, and tennis eliminated much of his gawkiness.

At 13, Alcindor stood 6-8 and weighed 200 pounds. A friend, Art Kenny, brought him to the attention of John Donohue, the basketball coach at Power Memorial Academy. Donohue arranged a scholarship for Alcindor, and his fantastic high school career began.

He led Power to 71 straight victories before the Panthers bowed, 46–43, to powerful DeMatha High School of Hyattsville, Maryland. Mr. A, as his teammates called him, scored 2,067 points and collected 2,002 rebounds in his high school career. Both were New York City schoolboy records.

Large Lewie was sought by every college in the country. One coach, deep in the South, said, "Get me Alcindor and I'll integrate. They'll forget his color when he makes us national champions."

Coach Donohue screened all the offers and kept the press, the recruiters, and the public away from his prodigy. The decision narrowed down to New York University, St. John's, Michigan, and UCLA. Ralph Bunche, a UCLA alumnus, left his United Nations post one afternoon to visit Alcindor. Jackie Robinson, another UCLA alumnus, also paid a courtesy call on Alcindor.

On May 3, 1965, in front of television cameras, microphones, his proud mother, and a swarm of reporters in the Power gym, Alcindor announced, "This fall I'll be attending UCLA."

So Alcindor went west. He led the freshmen to an undefeated season, then paced the varsity to an undefeated season and the NCAA title. His shooting, effortless rebounding, ball-handling skill and tenacious defense were beautiful to see. He intimidated the opposition with his height and skills.

UCLA went 45 games without a loss into the middle of his junior year. Then Lew suffered an eye injury in a fight for a rebound and sat out two games which UCLA won.

He returned to action against the No. 2 team in the country, Houston. The largest indoor crowd in the history of basketball, 52,693, augmented by millions of others over television, watched this meeting of the titans in the Astrodome. Alcindor, suffering from double-vision and weak from a hospital stay, was just another man on the court. Houston's Elvin Hayes scored 39 points to 18 for Alcindor, and the UCLA streak was over.

"We'll just have to start another streak," said UCLA coach John Wooden. The Bruins didn't lose again as they went on to win their second straight NCAA title, beating Houston in the semi-finals.

In his senior year, Alcindor led UCLA to an unprecedented third straight NCAA championship, losing only one game en route. For the third time in a row, Lew was named

MVP in the tourney. He averaged 26.4 points a game during his three years and made 62.4 percent of his shots, an NCAA record.

The subject of a bidding war between the National Basketball Association and the fledgling American Basketball Association, Lew signed a contract for more than $1 million with the Milwaukee Bucks of the NBA.

VINCE BORYLA

The most vivid memory of the 1940s for many basketball fans is a picture of the husky figure of Vince Boryla, looking bulkier than his listed 210 pounds and shorter than 6-5, driving to the basket with his left arm in front of his body and his right arm arching for one of the most accurate hook shots ever seen.

Denver's Vince Boryla

Boryla could make a crowd gasp over his soft over-the-head hook. Many times the ball would float into the basket as Boryla was rolling on the floor from a push. No defense could stop his shot.

The memory is stronger and sharper because Boryla seemed to be around the college scene longer than any other man in history. Indeed, his college career spanned nearly a decade. He was 28 years old when he made most All-America teams in 1949 at the University of Denver.

Boryla was born in East Chicago, Indiana. After an exceptional high school career, he entered Notre Dame and was a star right from the beginning. Basketball had always been No. 2 to football at Notre Dame, and if Boryla didn't change that, he at least led the Irish to national basketball prominence.

After a season at Notre Dame, Boryla enlisted in the Army Air Corps, where he continued to play basketball at Lowry Air Force Base in Denver, Colorado.

When World War II ended, Boryla stayed on in Denver to play for the AAU Denver Nuggets. In 1948 he performed with the U.S. Olympic team in London. Following the Olympics, Boryla decided to return to college for his degree. He was 28 years old by this time, married with two sons and a daughter, but could still score with his deadly hook shot at Denver U.

The oldest man playing in the conference, Boryla broke the Skyline Six scoring record with 624 points in 33 games, including 379 in 20 league games. His top single game output was 39. Despite a slump in the final week of the season, Vince averaged 18.9 points a game. The Skyline runner-up, Vern Gardner of Utah, averaged 15.1 points. Boryla also was voted the outstanding visiting player in New York after scoring 36 points against St. John's in Madison Square Garden.

Vince's scoring, rebounding, and all-around court sense made him a natural for the professional ranks. He joined the New York Knickerbockers in time for the 1949–50 season and averaged 10 points a game in his rookie year. He improved that to 15 points a game the following season. He lasted three more years as a professional and retired after the 1953–54 season at the age of 34.

Boryla couldn't give up basketball completely, however. He became coach of the AAU Denver Central Bankers. He returned to New York as coach of the Knickerbockers for two-and-a-half seasons through 1957–58.

Vince retired from basketball to devote full time to his insurance and investment business in Denver. He was associated with the Denver Rockets of the American Basketball Association for a time, but finally limited his participation in the sport to Saturday morning backyard games with his sons and the neighborhood kids who wanted to see the most uncanny shot in the book come whizzing off a husky old man's ear.

HARRY BOYKOFF

A curly-headed mustachioed giant named Harry Boykoff was a major cause of one of the most drastic changes in the history of basketball.

Boykoff, who stood 6-9 and weighed 290 pounds at the end of his All-America career at St. John's University, was, despite his massive size, quick, agile, and devastating under the backboards. On offense he could dunk the ball with ease or hit from 25 feet away if he had to. But it was on defense that High-pockets Harry changed the game.

When an opponent would shoot from in close, Boykoff would leap to the backboard, flick his strong fingers at the ball and tap another potential enemy goal away from the basket.

"Harry would cut at least twenty or twenty-five points a game off the opposition's total with his fantastic ability to reach the ball before it would go in the basket," St. John's coach Joe Lapchick said.

With the coming of a few more giants of this type, the goal-tending rule was put into the game for the 1944–45 season. No player, regardless of size, would be allowed to hamper the ball on its downward arc to the basket.

Boykoff was born and raised in the tough Brownsville section of Brooklyn where many of the "graduates" went on to become members of the infamous Murder Inc. mob of the 1930s and 40s. Heshie Boykoff was one of the neighborhood kids, the gangling, shy, soft-spoken one who spent most of his time playing basketball in the schoolyard of P.S. 174.

St. John's Harry Boykoff

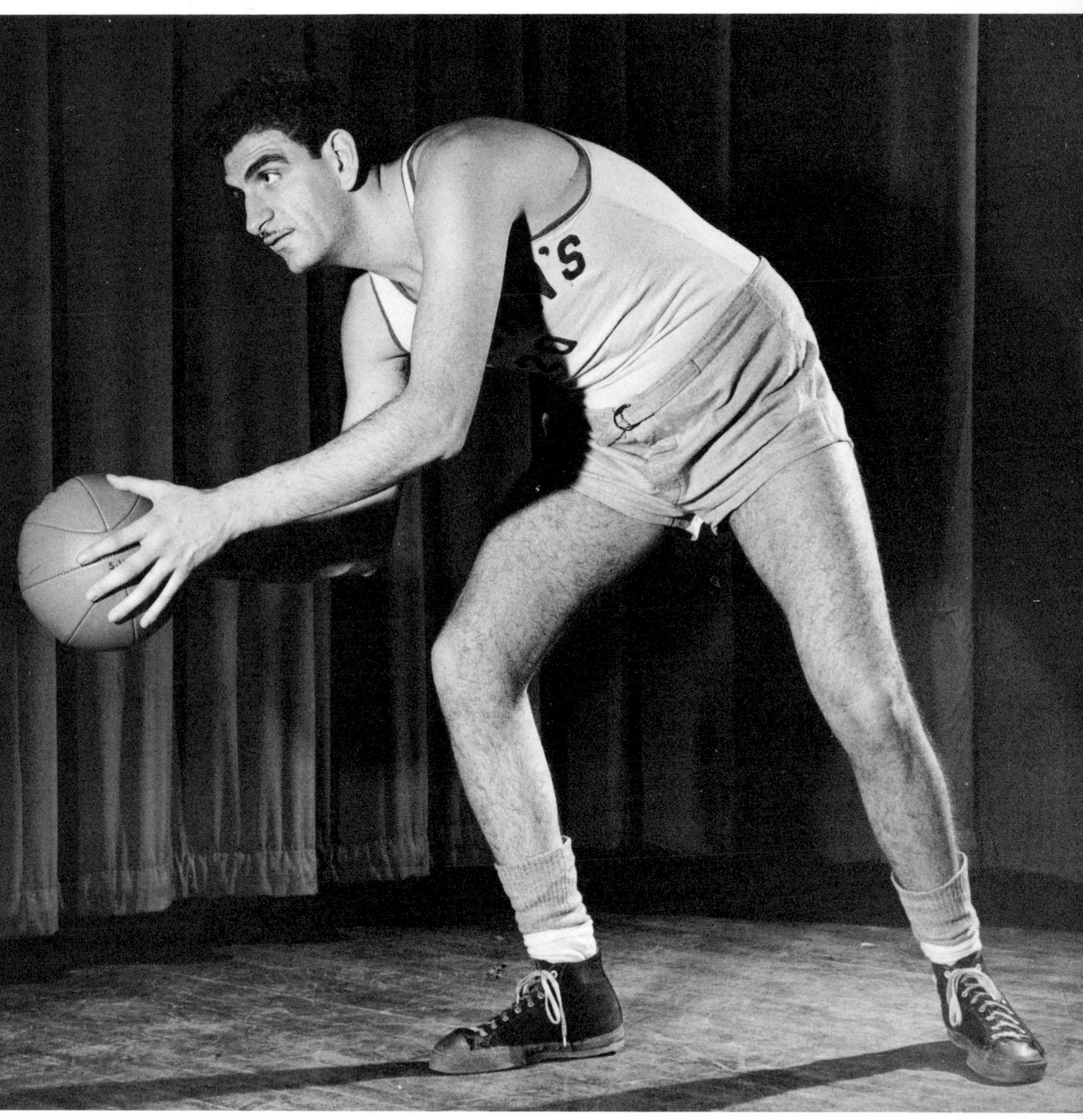

At Thomas Jefferson High School, Boykoff was fully grown, but awkward at 190 pounds. Through the efforts of his coach, Mac Hodesblatt, and his good friend, 5-6 playmaker Hy Gotkin, Boykoff became a polished player.

By the time he entered St. John's in the fall of 1941, he could dribble as well as many small men, shoot from in close or out, rebound better than any opponent and destroy foes with his goal-tending and shot-blocking.

As a sophomore he averaged 16.6 points a game in the days when the winning team rarely scored 50 points in a game. He led the Redmen to their first National Invitation Tournament title in Madison Square Garden after having broken the Garden scoring record earlier in the season with a 45-point outburst against St. Joseph's.

This was during World War II and Harry had been turned down several times by the military because of his height, but he was determined to serve. He asked the Army for still another physical. He straddled the scale instead of stepping on it, bent his knees and was measured at 6-5, the height limit. Boykoff the soldier served for two years as a physical training instructor at West Point.

Slowed by knee trouble and excess weight, Boykoff returned to St. John's without his old maneuverability. Still, he could rebound and score. On March 11, 1947, he broke the Garden scoring record with 54 points against St. Francis of Brooklyn. The final score was St. John's 71, St. Francis 52.

The gentle giant registered 1,129 points in three seasons and went into professional basketball with the Waterloo Hawks and the Boston Celtics.

After quitting basketball, Boykoff entered the laundromat business in Memphis, Tennessee, where there were no rules against his height.

BILL BRADLEY

Many of college basketball's greatest players have appeared in New York's Madison Square Garden. But none of them ever excited a crowd as Bill Bradley did on December 30, 1964. When Bradley fouled out of the semifinal game of the Holiday Festival that night, 18,499 fans gave him the longest ovation any basketball player had ever received in the history of the Garden.

Play was suspended for more than two minutes as the crowd showered its applause on the 6-5, 200-pound Princeton forward. Singlehandedly, Bradley had led Princeton to the brink of an incredible upset over Michigan, the country's top team. When Bradley fouled out, Princeton led, 75-63, with 4:37 remaining. Of Princeton's 75 points, Bradley had scored 41. He had popped in the Tigers' last twelve points of the first half to put them into the lead. He had nine rebounds, four assists, and on defense had held his man to only one point.

Michigan's Cazzie Russell, along with Bradley the season's most heralded college players, had been completely overshadowed. But without Bradley the Tigers were a different team. Over the next three minutes, Michigan outscored them, 17-1, and went on to an 80-78 victory.

Bradley had a capacity for inspiring his ordinary teammates to extraordinary heights. For many, Bradley, not only that night, but every time he played, was the closest thing to a perfect basketball player that they had ever seen. He moved with such effortless ease, shot with such uncanny perfection, that few realized just how much effort he put into the game.

As a youngster in Crystal City, Missouri, he practiced incessantly. "During the football season, I'd practice for about two hours a day," he recalled. "Then during the basketball season I'd always try to stay after practice for more work. During the summer was the toughest part because many days when it was hot, the perspiration would soak through your shoes and you'd have to quit because you'd start to slip out of your shoes."

Princeton's Bill Bradley

PRINCETON
42

At Princeton he continued practicing just as much. "I don't think I've ever seen a harder working boy," said Butch van Breda Kolff, his Princeton coach. After practice Bradley would stay in the gym for an extra hour, practicing his deadly jump shot.

All the hours of work paid off as Bradley won honor after honor for himself and his Ivy League school. In Bradley's three years the Tigers won three Ivy championships. He averaged 30.1 points a game and was an All-American all three seasons. In 1964, as the only college junior on the team, he paced the United States to the gold medal in basketball at the Tokyo Olympics.

Bradley closed his career with a personal high of 58 points in Princeton's 118-82 victory over Wichita in the consolation finals of the 1965 NCAA championship. This gave him a career total of 2,503 points, making him the fourth most prolific scorer in the history of college basketball.

In 1965 Bradley won the Sullivan Award, given annually by the Amateur Athletic Union to the nation's outstanding amateur athlete. He was the first basketball player ever to win the award.

Bradley was as outstanding academically at Princeton as he was athletically. Because the Ivy League schools do not award athletic scholarships, Bradley paid his own way at Princeton, when he could have had a basketball scholarship at nearly any other school in the country.

In his senior year Bradley was awarded a Rhodes Scholarship for postgraduate study at Oxford University in England. Although the professional New York Knickerbockers made him their first choice in the draft, Bradley turned them down to study abroad for two years.

On his return he reconsidered the professional game and finally signed a four-year contract with the Knicks for an estimated $500,000. This made him basketball's highest-paid rookie. But Bradley, who excelled at almost everything he ever attempted, insisted that it was not the money that had convinced him to sign. "I just wanted to see how I would do against the best players in the world. I just had to know," he said.

BOB DAVIES

There was no more spectacular sight on a basketball floor in 1942 than the handsome, blond, tousle-haired youngster from Seton Hall dribbling down the right side of the court, faking his man out of position, switching the ball behind his back and driving to the basket for a left-handed lay-up.

Bob Davies, who stood 6-3 and weighed 180 pounds, was a complete basketball player. He led the New Jersey institution to 43 straight victories and was extolled by all for his tremendous skills. He could shoot, he could pass, he could rebound. The flashy native of Harrisburg, Pennsylvania, earned the nickname "The Harrisburg Houdini" on the strength of his magnificent ball-control, dribbling, and behind-the-back maneuvers.

Davies was considered by many the best all-around basketball player since Stanford's Hank Luisetti, then considered the game's measure of excellence.

"Luisetti was a frontcourt player," said Nat Holman, the coach of City College of New York and one of the early greats of the game, "and Davies is equally as good anywhere on the court. His change of pace dribble is the best and trickiest there is. Davies is a team man, setting up plays and acting as leader. He's got color, coordination, speed, and stamina."

Surprisingly, Davies came to Seton Hall with a reputation as a fine baseball player but unheard of as a basketball player. The Seton Hall coach, Honey Russell, changed Davies' life after he saw him control a ball during one early basketball practice.

Davies said his behind-the-back dribble was just a natural part of his game. "I really never practiced it much," he said. "I found it

Seton Hall's Bob Davies

could throw the opposition off balance and I tried to save it for the right spot."

Davies had a flair for the dramatic, and the right spot would usually be a one-on-one situation with the game hanging on the next basket.

"He had such uncanny control of the ball behind his back," said Russell, "that it never concerned me. He made it look as easy as the conventional dribble."

The exciting maneuver was appreciated by the fans and wherever Seton Hall played, the crowds came to watch Davies and his acrobatic dribbles. The largest crowd ever to see a basketball game up to that time, 18,403, watched Davies and his Seton Hall teammates defeat Rhode Island in the quarter-finals of the National Invitation Tournament at Madison Square Garden on March 19, 1941.

Davies graduated in 1942 and enlisted in the Navy. He led the Great Lakes Naval Training Station team to a 34-3 record. He became an ensign in 1943 and took part in the invasions of Sicily and Normandy as an officer on a sub chaser.

He played professional basketball for ten years and was an all-league selection five times. He also coached Seton Hall to a 24-3 record while playing with the Rochester Royals in the National Basketball Association.

Davies went back to college coaching at Gettysburg for two seasons after he retired as a player. He retired from basketball in 1957 to take a position in sales and promotion with the Converse Rubber Company in Massachusetts.

Bob Davies never averaged more than 11.8 points a game in any of his three college seasons at Seton Hall but no player ever did more to make basketball a show as well as a game. The Harrisburg Houdini was indeed a master of hoop magic.

TOM GOLA

The surprising winner of the 1952 National Invitation Tournament in Madison Square Garden was LaSalle College of Philadelphia. Even more surprising was the name of Tom Gola as one of the co-winners of the tourney's Most Valuable Player award with teammate Norm Grekin.

Gola's play in the pressure-packed championships was especially noteworthy since the 6-6, 220-pound forward from Philadelphia was only a freshman. Coach Ken Loeffler said of Tom: "I have never seen a youngster with such poise. It is his greatest asset. Nothing rattles him. He can do everything and do it well."

Gola went at his work like a mechanic who is sure of his skills. His play was unspectacular, almost unnoticed, but he always scored the big basket, grabbed the vital rebound, set the tempo and pace of play for his team.

"I have never seen one player control a game by himself as well as Gola does," said Loeffler.

The other players on the LaSalle team didn't take too kindly to the appearance of Gola in the starting line-up as a freshman when the season began. Veteran players tend to downgrade inexperienced players until they can prove themselves. By mid-season, his teammates looked up to Gola as a leader. He scored 504 points in leading LaSalle to a 25-7 season, the NIT championship, and high national ranking.

Tom learned his basketball the hard way, in the three-man playground games in the lower-middle class section of Philadelphia where he grew up. He was one of seven children of a Philadelphia policeman. There was little extra money for recreation so young Tom found his own fun in the basketball games around home.

He scored 2,222 points for LaSalle High School in the Philadelphia Catholic League, was named a first-team high-school All-America and led the North to victory in the annual North-South high school all-star game.

After his stunning freshman season, Gola was a marked man. Although every defense was geared to stop him, none succeeded. In each of the next three seasons, the soft-spoken,

La Salle's Tom Gola

self-effacing youngster led the Explorers in scoring and improved his average from 17.4 per game as a freshman to 24.1 as a senior.

The handsome, dark-haired Gola excelled off the floor as well as on it. He finished in the upper third of his graduating class with a degree in accounting.

Following military service, Gola became a splendid professional player with the Philadelphia Warriors and the New York Knickerbockers. He retired after the 1965 season to concentrate on his business interests as the owner of a golf driving range, apartment buildings and various other investments, and to run for public office in Pennsylvania.

Gola became a Republican member of the Pennsylvania State Legislature and in the fall of 1968 he added still another hat when he returned to LaSalle, his alma mater, as head basketball coach.

DICK GROAT

Most college athletes who excel in one sport play another just for fun. But few ever make All-America teams in two sports. One notable exception was Dick Groat of Duke, a standout both on the basketball court and the baseball diamond. Groat is probably better remembered as the long-time shortstop of the Pittsburgh Pirates and several other major-league baseball teams. But it was as a collegiate basketball player that he first gained national prominence.

In his junior year, 1950–51, Groat led the nation in scoring. The 6-foot, 180-pound guard's 831 points in 31 games, a 25.2 average, set an NCAA single-season scoring record. That season and the following year, when he averaged 26.0 points, Groat earned All-America basketball honors. Besides leading the Blue Devils in scoring, Groat was also the team leader in assists for two years.

"If you tell Dick he's doing something wrong he goes out and practices until he does it perfectly. He's a real team man," said Hal Bradley, the Duke coach. And Gus Tebell, then director of athletics at Virginia, added, "He's the finest basketball player I've seen in the South in my twenty-seven years in the game."

Groat wound up at the North Carolina school even though he grew up in Swissvale, Pennsylvania, and three members of his family attended the nearby University of Pittsburgh. Dick went to Duke because it was a baseball-minded school, and he always considered baseball his best sport.

He received his introduction to basketball at the age of four when Pete Noon, who had been a teammate of two of Groat's brothers at Pitt, gave him a basketball as a present. Although Dick took to the game immediately, he didn't start taking it seriously until his high school days.

On the basketball court he was an outstanding faker and playmaker as well as a scorer. His favorite shot was a short jumper from the foul line, but he also could go all the way in for a lay-up. He credits Red Auerbach, then an assistant coach at Duke, with teaching him many of his feints. Carl Braun, a professional star with the New York Knicks, said that defense was Groat's only weakness. "But as for offense," Braun added, "I've never seen a better one anywhere."

At Duke, Groat broke most of the school's scoring records. Up until his time no Blue Devil player had ever scored more than 30

Duke's Dick Groat

points in a game. But in his junior year he exceeded 30 points nine times. His peak single-game output of 48 points came against North Carolina in his senior season. Dick also tallied 46 points against George Washington. He also set a national record by making 261 free throws in 1950–51.

Following his college career, Groat signed a contract with the Pittsburgh Pirates baseball team. Then he spent two years in the Army. Both as a collegiate basketball and baseball player, he had been considered extremely quick. But during his Army years he lost a lot of his speed. "I played a great deal of basketball in the Army and the hard floors wore my feet down," he said. Nevertheless, he became an outstanding major-league shortstop and in 1960 won the National League Most Valuable Player award and the batting championship.

He retired from baseball after the 1967 season and became manager of a golf course near Pittsburgh.

K. C. JONES

Joe Lapchick called the University of San Francisco teams of 1954–56 "the best college teams I have ever seen." The Dons swept through 60 consecutive games without a loss, and won two straight NCAA titles. Most of the credit went to Bill Russell, the team's skinny 6-9 center. Russell was the top scorer and rebounder and the man who intimidated opposing shooters with his long arms and fantastic reflexes.

But in many ways the heart of the team was not Russell but K.C. Jones, a 6-1 guard. Jones didn't score very many points, he wasn't much of a shooter, and although a good leaper for his size, he wasn't really an outstanding rebounder either.

All K.C. had to do was play defense, something he did like nobody else before. Lapchick described him as "the most challenging defensive player in the history of the college game." Jones always covered the other team's top player, and almost always held him well below his scoring average.

In the finals of the 1955 NCAA tournament, San Francisco faced LaSalle. Everyone thought that coach Phil Woolpert would assign Russell to cover Tom Gola, LaSalle's superscorer and the nation's Player of the Year. Instead, Woolpert had Jones cover the 6-6 Gola. And K.C. did the job. He held Gola completely scoreless for the first 21 minutes of the game, and the Dons won the national championship by a comfortable 14 points.

Despite the fame he achieved in basketball, for a long time K.C.'s first love was football. He had been an outstanding football player at San Francisco's Commerce High. But he had given no real thought to college, and had been considering applying for a post office job when San Francisco offered him a basketball scholarship.

In K.C.'s sophomore year at USF, the Dons were only mediocre. They had an 11-13 record and K.C. averaged 3.5 points a game. Jones played in only one game the next season before an emergency appendectomy operation finished him for the year. Because he only got into that one game, he still retained two years of college eligibility.

Over the next two seasons, the Dons, with K.C. and Russell leading the way, were unstoppable. Early in the 1954–55 season they lost to UCLA, 47-40. That was the last time they were to lose for the next two years. San Francisco played a slow, ball-control game, with Russell dominating the backboards and Jones setting up the plays. Russell described their roles by saying "The team was a slingshot. I was the fork. K.C. was the rubber band. He made us go."

Jones and Russell both played on the 1956 Olympic basketball team that won the gold medal at Melbourne.

The Los Angeles Rams football team, remembering K.C.'s days as a high school grid star and also noting his strength and quickness on the court, drafted him as a defensive back. After the Olympics, Jones spent two

San Francisco's K.C. Jones

years in the Army and then reported to the Rams. He looked good in exhibition games, but decided that basketball was what he really wanted. "I was sitting in a blackboard drill with the defensive backs, and I was dreaming about Big Bill and Cousy and the rest of the Celtics. I realized I was in the wrong sport."

The Celtics had drafted Jones as a basketball player and he decided to rejoin his old teammate, Bill Russell. Jones played in the pros just the way he had in college. He still couldn't shoot—in fact his teammates jokingly called him the poorest shooter in the NBA. But his playmaking and ball-hawking, coupled with his tremendous defensive talent, made him a star once again.

He played for the Celtics through the 1966–67 season, when he retired to become head coach at Brandeis University.

WALLACE "WAH WAH" JONES

For four seasons after World War II, no college basketball team in the country could match mighty Kentucky. Adolph Rupp's Wildcats won two NCAA titles and one NIT championship in that span. Center Alex Groza and guard Ralph Beard did most of the scoring, but some of the most important contributions were made by Wallace "Wah

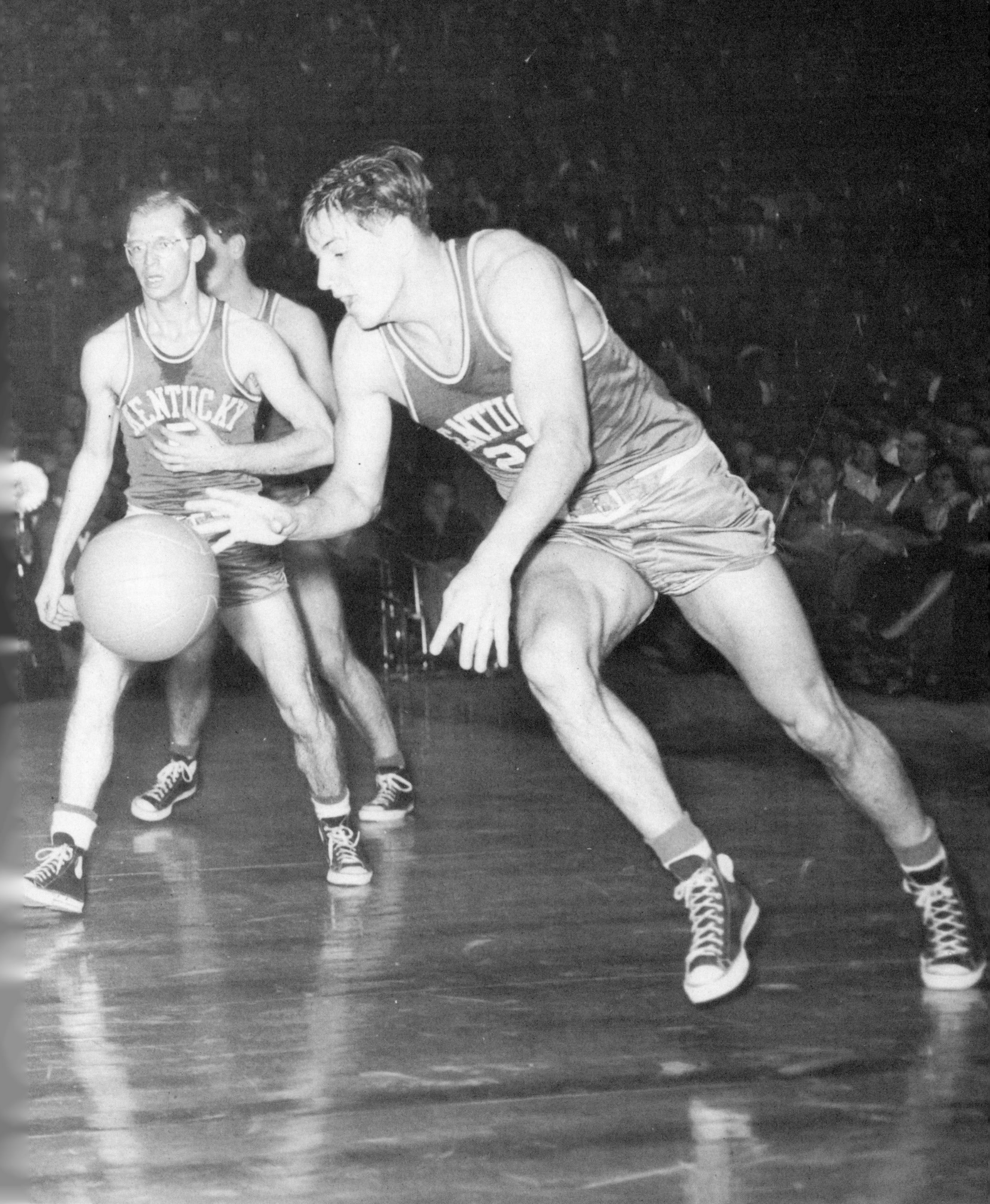

Kentucky's Wah Wah Jones

Wah" Jones, a 6-4, 200-pound forward.

"Wah Wah is the best man I have in the clutch," said Rupp during the 1946 NIT. "He may not get the most baskets, only the most important ones."

Besides being a tremendous basketball player, Wah Wah was probably the greatest all-around athlete in Kentucky's history. He earned four varsity letters in basketball, four in football, and three in baseball. He got involved with football only because at the time he entered Kentucky as a freshman in 1945, he found that he had seven weeks to wait before basketball practice was to begin. He won a starting spot for the first football game, although he had practiced for only three days.

But it was on the basketball court that Wah Wah earned his greatest fame. He began his career as a center, filling in for Alex Groza, who was in military service. When Groza returned to school the following year, Jones shifted to forward and stayed there.

As a scorer, he was only average. Over his college career he averaged less than 10 points and made fewer than a third of his shots. But he contributed in other ways: with his tough, tight defense, and, of course, his clutch shooting.

By his senior year, his contributions—the kind that can't always be measured in statistics—became fully recognized and Jones won All-America honors. That year the Wildcats won 32 games, lost only twice and captured the NCAA championship.

If Wah Wah was merely outstanding during the regular season, he became brilliant in the post-season championships. Along with teammate Ralph Beard, Jones set a record by being named to the All-Southeast Conference tournament team four straight years.

For a time though, it looked as if Jones wouldn't even attend Kentucky. As a high school star at Harlan (Kentucky) High, he had scored a national record 2,398 points in his four years, and nearly every college in the country was trying to recruit him. Wah Wah leaned toward Tennessee because his brother went there. But Alva Bell, a smart Kentucky businessman, introduced Wah Wah to his pretty daughter, Edna, who just happened to be a student at Kentucky. Wah Wah not only changed his college plans but went on to marry Edna after his college graduation.

Wah Wah played for a while with the professional Indianapolis Olympians. But he decided against pro ball as a career and went into publishing, editing a magazine. In addition, he does the color commentary on the radio broadcasts of Kentucky basketball games. Wah Wah also ventured into politics, serving a term as the sheriff of Fayette County, Kentucky in 1953.

BOB KURLAND

Hank Iba, the coach at Oklahoma A&M, always believed that the key to basketball success was good defense, and his theory paid off when the Aggies won consecutive NCAA championships in 1945 and 1946. The biggest part of the Aggie defense was Bob "Foothills" Kurland, the first of basketball's well-coordinated seven-footers.

Oklahoma A&M (today Oklahoma State University) played a slow, ball-control game and Kurland made that style of play work. He used his height and strength to control the backboards and to frustrate opponents' offensive maneuvers. "Kurland made our type of game go. We knew he would get us the ball so we never had to rush into a bad shot," Iba said.

Kurland had agility for a man of his size, but not much speed. In Iba's style of play it didn't matter. After grabbing a rebound, Kurland would pass the ball to a teammate, and while the big center moved up court, the rest of the team would work the ball in a weave. With Kurland in position, the Aggies could either pass into him under the basket, cut off him for a lay-up, or use his huge body for a screen on a shot.

But Bob's greatest contributions came on defense. He was an adept shot-blocker and perfected the goal-tending technique, in which he would knock away a shot just before it reached the basket. Coach Iba disliked this maneuver, though, and rarely allowed Kurland to practice it. By his senior year, the NCAA, influenced by the play of Kurland, George Mikan of DePaul, and Harry Boykoff at St. John's, outlawed goal-tending.

As a freshman, Kurland was a little-used varsity substitute and averaged only 2.5 points a game. Over the next three seasons he came into his own and in 1945–46 led the nation in scoring with 643 points, a 19.5 average. In his final three college seasons he was an All-America selection and in both 1945 and 1946 was voted the outstanding player in the NCAA tournament.

Usually Kurland was content to concentrate on defense and passing off, but on February 22, 1946, in his last home game, Iba told him to go all-out in scoring. That night he scored 58 points against St. Louis University, the highest single-game total of his career.

The Oklahoma A&M star had a series of classic confrontations with Mikan, DePaul's 6-10 center. The two met several times in their college careers, but neither of the big centers was able to establish clear superiority over the other. In the most publicized of their battles, a Red Cross benefit game in Madison Square Garden in March, 1945, Kurland outscored Mikan, 14-9, as Oklahoma A&M won, 52-44.

Kurland passed up large bonus offers from the pros after his graduation and instead went to work for Phillips Petroleum, of Bartlesville, Oklahoma, and played for the famous Phillips 66ers AAU team. During his amateur career, he became the first American to play on two Olympic basketball teams. Kurland was a member of the victorious United States squads in the 1948 Games at London and in 1952 at Helsinki.

After his retirement as a player, he remained with Phillips and went on to become president of Phillips Films Co., a subsidiary of Phillips Petroleum.

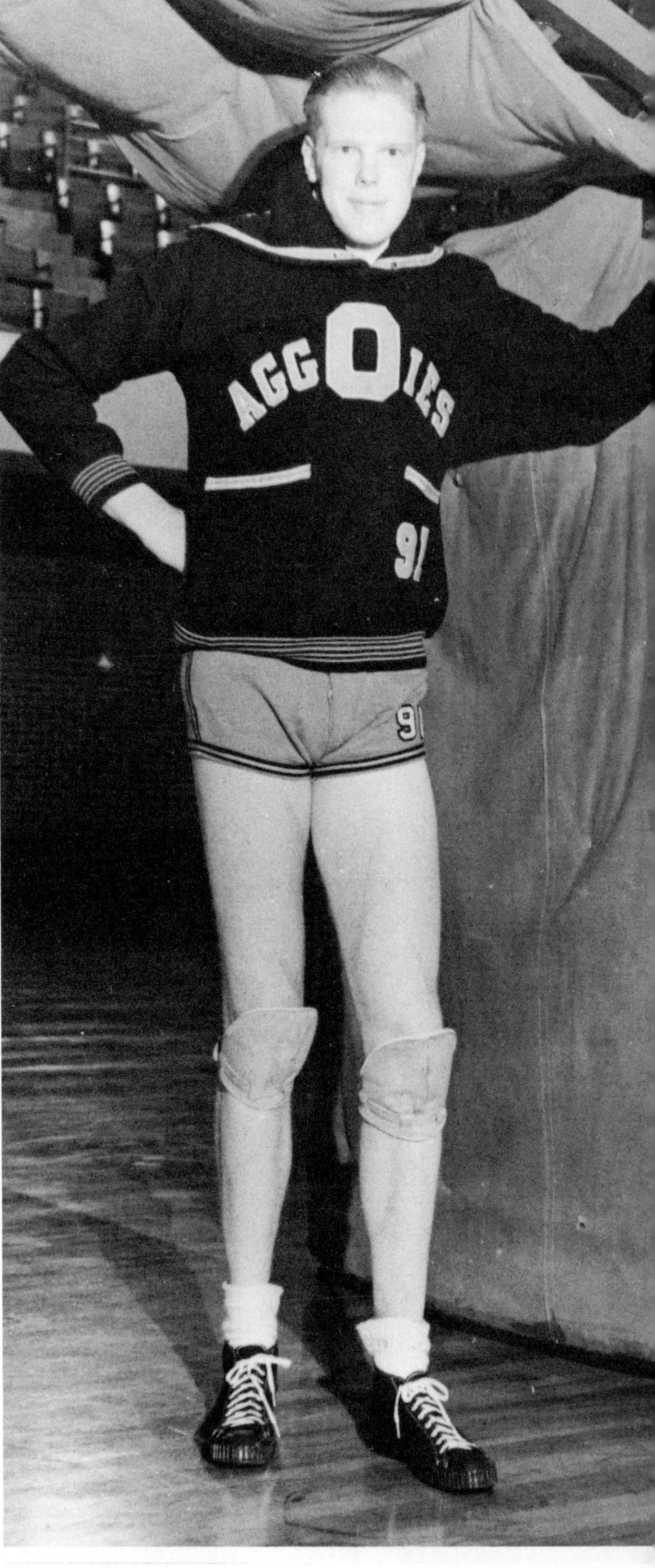

Oklahoma A&M's Bob Kurland

CLYDE LOVELLETTE

The era of gigantic high-scoring centers dates from the early 1950s, with one player responsible for the trend. He was Clyde Lovellette, the 6-9 center from Kansas University.

Before Lovellette came to Kansas, huge centers were used mainly to get the ball off the backboard for their mates, harass the opposition on defense and use their size to block out opposing players as their teammates drove to the basket.

Coach Phog Allen of Kansas changed all that when he designed an offense around Lovellette and encouraged him to shoot and score. "He is closer to the basket than anyone else on the floor," said Allen, "so I'd rather see him go for it than anyone else."

Lovellette was not a very graceful man and at the end of his college career he weighed nearly 280 pounds. But he was still able to stuff the ball into the basket.

Lovellette was from Terre Haute, Indiana, one of the great hotbeds of high school basketball. He was huge, but his game was only average as a high school player because his great size hampered rather than helped him. Coach Allen knew he could develop the boy after supervising his diet, his practices, and his exercising while Lovellette was a freshman at Kansas. When he joined the Jayhawk varsity in 1949, Lovellette was ready to show the world he could play with the best.

"I knew I had the ability," said Lovellette. "The only thing I was lacking was self-confidence."

Lovellette started his first game at center on the varsity and scored 21 points. From that time on, there was no stopping the husky Hoosier. In his sophomore year Lovellette led Kansas to a 14-11 record and he won the Big Eight scoring title. The Jayhawks finished in a tie with Kansas State and Nebraska for the conference championship, but lost the playoff and an NCAA berth with it.

As a junior, Lovellette was again the lead-

Kansas' Clyde Lovellette

ing scorer in the conference, averaging 22.8 points a game as Kansas finished second with a 16-8 record. In his final season Kansas won the NCAA championship with Lovellette scoring 141 points in four games for a tournament record. Forty-four of those points came against St. Louis for a new single-game NCAA tournament record.

His career total of 1,888 points in 1952 was a national record, while his 795 points that season was a conference standard.

The influence of Lovellette made many coaches around the country anxious for large centers of their own who could score more easily than the smaller players. Kansas followed its own tradition when it came up with Wilt Chamberlain several years later.

Lovellette played AAU basketball for a season after graduation and then enjoyed a long career in the National Basketball Association with the Minneapolis Lakers, Cincinnati Royals, St. Louis Hawks, and Boston Celtics. When he retired he was elected sheriff in his home town of Terre Haute.

JERRY LUCAS

When Jerry Lucas played high school basketball in Middletown, Ohio, his team won 76 consecutive games and two Ohio state championships. During his three varsity years at Ohio State University, 1959–62, the Buckeyes didn't quite match that record, but nobody complained.

During the Lucas era, Ohio State won three Big Ten championships, one NCAA title, and finished second in the NCAA tournament twice. Overall they won 78 games and lost only six. Playing on a team loaded with outstanding basketball talent—four of his teammates went on to play pro ball—Lucas clearly established himself as the outstanding college player of his time.

Unlike so many point-hungry stars, Lucas, a 6-8, 230-pound pivotman, would just as soon pass the ball to an open teammate as shoot. Over his varsity career he averaged 24.3 points a game, while taking only about 16 shots a contest. His shooting percentage ranged from an unbelievable .637 as a sophomore to a merely phenomenal .611 as a senior. He led the nation in field-goal accuracy all three seasons.

A total team player, Lucas could shoot, rebound, pass, dribble, and play defense. "He has the ideal attitude. He'll play the post and he'll pass off all day. When he has to score, he'll do it. Whenever it looked as though Ohio State needed points, he got them. The rest of the time he passed off," said Frank McGuire, who coached North Carolina to a national championship.

When he had to score points, Lucas frequently used a deadly hook shot, which he could launch with either hand. But he could also score on jumpers from the corner, driving lay-ups or tip-ins of rebounds.

As a schoolboy sensation at Middletown High, Lucas had attracted college offers from schools around the nation. He finished his scholastic career with 2,466 points, breaking Wilt Chamberlain's high school scoring record by more than 200 points.

The only blemish on Lucas' high school record came in his senior year, when Columbus North defeated Middletown, 63-62, in the semifinals of the state tournament. But he couldn't be too bitter about the defeat, since it was there that he met his future wife, Treva Geib, one of the Columbus cheerleaders.

Lucas turned down an estimated 150 scholarship offers—some including such incentives as cars, houses, and even jobs for his father—to accept an academic scholarship at Ohio State. At OSU he excelled as a student as well as an athlete. Lucas was elected to the national honor fraternity for commerce students.

In his first varsity season, the Buckeyes went all the way to the NCAA title, crushing California, 75-55, in the championship game. Lucas held Darrall Imhoff, California's All-America center, to eight points, the lowest total of his career. The next two seasons,

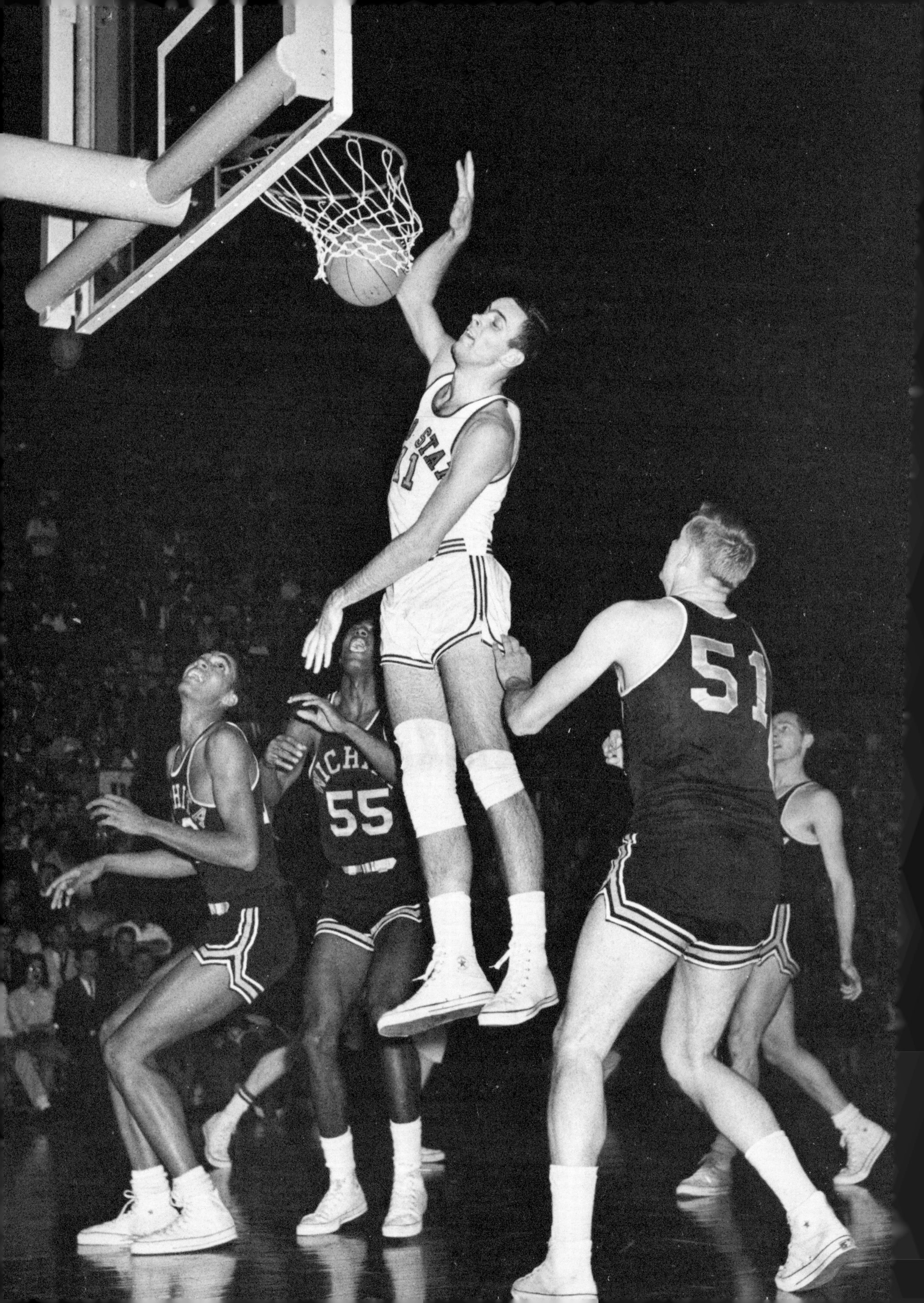
11
55
51

Ohio State lost to Cincinnati in the NCAA championship games.

Following his freshman year, Lucas played on the United States Olympic basketball team and led it to the gold medal in Rome. Pete Newell, who coached the Olympic squad, called Lucas "the best player I have ever coached." This was quite a tribute, since the Olympic team also included Oscar Robertson, Jerry West, Walt Bellamy, and Terry Dischinger.

Throughout his career, Lucas continually insisted that he wouldn't play professional basketball. And after his graduation in 1962, he did pursue graduate studies at Ohio State for a year. But the Cincinnati Royals persuaded him to turn pro the next season with a long-term contract and bonus, and Lucas went on to become one of the NBA's outstanding forwards.

HANK LUISETTI

The fastest gun in the West, Hank Luisetti, came east to Madison Square Garden with his Stanford team in December, 1936, to end Long Island University's 43-game winning streak and leave a lasting imprint on the court game. Luisetti broke up the game and changed basketball forever with his one-handed off-the-ear running shots.

Until Luisetti revolutionized basketball offense, there were two major types of shots, the driving lay-up and the two-handed set shot with feet firmly planted on the ground.

"Two years after Luisetti's appearance in the Garden," wrote his biographer, Dick Friendlich, "every school kid coming to an Eastern college was firing one-handed shots off his ears."

Luisetti's one-handed shot was his most memorable contribution to the game, but his floor play, his playmaking and his court generalship made his name a standard of excellence.

Ohio State's Jerry Lucas

Stanford's Hank Luisetti

The Stanford star finished second to George Mikan of DePaul as the best basketball player in the first half of the century in an Associated Press poll. This was a notable achievement considering that Luisetti's career ended 15 years before the poll was taken, many voters had never seen him play, and Luisetti's career had been in the era of the center jump.

The dark-haired San Franciscan broke the national scoring record in his four seasons at Stanford with 1,596 points and still holds the school record for most points in a single game with 50 against Duquesne on January 1, 1938.

Angelo "Hank" Luisetti was a lanky 6-2 kid when he was first introduced to the one-handed shot at San Francisco's Galileo High School by his coach, Tommy DeNike.

"Several of my players were using it in practice and in a game once in a while," said DeNike, "but nobody took it like Hank."

Mostly he took the shot from just behind the foul line since he was able to drive past his guarding man and loft it over the last defender's head.

Stanford won three Pacific Coast Conference basketball championships during Luisetti's collegiate career. Despite his brilliant shooting, Luisetti was a team man who constantly looked for the open man on the floor.

After graduation from Stanford, Luisetti played and coached club and AAU basketball and became an executive with an automobile and a travel company. He also served three years in the Navy during World War II.

While in service he led St. Mary's Pre-Flight School to several impressive basketball victories over a Coast Guard team led by Jim Pollard, a 1942 Stanford star and later a member of the professional Minneapolis Lakers.

Luisetti's basketball fame in college was such that after graduation he was paid $10,000 to portray a college basketball player in a movie. The picture, called "Campus Confessions," was one of the most forgettable films ever made.

ANDY PHILLIP

One or two sophomores on the starting team of any college basketball squad is not considered unusual. The juniors and seniors carry the sophomores until the youngsters mature. Mistakes are the price the coach must pay as his sophomores learn the game.

Illinois coach Doug Mills shocked the Big Ten in the 1941–42 season when he put five sophomores on the starting five. The best of the baby bunch was a 6-2½ scorer from Granite City, Illinois, Andy Phillip He was the best shooter on the team, a fine dribbler, and an outstanding defensive player who normally drew the other team's biggest and best player. He consistently out-rebounded taller men.

These sophomores blazed through the first season with a 13-2 Big Ten record and an 18-5 overall mark. Their poise surprised all opponents and they soon earned a nickname that was to stay with them throughout their careers, "The Whiz Kids."

The Whiz Kids—Phillip, Gene Vance, Art Mathisen, Jack Smiley, and Ken Menke—opened the season with an easy triumph over Marquette. They lost to Chanute Field at a time when the strongest teams in the country were military teams. They followed that loss with 11 straight victories.

They made it to the NCAA tournament and lost to Kentucky, 46-44, in the first round. Phillip ended the year by being selected Illinois' Most Valuable Player and a unanimous All-Big Ten choice.

The 1942–43 season was even better. Illinois won 17 of 18 games, with Phillip showing the way as the leading scorer and playmaker. He set conference season marks for most points (255), most field goals (111), and most points in a single game (40). He ended the the season with 305 points in 18 games.

Although Phillip had come to be the best player on the Whiz Kids, it didn't always look as though he would be. "When he joined us as an all-state player from Granite City,"

Illinois' Andy Phillip

Coach Mills said, "he wasn't yet a great player. He had to work as hard as any of the Whiz Kids to reach the point he did."

Phillip was considered a tremendous competitor, playing his best in the toughest games. His face was never expressive on the court. His quick hands were the most noticeable feature of his play, with his long fingers guiding the ball to a teammate or into the basket on a long set shot or driving lay-up.

Phillip was a two-sport athlete at Illinois with three varsity letters in basketball and three more in baseball as a pitcher, first baseman, and outfielder. Following the 1943 season, he was called into active duty with the Marine Corps and served as a lieutenant in the Pacific.

At 24, he returned to college with three other members of the Whiz Kids—Smiley, Vance, and Menke—to team with Fred Green as Illinois finished second in the Big Ten with an 8-4 conference mark and 14-6 overall.

After his college days, Phillip played ten years of professional basketball and was considered one of the finest guards in the game. He retired in 1957 to go into business in California.

OSCAR ROBERTSON

"There's never been one like him. Fabulous! Until this kid came along, I thought Tom Gola was the best soph I'd ever seen. I was wrong," said Joe Lapchick, who had been watching young men play basketball for more than 50 years. "This kid" is Oscar Palmer Robertson, the Big O, and quite possibly the greatest player in the history of college basketball.

In his three varsity seasons at the University of Cincinnati, Robertson scored more points, 2,973, than any major college player had before. When he graduated in 1960, the Big O held 14 NCAA University Division records. A three-time consensus All-American and Player of the Year all three years, Robertson led the Bearcats to records of 25-3, 26-4 and 28-2.

At 6-5 and 215 pounds, Robertson didn't score his points merely by being bigger than everyone else on the court. Instead, he so perfectly mastered the skills of shooting, dribbling, rebounding, and passing, that coach Phog Allen of Kansas was moved to comment, "Oscar Robertson is the greatest player of all time for a fellow of his size."

Early in his sophomore season, Cincinnati came into New York's Madison Square Garden to take on Seton Hall. For many heralded sophomores, the pressure of playing on basketball's most famous court simply proves too much. But not for Oscar. He scored 56 points that night. The entire Seton Hall team scored 54, and Cincinnati won, 118-54. In the history of the Garden, no basketball player—high school, college, or professional—had ever scored more points. He hit on 22 of 32 shots from the floor, made all 12 free throws he attempted, grabbed 15 rebounds, and added six assists.

Robertson went on to have many more big nights, leading the Bearcats in scoring in nearly every game and usually leading them in rebounds and assists as well. He finished his career with a 33.8 scoring average, the highest in collegiate history, and reached a single-game peak of 62 against North Texas State in his senior year.

The first indications of just how good a basketball player the Big O would be came in his junior year at Crispus Attucks High School in Indianapolis, Indiana. As a sophomore he had been good but not great, averaging 12 points a game. But as a junior he led Crispus Attucks to an undefeated season—the first in Indiana high school history—and the state championship. Attucks extended its winning streak to 45 games the next season before finally losing, and again won the state title.

Robertson graduated in the upper tenth of his class and was elected to the National Honor Society. Coupling this with his extraordinary basketball talent, he had his choice of virtually any college in the country. He chose Cincinnati, partly because of a co-op program which allowed students to alternate classroom work with on-the-job training.

Although he was the first Negro basketball player in the school's history, Robertson insisted that he didn't want to be a crusader for civil rights. "A lot of people thought that I should open doors. But I didn't feel that it was up to me to do it. It's for everybody to do, Negroes, whites, everybody," he said. As a Negro, Robertson frequently found himself singled out for insults. During the Dixie Classic at Raleigh, North Carolina, the fans showered him with racial epithets and Oscar wound up in a wrestling match on the floor with a Wake Forest player.

But none of this could stop Robertson. With some of the quickest reflexes and finest moves ever seen on the court, he completely dominated any game and seemed capable of scoring almost at will. He continued his basketball career with the Cincinnati Royals and

Cincinnati's Oscar Robertson

became one of the all-time pro stars. When the state of Ohio awarded him a license plate that read simply "O", it recognized what basketball fans had known for a long time: There was only one Big O.

GUY RODGERS

Guy Rodgers was one of the fastest, flashiest backcourt operators ever to lace on a pair of basketball shoes. In an era when big men were dominating the game, Rodgers came along, stretched himself fully to reach six feet, and showed the basketball world there was still a place for the small man if he could move the ball like he did, shoot like him or destroy the best defensive plans of the opposition.

Guy learned his basketball in half-court games in South Philadelphia, the spawning ground of many of that city's finest players. "In those games," he later said, "I had to be quick because most of the fellows I played with were taller, tougher and stronger than I was. I knew I couldn't go through them to the basket so I had to learn how to go around them."

After an All-City high school career, Rodgers enrolled at Temple University in Philadelphia, but was still an uncertain pros-

Temple's Guy Rodgers

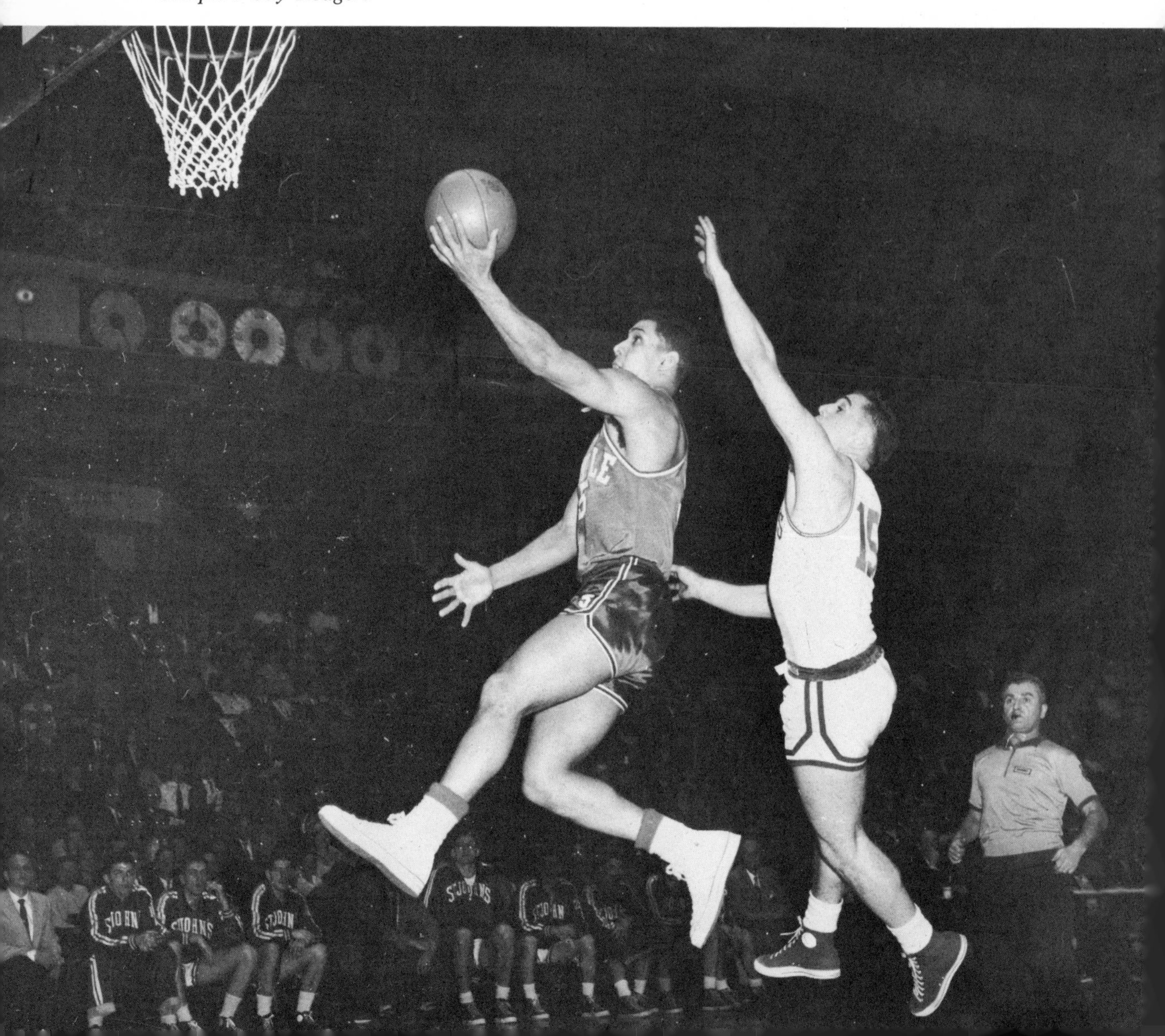

pect because of his size. "All my life I had to prove to coaches that I could play well enough to make their teams. It never bothered me. I always had the confidence," he said.

Coach Harry Litwack of Temple recognized Rodgers' skills almost immediately and gave him the floor leadership of the Owls as a sophomore. Rodgers was on his way. He led the Owls to a record of 27 victories and only four losses in the 1955–56 season and a third-place finish in the NCAA tourney. He was the team leader in assists as well as the high scorer with 573 points. Temple was 20-9 in his second season as Rodgers again led the team in scoring with 591 points. That year the Owls finished third in the NIT.

In Guy's senior year, Temple won 27 games, lost three, and finished third in the NCAA tournament. The Owls also won the Holiday Festival in New York's Madison Square Garden. Rodgers finished the season with school records for scoring, field goals, and assists. He had 15 assists in a single game against Manhattan College. Rodgers was always a crowd favorite. He could pass a ball behind his back and was a master ball-handler.

Upon graduation from Temple, he led a touring team of college all-stars against the famed Harlem Globetrotters. The Globetrotters tried to get Rodgers to play with them after the tour ended but he decided to try his hand in the National Basketball Association. "I wanted to see if a small man could play in the big league," he said.

Rodgers certainly could. He teamed with another Philadelphian, Wilt Chamberlain, to make the Philadelphia Warriors one of the best teams in the professional game. Guy later played with Chicago, Cincinnati, and Milwaukee.

An extremely personable and witty fellow, Rodgers was successful as a banquet speaker. He also did some part-time teaching and basketball coaching at school clinics during his time off from professional play.

Because he was barely six feet, Guy Rodgers was an inspiring model for all small basketball players.

CAZZIE RUSSELL

Football was king at the University of Michigan at Ann Arbor. Talk of the Rose Bowl was everywhere. This was 1963 and only eleven season tickets had been sold for the Wolverines' basketball games. This all changed with the arrival on campus of a burly 6-5 basketball player from Chicago, Cazzie Lee Russell, Jr.

In three seasons at Michigan, Russell elevated the court game to prominence on campus, raised Michigan to the top of the national ratings, and electrified crowds all over the country with his exciting, aggressive style of play.

Russell began his basketball career at Carver High School on Chicago's South Side. His coach, Larry Hawkins, saw the potential in the gangling six-footer and worked for hours to perfect his skills.

"Another thing that helped my career," said Russell, "were some friendly janitors." When Russell was a freshman at the high school he persuaded the janitors to let him into the locked school building, keep the lights on late in the gymnasium and practice for hours on end.

"If it weren't for them letting me practice," Russell claimed, "I might have wound up driving a cab or working in the steel mills or pushing rocks on a construction gang."

Russell became an all-state basketball player at Carver. Soon the college offers poured in. Oscar Robertson advised Cazzie to go to his alma mater, Cincinnati. More than 75 schools put in their bids. Finally the choice narrowed to Cincinnati and Michigan.

"I chose Michigan because I always had some feeling for the underdog. Michigan's basketball team was down and Cincinnati's was up. I thought I just might be only another player at Cincinnati. At Michigan I had a chance to be a star," Russell said.

In his first year Cazzie led Michigan to a 23-5 record, the Holiday Festival championship (in a memorable triumph over Princeton

MICHIGAN
33
41

after Bill Bradley had fouled out), the Big Ten title, and third place in the NCAA tournament.

With Cazzie's heroics, basketball interest zoomed on campus. By his fifth game, students were lining up at 1 a.m. to buy tickets that didn't go on sale until 8 a.m.

Russell moved from backcourt to forecourt with ease. He was quick enough to set up the offense, guard the small man on defense and move the team. He was big enough to drive and shoot from the corners, help out with rebounding, and lead the Wolverine offense from in close.

Russell averaged nearly 25 points a game as a sophomore and was named to the All-Big Ten team and several All-America squads. He missed making the 1964 Olympic team when he sustained an ankle injury.

The following season was even better. Cazzie averaged 25.7 points a game, was a unanimous All-Big Ten selection, and made every All-America team. In his senior year, Cazzie averaged 30.8 points a game (the whole team averaged 91), led the Wolverines to a third-place NCAA tourney finish and was named Player of the Year.

The New York Knickerbockers made Cazzie the first choice in the annual pro draft and signed him to a three-year contract for a reported salary and bonus of $200,000. His contract set the pattern of huge bonuses for top NBA rookies.

MAURICE STOKES

At 6-7 and 240 pounds, Maurice Stokes was a basketball coach's dream. He had the speed and agility of a small man, coupled with the size and strength of a huge center. Maurice the Magnificent, as the newspapers called him, could shoot, drive, and pass off. He could do so much on the basketball court, in fact, that many who saw him play consider him the greatest all-around player of his time.

Michigan's Cazzie Russell

Certainly nobody who saw Stokes in the 1955 National Invitation Tournament in New York's Madison Square Garden is likely to argue that evaluation. Stokes, the tournament's Most Valuable Player, put on one of the most stunning individual exhibitions ever in the Garden and almost led his school, tiny St. Francis College of Loretto, Pennsylvania, into the finals of the NIT. That the Frankies fell short was no fault of Stokes, who by himself almost outplayed an entire Dayton team.

On the night of March 17, 1955, Stokes in 45 minutes scored 43 points, got 19 rebounds against a Dayton team that had four men taller than he, intercepted numerous passes, and generally frustrated the Flyers on defense. Despite these heroics, Dayton won in overtime, 79-73, but only after Stokes' teammates had missed three unobstructed layups on his perfect lead passes in the last few minutes of the game.

Walter McLaughlin, the St. John's athletic director and chairman of the NIT selection committee, said, "This is the greatest performance I have ever seen. There have been other great players here but what they did pales by comparison." Sports writers, marveling at Stokes' play, wondered in print how he had previously failed to make the All-America teams.

The answer was obvious. Stokes played for a small school that played many of its games against obscure opponents. As a result he didn't receive much national publicity. Nevertheless, his college statistics were impressive. Because of St. Francis' small size, freshmen were eligible for varsity competition and Stokes didn't waste any time showing what he could do. In his third varsity game, against Villanova, he scored 32 points, and Al Severance, the Villanova coach, commented, "He's the best freshman player I've ever seen."

Stokes finished his freshman season with a 16.7 average. That year the Frankies played 30 games, but after having seen the burly Stokes in action, some opposing schools decided not to reschedule St. Francis—at least

26
26

not until Stokes graduated. His scoring average increased each season and in his senior year, 1954–55, he averaged 26.6 a game.

The scouts saw Stokes as a natural pro. They were awed by his shooting touch and tremendous strength off the boards. The Rochester Royals made him their first choice in the annual draft, and Stokes, who had turned down an offer from the Harlem Globetrotters, became the NBA's Rookie of the Year. The next season he was even better, making the All-NBA second team.

But the following year, 1957–58, the world that Stokes had built through basketball, collapsed. Encephalitis, a crippling brain disease, turned Stokes into an invalid. For months he was in a coma, but he fought against the illness with the same tenacity that he used to fight for rebounds under the boards. Jack Twyman, his teammate on the Royals, became Stokes' guardian and with his help Maurice began a long and painful period of rehabilitation.

Today he is still confined to a wheelchair and his speech is hard to understand, although his mind is unaffected. But he has never stopped his struggle toward regaining the use of his body. And those who once saw him play basketball can only watch him in his greatest battle and remember what a player he once was.

ERNIE VANDEWEGHE

One of the classic all-star basketball games in Madison Square Garden history was the annual East-West encounter for the *Herald Tribune* Fresh Air Fund. The first of the series was played in 1946 and more than 18,000 people jammed the Garden to watch the best college players in the land, led by Bob Kurland, Kenny Sailors, Don Otten, and Charley Black.

When the Garden smoke had cleared, the East was a surprising winner, 60-59, and the Most Valuable Player was a gangling, large-eared 17-year-old Colgate freshman, Ernie Vandeweghe.

St. Francis' Maurice Stokes

Vandeweghe helped double-team the 7-foot Kurland, scored 16 points, set the East's offense, and controlled the pace of the game. Three years later, as a senior, Vandeweghe was again invited to play in the game.

Vandeweghe's career at Colgate spanned 1945–49, the post-World War II seasons when GIs returned to college and dominated the game. Vandeweghe was usually the youngest player on the floor when Colgate met its opposition. Even when he graduated in 1949 at 20, he was still one of the youngest players on his own team, which he had captained in his junior and senior years.

The 6-4 Vandeweghe was born in Montreal, Canada, where his father was a semi-professional basketball player by avocation and a furrier by vocation.

"I was a spoiled little boy," remembers Vandeweghe. "I had everything I wanted, especially when it came to athletic equipment. I had a hockey rink in my back yard, a basketball court, a motorboat, skates, hunting guns, and a horse. That's when I thought I would be a jockey."

He soon grew out of the jockey stage and began concentrating on basketball, soccer, and skating. His family moved to Oceanside, New York, when Ernie was in sixth grade. In the summer he spent his time between games running a lawn-mowing enterprise with a friend.

Vandeweghe earned eight varsity letters in high school in football, basketball, baseball, and track. He entered his father's alma mater, Colgate, in 1945. He gave up football because of a back injury and devoted himself to basketball.

One day he came home from college driving a convertible, a gift from his dad for good grades. A friend asked if the college gave him that car for his basketball playing. "No," said Ernie, "The only thing I get from Colgate is applause."

The applause was loud and clear as

Colgate's Ernie Vandeweghe

Vandeweghe led the Red Raiders in scoring four straight years with a career total of 1,377 for a Colgate record. He made the first team on most All-America squads along with Ed Macauley, Alex Groza, Tony Lavelli and Vince Boryla.

From the time he had written a high school paper on Louis Pasteur, Vandeweghe wanted to be a doctor. He entered medical school upon graduation and played basketball for the New York Athletic Club.

While playing golf one day with coach Joe Lapchick of the New York Knickerbockers, Lapchick suggested the possibility of combining medical studies with professional basketball. For four years Vandeweghe was one of the Knicks' finest guards while he continued his medical studies. When he completed his schooling he retired from basketball to devote full time to his profession.

Vandeweghe married a former Miss America, Colleen Kay Hutchins, sister of Mel Hutchins, who played for the Milwaukee Hawks. The Vandeweghes now make their home in Los Angeles where Ernie is a pediatrician.

JIMMY WALKER

Some days you never know who you may find in the playground basketball games in the city of Boston. One day it might be a local college hotshot out for some summer fun, or it might be a talented high school senior getting ready for college. It might even be a professional star like Sam Jones of the Boston Celtics.

"I was just out for some exercise," remembers Jones, "and this skinny kid gave me all I could handle."

Jimmy Walker, the skinny kid, grew up to be a 6-3, strong-legged 210-pounder who, with the help of his new-found friend, Sam Jones, was to discover a new world, become a college sensation and move into the professional basketball ranks.

"When I first played against Sam in the playground I had no ideas about college," Walker recalled. "I liked basketball and I wanted to go on but I certainly couldn't afford college."

Jones convinced Walker that he could continue both his education and his basketball career if he entered Laurinberg (N.C.) Prep School. Jones arranged for a scholarship and Walker went south from his Boston home to acquire the necessary credits for college admission and, at the same time, smooth out his basketball style.

In the fall of 1963, Walker entered Providence College in Rhode Island on a scholarship. As a freshman basketball player he averaged 22 points a game and gave all signs of being an exceptional star for the school that has a long history of outstanding basket-

Providence's Jimmy Walker

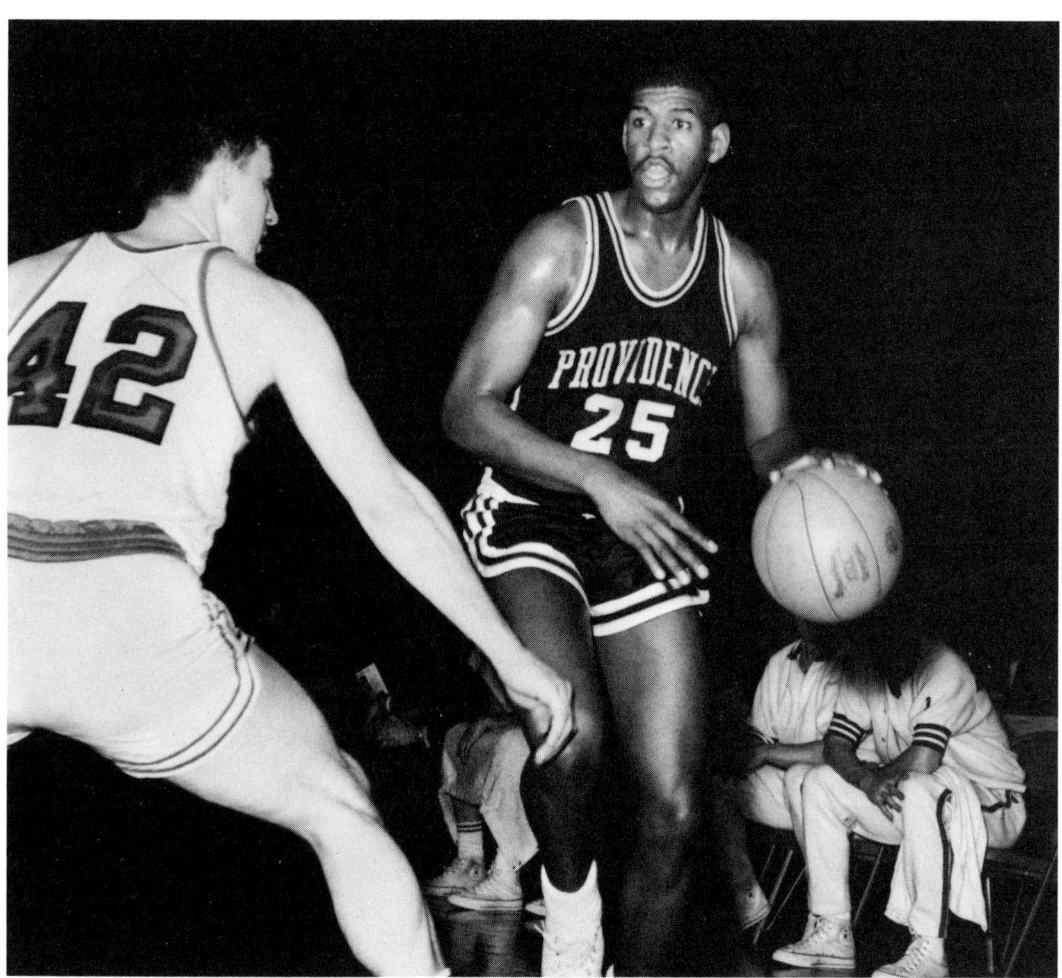

ball players, including Len Wilkens, John Egan, and Vinnie Ernst.

As a sophomore, Walker averaged 20.5 points a game and gained many All-America nominations. He was an outstanding scorer, especially in the clutch, and deadly when he got his man in a driving one-on-one situation.

"The thing I like about Jim most," said his coach, Joe Mullaney, "is he does just what you tell him to help the team win. I remember one game when he scored four points against St. Francis. We used him as a decoy and he took only three shots all night. He was just happy that we won."

As a junior he was selected as the Most Valuable Player in the Holiday Festival at Madison Square Garden and the outstanding player to appear at the Garden all season. He scored 622 points in 27 games and became the first Providence player to score more than 1,000 points before finishing his junior year.

In the final Festival game against Bob Cousy's Boston College team, Walker scored 50 points for the Friars and prompted Cousy to acclaim him as "The nearest thing to Oscar Robertson I've ever seen in college."

Oscar—and Cousy before him—were the standards by which all college backcourt players were measured. Walker was an exciting performer with his aggressive drives to the basket, his uncanny jump-shooting, his ferocious rebounding against taller men, and the amazing way he controlled the tempo of a game.

"He is a tremendous crowd-pleaser," said Joe Lapchick, "and he never lets the crowd down with his performance."

Walker capped his career with unanimous All-America selections, a repeat as MVP in the Holiday Festival, and the scoring leadership of the nation with an average of 30.4 points a game. He tallied 851 points in his final season at Providence.

Jim was named Player of the Year, and was the first choice in the professional basketball draft, being selected by the Detroit Pistons. He started slowly as a professional, but most people felt sure he would be ranked with the greats before his career was over.

5: THE COACHES

They throw towels, they argue, they suffer on the bench. If they win they are lauded. If they lose too frequently, they sometimes find themselves out of a job. But they are the lifeblood of the game. They are the coaches.

Players come and players go, but coaches remain to teach, to improve the game, and to serve as public relations officers and goodwill ambassadors for their beloved sport.

The following is a list of coaches whose contributions have had a vital impact on college basketball. They are not necessarily the coaches with the best won-lost records. They are the coaches who have contributed something of permanent value to the sport, something that has transcended the mere winning of games.

The coaches, such as Pitt's Doc Carlson, pointed to basketball's modern era.

DR. FORREST C. (PHOG) ALLEN

While still a student at the University of Kansas in 1908, Allen took over as coach from Dr. James Naismith, the game's inventor. Almost a half-century later, Allen retired with 771 victories. Only one coach has won more games—Adolph Rupp of Kentucky, who was Allen's pupil. In his 39 seasons at Kansas, Allen's teams won 24 conference championships, climaxed by the NCAA

Phog Allen

crown in 1952. His teams were always distinguished for outstanding defense and they typified the ball-control style of basketball. Allen founded the National Association of Basketball Coaches in 1927 and was later instrumental in having basketball included in the Olympic Games.

CLAIR BEE

This dynamic, intense little man who stood so tall as coach of Long Island University is a foremost clinician, teacher, strategist, and author of basketball books for boys and coaches. In constant demand at coaching clinics, Bee used to spread his coaching gospel

Clair Bee

all over the country. As a coach, Bee was a master at capitalizing on opponents' weaknesses. He originated the 1-3-1 zone defense and helped with the development of the 24-second clock, the salvation of the pro game. In 18 seasons at LIU, Bee's teams won 327 games, including winning streaks of 43, 38, 28 and 26, and they lost only 67. Bee is a member of the Hall of Fame.

JOHN H. BUNN

The most significant change in offensive basketball in the past 50 years was the perfection of one-handed shooting. In 1936 Bunn brought his Stanford five into New York's Madison Square Garden to play LIU, which had won 43 straight games. New York, for the first time, saw one-handed shooting, an art perfectly exemplified by Bunn's prize player, Hank Luisetti. Stanford broke LIU's streak, and soon most college players were firing with one hand. Bunn later coached at Springfield and Colorado State, and was elected to the Hall of Fame.

John Bunn

DR. H. CLIFFORD CARLSON

A charter member of the Hall of Fame, Doc Carlson coached Pitt for 31 years, winning 370 games, losing 246. His 1927–28 and 1929–30 teams were acclaimed unofficial national champions. He was the first coach to take an eastern team to the West Coast, in 1931–32. Doc is credited with having originated the first patterned offense, the "figure eight." While coaching he maintained a medical practice.

Doc Carlson

ED DIDDLE

Third on the all-time list of winning coaches with 759 victories and 302 defeats at Western Kentucky, Diddle used to delight the audience with his towel act. When unhappy with an official's decision, the performance of his players or anything else, Ed would heave his omnipresent towel to the floor. An advocate of race-horse basketball, Diddle employed the fast break with great success. One of his regrets was that his teams never fared well in New York. But they did very well everywhere else.

Ed Diddle

PAUL (TONY) HINKLE

Although coaching at a small school, Butler, Hinkle rates with the giants. He scheduled the best opponents and beat Big Ten schools

Tony Hinkle

with amazing regularity. Through the 1967–68 season he had won 534 games and lost 366 in 39 years. Tony was elected to the Hall of Fame in 1965.

NAT HOLMAN

Known as "Mr. Basketball" at City College of New York, Holman was a master teacher and innovator who brought a certain class and sophistication to the game. The erudite Holman was credited with being the brains of the Original Celtics, and he was a natural as a coach. As a player he improvised all sorts of individual moves that eventually became the foundation for "New York basketball," recognized the country over as connoting guile and finesse. Holman, like Clair Bee, was in great demand as a lecturer and wrote several books on basketball techniques. His greatest coaching achievement came in 1949–50, when CCNY's Beavers achieved the Grand Slam of college basketball, winning both major post-season tournaments—the National Invitation Tournament and the NCAA. No other coach accomplished the feat. Holman was elected to the Hall of Fame in 1967.

HENRY P. (HANK) IBA

Patience is not just a virtue for Hank Iba, it's a way of life. Discipline and ball control are his obsession. Iba's Oklahoma State (formerly

Nat Holman

Hank Iba

A&M) teams shoot only when absolutely necessary, when there is nothing else to do with the ball. Iba makes patience an absolute necessity as far as shot-taking. His contributions to the game are many and one of the most noteworthy was his use of basketball's first good 7-footer, Bob Kurland, who became an All-American, a Hall of Famer, and helped make the word "goon" disappear from the jargon of basketball. Iba's rewards have been many. His 741 victories through 1968 place him fourth on the all-time winning list. He won back-to-back NCAA championships in 1944–45 and 1945–46 and he has served as U.S. Olympic coach in 1964 at Tokyo and in 1968 at Mexico City. His Olympians maintained the unbeaten U.S. record that began with the introduction of basketball to the Olympic program in 1936. Iba's son, Moe, is basketball coach at Memphis State.

GEORGE E. KEOGAN

From 1923 to 1943, Keogan gave Notre Dame a basketball team that rivalled football at South Bend, if not in prestige and fame, at least in performance. In that span, the Irish won 327 games and lost 96, a fantastic .773 percentage. He studied dentistry, but gave up that career to concentrate on coaching and was elected to the Basketball Hall of Fame in 1961. Keogan is credited with creating the shifting man-to-man defense. A student of the game, he followed professional ball and learned from the pros, particularly the Original Celtics and their pivot man, Dutch Dehnert. From Dehnert, he adopted the successful use of pivots and cuts.

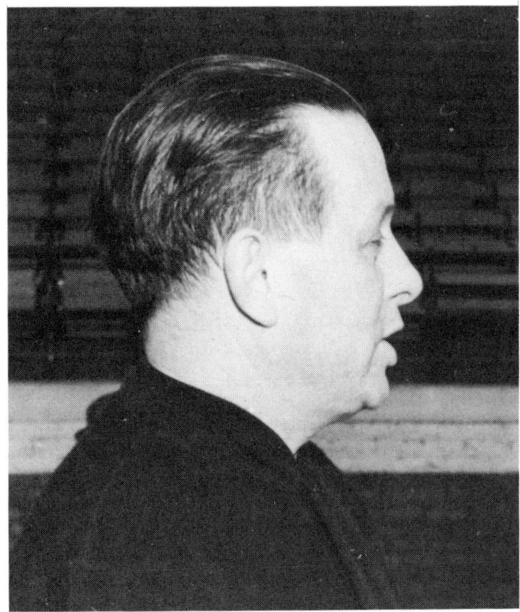

George Keogan

WARD L. (PIGGY) LAMBERT

He helped put the Big Ten on the basketball map with his powerful Purdue teams, which gained national recognition in the 20s and 30s. In 29 years as coach, his teams won or shared 11 Big Ten titles and posted 371 victories. He pioneered the fast break style of basketball and his teams were noted for their sustained speed. There was nothing mechanical about their play. "Basketball," he was fond of saying, "is a mental game." Lambert died in 1958. Two years later he was elected to the Hall of Fame.

Piggy Lambert

JOE LAPCHICK

The game's greatest goodwill ambassador, highly respected as a coach and dedicated contributor to college basketball, Lapchick has viewed 50 years of the sport as a player, college coach, professional coach, and college coach again. He was the game's first big man as the 6-5 center of the famed Original Celtics, then helped make St. John's "The Notre Dame of college basketball," according to a

Joe Lapchick

rival coach. Lapchick's teams were characterized by their patience, intelligence, ball control, and defense. He was an inspirational coach whose fatherly approach got tremendous mileage out of his players. More than a dozen of his pupils became pro or college coaches themselves. An habitual walker with countless trips to the water cooler during a game, Lapchick was able to adjust and keep pace with the times as the college game changed through the years. He capped a brilliant career in his final game in 1965 by becoming the only coach to win the National Invitation Tournament four times. In 17 seasons Lapchick's Redmen won 291 games, lost 95.

BRANCH McCRACKEN

The fast break was McCracken's forte, and he employed it successfully to produce some of the highest scoring teams in collegiate history.

Branch McCracken

His Indiana teams won national championships in 1939–40 and 1952–53, and McCracken was twice selected to conduct clinics for coaches of armed forces teams overseas, once in Europe, once in Japan. McCracken was voted into the Hall of Fame in 1960. Upon his retirement following the 1964–65 season, he had won 451 games and lost only 277, while competing in the tough and highly competitive Big Ten. His 451 victories place him 12th on the all-time winning list.

JOHN McLENDON

In more than 20 years of coaching at North Carolina College, Hampton Institute, Tennessee State, Kentucky State, and Cleveland State, McLendon's teams won over 650 games. His winning percentage of nearly .800 is among the highest of all modern coaches. McLendon's Tennessee State teams won three consecutive NAIA championships in 1957–59.

John McLendon

Adolph Rupp

Among McLendon's players who have gone on to the pros are NBA stars Sam Jones, Dick Barnett, John Barnhill, and Ben Warley. When he was appointed head coach of the Cleveland Pipers of the short-lived American Basketball League in 1960, McLendon became the first Negro coach to reach so high a level in professional sports.

ADOLPH (THE BARON) RUPP

Kentucky's controversial and outspoken Baron is No. 1 on the all-time list of winning coaches, having been on the winning side 782 times in 952 games, a sensational .820 winning percentage through 1968, his 38th year on the job. Rupp is a strong-willed individual who has never been afraid to voice his opinion, even if it is a minority and unpopular one. He is a strange mixture of vanity and humility. He developed a mode of operation based on set offenses and made it stand up, never deviating from it regardless of the opposition's style of play. Much of his success has depended on the employment of a stiff man-to-man defense. He produced some of the college game's greatest teams and usually sacrificed height for speed and ruggedness. He once said, "I know I have plenty of enemies, but I'd rather be the most hated winning coach in the country than the most popular losing one." Rupp has been Coach of the Year four times, has produced 24 All-Americans, has won four national championships, and has made more appearances in the NCAA tournament (15) than any other coach—a record of achievement unmatched in college basketball.

JOHN WOODEN

The record acknowledges scholarly and soft-spoken John Wooden as a coaching great. He won five NCAA championships and in a 32-year career as a high school and college coach, Wooden's teams have won almost 80 per cent of their games and never had a losing season. Through 1969, he had won 496 college games, lost only 151, and was tenth on the all-time winning list. Wooden is another exponent of deliberate basketball. His teams are characterized by conditioning, fundamentals of speed, quickness and basketball sense, which Wooden describes as "the ability to be in the right place at the right time."

John Wooden

Phil Woolpert

Wooden was voted into the Hall of Fame in 1960.

PHIL WOOLPERT

The measure of Woolpert as a coach is in his 60 consecutive victories at the University of San Francisco in 1954–55 and 1955–56. In those two years he established himself as a genius of defensive basketball. Woolpert had always been violently opposed to fast break, race-horse basketball. "It just isn't good basketball," he once said. "I wouldn't know how to go about coaching it. You can't expect to execute scoring plays when you're racing up and down the court like madmen." Woolpert's teams spent 60 per cent of their practice time on defense, but theory means nothing if you do not have the players to do the execution. In those two years he had the players—rather he made the players. The center was a tall, lanky kid who had been the sixth man on his high school team. Bill Russell was his name. And one guard had been a football player in high school. K.C. Jones was his name. They were the stalwarts on a team that won two successive NCAA titles and completed two seasons without losing a game. "The best college team I ever saw," says Joe Lapchick. "They played a defense I never saw before."

There are many others, past and present, who can claim a place on the coaching honor roll. They include:

Harold Anderson, Toledo and Bowling Green; **Tom Blackburn,** Dayton; **Al Brightman,** Seattle; **Vic Bubas,** Duke; **Howard Cann,** NYU; **Ben Carnevale,** Navy; **Ev Case,** North Carolina State; **Chick Davies,** Duquesne; **Everett Dean,** Indiana and Stanford; **Lefty Driesell,** Davidson; **Fred Enke,** Arizona; **Harold "Bud" Foster,** Wisconsin; **Jack Friel,** Washington State; **Taps Gallagher,** Niagara; **Jack Gardner,** Utah State; **Zip Gayles,** Langston; **Slats Gill,** Oregon State; **Bruce Hale,** Miami (Fla.); **Jack Hartman,** Southern Illinois; **Ed Hickey,** Creighton, St. Louis, and Marquette; **Peck Hickman,** Louisville; **Fred Hobdy,** Grambling; and **Howard Hobson,** Oregon and Yale.

Also **George Ireland,** Loyola (Ill.); **Ed Jucker,** Cincinnati; **Alvin "Doggy" Julian,** Holy Cross and Dartmouth; **Bob King,** New Mexico; **Frank Keaney,** Rhode Island; **Jack Kraft,** Villanova; **Guy Lewis,** Houston; **Harry Litwack,** Temple; **Ken Loeffler,** LaSalle; **Dutch Lonberg,** Northwestern; **Arad McCutchan,** Evansville; **Frank McGuire,** St. John's, North Carolina, and South Carolina; **Ray Mears,** Tennessee; **Ray Meyer,** DePaul; **Dudey Moore,** Duquesne; **Joe Mullaney,** Providence; **Pete Newell,** California; **Vadal Peterson,** Utah; **Nibs Price,** California; **Jack Ramsay,** St. Joseph's; **Elmer Ripley,** Georgetown and Army; **John "Honey" Russell,** Seton Hall; **Dean Smith,** North Carolina; **Bill van Breda Kolff,** Princeton; **Stan Watts,** Brigham Young; **Tex Winter,** Marquette and Kansas State.

6: THE MAJOR COLLEGES

The following year-by-year records cover the "major colleges" as classified by the National Collegiate Athletic Association. According to the NCAA's Service Bureau, these University Division teams "represent the field of so-called big-time college basketball as judged by the class of competition rather than seasonal records."

In keeping with the theme of a "Modern Encyclopedia," the editors chose the 1937–38 season —which culminated with the first National Invitation Tournament—as the starting point for these annual records.

A variety of circumstances accounts for any omission in a given year. World War II, for example, forced some schools to cancel their schedules. In several instances records were destroyed by fire or otherwise lost to the historians. Records for schools that were at one time junior or women's colleges are listed only from the dates when they became four-year or co-educational institutions.

Yr.	W	L	Coach

AIR FORCE ACADEMY

Air Force Academy, Colorado

Falcons — *Silver and Blue*

Yr.	W	L	Coach
1957	11	10	Bob Spear
1958	17	6	Bob Spear
1959	14	9	Bob Spear
1960	12	10	Bob Spear
1961	12	12	Bob Spear
1962	16	7	Bob Spear
1963	10	12	Bob Spear
1964	11	12	Bob Spear
1965	9	14	Bob Spear
1966	14	12	Bob Spear
1967	7	18	Bob Spear
1968	9	15	Bob Spear
Totals	142	137	

ALABAMA, UNIVERSITY OF

Tuscaloosa, Alabama

Crimson Tide — *Crimson and White*

Yr.	W	L	Coach
1938	4	13	Henry Crisp
1939	16	5	Henry Crisp
1940	18	6	Henry Crisp
1941	14	8	Henry Crisp
1942	18	6	Henry Crisp
1943	10	10	Paul Burnum
1944	—	—	
1945	10	5	Malcolm Laney
1946	11	5	Henry Crisp
1947	16	6	Floyd Burdette
1948	15	12	Floyd Burdette
1949	13	12	Floyd Burdette
1950	9	12	Floyd Burdette
1951	15	8	Floyd Burdette
1952	13	9	Floyd Burdette
1953	10	9	Johnny Dee
1954	16	8	Johnny Dee
1955	19	5	Johnny Dee
1956	21	3	Johnny Dee
1957	15	11	Dr. Eugene Lambert
1958	17	9	Dr. Eugene Lambert
1959	10	12	Dr. Eugene Lambert
1960	7	17	Dr. Eugene Lambert
1961	7	18	Hayden Riley
1962	11	15	Hayden Riley
1963	14	11	Hayden Riley
1964	14	12	Hayden Riley
1965	17	9	Hayden Riley
1966	16	10	Hayden Riley
1967	13	13	Hayden Riley
1968	10	16	Hayden Riley
Totals	399	295	

AMERICAN UNIVERSITY

Washington, D. C.

Eagles — *Red, White and Blue*

Yr.	W	L	Coach
1938	8	6	Cassell
1939	10	7	Cassell
1940	10	6	Cassell
1941	8	7	Cassell
1942	9	7	Cassell
1943	7	12	Kalijarvi
1944	6	12	Kalijarvi
1945	15	1	Boyd
1946	16	4	Boyd
1947	15	12	Cassell
1948	17	11	Cassell
1949	17	9	Cassell
1950	22	7	Cassell
1951	18	10	Cassell
1952	18	7	Cassell
1953	15	8	Schulze
1954	12	13	Schulze
1955	8	19	Schulze
1956	11	11	Schulze
1957	10	14	Dave Carrasco
1958	22	6	Dave Carrasco
1959	22	7	Dave Carrasco
1960	23	6	Dave Carrasco
1961	23	6	Dave Carrasco
1962	10	11	Carrasco, J. Williams
1963	10	14	Jim Williams
1964	6	18	Jim Williams
1965	4	19	Jim Williams
1966	8	14	Alan Kyber
1967	16	8	Alan Kyber
1968	14	12	Alan Kyber
Totals	410	304	

ARIZONA, UNIVERSITY OF

Tucson, Arizona

Wildcats — *Navy Blue and Cardinal Red*

Yr.	W	L	Coach
1938	13	8	Fred Enke
1939	12	11	Fred Enke
1940	15	10	Fred Enke
1941	11	7	Fred Enke
1942	9	13	Fred Enke
1943	20	2	Fred Enke
1944	12	2	Fred Enke
1945	7	11	Fred Enke
1946	25	5	Fred Enke
1947	21	3	Fred Enke
1948	19	10	Fred Enke
1949	18	11	Fred Enke
1950	29	5	Fred Enke
1951	24	6	Fred Enke
1952	11	16	Fred Enke
1953	14	13	Fred Enke
1954	14	10	Fred Enke
1955	8	17	Fred Enke
1956	11	15	Fred Enke
1957	13	13	Fred Enke
1958	10	16	Fred Enke
1959	4	22	Fred Enke
1960	10	14	Fred Enke
1961	11	15	Fred Enke
1962	12	14	Bruce Larson
1963	13	13	Bruce Larson
1964	15	11	Bruce Larson
1965	17	9	Bruce Larson
1966	15	11	Bruce Larson
1967	8	17	Bruce Larson
1968	11	13	Bruce Larson
Totals	432	343	

Yr.	W	L	Coach

ARIZONA STATE UNIVERSITY

Tempe, Arizona

Sun Devils — *Maroon and Gold*

Yr.	W	L	Coach
1938	13	13	Earl Pomeroy
1939	13	13	Earl Pomeroy
1940	8	11	Earl Pomeroy
1941	8	13	Earl Pomeroy
1942	10	6	Rudolph Lavik
1943	9	9	Rudolph Lavik
1944	—	—	
1945	—	—	
1946	12	16	Rudolph Lavik
1947	7	13	Rudolph Lavik
1948	13	11	Rudolph Lavik
1949	12	16	Rudolph Lavik
1950	12	14	Rudolph Lavik
1951	7	17	Bill Kajikawa
1952	8	16	Bill Kajikawa
1953	13	12	Bill Kajikawa
1954	5	18	Bill Kajikawa
1955	10	14	Bill Kajikawa
1956	11	15	Bill Kajikawa
1957	10	15	Bill Kajikawa
1958	13	13	Ned Wulk
1959	17	9	Ned Wulk
1960	18	7	Ned Wulk
1961	23	6	Ned Wulk
1962	23	4	Ned Wulk
1963	26	3	Ned Wulk
1964	16	11	Ned Wulk
1965	13	14	Ned Wulk
1966	12	14	Ned Wulk
1967	5	21	Ned Wulk
1968	11	17	Ned Wulk
Totals	358	361	

ARKANSAS, UNIVERSITY OF

Fayetteville, Arkansas

Razorbacks — *Cardinal and White*

Yr.	W	L	Coach
1938	20	2	Glen Rose
1939	18	5	Glen Rose
1940	12	10	Glen Rose
1941	20	3	Glen Rose
1942	19	4	Glen Rose
1943	19	7	Eugene Lambert
1944	16	7	Eugene Lambert
1945	17	9	Eugene Lambert
1946	16	7	Eugene Lambert
1947	14	10	Eugene Lambert
1948	16	8	Eugene Lambert
1949	15	11	Eugene Lambert
1950	12	12	Presley Askew
1951	13	11	Presley Askew
1952	10	14	Presley Askew
1953	10	11	Glen Rose
1954	13	10	Glen Rose
1955	14	10	Glen Rose
1956	11	13	Glen Rose
1957	11	12	Glen Rose
1958	17	10	Glen Rose
1959	9	14	Glen Rose
1960	12	11	Glen Rose
1961	16	7	Glen Rose
1962	14	10	Glen Rose
1963	13	11	Glen Rose
1964	9	14	Glen Rose
1965	9	14	Glen Rose
1966	13	10	Glen Rose
1967	6	17	P. T. (Duddy) Waller
1968	10	14	P. T. (Duddy) Waller
Totals	424	308	

ARMY (U. S. M. A.)

West Point, New York

Cadets — *Black, Gold and Gray*

Yr.	W	L	Coach
1938	12	2	Leo Novak
1939	13	2	Leo Novak
1940	11	4	Valentine Lentz
1941	5	11	Valentine Lentz
1942	10	6	Valentine Lentz
1943	5	10	Valentine Lentz
1944	15	0	Edward A. Kelleher
1945	14	1	Edward A. Kelleher
1946	9	6	Stewart K. Holcomb
1947	9	7	Stewart K. Holcomb
1948	8	9	John W. Mauer
1949	7	10	John W. Mauer
1950	9	8	John W. Mauer
1951	9	8	John W. Mauer
1952	8	9	Elmer Ripley
1953	11	8	Elmer Ripley
1954	15	7	Robert Vanatta
1955	19	9	Orvis Sigler
1956	10	13	Orvis Sigler
1957	7	13	Orvis Sigler
1958	13	12	Orvis Sigler
1959	14	10	George Hunter
1960	14	9	George Hunter
1961	17	6	George Hunter
1962	10	11	George Hunter
1963	8	11	George Hunter
1964	19	7	Taylor (Tates) Locke
1965	21	8	Taylor (Tates) Locke
1966	18	8	Bobby Knight
1967	13	8	Bobby Knight
1968	20	5	Bobby Knight
Totals	373	238	

AUBURN UNIVERSITY

Auburn, Alabama

Tigers — *Orange and Black*

Yr.	W	L	Coach
1938	14	5	Ralph Jordan
1939	14	5	Ralph Jordan
1940	7	9	Ralph Jordan
1941	13	6	Ralph Jordan
1942	11	6	Ralph Jordan
1943	1	14	Robert K. Evans
1944	—	—	

Yr.	W	L	Coach
1945	3	14	Robert K. Evans
1946	7	9	Ralph Jordan
1947	3	18	V. J. Edney
1948	12	10	Daniel Doyle
1949	9	15	Daniel Doyle
1950	17	7	Joel Eaves
1951	12	10	Joel Eaves
1952	14	12	Joel Eaves
1953	13	8	Joel Eaves
1954	16	8	Joel Eaves
1955	11	9	Joel Eaves
1956	11	10	Joel Eaves
1957	13	8	Joel Eaves
1958	16	6	Joel Eaves
1959	20	2	Joel Eaves
1960	19	3	Joel Eaves
1961	15	7	Joel Eaves
1962	18	6	Joel Eaves
1963	18	4	Joel Eaves
1964	11	12	Joel Eaves
1965	16	9	Joel Eaves
1966	16	10	Bill Lynn
1967	17	8	Bill Lynn
1968	13	13	Bill Lynn
Totals	380	263	

AUSTIN PEAY STATE UNIVERSITY

Clarksville, Tennessee

Governors — *Scarlet and White*

Yr.	W	L	Coach
1938	11	6	Fred Brown
1939	11	7	Fred Brown
1940	19	0	Fred Brown
1941	17	5	Fred Brown
1942	9	10	Fred Brown
1943	1	6	Fred Brown
1944	—	—	
1945	—	—	
1946	2	19	Bee Lowe
1947	23	5	David Aaron
1948	16	9	David Aaron
1949	17	3	David Aaron
1950	14	11	David Aaron
1951	13	12	David Aaron
1952	11	17	David Aaron
1953	14	12	David Aaron
1954	14	13	David Aaron
1955	7	17	David Aaron
1956	16	11	David Aaron
1957	24	9	David Aaron
1958	17	9	David Aaron
1959	14	10	David Aaron
1960	22	5	David Aaron
1961	22	9	David Aaron
1962	14	12	David Aaron
1963	18	11	George Fisher
1964	14	9	George Fisher
1965	4	17	George Fisher
1966	7	14	George Fisher
1967	14	9	George Fisher
1968	8	16	George Fisher
Totals	393	293	

BAYLOR UNIVERSITY

Waco, Texas

Bears — *Green and Gold*

Yr.	W	L	Coach
1938	8	8	Ralph Wolf
1939	14	7	Ralph Wolf
1940	12	9	Ralph Wolf
1941	10	12	Ralph Wolf
1942	11	9	R. E. "Bill" Henderson
1943	6	14	R. E. "Bill" Henderson
1944	6	12	M. T. "Van" Sweet
1945	0	14	Sweet and Henderson
1946	24	5	R. E. "Bill" Henderson
1947	11	11	R. E. "Bill" Henderson
1948	24	8	R. E. "Bill" Henderson
1949	14	10	R. E. "Bill" Henderson
1950	14	13	R. E. "Bill" Henderson
1951	8	16	R. E. "Bill" Henderson
1952	6	18	R. E. "Bill" Henderson
1953	10	11	R. E. "Bill" Henderson
1954	12	11	R. E. "Bill" Henderson
1955	13	11	R. E. "Bill" Henderson
1956	6	17	R. E. "Bill" Henderson
1957	9	15	R. E. "Bill" Henderson
1958	5	19	R. E. "Bill" Henderson
1959	11	13	R. E. "Bill" Henderson
1960	12	12	R. E. "Bill" Henderson
1961	4	20	R. E. "Bill" Henderson
1962	4	20	Bill Menefee
1963	7	17	Bill Menefee
1964	7	17	Bill Menefee
1965	15	9	Bill Menefee
1966	8	16	Bill Menefee
1967	14	10	Bill Menefee
1968	15	9	Bill Menefee
Totals	320	393	

BOSTON COLLEGE

Chestnut Hill, Massachusetts

Eagles — *Maroon and Gold*

Yr.	W	L	Coach
1946	3	11	Albert McClellan
1947	11	11	Albert McClellan
1948	13	10	Albert McClellan
1949	9	9	Albert McClellan
1950	11	9	Albert McClellan
1951	17	11	Albert McClellan
1952	22	5	Albert McClellan
1953	7	15	Albert McClellan
1954	11	11	Donald Martin
1955	8	18	Donald Martin
1956	6	17	Donald Martin
1957	13	12	Donald Martin
1958	15	6	Donald Martin
1959	17	9	Donald Martin
1960	11	14	Donald Martin
1961	14	9	Donald Martin
1962	15	7	Donald Martin
1963	10	16	Frank Power
1964	10	11	Bob Cousy
1965	21	7	Bob Cousy
1966	21	5	Bob Cousy
1967	21	3	Bob Cousy
1968	17	8	Bob Cousy
Totals	303	234	

BOSTON UNIVERSITY

Boston, Massachusetts

Terriers — *Scarlet and White*

Yr.	W	L	Coach
1938	10	6	Merrel Collard
1939	10	4	Merrel Collard
1940	6	6	Merrel Collard
1941	13	3	Merrel Collard
1942	8	4	Merrel Collard
1943	3	10	Merrel Collard
1944	4	5	Russell Peterson
1945	—	—	
1946	11	2	Russell Peterson
1947	14	7	Russell Peterson
1948	10	9	Russell Peterson
1949	6	12	Charles Cummings
1950	7	9	Vincent Cronin
1951	7	11	Vincent Cronin
1952	9	8	Vincent Cronin
1953	10	10	Matthew Zunic
1954	9	11	Matthew Zunic
1955	13	9	Matthew Zunic
1956	17	6	Matthew Zunic
1957	13	10	Matthew Zunic
1958	15	5	Matthew Zunic
1959	20	7	Matthew Zunic
1960	14	10	John Burke
1961	9	14	John Burke
1962	5	15	John Burke
1963	10	9	John Burke
1964	16	7	John Burke
1965	10	10	John Burke
1966	4	19	John Burke
1967	4	18	Charles Luce
1968	10	14	Charles Luce
Totals	297	270	

BOWLING GREEN STATE UNIVERSITY

Bowling Green, Ohio

Falcons — *Burnt Orange and Seal Brown*

Yr.	W	L	Coach
1938	16	4	Paul Landis
1939	12	7	Paul Landis
1940	16	5	Paul Landis
1941	10	12	Paul Landis
1942	8	12	Paul Landis
1943	18	5	Harold Anderson
1944	22	4	Harold Anderson
1945	24	4	Harold Anderson
1946	27	5	Harold Anderson
1947	28	7	Harold Anderson
1948	27	6	Harold Anderson
1949	24	7	Harold Anderson
1950	19	11	Harold Anderson
1951	15	12	Anderson, G. Muellich
1952	17	10	Harold Anderson
1953	12	15	Harold Anderson
1954	17	7	Harold Anderson
1955	6	16	Harold Anderson
1956	4	19	Harold Anderson
1957	14	9	Harold Anderson
1958	15	8	Harold Anderson
1959	18	8	Harold Anderson
1960	10	14	Harold Anderson
1961	10	14	Harold Anderson
1962	21	4	Harold Anderson
1963	19	8	Harold Anderson
1964	14	9	Harold Anderson
1965	9	15	Harold Anderson
1966	9	15	Warren Scholler
1967	11	13	Warren Scholler
1968	18	7	Bill Fitch
Totals	490	292	

BRADLEY UNIVERSITY

Peoria, Illinois

Braves — *Red and White*

Yr.	W	L	Coach
1938	18	2	Alfred Robertson
1939	19	3	Alfred Robertson
1940	14	6	Alfred Robertson
1941	16	4	Alfred Robertson
1942	15	5	Alfred Robertson
1943	8	11	Alfred Robertson
1944	—	—	
1945	—	—	
1946	11	12	Alfred Robertson
1947	25	7	Alfred Robertson
1948	28	3	Alfred Robertson
1949	27	8	Forrest Anderson
1950	32	5	Forrest Anderson
1951	32	6	Forrest Anderson
1952	17	12	Forrest Anderson
1953	15	12	Forrest Anderson
1954	19	13	Forrest Anderson
1955	9	20	Bob Vanatta
1956	13	13	Bob Vanatta
1957	22	7	Chuck Orsborn
1958	20	7	Chuck Orsborn
1959	25	4	Chuck Orsborn
1960	27	2	Chuck Orsborn
1961	21	5	Chuck Orsborn
1962	21	7	Chuck Orsborn
1963	17	9	Chuck Orsborn
1964	23	6	Chuck Orsborn
1965	18	9	Chuck Orsborn
1966	20	6	Joe Stowell
1967	17	9	Joe Stowell
1968	19	9	Joe Stowell
Totals	568	222	

BRIGHAM YOUNG UNIVERSITY

Provo, Utah

Cougars — *Royal Blue and White*

Yr.	W	L	Coach
1938	8	13	Fred Dixon
1939	12	11	Fred Dixon
1940	15	8	Floyd Millett
1941	12	9	Floyd Millett
1942	17	3	Floyd Millett
1943	15	7	Floyd Millett
1944	3	2	Floyd Millett

Yr.	W	L	Coach
1945	11	7	Floyd Millett
1946	13	12	Floyd Millett
1947	9	13	Floyd Millett
1948	16	10	Floyd Millett
1949	22	14	Floyd Millett
1950	22	12	Stan Watts
1951	26	10	Stan Watts
1952	14	10	Stan Watts
1953	22	8	Stan Watts
1954	18	11	Stan Watts
1955	13	13	Stan Watts
1956	18	8	Stan Watts
1957	19	9	Stan Watts
1958	13	13	Stan Watts
1959	15	11	Stan Watts
1960	8	17	Stan Watts
1961	15	11	Stan Watts
1962	10	16	Stan Watts
1963	12	14	Stan Watts
1964	13	12	Stan Watts
1965	21	7	Stan Watts
1966	20	5	Stan Watts
1967	14	10	Stan Watts
1968	13	12	Stan Watts
Totals	459	318	

BROWN UNIVERSITY

Providence, Rhode Island

Bruins			*Seal Brown and White*
1938	8	11	Arthur Kahler
1939	17	4	George Allen
1940	14	6	George Allen
1941	11	10	George Allen
1942	11	7	William "Tippy" Dye
1943	9	11	Charles "Rip" Engle
1944	10	14	Charles "Rip" Engle
1945	15	4	Charles "Rip" Engle
1946	5	15	Charles "Rip" Engle
1947	8	12	Wilbur "Weeb" Ewbank
1948	6	14	Robert Morris
1949	13	8	Robert Morris
1950	11	14	Robert Morris
1951	8	11	Robert Morris
1952	5	15	Robert Morris
1953	5	14	Robert Morris
1954	13	12	Robert Morris
1955	7	18	L. Stanley Ward
1956	7	18	L. Stanley Ward
1957	8	16	L. Stanley Ward
1958	11	14	L. Stanley Ward
1959	11	13	L. Stanley Ward
1960	13	12	L. Stanley Ward
1961	11	14	L. Stanley Ward
1962	11	14	L. Stanley Ward
1963	11	13	L. Stanley Ward
1964	6	19	L. Stanley Ward
1965	7	17	L. Stanley Ward
1966	9	17	L. Stanley Ward
1967	10	16	L. Stanley Ward
1968	9	16	L. Stanley Ward
Totals	300	399	

Yr.	W	L	Coach

BUCKNELL UNIVERSITY

Lewisburg, Pennsylvania

Bisons			*Orange and Blue*
1938	7	6	Malcolm Musser
1939	8	8	Malcolm Musser
1940	13	7	Malcolm Musser
1941	10	7	Malcolm Musser
1942	9	9	Malcolm Musser
1943	5	8	John Sitarski
1944	9	3	J. Lewood Ludwig
1945	10	7	J. Lewood Ludwig
1946	6	11	J. Lewood Ludwig
1947	11	8	J. Lewood Ludwig
1948	5	17	Jack Guy
1949	2	18	Jack Guy
1950	5	16	Jack Guy
1951	9	13	Jack Guy
1952	8	16	Jack Guy
1953	3	16	Benton Kribbs
1954	4	16	Benton Kribbs
1955	3	18	Benton Kribbs
1956	10	14	Benton Kribbs
1957	16	8	Benton Kribbs
1958	16	8	Benton Kribbs
1959	16	7	Benton Kribbs
1960	10	11	Benton Kribbs
1961	12	11	Benton Kribbs
1962	7	15	Benton Kribbs
1963	7	15	Gene Evans
1964	8	13	Gene Evans
1965	11	13	Gene Evans
1966	15	10	Don Smith
1967	11	11	Don Smith
1968	12	11	Don Smith
Totals	278	351	

BUTLER UNIVERSITY

Indianapolis, Indiana

Bulldogs			*Royal Blue and White*
1938	11	12	Tony Hinkle
1939	14	6	Tony Hinkle
1940	17	6	Tony Hinkle
1941	13	9	Tony Hinkle
1942	13	9	Tony Hinkle
1943	4	9	Frank "Pop" Hedden
1944	—	—	
1945	14	6	Frank "Pop" Hedden
1946	12	8	Tony Hinkle
1947	16	7	Tony Hinkle
1948	14	7	Tony Hinkle
1949	18	5	Tony Hinkle
1950	12	12	Tony Hinkle
1951	5	19	Tony Hinkle
1952	12	12	Tony Hinkle
1953	14	9	Tony Hinkle
1954	13	12	Tony Hinkle
1955	10	14	Tony Hinkle
1956	14	9	Tony Hinkle
1957	11	14	Tony Hinkle
1958	15	10	Tony Hinkle
1959	19	9	Tony Hinkle
1960	15	11	Tony Hinkle

Yr.	W	L	Coach
1961	15	11	Tony Hinkle
1962	22	6	Tony Hinkle
1963	16	10	Tony Hinkle
1964	13	13	Tony Hinkle
1965	11	15	Tony Hinkle
1966	16	10	Tony Hinkle
1967	10	17	Tony Hinkle
1968	11	14	Tony Hinkle
Totals	400	311	

CALIFORNIA, UNIVERSITY OF

Berkeley, California

Golden Bears — *Blue and Gold*

Yr.	W	L	Coach
1938	18	11	Nibs Price
1939	24	8	Nibs Price
1940	15	17	Nibs Price
1941	15	12	Nibs Price
1942	11	19	Nibs Price
1943	9	15	Nibs Price
1944	7	3	Nibs Price
1945	7	8	Nibs Price
1946	30	6	Nibs Price
1947	20	11	Nibs Price
1948	25	9	Nibs Price
1949	14	19	Nibs Price
1950	10	17	Nibs Price
1951	16	16	Nibs Price
1952	17	13	Nibs Price
1953	16	10	Nibs Price
1954	18	9	Nibs Price
1955	9	16	Pete Newell
1956	17	8	Pete Newell
1957	21	5	Pete Newell
1958	19	9	Pete Newell
1959	24	4	Pete Newell
1960	28	2	Pete Newell
1961	13	9	Rene Herrerias
1962	8	17	Rene Herrerias
1963	13	11	Rene Herrerias
1964	11	13	Rene Herrerias
1965	8	15	Rene Herrerias
1966	9	16	Rene Herrerias
1967	15	10	Rene Herrerias
1968	15	9	Rene Herrerias
Totals	482	347	

CANISIUS COLLEGE

Buffalo, New York

Griffins — *Blue and Gold*

Yr.	W	L	Coach
1938	8	9	Allie Seelbach
1939	1	13	Allie Seelbach
1940	8	9	James Wilson
1941	11	9	Allie Seelbach
1942	11	7	Allie Seelbach
1943	11	9	Allie Seelbach
1944	15	6	Allie Seelbach
1945	13	11	Arthur Powell
1946	8	11	Arthur Powell
1947	18	13	Earl Brown
1948	10	15	Brown, J. Niland
1949	16	12	Joseph Niland
1950	17	8	Joseph Niland
1951	15	10	Joseph Niland
1952	15	9	Joseph Niland
1953	9	14	Joseph Niland
1954	9	14	Joseph Curran
1955	18	7	Joseph Curran
1956	19	7	Joseph Curran
1957	22	6	Joseph Curran
1958	2	19	Joseph Curran
1959	7	16	Curran, R. MacKinnon
1960	10	13	Robert MacKinnon
1961	13	10	Robert MacKinnon
1962	12	9	Robert MacKinnon
1963	19	7	Robert MacKinnon
1964	10	14	Robert MacKinnon
1965	10	12	Robert MacKinnon
1966	7	15	Robert MacKinnon
1967	15	10	Robert MacKinnon
1968	7	17	Robert MacKinnon
Totals	366	341	

CENTENARY COLLEGE

Shreveport, Louisiana

Gentlemen — *Maroon and White*

Yr.	W	L	Coach
1938	13	1	Curtis Parker
1939	10	13	Curtis Parker
1940	15	8	Elmer Smith
1941	8	15	Elmer Smith
1942	1	0	Elmer Smith
1943	—	—	
1944	—	—	
1945	—	—	
1946	—	—	
1947	22	7	Jack Clayton
1948	11	21	A. B. Young
1949	21	15	A. B. Young
1950	16	12	F. H. "Buss" Delaney
1951	16	13	F. H. "Buss" Delaney
1952	17	17	F. H. "Buss" Delaney
1953	21	10	F. H. "Buss" Delaney
1954	13	12	F. H. "Buss" Delaney
1955	14	12	F. H. "Buss" Delaney
1956	20	7	Harold Mooty
1957	16	9	Harold Mooty
1958	13	10	Harold Mooty
1959	14	14	Orvis Sigler
1960	12	12	Orvis Sigler
1961	14	12	Orvis Sigler
1962	17	9	Orvis Sigler
1963	12	14	Orvis Sigler
1964	16	8	Orvis Sigler
1965	13	11	Orvis Sigler
1966	12	14	Orvis Sigler
1967	9	17	Orvis Sigler
1968	3	23	Orvis Sigler
Totals	369	316	

CINCINNATI, UNIVERSITY OF

Cincinnati, Ohio

Bearcats — *Red and Black*

Yr.	W	L	Coach
1938	6	11	Walter Van Winkle
1939	12	15	Walter Van Winkle
1940	9	9	Clark Ballard
1941	6	12	Clark Ballard
1942	10	10	Clark Ballard

Yr.	W	L	Coach
1943	9	10	Robert Reuss
1944	6	5	Robert Reuss
1945	8	9	Ray Farnham
1946	8	13	Ray Farnham
1947	17	9	John Wiethe
1948	17	7	John Wiethe
1949	23	5	John Wiethe
1950	20	6	John Wiethe
1951	18	4	John Wiethe
1952	11	16	John Wiethe
1953	11	13	George Smith
1954	11	10	George Smith
1955	21	8	George Smith
1956	17	7	George Smith
1957	15	9	George Smith
1958	25	3	George Smith
1959	26	4	George Smith
1960	28	2	George Smith
1961	27	3	Ed Jucker
1962	29	2	Ed Jucker
1963	26	2	Ed Jucker
1964	17	9	Ed Jucker
1965	14	12	Ed Jucker
1966	21	7	Tay Baker
1967	17	9	Tay Baker
1968	18	8	Tay Baker
Totals	503	249	

THE CITADEL

Charleston, South Carolina

Bulldogs — *Blue and White*

Yr.	W	L	Coach
1938	13	4	A. W. Norman
1939	13	6	A. W. Norman
1940	8	8	A. W. Norman
1941	5	13	Benjamin Parker
1942	2	14	Benjamin Parker
1943	9	4	E. H. Sherman
1944	4	3	Benjamin Clemons
1945	16	7	Ernest Wehman
1946	7	12	Eugene Clark
1947	5	11	H. W. Piro
1948	8	9	Bernard S. O'Neil
1949	1	17	Bernard S. O'Neil
1950	4	16	Bernard S. O'Neil
1951	6	11	Bernard S. O'Neil
1952	8	20	Bernard S. O'Neil
1953	4	14	Leo A. Zack
1954	1	18	Leo A. Zack
1955	1	22	Leo A. Zack
1956	2	19	Henry Witt
1957	11	14	Norman Sloan
1958	16	11	Norman Sloan
1959	15	5	Norman Sloan
1960	15	8	Norman Sloan
1961	17	8	Mel Thompson
1962	8	15	Mel Thompson
1963	3	20	Mel Thompson
1964	11	10	Mel Thompson
1965	13	11	Mel Thompson
1966	7	16	Mel Thompson
1967	8	17	Mel Thompson
1968	11	14	Dick Campbell
Totals	252	377	

CITY COLLEGE OF NEW YORK (C.C.N.Y.)

New York, New York

Beavers — *Lavender and Black*

Yr.	W	L	Coach
1938	13	3	Nat Holman
1939	11	6	Nat Holman
1940	8	8	Nat Holman
1941	17	5	Nat Holman
1942	16	3	Nat Holman
1943	8	10	Nat Holman
1944	6	11	Nat Holman
1945	12	14	Nat Holman
1946	14	4	Nat Holman
1947	16	6	Nat Holman
1948	18	3	Nat Holman
1949	17	8	Nat Holman
1950	24	5	Nat Holman
1951	12	7	Nat Holman
1952	8	11	Nat Holman
1953	10	6	Dave Polansky
1954	10	8	Dave Polansky
1955	8	10	Nat Holman
1956	4	14	Nat Holman
1957	11	8	Dave Polansky
1958	9	8	Dave Polansky
1959	6	12	Nat Holman
1960	4	14	Holman, Polansky
1961	7	10	Dave Polansky
1962	9	9	Dave Polansky
1963	8	10	Dave Polansky
1964	9	9	Dave Polansky
1965	10	8	Dave Polansky
1966	12	6	Dave Polansky
1967	13	6	Dave Polansky
1968	5	13	Dave Polansky
Totals	335	255	

CLEMSON UNIVERSITY

Clemson, South Carolina

Tigers — *Purple and Burnt Orange*

Yr.	W	L	Coach
1938	16	7	Joe Davis
1939	16	6	Joe Davis
1940	9	12	Joe Davis
1941	8	14	Rock Norman
1942	3	14	Rock Norman
1943	3	13	Rock Norman
1944	2	13	Rock Norman
1945	8	12	Rock Norman
1946	9	11	Rock Norman
1947	7	16	Banks McFadden
1948	6	17	Banks McFadden
1949	10	11	Banks McFadden
1950	10	10	Banks McFadden
1951	11	6	Banks McFadden
1952	17	7	Banks McFadden
1953	8	10	Banks McFadden
1954	5	18	Banks McFadden
1955	2	21	Banks McFadden
1956	9	17	Banks McFadden
1957	7	17	Press Maravich
1958	8	16	Press Maravich
1959	8	16	Press Maravich
1960	10	16	Press Maravich

Yr.	W	L	Coach
1961	10	16	Press Maravich
1962	12	15	Press Maravich
1963	12	13	Bobby Roberts
1964	13	12	Bobby Roberts
1965	8	15	Bobby Roberts
1966	15	10	Bobby Roberts
1967	17	8	Bobby Roberts
1968	4	20	Bobby Roberts
Totals	283	409	

COLGATE UNIVERSITY
Hamilton, New York

Red Raiders — *Maroon and White*

Yr.	W	L	Coach
1938	10	9	John E. Galloway
1939	6	13	John E. Galloway
1940	12	6	Paul O. Bixler
1941	9	6	Paul O. Bixler
1942	5	9	Karl J. Lawrence
1943	5	7	Karl J. Lawrence
1944	11	5	Karl J. Lawrence
1945	5	10	Karl J. Lawrence
1946	12	6	Karl J. Lawrence
1947	11	6	Karl J. Lawrence
1948	14	8	Karl J. Lawrence
1949	12	7	Karl J. Lawrence
1950	11	8	Howard Hartman
1951	13	10	Howard Hartman
1952	11	12	Howard Hartman
1953	12	9	Howard Hartman
1954	5	12	Howard Hartman
1955	11	10	Howard Hartman
1956	18	9	Howard Hartman
1957	14	10	Howard Hartman
1958	6	16	Howard Hartman
1959	7	12	Howard Hartman
1960	11	12	Howard Hartman
1961	14	12	Howard Hartman
1962	8	15	Howard Hartman
1963	5	13	Howard Hartman
1964	7	16	Howard Hartman
1965	7	16	Robert Duffy
1966	8	14	Robert Duffy
1967	10	13	Robert Duffy
1968	10	16	Edward J. Ashnault
Totals	300	327	

COLORADO, UNIVERSITY OF
Boulder, Colorado

Buffaloes — *Silver and Gold*

Yr.	W	L	Coach
1938	15	6	Frosty Cox
1939	14	4	Frosty Cox
1940	17	4	Frosty Cox
1941	10	6	Frosty Cox
1942	16	2	Frosty Cox
1943	—	—	
1944	—	—	
1945	13	3	Frosty Cox
1946	12	6	Frosty Cox
1947	7	11	Frosty Cox
1948	7	14	Frosty Cox
1949	6	12	Frosty Cox
1950	14	8	Frosty Cox
1951	4	20	Horace B. "Bebe" Lee
1952	8	16	Horace B. "Bebe" Lee
1953	10	11	Horace B. "Bebe" Lee
1954	11	11	Horace B. "Bebe" Lee
1955	19	6	Horace B. "Bebe" Lee
1956	11	10	Horace B. "Bebe" Lee
1957	14	9	Russell "Sox" Walseth
1958	8	15	Russell "Sox" Walseth
1959	14	10	Russell "Sox" Walseth
1960	13	11	Russell "Sox" Walseth
1961	19	7	Russell "Sox" Walseth
1962	15	10	Russell "Sox" Walseth
1963	19	7	Russell "Sox" Walseth
1964	15	10	Russell "Sox" Walseth
1965	13	12	Russell "Sox" Walseth
1966	12	13	Russell "Sox" Walseth
1967	17	8	Russell "Sox" Walseth
1968	9	16	Russell "Sox" Walseth
Totals	362	278	

COLORADO STATE UNIVERSITY
Fort Collins, Colorado

Rams — *Green and Gold*

Yr.	W	L	Coach
1938	7	9	John Davis
1939	2	14	John Davis
1940	6	12	John Davis
1941	10	9	John Davis
1942	3	16	John Davis
1943	7	9	John Davis
1944	—	—	
1945	7	11	John Davis
1946	15	9	E. D. Taylor
1947	3	18	E. D. Taylor
1948	6	15	E. D. Taylor
1949	14	21	E. D. Taylor
1950	7	23	H. B. Lee
1951	13	20	Bill Strannigan
1952	13	15	Bill Strannigan
1953	12	14	Bill Strannigan
1954	22	7	Bill Strannigan
1955	12	11	Jim Williams
1956	12	13	Jim Williams
1957	9	16	Jim Williams
1958	14	11	Jim Williams
1959	8	14	Jim Williams
1960	13	10	Jim Williams
1961	17	9	Jim Williams
1962	18	9	Jim Williams
1963	18	5	Jim Williams
1964	16	9	Jim Williams
1965	14	8	Jim Williams
1966	16	8	Jim Williams
1967	14	10	Jim Williams
1968	11	13	Jim Williams
Totals	339	368	

COLUMBIA UNIVERSITY
New York, New York

Lions — *Light Blue and White*

Yr.	W	L	Coach
1938	11	8	Paul Mooney
1939	12	5	Paul Mooney
1940	5	13	Paul Mooney
1941	12	5	Paul Mooney
1942	2	13	Paul Mooney

Yr.	W	L	Coach
1943	10	8	Cliff Battles
1944	8	10	Elmer Ripley
1945	9	11	Elmer Ripley
1946	11	9	Paul Mooney
1947	15	5	Gordon Ridings
1948	21	3	Gordon Ridings
1949	14	6	Gordon Ridings
1950	22	7	Gordon Ridings
1951	22	1	Lou Rossini
1952	16	10	Lou Rossini
1953	17	6	Lou Rossini
1954	11	13	Lou Rossini
1955	17	8	Lou Rossini
1956	15	9	Lou Rossini
1957	18	6	Lou Rossini
1958	6	18	Lou Rossini
1959	3	21	Archie Oldham
1960	9	14	Archie Oldham
1961	8	15	Oldham, K. Hunter
1962	3	21	John P. Rohan
1963	10	12	John P. Rohan
1964	11	12	John P. Rohan
1965	7	15	John P. Rohan
1966	18	6	John P. Rohan
1967	11	14	John P. Rohan
1968	23	5	John P. Rohan
Totals	377	309	

CONNECTICUT, UNIVERSITY OF

Storrs, Connecticut

Huskies — *Blue and White*

Yr.	W	L	Coach
1938	13	5	Donald White
1939	12	6	Donald White
1940	9	7	Donald White
1941	14	2	Donald White
1942	12	5	Donald White
1943	8	7	Donald White
1944	10	9	Donald White
1945	5	11	Donald White
1946	11	6	Blair Gullion
1947	16	2	Gullion, Hugh Greer
1948	17	6	Hugh Greer
1949	19	6	Hugh Greer
1950	17	8	Hugh Greer
1951	22	4	Hugh Greer
1952	20	7	Hugh Greer
1953	17	4	Hugh Greer
1954	23	3	Hugh Greer
1955	20	5	Hugh Greer
1956	17	11	Hugh Greer
1957	17	8	Hugh Greer
1958	17	10	Hugh Greer
1959	17	7	Hugh Greer
1960	17	9	Hugh Greer
1961	11	13	Hugh Greer
1962	16	8	Hugh Greer
1963	18	7	Fred Shabel
1964	16	11	Fred Shabel
1965	23	3	Fred Shabel
1966	16	8	Fred Shabel
1967	17	7	Burr Carlson
1968	11	13	Burr Carlson
Totals	478	218	

CORNELL UNIVERSITY

Ithaca, New York

Big Red — *Carnelian and White*

Yr.	W	L	Coach
1938	11	7	John Rowland
1939	12	12	Blair Gullion
1940	10	13	Blair Gullion
1941	17	6	Blair Gullion
1942	9	12	Blair Gullion
1943	7	15	Emerald Wilson
1944	9	11	Emerald Wilson
1945	12	5	Emerald Wilson
1946	12	5	Emerald Wilson
1947	14	8	Royner Greene
1948	16	9	Royner Greene
1949	11	15	Royner Greene
1950	18	7	Royner Greene
1951	20	5	Royner Greene
1952	16	9	Royner Greene
1953	10	13	Royner Greene
1954	18	8	Royner Greene
1955	11	13	Royner Greene
1956	11	13	Royner Greene
1957	4	19	Royner Greene
1958	11	11	Royner Greene
1959	8	15	Royner Greene
1960	13	10	Sam MacNeil
1961	14	10	Sam MacNeil
1962	18	7	Sam MacNeil
1963	12	12	Sam MacNeil
1964	15	10	Sam MacNeil
1965	19	5	Sam MacNeil
1966	15	9	Sam MacNeil
1967	19	5	Sam MacNeil
1968	14	11	Sam MacNeil
Totals	406	310	

CREIGHTON UNIVERSITY

Omaha, Nebraska

Blue Jays — *White and Blue*

Yr.	W	L	Coach
1938	11	14	Eddie Hickey
1939	11	12	Eddie Hickey
1940	11	9	Eddie Hickey
1941	18	7	Eddie Hickey
1942	19	5	Eddie Hickey
1943	19	2	Eddie Hickey
1944	—	—	
1945	—	—	
1946	9	12	Julius Belford
1947	19	8	Eddie Hickey
1948	10	13	Julius Belford
1949	9	14	Julius Belford
1950	13	14	Julius Belford
1951	9	18	Julius Belford
1952	7	17	Julius Belford
1953	11	14	Sebastian "Subby" Salerno
1954	14	18	Sebastian "Subby" Salerno
1955	5	14	Sebastian "Subby" Salerno
1956	11	12	Theron "Tummy" Thomsen
1957	15	6	Theron "Tummy" Thomsen
1958	10	12	Theron "Tummy" Thomsen
1959	13	9	Theron "Tummy" Thomsen
1960	13	11	John J. "Red" McManus

Yr.	W	L	Coach
1961	8	17	John J. "Red" McManus
1962	21	5	John J. "Red" McManus
1963	14	13	John J. "Red" McManus
1964	22	7	John J. "Red" McManus
1965	13	10	John J. "Red" McManus
1966	14	12	John J. "Red" McManus
1967	12	13	John J. "Red" McManus
1968	8	17	John J. "Red" McManus
Totals	369	335	

DARTMOUTH COLLEGE
Hanover, New Hamshire

Indians, Big Green			*Oak Green*
1938	20	5	Osborne Cowles
1939	18	5	Osborne Cowles
1940	15	6	Osborne Cowles
1941	19	5	Osborne Cowles
1942	22	4	Osborne Cowles
1943	20	3	Osborne Cowles
1944	19	2	Earl Brown
1945	6	8	Albert "Dolly" Stark
1946	13	3	Albert "Dolly" Stark
1947	10	15	Elmer Lampe
1948	12	12	Elmer Lampe
1949	15	11	Elmer Lampe
1950	8	17	Elmer Lampe
1951	3	23	Alvin "Doggie" Julian
1952	11	19	Alvin "Doggie" Julian
1953	12	14	Alvin "Doggie" Julian
1954	13	13	Alvin "Doggie" Julian
1955	18	7	Alvin "Doggie" Julian
1956	18	11	Alvin "Doggie" Julian
1957	18	7	Alvin "Doggie" Julian
1958	22	5	Alvin "Doggie" Julian
1959	22	6	Alvin "Doggie" Julian
1960	14	9	Alvin "Doggie" Julian
1961	5	19	Alvin "Doggie" Julian
1962	6	18	Alvin "Doggie" Julian
1963	7	18	Alvin "Doggie" Julian
1964	2	23	Alvin "Doggie" Julian
1965	4	21	Alvin "Doggie" Julian
1966	3	21	Alvin "Doggie" Julian
1967	7	17	Alvin "Doggie" Julian
1968	8	18	Dick Gavitt
Totals	390	365	

DAVIDSON COLLEGE
Davidson, North Carolina

Wildcats			*Red and Black*
1938	6	9	Red Laird
1939	16	8	Norman Shepard
1940	8	13	Norman Shepard
1941	10	12	Norman Shepard
1942	12	13	Norman Shepard
1943	18	6	Norman Shepard
1944	16	7	Norman Shepard
1945	9	9	Norman Shepard
1946	13	12	Norman Shepard
1947	17	8	Norman Shepard
1948	19	9	Norman Shepard
1949	18	8	Norman Shepard
1950	10	16	Boydson Baird
1951	7	19	Boydson Baird

Yr.	W	L	Coach
1952	7	18	Boydson Baird
1953	4	16	Daniel Miller
1954	7	15	Daniel Miller
1955	8	13	Daniel Miller
1956	10	15	Dr. Thomas Scott
1957	7	20	Dr. Thomas Scott
1958	9	15	Dr. Thomas Scott
1959	9	15	Dr. Thomas Scott
1960	5	19	Dr. Thomas Scott
1961	9	14	C. G. "Lefty" Driesell
1962	14	11	C. G. "Lefty" Driesell
1963	20	7	C. G. "Lefty" Driesell
1964	22	4	C. G. "Lefty" Driesell
1965	24	2	C. G. "Lefty" Driesell
1966	21	7	C. G. "Lefty" Driesell
1967	15	12	C. G. "Lefty" Driesell
1968	24	5	C. G. "Lefty" Driesell
Totals	394	357	

DAYTON, UNIVERSITY OF
Dayton, Ohio

Flyers			*Red and Blue*
1938	7	10	Joe Holsinger
1939	2	12	Joe Holsinger
1940	4	17	James Carter
1941	9	14	James Carter
1942	12	6	James Carter
1943	9	8	James Carter
1944	—	—	
1945	—	—	
1946	3	13	James Carter
1947	4	17	James Carter
1948	12	14	Tom Blackburn
1949	16	14	Tom Blackburn
1950	24	8	Tom Blackburn
1951	27	5	Tom Blackburn
1952	28	5	Tom Blackburn
1953	16	13	Tom Blackburn
1954	25	7	Tom Blackburn
1955	25	4	Tom Blackburn
1956	25	4	Tom Blackburn
1957	19	9	Tom Blackburn
1958	25	4	Tom Blackburn
1959	14	12	Tom Blackburn
1960	21	7	Tom Blackburn
1961	20	9	Tom Blackburn
1962	24	6	Tom Blackburn
1963	16	10	Tom Blackburn
1964	15	10	Tom Blackburn
1965	22	7	Don Donoher
1966	23	6	Don Donoher
1967	25	6	Don Donoher
1968	21	9	Don Donoher
Totals	493	266	

DELAWARE, UNIVERSITY OF
Newark, Delaware

Blue Hens			*Blue and Gold*
1938	6	10	Lyal Clark
1939	9	7	Steven Grenda
1940	4	12	Steven Grenda
1941	7	9	F. L. Stewart

Yr.	W	L	Coach
1942	7	8	E. Emery Adkins
1943	7	13	E. Emery Adkins
1944	8	9	Edmund Price
1945	4	10	William D. Murray
1946	7	9	D. Kenneth Steers
1947	9	7	Joseph Brunansky
1948	10	8	Joseph Brunansky
1949	6	14	Joseph Brunansky
1950	8	8	Fred Emmerson
1951	13	7	Fred Emmerson
1952	17	6	Fred Emmerson
1953	18	7	Fred Emmerson
1954	9	13	Fred Emmerson
1955	6	16	Irv Wisniewski
1956	8	15	Irv Wisniewski
1957	8	16	Irv Wisniewski
1958	8	12	Irv Wisniewski
1959	9	13	Irv Wisniewski
1960	7	16	Irv Wisniewski
1961	8	11	Irv Wisniewski
1962	17	4	Irv Wisniewski
1963	14	8	Irv Wisniewski
1964	13	10	Irv Wisniewski
1965	3	17	Irv Wisniewski
1966	9	15	Irv Wisniewski
1967	15	9	Dan Peterson
1968	16	7	Dan Peterson
Totals	290	326	

DENVER, UNIVERSITY OF
Denver, Colorado

Pioneers			*Crimson and Gold*
1938	2	16	Clyde Hubbard
1939	5	13	Clyde Hubbard
1940	6	15	Clyde Hubbard
1941	8	9	Ellison Ketchum
1942	4	16	Ellison Ketchum
1943	19	8	Ketchum, Mark Ducan
1944	6	18	Arthur Quinlan
1945	7	16	Clifford Rock
1946	9	15	Ken Loeffler
1947	16	10	Ellison Ketchum
1948	18	11	Ellison Ketchum
1949	18	15	Ketchum, Hoyt Brawner
1950	18	13	Hoyt Brawner
1951	14	16	Hoyt Brawner
1952	11	15	Hoyt Brawner
1953	9	16	Hoyt Brawner
1954	6	21	Hoyt Brawner
1955	9	14	Hoyt Brawner
1956	13	12	Hoyt Brawner
1957	11	12	Hoyt Brawner
1958	13	12	Hoyt Brawner
1959	14	10	Hoyt Brawner
1960	13	11	Hoyt Brawner
1961	12	14	Hoyt Brawner
1962	8	17	Hoyt Brawner
1963	9	16	Troy Bledsoe
1964	6	20	Troy Bledsoe
1965	11	14	Troy Bledsoe
1966	14	11	Troy Bledsoe
1967	13	12	Troy Bledsoe
1968	11	14	Troy Bledsoe
Totals	333	432	

Yr.	W	L	Coach

DE PAUL UNIVERSITY
Chicago, Illinois

Blue Demons			*Scarlet and Blue*
1938	12	10	Thomas Haggerty
1939	15	7	Thomas Haggerty
1940	22	6	Thomas Haggerty
1941	13	8	William Wendt
1942	10	12	William Wendt
1943	19	5	Ray Meyer
1944	22	4	Ray Meyer
1945	21	3	Ray Meyer
1946	19	5	Ray Meyer
1947	16	9	Ray Meyer
1948	22	8	Ray Meyer
1949	16	9	Ray Meyer
1950	12	13	Ray Meyer
1951	13	12	Ray Meyer
1952	19	8	Ray Meyer
1953	19	9	Ray Meyer
1954	11	10	Ray Meyer
1955	16	6	Ray Meyer
1956	16	8	Ray Meyer
1957	8	14	Ray Meyer
1958	8	12	Ray Meyer
1959	13	11	Ray Meyer
1960	17	7	Ray Meyer
1961	17	8	Ray Meyer
1962	14	9	Ray Meyer
1963	15	8	Ray Meyer
1964	21	4	Ray Meyer
1965	17	10	Ray Meyer
1966	18	8	Ray Meyer
1967	17	8	Ray Meyer
1968	13	12	Ray Meyer
Totals	491	263	

DETROIT, UNIVERSITY OF
Detroit, Michigan

Titans			*Cardinal and White*
1938	16	4	Lloyd Brazil
1939	15	15	Lloyd Brazil
1940	15	9	Lloyd Brazil
1941	11	10	Lloyd Brazil
1942	13	8	Lloyd Brazil
1943	15	5	Lloyd Brazil
1944	12	6	Lloyd Brazil
1945	9	13	Lloyd Brazil
1946	15	8	Lloyd Brazil
1947	12	13	J. Shada
1948	7	15	J. Shada
1949	13	10	Robert Calihan
1950	20	6	Robert Calihan
1951	15	14	Robert Calihan
1952	14	12	Robert Calihan
1953	11	15	Robert Calihan
1954	11	17	Robert Calihan
1955	15	11	Robert Calihan
1956	13	12	Robert Calihan
1957	11	15	Robert Calihan
1958	13	12	Robert Calihan
1959	11	14	Robert Calihan
1960	20	7	Robert Calihan
1961	18	9	Robert Calihan

Yr.	W	L	Coach
1962	15	12	Robert Calihan
1963	14	12	Robert Calihan
1964	14	11	Robert Calihan
1965	20	8	Robert Calihan
1966	17	8	Robert Calihan
1967	10	15	Robert Calihan
1968	13	12	Robert Calihan
Totals	428	338	

DRAKE UNIVERSITY

Des Moines, Iowa

Bulldogs			*White and Blue*
1938	14	6	Bill Williams
1939	14	7	Bill Williams
1940	13	12	Bill Williams
1941	9	11	Bill Williams
1942	2	13	Bill Williams
1943	8	9	Bill Williams
1944	7	13	William Easton
1945	11	13	V.J. Green
1946	10	16	V.J. Green
1947	18	11	Forrest Anderson
1948	14	12	Forrest Anderson
1949	13	13	Jack McClelland
1950	14	12	Jack McClelland
1951	11	14	Jack McClelland
1952	13	12	Jack McClelland
1953	13	12	Jack McClelland
1954	7	16	Jack McClelland
1955	9	12	Jack McClelland
1956	10	14	Jack McClelland
1957	8	16	John Benington
1958	13	12	John Benington
1959	9	15	Maurice John
1960	11	14	Maurice John
1961	19	7	Maurice John
1962	16	8	Maurice John
1963	11	14	Maurice John
1964	21	7	Maurice John
1965	15	10	Maurice John
1966	13	12	Maurice John
1967	9	16	Maurice John
1968	18	8	Maurice John
Totals	373	377	

DUKE UNIVERSITY

Durham, North Carolina

Blue Devils			*Blue and White*
1938	15	9	Eddie Cameron
1939	10	12	Eddie Cameron
1940	19	7	Eddie Cameron
1941	14	8	Eddie Cameron
1942	22	2	Eddie Cameron
1943	20	6	Gerry Gerard
1944	13	13	Gerry Gerard
1945	13	9	Gerry Gerard
1946	21	6	Gerry Gerard
1947	19	8	Gerry Gerard
1948	17	12	Gerry Gerard
1949	13	9	Gerry Gerard
1950	15	15	Gerry Gerard
1951	20	13	Harold Bradley

Yr.	W	L	Coach
1952	24	6	Harold Bradley
1953	18	8	Harold Bradley
1954	22	6	Harold Bradley
1955	20	8	Harold Bradley
1956	19	7	Harold Bradley
1957	13	11	Harold Bradley
1958	18	7	Harold Bradley
1959	13	12	Harold Bradley
1960	17	11	Vic Bubas
1961	22	6	Vic Bubas
1962	20	5	Vic Bubas
1963	27	3	Vic Bubas
1964	26	5	Vic Bubas
1965	20	5	Vic Bubas
1966	26	4	Vic Bubas
1967	18	9	Vic Bubas
1968	22	6	Vic Bubas
Totals	576	248	

DUQUESNE UNIVERSITY

Pittsburgh, Pennsylvania

Dukes			*Red and Blue*
1938	6	11	Charles "Chick" Davies
1939	14	4	Charles "Chick" Davies
1940	20	3	Charles "Chick" Davies
1941	17	3	Charles "Chick" Davies
1942	15	6	Charles "Chick" Davies
1943	12	7	Charles "Chick" Davies
1944	—	—	
1945	—	—	
1946	—	—	
1947	20	2	Charles "Chick" Davies
1948	17	6	Charles "Chick" Davies
1949	17	5	Donald "Dudey" Moore
1950	23	6	Donald "Dudey" Moore
1951	16	11	Donald "Dudey" Moore
1952	23	4	Donald "Dudey" Moore
1953	21	8	Donald "Dudey" Moore
1954	26	3	Donald "Dudey" Moore
1955	22	4	Donald "Dudey" Moore
1956	17	10	Donald "Dudey" Moore
1957	16	7	Donald "Dudey" Moore
1958	10	12	Donald "Dudey" Moore
1959	13	11	John "Red" Manning
1960	8	15	John "Red" Manning
1961	15	7	John "Red" Manning
1962	22	7	John "Red" Manning
1963	13	9	John "Red" Manning
1964	16	7	John "Red" Manning
1965	14	10	John "Red" Manning
1966	14	9	John "Red" Manning
1967	7	15	John "Red" Manning
1968	18	7	John "Red" Manning
Totals	452	209	

EAST CAROLINA UNIVERSITY

Greenville, North Carolina

Pirates			*Purple and Gold*
1946	14	8	Earl Smith
1951	16	6	Howard Porter
1952	11	10	Howard Porter

Yr.	W	L	Coach
1953	15	7	Howard Porter
1954	13	8	Howard Porter
1955	21	1	Howard Porter
1956	12	10	Howard Porter
1957	17	11	Howard Porter
1958	15	8	Howard Porter
1959	14	9	Howard Porter
1960	16	8	Earl Smith
1961	12	9	Earl Smith
1962	15	12	Earl Smith
1963	12	10	Earl Smith
1964	9	15	Wendell Carr
1965	12	10	Wendell Carr
1966	11	15	Wendell Carr
1967	7	17	Tom Quinn
1968	9	16	Tom Quinn
Totals	251	190	

EASTERN KENTUCKY STATE COLLEGE

Richmond, Kentucky

Maroons — *Maroon and White*

Yr.	W	L	Coach
1938	13	6	Rome Rankin
1939	11	4	Rome Rankin
1940	17	1	Rome Rankin
1941	10	4	Rome Rankin
1942	14	8	Rome Rankin
1943	—	—	
1944	—	—	
1945	20	5	Rome Rankin
1946	20	5	Rome Rankin
1947	21	4	Paul McBrayer
1948	17	7	Paul McBrayer
1949	17	4	Paul McBrayer
1950	16	6	Paul McBrayer
1951	18	8	Paul McBrayer
1952	13	11	Paul McBrayer
1953	16	9	Paul McBrayer
1954	7	16	Paul McBrayer
1955	15	8	Paul McBrayer
1956	9	16	Paul McBrayer
1957	7	15	Paul McBrayer
1958	8	11	Paul McBrayer
1959	16	6	Paul McBrayer
1960	14	8	Paul McBrayer
1961	15	9	Paul McBrayer
1962	10	6	McBrayer, Jim Baechtold
1963	9	12	Jim Baechtold
1964	15	9	Jim Baechtold
1965	19	6	Jim Baechtold
1966	16	9	Jim Baechtold
1967	5	18	Jim Baechtold
1968	10	14	Guy Strong
Totals	398	245	

EAST TENNESSEE STATE UNIVERSITY

Johnson City, Tennessee

Buccaneers — *Blue and Gold*

Yr.	W	L	Coach
1945	9	2	Gene McMurray
1946	10	1	Gene McMurray
1947	13	3	Gene McMurray
1948	11	8	L.T. Roberts
1949	19	6	J. Madison Brooks
1950	17	6	J. Madison Brooks
1951	23	9	J. Madison Brooks
1952	22	9	J. Madison Brooks
1953	23	6	J. Madison Brooks
1954	23	4	J. Madison Brooks
1955	16	7	J. Madison Brooks
1956	19	8	J. Madison Brooks
1957	17	11	J. Madison Brooks
1958	7	17	J. Madison Brooks
1959	13	10	J. Madison Brooks
1960	9	14	J. Madison Brooks
1961	9	15	J. Madison Brooks
1962	11	14	J. Madison Brooks
1963	14	8	J. Madison Brooks
1964	12	10	J. Madison Brooks
1965	6	17	J. Madison Brooks
1966	7	14	J. Madison Brooks
1967	17	9	J. Madison Brooks
1968	19	8	J. Madison Brooks
Totals	346	216	

FAIRFIELD UNIVERSITY

Fairfield, Connecticut

Stags — *Cardinal Red and White*

Yr.	W	L	Coach
1949	9	14	John Dunn
1950	5	16	Bob Noonan
1951	16	11	Jim Hanrahan
1952	9	9	Jim Hanrahan
1953	10	9	Jim Hanrahan
1954	12	8	Jim Hanrahan
1955	12	8	Jim Hanrahan
1956	6	10	Jim Hanrahan
1957	5	16	Jim Hanrahan
1958	12	9	Jim Hanrahan
1959	11	11	George Bisacca
1960	17	9	George Bisacca
1961	17	7	George Bisacca
1962	20	5	George Bisacca
1963	11	13	George Bisacca
1964	14	11	George Bisacca
1965	14	7	George Bisacca
1966	19	5	George Bisacca
1967	12	9	George Bisacca
1968	16	10	George Bisacca
Totals	247	197	

FAIRLEIGH DICKINSON UNIVERSITY

Rutherford, New Jersey

Knights — *Maroon and White*

Yr.	W	L	Coach
1950	10	7	Dick Holub
1951	16	6	Dick Holub
1952	22	4	Dick Holub
1953	20	1	Dick Holub
1954	17	3	Dick Holub
1955	10	14	Dick Holub
1956	9	15	Dick Holub
1957	12	12	Dick Holub
1958	9	15	Dick Holub
1959	17	11	Dick Holub
1960	14	11	Dick Holub
1961	13	10	Dick Holub
1962	12	11	Dick Holub

Yr.	W	L	Coach
1963	16	12	Dick Holub
1964	12	10	Dick Holub
1965	9	15	Dick Holub
1966	15	10	Dick Holub
1967	4	19	Jack Devine
1968	10	12	Jack Devine
Totals	247	198	

Yr.	W	L	Coach
1963	15	10	J.K. "Bud" Kennedy
1964	14	14	J.K. "Bud" Kennedy
1965	16	10	J.K. "Bud" Kennedy
1966	15	11	J.K. "Bud" Kennedy
1967	11	15	Hugh Durham
1968	19	8	Hugh Durham
Totals	272	244	

FLORIDA, UNIVERSITY OF

Gainesville, Florida

Gators			*Orange and Blue*
1938	11	9	Sam McAllister
1939	9	6	Sam McAllister
1940	13	9	Sam McAllister
1941	15	3	Sam McAllister
1942	8	9	Sam McAllister
1943	8	7	Spurgeon Cherry
1944	—	—	
1945	7	12	Spurgeon Cherry
1946	7	14	Spurgeon Cherry
1947	17	9	Sam McAllister
1948	15	10	Sam McAllister
1949	11	15	Sam McAllister
1950	9	14	Sam McAllister
1951	11	12	Sam McAllister
1952	15	9	John Mauer
1953	13	6	John Mauer
1954	7	15	John Mauer
1955	12	10	John Mauer
1956	11	12	John Mauer
1957	14	10	John Mauer
1958	12	9	John Mauer
1959	8	15	John Mauer
1960	6	16	John Mauer
1961	15	11	Norman Sloan
1962	12	11	Norman Sloan
1963	12	14	Norman Sloan
1964	12	10	Norman Sloan
1965	18	7	Norman Sloan
1966	16	10	Norman Sloan
1967	21	4	Tommy Bartlett
1968	15	10	Tommy Bartlett
Totals	360	308	

FLORIDA STATE UNIVERSITY

Tallahassee, Florida

Seminoles			*Garnet and Gold*
1948	5	13	Don Loucks
1949	12	12	J.K. "Bud" Kennedy
1950	15	10	J.K. "Bud" Kennedy
1951	18	9	J.K. "Bud" Kennedy
1952	5	20	J.K. "Bud" Kennedy
1953	11	11	J.K. "Bud" Kennedy
1954	13	7	J.K. "Bud" Kennedy
1955	22	4	J.K. "Bud" Kennedy
1956	16	9	J.K. "Bud" Kennedy
1957	9	17	J.K. "Bud" Kennedy
1958	9	16	J.K. "Bud" Kennedy
1959	8	15	J.K. "Bud" Kennedy
1960	10	15	J.K. "Bud" Kennedy
1961	14	10	J.K. "Bud" Kennedy
1962	15	8	J.K. "Bud" Kennedy

FORDHAM UNIVERSITY

Bronx, New York

Rams			*Maroon*
1938	9	10	Vincent Cavanaugh
1939	10	8	Edward Kelleher
1940	10	8	Edward Kelleher
1941	12	8	Edward Kelleher
1942	11	7	Edward Kelleher
1943	16	5	Edward Kelleher
1944	—	—	
1945	3	14	Frank Adams
1946	2	17	Frank Adams
1947	18	5	Frank Adams
1948	17	6	Frank Adams
1949	9	15	Frank Adams
1950	15	12	John Bach
1951	15	12	John Bach
1952	19	8	John Bach
1953	18	8	John Bach
1954	18	6	John Bach
1955	18	9	John Bach
1956	11	14	John Bach
1957	16	10	John Bach
1958	15	9	John Bach
1959	17	8	John Bach
1960	8	18	John Bach
1961	7	16	John Bach
1962	10	14	John Bach
1963	18	8	John Bach
1964	9	11	John Bach
1965	15	12	John Bach
1966	10	15	John Bach
1967	14	11	John Bach
1968	19	8	John Bach
Totals	389	312	

FURMAN UNIVERSITY

Greenville, South Carolina

Paladins			*Purple and White*
1946	15	4	Lyles Alley
1947	9	9	Lyles Alley
1948	11	16	Lyles Alley
1949	8	14	Lyles Alley
1950	9	12	Melvin Bell
1951	3	20	Lyles Alley
1952	18	6	Lyles Alley
1953	21	6	Lyles Alley
1954	20	9	Lyles Alley
1955	17	10	Lyles Alley
1956	12	16	Lyles Alley
1957	10	17	Lyles Alley
1958	12	14	Lyles Alley
1959	14	12	Lyles Alley
1960	9	16	Lyles Alley

Yr.	W	L	Coach
1961	15	11	Lyles Alley
1962	15	11	Lyles Alley
1963	14	14	Lyles Alley
1964	11	15	Lyles Alley
1965	6	19	Lyles Alley
1966	9	17	Lyles Alley
1967	9	15	Frank Selvy
1968	13	14	Frank Selvy
Totals	280	297	

GEORGETOWN UNIVERSITY

Washington, D. C.

Hoyas			*Blue and Gray*
1938	7	11	Fred Mesmer
1939	13	9	Elmer Ripley
1940	8	10	Elmer Ripley
1941	16	4	Elmer Ripley
1942	9	11	Elmer Ripley
1943	22	5	Elmer Ripley
1944	—	—	
1945	—	—	
1946	11	9	Ken Engles
1947	19	7	Elmer Ripley
1948	13	15	Elmer Ripley
1949	9	15	Elmer Ripley
1950	11	12	Buddy O'Grady
1951	8	14	Buddy O'Grady
1952	15	9	Buddy O'Grady
1953	13	7	Buddy Jeannette
1954	11	18	Buddy Jeannette
1955	13	12	Buddy Jeannette
1956	13	11	Buddy Jeannette
1957	11	11	Tom Nolan
1958	10	11	Tom Nolan
1959	9	14	Tom Nolan
1960	11	12	Tom Nolan
1961	11	10	Tom O'Keefe
1962	14	9	Tom O'Keefe
1963	13	13	Tom O'Keefe
1964	15	10	Tom O'Keefe
1965	13	10	Tom O'Keefe
1966	16	8	Tom O'Keefe
1967	12	11	Jack Magee
1968	11	12	Jack Magee
Totals	357	310	

GEORGE WASHINGTON UNIVERSITY

Washington, D. C.

Colonials			*Buff and Blue*
1938	12	5	Bill Reinhart
1939	13	8	Bill Reinhart
1940	13	6	Bill Reinhart
1941	16	5	Bill Reinhart
1942	10	9	Bill Reinhart
1943	17	6	Otis Zahn
1944	—	—	
1945	—	—	
1946	5	9	Otis Zahn
1947	21	7	Otis Zahn
1948	19	7	Otis Zahn
1949	18	8	Otis Zahn
1950	17	8	Bill Reinhart

Yr.	W	L	Coach
1951	12	12	Bill Reinhart
1952	15	9	Bill Reinhart
1953	15	7	Bill Reinhart
1954	23	3	Bill Reinhart
1955	24	6	Bill Reinhart
1956	19	7	Bill Reinhart
1957	3	21	Bill Reinhart
1958	12	11	Bill Reinhart
1959	14	11	Bill Reinhart
1960	15	11	Bill Reinhart
1961	9	17	Bill Reinhart
1962	9	15	Bill Reinhart
1963	8	15	Bill Reinhart
1964	11	15	Bill Reinhart
1965	10	13	Bill Reinhart
1966	3	18	Bill Reinhart
1967	6	18	James "Babe" McCarthy
1968	5	19	Wayne Dobbs
Totals	374	306	

GEORGIA, UNIVERSITY OF

Athens, Georgia

Bulldogs			*Red and Black*
1938	12	10	Frank Johnson
1939	9	3	Elmer Lampe
1940	20	5	Elmer Lampe
1941	8	6	Elmer Lampe
1942	5	9	Elmer Lampe
1943	3	13	Elmer Lampe
1944	5	9	Elmer Lampe
1945	5	15	Elmer Lampe
1946	12	9	Elmer Lampe
1947	5	14	Ralph Jordan
1948	18	10	Ralph Jordan
1949	17	13	Ralph Jordan
1950	15	9	Jordan, J. Whatley
1951	13	11	James Whatley
1952	3	22	Harbin "Red" Lawson
1953	7	18	Harbin "Red" Lawson
1954	7	18	Harbin "Red" Lawson
1955	9	16	Harbin "Red" Lawson
1956	3	21	Harbin "Red" Lawson
1957	8	16	Harbin "Red" Lawson
1958	7	19	Harbin "Red" Lawson
1959	11	15	Harbin "Red" Lawson
1960	12	13	Harbin "Red" Lawson
1961	8	18	Harbin "Red" Lawson
1962	8	16	Harbin "Red" Lawson
1963	8	18	Harbin "Red" Lawson
1964	12	14	Harbin "Red" Lawson
1965	8	18	Harbin "Red" Lawson
1966	10	15	Ken Rosemond
1967	9	17	Ken Rosemond
1968	17	8	Ken Rosemond
Totals	294	418	

GEORGIA INSTITUTE OF TECHNOLOGY

Atlanta, Georgia

Yellow Jackets			*White and Gold*
1938	18	2	Roy Mundorff
1939	6	9	Roy Mundorff
1940	7	8	Roy Mundorff
1941	8	11	Roy Mundorff

Yr.	W	L	Coach
1942	8	8	Dwight Keith
1943	11	5	Dwight Keith
1944	14	4	Dwight Keith
1945	11	6	Dwight Keith
1947	12	11	Dwight Keith
1948	12	16	Roy McArthur
1949	11	13	Roy McArthur
1950	14	13	Roy McArthur
1951	8	19	Roy McArthur
1952	7	16	John "Whack" Hyder
1953	5	17	John "Whack" Hyder
1954	2	22	John "Whack" Hyder
1955	12	13	John "Whack" Hyder
1956	12	11	John "Whack" Hyder
1957	18	8	John "Whack" Hyder
1958	15	11	John "Whack" Hyder
1959	17	9	John "Whack" Hyder
1960	22	6	John "Whack" Hyder
1961	13	13	John "Whack" Hyder
1962	10	16	John "Whack" Hyder
1963	21	5	John "Whack" Hyder
1964	17	9	John "Whack" Hyder
1965	14	11	John "Whack" Hyder
1966	13	13	John "Whack" Hyder
1967	17	9	John "Whack" Hyder
1968	12	13	John "Whack" Hyder
Totals	367	327	

GETTYSBURG COLLEGE

Gettysburg, Pennsylvania

Bullets			*Orange and Blue*
1938	10	2	Henry Bream
1939	17	2	Henry Bream
1940	10	8	Henry Bream
1941	9	9	Henry Bream
1942	14	5	Henry Bream
1943	9	8	Henry Bream
1944	—	—	
1945	—	—	
1946	11	6	Henry Bream
1947	7	14	Henry Bream
1948	10	10	Henry Bream
1949	16	10	Henry Bream
1950	12	12	Henry Bream
1951	15	7	Henry Bream
1952	13	8	Henry Bream
1953	13	9	Henry Bream
1954	14	8	Henry Bream
1955	9	12	Henry Bream
1956	11	11	Robert Davies
1957	17	8	Robert Davies
1958	9	15	Robert Hulton
1959	13	13	Robert Hulton
1960	15	11	Robert Hulton
1961	19	6	Robert Hulton
1962	18	8	Robert Hulton
1963	16	9	Robert Hulton
1964	15	9	Robert Hulton
1965	12	11	Robert Hulton
1966	14	11	Robert Hulton
1967	9	15	Robert Hulton
1968	12	10	Robert Hulton
Totals	369	267	

Yr.	W	L	Coach

GONZAGA UNIVERSITY

Spokane, Washington

Bulldogs			*Columbia Blue and White*
1938	0	2	Claude McGrath
1939	7	10	Claude McGrath
1940	9	15	Claude McGrath
1941	13	14	Claude McGrath
1942	16	13	Claude McGrath
1943	2	9	— —
1944	22	4	Charles Henry
1945	12	19	Eugene Wozny
1946	6	14	Eugene Wozny
1947	20	9	Claude McGrath
1948	24	11	Claude McGrath
1949	17	12	Claude McGrath
1950	18	11	Bill Underwood
1951	8	22	Bill Underwood
1952	20	17	Hank Anderson
1953	15	14	Hank Anderson
1954	14	13	Hank Anderson
1955	15	11	Hank Anderson
1956	13	15	Hank Anderson
1957	11	16	Hank Anderson
1958	15	10	Hank Anderson
1959	11	15	Hank Anderson
1960	14	12	Hank Anderson
1961	11	15	Hank Anderson
1962	14	12	Hank Anderson
1963	14	12	Hank Anderson
1964	10	15	Hank Anderson
1965	18	6	Hank Anderson
1966	9	15	Hank Anderson
1967	19	6	Hank Anderson
1968	9	17	Hank Anderson
Totals	406	386	

HARDIN-SIMMONS UNIVERSITY

Abilene, Texas

Cowboys			*Purple and Gold*
1938	3	12	Frank Kimbrough
1939	3	12	Frank Kimbrough
1940	2	12	Frank Kimbrough
1941	—	—	
1942	6	10	— —
1943	1	9	— —
1944	—	—	
1945	7	23	Warren Woodson
1946	2	11	Warren Woodson
1947	8	26	Westley Bradshaw
1948	7	17	Westley Bradshaw
1949	13	10	Jack Martin
1950	15	10	Jack Martin
1951	13	15	Jack Martin
1952	17	15	Bill Scott
1953	19	12	Bill Scott
1954	7	17	Bill Scott
1955	9	15	Bill Scott
1956	7	18	Bill Scott
1957	17	9	Bill Scott
1958	11	14	Bill Scott
1959	14	12	Bill Scott
1960	8	18	Bill Scott

Yr.	W	L	Coach
1961	12	14	Bill Scott
1962	8	17	Bill Scott
1963	10	16	Lou Henson
1964	20	6	Lou Henson
1965	12	8	Lou Henson
1966	20	6	Paul Lambert
1967	17	9	Paul Lambert
1968	10	16	Paul Lambert
Totals	298	389	

HARVARD UNIVERSITY

Cambridge, Massachusetts

Crimson			*Crimson*
1938	13	5	Wes Fesler
1939	5	14	Wes Fesler
1940	5	14	Wes Fesler
1941	9	10	Wes Fesler
1942	8	16	Earl Brown
1943	12	14	Earl Brown
1944	2	12	Floyd Stahl
1945	2	13	Floyd Stahl
1946	19	3	Floyd Stahl
1947	16	9	William Barclay
1948	5	20	William Barclay
1949	3	20	William Barclay
1950	9	15	Norman Shepard
1951	8	18	Norman Shepard
1952	5	17	Norman Shepard
1953	7	16	Norman Shepard
1954	9	16	Norman Shepard
1955	6	17	Floyd Wilson
1956	8	16	Floyd Wilson
1957	12	9	Floyd Wilson
1958	16	9	Floyd Wilson
1959	10	15	Floyd Wilson
1960	12	11	Floyd Wilson
1961	11	13	Floyd Wilson
1962	10	14	Floyd Wilson
1963	6	15	Floyd Wilson
1964	12	10	Floyd Wilson
1965	11	12	Floyd Wilson
1966	10	14	Floyd Wilson
1967	11	14	Floyd Wilson
1968	7	14	Floyd Wilson
Totals	279	415	

HOFSTRA UNIVERSITY

Hempstead, New York

Flying Dutchmen			*Blue and Gold*
1939	10	8	Jack MacDonald
1940	14	8	Jack MacDonald
1941	13	7	Jack MacDonald
1942	15	6	Jack MacDonald
1943	15	6	Jack MacDonald
1944	—	—	
1945	—	—	
1946	12	7	Jack Smith
1947	18	6	Jack MacDonald
1948	13	6	Jack MacDonald
1949	18	8	Frank Reilly
1950	17	9	Frank Reilly
1951	18	11	Frank Reilly
1952	26	3	Frank Reilly

Yr.	W	L	Coach
1953	20	7	Frank Reilly
1954	15	9	Frank Reilly
1955	19	7	Frank Reilly
1956	22	4	Bill van Breda Kolff
1957	11	15	Bill van Breda Kolff
1958	15	8	Bill van Breda Kolff
1959	20	7	Bill van Breda Kolff
1960	23	1	Bill van Breda Kolff
1961	21	4	Bill van Breda Kolff
1962	24	4	Bill van Breda Kolff
1963	23	7	Paul Lynner
1964	23	6	Paul Lynner
1965	11	14	Paul Lynner
1966	16	10	Paul Lynner
1967	12	13	Paul Lynner
1968	13	12	Paul Lynner
Totals	477	213	

HOLY CROSS COLLEGE

Worcester, Massachusetts

Crusaders			*Royal Purple*
1940	2	3	Edward "Moose" Krause
1941	4	7	Edward "Moose" Krause
1942	5	4	Edward "Moose" Krause
1943	1	5	Albert Riopel
1944	6	8	Albert Riopel
1945	5	8	Albert Riopel
1946	12	3	Alvin "Doggie" Julian
1947	27	3	Alvin "Doggie" Julian
1948	26	4	Alvin "Doggie" Julian
1949	19	8	Lester "Buster" Sheary
1950	27	4	Lester "Buster" Sheary
1951	20	5	Lester "Buster" Sheary
1952	24	4	Lester "Buster" Sheary
1953	20	6	Lester "Buster" Sheary
1954	26	2	Lester "Buster" Sheary
1955	19	7	Lester "Buster" Sheary
1956	22	5	Roy Leenig
1957	11	12	Roy Leenig
1958	15	9	Roy Leenig
1959	14	11	Roy Leenig
1960	20	6	Roy Leenig
1961	21	5	Roy Leenig
1962	20	6	Frank A. Oftring
1963	16	9	Frank A. Oftring
1964	15	8	Frank A. Oftring
1965	13	10	Frank A. Oftring
1966	10	13	Jack Donahue
1967	19	6	Jack Donahue
1968	15	8	Jack Donahue
Totals	454	189	

HOUSTON, UNIVERSITY OF

Houston, Texas

Cougars			*Scarlet and White*
1946	11	7	Alden Pasche
1947	17	8	Alden Pasche
1948	10	12	Alden Pasche
1949	11	11	Alden Pasche
1950	16	7	Alden Pasche
1951	11	17	Alden Pasche
1952	7	14	Alden Pasche

Yr.	W	L	Coach
1953	9	13	Alden Pasche
1954	11	15	Alden Pasche
1955	15	10	Alden Pasche
1956	19	7	Alden Pasche
1957	10	16	Guy V. Lewis
1958	9	16	Guy V. Lewis
1959	12	14	Guy V. Lewis
1960	13	12	Guy V. Lewis
1961	17	11	Guy V. Lewis
1962	21	6	Guy V. Lewis
1963	15	11	Guy V. Lewis
1964	16	10	Guy V. Lewis
1965	19	10	Guy V. Lewis
1966	23	6	Guy V. Lewis
1967	27	4	Guy V. Lewis
1968	31	2	Guy V. Lewis
Totals	350	239	

IDAHO, UNIVERSITY OF

Moscow, Idaho

Vandals			*Silver and Gold*
1938	22	11	Forrest Twogood
1939	12	19	Forrest Twogood
1940	13	15	Forrest Twogood
1941	15	14	Forrest Twogood
1942	12	16	Guy Wicks
1943	8	18	Babe Brown
1944	7	16	Babe Brown
1945	11	20	Babe Brown
1946	26	10	Babe Brown
1947	4	24	Guy Wicks
1948	12	18	Charles Finley
1949	17	15	Charles Finley
1950	15	17	Charles Finley
1951	15	14	Charles Finley
1952	19	13	Charles Finley
1953	14	11	Charles Finley
1954	15	8	Charles Finley
1955	8	18	Harlan Hodges
1956	6	19	Harlan Hodges
1957	10	16	Harlan Hodges
1958	17	9	Harlan Hodges
1959	11	15	Harlan Hodges
1960	11	15	Dave Strack
1961	10	16	Joe Cipriano
1962	13	13	Joe Cipriano
1963	20	6	Joe Cipriano
1964	7	19	Joe Cipriano
1965	6	19	Joe Cipriano
1966	12	14	Jim Goddard
1967	14	11	Jim Goddard
1968	15	11	Wayne Anderson
Totals	397	460	

IDAHO STATE UNIVERSITY

Pocatello, Idaho

Bengals			*Gold and Black*
1948	12	16	Walter Carte
1949	11	16	Ed Willett
1950	5	25	Ed Willett
1951	17	12	Steve Belko
1952	16	11	Steve Belko

Yr.	W	L	Coach
1953	18	7	Steve Belko
1954	22	5	Steve Belko
1955	18	8	Steve Belko
1956	18	8	Steve Belko
1957	25	4	John Grayson
1958	23	6	John Grayson
1959	21	7	John Grayson
1960	21	5	John Evans
1961	13	12	John Evans
1962	17	9	John Evans
1963	9	15	John Evans
1964	11	13	John Evans
1965	7	19	James L. Nau
1966	7	19	Claude Retherford
1967	11	14	Claude Retherford
1968	13	13	Claude Retherford
Totals	315	244	

ILLINOIS, UNIVERSITY OF

Champaign, Illinois

Illini			*Orange and Blue*
1938	9	9	Doug Mills
1939	14	5	Doug Mills
1940	14	6	Doug Mills
1941	13	7	Doug Mills
1942	18	5	Doug Mills
1943	17	1	Doug Mills
1944	11	9	Doug Mills
1945	13	7	Doug Mills
1946	14	7	Doug Mills
1947	14	6	Doug Mills
1948	15	5	Harry Combes
1949	21	4	Harry Combes
1950	14	8	Harry Combes
1951	22	5	Harry Combes
1952	22	4	Harry Combes
1953	18	4	Harry Combes
1954	17	5	Harry Combes
1955	17	5	Harry Combes
1956	18	4	Harry Combes
1957	14	8	Harry Combes
1958	11	11	Harry Combes
1959	12	10	Harry Combes
1960	16	7	Harry Combes
1961	9	15	Harry Combes
1962	15	8	Harry Combes
1963	20	6	Harry Combes
1964	13	11	Harry Combes
1965	18	6	Harry Combes
1966	12	12	Harry Combes
1967	12	12	Harry Combes
1968	11	13	Harvey Schmidt
Totals	464	225	

INDIANA UNIVERSITY

Bloomington, Indiana

Hoosiers			*Cream and Crimson*
1938	10	10	Everett Dean
1939	17	3	Branch McCracken
1940	20	3	Branch McCracken

Yr.	W	L	Coach
1941	16	4	Branch McCracken
1942	15	6	Branch McCracken
1943	18	2	Harry Gold
1944	7	15	Harry Gold
1945	10	11	Harry Gold
1946	18	3	Branch McCracken
1947	12	8	Branch McCracken
1948	8	12	Branch McCracken
1949	14	8	Branch McCracken
1950	17	5	Branch McCracken
1951	19	3	Branch McCracken
1952	16	6	Branch McCracken
1953	23	3	Branch McCracken
1954	20	4	Branch McCracken
1955	8	14	Branch McCracken
1956	13	9	Branch McCracken
1957	14	8	Branch McCracken
1958	13	11	Branch McCracken
1959	11	11	Branch McCracken
1960	20	4	Branch McCracken
1961	15	9	Branch McCracken
1962	13	11	Branch McCracken
1963	13	11	Branch McCracken
1964	9	15	Branch McCracken
1965	19	5	Branch McCracken
1966	8	16	Lou Watson
1967	18	8	Lou Watson
1968	10	14	Lou Watson
Totals	444	252	

IONA COLLEGE

New Rochelle, New York

Gaels — *Maroon and Gold*

Yr.	W	L	Coach
1941	17	5	A. A. Loftus
1942	19	4	A. A. Loftus
1943	—	—	
1944	—	—	
1945	—	—	
1946	17	5	A. A. Loftus
1947	15	8	Peter Caruso
1948	12	11	Jim McDermott
1949	17	8	Jim McDermott
1950	21	2	Jim McDermott
1951	16	6	Jim McDermott
1952	19	9	Jim McDermott
1953	18	3	Jim McDermott
1954	11	10	Jim McDermott
1955	10	11	Jim McDermott
1956	9	15	Jim McDermott
1957	13	7	Jim McDermott
1958	18	6	Jim McDermott
1959	14	7	Jim McDermott
1960	13	5	Jim McDermott
1961	10	11	Jim McDermott
1962	8	11	Jim McDermott
1963	12	7	Jim McDermott
1964	15	5	Jim McDermott
1965	12	11	Jim McDermott
1966	5	16	Jim McDermott
1967	11	10	Jim McDermott
1968	13	9	Jim McDermott
Totals	345	202	

IOWA, UNIVERSITY OF

Iowa City, Iowa

Hawkeyes — *Gold and Black*

Yr.	W	L	Coach
1938	10	9	Rollie Williams
1939	8	11	Rollie Williams
1940	9	12	Rollie Williams
1941	12	8	Rollie Williams
1942	12	8	Rollie Williams
1943	7	10	Pops Harrison
1944	14	4	Pops Harrison
1945	17	1	Pops Harrison
1946	14	4	Pops Harrison
1947	12	7	Pops Harrison
1948	15	4	Pops Harrison
1949	10	10	Pops Harrison
1950	15	7	Bucky O'Connor
1951	15	7	Rollie Williams
1952	19	3	Bucky O'Connor
1953	12	10	Bucky O'Connor
1954	17	5	Bucky O'Connor
1955	19	7	Bucky O'Connor
1956	20	6	Bucky O'Connor
1957	8	14	Bucky O'Connor
1958	13	9	Bucky O'Connor
1959	10	12	Milt Scheuerman
1960	14	10	Milt Scheuerman
1961	18	6	Milt Scheuerman
1962	13	11	Milt Scheuerman
1963	9	15	Milt Scheuerman
1964	8	15	Milt Scheuerman
1965	14	10	Ralph Miller
1966	17	7	Ralph Miller
1967	16	8	Ralph Miller
1968	16	9	Ralph Miller
Totals	413	259	

IOWA STATE UNIVERSITY

Ames, Iowa

Cyclones — *Cardinal and Gold*

Yr.	W	L	Coach
1938	6	9	Louis Menze
1939	8	9	Louis Menze
1940	9	9	Louis Menze
1941	15	4	Louis Menze
1942	11	6	Louis Menze
1943	7	9	Louis Menze
1944	14	4	Louis Menze
1945	11	5	Louis Menze
1946	8	8	Louis Menze
1947	7	14	Louis Menze
1948	15	8	Clayton Sutherland
1949	8	14	Clayton Sutherland
1950	6	17	Clayton Sutherland
1951	10	11	Clayton Sutherland
1952	10	11	Clayton Sutherland
1953	10	11	Clayton Sutherland
1954	6	15	Clayton Sutherland
1955	11	10	Bill Strannigan
1956	18	5	Bill Strannigan
1957	16	7	Bill Strannigan
1958	15	8	Bill Strannigan
1959	9	16	Bill Strannigan
1960	15	9	Glen Anderson

Yr.	W	L	Coach
1961	12	13	Glen Anderson
1962	13	12	Glen Anderson
1963	14	11	Glen Anderson
1964	9	16	Glen Anderson
1965	9	16	Glen Anderson
1966	11	14	Glen Anderson
1967	13	12	Glen Anderson
1968	12	13	Glen Anderson
Totals	338	329	

JACKSONVILLE UNIVERSITY

Jacksonville, Florida

Dolphins — *Kelly Green and White*

Yr.	W	L	Coach
1959	11	8	Rollie Rourke
1960	11	10	Rollie Rourke
1961	12	11	Dick Kendall
1962	12	13	Dick Kendall
1963	14	12	Dick Kendall
1964	13	13	Dick Kendall
1965	15	10	Joe Williams
1966	12	11	Joe Williams
1967	8	17	Joe Williams
1968	13	13	Joe Williams
Totals	121	118	

KANSAS, UNIVERSITY OF

Lawrence, Kansas

Jayhawks — *Crimson and Blue*

Yr.	W	L	Coach
1938	18	2	Dr. Forest "Phog" Allen
1939	13	7	Dr. Forest "Phog" Allen
1940	19	6	Dr. Forest "Phog" Allen
1941	12	6	Dr. Forest "Phog" Allen
1942	17	5	Dr. Forest "Phog" Allen
1943	22	6	Dr. Forest "Phog" Allen
1944	17	9	Dr. Forest "Phog" Allen
1945	12	5	Dr. Forest "Phog" Allen
1946	19	2	Dr. Forest "Phog" Allen
1947	16	11	Allen, H. Engleman
1948	9	15	Dr. Forest "Phog" Allen
1949	12	12	Dr. Forest "Phog" Allen
1950	14	11	Dr. Forest "Phog" Allen
1951	16	8	Dr. Forest "Phog" Allen
1952	28	3	Dr. Forest "Phog" Allen
1953	19	6	Dr. Forest "Phog" Allen
1954	16	5	Dr. Forest "Phog" Allen
1955	11	10	Dr. Forest "Phog" Allen
1956	14	9	Dr. Forest "Phog" Allen
1957	24	3	Dick Harp
1958	18	5	Dick Harp
1959	11	14	Dick Harp
1960	19	9	Dick Harp
1961	17	8	Dick Harp
1962	7	18	Dick Harp
1963	12	13	Dick Harp
1964	13	12	Dick Harp
1965	17	8	Ted Owens
1966	23	4	Ted Owens
1967	23	4	Ted Owens
1968	22	8	Ted Owens
Totals	510	244	

KANSAS STATE UNIVERSITY

Manhattan, Kansas

Wildcats — *Purple and White*

Yr.	W	L	Coach
1938	7	11	Frank Root
1939	5	14	Frank Root
1940	6	12	Jack Gardner
1941	6	12	Jack Gardner
1942	8	10	Jack Gardner
1943	6	14	Chili Cochrane
1944	7	15	Cliff Rock
1945	10	13	Fritz Knorr
1946	4	20	Fritz Knorr
1947	14	10	Jack Gardner
1948	22	6	Jack Gardner
1949	13	11	Jack Gardner
1950	17	7	Jack Gardner
1951	25	4	Jack Gardner
1952	19	5	Jack Gardner
1953	17	4	Jack Gardner
1954	11	10	Tex Winter
1955	11	10	Tex Winter
1956	17	8	Tex Winter
1957	15	8	Tex Winter
1958	22	5	Tex Winter
1959	25	2	Tex Winter
1960	16	10	Tex Winter
1961	22	5	Tex Winter
1962	22	3	Tex Winter
1963	16	9	Tex Winter
1964	22	7	Tex Winter
1965	12	13	Tex Winter
1966	14	11	Tex Winter
1967	17	8	Tex Winter
1968	19	9	Tex Winter
Totals	447	296	

KENT STATE UNIVERSITY

Kent, Ohio

Golden Flashes — *Blue and Gold*

Yr.	W	L	Coach
1938	10	13	— —
1939	12	11	— —
1940	13	10	— —
1941	12	10	— —
1942	14	11	G. N. Starn
1943	12	12	G. N. Starn
1944	—	—	
1945	3	12	William Satterlee
1946	10	10	Harry Adams
1947	13	11	Harry Adams
1948	15	8	Harry Adams
1949	20	8	David McDowell
1950	18	4	David McDowell
1951	18	8	David McDowell
1952	14	10	Clarence Haerr
1953	7	15	Clarence Haerr
1954	8	13	Clarence Haerr
1955	8	14	Clarence Haerr
1956	10	11	David McDowell
1957	5	18	William Bertka
1958	9	14	William Bertka
1959	11	13	William Bertka
1960	7	16	William Bertka

Yr.	W	L	Coach
1961	9	14	William Bertka
1962	2	19	Bob Doll
1963	3	18	Bob Doll
1964	11	13	Bob Doll
1965	8	12	Bob Doll
1966	8	16	Bob Doll
1967	5	19	Frank Truitt
1968	9	15	Frank Truitt
Totals	304	368	

KENTUCKY, UNIVERSITY OF

Lexington, Kentucky

Wildcats			*Blue and White*
1938	13	5	Adolph Rupp
1939	16	4	Adolph Rupp
1940	15	6	Adolph Rupp
1941	17	8	Adolph Rupp
1942	19	6	Adolph Rupp
1943	17	6	Adolph Rupp
1944	19	2	Adolph Rupp
1945	22	4	Adolph Rupp
1946	28	2	Adolph Rupp
1947	34	3	Adolph Rupp
1948	36	3	Adolph Rupp
1949	32	2	Adolph Rupp
1950	25	5	Adolph Rupp
1951	32	2	Adolph Rupp
1952	29	3	Adolph Rupp
1953	—	—	
1954	25	0	Adolph Rupp
1955	23	3	Adolph Rupp
1956	20	6	Adolph Rupp
1957	23	5	Adolph Rupp
1958	23	6	Adolph Rupp
1959	24	3	Adolph Rupp
1960	18	7	Adolph Rupp
1961	19	9	Adolph Rupp
1962	23	3	Adolph Rupp
1963	16	9	Adolph Rupp
1964	21	6	Adolph Rupp
1965	15	10	Adolph Rupp
1966	27	2	Adolph Rupp
1967	13	13	Adolph Rupp
1968	22	5	Adolph Rupp
Totals	666	148	

LAFAYETTE COLLEGE

Easton, Pennsylvania

Leopards			*Maroon and White*
1938	9	8	Michael Michalske
1939	6	11	R. C. Madison
1940	11	8	R. C. Madison
1941	8	10	R. C. Madison
1942	4	12	R. C. Madison
1943	7	6	A. R. Winters
1944	7	3	A. R. Winters
1945	16	2	A. R. Winters
1946	17	3	Ray Stanley
1947	15	7	Ray Stanley
1948	12	9	Ray Stanley
1949	20	9	Ray Stanley
1950	19	6	Ray Stanley
1951	14	11	Ray Stanley

Yr.	W	L	Coach
1952	15	9	Bill van Breda Kolff
1953	13	12	Bill van Breda Kolff
1954	17	10	Bill van Breda Kolff
1955	24	3	Bill van Breda Kolff
1956	20	7	George Davidson
1957	22	5	George Davidson
1958	16	10	George Davidson
1959	13	8	George Davidson
1960	12	13	George Davidson
1961	16	8	George Davidson
1962	18	6	George Davidson
1963	13	11	George Davidson
1964	15	8	George Davidson
1965	12	8	George Davidson
1966	9	11	George Davidson
1967	4	21	George Davidson
1968	5	19	Hal Wissel
Totals	409	274	

LASALLE COLLEGE

Philadelphia, Pennsylvania

Explorers			*Blue and Gold*
1938	9	8	Leonard Tanseer
1939	12	6	Leonard Tanseer
1940	12	8	Leonard Tanseer
1941	9	8	Leonard Tanseer
1942	12	10	Obie O'Brien
1943	13	10	Obie O'Brien
1944	8	8	Joseph Meehan
1945	11	8	Joseph Meehan
1946	10	13	Joseph Meehan
1947	20	6	Charles McGlone
1948	20	4	Charles McGlone
1949	20	7	Charles McGlone
1950	21	4	Ken Loeffler
1951	22	7	Ken Loeffler
1952	25	7	Ken Loeffler
1953	25	3	Ken Loeffler
1954	26	4	Ken Loeffler
1955	26	5	Ken Loeffler
1956	15	10	Jim Pollard
1957	17	9	Jim Pollard
1958	16	9	Jim Pollard
1959	16	7	Donald "Dudey" Moore
1960	16	6	Donald "Dudey" Moore
1961	15	7	Donald "Dudey" Moore
1962	16	9	Donald "Dudey" Moore
1963	16	8	Donald "Dudey" Moore
1964	16	9	Donald "Dudey" Moore
1965	15	8	Donald "Dudey" Moore
1966	10	15	Robert W. Walters
1967	14	12	Joe Heyer
1968	20	8	Jim Harding
Totals	503	243	

LEHIGH UNIVERSITY

Bethlehem, Pennsylvania

Engineers			*Brown and White*
1938	7	8	Paul Calvert
1939	10	5	Paul Calvert
1940	5	10	Paul Calvert
1941	5	12	Paul Calvert
1942	7	8	Marty Westerman

Yr.	W	L	Coach
1943	5	10	James Gordon
1944	4	12	Leo Prendergast
1945	2	14	Leo Prendergast
1946	3	13	Leo Prendergast
1947	5	13	Daniel Yarbo
1948	2	16	Daniel Yarbo
1949	7	11	Daniel Yarbo
1950	4	14	Daniel Yarbo
1951	6	13	Tony Packer
1952	7	12	Tony Packer
1953	12	8	Tony Packer
1954	8	12	Tony Packer
1955	10	11	Tony Packer
1956	7	11	Tony Packer
1957	8	10	Tony Packer
1958	8	10	Tony Packer
1959	6	16	Tony Packer
1960	6	16	Tony Packer
1961	5	16	Tony Packer
1962	7	12	Tony Packer
1963	6	19	Tony Packer
1964	5	17	Tony Packer
1965	7	13	Tony Packer
1966	4	17	Tony Packer
1967	11	12	Pete Carrill
1968	12	11	Roy Heckman
Totals	201	382	

LONG ISLAND UNIVERSITY

Brooklyn, New York

Blackbirds — *Blue and White*

Yr.	W	L	Coach
1938	23	4	Clair Bee
1939	25	0	Clair Bee
1940	20	4	Clair Bee
1941	25	2	Clair Bee
1942	25	4	Clair Bee
1943	14	6	Clair Bee
1944	12	3	George Wolfe
1945	15	5	George Wolfe
1946	14	9	Clair Bee
1947	19	4	Clair Bee
1948	18	4	Clair Bee
1949	19	12	Clair Bee
1950	20	5	Clair Bee
1951	20	4	Clair Bee
1952	—	—	
1953	—	—	
1954	—	—	
1955	—	—	
1956	—	—	
1957	—	—	
1958	12	6	Buck Lai
1959	7	14	Buck Lai
1960	12	9	Buck Lai
1961	13	10	Buck Lai
1962	12	9	Roy Rubin
1963	10	14	Roy Rubin
1964	14	9	Roy Rubin
1965	16	7	Roy Rubin
1966	22	4	Roy Rubin
1967	22	7	Roy Rubin
1968	22	2	Roy Rubin
Totals	431	157	

LOUISIANA STATE UNIVERSITY

Baton Rouge, Louisiana

Tigers — *Purple and Gold*

Yr.	W	L	Coach
1938	10	10	Harry Rabenhorst
1939	13	7	Harry Rabenhorst
1940	10	8	Harry Rabenhorst
1941	9	9	Harry Rabenhorst
1942	8	7	Harry Rabenhorst
1943	18	4	Dale Morey
1944	10	15	Dale Morey
1945	15	9	J. Fatheree, A. L. Swanson
1946	18	3	Harry Rabenhorst
1947	17	4	Harry Rabenhorst
1948	8	18	Harry Rabenhorst
1949	15	10	Harry Rabenhorst
1950	13	12	Harry Rabenhorst
1951	10	14	Harry Rabenhorst
1952	17	7	Harry Rabenhorst
1953	24	3	Harry Rabenhorst
1954	21	5	Harry Rabenhorst
1955	6	18	Harry Rabenhorst
1956	7	17	Harry Rabenhorst
1957	6	19	Harry Rabenhorst
1958	7	18	Jay McCreary
1959	10	15	Jay McCreary
1960	5	18	Jay McCreary
1961	11	14	Jay McCreary
1962	13	11	Jay McCreary
1963	12	12	Jay McCreary
1964	12	13	Jay McCreary
1965	12	14	Jay McCreary
1966	6	20	Frank Truitt
1967	3	23	Press Maravich
1968	14	12	Press Maravich
Totals	360	369	

LOUISVILLE, UNIVERSITY OF

Louisville, Kentucky

Cardinals — *Red and Black*

Yr.	W	L	Coach
1938	5	11	Lawrence Apitz
1939	1	16	Lawrence Apitz
1940	2	18	Lawrence Apitz
1941	3	14	John Heldman
1942	8	10	John Heldman
1943	—	—	
1944	10	10	H. Church, W. Casey
1945	16	3	Bernard "Peck" Hickman
1946	22	6	Bernard "Peck" Hickman
1947	17	6	Bernard "Peck" Hickman
1948	29	6	Bernard "Peck" Hickman
1949	23	10	Bernard "Peck" Hickman
1950	21	11	Bernard "Peck" Hickman
1951	19	7	Bernard "Peck" Hickman
1952	20	6	Bernard "Peck" Hickman
1953	22	6	Bernard "Peck" Hickman
1954	22	7	Bernard "Peck" Hickman
1955	19	8	Bernard "Peck" Hickman
1956	26	3	Bernard "Peck" Hickman
1957	21	5	Bernard "Peck" Hickman
1958	13	12	Bernard "Peck" Hickman
1959	19	12	Bernard "Peck" Hickman
1960	15	11	Bernard "Peck" Hickman

Yr.	W	L	Coach
1961	21	8	Bernard "Peck" Hickman
1962	15	10	Bernard "Peck" Hickman
1963	14	11	Bernard "Peck" Hickman
1964	15	10	Bernard "Peck" Hickman
1965	15	10	Bernard "Peck" Hickman
1966	16	10	Bernard "Peck" Hickman
1967	23	5	Bernard "Peck" Hickman
1968	21	7	John Dromo
Totals	493	269	

LOYOLA UNIVERSITY
Los Angeles, California

Lions			*Crimson and Gray*
1946	12	15	Scotty McDonald
1947	13	20	Scotty McDonald
1948	22	14	Scotty McDonald
1949	9	17	Scotty McDonald
1950	14	11	Scotty McDonald
1951	12	14	Scotty McDonald
1952	15	14	Edwin Powell
1953	14	16	Bill Donovan
1954	16	9	Bill Donovan
1955	13	12	Bill Donovan
1956	11	16	Bill Donovan
1957	6	18	Bill Donovan
1958	8	15	Bill Donovan
1959	19	8	Bill Donovan
1960	20	7	Bill Donovan
1961	16	8	John Arndt
1963	9	17	John Arndt
1964	12	13	John Arndt
1965	6	20	John Arndt
1966	11	15	John Arndt
1967	16	10	John Arndt
1968	19	6	John Arndt
Totals	293	295	

LOYOLA UNIVERSITY
Chicago, Illinois

Ramblers			*Maroon and Gold*
1938	12	8	Leonard Sachs
1939	21	1	Leonard Sachs
1940	5	14	Leonard Sachs
1941	13	8	Leonard Sachs
1942	17	6	Leonard Sachs
1943	12	10	John Connelly
1944	—	—	
1945	4	8	Alex Wilson
1946	23	4	Thomas Haggerty
1947	20	9	Thomas Haggerty
1948	26	9	Thomas Haggerty
1949	25	6	Thomas Haggerty
1950	17	13	Thomas Haggerty
1951	15	14	John Jordan
1952	17	8	George Ireland
1953	8	15	George Ireland
1954	7	15	George Ireland
1955	13	11	George Ireland
1956	10	14	George Ireland
1957	14	10	George Ireland
1958	16	8	George Ireland
1959	11	13	George Ireland

Yr.	W	L	Coach
1960	10	12	George Ireland
1961	15	8	George Ireland
1962	23	4	George Ireland
1963	29	2	George Ireland
1964	22	6	George Ireland
1965	11	14	George Ireland
1966	22	3	George Ireland
1967	14	9	George Ireland
1968	15	9	George Ireland
Totals	467	271	

LOYOLA UNIVERSITY
New Orleans, Louisiana

Wolfpack			*Maroon and Gold*
1942	14	2	Jack Orsley
1943	21	3	Jack Orsley
1944	25	5	Jack Orsley
1945	22	11	Jack Orsley
1946	16	9	Jack Orsley
1947	20	10	Jack Orsley
1948	11	16	Jack Orsley
1949	7	18	J. Orsley, J. McCafferty
1950	15	11	Tom Haggerty
1951	20	14	Tom Haggerty
1952	14	13	Tom Haggerty
1953	15	9	T. Haggerty, J. McCafferty
1954	13	10	Jim McCafferty
1955	11	14	Jim McCafferty
1956	14	12	Jim McCafferty
1957	16	9	Jim Harding
1958	10	16	Henry Kuzma
1959	12	13	Bill Gardiner
1960	6	18	Bill Gardiner
1961	11	12	Bill Gardiner
1963	12	11	Bill Gardiner
1964	12	12	Bill Gardiner
1965	8	16	Bill Gardiner
1966	9	17	Bill Gardiner
1967	12	10	Bill Gardiner
1968	11	14	Ron Greene
Totals	357	305	

MAINE, UNIVERSITY OF
Orono, Maine

Black Bears			*Blue and White*
1938	4	9	William Kenyon
1939	8	4	H. Woodbury, W. Kenyon
1940	3	9	William Kenyon
1941	4	8	William Kenyon
1942	7	7	William Kenyon
1943	9	6	Samuel Sezak
1944	4	6	Samuel Sezak
1945	4	8	William Kenyon
1946	10	4	Eck Allen
1947	9	8	Eck Allen
1948	11	7	Eck Allen
1949	4	14	Eck Allen
1950	13	6	Rome Rankin
1951	5	13	Rome Rankin
1952	7	12	Rome Rankin
1953	7	10	Rome Rankin
1954	6	12	Rome Rankin

Yr.	W	L	Coach
1955	4	13	Russell DeVette
1956	6	12	Harold Woodbury
1957	6	14	Harold Woodbury
1958	8	12	Harold Woodbury
1959	15	7	Brian McCall
1960	19	4	Brian McCall
1961	18	5	Brian McCall
1962	11	13	Brian McCall
1963	8	15	Brian McCall
1964	12	11	Brian McCall
1965	13	10	Brian McCall
1966	9	13	Brian McCall
1967	8	12	Brian McCall
1968	7	17	Brian McCall
Totals	259	301	

MANHATTAN COLLEGE

Bronx, New York

Jaspers			*Green and White*
1938	12	6	Neil Cohalan
1939	12	5	Neil Cohalan
1940	14	9	Neil Cohalan
1941	11	7	Neil Cohalan
1942	10	10	Neil Cohalan
1943	18	3	Joseph Daher
1944	—	—	
1945	—	—	
1946	15	8	John "Honey" Russell
1947	13	13	Ken Norton
1948	23	6	Ken Norton
1949	18	8	Ken Norton
1950	13	11	Ken Norton
1951	16	6	Ken Norton
1952	12	9	Ken Norton
1953	20	6	Ken Norton
1954	15	11	Ken Norton
1955	18	5	Ken Norton
1956	16	8	Ken Norton
1957	15	9	Ken Norton
1958	16	10	Ken Norton
1959	15	6	Ken Norton
1960	13	11	Ken Norton
1961	8	11	Ken Norton
1962	12	10	Ken Norton
1963	9	14	Ken Norton
1964	11	11	Ken Norton
1965	13	9	Ken Norton
1966	13	9	Ken Norton
1967	13	8	Ken Norton
1968	8	14	Ken Norton
Totals	402	253	

MARQUETTE UNIVERSITY

Milwaukee, Wisconsin

Warriors			*Blue and Gold*
1938	14	5	William Chandler
1939	12	5	William Chandler
1940	7	9	William Chandler
1941	2	13	William Chandler
1942	6	11	William Chandler
1943	9	10	William Chandler
1944	8	6	William Chandler
1945	7	10	William Chandler
1946	11	7	William Chandler
1947	9	14	William Chandler
1948	9	15	William Chandler
1949	8	13	William Chandler
1950	6	17	William Chandler
1951	8	14	William Chandler
1952	12	14	Tex Winter
1953	13	11	Tex Winter
1954	11	15	Jack Nagle
1955	24	3	Jack Nagle
1956	13	11	Jack Nagle
1957	10	15	Jack Nagle
1958	11	11	Jack Nagle
1959	23	6	Eddie Hickey
1960	13	12	Eddie Hickey
1961	16	11	Eddie Hickey
1962	15	11	Eddie Hickey
1963	20	9	Eddie Hickey
1964	5	21	Eddie Hickey
1965	8	18	Al McGuire
1966	14	12	Al McGuire
1967	21	9	Al McGuire
1968	23	6	Al McGuire
Totals	368	344	

MARSHALL UNIVERSITY

Huntington, West Virginia

Big Green, Thundering Herd			*Green and White*
1939	22	5	Cam Henderson
1940	25	4	Cam Henderson
1941	14	9	Cam Henderson
1942	14	9	Cam Henderson
1943	10	6	Cam Henderson
1944	15	7	Cam Henderson
1945	16	9	Cam Henderson
1946	25	9	Cam Henderson
1947	32	5	Cam Henderson
1948	22	11	Cam Henderson
1949	16	12	Cam Henderson
1950	15	9	Cam Henderson
1951	13	13	Cam Henderson
1952	15	11	Cam Henderson
1953	20	4	Cam Henderson
1954	12	9	Cam Henderson
1955	17	4	Cam Henderson
1956	18	5	Jule Rivlin
1957	15	9	Jule Rivlin
1958	17	7	Jule Rivlin
1959	12	12	Jule Rivlin
1960	10	13	Jule Rivlin
1961	11	13	Jule Rivlin
1962	10	13	Jule Rivlin
1963	7	16	Jule Rivlin
1964	6	17	Ellis Johnson
1965	4	20	Ellis Johnson
1966	12	12	Ellis Johnson
1967	20	8	Ellis Johnson
1968	17	8	Ellis Johnson
Totals	462	289	

MARYLAND, UNIVERSITY OF

College Park, Maryland

Terrapins, Terps — *Red and White*

Yr.	W	L	Coach
1938	15	9	H. Burton Shipley
1939	15	9	H. Burton Shipley
1940	14	9	H. Burton Shipley
1941	1	21	H. Burton Shipley
1942	7	15	H. Burton Shipley
1943	8	8	H. Burton Shipley
1944	4	14	H. Burton Shipley
1945	2	14	H. Burton Shipley
1946	9	12	H. Burton Shipley
1947	14	10	H. Burton Shipley
1948	11	14	Flucie Stewart
1949	9	18	Flucie Stewart
1950	7	18	Flucie Stewart
1951	16	11	H.A. "Bud" Millikan
1952	13	9	H.A. "Bud" Millikan
1953	15	8	H.A. "Bud" Millikan
1954	23	7	H.A. "Bud" Millikan
1955	17	7	H.A. "Bud" Millikan
1956	14	10	H.A. "Bud" Millikan
1957	15	9	H.A. "Bud" Millikan
1958	22	7	H.A. "Bud" Millikan
1959	10	13	H.A. "Bud" Millikan
1960	15	8	H.A. "Bud" Millikan
1961	14	12	H.A. "Bud" Millikan
1962	8	17	H.A. "Bud" Millikan
1963	8	13	H.A. "Bud" Millikan
1964	9	17	H.A. "Bud" Millikan
1965	18	8	H.A. "Bud" Millikan
1966	14	11	H.A. "Bud" Millikan
1967	11	14	H.A. "Bud" Millikan
1968	8	16	Frank Fellows
Totals	366	368	

MASSACHUSETTS, UNIVERSITY OF

Amherst, Mass.

Redmen — *Maroon and White*

Yr.	W	L	Coach
1938	8	6	Wilho Frigard
1939	7	7	Wilho Frigard
1940	1	14	Wilho Frigard
1941	5	9	F. Ellert, L. Bush
1942	8	6	Walter Hargesheimer
1943	5	8	Walter Hargesheimer
1944	—	—	
1945	—	—	
1946	4	8	L. Ball, T. Eck
1947	4	12	Lorin Ball
1948	2	14	Lorin Ball
1949	6	12	Lorin Ball
1950	8	11	Lorin Ball
1951	6	15	Lorin Ball
1952	4	17	Lorin Ball
1953	4	15	Robert Curran
1954	13	9	Robert Curran
1955	10	14	Robert Curran
1956	17	6	Robert Curran
1957	13	11	Robert Curran
1958	13	12	Robert Curran
1959	11	13	Robert Curran
1960	14	10	Matt Zunic
1961	16	10	Matt Zunic
1962	15	9	Matt Zunic
1963	12	12	Matt Zunic
1964	15	9	Johnny Orr
1965	13	11	Johnny Orr
1966	11	13	Johnny Orr
1967	11	14	Jack Leamen
1968	14	11	Jack Leamen
Totals	270	318	

MEMPHIS STATE UNIVERSITY

Memphis, Tenn.

Tigers — *Blue and Gray*

Yr.	W	L	Coach
1947	10	7	Zack Curlin
1948	13	10	Zack Curlin
1949	11	10	McCoy Tarry
1950	12	9	McCoy Tarry
1951	17	8	McCoy Tarry
1952	25	10	Eugene Lambert
1953	10	14	Eugene Lambert
1954	15	9	Eugene Lambert
1955	17	5	Eugene Lambert
1956	20	7	Eugene Lambert
1957	24	6	Bob Vanatta
1958	15	7	Bob Vanatta
1959	17	6	Bob Vanatta
1960	18	5	Bob Vanatta
1961	20	3	Bob Vanatta
1962	15	7	Bob Vanatta
1963	19	7	Dean Ehlers
1964	14	11	Dean Ehlers
1965	10	14	Dean Ehlers
1966	10	15	Dean Ehlers
1967	17	9	Dean Ehlers
1968	8	17	Moe Iba
Totals	337	196	

MIAMI, UNIVERSITY OF

Coral Gables, Florida

Hurricanes — *Orange, Green and White*

Yr.	W	L	Coach
1939	4	6	Hart Morris
1940	4	12	Hart Morris
1941	10	6	Hart Morris
1942	9	7	Hart Morris
1943	—	—	
1944	—	—	
1945	—	—	
1946	8	5	W.H. Steers
1947	20	7	Hart Morris
1948	11	7	Hart Morris
1949	19	8	Hart Morris
1950	14	9	Hart Morris
1951	10	12	Hart Morris
1952	14	8	Hart Morris
1953	9	12	Hart Morris
1954	5	10	David Wike
1955	9	11	Bruce Hale
1956	14	12	Bruce Hale
1957	13	13	Bruce Hale
1958	14	8	Bruce Hale
1959	18	7	Bruce Hale

Yr.	W	L	Coach
1960	23	4	Bruce Hale
1961	20	7	Bruce Hale
1962	14	12	Bruce Hale
1963	23	5	Bruce Hale
1964	20	7	Bruce Hale
1965	22	4	Bruce Hale
1966	15	11	Bruce Hale
1967	15	11	Dick Hickcox
1968	17	11	Ron Godfrey
Totals	374	232	

MIAMI, UNIVERSITY OF

Oxford, Ohio

Redskins			*Red and White*
1938	11	5	John Mauer
1939	5	13	Wilber "Weeb" Ewbank
1940	12	6	Rip Van Winkle
1941	10	7	Rip Van Winkle
1942	16	9	Rip Van Winkle
1943	11	5	W.J. "Blue" Foster
1944	10	2	W.J. "Blue" Foster
1945	8	7	W.J. "Blue" Foster
1946	10	9	W.J. "Blue" Foster
1947	15	7	W.J. "Blue" Foster
1948	13	15	W.J. "Blue" Foster
1949	8	13	W.J. "Blue" Foster
1950	5	15	John Brickels
1951	10	13	John Brickels
1952	19	6	Bill Rohr
1953	17	6	Bill Rohr
1954	12	10	Bill Rohr
1955	14	9	Bill Rohr
1956	12	8	Bill Rohr
1957	17	8	Bill Rohr
1958	18	9	Dick Shrider
1959	14	11	Dick Shrider
1960	8	16	Dick Shrider
1961	12	12	Dick Shrider
1962	7	17	Dick Shrider
1963	12	12	Dick Shrider
1964	17	7	Dick Shrider
1965	20	5	Dick Shrider
1966	18	7	Dick Shrider
1967	14	10	Taylor "Tates" Locke
1968	11	12	Taylor "Tates" Locke
Totals	386	291	

MICHIGAN, UNIVERSITY OF

Ann Arbor, Michigan

Wolverines			*Maize and Blue*
1938	13	7	Franklin Cappon
1939	11	9	Bennie Oosterbaan
1940	13	7	Bennie Oosterbaan
1941	9	10	Bennie Oosterbaan
1942	6	14	Bennie Oosterbaan
1943	10	8	Bennie Oosterbaan
1944	8	10	Bennie Oosterbaan
1945	12	7	Bennie Oosterbaan
1946	12	7	Bennie Oosterbaan
1947	12	8	Osborne Cowles
1948	15	6	Osborne Cowles
1949	16	6	Ernest McCoy

Yr.	W	L	Coach
1950	11	11	Ernest McCoy
1951	7	15	Ernest McCoy
1952	7	15	Ernest McCoy
1953	6	16	William Perigo
1954	9	13	William Perigo
1955	11	11	William Perigo
1956	9	13	William Perigo
1957	13	9	William Perigo
1958	11	11	William Perigo
1959	15	7	William Perigo
1960	4	20	Dave Strack
1961	6	18	Dave Strack
1962	7	17	Dave Strack
1963	16	8	Dave Strack
1964	23	5	Dave Strack
1965	24	4	Dave Strack
1966	18	8	Dave Strack
1967	8	16	Dave Strack
1968	11	13	Dave Strack
Totals	353	329	

MICHIGAN STATE UNIVERSITY

East Lansing, Michigan

Spartans			*Green and White*
1938	9	8	Benjamin F. VanAlstyne
1939	9	8	Benjamin F. VanAlstyne
1940	14	6	Benjamin F. VanAlstyne
1941	11	6	Benjamin F. VanAlstyne
1942	15	6	Benjamin F. VanAlstyne
1943	2	14	Benjamin F. VanAlstyne
1944	—	—	
1945	10	7	Benjamin F. VanAlstyne
1946	12	9	Benjamin F. VanAlstyne
1947	11	10	Benjamin F. VanAlstyne
1948	12	10	Benjamin F. VanAlstyne
1949	9	12	Benjamin F. VanAlstyne
1950	4	18	Alton S. Kircher
1951	10	11	Peter F. Newell
1952	13	9	Peter F. Newell
1953	13	9	Peter F. Newell
1954	9	13	Peter F. Newell
1955	13	9	Forrest A. Anderson
1956	13	9	Forrest A. Anderson
1957	16	10	Forrest A. Anderson
1958	16	6	Forrest A. Anderson
1959	19	4	Forrest A. Anderson
1960	10	11	Forrest A. Anderson
1961	7	17	Forrest A. Anderson
1962	8	14	Forrest A. Anderson
1963	4	16	Forrest A. Anderson
1964	14	10	Forrest A. Anderson
1965	5	18	Forrest A. Anderson
1966	17	7	John E. Benington
1967	16	7	John E. Benington
1968	12	12	John E. Benington
Totals	333	306	

MIDDLE TENNESSEE STATE COLLEGE

Murfreesboro, Tennessee

Blue Raiders			*Blue and White*
1938	6	10	John Floyd
1939	5	8	John Floyd

Yr.	W	L	Coach
1940	9	12	Edwin Midgett
1941	7	14	Edwin Midgett
1942	9	9	Edwin Midgett
1943	—	—	
1944	—	—	
1945	—	—	
1946	4	0	Otis Freeman
1947	14	8	Elbert Patty
1948	10	11	Elbert Patty
1949	11	12	Charles Murphy
1950	14	13	Charles Greer
1951	8	14	Charles Greer
1952	19	12	Charles Greer
1953	7	16	Charles Greer
1954	11	17	Charles Greer
1955	11	16	Charles Greer
1956	6	15	Charles Greer
1957	12	13	Edgar Diddle, Jr.
1958	11	10	Edgar Diddle, Jr.
1959	9	17	Edgar Diddle, Jr.
1960	9	14	Edgar Diddle, Jr.
1961	9	14	Edgar Diddle, Jr.
1962	6	12	Edgar Diddle, Jr.
1963	9	15	William M. Stokes
1964	11	10	William M. Stokes
1965	6	18	William M. Stokes
1966	7	17	Ken Trickey
1967	10	15	Ken Trickey
1968	15	9	Ken Trickey
Totals	265	351	

MINNESOTA, UNIVERSITY OF

Minneapolis, Minnesota

Gophers			*Maroon and Gold*
1938	16	4	David MacMillan
1939	14	6	David MacMillan
1940	12	8	David MacMillan
1941	11	9	David MacMillan
1942	15	6	David MacMillan
1943	10	9	David MacMillan
1944	7	14	Carl Nordly
1945	8	13	Carl Nordly
1946	14	7	Weston Mitchell
1947	14	7	David MacMillan
1948	10	10	David MacMillan
1949	18	3	Osborne Cowles
1950	13	9	Osborne Cowles
1951	13	9	Osborne Cowles
1952	15	7	Osborne Cowles
1953	14	8	Osborne Cowles
1954	17	5	Osborne Cowles
1955	15	7	Osborne Cowles
1956	11	11	Osborne Cowles
1957	14	8	Osborne Cowles
1958	10	12	Osborne Cowles
1959	8	14	Osborne Cowles
1960	12	12	John Kundla
1961	10	14	John Kundla
1962	10	14	John Kundla
1963	12	12	John Kundla
1964	17	7	John Kundla
1965	19	5	John Kundla
1966	14	10	John Kundla
1967	9	15	John Kundla
1968	7	17	John Kundla
Totals	389	292	

MISSISSIPPI, UNIVERSITY OF

University, Mississippi

Rebels			*Red and Blue*
1938	19	10	Ed Walker
1939	9	15	Frank Johnson
1940	9	10	Frank Johnson
1941	2	17	Charles Jaskwhich
1942	4	14	Charles Jaskwhich
1943	9	9	Charles Jaskwhich
1944	—	—	
1945	13	10	E. W. Hale
1946	7	11	E. W. Hale
1947	7	14	James Whitney
1948	11	12	James Whitney
1949	8	13	James Whitney
1950	8	17	James Whitney
1951	12	12	Bonnie Graham
1952	15	11	Bonnie Graham
1953	14	11	Bonnie Graham
1954	12	12	Bonnie Graham
1955	8	15	Bonnie Graham
1956	10	13	Bonnie Graham
1957	9	12	Bonnie Graham
1958	12	12	Bonnie Graham
1959	7	17	Bonnie Graham
1960	15	9	Bonnie Graham
1961	10	14	Bonnie Graham
1962	12	13	Bonnie Graham
1963	7	17	Edward S. Crawford
1964	10	12	Edward S. Crawford
1965	4	21	Edward S. Crawford
1966	5	18	Edward S. Crawford
1967	13	12	Howard Crawford
1968	7	17	Howard Crawford
Totals	288	400	

MISSISSIPPI STATE UNIVERSITY

State College, Mississippi

Maroons			*Maroon and White*
1938	9	11	Frank Carideo
1939	8	11	Frank Carideo
1940	9	5	Frank Carideo
1941	12	9	Dick Hitt
1942	13	7	Dick Hitt
1943	14	8	Dick Hitt
1944	—	—	
1945	4	14	Dick Hitt
1946	5	14	Dick Hitt
1947	10	11	Dick Hitt
1948	6	12	Paul Gregory
1949	4	13	Paul Gregory
1950	7	11	Paul Gregory
1951	3	16	Paul Gregory
1952	12	11	Paul Gregory
1953	9	10	Paul Gregory
1954	11	10	Paul Gregory
1955	6	17	Paul Gregory
1956	12	12	Babe McCarthy
1957	17	8	Babe McCarthy

Yr.	W	L	Coach
1958	20	5	Babe McCarthy
1959	24	1	Babe McCarthy
1960	12	13	Babe McCarthy
1961	19	6	Babe McCarthy
1962	24	1	Babe McCarthy
1963	22	6	Babe McCarthy
1964	9	17	Babe McCarthy
1965	10	16	Babe McCarthy
1966	14	11	Joe Dan Gold
1967	14	11	Joe Dan Gold
1968	9	17	Joe Dan Gold
Totals	348	314	

MISSOURI, UNIVERSITY OF

Columbia, Missouri

Tigers — *Black and Gold*

Yr.	W	L	Coach
1938	9	9	George Edwards
1939	12	6	George Edwards
1940	13	6	George Edwards
1941	6	10	George Edwards
1942	6	12	George Edwards
1943	7	10	George Edwards
1944	10	9	George Edwards
1945	8	10	George Edwards
1946	6	11	George Edwards
1947	15	10	Wilbur "Sparky" Stalcup
1948	14	10	Wilbur "Sparky" Stalcup
1949	11	13	Wilbur "Sparky" Stalcup
1950	14	10	Wilbur "Sparky" Stalcup
1951	16	8	Wilbur "Sparky" Stalcup
1952	14	10	Wilbur "Sparky" Stalcup
1953	12	9	Wilbur "Sparky" Stalcup
1954	11	10	Wilbur "Sparky" Stalcup
1955	16	5	Wilbur "Sparky" Stalcup
1956	15	7	Wilbur "Sparky" Stalcup
1957	10	13	Wilbur "Sparky" Stalcup
1958	9	13	Wilbur "Sparky" Stalcup
1959	6	19	Wilbur "Sparky" Stalcup
1960	12	13	Wilbur "Sparky" Stalcup
1961	9	15	Wilbur "Sparky" Stalcup
1962	9	16	Wilbur "Sparky" Stalcup
1963	10	15	Bob Vanatta
1964	13	11	Bob Vanatta
1965	13	11	Bob Vanatta
1966	3	21	Bob Vanatta
1967	3	22	Bob Vanatta
1968	10	16	Norm Stewart
Totals	322	360	

MONTANA, UNIVERSITY OF

Missoula, Montana

Grizzlies — *Silver, Copper and Gold*

Yr.	W	L	Coach
1938	10	19	George Dahlberg
1939	17	13	George Dahlberg
1940	17	8	George Dahlberg
1941	14	14	George Dahlberg
1942	14	10	George Dahlberg
1943	15	9	C. Carpenter, E. Chinske
1944	2	10	Ed Buzzetti
1945	7	23	George Dahlberg
1946	13	16	George Dahlberg
1947	12	16	George Dahlberg
1948	21	11	George Dahlberg
1949	12	13	George Dahlberg
1950	27	4	George Dahlberg
1951	13	18	George Dahlberg
1952	12	14	George Dahlberg
1953	14	11	George Dahlberg
1954	7	20	George Dahlberg
1955	12	14	George Dahlberg
1956	14	12	Frosty Cox
1957	13	9	Frosty Cox
1958	12	10	Frosty Cox
1959	10	14	Frosty Cox
1960	7	17	Frosty Cox
1961	14	9	Frosty Cox
1962	10	14	Frosty Cox
1963	6	18	Ron Nord
1964	6	17	Ron Nord
1965	18	6	Ron Nord
1966	14	10	Ron Nord
1967	6	18	Ron Nord
1968	8	17	Ron Nord
Totals	377	414	

MONTANA STATE UNIVERSITY

Bozeman, Montana

Bobcats — *Blue and Gold*

Yr.	W	L	Coach
1938	22	5	John Breeden
1939	18	11	John Breeden
1940	10	16	John Breeden
1941	13	12	John Breeden
1942	14	8	John Breeden
1943	17	5	John Breeden
1944	—	—	
1945	10	14	John Breeden
1946	17	10	John Breeden
1947	25	11	John Breeden
1948	18	9	Max Worthington
1949	14	15	John Breeden
1950	20	12	John Breeden
1951	24	12	John Breeden
1952	22	14	John Breeden
1953	11	24	John Breeden
1954	18	11	John Breeden
1955	11	16	Wally Lemm
1956	15	14	Keith Lambert
1957	12	13	Keith Lambert
1958	18	8	Keith Lambert
1959	12	13	Keith Lambert
1960	11	14	Keith Lambert
1961	10	15	Keith Lambert
1962	10	13	Keith Lambert
1963	13	13	Roger Craft
1964	16	9	Roger Craft
1965	15	10	Roger Craft
1966	7	17	Roger Craft
1967	14	11	Roger Craft
1968	10	15	Roger Craft
Totals	447	370	

MOREHEAD STATE COLLEGE

Morehead, Kentucky

Eagles — *Blue and Gold*

Yr.	W	L	Coach
1938	5	8	Ellis Johnson
1939	16	6	Ellis Johnson

Yr.	W	L	Coach
1940	8	14	Ellis Johnson
1941	10	6	Ellis Johnson
1942	12	10	Ellis Johnson
1943	—	—	
1944	12	5	Leonard Miller
1945	14	7	Leonard Miller
1946	13	9	Leonard Miller
1947	13	16	Ellis Johnson
1948	10	18	Ellis Johnson
1949	13	10	Ellis Johnson
1950	12	10	Ellis Johnson
1951	13	11	Ellis Johnson
1952	10	14	Ellis Johnson
1953	13	12	Ellis Johnson
1954	16	7	Robert Laughlin
1955	14	10	Robert Laughlin
1956	19	10	Robert Laughlin
1957	19	8	Robert Laughlin
1958	13	10	Robert Laughlin
1959	11	12	Robert Laughlin
1960	5	14	Robert Laughlin
1961	19	12	Robert Laughlin
1962	14	8	Robert Laughlin
1963	13	7	Robert Laughlin
1964	10	11	Robert Laughlin
1965	13	10	Robert Laughlin
1966	12	12	Bob Wright
1967	16	8	Bob Wright
1968	12	9	Bob Wright
Totals	380	304	

MURRAY STATE COLLEGE

Murray, Kentucky

Thoroughbreds			*Blue and Gold*
1938	27	4	Carlisle Cutchin
1939	13	8	Carlisle Cutchin
1940	14	9	Carlisle Cutchin
1941	25	5	Carlisle Cutchin
1942	18	4	Rice Mountjoy
1943	23	5	John Miller
1944	5	9	John Miller
1945	12	10	John Miller
1946	10	13	John Miller
1947	14	11	John Miller
1948	13	11	Carlisle Cutchin
1949	13	11	Harlan Hodges
1950	18	13	Harlan Hodges
1951	21	6	Harlan Hodges
1952	24	10	Harlan Hodges
1953	18	9	Harlan Hodges
1954	15	6	Harlan Hodges
1955	11	15	Rex Alexander
1956	15	10	Rex Alexander
1957	11	13	Rex Alexander
1958	8	16	Rex Alexander
1959	10	15	Cal Luther
1960	12	11	Cal Luther
1961	13	10	Cal Luther
1962	13	12	Cal Luther
1963	13	9	Cal Luther
1964	16	9	Cal Luther
1965	19	7	Cal Luther
1966	13	10	Cal Luther
1967	14	9	Cal Luther
1968	16	7	Cal Luther
Totals	467	297	

NAVY (U. S. N. A.)

Annapolis, Maryland

Midshipmen			*Navy Blue and Gold*
1938	11	3	John Wilson
1939	8	6	John Wilson
1940	3	11	John Wilson
1941	9	5	John Wilson
1942	8	6	John Wilson
1943	6	8	John Wilson
1944	10	4	John Wilson
1945	12	2	John Wilson
1946	12	3	John Wilson
1947	16	3	Ben Carnevale
1948	10	7	Ben Carnevale
1949	12	9	Ben Carnevale
1950	14	7	Ben Carnevale
1951	16	6	Ben Carnevale
1952	16	7	Ben Carnevale
1953	16	5	Ben Carnevale
1954	18	8	Ben Carnevale
1955	11	9	Ben Carnevale
1956	10	9	Ben Carnevale
1957	15	8	Ben Carnevale
1958	10	10	Ben Carnevale
1959	18	6	Ben Carnevale
1960	16	6	Ben Carnevale
1961	10	9	Ben Carnevale
1962	13	8	Ben Carnevale
1963	9	9	Ben Carnevale
1964	10	12	Ben Carnevale
1965	10	10	Ben Carnevale
1966	7	12	Ben Carnevale
1967	8	10	Dave Smalley
1968	9	11	Dave Smalley
Totals	353	229	

NEBRASKA, UNIVERSITY OF

Lincoln, Nebraska

Cornhuskers			*Scarlet and Cream*
1938	9	11	W. H. Browne
1939	7	13	W. H. Browne
1940	6	12	W. H. Browne
1941	8	10	A. J. Lewandowski
1942	6	13	A. J. Lewandowski
1943	6	10	A. J. Lewandowski
1944	2	13	A. J. Lewandowski
1945	2	17	A. J. Lewandowski
1946	7	13	L. F. Klein
1947	10	14	Harry Good
1948	11	13	Harry Good
1949	16	10	Harry Good
1950	16	7	Harry Good
1951	11	14	Harry Good
1952	7	17	Harry Good
1953	9	11	Harry Good
1954	8	13	Harry Good
1955	9	12	Gerard Bush
1956	7	16	Gerard Bush

Yr.	W	L	Coach
1957	11	12	Gerard Bush
1958	10	13	Gerard Bush
1959	12	13	Gerard Bush
1960	8	17	Gerard Bush
1961	10	14	Gerard Bush
1962	9	16	Gerard Bush
1963	6	19	Gerard Bush
1964	8	17	Gerard Bush
1965	10	15	Gerard Bush
1966	20	5	Joe Cipriano
1967	16	9	Joe Cipriano
1968	15	10	Joe Cipriano
Totals	292	399	

NEW HAMPSHIRE, UNIVERSITY OF

Durham, New Hampshire

Wildcats — *White and Blue*

Yr.	W	L	Coach
1938	12	6	Henry Swasey
1939	3	14	Henry Swasey
1940	5	10	Henry Swasey
1941	9	8	Henry Swasey
1942	4	15	Henry Swasey
1943	4	14	Henry Swasey
1944	—	—	
1945	—	—	
1946	3	7	Ed Stanczyk
1947	6	11	Ed Stanczyk
1948	5	12	Ed Stanczyk
1949	7	10	Ed Stanczyk
1950	4	11	Ed Stanczyk
1951	4	12	Andy Morradian
1952	11	9	Dale Hall
1953	8	10	Robert Kerr
1954	8	10	Robert Kerr
1955	4	14	Robert Kerr
1956	2	15	Robert Kerr
1957	2	15	Bill Olson
1958	10	12	Bill Olson
1959	9	14	Bill Olson
1960	9	14	Bill Olson
1961	6	18	Bill Olson
1962	3	20	Bill Olson
1963	7	17	Bill Olson
1964	8	15	Bill Olson
1965	2	19	Bill Olson
1966	3	21	Bill Olson
1967	10	12	F. William Haubrich
1968	1	22	F. William Haubrich
Totals	169	387	

NEW MEXICO, UNIVERSITY OF

Albuquerque, New Mexico

Lobos — *Cherry and Silver*

Yr.	W	L	Coach
1938	8	12	Roy Johnson
1939	4	19	Roy Johnson
1940	3	22	Roy Johnson
1941	5	18	Roy Johnson
1942	9	13	Willis Barnes
1943	3	11	Willis Barnes
1944	12	2	Willis Barnes
1945	15	2	Woodrow Clements
1946	16	9	Woodrow Clements
1947	11	8	Woodrow Clements
1948	14	15	Woodrow Clements
1949	9	11	Woodrow Clements
1950	5	19	Woodrow Clements
1951	13	11	Woodrow Clements
1952	6	19	Berl Huffman
1953	10	15	Woodrow Clements
1954	11	11	Woodrow Clements
1955	7	17	Woodrow Clements
1956	6	16	William Stockton
1957	5	21	William Stockton
1958	3	21	William Stockton
1959	3	19	Robert Sweeney
1960	6	19	Robert Sweeney
1961	6	17	Robert Sweeney
1962	6	20	Robert Sweeney
1963	16	9	Bob King
1964	23	6	Bob King
1965	19	8	Bob King
1966	16	8	Bob King
1967	19	8	Bob King
1968	23	5	Bob King
Totals	312	411	

NEW MEXICO STATE UNIVERSITY

Las Cruces, New Mexico

Aggies — *Crimson and White*

Yr.	W	L	Coach
1938	8	2	Jerry Hines
1939	16	0	Jerry Hines
1940	7	1	Jerry Hines
1941	11	3	Jerry Hines
1942	8	2	Julius Johnson
1943	7	6	Julius Johnson
1944	—	—	
1945	—	—	
1946	—	—	
1947	—	—	
1948	3	12	Raymond Curfman
1949	10	11	Raymond Curfman
1950	15	12	George McCarty
1951	16	11	George McCarty
1952	22	11	George McCarty
1953	7	14	George McCarty
1954	7	12	Presley Askew
1955	6	13	Presley Askew
1956	15	7	Presley Askew
1957	6	18	Presley Askew
1958	14	9	Presley Askew
1959	17	11	Presley Askew
1960	20	7	Presley Askew
1961	19	5	Presley Askew
1962	10	14	Presley Askew
1963	4	17	Presley Askew
1964	8	15	Presley Askew
1965	8	18	Presley Askew
1966	4	22	Jim McGregor
1967	15	11	Louis Henson
1968	23	6	Louis Henson
Totals	306	270	

Yr.	W	L	Coach

NEW YORK UNIVERSITY

New York, New York

Violets — *Violet and White*

Yr.	W	L	Coach
1938	16	8	Howard Cann
1939	11	11	Howard Cann
1940	18	1	Howard Cann
1941	13	6	Howard Cann
1942	12	7	Howard Cann
1943	16	6	Howard Cann
1944	7	7	Howard Cann
1945	14	7	Howard Cann
1946	19	3	Howard Cann
1947	12	9	Howard Cann
1948	22	4	Howard Cann
1949	12	8	Howard Cann
1950	8	11	Howard Cann
1951	12	4	Howard Cann
1952	17	8	Howard Cann
1953	9	11	Howard Cann
1954	9	9	Howard Cann
1955	7	13	Howard Cann
1956	10	8	Howard Cann
1957	8	13	Howard Cann
1958	10	11	Howard Cann
1959	15	8	Lou Rossini
1960	22	5	Lou Rossini
1961	12	11	Lou Rossini
1962	20	5	Lou Rossini
1963	18	5	Lou Rossini
1964	17	10	Lou Rossini
1965	16	10	Lou Rossini
1966	18	10	Lou Rossini
1967	10	16	Lou Rossini
1968	8	16	Lou Rossini
Totals	418	261	

NIAGARA UNIVERSITY

Niagara Falls, N. Y.

Purple Eagles — *Purple and White*

Yr.	W	L	Coach
1938	8	13	Taps Gallagher
1939	11	8	Taps Gallagher
1940	12	7	Taps Gallagher
1941	13	7	Taps Gallagher
1942	16	6	Taps Gallagher
1943	20	6	Taps Gallagher
1944	—	—	
1945	7	6	Edward Flynn
1946	11	8	Edward Flynn
1947	13	8	Taps Gallagher
1948	15	9	Taps Gallagher
1949	23	8	Taps Gallagher
1950	20	7	Taps Gallagher
1951	18	10	Taps Gallagher
1952	8	21	Taps Gallagher
1953	22	6	Taps Gallagher
1954	24	6	Taps Gallagher
1955	20	6	Taps Gallagher
1956	20	7	Taps Gallagher
1957	12	13	Taps Gallagher
1958	18	7	Taps Gallagher
1959	15	7	Taps Gallagher
1960	12	12	Taps Gallagher
1961	16	5	Taps Gallagher
1962	16	8	Taps Gallagher
1963	14	4	Taps Gallagher
1964	8	12	Taps Gallagher
1965	4	17	Taps Gallagher
1966	11	12	Jim Maloney
1967	12	13	Jim Maloney
1968	12	12	Jim Maloney
Totals	431	271	

NORTH CAROLINA, UNIVERSITY OF

Chapel Hill, North Carolina

Tar Heels — *Carolina Blue and White*

Yr.	W	L	Coach
1938	16	5	Walter Skidmore
1939	10	11	Walter Skidmore
1940	18	3	Bill Lange
1941	15	8	Bill Lange
1942	10	7	Bill Lange
1943	12	10	Bill Lange
1944	15	9	Bill Lange
1945	9	6	Ben Carnevale
1946	29	5	Ben Carnevale
1947	19	8	Tom Scott
1948	20	7	Tom Scott
1949	19	6	Tom Scott
1950	17	12	Tom Scott
1951	12	15	Tom Scott
1952	12	15	Tom Scott
1953	17	10	Frank McGuire
1954	11	10	Frank McGuire
1955	10	11	Frank McGuire
1956	18	5	Frank McGuire
1957	32	0	Frank McGuire
1958	19	7	Frank McGuire
1959	20	5	Frank McGuire
1960	18	6	Frank McGuire
1961	19	4	Frank McGuire
1962	8	9	Dean Smith
1963	15	6	Dean Smith
1964	12	12	Dean Smith
1965	15	9	Dean Smith
1966	16	11	Dean Smith
1967	26	6	Dean Smith
1968	28	4	Dean Smith
Totals	517	242	

NORTH CAROLINA STATE UNIVERSITY

Raleigh, North Carolina

Wolfpack — *Red and White*

Yr.	W	L	Coach
1938	15	5	R. R. Sermon
1939	11	6	R. R. Sermon
1940	6	11	R. R. Sermon
1941	6	8	Bob Warren
1942	12	5	Bob Warren
1943	9	7	Leroy Jay
1944	3	15	Leroy Jay
1945	8	11	Leroy Jay
1946	7	10	Leroy Jay
1947	26	5	Everett Case
1948	29	3	Everett Case
1949	25	8	Everett Case
1950	27	6	Everett Case

Yr.	W	L	Coach
1951	30	7	Everett Case
1952	24	10	Everett Case
1953	26	6	Everett Case
1954	26	7	Everett Case
1955	28	4	Everett Case
1956	24	4	Everett Case
1957	15	11	Everett Case
1958	18	6	Everett Case
1959	22	4	Everett Case
1960	11	15	Everett Case
1961	16	9	Everett Case
1962	11	6	Everett Case
1963	10	11	Everett Case
1964	8	11	Everett Case
1965	21	5	Press Maravich
1966	18	9	Press Maravich
1967	7	19	Norman Sloan
1968	16	10	Norman Sloan
Totals	515	254	

NORTHERN ILLINOIS UNIVERSITY

DeKalb, Illinois

Huskies — *Cardinal and Black*

Yr.	W	L	Coach
1939	12	6	George Evans
1940	12	10	George Evans
1941	16	3	Ralph McKinzie
1942	11	9	Ralph McKinzie
1943	9	8	Ralph McKinzie
1944	7	7	Ralph McKinzie
1945	15	1	Ralph McKinzie
1946	11	8	Ralph McKinzie
1947	11	8	Ralph McKinzie
1948	14	12	Ralph McKinzie
1949	10	10	Gene Fekete
1950	4	17	Gil Wilson
1951	12	7	Gil Hertz
1952	6	16	Gil Hertz
1953	13	7	Gil Hertz
1954	5	14	Gil Hertz
1955	9	10	Bill Healey
1956	5	14	Bill Healey
1957	7	13	Bill Healey
1958	9	11	Bill Healey
1959	11	11	Bill Healey
1960	14	7	Bill Healey
1961	14	8	Bill Healey
1962	11	10	Bill Healey
1963	15	8	Bill Healey
1964	11	11	Ev Cochran
1965	12	10	Ev Cochran
1966	10	13	Ev Cochran
1967	8	12	Tom Jorgensen
1968	10	14	Tom Jorgensen
Totals	314	295	

NORTH TEXAS STATE UNIVERSITY

Denton, Texas

Eagles — *Green and White*

Yr.	W	L	Coach
1938	15	8	Pete Shands
1939	13	11	Pete Shands
1940	10	16	Pete Shands
1941	6	14	Pete Shands
1942	13	7	Daniel Yarbo
1943	15	15	Lloyd Russell
1944	—	—	
1945	—	—	
1946	—	—	
1947	13	10	Pete Shands
1948	16	9	Pete Shands
1949	10	13	Pete Shands
1950	9	17	Pete Shands
1951	13	13	Pete Shands
1952	15	8	Pete Shands
1953	20	5	Pete Shands
1954	19	9	Pete Shands
1955	8	16	Pete Shands
1956	9	13	Pete Shands
1957	3	20	Pete Shands
1958	3	18	Pete Shands
1959	6	18	Pete Shands
1960	7	19	Charles Johnson
1961	2	22	Charles Johnson
1962	3	23	Charles Johnson
1963	10	14	Charles Johnson
1964	7	17	Charles Johnson
1965	7	19	Charles Johnson
1966	5	20	Dan Spike
1967	12	13	Dan Spike
1968	8	18	Dan Spike
Totals	277	405	

NORTHWESTERN UNIVERSITY

Evanston, Illinois

Wildcats — *Purple and White*

Yr.	W	L	Coach
1938	10	10	Dutch Lonborg
1939	7	13	Dutch Lonborg
1940	13	7	Dutch Lonborg
1941	7	11	Dutch Lonborg
1942	8	13	Dutch Lonborg
1943	8	9	Dutch Lonborg
1944	12	7	Dutch Lonborg
1945	7	12	Dutch Lonborg
1946	15	5	Dutch Lonborg
1947	15	5	Dutch Lonborg
1948	6	14	Dutch Lonborg
1949	5	16	Dutch Lonborg
1950	10	12	Dutch Lonborg
1951	12	10	Harold Olson
1952	7	15	Harold Olson
1953	6	16	Waldo Fisher
1954	9	13	Waldo Fisher
1955	12	10	Waldo Fisher
1956	2	20	Waldo Fisher
1957	6	16	Waldo Fisher
1958	13	9	William Rohr
1959	15	7	William Rohr
1960	11	12	William Rohr
1961	10	12	William Rohr
1962	8	15	William Rohr
1963	9	15	William Rohr
1964	8	13	Larry Glass
1965	7	17	Larry Glass
1966	12	12	Larry Glass
1967	11	11	Larry Glass
1968	13	10	Larry Glass
Totals	294	367	

Yr.	W	L	Coach

NOTRE DAME, UNIVERSITY OF
South Bend, Indiana

Fighting Irish — *Gold and Blue*

Yr.	W	L	Coach
1938	20	3	George Koegan
1939	15	6	George Koegan
1940	15	6	George Koegan
1941	17	5	George Koegan
1942	16	6	George Koegan
1943	18	2	Koegan, Ed Krause
1944	10	9	Koegan, Ed Krause
1945	15	5	Clem Crowe
1946	17	4	Elmer Ripley
1947	20	4	Ed "Moose" Krause
1948	17	7	Ed "Moose" Krause
1949	17	7	Ed "Moose" Krause
1950	15	9	Ed "Moose" Krause
1951	13	11	Ed "Moose" Krause
1952	16	10	John Jordan
1953	19	5	John Jordan
1954	22	3	John Jordan
1955	14	10	John Jordan
1956	9	15	John Jordan
1957	20	8	John Jordan
1958	24	5	John Jordan
1959	12	13	John Jordan
1960	17	9	John Jordan
1961	12	14	John Jordan
1962	8	15	John Jordan
1963	17	9	John Jordan
1964	10	14	John Jordan
1965	15	12	Johnny Dee
1966	5	20	Johnny Dee
1967	14	12	Johnny Dee
1968	21	9	Johnny Dee
Totals	480	267	

OHIO STATE UNIVERSITY
Columbus, Ohio

Buckeyes — *Scarlet and Gray*

Yr.	W	L	Coach
1938	12	8	Harold Olsen
1939	16	7	Harold Olsen
1940	13	7	Harold Olsen
1941	10	10	Harold Olsen
1942	6	14	Harold Olsen
1943	7	10	Harold Olsen
1944	14	7	Harold Olsen
1945	15	5	Harold Olsen
1946	16	5	Harold Olsen
1947	7	13	Tippy Dye
1948	10	10	Tippy Dye
1949	14	7	Tippy Dye
1950	22	4	Tippy Dye
1951	6	16	Floyd Stahl
1952	8	14	Floyd Stahl
1953	10	12	Floyd Stahl
1954	11	11	Floyd Stahl
1955	10	12	Floyd Stahl
1956	16	6	Floyd Stahl
1957	14	8	Floyd Stahl
1958	9	13	Floyd Stahl
1959	11	11	Fred Taylor
1960	25	3	Fred Taylor
1961	27	1	Fred Taylor
1962	26	2	Fred Taylor
1963	20	4	Fred Taylor
1964	16	8	Fred Taylor
1965	12	12	Fred Taylor
1966	11	13	Fred Taylor
1967	13	11	Fred Taylor
1968	21	8	Fred Taylor
Totals	428	272	

OHIO UNIVERSITY
Athens, Ohio

Bobcats — *Green and White*

Yr.	W	L	Coach
1938	12	8	Brandon Glover
1939	12	8	William Trautwein
1940	19	6	William Trautwein
1941	18	4	William Trautwein
1942	12	9	William Trautwein
1943	11	7	William Trautwein
1944	9	7	William Trautwein
1945	10	9	William Trautwein
1946	15	5	William Trautwein
1947	13	10	William Trautwein
1948	10	10	William Trautwein
1949	6	16	William Trautwein
1950	6	14	James Snyder
1951	13	11	James Snyder
1952	12	12	James Snyder
1953	9	13	James Snyder
1954	12	10	James Snyder
1955	16	5	James Snyder
1956	13	11	James Snyder
1957	15	8	James Snyder
1958	16	8	James Snyder
1959	14	10	James Snyder
1960	17	8	James Snyder
1961	17	7	James Snyder
1962	13	10	James Snyder
1963	12	13	James Snyder
1964	21	6	James Snyder
1965	19	7	James Snyder
1966	13	10	James Snyder
1967	8	15	James Snyder
1968	7	16	James Snyder
Totals	400	293	

OKLAHOMA CITY UNIVERSITY
Oklahoma City, Oklahoma

Chiefs — *Blue and White*

Yr.	W	L	Coach
1938	7	15	Melvin Binford
1939	10	8	Melvin Binford
1940	6	13	Faye Ferguson
1941	7	11	Faye Ferguson
1942	5	11	Merle Rousey
1943	—	—	
1944	—	—	
1945	—	—	
1946	—	—	
1947	7	9	Bo Sherman
1948	18	13	Doyle Parrack
1949	20	6	Doyle Parrack
1950	19	5	Doyle Parrack
1951	16	14	Doyle Parrack

Yr.	W	L	Coach
1952	18	9	Doyle Parrack
1953	18	6	Doyle Parrack
1954	18	7	Doyle Parrack
1955	9	18	Doyle Parrack
1956	20	7	Abe Lemons
1957	9	19	Abe Lemons
1958	14	12	Abe Lemons
1959	20	7	Abe Lemons
1960	12	13	Abe Lemons
1961	14	12	Abe Lemons
1962	14	12	Abe Lemons
1963	19	10	Abe Lemons
1964	15	11	Abe Lemons
1965	21	10	Abe Lemons
1966	24	5	Abe Lemons
1967	16	10	Abe Lemons
1968	20	7	Abe Lemons
Totals	396	280	

OKLAHOMA, UNIVERSITY OF

Norman, Oklahoma

Sooners — *Red and White*

Yr.	W	L	Coach
1938	14	4	Hugh McDermott
1939	12	9	Bruce Drake
1940	12	7	Bruce Drake
1941	6	12	Bruce Drake
1942	11	7	Bruce Drake
1943	18	9	Bruce Drake
1944	15	8	Bruce Drake
1945	12	13	Bruce Drake
1946	11	10	Bruce Drake
1947	24	7	Bruce Drake
1948	13	9	Bruce Drake
1949	14	9	Bruce Drake
1950	12	10	Bruce Drake
1951	14	10	Bruce Drake
1952	7	17	Bruce Drake
1953	8	13	Bruce Drake
1954	8	13	Bruce Drake
1955	3	18	Bruce Drake
1956	4	19	Doyle Parrack
1957	8	15	Doyle Parrack
1958	13	10	Doyle Parrack
1959	15	10	Doyle Parrack
1960	14	11	Doyle Parrack
1961	10	15	Doyle Parrack
1962	7	17	Doyle Parrack
1963	12	13	Bob Stevens
1964	7	18	Bob Stevens
1965	8	17	Bob Stevens
1966	11	14	Bob Stevens
1967	8	17	Bob Stevens
1968	13	13	John McLeod
Totals	344	374	

OKLAHOMA STATE UNIVERSITY

Stillwater, Oklahoma

Cowboys — *Orange and Black*

Yr.	W	L	Coach
1938	25	3	Hank Iba
1939	19	8	Hank Iba
1940	26	3	Hank Iba
1941	18	7	Hank Iba
1942	20	6	Hank Iba
1943	14	10	Hank Iba
1944	27	6	Hank Iba
1945	27	4	Hank Iba
1946	31	2	Hank Iba
1947	24	8	Hank Iba
1948	27	4	Hank Iba
1949	23	5	Hank Iba
1950	18	9	Hank Iba
1951	29	6	Hank Iba
1952	19	8	Hank Iba
1953	23	7	Hank Iba
1954	24	5	Hank Iba
1955	12	13	Hank Iba
1956	18	9	Hank Iba
1957	17	9	Hank Iba
1958	21	8	Hank Iba
1959	11	14	Hank Iba
1960	10	15	Hank Iba
1961	14	11	Hank Iba
1962	14	11	Hank Iba
1963	16	9	Hank Iba
1964	15	10	Hank Iba
1965	20	7	Hank Iba
1966	4	21	Hank Iba
1967	7	18	Hank Iba
1968	10	16	Hank Iba
Totals	583	272	

OREGON, UNIVERSITY OF

Eugene, Oregon

Webfoots — *Yellow and Green*

Yr.	W	L	Coach
1938	25	8	Howard Hobson
1939	29	5	Howard Hobson
1940	19	12	Howard Hobson
1941	18	18	Howard Hobson
1942	12	15	Howard Hobson
1943	19	10	Howard Hobson
1944	16	10	Howard Hobson
1945	30	13	Howard Hobson
1946	16	17	Howard Hobson
1947	18	9	Howard Hobson
1948	18	11	John Warren
1949	12	18	John Warren
1950	9	19	John Warren
1951	18	13	John Warren
1952	14	16	Bill Borcher
1953	14	14	Bill Borcher
1954	17	10	Bill Borcher
1955	13	13	Bill Borcher
1956	11	15	Bill Borcher
1957	4	21	Steve Belko
1958	13	11	Steve Belko
1959	9	16	Steve Belko
1960	19	10	Steve Belko
1961	15	12	Steve Belko
1962	9	17	Steve Belko
1963	11	15	Steve Belko
1964	14	12	Steve Belko
1965	9	17	Steve Belko
1966	13	13	Steve Belko
1967	9	17	Steve Belko
1968	7	19	Steve Belko
Totals	460	426	

Yr.	W	L	Coach

OREGON STATE UNIVERSITY

Corvallis, Oregon

Beavers *Orange and Black*

Yr.	W	L	Coach
1938	17	16	Slats Gill
1939	13	11	Slats Gill
1940	27	11	Slats Gill
1941	19	9	Slats Gill
1942	18	9	Slats Gill
1943	19	9	Slats Gill
1944	8	16	Slats Gill
1945	20	8	Slats Gill
1946	13	11	Slats Gill
1947	28	5	Slats Gill
1948	21	13	Slats Gill
1949	24	12	Slats Gill
1950	13	14	Slats Gill
1951	14	18	Slats Gill
1952	9	19	Slats Gill
1953	11	18	Slats Gill
1954	19	10	Slats Gill
1955	22	8	Slats Gill
1956	8	18	Slats Gill
1957	11	15	Slats Gill
1958	20	6	Slats Gill
1959	13	13	Slats Gill
1960	15	11	Gill, Paul Valenti
1961	14	12	Slats Gill
1962	24	5	Slats Gill
1963	22	9	Slats Gill
1964	25	4	Slats Gill
1965	16	10	Paul Valenti
1966	21	7	Paul Valenti
1967	14	14	Paul Valenti
1968	12	13	Paul Valenti
Totals	530	354	

PACIFIC, UNIVERSITY OF THE

Stockton, California

Tigers *Orange and Black*

Yr.	W	L	Coach
1938	9	11	Ralph Francis
1939	7	13	Ralph Francis
1940	—	—	
1941	12	6	Ralph Francis
1942	—	—	
1943	—	—	
1944	—	—	
1945	17	6	Chris Jeldsen
1946	12	13	Chris Jeldsen
1947	16	8	Chris Jeldsen
1948	9	14	Chris Jeldsen
1949	12	13	Chris Jeldsen
1950	7	15	Chris Jeldsen
1951	19	11	Chris Jeldsen
1952	10	14	Chris Jeldsen
1953	3	20	Van Sweet
1954	9	17	Van Sweet
1955	11	15	Van Sweet
1956	15	11	Van Sweet
1957	9	17	Van Sweet
1958	9	15	Van Sweet
1959	11	15	Van Sweet
1960	9	17	Van Sweet
1961	5	21	Van Sweet
1962	9	15	Van Sweet
1963	4	22	Van Sweet
1964	15	11	Dick Edwards
1965	13	12	Dick Edwards
1966	22	6	Dick Edwards
1967	24	4	Dick Edwards
1968	17	9	Dick Edwards
Totals	315	351	

PENNSYLVANIA, UNIVERSITY OF

Philadelphia, Pennsylvania

Quakers *Red and Blue*

Yr.	W	L	Coach
1938	8	10	Lon Jourdet
1939	7	11	Lon Jourdet
1940	5	13	Lon Jourdet
1941	5	12	Lon Jourdet
1942	9	9	Lon Jourdet
1943	14	7	Lon Jourdet
1944	10	4	Don Kellett
1945	12	5	Don Kellett
1946	7	10	Robert Dougherty
1947	14	8	Don Kellett
1948	10	14	Don Kellett
1949	15	8	Howie Dallmar
1950	11	14	Howie Dallmar
1951	19	8	Howie Dallmar
1952	21	8	Howie Dallmar
1953	22	5	Howie Dallmar
1954	17	8	Howie Dallmar
1955	19	6	Ray Stanley
1956	12	13	Ray Stanley
1957	7	19	Jack McCloskey
1958	13	12	Jack McCloskey
1959	12	14	Jack McCloskey
1960	14	11	Jack McCloskey
1961	16	9	Jack McCloskey
1962	17	8	Jack McCloskey
1963	19	6	Jack McCloskey
1964	14	10	Jack McCloskey
1965	15	10	Jack McCloskey
1966	19	6	Jack McCloskey
1967	11	14	Dick Harter
1968	9	17	Dick Harter
Totals	403	309	

PENNSYLVANIA STATE UNIVERSITY

University Park, Pennsylvania

Nittany Lions *Blue and White*

Yr.	W	L	Coach
1938	13	5	John Lawther
1939	13	10	John Lawther
1940	15	8	John Lawther
1941	15	5	John Lawther
1942	18	3	John Lawther
1943	15	4	John Lawther
1944	8	7	John Lawther
1945	10	7	John Lawther
1946	7	9	John Lawther
1947	10	8	John Lawther
1948	9	10	John Lawther
1949	7	10	John Lawther
1950	13	10	Elmer Gross

Yr.	W	L	Coach
1951	14	9	Elmer Gross
1952	20	6	Elmer Gross
1953	15	9	Elmer Gross
1954	18	6	Elmer Gross
1955	18	10	John Egli
1956	12	14	John Egli
1957	15	10	John Egli
1958	8	11	John Egli
1959	11	9	John Egli
1960	11	11	John Egli
1961	11	13	John Egli
1962	12	11	John Egli
1963	15	5	John Egli
1964	17	8	John Egli
1965	20	4	John Egli
1966	18	6	John Egli
1967	10	14	John Egli
1968	10	10	John Egli
Totals	408	262	

PEPPERDINE COLLEGE
Los Angeles, California

Waves			*Blue and Orange*
1939	17	12	Dr. Wade Ruby
1940	14	12	Dr. Wade Ruby
1941	11	13	Dr. Wade Ruby
1942	14	6	Dr. Wade Ruby
1943	23	8	Dr. Wade Ruby
1944	21	13	Dr. Wade Ruby
1945	24	12	Dr. Wade Ruby
1946	26	9	Dr. Wade Ruby
1947	14	13	Dr. Wade Ruby
1948	22	11	Dr. Wade Ruby
1949	19	11	R. L. "Duck" Dowell
1950	21	12	R. L. "Duck" Dowell
1951	25	8	R. L. "Duck" Dowell
1952	20	5	R. L. "Duck" Dowell
1953	18	8	R. L. "Duck" Dowell
1954	14	10	R. L. "Duck" Dowell
1955	16	9	R. L. "Duck" Dowell
1956	2	24	R. L. "Duck" Dowell
1957	7	18	R. L. "Duck" Dowell
1958	15	11	R. L. "Duck" Dowell
1959	16	8	R. L. "Duck" Dowell
1960	14	11	R. L. "Duck" Dowell
1961	9	16	R. L. "Duck" Dowell
1962	20	7	R. L. "Duck" Dowell
1963	14	11	R. L. "Duck" Dowell
1964	6	19	R. L. "Duck" Dowell
1965	6	19	R. L. "Duck" Dowell
1966	2	24	R. L. "Duck" Dowell
1967	9	17	R. L. "Duck" Dowell
1968	9	17	R. L. "Duck" Dowell
Totals	448	374	

PITTSBURGH, UNIVERSITY OF
Pittsburgh, Pennsylvania

Panthers			*Blue and Gold*
1938	9	12	Dr. Harold Carlson
1939	10	8	Dr. Harold Carlson
1940	8	9	Dr. Harold Carlson
1941	13	6	Dr. Harold Carlson
1942	5	10	Dr. Harold Carlson

Yr.	W	L	Coach
1943	10	5	Dr. Harold Carlson
1944	7	7	Dr. Harold Carlson
1945	8	4	Dr. Harold Carlson
1946	7	7	Dr. Harold Carlson
1947	8	10	Dr. Harold Carlson
1948	10	11	Dr. Harold Carlson
1949	12	13	Dr. Harold Carlson
1950	4	14	Dr. Harold Carlson
1951	9	17	Dr. Harold Carlson
1952	10	12	Dr. Harold Carlson
1953	12	11	Dr. Harold Carlson
1954	9	14	Bob Timmons
1955	10	16	Bob Timmons
1956	15	10	Bob Timmons
1957	16	11	Bob Timmons
1958	18	7	Bob Timmons
1959	10	14	Bob Timmons
1960	11	14	Bob Timmons
1961	12	11	Bob Timmons
1962	12	11	Bob Timmons
1963	19	6	Bob Timmons
1964	16	7	Bob Timmons
1965	7	16	Bob Timmons
1966	5	17	Bob Timmons
1967	6	19	Bob Timmons
1968	7	15	Bob Timmons
Totals	315	344	

PORTLAND, UNIVERSITY OF
Portland, Oregon

Pilots			*Purple and White*
1938	8	10	Edwin Fitzpatrick
1939	13	9	Edwin Fitzpatrick
1940	16	4	Edwin Fitzpatrick
1941	15	9	Edwin Fitzpatrick
1942	14	7	Edwin Fitzpatrick
1943	16	8	R. Mathews
1944	—	—	
1945	—	—	
1946	8	7	Leonard Yandle
1947	13	18	Mush Torson
1948	15	19	Mush Torson
1949	22	11	Mush Torson
1950	19	12	Mush Torson
1951	23	6	Mush Torson
1952	24	11	Mush Torson
1953	16	14	Mush Torson
1954	9	19	Mush Torson
1955	9	13	A. McLarney, M. Tichy
1956	20	8	Al Negratti
1957	18	12	Al Negratti
1958	18	11	Al Negratti
1959	19	8	Al Negratti
1960	11	15	Al Negratti
1961	16	9	Al Negratti
1962	8	18	Al Negratti
1963	8	18	Al Negratti
1964	17	9	Al Negratti
1965	12	13	Al Negratti
1966	6	19	Al Negratti
1967	10	16	Al Negratti
1968	5	21	Bill Turner
Totals	408	354	

Yr.	W	L	Coach

PRINCETON UNIVERSITY
Princeton, New Jersey

Tigers — *Orange and Black*

Yr.	W	L	Coach
1938	10	10	Ken Fairman
1939	10	9	Franklin Cappon
1940	14	8	Franklin Cappon
1941	10	13	Franklin Cappon
1942	16	5	Franklin Cappon
1943	14	6	Cappon & William Logan
1944	6	12	William Logan
1945	7	12	Wm. Logan, L. Hettinger
1946	7	12	Wes Fesler
1947	7	16	Franklin Cappon
1948	12	11	Franklin Cappon
1949	13	9	Franklin Cappon
1950	14	9	Franklin Cappon
1951	15	7	Franklin Cappon
1952	16	11	Franklin Cappon
1953	9	14	Franklin Cappon
1954	16	9	Franklin Cappon
1955	13	12	Franklin Cappon
1956	11	13	Franklin Cappon
1957	14	9	Franklin Cappon
1958	15	8	Franklin Cappon
1959	19	5	Franklin Cappon
1960	15	9	Franklin Cappon
1961	18	8	Cappon, J. L. McCandless
1962	13	10	J. L. McCandless
1963	19	6	Bill van Breda Kolff
1964	20	9	Bill van Breda Kolff
1965	23	6	Bill van Breda Kolff
1966	16	7	Bill van Breda Kolff
1967	25	3	Bill van Breda Kolff
1968	20	6	Pete Carrill
Totals	437	284	

PROVIDENCE COLLEGE
Providence, Rhode Island

Friars — *Black and White*

Yr.	W	L	Coach
1938	7	9	Albert McClellan
1939	4	7	Edward Crotty
1940	5	9	Edward Crotty
1941	11	6	Edward Crotty
1942	13	7	Edward Crotty
1943	15	5	Edward Crotty
1944	—	—	
1945	5	7	Edward Crotty
1946	5	12	Edward Crotty
1947	8	11	Lawrence Drew
1948	10	10	Lawrence Drew
1949	7	19	Lawrence Drew
1950	14	9	James Cuddy
1951	14	10	James Cuddy
1952	14	9	James Cuddy
1953	11	11	James Cuddy
1954	13	13	James Cuddy
1955	9	12	James Cuddy
1956	14	8	Joe Mullaney
1957	15	9	Joe Mullaney
1958	18	6	Joe Mullaney
1959	20	7	Joe Mullaney
1960	24	5	Joe Mullaney
1961	24	5	Joe Mullaney
1962	20	6	Joe Mullaney
1963	24	4	Joe Mullaney
1964	20	6	Joe Mullaney
1965	24	2	Joe Mullaney
1966	22	5	Joe Mullaney
1967	21	7	Joe Mullaney
1968	11	14	Joe Mullaney
Totals	422	250	

PURDUE UNIVERSITY
Lafayette, Indiana

Boilermakers — *Old Gold and Black*

Yr.	W	L	Coach
1938	18	2	Ward "Piggy" Lambert
1939	12	7	Ward "Piggy" Lambert
1940	16	4	Ward "Piggy" Lambert
1941	13	7	Ward "Piggy" Lambert
1942	14	7	Ward "Piggy" Lambert
1943	9	11	Ward "Piggy" Lambert
1944	11	10	Ward "Piggy" Lambert
1945	9	11	Ward "Piggy" Lambert
1946	10	11	Lambert, Mel Taube
1947	9	11	Mel Taube
1948	11	9	Mel Taube
1949	13	9	Mel Taube
1950	9	13	Mel Taube
1951	8	14	Ray Eddy
1952	8	14	Ray Eddy
1953	4	18	Ray Eddy
1954	9	13	Ray Eddy
1955	12	10	Ray Eddy
1956	16	6	Ray Eddy
1957	15	7	Ray Eddy
1958	14	8	Ray Eddy
1959	15	7	Ray Eddy
1960	11	12	Ray Eddy
1961	16	7	Ray Eddy
1962	17	7	Ray Eddy
1963	7	17	Ray Eddy
1964	12	12	Ray Eddy
1965	12	12	Ray Eddy
1966	8	16	George King
1967	15	9	George King
1968	15	9	George King
Totals	368	310	

RHODE ISLAND, UNIVERSITY OF
Kingston, Rhode Island

Rams — *Blue and White*

Yr.	W	L	Coach
1938	19	2	Frank Keaney
1939	17	4	Frank Keaney
1940	19	3	Frank Keaney
1941	21	4	Frank Keaney
1942	18	4	Frank Keaney
1943	16	3	Frank Keaney
1944	14	6	Frank Keaney
1945	20	5	Frank Keaney
1946	21	3	Frank Keaney
1947	17	3	Frank Keaney
1948	17	6	Frank Keaney
1949	16	6	Robert Haire
1950	18	8	Robert Haire
1951	13	15	Robert Haire

Yr.	W	L	Coach
1952	10	13	Robert Haire
1953	13	10	Jack Guy
1954	8	14	Jack Guy
1955	17	10	Jack Guy
1956	11	14	Jack Guy
1957	11	11	Jack Guy
1958	4	17	Ernie Calverley
1959	8	12	Ernie Calverley
1960	12	14	Ernie Calverley
1961	18	9	Ernie Calverley
1962	14	12	Ernie Calverley
1963	15	11	Ernie Calverley
1964	19	8	Ernie Calverley
1965	15	11	Ernie Calverley
1966	20	8	Ernie Calverley
1967	14	12	Ernie Calverley
1968	15	11	Ernie Calverley
Totals	470	269	

RICE UNIVERSITY

Houston, Texas

Owls			*Blue and Gray*
1938	2	10	James Kitts
1939	12	12	James Kitts
1940	21	3	Buster Brannon
1941	18	6	Buster Brannon
1942	22	5	Buster Brannon
1943	17	9	Joe Davis
1944	15	5	Joe Davis
1945	20	1	Joe Davis
1946	10	11	Buster Brannon
1947	7	17	Joe Davis
1948	10	14	Jess Neely
1949	13	11	Don Suman
1950	8	15	Don Suman
1951	8	15	Don Suman
1952	9	15	Don Suman
1953	15	6	Don Suman
1954	23	5	Don Suman
1955	10	12	Don Suman
1956	19	5	Don Suman
1957	16	8	Don Suman
1958	13	11	Don Suman
1959	11	13	Don Suman
1960	4	20	John Frankie
1961	11	12	John Frankie
1962	12	11	John Frankie
1963	12	11	John Frankie
1964	15	9	George Carlisle
1965	2	22	George Carlisle
1966	1	22	George Carlisle
1967	7	17	Don Knodel
1968	8	16	Don Knodel
Totals	371	349	

RICHMOND, UNIVERSITY OF

Richmond, Virginia

Spiders			*Red and Blue*
1938	15	5	Malcolm U. Pitt
1939	10	10	Malcolm U. Pitt
1940	11	6	Malcolm U. Pitt
1941	11	10	Malcolm U. Pitt
1942	9	9	Malcolm U. Pitt
1943	11	5	Malcolm U. Pitt
1944	7	6	Malcolm U. Pitt
1945	3	4	Malcolm U. Pitt
1946	8	12	Malcolm U. Pitt
1947	17	9	Malcolm U. Pitt
1948	8	14	Malcolm U. Pitt
1949	8	15	Malcolm U. Pitt
1950	8	16	Malcolm U. Pitt
1951	7	14	Malcolm U. Pitt
1952	7	15	Malcolm U. Pitt
1953	20	7	H. Lester Hooker, Jr.
1954	23	8	H. Lester Hooker, Jr.
1955	19	9	H. Lester Hooker, Jr.
1956	16	13	H. Lester Hooker, Jr.
1957	15	11	H. Lester Hooker, Jr.
1958	14	12	H. Lester Hooker, Jr.
1959	11	11	H. Lester Hooker, Jr.
1960	7	18	H. Lester Hooker, Jr.
1961	9	14	H. Lester Hooker, Jr.
1962	6	21	H. Lester Hooker, Jr.
1963	7	18	H. Lester Hooker, Jr.
1964	6	16	Lewis Mills
1965	10	16	Lewis Mills
1966	12	13	Lewis Mills
1967	11	12	Lewis Mills
1968	12	13	Lewis Mills
Totals	338	362	

RIDER COLLEGE

Trenton, New Jersey

Broncs, Roughriders			*Purple and Gold*
1938	9	7	Frank Donlon
1939	10	6	Frank Donlon
1940	12	5	Frank Donlon
1941	10	7	Rex Ellis
1942	10	13	Rex Ellis
1943	13	16	Tom Leyden
1944	3	12	Frank Donlon
1945	5	12	Frank Donlon
1946	11	7	Frank Donlon
1947	13	12	Thomas Leyden
1948	14	6	Thomas Leyden
1949	14	9	Thomas Leyden
1950	11	9	Thomas Leyden
1951	6	13	Thomas Leyden
1952	9	5	Thomas Leyden
1953	9	10	Thomas Leyden
1954	12	12	Thomas Leyden
1955	9	15	Thomas Leyden
1956	16	7	Thomas Leyden
1957	20	7	Thomas Leyden
1958	17	8	Thomas Leyden
1959	12	14	Thomas Leyden
1960	12	14	Thomas Leyden
1961	13	12	Glenn Leach
1962	12	13	Glenn Leach
1963	20	8	Robert Greenwood
1964	15	10	Robert Greenwood
1965	13	11	Robert Greenwood
1966	16	9	Richard Harter
1967	11	12	John Carpenter
1968	9	15	John Carpenter
Totals	366	316	

Yr.	W	L	Coach

RUTGERS UNIVERSITY

New Brunswick, New Jersey

Scarlet Knights			*Scarlet*
1938	11	4	Frank Hill
1939	8	6	Frank Hill
1940	5	14	Frank Hill
1941	5	14	Frank Hill
1942	8	12	Frank Hill
1943	7	9	Frank Hill
1944	—	—	
1945	10	3	Thomas Kenneally
1946	13	7	Donald White
1947	7	12	Donald White
1948	14	9	Donald White
1949	14	12	Donald White
1950	13	15	Donald White
1951	7	14	Donald White
1952	6	13	Donald White
1953	8	13	Donald White
1954	11	13	Donald White
1955	2	22	Donald White
1956	3	15	Donald White
1957	8	15	Warren Harris
1958	7	15	Warren Harris
1959	9	15	Warren Harris
1960	11	14	Anthony Kuolt
1961	11	10	Anthony Kuolt
1962	10	13	Anthony Kuolt
1963	7	16	Donald White
1964	5	17	William Foster
1965	12	12	William Foster
1966	17	7	William Foster
1967	22	7	William Foster
1968	14	10	William Foster
Totals	285	358	

ST. BONAVENTURE UNIVERSITY

St. Bonaventure, New York

Indians			*Brown and White*
1938	9	0	Carroll Reilly
1939	10	7	Carroll Reilly
1940	11	6	Carroll Reilly
1941	12	5	Carroll Reilly
1942	12	8	Carroll Reilly
1943	8	9	Carroll Reilly
1944	—	—	
1945	3	7	Rev. Anselm Krieger
1946	12	3	Rev. Anselm Krieger
1947	10	11	Harry Singleton
1948	12	10	Edward Melvin
1949	18	8	Edward Melvin
1950	17	5	Edward Melvin
1951	19	6	Edward Melvin
1952	21	6	Edward Melvin
1953	11	11	Edward Melvin
1954	12	11	Edward Donovan
1955	13	10	Edward Donovan
1956	11	12	Edward Donovan
1957	17	7	Edward Donovan
1958	21	5	Edward Donovan
1959	20	3	Edward Donovan
1960	21	5	Edward Donovan
1961	24	4	Edward Donovan
1962	14	7	Larry Weise
1963	13	12	Larry Weise
1964	16	8	Larry Weise
1965	15	8	Larry Weise
1966	16	7	Larry Weise
1967	13	9	Larry Weise
1968	23	2	Larry Weise
Totals	434	212	

ST. FRANCIS COLLEGE

Brooklyn, N. Y.

Terriers			*Red and Blue*
1938	15	8	Rody Cooney
1939	16	7	Rody Cooney
1940	14	5	Rody Cooney
1941	10	9	Rody Cooney
1942	17	2	Joseph Brennan
1943	14	7	Joseph Brennan
1944	11	6	Joseph Brennan
1945	10	9	Joseph Brennan
1946	13	6	Joseph Brennan
1947	15	7	Joseph Brennan
1948	16	9	Joseph Brennan
1949	21	12	Daniel Lynch
1950	8	19	Daniel Lynch
1951	19	11	Daniel Lynch
1952	20	8	Daniel Lynch
1953	20	7	Daniel Lynch
1954	22	5	Daniel Lynch
1955	21	8	Daniel Lynch
1956	21	4	Daniel Lynch
1957	12	14	Daniel Lynch
1958	14	9	Daniel Lynch
1959	5	18	Daniel Lynch
1960	13	8	Daniel Lynch
1961	10	10	Daniel Lynch
1962	8	15	Daniel Lynch
1963	16	7	Daniel Lynch
1964	9	12	Daniel Lynch
1965	11	9	Daniel Lynch
1966	5	17	Daniel Lynch
1967	14	8	Daniel Lynch
1968	7	16	Daniel Lynch
Totals	427	292	

ST. FRANCIS COLLEGE

Loretto, Pennsylvania

Red Flash			*Red and White*
1946	1	9	Dr. "Skip" Hughes
1947	11	8	Dr. "Skip" Hughes
1948	15	8	Dr. "Skip" Hughes
1949	16	11	Dr. "Skip" Hughes
1950	17	9	Dr. "Skip" Hughes
1951	19	4	Dr. "Skip" Hughes
1952	23	7	Dr. "Skip" Hughes
1953	13	5	Dr. "Skip" Hughes
1954	21	5	Dr. "Skip" Hughes
1955	21	7	Dr. "Skip" Hughes
1956	10	14	Dr. "Skip" Hughes
1957	12	12	Dr. "Skip" Hughes
1958	20	5	Dr. "Skip" Hughes

Yr.	W	L	Coach
1959	20	5	Dr. "Skip" Hughes
1960	14	9	Dr. "Skip" Hughes
1961	6	19	Dr. "Skip" Hughes
1962	14	8	Dr. "Skip" Hughes
1963	10	13	Dr. "Skip" Hughes
1964	10	14	Dr. "Skip" Hughes
1965	10	15	Dr. "Skip" Hughes
1966	8	18	Dr. "Skip" Hughes
1967	20	6	John Clark
1968	19	6	John Clark
Totals	330	217	

ST. JOHN'S UNIVERSITY

Jamaica, New York

Redmen — *Red and White*

Yr.	W	L	Coach
1938	15	4	Joe Lapchick
1939	18	4	Joe Lapchick
1940	15	4	Joe Lapchick
1941	11	6	Joe Lapchick
1942	16	5	Joe Lapchick
1943	21	3	Joe Lapchick
1944	18	5	Joe Lapchick
1945	21	3	Joe Lapchick
1946	17	6	Joe Lapchick
1947	16	7	Joe Lapchick
1948	12	11	Frank McGuire
1949	16	9	Frank McGuire
1950	24	5	Frank McGuire
1951	26	5	Frank McGuire
1952	25	5	Frank McGuire
1953	17	6	Alfred DeStefano
1954	9	11	Alfred DeStefano
1955	11	9	Alfred DeStefano
1956	12	12	Alfred DeStefano
1957	14	9	Joe Lapchick
1958	18	8	Joe Lapchick
1959	20	6	Joe Lapchick
1960	17	8	Joe Lapchick
1961	20	5	Joe Lapchick
1962	21	5	Joe Lapchick
1963	9	15	Joe Lapchick
1964	14	11	Joe Lapchick
1965	21	8	Joe Lapchick
1966	18	8	Lou Carnesecca
1967	23	5	Lou Carnesecca
1968	19	8	Lou Carnesecca
Totals	534	216	

ST. JOSEPH'S COLLEGE

Philadelphia, Pennsylvania

Hawks — *Crimson and Gray*

Yr.	W	L	Coach
1938	13	5	William Ferguson
1939	10	12	William Ferguson
1940	10	5	William Ferguson
1941	12	6	William Ferguson
1942	12	6	William Ferguson
1943	18	4	William Ferguson
1944	18	7	William Ferguson
1945	12	11	William Ferguson
1946	9	11	William Ferguson
1947	16	6	William Ferguson
1948	12	11	William Ferguson
1949	12	11	William Ferguson
1950	10	15	William Ferguson
1951	13	14	William Ferguson
1952	20	7	William Ferguson
1953	14	11	William Ferguson
1954	14	9	John McMenamin
1955	12	14	John McMenamin
1956	23	6	Jack Ramsey
1957	17	7	Jack Ramsey
1958	18	9	Jack Ramsey
1959	22	5	Jack Ramsey
1960	20	7	Jack Ramsey
1961	25	5	Jack Ramsey
1962	18	10	Jack Ramsey
1963	23	5	Jack Ramsey
1964	18	10	Jack Ramsey
1965	26	3	Jack Ramsey
1966	24	5	Jack Ramsey
1967	16	10	Jack McKinney
1968	17	9	Jack McKinney
Totals	504	256	

ST. LOUIS UNIVERSITY

St. Louis, Missouri

Billikens — *Blue and White*

Yr.	W	L	Coach
1938	9	20	Ed Davidson
1939	5	16	Jack Sterrett
1940	4	14	Jack Sterrett
1941	3	14	Robert Klenck
1942	8	12	Robert Klenck
1943	11	10	Robert Klenck
1944	—	—	
1945	10	4	Dukes Duford
1946	13	11	John Flanigan
1947	18	11	John Flanigan
1948	24	3	Eddie Hickey
1949	22	4	Eddie Hickey
1950	17	9	Eddie Hickey
1951	22	8	Eddie Hickey
1952	23	8	Eddie Hickey
1953	16	11	Eddie Hickey
1954	14	12	Eddie Hickey
1955	20	8	Eddie Hickey
1956	18	7	Eddie Hickey
1957	19	9	Eddie Hickey
1958	16	10	Eddie Hickey
1959	20	6	John Benington
1960	19	8	John Benington
1961	21	9	John Benington
1962	11	15	John Benington
1963	16	12	John Benington
1964	13	12	John Benington
1965	18	9	John Benington
1966	15	10	Joe Brehmer
1967	13	13	Joe Brehmer
1968	15	11	Joe Brehmer
Totals	453	306	

ST. MARY'S COLLEGE

St. Mary's, California

Gaels — *Red and Blue*

Yr.	W	L	Coach
1938	24	6	Harlan Dykes

Yr.	W	L	Coach
1939	20	11	Harlan Dykes
1940	12	12	Jack Otten
1941	6	11	Louis Conlan
1942	—	—	
1943	12	9	Louis Conlan
1944	—	—	
1945	—	—	
1946	10	5	Clarence Andersen
1947	13	17	Clarence Andersen
1948	11	13	Benjamin Neff
1949	13	17	Benjamin Neff
1950	3	22	Benjamin Neff
1951	9	11	Thomas Foley
1952	17	10	Thomas Foley
1953	9	11	Thomas Foley
1954	10	14	Thomas Foley
1955	6	19	Thomas Foley
1956	16	10	James Weaver
1957	17	9	James Weaver
1958	11	15	James Weaver
1959	19	6	James Weaver
1960	15	11	James Weaver
1961	19	7	James Weaver
1962	13	11	James Weaver
1963	14	11	Mike Cimino
1964	7	19	Mike Cimino
1965	8	18	Mike Cimino
1966	8	17	Mike Cimino
1967	4	21	Mike Cimino
1968	4	20	Mike Cimino
Totals	330	363	

ST. PETER'S COLLEGE

Jersey City, New Jersey

Peacocks — *Blue and White*

Yr.	W	L	Coach
1938	6	15	H. M. Sweetman
1939	7	13	H. M. Sweetman
1940	4	10	H. M. Sweetman
1941	9	8	H. M. Sweetman
1942	5	11	H. M. Sweetman
1943	5	7	Thomas O'Brien
1944	—	—	
1945	—	—	
1946	—	—	
1947	5	15	George Babich
1948	16	5	George Babich
1949	18	5	George Babich
1950	13	11	Pete Caruso
1951	11	14	Don Kennedy
1952	14	8	Don Kennedy
1953	18	8	Don Kennedy
1954	17	7	Don Kennedy
1955	12	11	Don Kennedy
1956	14	7	Don Kennedy
1957	18	4	Don Kennedy
1958	20	4	Don Kennedy
1959	15	6	Don Kennedy
1960	15	6	Don Kennedy
1961	16	9	Don Kennedy
1962	13	10	Don Kennedy
1963	12	11	Don Kennedy
1964	13	9	Don Kennedy
1965	10	10	Don Kennedy
1966	11	12	Don Kennedy
1967	18	6	Don Kennedy
1968	24	4	Don Kennedy
Totals	359	246	

SAN FRANCISCO, UNIVERSITY OF

San Francisco, California

Dons — *Green and Gold*

Yr.	W	L	Coach
1938	10	12	Scotty Cameron
1939	7	10	Scotty Cameron
1940	9	8	Scotty Cameron
1941	2	13	Scotty Cameron
1942	14	10	Scotty Cameron
1943	13	9	James Needles
1944	8	11	James Needles
1945	—	—	
1946	9	12	William Bussenius
1947	13	14	Pete Newell
1948	13	11	Pete Newell
1949	25	5	Pete Newell
1950	19	7	Pete Newell
1951	9	17	Phil Woolpert
1952	11	13	Phil Woolpert
1953	10	11	Phil Woolpert
1954	14	7	Phil Woolpert
1955	28	1	Phil Woolpert
1956	29	0	Phil Woolpert
1957	21	7	Phil Woolpert
1958	25	2	Phil Woolpert
1959	6	20	Phil Woolpert
1960	8	17	Ross Giudice
1961	17	11	Peter P. Peletta
1962	10	15	Peter P. Peletta
1963	18	9	Peter P. Peletta
1964	23	5	Peter P. Peletta
1965	24	5	Peter P. Peletta
1966	22	6	Peter P. Peletta
1967	13	12	Phil Vukievich
1968	14	8	Phil Vukievich
Totals	444	288	

SAN JOSE STATE COLLEGE

San Jose, California

Spartans — *Gold and White*

Yr.	W	L	Coach
1938	19	4	Wilbur Hubbard
1939	12	8	Wilbur Hubbard
1940	14	10	Wilbur Hubbard
1941	19	8	Walter McPherson
1942	4	11	Walter McPherson
1943	11	13	T. E. Blesh
1944	—	—	
1945	8	14	Wilbur Hubbard
1946	17	14	Walter McPherson
1947	19	9	Walter McPherson
1948	13	9	Walter McPherson
1949	22	13	Walter McPherson
1950	21	7	Walter McPherson
1951	18	12	Walter McPherson
1952	15	10	Walter McPherson
1953	15	11	Walter McPherson
1954	12	15	Walter McPherson
1955	16	9	Walter McPherson

Yr.	W	L	Coach
1956	15	10	Walter McPherson
1957	13	12	Walter McPherson
1958	13	13	Walter McPherson
1959	5	19	Walter McPherson
1960	6	19	Walter McPherson
1961	11	14	Stu Inman
1962	2	22	Stu Inman
1963	14	10	Stu Inman
1964	14	10	Stu Inman
1965	14	10	Stu Inman
1966	11	13	Stu Inman
1967	9	15	Dan Glines
1968	12	13	Dan Glines
Totals	394	357	

SANTA CLARA, UNIVERSITY OF

Santa Clara, California

Broncos — *Cardinal and White*

Yr.	W	L	Coach
1938	10	6	George Barsi
1939	15	5	George Barsi
1940	17	3	George Barsi
1941	15	7	George Barsi
1942	10	9	George Barsi
1943	10	9	George Barsi
1944	—	—	
1945	—	—	
1946	9	6	George Barsi
1947	21	4	Ray Pesco
1948	11	11	Ray Pesco
1949	8	15	Ray Pesco
1950	14	8	Ray Pesco
1951	9	15	Bob Feerick
1952	17	12	Bob Feerick
1953	20	7	Bob Feerick
1954	21	7	Bob Feerick
1955	13	11	Bob Feerick
1956	8	16	Bob Feerick
1957	15	7	Bob Feerick
1958	13	11	Bob Feerick
1959	16	9	Bob Feerick
1960	18	9	Bob Feerick
1961	18	9	Bob Feerick
1962	19	6	Bob Feerick
1963	16	9	Dick Garibaldi
1964	6	20	Dick Garibaldi
1965	14	12	Dick Garibaldi
1966	16	11	Dick Garibaldi
1967	13	13	Dick Garibaldi
1968	22	4	Dick Garibaldi
Totals	414	271	

SEATTLE UNIVERSITY

Seattle, Washington

Chieftains — *Maroon and White*

Yr.	W	L	Coach
1946	8	22	Joseph Budnick
1947	18	13	Budnick, Fenton, Ryan
1948	10	16	Leonard Yandle
1949	12	14	Al Brightman
1950	12	17	Al Brightman
1951	32	5	Al Brightman
1952	29	8	Al Brightman
1953	29	4	Al Brightman
1954	26	2	Al Brightman
1955	22	7	Al Brightman
1956	18	11	Al Brightman
1957	24	3	John Castellani
1958	24	7	John Castellani
1959	23	6	Vince Cazzetta
1960	16	10	Vince Cazzetta
1961	18	8	Vince Cazzetta
1962	18	9	Vince Cazzetta
1963	21	6	Vince Cazzetta
1964	22	6	Clair Markey
1965	19	7	W. R. "Bob" Boyd
1966	16	10	Lionel Purcell
1967	18	8	Lionel Purcell
1968	14	13	Morris Buckwalter
Totals	449	212	

SETON HALL UNIVERSITY

South Orange, New Jersey

Pirates — *Blue and White*

Yr.	W	L	Coach
1938	10	8	John "Honey" Russell
1939	15	7	John "Honey" Russell
1940	19	0	John "Honey" Russell
1941	20	2	John "Honey" Russell
1942	16	2	John "Honey" Russell
1943	15	3	John "Honey" Russell
1944	—	—	
1945	—	—	
1946	—	—	
1947	24	3	Robert Davies
1948	18	4	John Reitemeier
1949	16	8	John Reitemeier
1950	11	15	John "Honey" Russell
1951	24	7	John "Honey" Russell
1952	25	3	John "Honey" Russell
1953	31	2	John "Honey" Russell
1954	13	10	John "Honey" Russell
1955	17	9	John "Honey" Russell
1956	20	5	John "Honey" Russell
1957	17	10	John "Honey" Russell
1958	7	19	John "Honey" Russell
1959	7	19	John "Honey" Russell
1960	16	7	John "Honey" Russell
1961	15	9	Richie Regan
1962	15	9	Richie Regan
1963	17	6	Richie Regan
1964	13	12	Richie Regan
1965	12	13	Richie Regan
1966	6	18	Richie Regan
1967	7	17	Richie Regan
1968	9	15	Richie Regan
Totals	435	242	

SOUTH CAROLINA, UNIVERSITY OF

Columbia, South Carolina

Gamecocks — *Garnet and Black*

Yr.	W	L	Coach
1938	3	20	Ted Petoskey
1939	5	18	Ted Petoskey
1940	5	13	Ted Petoskey
1941	15	9	Frank Johnson
1942	12	9	Frank Johnson
1943	9	5	Frank Johnson

Yr.	W	L	Coach
1944	13	2	Henry Findley
1945	19	3	John McMillan
1946	9	11	Frank Johnson
1947	15	9	Frank Johnson
1948	12	11	Frank Johnson
1949	10	12	Frank Johnson
1950	13	9	Frank Johnson
1951	13	12	Frank Johnson
1952	14	10	Frank Johnson
1953	11	13	Frank Johnson
1954	10	16	Frank Johnson
1955	10	17	Frank Johnson
1956	9	14	Frank Johnson
1957	17	12	Frank Johnson
1958	5	19	Frank Johnson
1959	4	20	Walt Hambrick
1960	10	16	Bob Stevens
1961	9	17	Bob Stevens
1962	15	12	Bob Stevens
1963	9	15	Chuck Noe
1964	10	14	C. Noe, D. Morrison
1965	6	17	Frank McGuire
1966	11	13	Frank McGuire
1967	16	7	Frank McGuire
1968	15	7	Frank McGuire
Totals	334	382	

SOUTHERN CALIFORNIA, UNIVERSITY OF

Los Angeles, California

Trojans — *Cardinal and Gold*

Yr.	W	L	Coach
1938	17	9	Sam Barry
1939	20	5	Sam Barry
1940	20	3	Sam Barry
1941	15	10	Sam Barry
1942	12	8	Julie Bescos
1943	23	5	Ernest Holbrook
1944	9	12	Holbrook, Robert Muth
1945	16	9	Robert Muth
1946	14	9	Sam Barry
1947	10	14	Sam Barry
1948	14	10	Sam Barry
1949	14	10	Sam Barry
1950	16	8	Sam Barry
1951	21	6	Forrest Twogood
1952	16	14	Forrest Twogood
1953	18	6	Forrest Twogood
1954	19	14	Forrest Twogood
1955	15	11	Forrest Twogood
1956	14	12	Forrest Twogood
1957	16	12	Forrest Twogood
1958	12	13	Forrest Twogood
1959	15	11	Forrest Twogood
1960	16	11	Forrest Twogood
1961	21	8	Forrest Twogood
1962	14	11	Forrest Twogood
1963	20	9	Forrest Twogood
1964	10	16	Forrest Twogood
1965	14	12	Forrest Twogood
1966	13	13	Forrest Twogood
1967	13	12	Bob Boyd
1968	18	8	Bob Boyd
Totals	485	311	

SOUTHERN ILLINOIS UNIVERSITY

Carbondale, Illinois

Salukis — *Maroon and White*

Yr.	W	L	Coach
1938	13	4	William McAndrew
1939	11	9	William McAndrew
1940	20	3	William McAndrew
1941	11	12	William McAndrew
1942	8	9	William McAndrew
1943	9	9	William McAndrew
1944	8	7	Abe Martin
1945	15	7	Abe Martin
1946	20	6	Abe Martin
1947	19	10	Lynn Holder
1948	22	4	Lynn Holder
1949	13	11	Lynn Holder
1950	21	6	Lynn Holder
1951	13	13	Lynn Holder
1952	13	11	Lynn Holder
1953	13	11	Lynn Holder
1954	12	11	Lynn Holder
1955	10	13	Lynn Holder
1956	14	11	Lynn Holder
1957	13	11	Lynn Holder
1958	13	11	Lynn Holder
1959	17	10	Harry Gallatin
1960	20	9	Harry Gallatin
1961	21	6	Harry Gallatin
1962	21	10	Harry Gallatin
1963	20	10	Jack Hartman
1964	16	10	Jack Hartman
1965	20	6	Jack Hartman
1966	22	7	Jack Hartman
1967	24	2	Jack Hartman
1968	13	11	Jack Hartman
Totals	485	270	

SOUTHERN METHODIST UNIVERSITY

Dallas, Texas

Mustangs — *Cardinal Red and Royal Blue*

Yr.	W	L	Coach
1938	9	6	Whitey Baccus
1939	14	8	Whitey Baccus
1940	7	13	Whitey Baccus
1941	10	10	Whitey Baccus
1942	3	16	Whitey Baccus
1943	10	8	James Stewart
1944	8	9	James Stewart
1945	11	10	Roy "Rusty" Baccus
1946	7	16	Whitey Baccus
1947	14	8	Whitey Baccus
1948	13	10	E. O. "Doc" Hayes
1949	11	13	E. O. "Doc" Hayes
1950	10	13	E. O. "Doc" Hayes
1951	14	10	E. O. "Doc" Hayes
1952	11	13	E. O. "Doc" Hayes
1953	8	12	E. O. "Doc" Hayes
1954	13	9	E. O. "Doc" Hayes
1955	15	11	E. O. "Doc" Hayes
1956	25	4	E. O. "Doc" Hayes
1957	22	4	E. O. "Doc" Hayes
1958	15	10	E. O. "Doc" Hayes
1959	16	8	E. O. "Doc" Hayes
1960	17	7	E. O. "Doc" Hayes

Yr.	W	L	Coach
1961	12	12	E. O. "Doc" Hayes
1962	18	7	E. O. "Doc" Hayes
1963	9	15	E. O. "Doc" Hayes
1964	12	12	E. O. "Doc" Hayes
1965	17	10	E. O. "Doc" Hayes
1966	17	9	E. O. "Doc" Hayes
1967	20	6	E. O. "Doc" Hayes
1968	6	18	Bob Prewitt
Totals	394	317	

STANFORD UNIVERSITY
Palo Alto, California

Indians			*Cardinal and White*
1938	21	3	John Bunn
1939	16	9	Everett Dean
1940	14	9	Everett Dean
1941	21	5	Everett Dean
1942	27	4	Everett Dean
1943	10	11	Everett Dean
1944	—	—	
1945	—	—	
1946	6	18	Everett Dean
1947	15	16	Everett Dean
1948	15	11	Everett Dean
1949	19	9	Everett Dean
1950	11	14	Everett Dean
1951	12	14	Everett Dean
1952	19	9	Robert Burnett
1953	7	20	Robert Burnett
1954	15	10	Robert Burnett
1955	17	8	Howard Dallmar
1956	18	6	Howard Dallmar
1957	11	15	Howard Dallmar
1958	12	13	Howard Dallmar
1959	16	9	Howard Dallmar
1960	11	14	Howard Dallmar
1961	7	17	Howard Dallmar
1962	16	6	Howard Dallmar
1963	16	9	Howard Dallmar
1964	15	10	Howard Dallmar
1965	12	13	Howard Dallmar
1966	13	12	Howard Dallmar
1967	15	11	Howard Dallmar
1968	11	15	Howard Dallmar
Totals	418	320	

SYRACUSE UNIVERSITY
Syracuse, New York

Orangemen			*Orange*
1938	13	5	Lew Andreas
1939	14	4	Lew Andreas
1940	10	8	Lew Andreas
1941	13	5	Lew Andreas
1942	14	6	Lew Andreas
1943	8	10	Lew Andreas
1944	—	—	
1945	7	12	Lew Andreas
1946	23	4	Lew Andreas
1947	19	6	Lew Andreas
1948	11	13	Lew Andreas
1949	18	7	Lew Andreas
1950	18	9	Lew Andreas
1951	19	9	Marc Guley
1952	14	6	Marc Guley
1953	7	11	Marc Guley
1954	10	9	Marc Guley
1955	10	11	Marc Guley
1956	14	8	Marc Guley
1957	18	7	Marc Guley
1958	11	10	Marc Guley
1959	14	9	Marc Guley
1960	13	8	Marc Guley
1961	4	19	Marc Guley
1962	2	22	Marc Guley
1963	8	13	Fred Lewis
1964	17	8	Fred Lewis
1965	13	10	Fred Lewis
1966	22	6	Fred Lewis
1967	20	6	Fred Lewis
1968	11	14	Fred Lewis
Totals	395	275	

TEMPLE UNIVERSITY
Philadelphia, Pennsylvania

Owls			*Cherry and White*
1938	23	2	James Usilton
1939	10	12	James Usilton
1940	13	10	Ernest Messikomer
1941	12	9	Ernest Messikomer
1942	10	8	Ernest Messikomer
1943	11	11	Josh Cody
1944	14	9	Josh Cody
1945	16	7	Josh Cody
1946	12	8	Josh Cody
1947	8	12	Josh Cody
1948	12	11	Josh Cody
1949	14	9	Josh Cody
1950	14	10	Josh Cody
1951	12	13	Josh Cody
1952	9	15	Josh Cody
1953	16	10	Harry Litwack
1954	15	12	Harry Litwack
1955	11	10	Harry Litwack
1956	27	4	Harry Litwack
1957	20	9	Harry Litwack
1958	27	3	Harry Litwack
1959	6	19	Harry Litwack
1960	17	9	Harry Litwack
1961	20	8	Harry Litwack
1962	18	9	Harry Litwack
1963	15	7	Harry Litwack
1964	17	8	Harry Litwack
1965	14	10	Harry Litwack
1966	21	7	Harry Litwack
1967	20	8	Harry Litwack
1968	19	9	Harry Litwack
Totals	473	288	

TENNESSEE, UNIVERSITY OF
Knoxville, Tennessee

Volunteers			*Orange and White*
1938	15	8	Blair Gullion
1939	14	7	John Mauer
1940	14	7	John Mauer
1941	17	5	John Mauer
1942	19	3	John Mauer

Yr.	W	L	Coach
1943	14	5	John Mauer
1944	—	—	
1945	18	4	John Mauer
1946	14	6	John Mauer
1947	16	5	John Mauer
1948	20	5	Emmett Lowery
1949	19	7	Emmett Lowery
1950	15	11	Emmett Lowery
1951	10	13	Emmett Lowery
1952	13	9	Emmett Lowery
1953	13	8	Emmett Lowery
1954	11	12	Emmett Lowery
1955	15	7	Emmett Lowery
1956	10	14	Emmett Lowery
1957	13	9	Emmett Lowery
1958	16	7	Emmett Lowery
1959	14	8	Emmett Lowery
1960	12	11	John Sines
1961	10	15	John Sines
1962	4	19	John Sines
1963	13	11	Ray Mears
1964	16	8	Ray Mears
1965	20	5	Ray Mears
1966	18	8	Ray Mears
1967	21	7	Ray Mears
1968	20	6	Ray Mears
Totals	444	250	

TENNESSEE POLYTECHNIC INSTITUTE

Cookeville, Tennessee

Golden Eagles			*Purple and Gold*
1938	11	6	P. V. Overall
1939	10	4	P. V. Overall
1940	9	7	P. V. Overall
1941	6	10	P. V. Overall
1942	9	7	Hooper Eblen
1943	10	9	Hooper Eblen
1944	3	13	Overall, Eblen
1945	6	5	Overall, Eblen
1946	6	8	Overall, Eblen
1947	20	5	Hooper Eblen
1948	18	7	Ray Brown
1949	10	10	Ray Brown
1950	9	12	Ray Brown
1951	12	9	Ray Brown
1952	9	13	Ray Brown
1953	14	11	Ray Brown
1954	12	10	Ray Brown
1955	9	11	Ray Brown
1956	14	7	John Oldham
1957	9	11	John Oldham
1958	17	9	John Oldham
1959	16	9	John Oldham
1960	13	9	John Oldham
1961	6	13	John Oldham
1962	16	6	John Oldham
1963	16	8	John Oldham
1964	11	11	John Oldham
1965	14	11	Kenny Sidwell
1966	17	8	Kenny Sidwell
1967	12	11	Kenny Sidwell
1968	10	16	Kenny Sidwell
Totals	354	286	

TEXAS, UNIVERSITY OF

Austin, Texas

Yr.	W	L	Coach
Longhorns			*Orange and White*
1938	10	12	Jack Gray
1939	19	6	Jack Gray
1940	18	5	Jack Gray
1941	15	9	Jack Gray
1942	14	9	Jack Gray
1943	19	7	H.C. Gilstrap
1944	14	11	H.C. Gilstrap
1945	10	10	H.C. Gilstrap
1946	16	7	Jack Gray
1947	26	2	Jack Gray
1948	20	5	Jack Gray
1949	17	7	Jack Gray
1950	13	11	Jack Gray
1951	13	14	Jack Gray
1952	16	8	Thurman Hull
1953	12	9	Thurman Hull
1954	16	9	Thurman Hull
1955	4	20	Thurman Hull
1956	12	12	Thurman Hull
1957	11	13	Marshall Hughes
1958	10	13	Marshall Hughes
1959	4	20	Marshall Hughes
1960	18	8	Harold Bradley
1961	14	10	Harold Bradley
1962	16	8	Harold Bradley
1963	20	7	Harold Bradley
1964	15	9	Harold Bradley
1965	16	9	Harold Bradley
1966	12	12	Harold Bradley
1967	14	10	Harold Bradley
1968	11	13	Leon Black
Totals	445	305	

TEXAS A&M UNIVERSITY

College Station, Texas

Aggies			*Maroon and White*
1938	10	8	H. R. McQuillan
1939	7	16	H. R. McQuillan
1940	11	11	H. R. McQuillan
1941	7	13	H. R. McQuillan
1942	8	16	Marty Karow
1943	11	11	Manning Smith
1944	2	15	Manning Smith
1945	3	18	Manning Smith
1946	9	14	Marty Karow
1947	8	17	Marty Karow
1948	7	17	Marty Karow
1949	5	19	Marty Karow
1950	10	14	Marty Karow
1951	17	12	John Floyd
1952	9	15	John Floyd
1953	6	15	John Floyd
1954	2	20	John Floyd
1955	4	20	John Floyd
1956	6	18	Ken Loeffler
1957	7	17	Ken Loeffler
1958	11	13	Bob Rogers
1959	15	9	Bob Rogers
1960	19	5	Bob Rogers

Yr.	W	L	Coach
1961	16	8	Bob Rogers
1962	15	9	Bob Rogers
1963	16	8	Bob Rogers
1964	18	7	Shelby Metcalf
1965	14	10	Shelby Metcalf
1966	15	9	Shelby Metcalf
1967	6	18	Shelby Metcalf
1968	14	10	Shelby Metcalf
Totals	308	420	

TEXAS CHRISTIAN UNIVERSITY

Fort Worth, Texas

Horned Frogs — *Purple and White*

Yr.	W	L	Coach
1938	1	11	Mike Brumbelow
1939	0	12	Mike Brumbelow
1940	1	11	Mike Brumbelow
1941	0	12	Mike Brumbelow
1942	6	6	Hugh McQuillan
1943	18	9	Hugh McQuillan
1944	9	12	Hugh McQuillan
1945	9	20	Hugh McQuillan
1946	13	11	Hugh McQuillan
1947	1	23	Hugh McQuillan
1948	3	20	Hugh McQuillan
1949	5	19	Buster Brannon
1950	13	11	Buster Brannon
1951	16	9	Buster Brannon
1952	24	4	Buster Brannon
1953	15	8	Buster Brannon
1954	10	14	Buster Brannon
1955	17	7	Buster Brannon
1956	4	20	Buster Brannon
1957	14	10	Buster Brannon
1958	17	7	Buster Brannon
1959	20	6	Buster Brannon
1960	7	17	Buster Brannon
1961	5	19	Buster Brannon
1962	5	19	Buster Brannon
1963	4	20	Buster Brannon
1964	4	20	Buster Brannon
1965	6	18	Buster Brannon
1966	8	16	Buster Brannon
1967	10	14	Buster Brannon
1968	15	11	Johnny Swaim
Totals	280	416	

TEXAS, UNIVERSITY OF (U. T. E. P.)

El Paso, Texas

Miners — *Orange and White*

Yr.	W	L	Coach
1938	2	16	Marshall Pennington
1939	3	11	Marshall Pennington
1940	6	12	Marshall Pennington
1941	13	11	Marshall Pennington
1942	11	13	Marshall Pennington
1943	—	—	
1944	—	—	
1945	10	13	Charles L. Finley
1946	13	12	Jack Curtice
1947	12	8	Dale Waters
1948	13	16	Ross Moore
1949	7	11	Dale Waters
1950	17	13	Dale Waters
1951	10	15	Dale Waters
1952	8	17	Dale Waters
1953	4	21	Dale Waters
1954	8	14	George McCarty
1955	13	8	George McCarty
1956	12	10	George McCarty
1957	15	8	George McCarty
1958	14	9	George McCarty
1959	14	9	George McCarty
1960	6	19	Harold Davis
1961	10	12	Harold Davis
1962	18	6	Don Haskins
1963	19	7	Don Haskins
1964	25	3	Don Haskins
1965	17	9	Don Haskins
1966	28	1	Don Haskins
1967	22	6	Don Haskins
1968	14	9	Don Haskins
Totals	364	319	

TEXAS TECHNOLOGICAL COLLEGE

Lubbock, Texas

Red Raiders — *Scarlet and Black*

Yr.	W	L	Coach
1938	8	13	Berl Hoffman
1939	13	6	Berl Hoffman
1940	22	6	Berl Hoffman
1941	19	6	Berl Hoffman
1942	16	11	Berl Hoffman
1943	13	11	Polk Robison
1944	5	17	Polk Robison
1945	10	14	Polk Robison
1946	15	10	Polk Robison
1947	10	12	Berl Hoffman
1948	16	12	Polk Robison
1949	21	9	Polk Robison
1950	14	12	Polk Robison
1951	14	14	Polk Robison
1952	14	10	Polk Robison
1953	12	10	Polk Robison
1954	20	5	Polk Robison
1955	18	7	Polk Robison
1956	13	12	Polk Robison
1957	12	11	Polk Robison
1958	15	8	Polk Robison
1959	15	9	Polk Robison
1960	10	14	Polk Robison
1961	15	10	Polk Robison
1962	19	8	Gene Gibson
1963	6	17	Gene Gibson
1964	16	7	Gene Gibson
1965	17	6	Gene Gibson
1966	13	11	Gene Gibson
1967	9	15	Gene Gibson
1968	9	15	Gene Gibson
Totals	429	328	

TOLEDO, UNIVERSITY OF

Toledo, Ohio

Rockets — *Midnight Blue and Gold*

Yr.	W	L	Coach
1938	14	6	Harold Anderson
1939	17	10	Harold Anderson
1940	24	6	Harold Anderson
1941	21	3	Harold Anderson
1942	23	5	Harold Anderson

Yr.	W	L	Coach
1943	22	4	Berle Friddle
1944	5	13	Berle Friddle
1945	9	4	Rollie Boldt
1946	20	7	Rollie Boldt
1947	18	6	Bill Orwig
1948	21	5	Jerry Bush
1949	13	12	Jerry Bush
1950	23	6	Jerry Bush
1951	23	8	Jerry Bush
1952	20	11	Jerry Bush
1953	16	7	Jerry Bush
1954	13	10	Jerry Bush
1955	5	17	Eddie Melvin
1956	9	13	Eddie Melvin
1957	5	19	Eddie Melvin
1958	9	14	Eddie Melvin
1959	11	13	Eddie Melvin
1960	18	6	Eddie Melvin
1961	15	8	Eddie Melvin
1962	14	10	Eddie Melvin
1963	13	11	Eddie Melvin
1964	13	11	Eddie Melvin
1965	13	11	Eddie Melvin
1966	13	11	Bob Nichols
1967	23	2	Bob Nichols
1968	16	8	Bob Nichols
Totals	479	277	

TULANE UNIVERSITY
New Orleans, Louisiana

Green Wave — *Olive and Blue*

Yr.	W	L	Coach
1938	8	10	Ray Dauber
1939	5	12	Claude Simons
1940	2	12	Claude Simons
1941	8	5	Claude Simons
1942	4	12	Claude Simons
1943	4	9	Vernon Haynes
1944	16	6	Vernon Haynes
1945	6	10	Vernon Haynes
1946	15	7	Cliff Wells
1947	22	9	Cliff Wells
1948	23	3	Cliff Wells
1949	24	4	Cliff Wells
1950	15	7	Cliff Wells
1951	12	12	Cliff Wells
1952	12	12	Cliff Wells
1953	12	6	Cliff Wells
1954	15	8	Cliff Wells
1955	14	6	Cliff Wells
1956	12	12	Cliff Wells
1957	15	9	Cliff Wells
1958	8	15	Cliff Wells
1959	13	11	Cliff Wells
1960	13	11	Cliff Wells
1961	11	13	Cliff Wells
1962	12	10	Cliff Wells
1963	6	16	Cliff Wells
1964	1	22	Ted Lenhardt
1965	3	22	Ted Lenhardt
1966	9	16	Ralph Pedersen
1967	14	10	Ralph Pedersen
1968	12	12	Ralph Pedersen
Totals	346	329	

TULSA, UNIVERSITY OF
Tulsa, Oklahoma

Hurricanes — *Blue, Crimson and Gold*

Yr.	W	L	Coach
1938	12	10	Chester Benefiel
1939	15	8	Chester Benefiel
1940	12	15	Benefiel, "Tex" Ryon
1941	12	9	Jack Sterrett
1942	3	13	"Tex" Ryon
1943	0	10	W. S. Milligan
1944	5	3	W. W. West
1945	4	8	P. J. Alyea
1946	6	12	Don Shields
1947	4	20	Don Shields
1948	7	17	John Garrison
1949	4	20	John Garrison
1950	12	11	Clarence Iba
1951	10	18	Clarence Iba
1952	14	10	Clarence Iba
1953	15	10	Clarence Iba
1954	15	14	Clarence Iba
1955	21	7	Clarence Iba
1956	16	10	Clarence Iba
1957	8	17	Clarence Iba
1958	7	19	Clarence Iba
1959	10	15	Clarence Iba
1960	9	17	Clarence Iba
1961	8	17	Joe Swank
1962	7	19	Joe Swank
1963	17	8	Joe Swank
1964	10	15	Joe Swank
1965	14	11	Joe Swank
1966	16	13	Joe Swank
1967	19	8	Joe Swank
1968	11	12	Joe Swank
Totals	323	396	

UNIVERSITY OF CALIFORNIA AT LOS ANGELES (U. C. L. A.)
Los Angeles, California

Bruins — *Navy Blue and Gold*

Yr.	W	L	Coach
1938	4	20	Caddy Works
1939	7	20	Caddy Works
1940	8	17	Wilbur Johns
1941	6	20	Wilbur Johns
1942	5	18	Wilbur Johns
1943	14	7	Wilbur Johns
1944	10	10	Wilbur Johns
1945	11	12	Wilbur Johns
1946	8	16	Wilbur Johns
1947	18	7	Wilbur Johns
1948	12	13	Wilbur Johns
1949	22	7	John R. Wooden
1950	24	7	John R. Wooden
1951	19	10	John R. Wooden
1952	19	12	John R. Wooden
1953	16	8	John R. Wooden
1954	18	7	John R. Wooden
1955	21	5	John R. Wooden
1956	22	6	John R. Wooden
1957	22	4	John R. Wooden
1958	16	10	John R. Wooden
1959	16	9	John R. Wooden

Yr.	W	L	Coach
1960	14	12	John R. Wooden
1961	18	8	John R. Wooden
1962	18	11	John R. Wooden
1963	20	9	John R. Wooden
1964	30	0	John R. Wooden
1965	28	2	John R. Wooden
1966	18	8	John R. Wooden
1967	30	0	John R. Wooden
1968	29	1	John R. Wooden
Totals	523	296	

UNIVERSITY OF CALIFORNIA AT SANTA BARBARA (U. C. S. B.)

Santa Barbara, California

Gauchos — *Blue and Gold*

Yr.	W	L	Coach
1938	8	12	Wilton
1939	11	9	Wilton
1940	21	9	Wilton
1941	20	10	Wilton
1942	10	10	Wilton
1943	10	6	Wilton
1944	—	—	
1945	—	—	
1946	—	—	
1947	17	8	Wilton
1948	17	8	Wilton
1949	11	9	Wilton
1950	14	14	Wilton
1951	14	15	Wilton
1952	7	20	Findlay
1953	5	16	Wilton
1954	16	10	Wilton
1955	18	7	Wilton
1956	18	8	Wilton
1957	8	16	Wilton
1958	13	12	Gallon
1959	4	19	Gallon
1960	18	7	Gallon
1961	20	8	Gallon
1962	12	12	Gallon
1963	16	9	Gallon
1964	18	11	Gallon
1965	12	14	Gallon
1966	10	16	Ralph Barkey
1967	10	16	Ralph Barkey
1968	9	17	Ralph Barkey
Totals	367	328	

UTAH, UNIVERSITY OF

Salt Lake City, Utah

Redskins — *Crimson and White*

Yr.	W	L	Coach
1938	17	4	Vadal Peterson
1939	12	7	Vadal Peterson
1940	18	4	Vadal Peterson
1941	14	7	Vadal Peterson
1942	13	7	Vadal Peterson
1943	10	12	Vadal Peterson
1944	21	4	Vadal Peterson
1945	17	4	Vadal Peterson
1946	12	8	Vadal Peterson
1947	19	5	Vadal Peterson
1948	11	9	Vadal Peterson
1949	24	8	Vadal Peterson
1950	25	19	Vadal Peterson
1951	23	13	Vadal Peterson
1952	19	9	Vadal Peterson
1953	10	14	Vadal Peterson
1954	12	14	Jack Gardner
1955	24	4	Jack Gardner
1956	22	6	Jack Gardner
1957	19	8	Jack Gardner
1958	20	7	Jack Gardner
1959	21	7	Jack Gardner
1960	26	3	Jack Gardner
1961	23	8	Jack Gardner
1962	23	3	Jack Gardner
1963	12	4	Jack Gardner
1964	19	9	Jack Gardner
1965	17	9	Jack Gardner
1966	23	8	Jack Gardner
1967	15	11	Jack Gardner
1968	14	11	Jack Gardner
Totals	555	246	

UTAH STATE UNIVERSITY

Logan, Utah

Aggies — *Blue and White*

Yr.	W	L	Coach
1938	11	9	Dick Romney
1939	—	—	
1940	—	—	
1941	2	16	Dick Romney
1942	6	10	R. W. Burnett
1943	14	7	Del Young
1944	—	—	
1945	9	10	Del Young
1946	7	12	"Beebe" Lee
1947	14	10	"Beebe" Lee
1948	8	16	Joseph Whitesides
1949	10	21	Joseph Whitesides
1950	18	16	Joseph Whitesides
1951	12	22	Cecil Baker
1952	19	14	Cecil Baker
1953	17	13	Cecil Baker
1954	14	13	Cecil Baker
1955	14	8	Cecil Baker
1956	13	13	Cecil Baker
1957	11	13	Cecil Baker
1958	4	20	Cecil Baker
1959	19	7	Cecil Baker
1960	24	5	Cecil Baker
1961	12	14	Cecil Baker
1962	22	7	LaDell Anderson
1963	20	7	LaDell Anderson
1964	21	8	LaDell Anderson
1965	13	12	LaDell Anderson
1966	12	14	LaDell Anderson
1967	20	6	LaDell Anderson
1968	14	11	LaDell Anderson
Totals	380	334	

VANDERBILT UNIVERSITY

Nashville, Tennessee

Commodores — *Gold and Black*

Yr.	W	L	Coach
1938	9	12	James Buford
1939	14	7	James Buford

Yr.	W	L	Coach
1940	10	12	James Buford
1941	8	9	James Buford
1942	7	9	Norman Cooper
1943	10	8	Norman Cooper
1944	11	4	Smokey Harper
1945	6	6	Gus Morrow
1946	3	10	Gus Morrow
1947	7	8	Norman Cooper
1948	8	14	Robert Polk
1949	14	8	Robert Polk
1950	17	8	Robert Polk
1951	19	8	Robert Polk
1952	18	9	Robert Polk
1953	10	9	Robert Polk
1954	12	10	Robert Polk
1955	16	6	Robert Polk
1956	19	4	Robert Polk
1957	17	5	Robert Polk
1958	14	11	Robert Polk
1959	14	10	Roy Skinner
1960	14	9	Robert Polk
1961	19	5	Robert Polk
1962	12	12	Roy Skinner
1963	16	7	Roy Skinner
1964	19	6	Roy Skinner
1965	24	4	Roy Skinner
1966	22	4	Roy Skinner
1967	21	5	Roy Skinner
1968	20	6	Roy Skinner
Totals	430	245	

VERMONT, UNIVERSITY OF

Burlington, Vermont

Catamounts			*Green and Gold*
1938	10	4	J. P. Sabo
1939	10	5	J. P. Sabo
1940	5	10	J. P. Sabo
1941	10	4	John Evans
1942	10	5	John Evans
1943	10	6	John Evans
1944	—	—	
1945	—	—	
1946	10	4	John Evans
1947	19	3	John Evans
1948	14	6	John Evans
1949	15	5	John Evans
1950	9	11	John Evans
1951	14	6	John Evans
1952	14	6	John Evans
1953	11	10	John Evans
1954	13	7	John Evans
1955	6	15	John Evans
1956	6	12	John Evans
1957	15	5	John Evans
1958	15	10	John Evans
1959	12	10	John Evans
1960	9	11	John Evans
1961	9	11	John Evans
1962	12	12	John Evans
1963	10	13	John Evans
1964	11	10	John Evans
1965	7	13	John Evans
1966	12	8	Art Loche
1967	10	15	Art Loche
1968	12	12	Art Loche
Totals	320	249	

VILLANOVA UNIVERSITY

Villanova, Pennsylvania

Wildcats			*Blue and White*
1938	25	5	Al Severance
1939	20	5	Al Severance
1940	17	2	Al Severance
1941	13	3	Al Severance
1942	13	9	Al Severance
1943	19	2	Al Severance
1944	9	11	Al Severance
1945	6	11	Al Severance
1946	10	13	Al Severance
1947	17	7	Al Severance
1948	15	9	Al Severance
1949	23	4	Al Severance
1950	25	4	Al Severance
1951	25	7	Al Severance
1952	19	8	Al Severance
1953	22	9	Al Severance
1954	20	11	Al Severance
1955	18	10	Al Severance
1956	14	12	Al Severance
1957	10	15	Al Severance
1958	12	11	Al Severance
1959	18	7	Al Severance
1960	20	6	Al Severance
1961	11	13	Al Severance
1962	21	7	Jack Kraft
1963	19	10	Jack Kraft
1964	24	4	Jack Kraft
1965	23	5	Jack Kraft
1966	18	11	Jack Kraft
1967	17	9	Jack Kraft
1968	19	9	Jack Kraft
Totals	542	249	

VIRGINIA, UNIVERSITY OF

Charlottesville, Virginia

Cavaliers			*Orange and Blue*
1938	6	10	Gus Tebell
1939	14	5	Gus Tebell
1940	16	5	Gus Tebell
1941	16	4	Gus Tebell
1942	6	10	Gus Tebell
1943	8	13	Gus Tebell
1944	11	8	Gus Tebell
1945	12	5	Gus Tebell
1946	12	5	Gus Tebell
1947	11	11	Gus Tebell
1948	16	10	Gus Tebell
1949	13	10	Gus Tebell
1950	12	13	Gus Tebell
1951	8	14	Gus Tebell
1952	11	13	Evan J. "Bus" Male
1953	10	13	Evan J. "Bus" Male
1954	16	11	Evan J. "Bus" Male
1955	14	15	Evan J. "Bus" Male
1956	10	17	Evan J. "Bus" Male

Yr.	W	L	Coach
1957	6	19	Evan J. "Bus" Male
1958	10	13	Billy McCann
1959	11	14	Billy McCann
1960	6	18	Billy McCann
1961	3	23	Billy McCann
1962	5	18	Billy McCann
1963	5	20	Billy McCann
1964	8	16	Bill Gibson
1965	7	18	Bill Gibson
1966	7	15	Bill Gibson
1967	9	17	Bill Gibson
1968	9	16	Bill Gibson
Totals	308	399	

VIRGINIA MILITARY INSTITUTE

Lexington, Virginia

Keydets — *Red, White and Yellow*

Yr.	W	L	Coach
1938	4	11	Pooley Hubert
1939	7	10	James Walker
1940	3	12	James Walker
1941	10	6	James Walker
1942	6	11	James Walker
1943	8	8	Pooley Hubert
1944	0	14	Pooley Hubert
1945	2	10	Joseph Daher
1946	1	10	Jay McWilliams
1947	3	16	Jay McWilliams
1948	3	16	Frank Summers
1949	3	16	Frank Summers
1950	4	17	William O'Hara
1951	3	18	William O'Hara
1952	3	21	William O'Hara
1953	5	19	Chuck Noe
1954	11	12	Chuck Noe
1955	8	15	Chuck Noe
1956	4	19	Jack Null
1957	4	22	Jack Null
1958	4	17	Jack Null
1959	5	13	Weenie Miller
1960	4	16	Weenie Miller
1961	5	17	Weenie Miller
1962	9	11	Weenie Miller
1963	6	15	Weenie Miller
1964	12	12	Weenie Miller
1965	8	13	Gary McPherson
1966	5	18	Gary McPherson
1967	5	16	Gary McPherson
1968	9	12	Gary McPherson
Totals	164	444	

VIRGINIA POLYTECHNIC INSTITUTE

Blacksburg, Virginia

Gobblers — *Orange and Maroon*

Yr.	W	L	Coach
1938	6	8	H. M. McEver
1939	3	14	H. M. McEver
1940	4	16	H. M. McEver
1941	7	14	H. M. McEver
1942	10	10	H. M. McEver
1943	7	7	H. M. McEver
1944	11	4	H. M. McEver
1945	6	8	G. S. "Gummy" Proctor
1946	11	8	G. S. "Gummy" Proctor
1947	13	13	G. S. "Gummy" Proctor
1948	14	8	G. F. "Red" Laird
1949	10	13	G. F. "Red" Laird
1950	15	9	G. F. "Red" Laird
1951	19	10	G. F. "Red" Laird
1952	4	16	G. F. "Red" Laird
1953	4	19	G. F. "Red" Laird
1954	3	24	G. F. "Red" Laird
1955	7	20	G. F. "Red" Laird
1956	14	11	Chuck Noe
1957	14	8	Chuck Noe
1958	11	8	Chuck Noe
1959	16	5	Chuck Noe
1960	20	6	Chuck Noe
1961	15	7	Chuck Noe
1962	19	6	Chuck Noe
1963	12	12	Bill Matthews
1964	16	7	Bill Matthews
1965	13	10	Howard Shannon
1966	19	5	Howard Shannon
1967	20	7	Howard Shannon
1968	14	7	Howard Shannon
Totals	357	320	

WAKE FOREST COLLEGE

Winston-Salem, North Carolina

Demon Deacons — *Old Gold and Black*

Yr.	W	L	Coach
1938	7	12	Murray Greason
1939	18	6	Murray Greason
1940	13	9	Murray Greason
1941	9	9	Murray Greason
1942	16	7	Murray Greason
1943	1	10	Murray Greason
1944	—	—	Murray Greason
1945	3	14	Murray Greason
1946	12	6	Murray Greason
1947	11	13	Murray Greason
1948	18	11	Murray Greason
1949	11	13	Murray Greason
1950	14	16	Murray Greason
1951	16	14	Murray Greason
1952	10	19	Murray Greason
1953	22	7	Murray Greason
1954	17	12	Murray Greason
1955	17	10	Murray Greason
1956	19	9	Murray Greason
1957	19	9	Murray Greason
1958	6	17	Horace "Bones" McKinney
1959	10	14	Horace "Bones" McKinney
1960	21	7	Horace "Bones" McKinney
1961	19	11	Horace "Bones" McKinney
1962	22	9	Horace "Bones" McKinney
1963	16	10	Horace "Bones" McKinney
1964	16	11	Horace "Bones" McKinney
1965	12	15	Horace "Bones" McKinney
1966	8	18	Jack Murdocy
1967	9	18	Jack McCloskey
1968	5	21	Jack McCloskey
Totals	397	357	

WASHINGTON STATE UNIVERSITY

Pullman, Washington

Cougars — *Crimson and Gray*

Yr.	W	L	Coach
1938	19	11	John Friel
1939	24	9	John Friel

Yr.	W	L	Coach
1940	23	10	John Friel
1941	26	6	John Friel
1942	21	8	John Friel
1943	19	11	John Friel
1944	8	18	John Friel
1945	22	12	John Friel
1946	16	13	John Friel
1947	23	10	John Friel
1948	19	10	John Friel
1949	21	9	John Friel
1950	19	13	John Friel
1951	17	15	John Friel
1952	19	16	John Friel
1953	6	27	John Friel
1954	10	17	John Friel
1955	11	15	John Friel
1956	4	22	John Friel
1957	8	18	John Friel
1958	7	19	John Friel
1959	10	16	Marv Harshman
1960	13	13	Marv Harshman
1961	10	16	Marv Harshman
1962	8	18	Marv Harshman
1963	5	20	Marv Harshman
1964	5	21	Marv Harshman
1965	9	17	Marv Harshman
1966	15	11	Marv Harshman
1967	15	11	Marv Harshman
1968	16	9	Marv Harshman
Totals	405	421	

WASHINGTON, UNIVERSITY OF

Seattle, Washington

Huskies			*Purple and Gold*
1938	21	7	Hec Edmundson
1939	20	5	Hec Edmundson
1940	10	15	Hec Edmundson
1941	12	13	Hec Edmundson
1942	18	7	Hec Edmundson
1943	24	7	Hec Edmundson
1944	26	6	Hec Edmundson
1945	22	18	Hec Edmundson
1946	13	14	Hec Edmundson
1947	16	8	Hec Edmundson
1948	23	11	Arthur McLarney
1949	11	15	Arthur McLarney
1950	19	10	Arthur McLarney
1951	24	6	Tippy Dye
1952	25	6	Tippy Dye
1953	30	3	Tippy Dye
1954	8	18	Tippy Dye
1955	13	12	Tippy Dye
1956	15	11	Tippy Dye
1957	17	9	Tippy Dye
1958	8	18	Tippy Dye
1959	18	8	Tippy Dye
1960	15	13	John Grayson
1961	13	13	John Grayson
1962	16	10	John Grayson
1963	13	13	John Grayson
1964	9	17	John Grayson
1965	9	16	John Grayson
1966	10	15	Mac Duckworth
1967	13	12	Mac Duckworth
1968	12	14	Mac Duckworth
Totals	503	350	

WEBER STATE COLLEGE

Ogden, Utah

Wildcats			*Purple and White*
1963	22	4	Dick Motta
1964	17	8	Dick Motta
1965	22	3	Dick Motta
1966	20	5	Dick Motta
1967	18	7	Dick Motta
1968	21	6	Dick Motta
Totals	120	33	

WESTERN KENTUCKY STATE COLLEGE

Bowling Green, Kentucky

Hilltoppers			*Scarlet and White*
1938	30	3	Ed Diddle
1939	22	3	Ed Diddle
1940	24	6	Ed Diddle
1941	22	4	Ed Diddle
1942	29	5	Ed Diddle
1943	24	3	Ed Diddle
1944	13	9	Ed Diddle
1945	17	10	Ed Diddle
1946	15	19	Ed Diddle
1947	25	4	Ed. Diddle
1948	28	2	Ed Diddle
1949	25	4	Ed Diddle
1950	25	6	Ed Diddle
1951	19	10	Ed Diddle
1952	26	5	Ed Diddle
1953	25	6	Ed Diddle
1954	29	3	Ed Diddle
1955	18	10	Ed Diddle
1956	16	12	Ed Diddle
1957	17	9	Ed Diddle
1958	14	11	Ed Diddle
1959	16	10	Ed Diddle
1960	21	7	Ed Diddle
1961	18	8	Ed Diddle
1962	17	10	Ed Diddle
1963	5	16	Ed Diddle
1964	5	16	Ed Diddle
1965	22	3	John Oldham
1966	25	3	John Oldham
1967	23	3	John Oldham
1968	18	7	John Oldham
Totals	633	227	

WESTERN MICHIGAN UNIVERSITY

Kalamazoo, Michigan

Broncos			*Brown and Gold*
1938	5	13	Buck Read
1939	7	10	Buck Read
1940	10	9	Buck Read
1941	10	8	Buck Read
1942	12	8	Buck Read
1943	15	4	Buck Read
1944	15	4	Buck Read

Yr.	W	L	Coach
1945	8	10	Buck Read
1946	15	7	Buck Read
1947	17	7	Buck Read
1948	12	10	Buck Read
1949	12	10	Buck Read
1950	12	10	William Perigo
1951	13	9	William Perigo
1952	16	8	William Perigo
1953	12	9	Joseph Hoy
1954	10	11	Joseph Hoy
1955	12	10	Joseph Hoy
1956	13	9	Joseph Hoy
1957	9	13	Joseph Hoy
1958	5	19	Joseph Hoy
1959	2	20	Donald Boven
1960	13	11	Donald Boven
1961	10	14	Donald Boven
1962	13	11	Donald Boven
1963	12	12	Donald Boven
1964	10	14	Donald Boven
1965	8	16	Donald Boven
1966	8	14	Donald Boven
1967	10	14	Sonny Means
1968	11	13	Sonny Means
Totals	337	337	

WEST TEXAS STATE COLLEGE

Canyon, Texas

Buffaloes — *Maroon and White*

Yr.	W	L	Coach
1938	27	6	Al Baggett
1939	21	9	Al Baggett
1940	26	8	Al Baggett
1941	29	6	Al Baggett
1942	28	3	Al Baggett
1943	15	7	Gus Miller
1944	—	—	
1945	16	10	Gus Miller
1946	19	8	Gus Miller
1947	13	11	Gus Miller
1948	11	13	Gus Miller
1949	18	6	Gus Miller
1950	19	10	Gus Miller
1951	14	12	Gus Miller
1952	19	9	Gus Miller
1953	8	13	Gus Miller
1954	13	7	Gus Miller
1955	15	7	Gus Miller
1956	12	10	Gus Miller
1957	6	14	Gus Miller
1958	3	15	Gus Miller
1959	6	16	Borden Price
1960	11	9	Metz LaFollette
1961	7	16	Metz LaFollette
1962	5	18	Metz LaFollette
1963	6	18	James Viramontes
1964	13	9	James Viramontes
1965	16	9	James Viramontes
1966	6	17	James Viramontes
1967	1	18	James Viramontes
1968	10	11	Dennis Walling
Totals	413	325	

WEST VIRGINIA UNIVERSITY

Morgantown, West Virginia

Mountaineers — *Old Gold and Blue*

Yr.	W	L	Coach
1938	6	13	Marshall Glen
1939	10	9	Dyke Raese
1940	13	6	Dyke Raese
1941	13	10	Dyke Raese
1942	19	4	Dyke Raese
1943	14	7	Rudy Baric
1944	8	11	Harry Lothes
1945	12	6	John Brickels
1946	24	3	Lee Patton
1947	19	3	Lee Patton
1948	17	3	Lee Patton
1949	18	6	Lee Patton
1950	13	11	Lee Patton
1951	18	9	Robert N. "Red" Brown
1952	23	4	Robert N. "Red" Brown
1953	19	7	Robert N. "Red" Brown
1954	12	11	Robert N. "Red" Brown
1955	19	11	Fred Schaus
1956	21	9	Fred Schaus
1957	25	5	Fred Schaus
1958	26	2	Fred Schaus
1959	29	5	Fred Schaus
1960	26	5	Fred Schaus
1961	23	4	George King
1962	24	6	George King
1963	23	8	George King
1964	18	10	George King
1965	14	15	George King
1966	19	9	Ray C. "Bucky" Waters
1967	19	9	Ray C. "Bucky" Waters
1968	19	9	Ray C. "Bucky" Waters
Totals	563	230	

WICHITA STATE UNIVERSITY

Wichita, Kansas

Shockers — *Yellow and Black*

Yr.	W	L	Coach
1938	10	14	William Hennigh
1939	9	12	William Hennigh
1940	11	7	William Hennigh
1941	9	11	William Hennigh
1942	5	15	Jack Sterrett
1943	12	7	Mel Binford
1944	—	—	
1945	14	4	Mel Binford
1946	14	8	Mel Binford
1947	8	17	Mel Binford
1948	12	13	Mel Binford
1949	10	17	Ken Gunning
1950	7	17	Ken Gunning
1951	9	16	Ken Gunning
1952	11	19	Ralph Miller
1953	16	11	Ralph Miller
1954	27	4	Ralph Miller
1955	17	9	Ralph Miller
1956	14	12	Ralph Miller
1957	15	11	Ralph Miller
1958	14	12	Ralph Miller
1959	14	12	Ralph Miller
1960	14	12	Ralph Miller

Yr.	W	L	Coach
1961	18	8	Ralph Miller
1962	18	9	Ralph Miller
1963	19	8	Ralph Miller
1964	23	6	Ralph Miller
1965	21	9	Gary Thompson
1966	17	10	Gary Thompson
1967	14	12	Gary Thompson
1968	12	14	Gary Thompson
Totals	414	336	

WILLIAM AND MARY, COLLEGE OF

Williamsburg, Virginia

Indians — *Green, Gold and Silver*

Yr.	W	L	Coach
1938	2	10	J. S. Kellison
1939	10	10	J. S. Kellison
1940	12	11	Dwight Stuessy
1941	16	9	Dwight Stuessy
1942	14	9	Dwight Stuessy
1943	11	10	Dwight Stuessy
1944	10	10	Rube McCray
1945	7	12	Rube McCray
1946	10	10	S. B. Holt
1947	14	12	Richard Gallagher
1948	13	10	Bernard Wilson
1949	24	10	Bernard Wilson
1950	23	9	Bernard Wilson
1951	20	11	Bernard Wilson
1952	15	13	Bernard Wilson
1953	9	13	Les Hooker
1954	9	14	Boydson Baird
1955	11	14	Boydson Baird
1956	12	14	Boydson Baird
1957	9	18	Boydson Baird
1958	15	14	Bill Chambers
1959	13	11	Bill Chambers
1960	15	11	Bill Chambers
1961	14	10	Bill Chambers
1962	7	17	Bill Chambers
1963	15	9	Bill Chambers
1964	9	13	Bill Chambers
1965	12	13	Bill Chambers
1966	13	12	Bill Chambers
1967	14	11	Warren Mitchell
1968	6	18	Warren Mitchell
Totals	384	368	

WISCONSIN, UNIVERSITY OF

Madison, Wisconsin

Badgers — *Cardinal and White*

Yr.	W	L	Coach
1938	10	10	Bud Foster
1939	10	10	Bud Foster
1940	5	15	Bud Foster
1941	20	3	Bud Foster
1942	14	7	Bud Foster
1943	12	9	Bud Foster
1944	12	9	Bud Foster
1945	10	11	Bud Foster
1946	4	17	Bud Foster
1947	16	6	Bud Foster
1948	12	8	Bud Foster
1949	12	10	Bud Foster
1950	17	5	Bud Foster
1951	10	12	Bud Foster
1952	10	12	Bud Foster
1953	13	9	Bud Foster
1954	12	10	Bud Foster
1955	10	12	Bud Foster
1956	6	16	Bud Foster
1957	5	17	Bud Foster
1958	8	14	Bud Foster
1959	3	19	Bud Foster
1960	8	16	John Erickson
1961	7	17	John Erickson
1962	17	7	John Erickson
1963	14	10	John Erickson
1964	8	16	John Erickson
1965	9	13	John Erickson
1966	11	13	John Erickson
1967	13	11	John Erickson
1968	13	11	John Erickson
Totals	331	355	

WYOMING, UNIVERSITY OF

Laramie, Wyoming

Cowboys — *Brown and Yellow*

Yr.	W	L	Coach
1938	12	5	Willard Witte
1939	10	11	Willard Witte
1940	7	10	Everett Shelton
1941	13	6	Everett Shelton
1942	15	5	Everett Shelton
1943	31	2	Everett Shelton
1944	—	—	
1945	10	17	Everett Shelton
1946	22	4	Everett Shelton
1947	22	6	Everett Shelton
1948	18	9	Everett Shelton
1949	25	10	Everett Shelton
1950	25	11	Everett Shelton
1951	26	11	Everett Shelton
1952	28	7	Everett Shelton
1953	20	10	Everett Shelton
1954	19	9	Everett Shelton
1955	17	9	Everett Shelton
1956	7	19	Everett Shelton
1957	6	19	Everett Shelton
1958	13	14	Everett Shelton
1959	4	22	Everett Shelton
1960	5	19	Bill Strannigan
1961	7	18	Bill Strannigan
1962	7	19	Bill Strannigan
1963	11	15	Bill Strannigan
1964	12	14	Bill Strannigan
1965	16	10	Bill Strannigan
1966	17	9	Bill Strannigan
1967	15	14	Bill Strannigan
1968	18	9	Bill Strannigan
Totals	458	343	

Yr.	W	L	Coach
		XAVIER UNIVERSITY	
		Cincinnati, Ohio	
Musketeers			*Royal Blue and White*
1938	10	9	C. Crowe
1939	13	7	C. Crowe
1940	7	16	C. Crowe
1941	13	9	C. Crowe
1942	10	8	C. Crowe
1943	6	10	C. Crowe
1944	—	—	
1945	—	—	
1946	3	16	E. Burns
1947	8	17	L. Hirt
1948	24	8	L. Hirt
1949	16	10	L. Hirt
1950	12	16	L. Hirt
1951	16	10	L. Hirt
1952	10	14	Ned Wulk
1953	11	12	Ned Wulk
1954	18	12	Ned Wulk
1955	13	13	Ned Wulk
1956	17	11	Ned Wulk
1957	20	8	Ned Wulk
1958	19	11	Jim McCafferty
1959	12	13	Jim McCafferty
1960	17	9	Jim McCafferty
1961	17	10	Jim McCafferty
1962	14	12	Jim McCafferty
1963	12	16	Jim McCafferty
1964	16	10	Jim McCafferty
1965	10	15	Jim McCafferty
1966	13	13	Donald Ruberg
1967	13	13	Donald Ruberg
1968	10	16	George Krajack
Totals	380	344	

Yr.	W	L	Coach
		YALE UNIVERSITY	
		New Haven, Connecticut	
Bulldogs			*Yale Blue*
1938	7	12	Ken Loeffler
1939	4	16	Ken Loeffler
1940	13	6	Ken Loeffler
1941	11	11	Ken Loeffler
1942	7	12	Ken Loeffler
1943	7	17	Robert "Red" Rolfe
1944	14	6	Robert "Red" Rolfe
1945	14	4	Robert "Red" Rolfe
1946	14	1	Robert "Red" Rolfe
1947	7	18	Ivy Williamson
1948	14	13	Howard Hobson
1949	22	8	Howard Hobson
1950	17	9	Howard Hobson
1951	14	13	Howard Hobson
1952	14	14	Howard Hobson
1953	10	15	Howard Hobson
1954	12	14	Howard Hobson
1955	3	21	Howard Hobson
1956	15	11	Howard Hobson
1957	18	8	Joe Vancisin
1958	14	10	Joe Vancisin
1959	10	13	Joe Vancisin
1960	6	17	Joe Vancisin
1961	12	12	Joe Vancisin
1962	18	6	Joe Vancisin
1963	13	10	Joe Vancisin
1964	16	8	Joe Vancisin
1965	10	12	Joe Vancisin
1966	9	12	Joe Vancisin
1967	14	7	Joe Vancisin
1968	15	9	Joe Vancisin
Totals	374	345	

7: THE SMALL COLLEGES

NCAA COLLEGE DIVISION

In 1957, in response to the request of smaller NCAA-member institutions for greater opportunity to compete at the national level, the NCAA divided its championship tournament into two divisions, University (for major colleges) and College (for smaller schools).

Although the College Division members are usually called small colleges, the caliber of competition and not the size of the institution is actually the determining factor in classification. The NCAA designates about 190 teams, playing most of their games against each other, as "major-college" teams. All other NCAA member schools (more than 400) comprise the College Division. Some so-called "small colleges" actually have much larger enrollments than schools that are classified as major college.

The championship round of the College Division tournament is held at Roberts Municipal Auditorium, Evansville, Ind. Host Evansville has captured four championships and Kentucky Wesleyan has won twice. The champions and runners-up with scores of the final games are as follows:

YEAR	CHAMPION	SCORE	RUNNER-UP
1957	Wheaton	89-65	Kentucky Wesleyan
1958	South Dakota	75-53	St. Michael's
1959	Evansville	83-67	Southwest Missouri
1960	Evansville	90-69	Chapman
1961	Wittenberg	42-38	Southeast Missouri
1962	Mount St. Mary's	58-57	Sacramento State
1963	South Dakota State	44-42	Wittenberg
1964	Evansville	72-59	Akron
1965	Evansville	85-82	Southern Illinois
1966	Kentucky Wesleyan	54-51	Southern Illinois
1967	Winston-Salem State	54-51	Akron
1968	Kentucky Wesleyan	63-52	Indiana State

NCAA COLLEGE DIVISION RECORDS

(Based on statistics from National Collegiate Sports Services)

INDIVIDUAL

Single Game

Most Points	113	Clarence "Bevo" Francis, Rio Grande (Ohio) vs Hillsdale (Michigan) 1954

Season

Most Points	1,329	Earl Monroe, Winston-Salem (North Carolina) 1967
Highest Average	46.5	Clarence "Bevo" Francis, Rio Grande (Ohio) 1954
Most F. G. Attempted	925	Jim Toombs, Stillman (Alabama) 1965
Most F. G. Made	509	Earl Monroe, Winston-Salem (North Carolina) 1967
Highest F. G. Percentage	.733	Edward Phillips, Alabama A&M 1968
		Harold Booker, Cheyney State (Pennsylvania) 1965
Most F. T. Attempted	510	Clarence "Bevo" Francis, Rio Grande (Ohio) 1954
Most F. T. Made	401	Joe Miller, Alderson-Broaddus (West Virginia) 1957
Highest F. T. Percentage		
(Minimum 100)	.920	Jim Sutton, South Dakota State 1957
(Minimum 200)	.913	Steve Nisenson, Hofstra (New York) 1964
Most Rebounds	733	Maurice Stokes, St. Francis (Pennsylvania) 1955
Highest Rebound Average	29.5	Tom Hart, Middlebury (Vermont) 1956

Career

Most Points	3,759	Bob Hopkins, Grambling (Louisiana) 1953–56
Highest Average	32.8	Florindo Vieira, Quinnipiac (Connecticut) 1954–57
Most Field Goals	1,403	Bob Hopkins, Grambling (Louisiana) 1953–56
Most Free Throws	1,130	Joe Miller, Alderson-Broaddus (West Virginia) 1954–57

TEAM

Season

Most Victories in Perfect Season	30	Central State (Ohio) 1965
Highest Scoring Average	114.2	Mississippi College 1960
Most Field Goals per game	46.9	Lincoln (Missouri) 1967
Highest F. G. Percentage	.582	South Carolina State 1968
Most Free Throws per game	36.1	Baltimore 1955
Highest F. T. Percentage	.798	Mississippi College 1965
Most Fouls per game	28.7	William Jewell (Missouri) 1952

NAIA

The National Association of Intercollegiate Athletics (NAIA) basketball tournament is the largest collegiate championship tournament in the United States. Thirty-two district champions representing more than 500 member institutions throughout the country play each March in Kansas City.

The NAIA, officially organized in 1940, is more than a basketball tournament, however, with a program including 13 national championships ranging from bowling to football. The formation of the organization grew out of a desire by some prominent Kansas City residents to have a championship basketball tournament after the AAU moved its tourney to Denver.

In 1937 these K.C. leaders got together with Dr. James Naismith, inventor of the game who was teaching at the University of Kansas, and Emil S. Liston, athletic director at Baker University in Baldwin, Kan. The result was an eight-team tournament of Midwest conference champions. The following year saw the first 32-team field entered in what was now the National Intercollegiate Basketball Championship tournament. The National Association of Intercollegiate Basketball (NAIB) was organized in 1940, changing its name in 1952 to the present NAIA.

The NAIA describes itself as an organization "whose primary and sole purpose is to champion the cause and promote the interests of the college of moderate enrollment and sound athletic philosophy and program."

The basketball tournament has served as a springboard to the professional ranks for a number of stars including Willis Reed of Grambling, Lucious Jackson of Pan American, Zelmo Beaty of Prairie View A&M, Al Tucker of Oklahoma Baptist and Dick Barnett, Ben Warley and John Barnhill of Tennessee A&I.

Willis Reed

Zelmo Beaty

Lucious Jackson

Clarence "Bevo" Francis

The tourney also served as the backdrop for the most publicized basketball collegian of the 1950s, Clarence "Bevo" Francis of little (96 students) Rio Grande College in Ohio. In his freshman year, 1954, Francis dominated the pre-tournament talk after averaging 50.1 points in 39 games and scoring 116 points in one outing against Ashland (Kentucky) College. The admiration of the fans for the 6-9 Francis was such that the tournament was sold out the first two nights, until Rio Grande was eliminated. But the coaches did not share the fans' admiration for Francis' exploits and purged the record book of all marks not set in games against schools which granted four-year degrees. Some of the teams Rio Grande played that year were Bliss Business College and Cincinnati Seminary.

The winners, runners-up and scores of NAIA championships:

YEAR	CHAMPION	SCORE	RUNNER-UP
1937	Central Missouri State	35-24	Morningside (Iowa)
1938	Central Missouri State	45-30	Roanoke (Virginia)
1939	Southwestern (Kansas)	32-31	San Diego State
1940	Tarkio (Missouri)	52-42	San Diego State
1941	San Diego State	36-32	Murray State (Kentucky)
1942	Hamline (Minnesota)	33-31	Southeastern Oklahoma
1943	Southeast Missouri State	34-32	Northwest Missouri State
1944	No Tournament		
1945	Loyola (Louisiana)	49-36	Pepperdine (California)
1946	Southern Illinois	49-40	Indiana State
1947	Marshall (West Virginia)	73-59	Mankato State (Minnesota)
1948	Louisville (Kentucky)	82-70	Hamline (Minnesota)
1949	Hamline (Minnesota)	57-46	Regis (Colorado)
1950	Indiana State	61-47	East Central Oklahoma

1951	Hamline (Minnesota)	69-61	Millikin (Illinois)
1952	Southwest Missouri State	73-64	Murray State (Kentucky)
1953	Southwest Missouri State	79-71	Hamline (Minnesota)
1954	St. Benedict's (Kansas)	62-56	Western Illinois
1955	East Texas State	71-54	Southeastern Oklahoma
1956	McNeese State (Louisiana)	60-55	Texas Southern
1957	Tennessee State	92-73	Southeastern Oklahoma
1958	Tennessee State	85-73	Western Illinois
1959	Tennessee State	97-87	Pacific Lutheran (Washington)
1960	Southwest Texas State	66-44	Westminster (Pennsylvania)
1961	Grambling (Louisiana)	95-75	Georgetown (Kentucky)
1962	Prairie View A&M (Texas)	62-53	Westminster (Pennsylvania)
1963	Pan American (Texas)	73-62	Western Carolina
1964	Rockhurst (Missouri)	66-56	Pan American (Texas)
1965	Central State (Ohio)	85-51	Oklahoma Baptist
1966	Oklahoma Baptist	88-59	Georgia Southern
1967	St. Benedict's (Kansas)	71-65	Oklahoma Baptist
1968	Central State (Ohio)	51-48	Fairmont (West Virginia)

NAIA ALL-TIME RECORDS

(Compiled by the NAIA)

INDIVIDUAL

Single Game

Most Points	113	Clarence "Bevo" Francis, Rio Grande (Ohio) vs Hillsdale (Michigan) 1954
Most Field Goals	38	Clarence "Bevo" Francis, Rio Grande (Ohio) vs Hillsdale (Michigan) 1954
Most Free Throws	37	Clarence "Bevo" Francis, Rio Grande (Ohio) vs Hillsdale (Michigan) 1954
Highest F. G. Percentage	1.000	(14 of 14) Bob Kauffman, Guilford (North Carolina) vs Catawba (North Carolina) 1966
Highest F. T. Percentage	1.000	(21 of 21) Chester Webb, Georgia Southern vs Stetson (Florida) 1956
Most Rebounds	36	Waymon Stewart, Lakeland (Wisconsin) vs Eureka (Illinois) 1966
	36	Phil Andros, New Haven (Connecticut) vs Bryant (Rhode Island) 1966
Most Assists	26	Don Adler, Georgia Southern vs Jacksonville (Florida) 1964

Season

Most Points	1,329	Earl Monroe, Winston-Salem (North Carolina) 1967
Highest Scoring Average	48.3	Clarence "Bevo" Francis, Rio Grande (Ohio) 1953
Most F. G. Attempted	915	Jim Toombs, Stillman (Alabama) 1965
Most F. G. Made	509	Earl Monroe, Winston-Salem (North Carolina) 1967
Highest F. G. Percentage	.747	Jack Brantley, Jacksonville State (Alabama) 1967

Most F. T. Attempted	529	Joe Miller, Alderson-Broaddus (West Virginia) 1957
Most F. T. Made	437	Joe Miller, Alderson-Broaddus (West Virginia) 1957
Highest F. T. Percentage	.938	(75 of 80) Jerry Lewis, Indiana Central 1959
Most Rebounds	738	Gene Hoyt, McKendree (Illinois) 1952
Highest Rebound Average	27.3	Gene Hoyt, McKendree (Illinois) 1952
Most Assists	223	Don Wallen, Georgia Southern 1955
		Jack Nisbet, New Haven (Connecticut) 1967

Career

Most Points	3,759	Bob Hopkins, Grambling (Louisiana) 1953-56
Most Field Goals	1,403	Bob Hopkins, Grambling (Louisiana) 1953-56
Highest F. G. Percentage	.602	Jim Ficek, Eastern Illinois 1963-65
		Isador Schmiesing, St. Cloud State (Minnesota) 1963-66
Most Free Throws	1,139	Joe Miller, Alderson-Broaddus (West Virginia) 1954-57
Highest F. T. Percentage	.873	Dwain Farmer, Tennessee Wesleyan 1955-58
Most Rebounds	2,191	Bob Hopkins, Grambling (Louisiana) 1953-56
Most Assists	541	Vasaco Walton, Indiana Central 1962-65

TEAM

Single Game

Most Points, One Team	169	Stillman (Alabama) vs Miles (Alabama) 1966
Most Points, Two Teams	257	New Mexico Highlands and Hiram Scott (Nebraska) 1966
Most Field Goals	68	Lakeland (Wisconsin) vs Judson (Illinois) 1967
Highest F. G. Percentage	.857	Huntingdon (Alabama) vs Troy State (Alabama) 1963
Most Free Throws	46	Northern Arizona vs Arizona University 1953
Highest F. T. Percentage	1.000	Southeastern Louisiana, 1950; Wartburg (Iowa) 1960; McNeese State (Louisiana), 1961; Kansas Wesleyan, 1965; Culver-Stockton (Missouri), 1966; Morningside (Iowa), 1966; Bloomsburg State (Pennsylvania), 1967; Alabama College, 1967
Largest Margin of Victory	80	Detroit Tech vs Cleary (Michigan) 1964
Largest Margin of Defeat (By NAIA member)	75	Lakeland (Wisconsin) by Youngstown (Ohio) 1964
Most Points Allowed	169	Miles (Alabama) vs Stillman (Alabama) 1966
Most Rebounds	102	North Park (Illinois) vs Carroll (Wisconsin) 1967

Season

Best Record	30-0	Central State (Ohio) 1965
Worst Record (Without a victory)	0-16	Morris Harvey (West Virginia) 1936
Worst Record (With a victory)	1-21	Detroit Tech 1965
Most Points	3,040	Pasadena (California) 1967
Highest Scoring Average	111.4	Stillman (Alabama) 1968
Widest Victory Margin Average	27.7	Western New England (Massachusetts) 1968

Most Consecutive Victories	30	Indiana Central 1939–43 Central State (Ohio) 1965
Most Consecutive Losses	26	St. Benedict's (Kansas) 1943–46
Most Field Goals	1,216	Morris Harvey (West Virginia) 1967
Highest F. G. Percentage	.609	Alabama State 1965
Most Free Throws	826	McNeese State (Louisiana) 1956
Highest F. T. Percentage	.827	Fisk (Tennessee) 1965
Most Consecutive Free Throws	32	Culver-Stockton (Missouri) 1966
Most Rebounds	1,944	St. Cloud State (Minnesota) 1966
Highest Percentage of Rebounds	.728	Western New England (Massachusetts) 1968

THE PROFESSIONALS

The 1902 Buffalo Germans: left to right, rear row, Maier and Burkhardt; middle row, Faust, Capt. Heerdt and Miller; front row, Redlein and Rohde.

8: THE PIVOTAL ERA

Professional basketball was born in the eastern United States just before the turn of the 20th century more as an economic necessity than as a profit-making venture.

When the young men at the various YMCAs along the eastern seaboard became converts to the sport invented by James Naismith in 1891, they played with such abandon that the Ys decided to drop basketball because of its growing roughness. That left the players no other choice than to rent halls in which to continue playing the sport. And to meet the rentals—and the guarantees for the visiting teams—admission charges had to be instituted.

Uncertainty surrounds the date and location of the first professional game. The strongest claim is for Trenton, New Jersey, in 1896. Attendance for a game at the Masonic Hall there was large enough so that after meeting expenses, the Trenton club had enough extra money to pay each player $15. Fred Cooper, the captain, received an extra dollar. A less substantiated claim has it that the first game was played in Herkimer, New York, in 1893. A group of local players supposedly rented the Fox Opera House in Herkimer and brought in a team from Utica. After paying the visiting team's expenses, there was only change left over for the Herkimer players.

The first professional league, the National Basketball League, was organized in 1898 in Philadelphia. The league disbanded after the 1902–03 season.

As the NBL broke up, the Philadelphia League came into being and welcomed a number of players from the original circuit. The Philadelphia League expanded in 1909 into the Eastern League and embraced teams from New Jersey and New York as well as Pennsylvania.

Professional leagues soon began to spring up elsewhere. The Central League got started in western Pennsylvania in 1906. The Hudson River League was formed in New York three years later. Other leagues established about that time were the New York State League, 1911; Western Pennsylvania League, 1912; Pennsylvania State League, 1914; Inter-State League, 1915; and the Metropolitan Basketball League, 1921. The American Basketball League was formed in 1926.

The Hudson River League and the New York State League were the showcases for the finest professional team of the era, Ed Wachter's Troy (New York) Trojans. Originally formed to challenge the famous Buffalo Germans, who claimed the national championship by virtue of their triumph at the Buffalo Exposition of 1901, the Trojans swept to two consecutive Hudson River League crowns before that league collapsed. The Trojans then became charter members of the New York State League and won three titles in four years before that circuit

CELTICS
CELTICS
CELTICS
CELTICS
CELTICS

also failed. Wachter took his team on tour after that and it won 38 straight games before he broke it up.

It was during the Trojans' second season in the Hudson River League that they were able to experiment with some of Wachter's new ideas for the game. Up to that time, passing consisted of short tosses caught on the fly by the receivers.

Wachter had his players adopt the bounce pass, which was much harder to intercept. Another of his innovations was the fast break. The fashion had been for everyone to scramble after the ball. But Wachter set his men in strategic places, with two pursuing the ball, prepared to throw it over the defense to an unguarded teammate in scoring position.

Wachter and the Trojans also anticipated the foul shot rule. All the Trojans were so good at shooting free throws that they encouraged a rule requiring the player to take the shot himself. Until then, each team used a specialist who shot all its free throws. The new rule, though, was not generally accepted for many years.

Early professional basketball was a rugged sport, with anything short of complete mayhem allowed. The rules depended mainly on what court the teams played on and who refereed the game. And there were other shortcomings as well. For example, the games were merely a sideshow for the dances usually held in conjunction with them. There would be dancing before the game, during halftime and after. The highly-waxed floors, excellent for dancing, were hardly conducive to quick starts and stops by the basketball players.

There was no such thing as an out-of-bounds ball because the courts, usually of 60′ x 40′ bandbox dimensions, were enclosed with chicken wire fences. Because the teams appeared caged in by the fences, the players soon received the nickname "cagers." Later the courts were enclosed with a netting of rope. The more adroit players used the ropes to their advantage, ricocheting in one direction or another.

Then, too, there was little stability among the professionals. Players sold their services to the highest bidder. They jumped from one club to another with impunity. A man would play with Troy one night and against them the next. The better players often played in several leagues at the same time. Under these conditions, team play didn't exist and coaching was almost nonexistent as well. Players relied on trial and error and sought advice from teammates on how to play a particular opponent.

Under these chaotic conditions the New York Celtics were organized in 1914 as a settlement house team in a tough neighborhood on the city's West Side. Among the best players on the club were John Whitty and Pete Barry. The Celtics played together for three seasons and broke up with the United States' entrance into the World War in 1917.

After the Armistice in 1918, Jim Furey, a New York promoter, and his brother Tom decided to reorganize the Celtics. However, Frank McCormack, who had been the founder of the first New York Celtics team, refused to give up the rights to the name. So the Fureys settled for the Original Celtics as the name of their new team. Whitty and Barry from the New York Celtics, and Ernie Reich, Joe Trippe, Eddie White and Mike Smolick made up the team. They were good, but far from the dominant team of their time.

The next season, Jim Furey turned the Celtics into a powerhouse by adding Swede Grimstead, Henry "Dutch" Dehnert and Johnny Beckman. Grimstead was a veteran and Dehnert and Beckman were two of the best young players. Beckman was considered the best foul shooter of the era and because of him the Celtics were unwilling to adopt the Troy Trojans' innovation requiring the player fouled to take the foul shot.

The other outstanding team of this time was the New York Whirlwinds, organized by

The Celtics, reborn for one last fling in the 1930s: left to right, rear, Pat Herlihy, Dutch Dehnert, Joe Lapchick; front, Paul Birch, Davey Banks, Nat Hickey.

Nat Holman

Dutch Dehnert

Chris Leonard

Pete Barry

Tex Rickard. The Whirlwinds included Barney Sedran, Nat Holman and Chris Leonard. The public naturally wanted to see the two teams meet. Neither the Celtics nor the Whirlwinds willingly recognized the other's existence, but a three-game series was finally arranged in 1921. The teams played in New York's 71st Regiment Armory. The Whirlwinds won the opening game, 40-27, before a crowd of 11,000, but the Celtics came back to win, 26-24, the following night. The third game was never played for fear of violence among the wrought-up partisans of the two teams.

At the end of the season, Furey persuaded Holman and Chris Leonard to jump from the Whirlwinds to the Celtics. In addition he signed all the Celtics to exclusive contracts with guaranteed salaries. With this move, wildcat basketball was on the way out. Furey wasn't content to stand pat and continually added the best players he could find. These included Joe Lapchick, Davey Banks, Horace "Horse" Haggerty, and Nat Hickey.

Beginning at the time Furey signed the Celtics to exclusive contracts for the 1922–23 season, the club totally dominated the game through the 1920s. The Celtics would travel anywhere and take on any opponent. They were paid comparatively well for the time, but money was never the most important thing to them. The Celtics had tremendous pride and always tried to win, although they seldom went out of their way to run up the score. At the same time they usually tried to have some fun, too.

Because the same players were together almost every night, the Celtics developed an almost uncanny sense of teamwork. Out of this came several of the great innovations in basketball strategy, including the pivot play, the switching defense and the give-and-go offense. The Celtics were so superior to most of the teams they played that they were able to perfect their new theories under actual game conditions without much fear of losing.

Davey Banks was an Original Celtic.

One night the Celtics ran up an early lead of 30-1 over a team in Miami, Florida. The Celts took the opportunity to practice their passing and set plays, but the other team's standing guard continually got in the way. The standing guard, common at the time, stood at the foul line and never moved downcourt, even when his own team had the ball.

Then an idea occurred to Dutch Dehnert. "I volunteered to stand in front of him with my back to the basket, so that instead of the guard breaking up our passes, they could pass to me and I could give it back to them. We tried this, and in an effort to bat the ball out of my hands, the standing guard moved around to my right side. All I had to do was pivot to my left, take one step and lay the ball up. This was the pivot play but we didn't even know it at the time."

Before the coming of the Celtics, basketball was strictly an individual game. Each player considered himself personally responsible for the player who lined up opposite him at the center jump. But the Celtics played as a team, and each player guarded the nearest man, regardless of whose personal opponent he was. Joe Lapchick, at 6-5 one of the big men of his time, had trouble adjusting to these defensive switches when he first joined the Celtics. Finally Johnny Whitty took him aside and explained the essential element of the Celtics' philosophy. "It isn't how many goals you get, Joe, or how often you get the tap. We know what you can do with the ball. It's how you are without the ball that determines how good a basketball player you are," Whitty said.

The Celtics were a confident bunch and were convinced that wherever they went they were the best. Always they knew that they were a marked team, that opponents and fans alike were out to get them. The players had to ignore such indignities as hatpins jabbed into their posteriors by courtside spectators. Holman, one of the smallest of the Celtics, was frequently a target. He was a brilliant passer and faker, and sometimes opposing players would vent their frustrations on Nat after being embarrassed by one of his clever moves. "Horse Haggerty was my personal bodyguard. Any time I got hit, and I got hit a lot in those early days, Haggerty would go over to the fellow who fouled me, give him a robust nudge in the ribs and say 'Now we're even.' They always knew what he meant, too," Nat recalled.

Haggerty, at 6-4 and 225 pounds, was truly a giant of a man and was quite capable of meeting any roughness on the court in kind. One night he was riled by a fan who had been continually insulting Holman. Horse beckoned the fan over and then knocked him cold with one punch. Another time he knocked out a referee when Horse thought his decisions too obviously favored the other team. Before Haggerty could get out of town that night, he was jumped by a gang of toughs, one of the few times he lost a fight.

As the Celtics were rolling over all opposition, winning about 90 percent of their games, George Preston Marshall, a Washington laundry tycoon, decided to organize a big-time professional league. His idea was sound but the independent Celtics refused to cooperate. They were too busy making money on their barnstorming tours to have any part of Marshall's American Basketball League. The Celtics added further insults by routing the league's teams in exhibition games.

Finally the ABL blacklisted the Celtics, forbidding any of the league's teams to play games against the Celtics. With their revenue sharply curtailed, the Celtics had no choice but to join the league, which they did midway through the 1926–27 season. The Celtics ran away with the second-half title, winning 19 of 20 games. The following year the Celtics easily won both halves of the ABL championship and then beat Fort Wayne in a playoff series.

Marshall, the owner of the Washington Palace Five, spent more than $65,000 in salaries trying to hire players good enough to beat the Celtics. But the spending didn't do his team any good. "We'll break you yet, George," Dehnert would yell to Marshall as the Celtics

Cleveland Rosenblums: left to right, Red Skurnick, Carl "Sox" Husta, Pete Barry, Ray Dickerson, Dutch Dehnert, George "Dink" Irwin, Dave Kerr and Joe Lapchick.

rolled over the Palace Five. The Celtics were so good, in fact, that fans around the league began to lose interest and attendance dropped. In a desperate attempt to restore competitive balance, the league decided to break up the Celtics and parcel out their players to the other teams.

Lapchick, Holman and Barry found their way to the Cleveland Rosenblums and stamped that team with the Celtics mold. The Rosenblums made such a shambles of the league opposition that the ABL had to cease operations in 1929 anyway. Thus the Celtics, whom the league had broken up for being too good, finally killed the circuit.

The Renaissance Big Five, an independent all-Negro team from New York, succeeded the Celtics as rulers of the basketball world. The Rens, as they were popularly known, took on all comers and from 1932 until 1936 unquestionably proved themselves the best team in the nation. The Rens would go on the road for about four months, playing one-night stands. They traveled in their own bus and often ended up sleeping in it since most hotels refused to offer them accommodations.

The Rens had been organized by Bob Douglas in New York's Harlem in 1922. Not until the 1925–26 season, though, did they capture the public's eye. That year Douglas acquired James "Pappy" Ricks, Clarence "Fat" Jenkins and Eyre "Bruiser" Saitch. Jenkins was also an outstanding outfielder in the Negro National Baseball League, but discrimination against Negroes prevented him from ever reaching the major leagues.

Douglas next added Charles "Tarzan" Cooper, Bill Yancey and John "Casey" Holt. In 1932 Douglas signed the seventh Ren, Wee Willie Smith, and the great years began. Over the next four seasons, the Rens compiled a record of 473-49. In their best year, 1933–34, they were 127-7, including an 88-game winning streak. In the four years the seven stars played together, the Rens claimed the world's championship each year without any serious dispute. In 1963 the team was elected to the Hall of Fame.

The American Basketball League, which the Celtics had put out of business, resumed play for the 1933–34 season after a lapse of four years. The Philadelphia Sphas, from the South Philadelphia Hebrew Association and coached by Eddie Gottlieb, emerged as the top team in the revived ABL. The Sphas won seven titles in 13 years. The New York Jewels, another of the league's good teams, were made up of the same men who had played for the St. John's "Wonder Five" during their college days.

In its later years, though, the ABL declined in stature and with the founding of the Basketball Association of America in 1946 lost recognition as a major league.

The National Basketball League began play in 1937. The NBL was organized by Lonnie Darling, who had formed the Oshkosh All-Stars a few years before. The Akron Goodyears won the first NBL title. The league had most of its franchises in smaller midwestern cities. Among the teams at one time or another were Oshkosh, Anderson, Tri-Cities, Flint, Youngstown, Toledo, Fort Wayne, Dayton, Waterloo and Hammond, as well as such larger cities as Detroit, Chicago, Denver, Minneapolis and Syracuse. With this assortment of franchises and few of its teams in the nation's largest cities, the NBL had difficulty achieving recognition as a truly major league.

The Rens: left to right, Clarence "Fat" Jenkins, Bill Yancey, John "Casey" Holt, James "Pappy" Ricks, Eyre "Bruiser" Saitch, Charles "Tarzan" Cooper, Wee Willie Smith. Inset: owner Bob Douglas.

9: BIG LEAGUE

In the summer of 1946 owners of some of the nation's largest sports arenas became convinced that the time was right to bring major league professional basketball to the biggest cities. With the conclusion of World War II, many fine collegiate players were discharged from the Armed Forces and became available to the pro teams. In addition, the lifting of wartime restrictions on the economy left Americans with more money for entertainment.

The group of arena owners, led by Walter Brown, president of the Boston Garden, and Al Sutphin, owner of the Cleveland Arena, all had successfully promoted such events as ice hockey, ice shows, boxing, rodeos and other sporting attractions. Encouraged by the drawing power of college basketball, they felt that a large potential audience for the professional game existed as well.

On June 6, 1946, these men met in New York City to organize a new major professional league, the Basketball Association of America. The owners chose Maurice Podoloff, a New Haven, Connecticut, lawyer, as president of the league. At the time Podoloff was president of the American Hockey League. Podoloff is given credit for holding the league together through its difficult early years. The BAA began play with teams in 11 cities: Boston, New York, Philadelphia, Providence, Toronto, Washington, Chicago, St. Louis, Cleveland, Detroit and Pittsburgh.

To encourage an offense-minded game, the new league outlawed all varieties of zone defense. Only man-to-man defenses were permitted.

The National Basketball League, with most of its franchises in smaller Midwestern cities, had been in operation since the 1937–38 season, and the two leagues immediately embarked on a struggle for supremacy in professional basketball. The BAA and NBL competed for the services of the best graduating college players each season. For 1947–48, Minneapolis of the NBL signed George Mikan, the 6-10 giant from DePaul who was basketball's greatest drawing card.

But before the 1948–49 season the BAA dealt the older league a crushing blow by picking up four of its best franchises, including Minneapolis with Mikan. A year later the war was over. The two leagues merged to form a new 17-team circuit called the National Basketball Association. Podoloff was elected president of the NBA and Ike W. Duffey, who had headed the NBL, became chairman of the new league's Executive Board.

Minneapolis' George Mikan (99) was the biggest man in the early NBA years.

NEW YO
18

A detailed year-by-year history of the modern era in professional basketball, dating from the establishment of the Basketball Association of America in the 1946–47 season, follows:

YEARLY ROUNDUPS

1946–47

The established National Basketball League and the brand-new Basketball Association of America each unveiled a high-powered scorer this season. And each of these stars led his team to victory in the playoffs.

The Philadelphia Warriors, paced by Joe Fulks, won the first championship in the BAA, and the Chicago American Gears, with 6-10 George Mikan, won the NBL playoffs, although Rochester emerged as the NBL champion.

The BAA began play with 11 teams, divided into two divisions. In the East, the Washington Capitols, coached by Arnold "Red" Auerbach, finished the regular season 14 games ahead of

Washington's Bones McKinney made the BAA's first All-Star team.

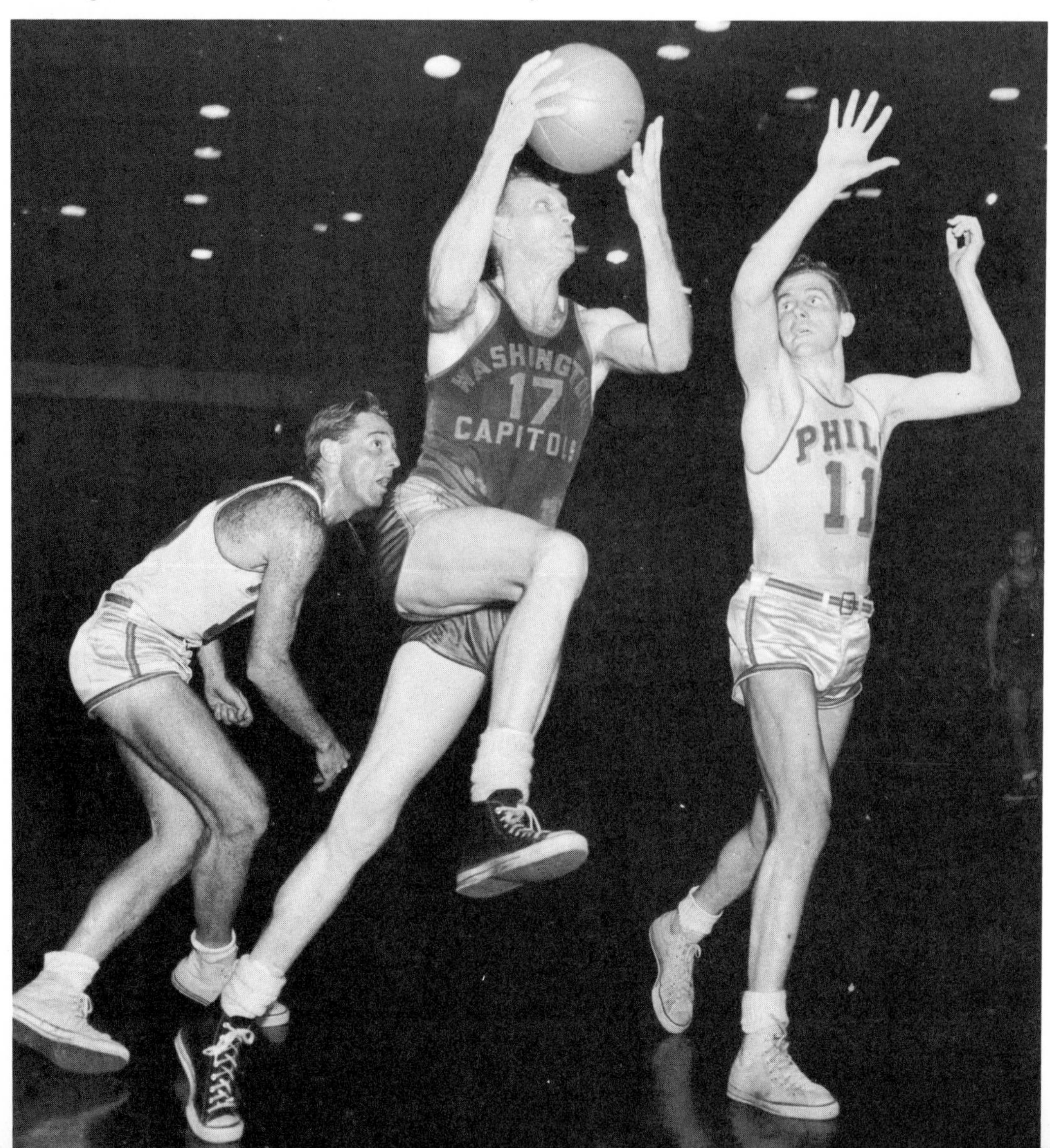

Eddie Gottlieb's Philadelphia Warriors. The New York Knickerbockers, Providence Steamrollers, Toronto Huskies and Boston Celtics followed.

The Western Division race was much closer, with the Chicago Stags finishing just one game ahead of the St. Louis Bombers. The Cleveland Rebels, Detroit Falcons and Pittsburgh Ironmen trailed. In the final series for the league championship, the Warriors crushed Chicago, four games to one. The crowd numbered 8,221 for the final playoff game in Philadelphia.

Fulks, a 6-6 ex-marine, was the BAA's top individual performer. He earned the nickname "Jumpin' Joe" as he averaged 23.1 points a game and consistently outleaped taller opponents. Jumpin' Joe scored 41 points against Toronto, the highest individual total in the BAA's first season.

Fulks shot more times (1,557)—and scored more baskets (475)—than anyone else in the league. He finished with a lead of more than 400 points over his nearest rival, Bob Feerick of Washington.

Other top players included little 5-10 Ernie Calverley of Providence and Max Zaslofsky of Chicago. Calverley, who had played on the famous "point-a-minute" teams at Rhode Island State, led the league in assists and also finished sixth in scoring with a 14.3 average. Zaslofsky, who ignored the jump shot in favor of a two-hand set, was the fifth-leading scorer with a 14.4 average. Many of his points came on shots from beyond the 30-foot mark.

The first BAA All-Star team included Fulks, who was a unanimous selection; Feerick, Zaslofsky, Stan Miasek of Detroit and Bones McKinney of Washington.

While Fulks was burning up the BAA, George Mikan, the giant from DePaul University, was making his pro debut with the NBL's Chicago Gears. The Gears, with player-coach Bobby McDermott and Mikan, who averaged 16.5 points, won the playoffs after finishing the regular season tied for third in the Western Division. A new league rule, however, gave the championship to the team with the best record for the entire season, and on this basis Rochester was declared the champion.

The NBL's All-Star team included Mikan, McDermott, Fred Lewis of Sheboygan, and Al Cervi and Bob Davies of the Rochester Royals. Cervi, one of the few pros in the league who didn't go to college, was the NBL's leading scorer with a 14.4 average.

STANDINGS

Eastern Division

	W.	L.	Pct.
Washington	49	11	.817
Philadelphia	35	25	.583
New York	33	27	.550
Providence	28	32	.467
Toronto	22	38	.367
Boston	22	38	.367

Western Division

	W.	L.	Pct.
Chicago	39	22	.639
St. Louis	38	23	.623
Cleveland	30	30	.500
Detroit	20	40	.333
Pittsburgh	15	45	.250

PLAYOFFS

First Round

Chicago defeated Washington 4 games to 2
Philadelphia defeated St. Louis 2 games to 1
New York defeated Cleveland 2 games to 1
Philadelphia defeated New York 2 games to 1

Championship

Philadelphia defeated Chicago 4 games to 1

TOP SCORERS

	Pts.	Ave.
Joe Fulks, Philadelphia	1389	23.2
Bob Feerick, Washington	926	16.8
Stan Miasek, Detroit	895	14.9
Ed Sadowski, Toronto-Cleveland	877	16.5
Max Zaslofsky, Chicago	877	14.4

LEADERS IN ASSISTS

	No.	Ave.
Ernie Calverley, Providence	202	3.4
Ken Sailors, Cleveland	134	2.3
Ossie Schectman, New York	109	2.0
Howie Dallmar, Philadelphia	104	1.7
Marv Rottner, Chicago	93	1.7

1947–48

The Basketball Association of America lost four of its original franchises and added one new team for its second season. And it was the Baltimore Bullets, the new team, which provided the biggest surprise by winning the league championship.

The entire Western Division finished in almost a dead heat. St. Louis was first, with a 29-19 record, and the other three teams, Baltimore, Chicago and Washington, finished in a three-way tie for second place, one game back. A special series of games had to be held to settle the final standings before the playoffs could get underway.

The Eastern Division race was close too, with the Philadelphia Warriors, the defending champions, finishing one game ahead of the New York Knicks. Toronto, Cleveland, Pittsburgh and Detroit, all BAA members in the league's first season, had folded before the second campaign began, making it an eight-team circuit.

New York rookie Carl Braun scored 47 points in one game.

Philadelphia's Howie Dallmar drives on New York's Dick Holub.

30
37

Baltimore came on in the playoffs and beat Philadelphia, four games to two, to win the league championship. Baltimore's player-coach, Buddy Jeanette, led the Bullets to the title with slick floor play and a 10.7 scoring average.

Philadelphia's Joe Fulks had the highest scoring average for the season, 22.1, but Chicago's Max Zaslofsky, with his long-range set shot, scored the most points, 1,009.

New York's Carl Braun, a 6-5 rookie from Colgate University, showed that he was a quick learner and one fine marksman when he shattered Fulks' single-game scoring mark of 41 points. Braun, a deadly outside shot, collected 47 points against Providence on December 6. Braun finished the season as the BAA's sixth-leading scorer with a 14.2 average.

Fulks, Max Zaslofsky of Chicago and Bob Feerick of Washington all repeated as All-BAA selections. They were joined by Howie Dallmar of Philadelphia, the league leader in assists, and Ed Sadowski of Boston.

In the National Basketball League, Minneapolis, with George Mikan, won the playoff for the league title. The Lakers had taken over the franchise of Detroit, which had won only four games the previous season, but the addition of Mikan and Jim Pollard converted them into champions. Mikan, the NBL's Most Valuable Player, broke virtually all the league's scoring records as he averaged 21.3 points a game and reached a peak of 42 points against Syracuse. In the final playoff series, Minneapolis defeated Rochester, the defending champion, three games to one.

The All-NBL team included Mikan and Pollard of Minneapolis, Rookie of the Year Marko Todorovich of Sheboygan and Al Cervi and Red Holzman of Rochester.

STANDINGS

Eastern Division

	W.	L.	Pct.
Philadelphia	27	21	.563
New York	26	22	.542
Boston	20	28	.417
Providence	6	42	.104

Western Division

	W.	L.	Pct.
St. Louis	29	19	.604
Baltimore	28	20	.583
Chicago	28	20	.583
Washington	28	20	.583

PLAYOFFS

First Round

Philadelphia defeated St. Louis 4 games to 3
Baltimore defeated New York 2 games to 1

Chicago defeated Boston 2 games to 1
Baltimore defeated Chicago 2 games to 0

Championship

Baltimore defeated Philadelphia 4 games to 2

TOP SCORERS

	Pts.	Ave.
Max Zaslofsky, Chicago	1007	21.0
Joe Fulks, Philadelphia	949	22.1
Ed Sadowski, Boston	910	19.4
Bob Feerick, Washington	775	16.1
Stan Miasek, Chicago	716	14.9

LEADERS IN ASSISTS

	No.	Ave.
Howie Dallmar, Philadelphia	120	2.5
Ernie Calverley, Providence	119	2.5
Jim Seminoff, Chicago	89	1.8
Chuck Gilmur, Chicago	77	1.6
Ed Sadowski, Boston	74	1.6

1948–49

Disaster struck the old National Basketball League in midsummer as four of its best franchises switched to the Basketball Association of America. The NBL lost the Minneapolis Lakers and George Mikan, their great 6-10 center; Rochester, the defending league champions; Fort Wayne and Indianapolis. These switches just about killed the NBL's chances for survival and left the pro basketball field virtually clear for the BAA.

Minneapolis and Mikan burst on the BAA scene with a vengeance. The Lakers won the league championship in their first season and Mikan used his tremendous strength and 240 pounds to great advantage. He dethroned Philadelphia's Joe Fulks, the BAA's resident scoring whiz, as the scoring champion. Mikan poured in an average of 28.3 points a game, comfortably ahead of Fulks' 26.0.

The Rochester Royals, with Arnie Risen and Bob Davies, finished a game ahead of the Lakers in the Western Division. But in the playoffs, Minneapolis eliminated Rochester in two straight games and went on to defeat Red Auerbach's Washington Capitols in six games for the BAA title. The Capitols had finished the season six games ahead of the New York Knicks and then eliminated the Knicks, two games to one, in the playoffs.

Minneapolis, with Mikan (99), won the title in its first year in the BAA.

Old NBL players dominated the All-BAA selections as Mikan and Jim Pollard of Minneapolis and Rochester's Davies, who had led the league in assists and averaged 15.1 points, all made the team. Mikan was a unanimous pick. Joining them were two familiar faces, Fulks, and Max Zaslofsky of Chicago, each making the all-league squad for the third consecutive year.

Fulks turned in the outstanding individual performance of the season by scoring 63 points against the Indianapolis Jets. His outburst totally eclipsed the league's old scoring high of 47 points, set by Carl Braun of New York the season before.

The Lakers played the famed Harlem Globetrotters twice and split the two games. One of the contests attracted a crowd of 20,046. The BAA's Philadelphia Warriors also took a game from the Globetrotters, winning 58-54.

The NBL, breathing its last, added Denver, Dayton, Hammond and Waterloo to make up for the loss of the four teams that jumped to the BAA and the disbanding of the Toledo and Flint franchises. The Anderson Duffey Packers finished first in the East and defeated the Oshkosh All-Stars, Western champions, in the playoffs. Don Otten of the Tri-Cities Blackhawks topped the NBL's scorers.

Otten, along with Dick Mehen of Waterloo, Al Cervi of Syracuse, Frank Brian of Anderson and Gene Englund of Oshkosh, made the All-NBL team.

STANDINGS

Eastern Division

	W.	L.	Pct.
Washington	38	22	.633
New York	32	28	.533
Baltimore	29	31	.483
Philadelphia	28	32	.467
Boston	25	35	.417
Providence	12	48	.200

Western Division

	W.	L.	Pct.
Rochester	45	15	.750
Minneapolis	44	16	.733
Chicago	38	22	.633
St. Louis	29	31	.483
Fort Wayne	22	38	.367
Indianapolis	18	42	.300

PLAYOFFS

First Round

Washington defeated Philadelphia 2 games to 0
New York defeated Baltimore 2 games to 1
Rochester defeated St. Louis 2 games to 0
Minneapolis defeated Chicago 2 games to 0

Semifinals

Minneapolis defeated Rochester 2 games to 0
Washington defeated New York 2 games to 1

Championship

Minneapolis defeated Washington 4 games to 2

TOP SCORERS

	Pts.	Ave.
George Mikan, Minneapolis	1698	28.3
Joe Fulks, Philadelphia	1560	26.0
Max Zaslofsky, Chicago	1197	20.6
Arnie Risen, Rochester	995	16.6
Ed Sadowski, Philadelphia	920	15.3

LEADERS IN ASSISTS

	No.	Ave.
Bob Davies, Rochester	321	5.4
Andy Phillip, Chicago	319	5.3
John Logan, St. Louis	276	4.8
Ernie Calverley, Providence	251	4.3
George Senesky, Philadelphia	233	3.9

1949–50

The war between the leagues came to an end as the BAA and the NBL merged to form the new National Basketball Association. The merger left an unwieldy 17-team league, divided into three divisions.

The Central Division included Minneapolis, Rochester, Fort Wayne, Chicago and St. Louis, BAA teams the year before. New York, Washington, Philadelphia, Boston and Philadelphia from the BAA and Syracuse of the NBL were in the Eastern Division. The West contained six former NBL teams, Indianapolis, Anderson, Tri-Cities, Sheboygan, Waterloo and Denver.

But despite all the new teams and new alignments, the league still had a familiar look as George Mikan and the Minneapolis Lakers won the championship. Mikan set all sorts of individual records, including the highest scoring average, 27.4 points a game; most field goals, 649, and most foul shots, 567 of 728 attempts. He rolled up the highest one-game scoring total of the season with 51 points against Rochester.

Even with Mikan, Jim Pollard, Vern Mikklesen, Arnie Ferrin and Slater Martin, the Lakers still had to beat Rochester in a special playoff after the two teams had tied for the Central title.

In the championship round of the playoffs, Minneapolis defeated Anderson, which had surprised Western champion Indianapolis, in two straight games and Syracuse, the Eastern champions, in a hard-fought six-game series.

The little man in the middle is Maurice Podoloff, first commissioner of the NBA.

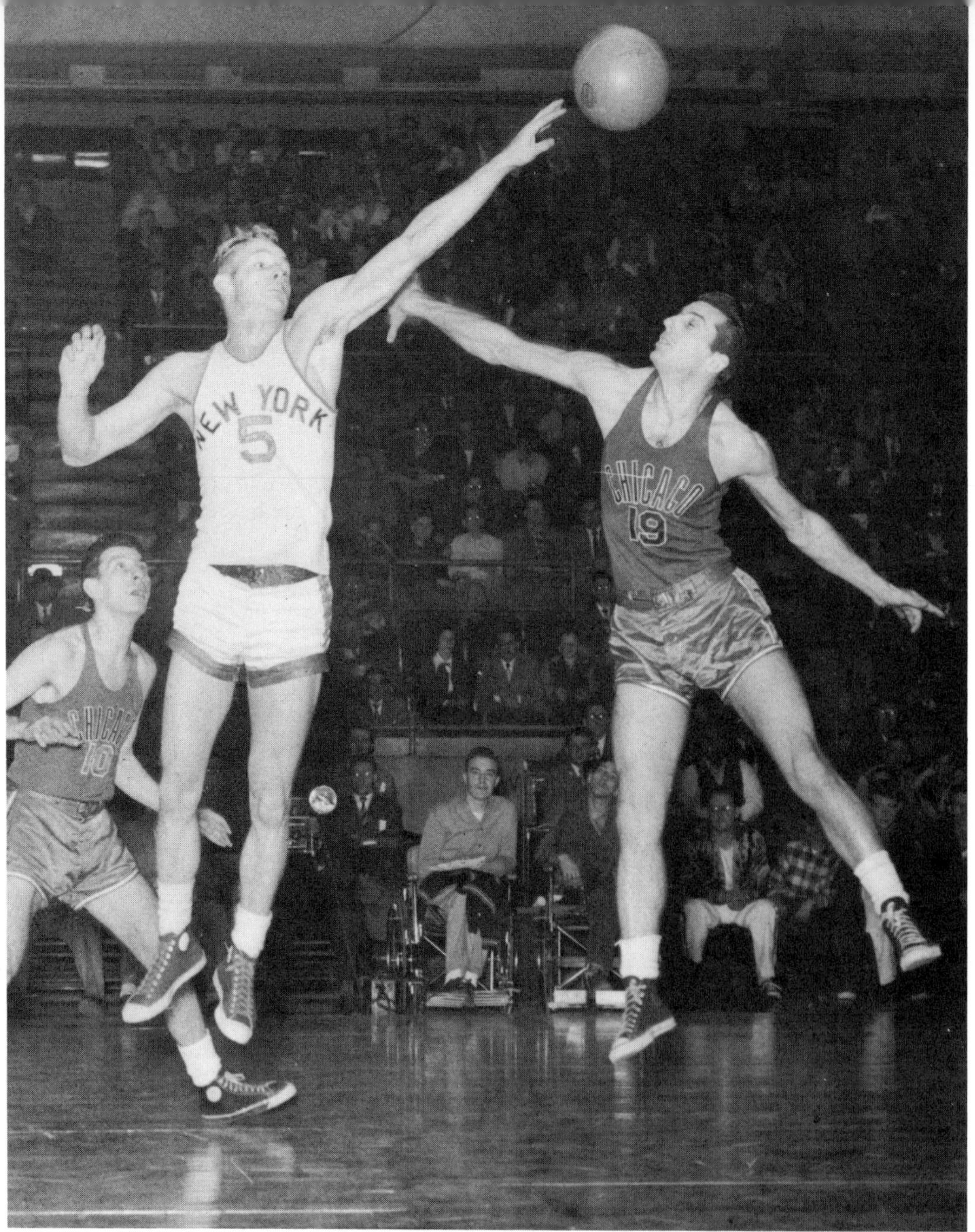

Chicago's Andy Phillip, second in NBA in assists, tries to stop New York's Paul Noel.

Two outstanding rookies, Ed Macauley with St. Louis and Alex Groza with Indianapolis, came into the league. Groza, who played his college ball at Kentucky, finished second to Mikan with a 23.4 scoring average and led the NBA in field-goal accuracy with a 47.8 mark. Macauley, a two-time All-American at St. Louis University, was fifth with a 16.1 average. Another rookie, Dick McGuire of the New York Knicks, topped the league in assists.

Mikan came within one vote of being a unanimous all-league pick for the second straight year. Joining him on the team were his teammate Jim Pollard; Max Zaslofsky of Chicago; Bobby Davies of Rochester and Groza.

The Lakers played the Harlem Globetrotters twice, winning both games. One of the games, in Chicago, attracted a crowd of 21,666.

STANDINGS

Eastern Division

	W.	L.	Pct.
Syracuse	51	13	.797
New York	40	28	.588
Washington	32	36	.471
Philadelphia	26	42	.382
Baltimore	25	43	.368
Boston	22	46	.324

Western Division

	W.	L.	Pct.
Indianapolis	39	25	.609
Anderson	37	27	.578
Tri-Cities	29	35	.453
Sheboygan	22	40	.355
Waterloo	19	43	.306
Denver	11	51	.177

Central Division

	W.	L.	Pct.
Minneapolis *	51	17	.750
Rochester	51	17	.750
Fort Wayne *	40	28	.588
Chicago	40	28	.588
St. Louis	26	42	.382

*Won playoff to break tie

PLAYOFFS

First Round

Syracuse defeated Philadelphia 2 games to 0
New York defeated Washington 2 games to 0

Minneapolis defeated Chicago 2 games to 0
Fort Wayne defeated Rochester 2 games to 0

Indianapolis defeated Sheboygan 2 games to 1
Anderson defeated Tri-Cities 2 games to 1

Second Round

Syracuse defeated New York 2 games to 1
Minneapolis defeated Fort Wayne 2 games to 0
Anderson defeated Indianapolis 2 games to 1

Third Round

Minneapolis defeated Anderson 2 games to 0

Championship

Minneapolis defeated Syracuse 4 games to 2

TOP SCORERS

	Pts.	Ave.
George Mikan, Minneapolis	1865	27.4
Alex Groza, Indianapolis	1496	23.4
Frank Brian, Anderson	1138	17.8
Max Zaslofsky, Chicago	1115	16.4
Ed Macauley, St. Louis	1081	16.1

LEADERS IN ASSISTS

	No.	Ave.
Dick McGuire, New York	386	5.7
Andy Phillip, Chicago	377	5.8
Bob Davies, Rochester	294	4.6
George Senesky, Philadelphia	264	3.9
Al Cervi, Syracuse	264	4.7

1950–51

When the Chicago franchise disbanded after the 1949–50 season, the remaining teams divided up the Stags' players. The Boston Celtics came up with Bob Cousy, a 6-1 guard who many other teams considered too small for the NBA. But this season, and for many seasons to come, Cousy would prove just how wrong were the skeptics. He averaged 15.6 points a game, ninth best in the league, and was named Rookie of the Year.

For the first time Negroes played in the NBA. The New York Knicks obtained Nat "Sweetwater" Clifton from the Harlem Globetrotters, and the Boston Celtics drafted Chuck Cooper of Duquesne. In general, though, rookies had trouble making the teams, with only 12 first-year men in the league.

The NBA got down to a more manageable size when six franchises—Chicago, St. Louis, Anderson, Waterloo, Sheboygan and Denver—dropped out. The remaining 11 teams were

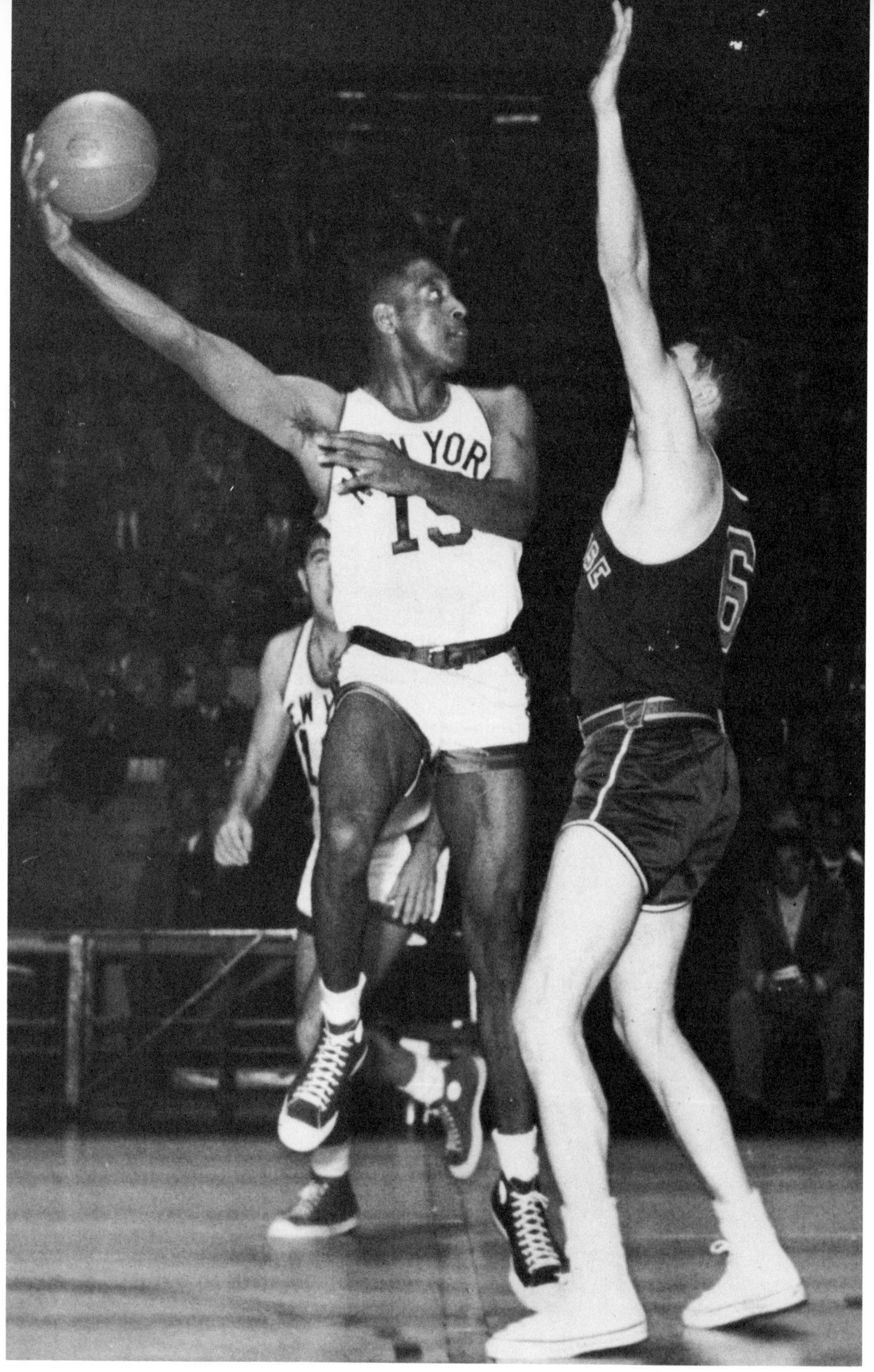

New York's Sweetwater Clifton, ex-Globetrotter, was one of the first Negroes in the NBA.

organized into two divisions. The collapse of the Washington Capitols on January 9, though, left the league with 10 teams for most of the season.

The Rochester Royals, with Arnie Risen, Bob Davies and Bob Wanzer, ended the Minneapolis Lakers' three-year reign as world champions. The Royals eliminated the Lakers, three games to one, in the playoff semifinals after having finished three games behind Minneapolis in the West. In the East, Philadelphia finished two-and-a-half games ahead of Boston, coached by Red Auerbach, and four games ahead of New York. But the Knicks won the Eastern playoffs before losing to Rochester, four games to three, for the championship.

Two highlights of the campaign were a 19-18 victory by Fort Wayne over Minneapolis in a stalling battle and a 75-73 triumph by Indianapolis over Rochester in six overtimes.

As he had every season since entering the league, George Mikan won the scoring title with a 28.4 average, Alex Groza of the Indianapolis Jets was second with a 21.7 mark, and "Easy Ed" Macauley of Boston was third with 20.4. For the second year in a row Groza was the NBA's most accurate shooter, connecting on 47.0 percent of his shots from the floor. Andy Phillip of Philadelphia led in assists and the Syracuse Nationals' Dolph Schayes topped the NBA in rebounding.

The league played its first All-Star Game in the Boston Garden on March 2 and 10,094 fans turned out to see the East down the West, 111-94. The winners' Macauley, MVP, led the scorers with 20 points and held Mikan to four field goals.

The All-NBA team included Mikan, a unanimous selection; Groza and Macauley, each in his second NBA season; Bob Davies of the champion Rochester Royals, and Ralph Beard of Indianapolis, who had been a college teammate of Groza at Kentucky.

STANDINGS

Eastern Division

	W.	L.	Pct.
Philadelphia	40	26	.606
Boston	39	30	.565
New York	36	30	.545
Syracuse	32	34	.485
Baltimore	24	42	.364
Washington*	10	25	.286

*Disbanded Jan. 10, 1951

Western Division

	W.	L.	Pct.
Minneapolis	44	24	.647
Rochester	41	27	.603
Fort Wayne	32	36	.471
Indianapolis	31	37	.456
Tri-Cities	25	43	.368

PLAYOFFS

First Round

New York defeated Boston 2 games to 0
Syracuse defeated Philadelphia 2 games to 0
Rochester defeated Fort Wayne 2 games to 1
Minneapolis defeated Indianapolis 2 games to 1

Semifinals

New York defeated Syracuse 3 games to 2
Rochester defeated Minneapolis 3 games to 1

Championship

Rochester defeated New York 4 games to 3

TOP SCORERS

	Pts.	Ave.
George Mikan, Minneapolis	1932	28.4
Alex Groza, Indianapolis	1429	21.7
Ed Macauley, Boston	1384	20.4
Joe Fulks, Philadelphia	1236	18.7
Frank Brian, Tri-Cities	1144	16.8

TOP REBOUNDERS

	No.	Ave.
Dolph Schayes, Syracuse	1080	16.4
George Mikan, Minneapolis	958	14.1
Harry Gallatin, New York	800	12.1
Arnie Risen, Rochester	795	12.0
Alex Groza, Indianapolis	709	10.7

LEADERS IN ASSISTS

	No.	Ave.
Andy Phillip, Philadelphia	414	6.3
Dick McGuire, New York	400	6.3
George Senesky, Philadelphia	342	5.3
Bob Cousy, Boston	341	4.9
Ralph Beard, Indianapolis	318	4.8

1951–52

Minneapolis regained the league championship, its second since the merger of the BAA and the NBL. The Lakers did it with big, strong scorers and rebounders in 6-10 George Mikan, 6-8 Vern Mikkelsen, and 6-3 Jim Pollard. The Laker stars weren't hampered by the wider free throw lanes, increased from six to twelve feet, designed to keep pivot men further from the basket by enlarging the three-second area.

For the first time in his NBA career, though, Mikan failed to lead the league in scoring. Instead the honors went to Paul Arizin, a 6-4 forward in his second pro season with the Philadelphia Warriors. Arizin finished with a 25.4 average, and Mikan was second with 23.8. Arizin led the NBA in field-goal accuracy with 44.8 percent, and also hit on 17 successive free throws, the longest streak of the season.

Mikan had the best single game of the year, scoring 61 points against Rochester on January

Knicks' Vince Boryla has Celtic Ed Macauley up in the air.

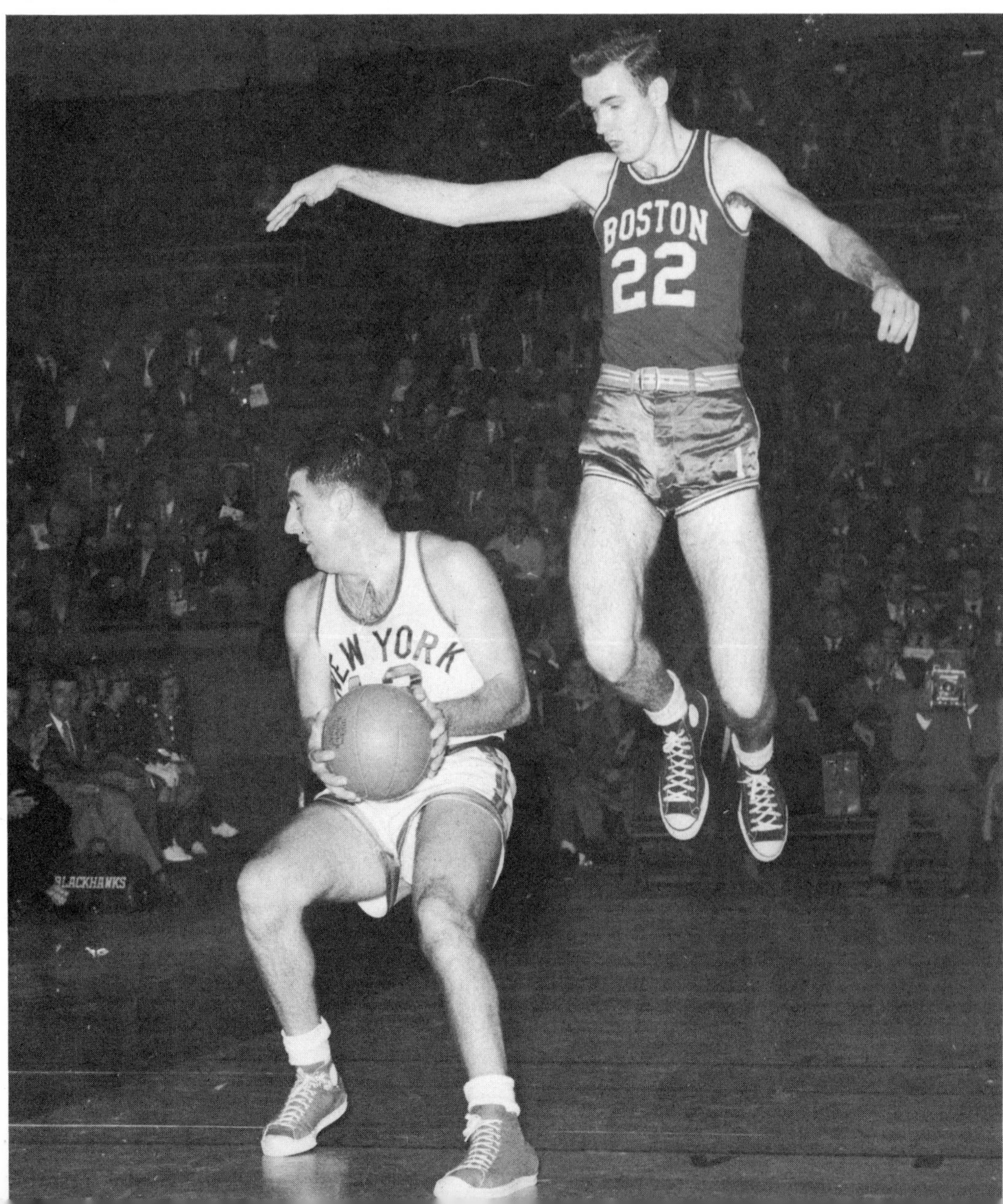

20. This was only two less than the NBA record set by Joe Fulks. Larry Foust of Fort Wayne and Mel Hutchins of Milwaukee tied for the rebounding lead.

The divisional races were the closest in the NBA's short history. Syracuse won by a single game over New York in the East, and Rochester, the defending NBA champion, by the same margin in the West. Neither of the first-place finishers made it to the playoff finals, however. The Knicks ousted Syracuse and Minneapolis eliminated Rochester. In the playoff finals, the Lakers beat the Knicks in a seven-game series for the title.

The league showed signs of increasing stability, with only one franchise shift. The Tri-Cities Blackhawks, one of the old NBL teams, moved to Milwaukee and became the Milwaukee Hawks. The change of scenery didn't help, though, as the team finished last in the West for the second straight year.

As usual Mikan headed the selections for the All-NBA team. The other members were Arizin; Boston's Bob Cousy, the third-leading scorer with a 25.7 average; Ed Macauley, Cousy's teammate and the NBA's fourth scorer with a 23.1 average; Bob Davies of Rochester, fifth with 21.1, and Dolph Schayes of Syracuse. Davies and Schayes shared the fifth spot on the team.

For the second consecutive year the All-Star Game was held in Boston and for the second time the East scored a convincing victory. Arizin led the East to a 108-91 triumph with 26 points and was named the game's Most Valuable Player. Mikan scored 26 for the West.

STANDINGS

Eastern Division

	W.	L.	Pct.
Syracuse	40	26	.606
Boston	39	27	.591
New York	37	29	.561
Philadelphia	33	33	.500
Baltimore	20	46	.303

Western Division

	W.	L.	Pct.
Rochester	41	25	.621
Minneapolis	40	26	.606
Indianapolis	34	32	.515
Fort Wayne	29	37	.439
Milwaukee	17	49	.258

PLAYOFFS

First Round

Syracuse defeated Philadelphia 2 games to 1
New York defeated Boston 2 games to 1
Minneapolis defeated Indianapolis 2 games to 0
Rochester defeated Fort Wayne 2 games to 0

Semifinals

New York defeated Syracuse 3 games to 1
Minneapolis defeated Rochester 3 games to 1

Championship

Minneapolis defeated New York 4 games to 3

TOP SCORERS

	Pts.	Ave.
Paul Arizin, Philadelphia	1674	25.4
George Mikan, Minneapolis	1523	23.8
Bob Cousy, Boston	1433	21.7
Ed Macauley, Boston	1264	19.2
Bob Davies, Rochester	1052	16.2

TOP REBOUNDERS

	No.	Ave.
Mel Hutchins, Milwaukee	880	13.3
Larry Foust, Fort Wayne	880	13.3
George Mikan, Minneapolis	866	13.5
Arnie Risen, Rochester	841	12.7
Dolph Schayes, Syracuse	773	12.3

LEADERS IN ASSISTS

	No.	Ave.
Andy Phillip, Philadelphia	539	8.2
Bob Cousy, Boston	441	6.7
Bob Davies, Rochester	390	6.0
Dick McGuire, New York	388	6.1
Fred Scolari, Baltimore	303	4.7

OSTON
14
14

1952–53

Bob Cousy, Boston's incredible guard, turned in the outstanding performance of the year when he scored 50 points against Syracuse in a playoff game on March 21. The game went into four overtimes before the Celtics finally won, 111-105. Cousy made good on 10 of 22 field-goal attempts, most of them from long range, and added a phenomenal 30 of 32 free throws. His 50 points were the most ever scored in a playoff game.

Despite Cousy's heroics, the playoffs had a familiar look as Minneapolis defeated New York for its second straight title and fourth in five seasons. The Knicks battled into the playoff finals for the third straight time and lost for the third consecutive year.

For the first time in its history the NBA opened the season with the same teams that had finished the year before. The Eastern division race was particularly close, with New York finishing half a game ahead of Syracuse and a game-and-a-half in front of the Celtics. In the West, Minneapolis wound up four games ahead of second-place Rochester.

Neil Johnston, Philadelphia's 6-8 center, won the scoring title with a 22.3 average. The Lakers' George Mikan, with a 20.6 mark, was second. Johnston was also the NBA's most accurate shooter, hitting on 45.2 percent of his shots. Mikan led in rebounds with a 14.4 average.

Seventeen individual and team records fell during the season. Boston's Cousy set new game (18) and season (547) records for assists and also tied the league record by making 15 of 15 free throws in a game.

Bill Sharman, Cousy's backcourt partner on the Celtics, made his first 11 shots from the floor against Philadelphia for a single-game mark. Another Celtic, Ed Macauley, and Mikan each scored 46 points in a game, high for the season. Mikan's performance was in a game against Baltimore in which he scored 32 points in the first half, 19 in the second quarter.

The West won its first All-Star Game in three tries, defeating the East, 79-75, before 10,322 fans in Fort Wayne. Mikan was the leading scorer with 22 points and was chosen MVP, but it was Bobby Davies of Rochester who broke the game open by scoring eight straight points for the West in the final five minutes of play.

Syracuse's Dolph Schayes was named to the All-NBA team with Mikan, Johnston, Cousy and Macauley.

STANDINGS

Eastern Division

	W.	L.	Pct.
New York	47	23	.671
Syracuse	47	24	.662
Boston	46	25	.648
Baltimore	16	54	.229
Philadelphia	12	57	.174

Western Division

	W.	L.	Pct.
Minneapolis	48	22	.686
Rochester	44	26	.629
Fort Wayne	36	33	.522
Indianapolis	28	43	.394
Milwaukee	27	44	.380

PLAYOFFS

First Round

New York defeated Baltimore 2 games to 0
Boston defeated Syracuse 2 games to 0
Fort Wayne defeated Rochester 2 games to 1
Minneapolis defeated Indianapolis 2 games to 0

Semifinals

New York defeated Boston 3 games to 1
Minneapolis defeated Fort Wayne 3 games to 2

Championship

Minneapolis defeated New York 4 games to 1

Playmaker Bob Cousy showed he could score, with a 50-point game.

TOP SCORERS

	Pts.	Ave.
Neil Johnston, Philadelphia	1564	22.3
George Mikan, Minneapolis	1442	20.6
Bob Cousy, Boston	1407	19.8
Ed Macauley, Boston	1402	20.3
Dolph Schayes, Syracuse	1262	17.8

TOP REBOUNDERS

	No.	Ave.
George Mikan, Minneapolis	1007	14.4
Neil Johnston, Philadelphia	976	13.9
Dolph Schayes, Syracuse	920	13.0
Harry Gallatin, New York	916	13.1
Mel Hutchins, Milwaukee	793	11.2

LEADERS IN ASSISTS

	No.	Ave.
Bob Cousy, Boston	547	7.7
Andy Phillip, Fort Wayne	397	5.7
George King, Syracuse	364	5.1
Dick McGuire, New York	296	4.9
Paul Seymour, Syracuse	294	4.4

1953–54

George Mikan, the magnificent 6-10 center, played his last season as a pro and led the Minneapolis Lakers to their third straight championship and fifth in six years in three leagues. Mikan, later named the greatest basketball player of the first half of the century in an Associated Press poll, averaged 18.4 points a game, fourth best in the league. He also was the all-league center, as he was in every year of his pro career.

Indianapolis dropped out of the league, leaving five teams in the East and four in the West. Both divisional races were close, with New York taking the Eastern crown by two games over Syracuse and Boston, and Minneapolis winning by two over Rochester in the West. Syracuse made it to the playoff finals but bowed to Minneapolis in a seven-game series for the championship.

The Philadelphia Warriors' Neil Johnston retained the scoring title with a 24.4 average. Bob Cousy of Boston was second with a 19.2 mark and his teammate Ed Macauley was third.

Warriors' Neil Johnston set a Madison Square Garden pro scoring mark with 50 points.

Macauley was the NBA's most accurate shooter from the floor with a .486 percentage, and Boston's Bill Sharman was tops from the free-throw line, making 84.4 percent of his shots. New York's Harry "The Horse" Gallatin hauled in a record-setting total of 1,098 rebounds, an average of 15.3 a game. What made his feat more remarkable was that, at 6-6, Gallatin was usually battling against taller men.

The East scored a 98-93 overtime victory in the annual All-Star Game, staged before a crowd of 16,478 in Madison Square Garden. Mikan tied the score at 84-all by hitting two free throws with no time left in regulation play. But Cousy, the game's MVP, scored 10 of the East's 14 points in the overtime period for the East's third victory in four games. Jim Pollard of Minneapolis led the West with 23 points.

The All-NBA team included Cousy, who was a unanimous pick; Johnston, Mikan, Dolph Schayes of Syracuse, and Gallatin. Ray Felix, a skinny 6-11 center from Long Island University, averaged 17.6 points a game for Baltimore and won Rookie of the Year honors.

STANDINGS

Eastern Division

	W.	L.	Pct.
New York	44	28	.611
Boston	42	30	.583
Syracuse	42	30	.583
Philadelphia	29	43	.403
Baltimore	16	56	.222

Western Division

	W.	L.	Pct.
Minneapolis	46	26	.639
Rochester	44	28	.611
Fort Wayne	40	32	.556
Milwaukee	21	51	.292

PLAYOFFS

First Round

Boston defeated New York 2 games to 0
Syracuse defeated New York 2 games to 0
Syracuse defeated Boston 2 games to 0
Rochester defeated Fort Wayne 2 games to 0
Minneapolis defeated Fort Wayne 2 games to 0
Minneapolis defeated Rochester 1 game to 0

Semifinals

Syracuse defeated Boston 2 games to 0
Minneapolis defeated Rochester 2 games to 1

Championship

Minneapolis defeated Syracuse 4 games to 3

TOP SCORERS

	Pts.	Ave.
Neil Johnston, Philadelphia	1759	24.4
Bob Cousy, Boston	1383	19.2
Ed Macauley, Boston	1344	18.9
George Mikan, Minneapolis	1306	18.1
Ray Felix, Baltimore	1269	17.6

TOP REBOUNDERS

	No.	Ave.
Harry Gallatin, New York	1098	15.3
George Mikan, Minneapolis	1028	14.3
Larry Foust, Fort Wayne	967	13.4
Ray Felix, Baltimore	958	13.3
Dolph Schayes, Syracuse	879	12.1

LEADERS IN ASSISTS

	No.	Ave.
Bob Cousy, Boston	578	7.2
Andy Phillip, Fort Wayne	449	6.3
Paul Seymour, Syracuse	364	5.1
Dick McGuire, New York	354	5.2
Bob Davies, Rochester	323	4.5

1954–55

The NBA made several important rules changes in an attempt to speed up play and eliminate excessive fouling. The most important was the introduction of the 24-second rule, requiring a team to shoot within 24 seconds of gaining possession of the ball. The league also decided to limit teams to six personal fouls a quarter. Any additional personals would be punished by a bonus foul shot.

LAKERS
17

The Syracuse Nationals won the league championship, defeating the Fort Wayne Pistons in the final playoff series. The Nats won the title when George King tossed in a foul shot with ten seconds remaining in the decisive seventh game to break a 91-91 deadlock.

Syracuse had won the Eastern Division title by five games over New York and Fort Wayne had finished three games ahead of the defending NBA champion, Minneapolis, in the West. The Lakers, champions in five of the last six seasons, had to get used to playing without George Mikan, their great center who had retired to attend law school.

The Baltimore Bullets disbanded early in the season after having played 14 games and their players were divided among the eight remaining teams.

Neil Johnston of Philadelphia continued his domination as the league's top point-maker, winning the scoring title for the third consecutive year. He averaged 22.7 points a game, beating out teammate Paul Arizin and Bob Cousy of Boston. Johnston also led in rebounding with a 15.1 average. Cousy was the league leader in assists, but Rochester's Bob Davies, playing his last season, set a single-game assist record of 20.

Several other outstanding individual performances highlighted the year. Johnston scored 45 points in a game against Rochester, and grabbed 39 rebounds against Syracuse. Boston's Bill Sharman, the league's best foul shooter, converted a record 50 consecutive free throws over a 10-game stretch.

The season's outstanding rookie was Bob Pettit, Milwaukee's 6-9 forward. Pettit, from Louisiana State, finished fourth in scoring with a 20.4 average. The Hawks also came up with another good rookie in Frank Selvy. Selvy came to Milwaukee after the collapse of the Baltimore franchise and wound up as the NBA's fifth-leading scorer with a 19.0 average. He reached a single-game peak of 42 against Minneapolis.

The East scored a 100-91 victory in the annual All-Star Game, played before 13,138 in Madison Square Garden. The Boston backcourt combination of Cousy and Sharman led the East, with Sharman picked as the game's MVP. He scored 15 points, Cousy 20.

Pettit, Johnston and Cousy made the All-NBA team, along with Dolph Schayes of Syracuse and Larry Foust of Fort Wayne. Schayes had averaged 18.8 points and 12.3 rebounds in leading the Nationals to the championship and Foust, a 6-9 center, was the NBA's leader in field-goal accuracy with a .487 percentage.

STANDINGS

Eastern Division

	W.	L.	Pct.
Syracuse	43	29	.597
New York	38	34	.528
Boston	36	36	.500
Philadelphia	33	39	.458

Western Division

	W.	L.	Pct.
Fort Wayne	43	29	.597
Minneapolis	40	32	.556
Rochester	29	43	.403
Milwaukee	29	46	.361

PLAYOFFS

First Round

Boston defeated New York 2 games to 1
Minneapolis defeated Rochester 2 games to 1

Semifinals

Syracuse defeated Boston 3 games to 1
Fort Wayne defeated Minneapolis 3 games to 1

Championship

Syracuse defeated Fort Wayne 4 games to 3

TOP SCORERS

	Pts.	Ave.
Neil Johnston, Philadelphia	1631	22.7
Paul Arizin, Philadelphia	1512	21.0
Bob Cousy, Boston	1504	21.2
Bob Pettit, Milwaukee	1466	20.4
Frank Selvy, Milwaukee	1348	19.0

Minneapolis' Jim Pollard captures rebound in face of Ft. Wayne's Paul Walther.

TOP REBOUNDERS

	No.	Ave.
Neil Johnston, Philadelphia	1085	15.1
Harry Gallatin, New York	995	13.8
Bob Pettit, Milwaukee	994	13.8
Dolph Schayes, Syracuse	887	12.3
Ray Felix, New York	818	11.4

LEADERS IN ASSISTS

	No.	Ave.
Bob Cousy, Boston	557	7.8
Dick McGuire, New York	542	7.6
Andy Phillip, Fort Wayne	491	7.7
Paul Seymour, Syracuse	483	6.7
Slater Martin, Minneapolis	427	5.9

1955-56

Bob Pettit, the NBA's Rookie of the Year a season ago, proved totally immune to the sophomore jinx. The 6-9 forward swept just about all the league's individual honors. He led the league in scoring, with a 25.7 average; in rebounding with a 16.2 average; won the Podoloff Cup as the NBA's Most Valuable Player, and was the outstanding player in the All-Star Game.

But despite Pettit's individual feats for the well-traveled Hawks, now in St. Louis, Philadelphia won the NBA championship, its first since the league's initial season. The Warriors won by six games over Boston in the East and Fort Wayne took the Western title by four games over Minneapolis. Both teams made it to the playoff finals, with Philadelphia defeating Fort Wayne, four games to one. Paul Arizin and Neil Johnston, the NBA's second- and third-leading scorers, led the Warriors to victory.

St. Louis Hawk Bob Pettit (9) was MVP, and a lot else.

The Hawks, who had started out as the Tri-Cities Blackhawks in the old NBL, moved from Milwaukee to St. Louis in the only franchise shift of the season. Another link to the past was broken when the Pistons' Max Zaslofsky, who had been on four all-league teams, was waived out of the circuit. This left Connie Simmons of Rochester as the only player who had been in the league since its founding as the Basketball Association of America a decade earlier.

Joe Lapchick, who had coached the New York Knickerbockers for nine seasons, retired in February and was succeeded by Vince Boryla, one of his former players.

The West, behind Pettit's brilliant all-around play, defeated the East, 108-94, in the annual All-Star Game at Rochester. Pettit scored 20 points and grabbed 24 rebounds on his way to MVP honors in the game. Philadelphia's Johnston scored 17 to pace the losers.

The All-NBA team included Pettit, the Warriors' Arizin and Johnston, and Cousy and Bill Sharman of Boston, who were the league's outstanding backcourt duo. Cousy broke his own record with 642 assists during the season and Sharman led the league in foul shooting for the fourth consecutive year with an .867 percentage. Johnston, with a .457 percentage, was the best shooter from the floor.

The Rochester Royals came up with two outstanding rookies, Maurice Stokes and Jack Twyman. Stokes, the NBA Rookie of the Year from tiny St. Francis of Loretto (Pa.) College, averaged 16.8 points a game and was second to Pettit in rebounding. Twyman averaged 14.4 points a game.

STANDINGS

Eastern Division

	W.	L.	Pct.
Philadelphia	45	27	.625
Boston	39	33	.542
Syracuse*	35	37	.486
New York	35	37	.486

*Won playoff to break tie

Western Division

	W.	L.	Pct.
Fort Wayne	37	35	.514
Minneapolis*	33	39	.458
St. Louis	33	39	.458
Rochester	31	41	.431

PLAYOFFS

First Round

Syracuse defeated Boston 2 games to 1
St. Louis defeated Minneapolis 2 games to 1

Semifinals

Philadelphia defeated Syracuse 3 games to 2
Fort Wayne defeated St. Louis 3 games to 2

Championship

Philadelphia defeated Fort Wayne 4 games to 1

TOP SCORERS

	Pts.	Ave.
Bob Pettit, St. Louis	1849	25.7
Paul Arizin, Philadelphia	1741	24.2
Neil Johnston, Philadelphia	1547	22.1
Clyde Lovellette, Minneapolis	1526	21.5
Dolph Schayes, Syracuse	1472	20.4

TOP REBOUNDERS

	No.	Ave.
Bob Pettit, St. Louis	1164	16.2
Maurice Stokes, Rochester	1094	16.3
Clyde Lovellette, Minneapolis	992	14.0
Neil Johnston, Philadelphia	872	12.5
Dolph Schayes, Syracuse	872	12.4

LEADERS IN ASSISTS

	No.	Ave.
Bob Cousy, Boston	642	8.9
Jack George, Philadelphia	457	6.3
Slater Martin, Minneapolis	445	6.2
Andy Phillip, Fort Wayne	410	5.9
George King, Syracuse	410	5.7

1956–57

Bill Russell came to the Boston Celtics and brought the key to the NBA championship with him. Russell, a skinny 6-10 rookie from the University of San Francisco, joined the Celtics in December after having led the United States to victory in the 1956 Olympic Games.

With his tremendous rebounding and defensive skills, Russell provided the missing ingredient in the Celtics' championship blend. On offense he made Boston's fast break work, getting the ball to Bob Cousy and Bill Sharman. And on defense his amazing shot-blocking talent intimidated opposing shooters.

Even with Russell, though, the Celtics had to struggle to win their first NBA title. The final playoff series with the St. Louis Hawks went the full seven games. Four of the games were decided by a single basket and two went into double overtime. In the decisive seventh game the lead changed hands 20 times before Frank Ramsey's 20-foot jump shot in the second overtime put Boston ahead, 124-122. The Celts held on to win, 125-123.

Boston won the Eastern title by a comfortable six-game margin over Syracuse, but in the West three teams tied for first. St. Louis, Minneapolis and Fort Wayne all finished with identical

Rookie Bill Russell (6) led ascension of Boston to its first NBA title.

BOSTON
6
NEW YORK
9
BOSTON
18
NEW YORK
12

34-38 marks. In special playoff games to sort out the Western teams, St. Louis beat the Lakers and Pistons.

Paul Arizin of Philadelphia, with a 25.6 average, dethroned St. Louis' Bob Pettit as the scoring champion. Pettit seemed headed for a second straight title until he broke his wrist in mid-February and had to play the rest of the season in a cast. He wound up second with a 24.7 average.

Neil Johnston of Philadelphia, the fourth-leading scorer, was the NBA's most accurate shooter with a .447 percentage from the floor. Bill Sharman, as usual, led in free-throw accuracy. Rochester's Maurice Stokes was the leading rebounder, although Russell, who missed a third of the season because of the Olympics, had the highest rebound average.

The East defeated the West, 109-97, in the All-Star Game at Boston. Cousy won the game MVP award for the second time with his brilliant floor play and Sharman stunned the crowd with a 70-foot field goal.

Cousy was the NBA's Most Valuable Player and was joined on the All-NBA team by Sharman, Arizin, Dolph Schayes of Syracuse and Pettit. Another Boston player, Tom Heinsohn, won Rookie of the Year honors, averaging 16.2 points a game.

STANDINGS

Eastern Division

	W.	L.	Pct.
Boston	44	28	.611
Syracuse	38	34	.528
Philadelphia	37	35	.514
New York	36	36	.500

Western Division

	W.	L.	Pct.
St. Louis*	34	38	.472
Minneapolis	34	38	.472
Fort Wayne	34	38	.472
Rochester	31	41	.431

*Won playoff with Minneapolis and Fort Wayne to break tie

PLAYOFFS

First Round

Syracuse defeated Philadelphia 2 games to 0
Minneapolis defeated Fort Wayne 2 games to 0

Semifinals

Boston defeated Syracuse 3 games to 0
St. Louis defeated Minneapolis 3 games to 0

Championship

Boston defeated St. Louis 4 games to 3

TOP SCORERS

	Pts.	Ave.
Paul Arizin, Philadelphia	1817	25.6
Bob Pettit, St. Louis	1755	24.7
Dolph Schayes, Syracuse	1617	22.5
Neil Johnston, Philadelphia	1575	22.8
George Yardley, Fort Wayne	1547	21.5

TOP REBOUNDERS

	No.	Ave.
Maurice Stokes, Rochester	1256	17.4
Bob Pettit, St. Louis	1037	14.6
Dolph Schayes, Syracuse	1008	14.0
Bill Russell, Boston	943	19.6
Clyde Lovellette, Minneapolis	932	13.5

LEADERS IN ASSISTS

	No.	Ave.
Bob Cousy, Boston	478	7.4
Jack McMahon, St. Louis	367	5.1
Maurice Stokes, Rochester	331	4.6
Jack George, Philadelphia	307	4.6
Slater Martin, St. Louis	269	4.1

1957–58

The St. Louis Hawks, behind the magnificent shooting of Bob Pettit, dethroned Boston in the playoffs and won their first NBA championship. The Hawks and Celtics met in the playoff finals for the second straight year, with St. Louis winning, four games to two. The Hawks' four triumphs came by a total of eight points.

George Yardley was top NBA scorer when Pistons moved to Detroit.

In the decisive sixth playoff game, Pettit scored 50 points, including 19 of the Hawks' last 21. The Hawks' victory gave the NBA its fifth different champion in five seasons.

Boston won by eight games over Syracuse in the East and St. Louis took the Western crown by the same margin over Detroit. The Celtics' hopes of repeating as league champions, though, were crushed when Bill Russell, their outstanding center, sprained his ankle in the third playoff game against St. Louis and had to miss the remainder of the series.

As part of the NBA's shift away from the smaller cities, the Rochester franchise moved to Cincinnati and the Fort Wayne Pistons relocated in Detroit.

George Yardley of Detroit captured the scoring title with a 27.8 average. His total of 2,001 points was a record, eclipsing the old mark of 1,932 set by George Mikan in the 1951–52 season. Yardley scored more than 50 points in a game twice, getting 51 against Boston on January 15 and topping that with 52 against Syracuse on February 4.

Dolph Schayes of Syracuse was second in scoring with a 24.9 average, followed by Pettit with 24.6. Jack Twyman of Cincinnati led the circuit in field-goal accuracy with a .452 percentage and Schayes, with a .904 percentage, dethroned perennial leader Bill Sharman of Boston as the best free-throw shooter. Russell topped the rebounders with a 22.7 average, and Cousy, averaging 7.1 assists a game, led in that department for the seventh straight season.

Harry Gallatin of Detroit, who played in his 682nd regular season game and 65th consecutive playoff contest, retired after ten years in the NBA.

The Hawks' Cliff Hagan and the Minneapolis Lakers' Dick Garmaker each scored 26 points in a single quarter, a league record.

In the All-Star Game at St. Louis, Cousy broke the game open with seven consecutive points to lead the East to a 130-118 victory. But Pettit, with 28 points and 26 rebounds, was the MVP.

Bill Russell won the Most Valuable Player award for the season in a vote of the players, but the annual poll of sportswriters only put him on the All-NBA second team. The first team included Schayes, Yardley, Pettit, Cousy and Sharman. Woody Sauldsberry of Philadelphia was the Rookie of the Year.

In a tragic development, Maurice Stokes, the 6-7 Cincinnati forward who had been the 1955–56 Rookie of the Year, was stricken with encephalitis. The crippling brain disease ended his career and put him in the hospital for extensive treatment.

STANDINGS

Eastern Division

	W.	L.	Pct.
Boston	49	23	.681
Syracuse	41	31	.569
Philadelphia	37	35	.514
New York	35	37	.486

Western Division

	W.	L.	Pct.
St. Louis	41	31	.569
Detroit	33	39	.458
Cincinnati	33	39	.458
Minneapolis	19	53	.264

PLAYOFFS

First Round

Philadelphia defeated Syracuse 2 games to 1
Detroit defeated Cincinnati 2 games to 0

Semifinals

Boston defeated Philadelphia 4 games to 1
St. Louis defeated Detroit 4 games to 1

Championship

St. Louis defeated Boston 4 games to 2

TOP SCORERS

	Pts.	Ave.
George Yardley, Detroit	2001	27.8
Dolph Schayes, Syracuse	1791	24.9
Bob Pettit, St. Louis	1719	24.6
Clyde Lovellette, Cincinnati	1659	23.4
Paul Arizin, Philadelphia	1406	20.7

TOP REBOUNDERS

	No.	Ave.
Bill Russell, Boston	1564	22.7
Bob Pettit, St. Louis	1216	17.4
Maurice Stokes, Cincinnati	1142	18.1
Dolph Schayes, Syracuse	1022	14.2
John Kerr, Syracuse	963	13.4

LEADERS IN ASSISTS

	No.	Ave.
Bob Cousy, Boston	463	7.1
Dick McGuire, Detroit	454	6.6
Maurice Stokes, Cincinnati	403	6.4
Carl Braun, New York	393	5.5
George King, Cincinnati	337	5.3

1958–59

Elgin Baylor, a 6-5 forward from Seattle University, made his pro debut with the Minneapolis Lakers and immediately became one of the NBA's brightest stars. He finished fourth in the individual scoring race with a 24.9 average and became only the third rookie in the history of the league to make the All-NBA team.

Alex Groza in 1949–50 and Bob Pettit in 1954–55 were the others to make the all-league squad in their first seasons.

Baylor boasted tremendous body control, some of the best inside moves ever seen in the

Detroit's Dick McGuire battles Boston's Bill Sharman.

DETROIT
15
PISTONS
ELTICS
21

league and an amazing capacity for seemingly hanging suspended in mid-air. His best scoring effort came against Cincinnati on February 25, when he tallied 55 points.

But it was Boston, with Bill Russell in the middle and Bob Cousy and Bill Sharman in backcourt, which won the NBA title, its second in three years. The Celtics coasted to a 12-game spread over New York in the East, Boston's 52 victories setting an NBA record. St. Louis, defending NBA champion, finished 16 games in front of Minneapolis in the West. But the Lakers, led by Baylor, eliminated the Hawks, four games to two in the playoffs. In the playoff finals Boston scored an unprecedented four-game sweep over the Lakers.

Financially, the league had its best season. Despite the runaways in the two divisional races, attendance reached an all-time high of over 1,449,000. The Knicks drew 18,376 fans in Madison Square Garden on December 25, and bettered that with a crowd of 18,496 on February 3. These were the two largest crowds in the history of the NBA.

Several individual records were set as well. The St. Louis Hawks' Bob Pettit won the scoring crown with a 29.2 average, the highest ever. His total of 2,105 points was also a new mark. Russell set a new standard with 1,612 rebounds for a 23.0 average. Cousy set a new record of 28 assists in a game against Minneapolis, with 19 in one half and 12 in one quarter. The Celtics set a scoring record in that game, bombing the Lakers, 173-139.

Kenny Sears of New York was the most accurate shooter with a .490 percentage from the floor and Sharman recaptured the foul-shooting title from Dolph Schayes with a phenomenal 92.9 percent. Cousy led in assists for the eighth straight year.

The West upset the East, 124-108, in the All-Star Game at Detroit. Elgin Baylor had 24 points and Bob Pettit 25 for the winners. The two were named co-winners of the MVP award.

Neil Johnston and Paul Arizin of Philadelphia, Sharman and Vern Mikkleson of Minneapolis all pushed their career scoring totals above 10,000 points during the season.

Pettit, the league's Most Valuable Player, headed the selections for the All-NBA team. He set a record by scoring over 50 points three times during the year. Joining him on the team were Baylor of the Lakers and Cousy, Sharman and Russell, the three leaders of the Celtics. Baylor, of course, won Rookie of the Year honors. But another rookie, Hal Greer of Syracuse, put on a phenomenal shooting exhibition by scoring 39 points in the first half, including 18 field goals, against Boston on February 14. He finished the game with 45 points.

STANDINGS

Eastern Division

	W.	L.	Pct.
Boston	52	20	.722
New York	40	32	.556
Syracuse	35	37	.486
Philadelphia	32	40	.444

Western Division

	W.	L.	Pct.
St. Louis	49	23	.681
Minneapolis	33	39	.458
Detroit	28	44	.389
Cincinnati	19	53	.264

PLAYOFFS

First Round

Syracuse defeated New York 2 games to 0
Minneapolis defeated Detroit 2 games to 1

Semifinals

Boston defeated Syracuse 4 games to 3
Minneapolis defeated St. Louis 4 games to 2

Championship

Boston defeated Minneapolis 4 games to 0

TOP SCORERS

	Pts.	Ave.
Bob Pettit, St. Louis	2105	29.2
Jack Twyman, Cincinnati	1857	25.8
Paul Arizin, Philadelphia	1851	26.4
Elgin Baylor, Minneapolis	1742	24.9
Cliff Hagan, St. Louis	1707	23.7

TOP REBOUNDERS

	No.	Ave.
Bill Russell, Boston	1612	23.0
Bob Pettit, St. Louis	1182	16.4
Elgin Baylor, Minneapolis	1050	15.0
John Kerr, Syracuse	1008	13.4
Dolph Schayes, Syracuse	962	13.4

LEADERS IN ASSISTS

	No.	Ave.
Bob Cousy, Boston	557	8.6
Dick McGuire, Detroit	443	6.2
Larry Costello, Syracuse	379	5.4
Richie Guerin, New York	364	5.1
Carl Braun, New York	349	4.8

1959–60

Wilt Chamberlain, the 7-1 center who had played two seasons of college basketball at Kansas and then toured for a year with the Harlem Globetrotters, signed with the Philadelphia Warriors. The Big Dipper had an unparalleled rookie season and quickly proved that he was the greatest offensive force in the league.

The Warrior star set numerous records, including most points, 2,707; highest scoring average, 37.6; most field goals attempted, 2,311; most field goals scored, 1,065; most rebounds, 1,941; highest rebound average, 26.9, and most games with 50 or more points, five.

But Wilt wasn't the only NBA performer to set records. Elgin Baylor, in his second season with Minneapolis, scored 64 points against Boston on November 8, breaking Joe Fulks' 11-year-old record of 63 points. Boston's Bill Russell set a record with 51 rebounds against Syracuse, and Dolph Schayes of Syracuse became the first player to score more than 15,000 points in his career. He finished the season with 15,798 points to move past George Mikan as the all-time scoring leader.

Cincinnati's Jack Twyman averaged 31.2 points, second only to Wilt Chamberlain.

It's Philadelphia's Chamberlain over Boston's Russell, but Celtics won the title again.

Boston became the first team in six seasons to repeat as league champion. The Celtics edged St. Louis, four games to three, in the playoff finals. Despite the scoring feats of Philadelphia's Chamberlain, Boston had won the Eastern title by 10 games over the second-place Warriors. Boston won 59 games, the most in the NBA's history, and tied a league record with 17 consecutive victories. In the West, St. Louis had an even easier time, breezing to a 16-game margin over the Detroit Pistons.

In the scoring race Cincinnati's Jack Twyman averaged 31.2 points a game. Although no other player had ever averaged over 30 points, Twyman's feat was completely overshadowed by Chamberlain's domination of the scoring statistics.

The Knicks' Kenny Sears led the league in field-goal accuracy with a .477 percentage and Schayes regained the free-throw title from Boston's Bill Sharman with an .892 percentage. The Celtics' Bob Cousy continued as the NBA's top playmaker, setting a season record with 715 assists and becoming the first to get more than 5,000 assists in his career.

The East trounced the West, 125-115, in the All-Star Game at Philadelphia, with Chamberlain scoring 23 points and winning the MVP award. Twyman had 26 for the West.

Chamberlain, the Rookie and Most Valuable Player of the Year headed the All-NBA team. He was joined by Baylor, Cousy, Gene Shue of Detriot and Bob Pettit of St. Louis. Pettit, along with New York's Carl Braun and St. Louis' Larry Foust, went over the 10,000-point mark for his career.

STANDINGS

Eastern Division

	W.	L.	Pct.
Boston	59	16	.787
Philadelphia	49	26	.653
Syracuse	45	30	.600
New York	27	48	.360

Western Division

	W.	L.	Pct.
St. Louis	46	29	.613
Detroit	30	45	.400
Minneapolis	25	50	.333
Cincinnati	19	56	.253

PLAYOFFS

First Round

Philadelphia defeated Syracuse 2 games to 1
Minneapolis defeated Detroit 2 games to 0

Semifinals

Boston defeated Philadelphia 4 games to 2
St. Louis defeated Minneapolis 4 games to 3

Championship

Boston defeated St. Louis 4 games to 3

TOP SCORERS

	Pts.	Ave.
Wilt Chamberlain, Philadelphia	2707	37.6
Jack Twyman, Cincinnati	2338	31.2
Elgin Baylor, Minneapolis	2074	29.6
Bob Pettit, St. Louis	1882	26.1
Cliff Hagan, St. Louis	1858	24.8

TOP REBOUNDERS

	No.	Ave.
Wilt Chamberlain, Philadelphia	1941	26.9
Bill Russell, Boston	1778	24.0
Bob Pettit, St. Louis	1221	16.9
Elgin Baylor, Minneapolis	1150	16.4
Dolph Schayes, Syracuse	959	12.8

LEADERS IN ASSISTS

	No.	Ave.
Bob Cousy, Boston	715	9.5
Guy Rodgers, Philadelphia	482	7.1
Richie Guerin, New York	468	6.3
Larry Costello, Syracuse	446	6.3
Tom Gola, Philadelphia	409	5.4

1960-61

The NBA became truly a national league when the Minneapolis Lakers moved to Los Angeles and brought professional basketball to the West Coast. The Lakers came up with an outstanding rookie, Jerry West of West Virginia University, to team with Elgin Baylor, their All-NBA forward.

Rookie Oscar Robertson of Cincinnati keeps Boston's K. C. Jones at arm's length.

But the most exciting rookie of the year was Oscar Robertson of the Cincinnati Royals. Robertson had led the nation in scoring for three years as a collegian at Cincinnati and quickly showed that he could score with equal ease in the pro game. The Big O averaged 30.5 points a game, fourth-best in the NBA, to become the highest-scoring guard in the league's history. Robertson excelled as a playmaker as well, taking over from Boston's Bob Cousy as the leader in assists. Robertson averaged 9.7 assists, the highest in history, and attendance in Cincinnati more than tripled.

Philadelphia's Wilt Chamberlain, who had set a basket of new scoring and rebounding records as a rookie, broke all of his own marks in his second season. He averaged 38.4 points a game and became the first player to score more than 3,000 points in a season, finishing with 3,033. He also set a record for rebounds with an average of 27.2 a game and led in field goal accuracy with a .505 percentage.

The Lakers' sensational Baylor erased his own NBA record by scoring 71 points against New York on November 15. He hit on 28 of 48 attempts and 15 of 19 free throws. In addition he grabbed 25 rebounds. Chamberlain produced the most impressive rebounding feat, though, hauling down a record 55 against Boston. Bill Sharman of Boston recaptured the free-throw title with a .921 percentage.

The Celtics established themselves as one of the finest teams in history by winning their third consecutive championship and fourth in five seasons. Boston won the Eastern title with ease, finishing 11 games ahead of the Chamberlain-led Philadelphia Warriors. St. Louis beat the Lakers by 15 games in the West. Boston crushed the Hawks, four games to one, in the playoff finals.

The West bombed the East, 153-131, in the All-Star Game at Syracuse. Bob Pettit of St. Louis, the league's second-highest scorer, posted 29 points for the West, but Oscar Robertson won the MVP award. The Big O had 23 points and 14 assists for the winners.

Bill Russell of Boston won his second Podoloff Cup as the NBA's Most Valuable Player in a vote of the players. But the sportswriters relegated him to the second All-NBA team in their poll. The All-NBA team included Pettit, Chamberlain, Baylor, Cousy and Robertson, the Rookie of the Year.

New York had the rather dubious distinction of losing a game by 62 points, the greatest margin of defeat in the league's history. The Knicks, who finished last in the East, absorbed a 162-100 beating at the hands of Syracuse on Christmas Day.

STANDINGS

Eastern Division

	W.	L.	Pct.
Boston	57	22	.722
Philadelphia	46	33	.582
Syracuse	38	41	.481
New York	21	58	.266

Western Division

	W.	L.	Pct.
St. Louis	51	28	.646
Los Angeles	36	43	.456
Detroit	34	45	.430
Cincinnati	33	46	.418

PLAYOFFS

First Round

Syracuse defeated Philadelphia 3 games to 0
Los Angeles defeated Detroit 3 games to 2

Semifinals

Boston defeated Syracuse 4 games to 1
St. Louis defeated Los Angeles 4 games to 3

Championship

Boston defeated St. Louis 4 games to 1

TOP SCORERS

	Pts.	Ave.
Wilt Chamberlain, Philadelphia	3033	38.4
Elgin Baylor, Los Angeles	2538	34.8
Oscar Robertson, Cincinnati	2165	30.5
Bob Pettit, St. Louis	2120	27.9
Jack Twyman, Cincinnati	1997	25.3

TOP REBOUNDERS

	No.	Ave.
Wilt Chamberlain, Philadelphia	2149	27.2
Bob Pettit, St. Louis	1540	20.3
Elgin Baylor, Los Angeles	1447	19.8
Bailey Howell, Detroit	1111	14.4
Willie Naulls, New York	1055	13.4

LEADERS IN ASSISTS

	No.	Ave.
Oscar Robertson, Cincinnati	690	9.7
Guy Rodgers, Philadelphia	677	8.9
Bob Cousy, Boston	591	7.8
Gene Shue, Detroit	530	6.8
Richie Guerin, New York	503	6.4

1961–62

Wilt Chamberlain, Philadelphia's mighty 7-1 center, dwarfed all past scoring feats by recording 100 points in a single game. Wilt's incredible performance came in the Warriors' 169-147 victory over New York in Hershey, Pennsylvania, on March 2. The 316 points the two teams scored also set an NBA record.

Chamberlain hit on 36 of 63 field-goal attempts and belied his reputation as the NBA's worst foul shooter by connecting on 28 of 32 shots from the free-throw line.

Bob Cousy, a 15,000-point man, shoots against Royals' Arlen Bockhorn and Oscar Robertson.

Wilt again obliterated all season scoring records. He averaged a phenomenal 50.4 points a game, nearly 19 points ahead of Chicago's Walt Bellamy, his nearest rival. In the 80 regular season games, Wilt scored 60 or more points 15 times and over 50 points 44 times. Los Angeles' Elgin Baylor and Jerry West each had 63-point games and Baylor also scored 61 points.

But all this scoring couldn't stop Boston, with a beautifully balanced attack and Bill Russell at center, from winning its fourth consecutive title and fifth in six seasons. The Celtics again made a shambles of the Eastern Division race, finishing 11 games ahead of Philadelphia. Tommy Heinsohn, Boston's best scorer, was no better than 11th in the league with a 22.3 average.

The NBA added a ninth team, the Chicago Packers, which joined the West and finished last. The division winner, Los Angeles, beat Cincinnati by 11 games as St. Louis, Western champions since 1957, dropped to fourth place. The final playoff series between the Lakers and Celtics went the full seven games, with Boston's Sam Jones scoring the winning basket with two seconds left in the deciding game.

Chamberlain won the rebounding title with a 25.6 average. Bellamy, a 6-11 rookie center from Indiana, was the most accurate shooter from the floor with a .513 percentage and Dolph Schayes of Syracuse was tops from the free-throw line with an .896 mark. Cincinnati's Oscar Robertson set a new record, averaging 11.4 assists a game. But Boston's Bob Cousy, who

Syracuse's Dolph Schayes slips past St. Louis' Cliff Hagan (16).

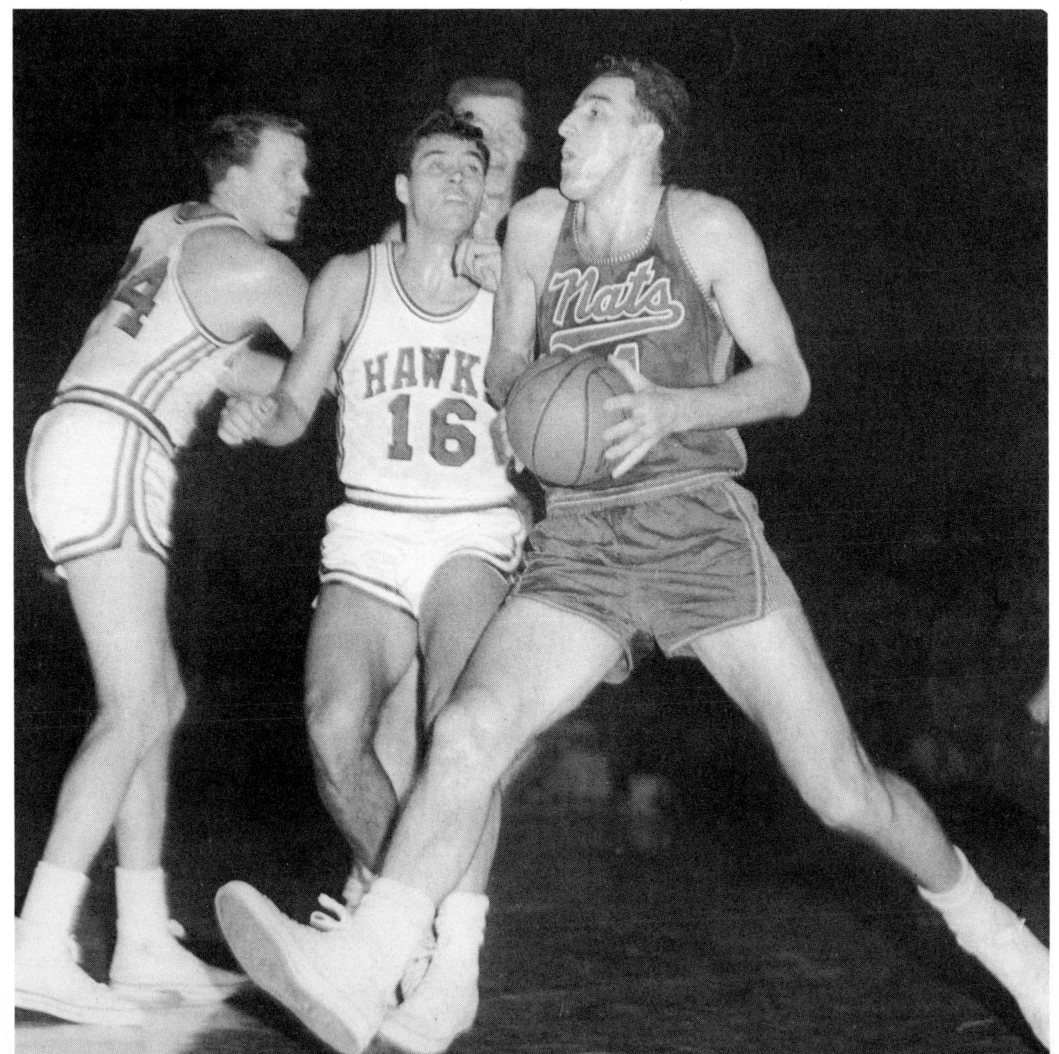

dropped to third in assists, became the first player to go over the 6,000 mark for his career.

Schayes broke Harry Gallatin's consecutive-game record of 682 but saw his own streak snapped at 706 when he suffered a fractured cheekbone on December 26.

Cousy, Bob Pettit of St. Louis and Paul Arizin of Philadelphia all passed the 15,000-point plateau for their careers.

The West scored a convincing 150-130 victory in the All-Star Game at St. Louis as Bob Pettit, with 27 rebounds and 25 points, took MVP honors for the third time. Wilt Chamberlain set an All-Star scoring record with 42 points for the losers.

Russell, the hub of the Celtics, won his second consecutive Most Valuable Player award but again did not make the All-NBA first team. The All-NBA team included Pettit, Baylor, Chamberlain, West and Robertson, with Chicago's Bellamy the Rookie of the Year.

STANDINGS

Eastern Division

	W.	L.	Pct.
Boston	60	20	.750
Philadelphia	49	31	.613
Syracuse	41	39	.513
New York	29	51	.363

Western Division

	W.	L.	Pct.
Los Angeles	54	26	.675
Cincinnati	43	37	.538
Detroit	37	43	.463
St. Louis	29	51	.363
Chicago	18	62	.225

PLAYOFFS

First Round

Philadelphia defeated Syracuse 3 games to 2
Detroit defeated Cincinnati 3 games to 1

Semifinals

Boston defeated Philadelphia 4 games to 3
Los Angeles defeated Detroit 4 games to 2

Championship

Boston defeated Los Angeles 4 games to 3

TOP SCORERS

	Pts.	Ave.
Wilt Chamberlain, Philadelphia	4029	50.4
Walt Bellamy, Chicago	2495	31.6
Oscar Robertson, Cincinnati	2432	30.3
Bob Pettit, St. Louis	2429	31.1
Jerry West, Los Angeles	2310	30.8

TOP REBOUNDERS

	No.	Ave.
Wilt Chamberlain, Philadelphia	2052	25.6
Bill Russell, Boston	1891	24.9
Walt Bellamy, Chicago	1500	19.0
Bob Pettit, St. Louis	1457	18.7
John Kerr, Syracuse	1176	14.7

LEADERS IN ASSISTS

	No.	Ave.
Oscar Robertson, Cincinnati	899	11.4
Guy Rodgers, Philadelphia	663	7.9
Bob Cousy, Boston	584	7.8
Richie Guerin, New York	539	6.9
Gene Shue, Detroit	465	5.8

1962–63

The NBA continued its march to the West as Eddie Gottlieb, a pioneer professional owner and former coach, sold the Philadelphia Warriors to a San Francisco group. Gottlieb, who was frequently said to have carried his office around in his hat, reportedly received $850,000 for the Warriors.

The Boston Celtics won their fifth consecutive title and sixth in seven years behind their incomparable team of Bob Cousy and Bill Russell. Cousy, generally regarded as the greatest guard in the history of the game, announced his retirement after 13 seasons. The only player to appear in all 13 All-Star Games, Cousy made the All-NBA first team 10 times and the second team twice.

Western champions Elgin Baylor, left, and Jerry West with Laker coach Fred Schaus.

Russell, the league's top defensive player, won his third straight Most Valuable Player award and returned to the All-NBA team after a two-year absence.

As usual, Boston made a runaway of the Eastern Division race. The Celts finished 10 games ahead of Syracuse. In the West, Los Angeles, with Elgin Baylor and Jerry West, successfully defended its divisional title, finishing five games ahead of St. Louis. Both division champions made it into the playoff finals, where Boston defeated the Lakers, four games to two.

San Francisco's Wilt Chamberlain won his fourth scoring title in four seasons in the NBA with a 44.8 average. Baylor finished second with a 34.0 average and Cincinnati's Oscar Robertson was third with 28.3. Chamberlain also led in rebounding with a 24.3 average and in field-goal accuracy, making 52.8 percent of his shots. San Francisco's Guy Rodgers led the league with 10.8 assists a game, most of them coming on passes to Chamberlain. Larry Costello of Syracuse was tops in free-throw accuracy with an .881 percentage.

Syracuse's Dolph Schayes, in his 15th professional season, played in his 1,000th game and scored his 19,000th point during the year. Bob Pettit of St. Louis broke the 17,000 barrier, and Richie Guerin of New York, Cliff Hagan of St. Louis, Tom Heinsohn of Boston, Chamberlain and Baylor all went over 10,000 points for their careers. Russell, who finished second to Chamberlain in rebounding, became the all-time rebound leader with 11,499.

The East won the All-Star Game at Los Angeles, 115-108, with Robertson scoring 21 points for the East and Pettit 25 for the West. But Russell, who dominated the backboards, won the game MVP award for the second consecutive year.

Baylor, Pettit, Robertson, Russell and West made the All-NBA team as Chamberlain was relegated to the second team for the first time in his career. Terry Dischinger, who two years before had played on the U.S. Olympic team as a college sophomore, won Rookie of the Year honors with Chicago. He averaged 25.5 points a game.

STANDINGS

Eastern Division

	W.	L.	Pct.
Boston	58	22	.725
Syracuse	48	32	.600
Cincinnati	42	38	.525
New York	21	59	.263

Western Division

	W.	L.	Pct.
Los Angeles	53	27	.663
St. Louis	48	32	.600
Detroit	34	46	.425
San Francisco	31	49	.388
Chicago	25	55	.313

PLAYOFFS

First Round

Cincinnati defeated Syracuse 3 games to 2
St. Louis defeated Detroit 3 games to 1

Semifinals

Boston defeated Cincinnati 4 games to 3
Los Angeles defeated St. Louis 4 games to 3

Championship

Boston defeated Los Angeles 4 games to 2

TOP SCORERS

	Pts.	Ave.
Wilt Chamberlain, San Francisco	3586	44.8
Elgin Baylor, Los Angeles	2719	34.0
Oscar Robertson, Cincinnati	2264	28.3
Bob Pettit, St. Louis	2241	28.4
Walt Bellamy, Chicago	2233	27.9

TOP REBOUNDERS

	No.	Ave.
Wilt Chamberlain, San Francisco	1946	24.3
Bill Russell, Boston	1843	23.6
Walt Bellamy, Chicago	1310	16.4
Bob Pettit, St. Louis	1195	15.1
Elgin Baylor, Los Angeles	1146	14.3

LEADERS IN ASSISTS

	No.	Ave.
Guy Rodgers, San Francisco	825	10.6
Oscar Robertson, Cincinnati	758	9.5
Bob Cousy, Boston	515	6.8
Sihugo Green, Chicago	422	5.8
Elgin Baylor, Los Angeles	386	4.8

1963-64

The Boston Celtics, playing without Bob Cousy who had retired to coach at Boston College, won their sixth consecutive NBA title and seventh in eight seasons. The Celtics dynasty, which began when Bill Russell joined the team in 1956-57, reached a new peak in the history of American sports.

The New York Yankees in baseball and the Montreal Canadiens in hockey had each won championships in five straight years, but never before had any major-league professional team won six consecutive titles.

Both divisional races were close. Boston won by five games over Cincinnati, which had Oscar Robertson and rookie sensation Jerry Lucas, and San Francisco, coached by Alex Hannum, held off St. Louis by two games in the West. The Celtics blasted San Francisco, four games to one, in the final playoff series.

Maurice Podoloff, who had served as president of the NBA since its founding 17 years before, retired at the close of the previous season. He was succeeded by Walter Kennedy, the original publicist of the NBA and a former mayor of Stamford, Connecticut. Financially the NBA enjoyed its best season, as attendance climbed above 2,000,000 for the first time. The Chicago franchise, after finishing last in the West for its two seasons of existence, moved to Baltimore. The team revived the nickname of Bullets, which had been used by an earlier Baltimore franchise in the league, and escaped the cellar with a fourth-place finish.

Bob Pettit of St. Louis closed the season with 19,756 career points, making him the most

Commissioner Walter Kennedy

Philadelphia's Johnny Kerr played in his 745th straight game.

productive scorer ever in the NBA. Dolph Schayes, the first man to score more than 19,000 points, had retired to coach the Philadelphia 76ers. The 76ers, actually the transplanted Syracuse Nationals, brought professional basketball back to Philadelphia after a two-year absence.

Philadelphia's Johnny Kerr played in his 745th consecutive regular season game and 62nd straight playoff contest. Kerr's 707th game in a row broke Schayes' record. An early-season eye injury halted Cincinnati's Jack Twyman's consecutive-game streak at 609.

Wilt Chamberlain won his fifth straight scoring title with a 36.5 average and scored 59 points three times during the year. Oscar Robertson of Cincinnati was second. Robertson also led the league in assists and field-goal accuracy. Cincinnati's Lucas, the Rookie of the Year, beat out Chamberlain as the leader in field goal accuracy with a .527 percentage and Boston's Russell took the rebounding title.

In the All-Star Game at Boston, Robertson led the East to a 111-107 triumph. The Big O, the MVP both in the game and for the season, scored 26 points. Robertson was a unanimous choice for the All-NBA team, and was joined by Pettit, Chamberlain, and Elgin Baylor and Jerry West of the Lakers.

After the season, the State Department sponsored an NBA All-Star team on a tour of Europe and the Middle East. The NBA stars swept all 21 games against teams in Poland, Rumania, Yugoslavia and Egypt.

STANDINGS

Eastern Division

	W.	L.	Pct.
Boston	59	21	.738
Cincinnati	55	25	.688
Philadelphia	34	46	.425
New York	22	58	.275

Western Division

	W.	L.	Pct.
San Francisco	48	32	.600
St. Louis	46	34	.575
Los Angeles	42	38	.525
Baltimore	31	49	.388
Detroit	23	57	.288

PLAYOFFS

First Round

Cincinnati defeated Philadelphia 3 games to 2
St. Louis defeated Los Angeles 3 games to 2

Semifinals

Boston defeated Cincinnati 4 games to 1
San Francisco defeated St. Louis 4 games to 3

Championship

Boston defeated San Francisco 4 games to 1

TOP SCORERS

	Pts.	Ave.
Wilt Chamberlain, San Francisco	2948	36.5
Oscar Robertson, Cincinnati	2480	31.4
Bob Pettit, St. Louis	2190	27.4
Walt Bellamy, Baltimore	2159	27.0
Jerry West, Los Angeles	2064	27.0

TOP REBOUNDERS

	No.	Ave.
Bill Russell, Boston	1930	24.7
Wilt Chamberlain, San Francisco	1687	21.1
Jerry Lucas, Cincinnati	1375	17.4
Walt Bellamy, Baltimore	1361	17.0
Bob Pettit, St. Louis	1224	15.3

LEADERS IN ASSISTS

	No.	Ave.
Oscar Robertson, Cincinnati	868	11.0
Guy Rodgers, San Francisco	556	7.0
K.C. Jones, Boston	407	5.1
Jerry West, Los Angeles	403	5.6
Wilt Chamberlain, San Francisco	403	5.0

Cincinnati's Jerry Lucas was Rookie of the Year.

1964–65

News of basketball's biggest trade rocked the NBA world on January 15, the night of the annual All-Star Game in St. Louis. At a post-midnight press conference, San Francisco owner Franklin Mieuli announced that he had traded Wilt Chamberlain, his 7-1 scoring machine, to the Philadelphia 76ers. In return the Warriors received three journeyman players, Connie Dierking, Paul Neuman, and Lee Shaffer, and an undisclosed amount of cash.

Neither the change in locale nor the change to a wider free throw lane (16 feet instead of 12) prevented Wilt from winning his sixth consecutive scoring title with a 34.7 average. Los Angeles' Jerry West was second with 31.0, and Cincinnati's Oscar Robertson was third with 30.4.

The seemingly invincible Boston Celtics won their seventh NBA title in a row and eighth in nine seasons. The Celtics, who won a record 62 games, finished 14 games ahead of Cincinnati in the East. Along the way, the Celtics posted winning streaks of 11 and 16 games.

Detroit player-coach Dave DeBusschere goes against Boston's Bill Russell.

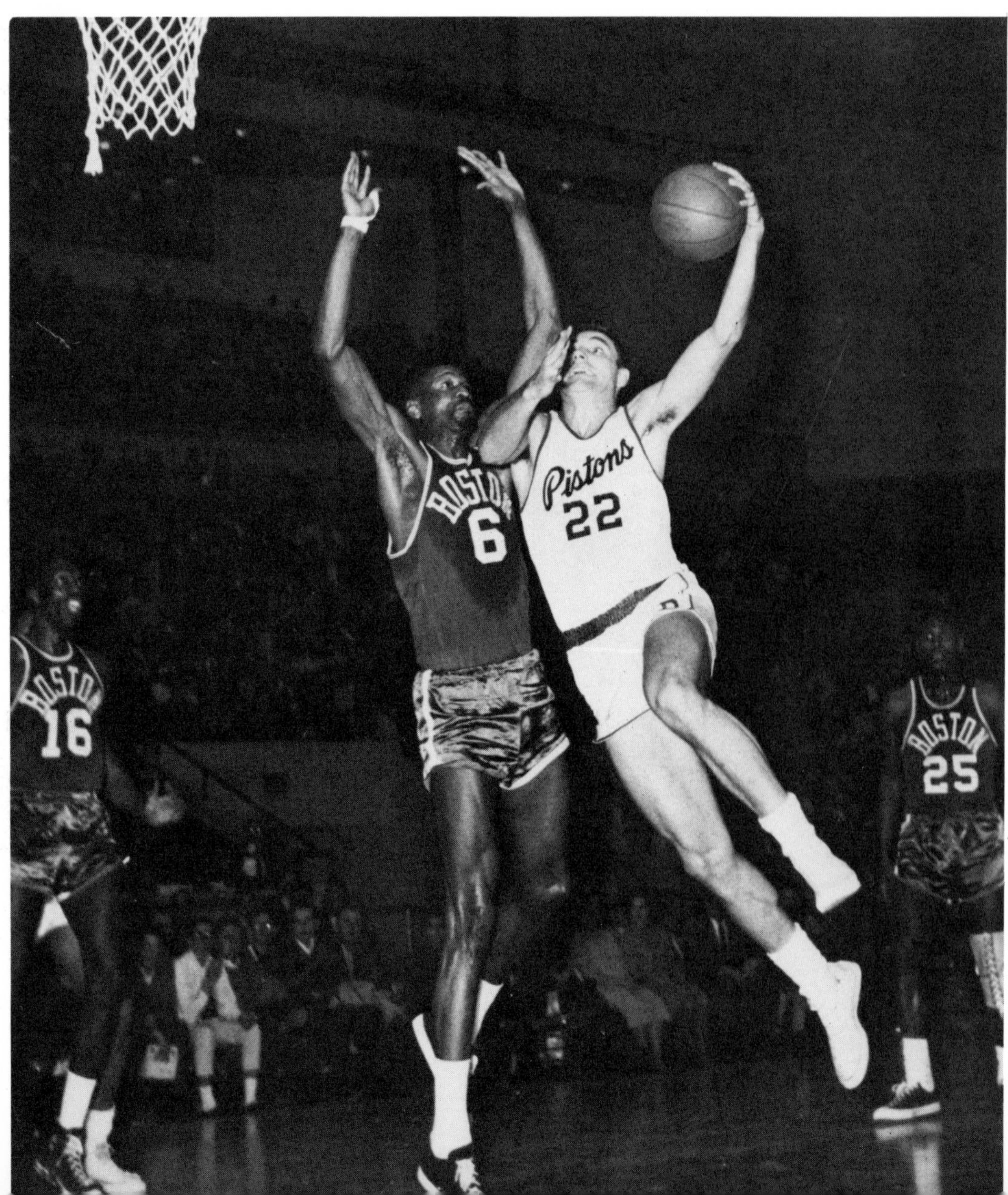

But it was Philadelphia, which had acquired Wilt in mid-season and finished third in the East, which gave Boston the greatest trouble. The 76ers extended Boston to the full seven games in the Eastern playoff finals. In the decisive final game, Boston's John Havlicek intercepted an in-bounds pass under the Philadelphia basket with five seconds remaining to preserve Boston's 110-109 victory.

The final playoff series came as something of an anticlimax, with Boston whipping Western champion Los Angeles in five games. The Lakers had won in the West by four games over St. Louis. Los Angeles' brilliant Elgin Baylor injured his ankle in the opening game of the Western playoff finals against Baltimore and missed the remainder of the playoffs. Even the fantastic play of the Lakers' Jerry West, who averaged 40.6 points a game during the playoffs, could not overcome Boston's balanced attack.

The Detroit Pistons made NBA history by naming Dave DeBusschere, their outstanding 24-year-old forward, as player-coach. He became the youngest coach in league annals. St. Louis also selected veteran guard Richie Guerin as player-coach.

Chamberlain led the league in field goal accuracy with a .510 percentage and his Philadelphia teammate, Larry Costello, led in free-throw accuracy with an .877 mark. The Big O was the top playmaker, averaging a record-shattering 11.5 assists a game, and Boston's Bill Russell was the top rebounder.

The East scored a 124-123 victory in the All-Star Game at St. Louis. Robertson scored 28 for the East and Gus Johnson of Baltimore had 25 for the West, but Cincinnati's Jerry Lucas won the MVP award for his outstanding rebounding and 25 points.

Bob Pettit of St. Louis, the most prolific scorer in NBA history, passed the 20,000-point mark for his career and later announced his retirement. Cincinnati's Jack Twyman went over the 15,000 mark, and Robertson, Russell and Los Angeles' Willie Naulls all topped 10,000 career points.

Russell, the NBA's MVP for the fifth time; Baylor, West, Lucas and Robertson made the All-NBA team. New York's Willis Reed was Rookie of the Year.

Walter Brown, the owner of the Boston Celtics, one of the founders of the NBA and the originator of the All-Star Game, died shortly before the start of the season. The Celtics wore a black strip of cloth on their uniforms in his memory throughout the campaign.

STANDINGS

Eastern Division

	W.	L.	Pct.
Boston	62	18	.715
Cincinnati	48	32	.600
Philadelphia	40	40	.500
New York	31	49	.388

Western Division

	W.	L.	Pct.
Los Angeles	49	31	.613
St. Louis	45	35	.563
Baltimore	37	43	.463
Detroit	31	49	.388
San Francisco	17	63	.213

PLAYOFFS

First Round

Philadelphia defeated Cincinnati 3 games to 1
Baltimore defeated St. Louis 3 games to 1

Semifinals

Boston defeated Philadelphia 4 games to 3
Los Angeles defeated Baltimore 4 games to 2

Championship

Boston defeated Los Angeles 4 games to 1

TOP SCORERS

	Pts.	Ave.
Wilt Chamberlain, San Francisco—Philadelphia	2534	34.7
Jerry West, Los Angeles	2292	31.0
Oscar Robertson, Cincinnati	2279	30.4
Sam Jones, Boston	2070	25.9
Elgin Baylor, Los Angeles	2009	27.1

TOP REBOUNDERS

	No.	Ave.
Bill Russell, Boston	1879	24.1
Wilt Chamberlain, San Francisco—Philadelphia	1673	22.9
Nate Thurmond, San Francisco	1395	18.1
Jerry Lucas, Cincinnati	1321	20.0
Willis Reed, New York	1175	14.7

LEADERS IN ASSISTS

	No.	Ave.
Oscar Robertson, Cincinnati	861	11.5
Guy Rodgers, San Francisco	565	7.3
K.C. Jones, Boston	437	5.6
Len Wilkens, St. Louis	431	5.5
Bill Russell, Boston	410	5.3

1965–66

For the first time in a decade, Boston failed to win the Eastern Division title. But the Celtics came back in the playoffs to win their eighth consecutive title and ninth in ten seasons.

The Philadelphia 76ers, with Wilt Chamberlain, Hal Greer and Chet Walker, won their last 11 games to finish a game ahead of Boston. But Boston easily ousted Philadelphia, four games to one in the Eastern playoff finals.

Los Angeles, with Elgin Baylor and Jerry West, won by seven games over Baltimore in the West and was the only team in the division to win more than half its games. In the playoff finals, Boston, despite the retirement of Tom Heinsohn, the high-scoring forward, beat the Lakers, four games to two.

Chamberlain won his seventh consecutive scoring title with a 33.5 average and also passed Bob Pettit as the all-time high scorer with a career total of 21,486 points in his seven NBA

Boston coach Red Auerbach, with the man who would succeed him, Bill Russell.

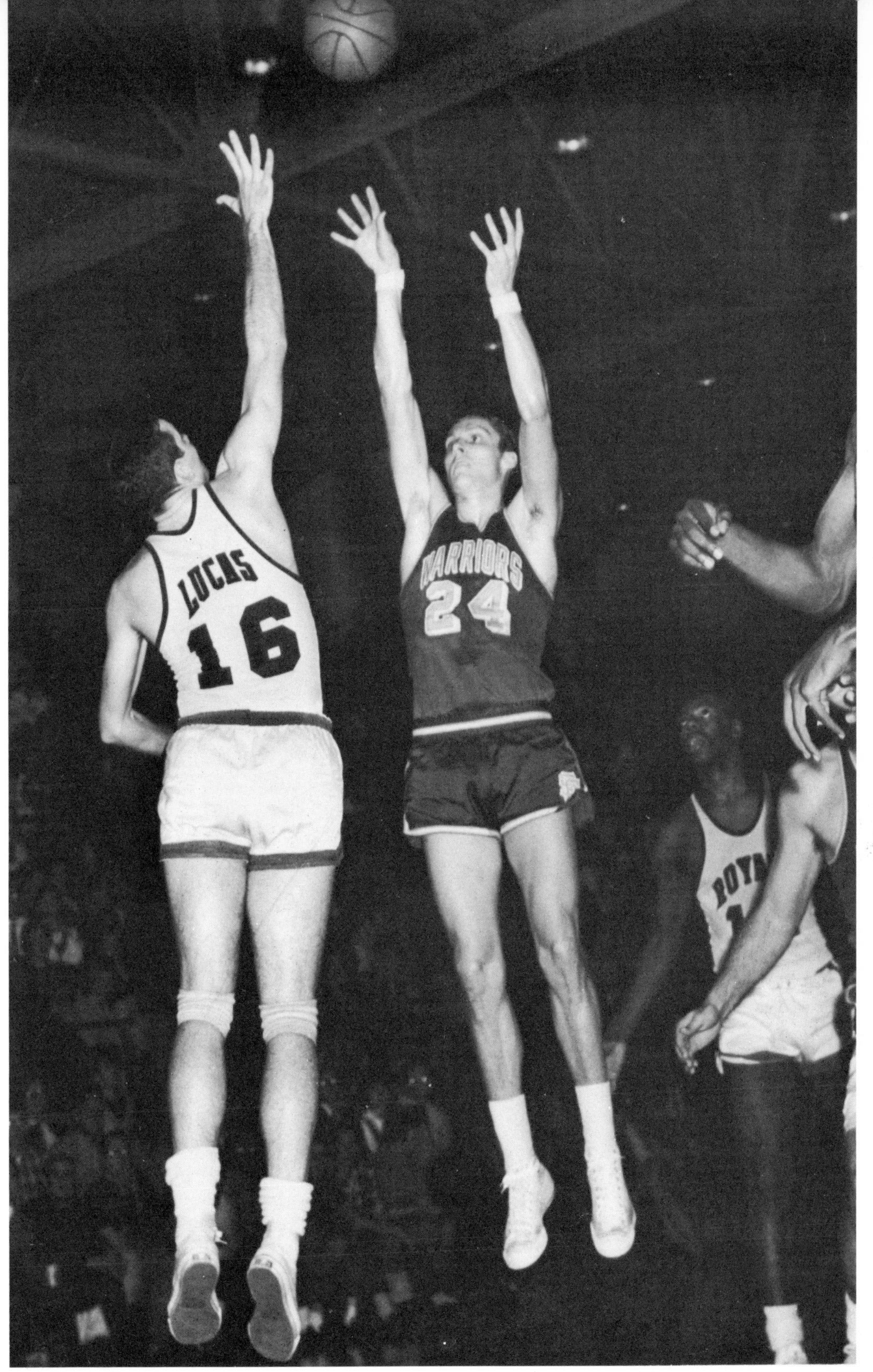

San Francisco's Rick Barry (24) scored more than 2,000 points in his rookie season.

seasons. In addition, Wilt led in field goal accuracy with a .540 percentage and rebounding with a 24.6 average. Chamberlain also won the Podoloff Cup as the league's Most Valuable Player and continued his streak of never having fouled out in his seven pro seasons.

San Francisco's Rick Barry, a 6-7 rookie from Miami (Fla.), was the season's outstanding rookie. He averaged 25.7 points, fourth best in the league, and reached a single-game high of 57 against New York. Barry joined Chamberlain, New York's Walt Bellamy and Cincinnati's Oscar Robertson as the only players to score more than 2,000 points in their first seasons.

Robertson retained his playmaking title with an average of 11.1 assists a game, and Boston's Larry Siegfried was the leading foul shooter with an .881 percentage.

Several all-time stars played their last season. They included Cincinnati's Jack Twyman, New York's Tom Gola, Los Angeles' Willie Naulls and Baltimore's John Kerr. Kerr had played in 844 consecutive games since entering the NBA in 1954 until an injury snapped his streak on November 5.

The East won its 11th All-Star Game in 16 tries, smashing the West, 137-94, at Cincinnati. Cincinnati's Adrian Smith, the last man selected for the game, led the East with 24 points and won MVP honors.

Chamberlain, Lucas, Robertson, Barry and West made the All-NBA team, with Boston's Bill Russell again back on the second five.

During the season West, Philadelphia's Hal Greer, Baltimore's Bailey Howell and Boston's Sam Jones all entered the exclusive 10,000-career-point club.

STANDINGS

Eastern Division

	W.	L.	Pct.
Philadelphia	55	25	.688
Boston	54	26	.675
Cincinnati	45	35	.563
New York	30	50	.375

Western Division

	W.	L.	Pct.
Los Angeles	45	35	.563
Baltimore	38	42	.475
St. Louis	36	44	.450
San Francisco	35	45	.438
Detroit	22	58	.275

PLAYOFFS

First Round

Boston defeated Cincinnati 3 games to 2
St. Louis defeated Baltimore 3 games to 0

Semifinals

Boston defeated Philadelphia 4 games to 1
Los Angeles defeated St. Louis 4 games to 3

Championship

Boston defeated Los Angeles 4 games to 3

TOP SCORERS

	Pts.	Ave.
Wilt Chamberlain, Philadelphia	2649	33.5
Jerry West, Los Angeles	2476	31.4
Oscar Robertson, Cincinnati	2378	31.3
Rick Barry, San Francisco	2059	25.7
Walt Bellamy, New York	1820	22.8

TOP REBOUNDERS

	No.	Ave.
Wilt Chamberlain, Philadelphia	1943	24.6
Bill Russell, Boston	1779	22.8
Jerry Lucas, Cincinnati	1668	21.8
Nate Thurmond, San Francisco	1312	18.0
Walt Bellamy, New York	1254	15.7

LEADERS IN ASSISTS

	No.	Ave.
Oscar Robertson, Cincinnati	847	11.1
Guy Rodgers, San Francisco	846	10.7
K.C. Jones, Boston	503	6.3
Jerry West, Los Angeles	480	6.1
Howard Komives, New York	426	5.3

1966–67

Sports' greatest success story ended when the Boston Celtics, NBA champions for the past eight seasons, yielded the league championship to Wilt Chamberlain and the Philadelphia 76ers. The 76ers won the most games (68), had the highest winning percentage (.840) in the history of the league and finished eight games ahead of the Celtics in the Eastern Division.

Before the season, Red Auerbach, the mastermind of Boston's phenomenal success, had retired and turned the coaching job over to Bill Russell. Russell, who continued as a player, became the first Negro head coach of a major league team in America. Auerbach closed out a 20-year coaching career with a record of 1,037 victories and 548 losses and nine NBA championships.

For the first time since coming into the league, Chamberlain failed to win the scoring title. But under the coaching of Alex Hannum, Chamberlain played the best all-around basketball of his career and excelled on defense and as a playmaker. San Francisco's Rick Barry, in his second pro season, took over as the scoring leader. Barry averaged 35.6 points a game and Chamberlain dropped to third behind Cincinnati's Oscar Robertson. Barry scored 50 or more points six times during the season.

Wilt Chamberlain's team finally bested Bill Russell's to win the NBA crown.

NEW YORK
14

Chamberlain won the Most Valuable Player award for the second straight year and established a record by hitting on 68.3 percent of his field goal attempts. He also led in rebounding with a 24.2 average.

Cincinnati's Adrian Smith led in foul-shooting with a .903 percentage, and Guy Rodgers of Chicago won his second assist title with an average of 11.1 a game.

The NBA returned to Chicago after a three-year absence and the new Chicago Bulls surprised everyone by making the playoffs in their very first season. Much of the credit went to John Kerr, who won Coach of the Year honors. Detroit finished below the Bulls in the West, and Dave DeBusschere, their player-coach, resigned as coach late in the season. He was replaced by Donnis Butcher.

San Francisco, with Barry and Nate Thurmond, won the Western title by five games over the St. Louis Hawks. Philadelphia ousted Boston, four games to one, in the Eastern finals and then downed the Warriors, four games to two, for the NBA championship.

Detroit's Dave Bing was top rookie.

The Knicks, with Cazzie Russell, made the playoffs.

The West, behind Barry, scored a 135-120 triumph in the All-Star Game at San Francisco. Barry scored 40 points on his way to MVP honors.

Barry, Chamberlain, Robertson, and Los Angeles' Elgin Baylor and Jerry West made the All-NBA team and Dave Bing of Detroit was named Rookie of the Year. Bing finished tenth in scoring with a 20.0 average.

New York, after seven years of failure, finally made it into the playoffs. But the Knicks' success was short-lived, as Boston eliminated them, three games to one, in the opening round.

After the season, the NBA, under pressure from the players, agreed to establish a major medical health insurance program and to institute a pension plan that would pay 10-year veterans of the league $600 a month when they reach age 65.

STANDINGS

Eastern Division

	W.	L.	Pct.
Philadelphia	68	13	.840
Boston	60	21	.741
Cincinnati	39	42	.481
New York	36	45	.444
Baltimore	20	61	.247

Western Division

	W.	L.	Pct.
San Francisco	44	37	.543
St. Louis	39	42	.481
Los Angeles	36	45	.444
Chicago	33	48	.470
Detroit	30	51	.370

PLAYOFFS

First Round

Philadelphia defeated Cincinnati 3 games to 1
Boston defeated New York 3 games to 1
San Francisco defeated Los Angeles 3 games to 0
St. Louis defeated Chicago 3 games to 0

Semifinals

Philadelphia defeated Boston 4 games to 1
San Francisco defeated St. Louis 4 games to 2

Championship

Philadelphia defeated San Francisco 4 games to 2

TOP SCORERS

	Pts.	Ave.
Rick Barry, San Francisco	2775	35.6
Oscar Robertson, Cincinnati	2412	30.5
Wilt Chamberlain, Philadelphia	1956	24.1
Jerry West, Los Angeles	1892	28.7
Elgin Baylor, Los Angeles	1862	26.6

TOP REBOUNDERS

	No.	Ave.
Wilt Chamberlain, Philadelphia	1957	24.2
Bill Russell, Boston	1700	21.0
Jerry Lucas, Cincinnati	1547	19.1
Nate Thurmond, San Francisco	1382	21.3
Bill Bridges, St. Louis	1190	15.1

LEADERS IN ASSISTS

	No.	Ave.
Guy Rodgers, Chicago	908	11.2
Oscar Robertson, Cincinnati	845	10.7
Wilt Chamberlain, Philadelphia	630	7.8
Bill Russell, Boston	472	5.8
Jerry West, Los Angeles	447	6.8

1967–68

Boston's tired old men battled back to recapture the NBA championship they had held for so long. The Celtics finished second in the East, eight games behind Philadelphia, the defending champion, and then fell behind the 76ers, three games to one, in the Eastern playoff finals.

But with Bill Russell, the 34-year-old player-coach, 35-year-old Sam Jones, 31-year-old Bailey Howell, and John Havlicek, a relative youngster at 28, Boston swept the next three games. The Celtics then went on to crush Los Angeles, four games to two, for their tenth champion-

Wilt Chamberlain soars in new Madison Square Garden.

ship in twelve seasons. Los Angeles had finished four games behind St. Louis in the West, but had eliminated the Hawks in four straight games to reach the playoff finals.

Rick Barry, the NBA's leading scorer a year ago, attempted to sign with Oakland of the new American Basketball Association. Bruce Hale, Barry's father-in-law, was the Oakland coach. But San Francisco brought legal action to stop Barry, and the former Warrior star was forced to sit out the season.

Dave Bing, the Rookie of the Year at Detroit in 1966–67, took over from Barry as the scoring leader. The Pistons' flashy guard averaged 27.1 points a game. Los Angeles' Elgin Baylor, who made an amazing recovery from a knee injury, was second.

Wilt Chamberlain, the NBA's leader in field goal percentage with a .595 mark, also became

Baltimore's Earl "The Pearl" Monroe, Rookie of Year, against Royals' Oscar Robertson.

Boston's John Havlicek rose from supersub to superstar.

the first center ever to lead the league in assists, averaging 8.6 a game. Wilt finished third in the scoring race, but did become the first player to reach a career mark of 25,000 points. Cincinnati's Oscar Robertson led in free-throw accuracy with an .873 percentage and Chamberlain, as usual, was the top rebounder, averaging 23.8 a game.

Bill Bradley, a three-time All-American at Princeton, finally made his pro debut with the New York Knickerbockers after spending two years at England's Oxford University as a Rhodes Scholar. Bradley joined the Knicks in mid-season and averaged only 8.0 points a game. The Knicks showed tremendous progress, though, and finished third in the East, their best showing in 10 years. Much of the improvement came after Red Holzman replaced Dick McGuire as coach in mid-season.

The NBA added two new franchises, San Diego and Seattle, to the Western Division, creating a 12-team league. The San Diego Rockets had the somewhat dubious distinction of losing 67 games, erasing a record of 63 losses set by San Francisco in 1964–65.

The East scored a 144-124 victory in the All-Star Game at New York, with Hal Greer of Philadelphia winning the MVP award. Greer tallied 21 points and Havlicek had 26 for the winners.

Chamberlain, the Most Valuable Player for the third consecutive year, headed the All-NBA team. He was joined by Russell, Bing, Robertson and Cincinnati's Jerry Lucas. Earl "The Pearl" Monroe, Baltimore's outstanding 6-3 guard, was Rookie of the Year. Monroe averaged

Ivy Leaguer and Rhodes scholar Bill Bradley made his debut with the Knicks.

24.3 points a game, fourth in the league, and proved an exciting playmaker and dribbler.

The league announced plans to expand to 14 teams for the 1968–69 season. The owners voted to locate new franchises in Phoenix and Milwaukee. The Phoenix team would be the first major league professional team ever in Arizona.

The NBA owners agreed that beginning with the 1968–69 season, rookies would be paid a minimum of $10,000 a year. This figure would be raised to a minimum of $13,000 for the 1970–71 season. The NBA also agreed to pay veteran players a minimum of $12,500 for 1968–69 and $13,500 the following year. The minimum pay scale was adopted at the urging of the NBA Players Association, whose president was Oscar Robertson.

STANDINGS

Eastern Division

	W.	L.	Pct.
Philadelphia	62	20	.756
Boston	54	28	.659
New York	43	39	.524
Detroit	40	42	.488
Cincinnati	39	43	.476
Baltimore	36	46	.439

Western Division

	W.	L.	Pct.
St. Louis	56	26	.683
Los Angeles	52	30	.634
San Francisco	43	39	.524
Chicago	29	53	.354
Seattle	23	59	.280
San Diego	15	67	.183

PLAYOFFS

First Round

Philadelphia defeated New York 4 games to 2
Boston defeated Detroit 4 games to 2
Los Angeles defeated Chicago 4 games to 1
San Francisco defeated St. Louis 4 games to 2

Semifinals

Boston defeated Philadelphia 4 games to 3
Los Angeles defeated San Francisco 4 games to 0

Championship

Boston defeated Los Angeles 4 games to 2

TOP SCORERS

	Pts.	Ave.
Dave Bing, Detroit	2142	27.1
Elgin Baylor, Los Angeles	2002	26.0
Wilt Chamberlain, Philadelphia	1992	24.3
Earl Monroe, Baltimore	1991	24.3
Hal Greer, Philadelphia	1976	24.1

TOP REBOUNDERS

	No.	Ave.
Wilt Chamberlain, Philadelphia	1952	23.8
Jerry Lucas, Cincinnati	1560	19.0
Bill Russell, Boston	1451	18.6
Clyde Lee, San Francisco	1141	13.9
Nate Thurmond, San Francisco	1121	22.0

LEADERS IN ASSISTS

	No.	Ave.
Wilt Chamberlain, Philadelphia	702	8.6
Len Wilkens, St. Louis	679	8.3
Oscar Robertson, Cincinnati	633	9.7
Dave Bing, Detroit	509	6.4
Walt Hazzard, Seattle	493	6.2

ALL-TIME NBA RECORDS

INDIVIDUAL

Single Game

Most Points	100	Wilt Chamberlain, Philadelphia, vs N.Y. at Hershey, Pa., March 2, 1962
Most F. G. Attempted	63	Wilt Chamberlain, Philadelphia, vs N.Y. at Hershey, Pa., March 2, 1962
Most F. G. Made	36	Wilt Chamberlain, Philadelphia, vs N.Y. at Hershey, Pa., March 2, 1962
Most F. T. Attempted	34	Wilt Chamberlain, Philadelphia, vs St. Louis at Philadelphia, Feb. 22, 1962
Most F. T. Made	28	Wilt Chamberlain, Philadelphia, vs N.Y. at Hershey, Pa., March 2, 1962
Most Rebounds	55	Wilt Chamberlain, Philadelphia, vs Boston at Philadelphia, Nov. 24, 1960
Most Assists	28	Bob Cousy, Boston, vs Minneapolis at Boston, Feb. 27, 1959
	28	Guy Rodgers, San Francisco, vs St. Louis at San Francisco, March 14, 1963

Most Personal Fouls	8	Don Otten, Tri-Cities, at Sheboygan, Nov. 24, 1949
Most Free Throws Missed	18	Wilt Chamberlain, Philadelphia, vs Syracuse, Nov. 17, 1960
Most Consecutive Points	32	Larry Costello, Syracuse vs Boston at Boston Dec. 8, 1961
Most Consecutive Free Throws	19	Bob Pettit, St. Louis, vs Boston Nov. 22, 1961

Season

Most Points	4,029	Wilt Chamberlain, Philadelphia, 1961-62
Highest Average	50.4	Wilt Chamberlain, Philadelphia, 1961-62
Most F. G. Attempted	3,159	Wilt Chamberlain, Philadelphia, 1961-62
Most F. G. Made	1,597	Wilt Chamberlain, Philadelphia, 1961-62
Highest F. G. Percentage	.683	Wilt Chamberlain, Philadelphia, 1966-67
Most F. T. Attempted	1,363	Wilt Chamberlain, Philadelphia, 1961-62
Most F. T. Made	840	Jerry West, Los Angeles, 1965-66
Highest F. T. Percentage	.932	Bill Sharman, Boston, 1958-59
Most Rebounds	2,149	Wilt Chamberlain, Philadelphia, 1960-61
Most Assists	908	Guy Rodgers, Chicago, 1966-67
Most Personal Fouls	366	Bill Bridges, St. Louis, 1967-68
Most Disqualifications	26	Don Meineke, Fort Wayne, 1952-53

Career

Most Points Scored	25,434	Wilt Chamberlain, Philadelphia Warriors, San Francisco Warriors, Philadelphia 76ers, 1959-68
Highest Scoring Average	36.0	Wilt Chamberlain, 1959-68
Most F. G. Attempted	19,617	Wilt Chamberlain, 1959-68
Most F. G. Made	10,321	Wilt Chamberlain, 1959-68
Highest F. G. Percentage	.526	Wilt Chamberlain, 1959-68
Most F. T. Attempted	9,196	Wilt Chamberlain, 1959-68
Most F. T. Made	6,979	Dolph Schayes, Syracuse, Philadelphia 76ers, 1948-64
Most F. T. Percentage	.883	Bill Sharman, Washington, Boston, 1950-61
Most Rebounds	20,237	Bill Russell, Boston, 1956-68
Most Assists	6,949	Bob Cousy, Boston, 1950-63
Most Minutes Played	37,435	Bill Russell, 1956-68
Most Personal Fouls	3,667	Dolph Schayes, 1948-64
Most Times Disqualified	127	Vern Mikkelsen, Minnesota, 1949-59

TEAM RECORDS

Single Game

Most Points, One Team	173	Boston vs Minneapolis at Boston, Feb. 27, 1959
Most Points, Two Teams	316	Philadelphia 169, New York 147 at Hershey, Pa., March 2, 1962
Most F. G. Attempted, One Team	153	Philadelphia vs Los Angeles at Philadelphia, Dec. 8, 1961
Most F. G. Attempted, Two Teams	291	Philadelphia 153, Los Angeles 138 at Philadelphia, Dec. 8, 1961

Most F. G. Made, One Team	72	Boston vs Minneapolis at Boston, Feb. 27, 1959
Most F. G. Made, Two Teams	125	Syracuse 69, San Francisco 56 at Syracuse, Mar. 10, 1963
Most F. T. Attempted, One Team	86	Syracuse vs Anderson at Syracuse (In 5 overtimes), Nov. 24, 1949
Most F. T. Attempted, Two Teams	160	Syracuse 86, Anderson 74 at Syracuse (In 5 overtimes), Nov. 24, 1949
Most F. T. Made, One Team	59	Syracuse vs Anderson at Syracuse (In 5 overtimes), Nov. 24, 1949
Most F. T. Made, Two Teams	116	Syracuse 59, Anderson 57 at Syracuse (In 5 overtimes), Nov. 24, 1949
Most Rebounds, One Team	112	Philadelphia vs Cincinnati at Philadelphia Nov. 8, 1959
	112	Boston vs Detroit at Boston, Dec. 24, 1960
Most Rebounds, Two Teams	215	Philadelphia 110, Los Angeles 105 at Philadelphia (In 3 overtimes), Dec. 8, 1961
Most Assists, One Team	60	Boston at Baltimore (In 1 overtime), Nov. 15, 1952
Most Assists, Two Teams	84	Rochester 49, Baltimore 35, Feb. 4, 1952
Most Personal Fouls, One Team	66	Anderson at Syracuse (In 5 overtimes), Nov. 24, 1949
Most Personal Fouls, Two Teams	122	Anderson 66, Syracuse 56 at Syracuse (In 5 overtimes), Nov. 24, 1949
Most Disqualifications, One Team	8	Syracuse vs Baltimore at Syracuse (In 1 overtime), Nov. 15, 1952
Most Disqualifications, Two Teams	13	Syracuse 8, Baltimore 5 at Syracuse (In 1 overtime), Nov. 15, 1952
Most Points in a Losing Game	148	Boston at Syracuse (In 1 overtime), Jan. 19, 1963
	148	San Francisco at Syracuse, Mar. 10, 1963
Widest Point Spread	62	Syracuse 162, New York 100, Dec. 25, 1960
Most Consecutive Points in a Game	24	Philadelphia vs Baltimore, Mar. 20, 1966

Season

Most Games Won	68	Philadelphia, 1966-67
Most Games Lost	67	San Diego, 1967-68
Longest Winning Streak	17	Washington, Nov. 16, 1946 to Dec. 30, 1946
	17	Boston, Nov. 28, 1959 to Dec. 30, 1959
Longest Losing Streak	17	San Francisco, Dec. 20, 1964 to Jan. 26, 1965
	17	San Diego, Jan. 17, 1968 to Feb. 18, 1968
Most Points Scored	10,143	Philadelphia, 1966-67
Most Points Allowed	10,261	Seattle, 1967-68
Highest Scoring Average	125.4	Philadelphia, 1961-62
Highest Average, Points Allowed	125.1	Seattle, 1967-68
Most F. G. Attempted	9,295	Boston, 1960-61
Most F. G. Made	3,965	Philadelphia, 1967-68
Highest F. G. Percentage	.483	Philadelphia, 1966-67
Most F. T. Attempted	3,411	Philadelphia, 1966-67
Most F. T. Made	2,408	Detroit, 1960-61
Highest F. T. Percentage	.794	Syracuse, 1956-57
Most Rebounds	6,131	Boston, 1960-61
Most Assists	2,197	Philadelphia, 1967-68

ALL-NBA TEAMS

1946–47

First	Second
Joe Fulks, Philadelphia	Ernie Calverley, Providence
Bob Feerick, Washington	Frank Baumholtz, Cleveland
Stan Miasek, Detroit	John Logan, St. Louis
Bones McKinney, Washington	Chuck Halbert, Chicago
Max Zaslofsky, Chicago	Fred Scolari, Washington

1947–48

First	Second
Joe Fulks, Philadelphia	John Logan, St. Louis
Max Zaslofsky, Chicago	Carl Braun, New York
Ed Sadowski, Boston	Stan Miasek, Chicago
Howie Dallmar, Philadelphia	Fred Scolari, Washington
Bob Feerick, Washington	Buddy Jeannette, Baltimore

1948–49

First	Second
George Mikan, Minneapolis	Arnie Risen, Rochester
Joe Fulks, Philadelphia	Bob Feerick, Washington
Bob Davies, Rochester	Bones McKinney, Washington
Max Zaslofsky, Chicago	Ken Sailors, Providence
Jim Pollard, Minneapolis	John Logan, St. Louis

1949–50

First	Second
George Mikan, Minneapolis	Frank Brian, Anderson
Jim Pollard, Minneapolis	Fred Schaus, Fort Wayne
Alex Groza, Indianapolis	Dolph Schayes, Syracuse
Bob Davies, Rochester	Al Cervi, Syracuse
Max Zaslofsky, Chicago	Ralph Beard, Indianapolis

1950–51

First	Second
George Mikan, Minneapolis	Dolph Schayes, Syracuse
Alex Groza, Indianapolis	Frank Brian, Tri-Cities
Ed Macauley, Boston	Vern Mikkelsen, Minneapolis
Bob Davies, Rochester	Joe Fulks, Philadelphia
Ralph Beard, Indianapolis	Dick McGuire, New York

1951–52

First	Second
George Mikan, Minneapolis	Larry Foust, Fort Wayne
Ed Macauley, Boston	Vern Mikkelsen, Minneapolis
Paul Arizin, Philadelphia	Jim Pollard, Minneapolis
Bob Cousy, Boston	Bob Wanzer, Rochester
{ Bob Davies, Rochester	Andy Phillip, Philadelphia
{ Dolph Schayes, Syracuse	

1952–53

First	Second
George Mikan, Minneapolis	Bill Sharman, Boston
Bob Cousy, Boston	Vern Mikkelsen, Minneapolis
Neil Johnston, Philadelphia	Bob Wanzer, Rochester
Ed Macauley, Boston	Bob Davies, Rochester
Dolph Schayes, Syracuse	Andy Phillip, Philadelphia

1953–54

First	Second
Bob Cousy, Boston	Ed Macauley, Boston
Neil Johnston, Philadelphia	Jim Pollard, Minneapolis
George Mikan, Minneapolis	Carl Braun, New York
Dolph Schayes, Syracuse	Bob Wanzer, Rochester
Harry Gallatin, New York	Paul Seymour, Syracuse

1954–55

First	Second
Neil Johnston, Philadelphia	Vern Mikkelsen, Minneapolis
Bob Cousy, Boston	Harry Gallatin, New York
Dolph Schayes, Syracuse	Paul Seymour, Syracuse
Bob Pettit, Milwaukee	Slater Martin, Minneapolis
Larry Foust, Fort Wayne	Bill Sharman, Boston

1955–56

Bob Pettit, St. Louis	Dolph Schayes, Syracuse
Paul Arizin, Philadelphia	Maurice Stokes, Rochester
Neil Johnston, Philadelphia	Clyde Lovellette, Minneapolis
Bob Cousy, Boston	Slater Martin, Minneapolis
Bill Sharman, Boston	Jack George, Philadelphia

1956–57

Paul Arizin, Philadelphia	George Yardley, Fort Wayne
Dolph Schayes, Syracuse	Maurice Stokes, Rochester
Bob Pettit, St. Louis	Neil Johnston, Philadelphia
Bob Cousy, Boston	Dick Garmaker, Minneapolis
Bill Sharman, Boston	Slater Martin, St. Louis

1957–58

Dolph Schayes, Syracuse	Cliff Hagan, St. Louis
George Yardley, Detroit	Maurice Stokes, Cincinnati
Bob Pettit, St. Louis	Bill Russell, Boston
Bob Cousy, Boston	Tom Gola, Philadelphia
Bill Sharman, Boston	Slater Martin, St. Louis

1958–59

Bob Pettit, St. Louis	Paul Arizin, Philadelphia
Elgin Baylor, Minneapolis	Cliff Hagan, St. Louis
Bill Russell, Boston	Dolph Schayes, Syracuse
Bob Cousy, Boston	Slater Martin, St. Louis
Bill Sharman, Boston	Richie Guerin, New York

1959–60

Bob Pettit, St. Louis	Jack Twyman, Cincinnati
Elgin Baylor, Minneapolis	Dolph Schayes, Syracuse
Wilt Chamberlain, Philadelphia	Bill Russell, Boston
Bob Cousy, Boston	Richie Guerin, New York
Gene Shue, Detroit	Bill Sharman, Boston

1960–61

Elgin Baylor, Los Angeles	Dolph Schayes, Syracuse
Bob Pettit, St. Louis	Tom Heinsohn, Boston
Wilt Chamberlain, Philadelphia	Bill Russell, Boston
Bob Cousy, Boston	Larry Costello, Syracuse
Oscar Robertson, Cincinnati	Gene Shue, Detroit

1961–62

Bob Pettit, St. Louis	Tom Heinsohn, Boston
Elgin Baylor, Los Angeles	Jack Twyman, Cincinnati
Wilt Chamberlain, Philadelphia	Bill Russell, Boston
Jerry West, Los Angeles	Richie Guerin, New York
Oscar Robertson, Cincinnati	Bob Cousy, Boston

1962–63

First	Second
Elgin Baylor, Los Angeles	Tom Heinsohn, Boston
Bob Pettit, St. Louis	Bailey Howell, Detroit
Bill Russell, Boston	Wilt Chamberlain, San Francisco
Oscar Robertson, Cincinnati	Bob Cousy, Boston
Jerry West, Los Angeles	Hal Greer, Syracuse

1963–64

First	Second
Bob Pettit, St. Louis	Tom Heinsohn, Boston
Elgin Baylor, Los Angeles	Jerry Lucas, Cincinnati
Wilt Chamberlain, San Francisco	Bill Russell, Boston
Oscar Robertson, Cincinnati	John Havlicek, Boston
Jerry West, Los Angeles	Hal Greer, Philadelphia

1964–65

First	Second
Elgin Baylor, Los Angeles	Bob Pettit, St. Louis
Jerry Lucas, Cincinnati	Gus Johnson, Baltimore
Bill Russell, Boston	Wilt Chamberlain, S. F.-Phila.
Oscar Robertson, Cincinnati	Sam Jones, Boston
Jerry West, Los Angeles	Hal Greer, Philadelphia

1965–66

First	Second
Rick Barry, San Francisco	John Havlicek, Boston
Jerry Lucas, Cincinnati	Gus Johnson, Boston
Wilt Chamberlain, Philadelphia	Bill Russell, Boston
Oscar Robertson, Cincinnati	Sam Jones, Boston
Jerry West, Los Angeles	Hal Greer, Philadelphia

1966–67

First	Second
Rick Barry, San Francisco	Willis Reed, New York
Elgin Baylor, Los Angeles	Jerry Lucas, Cincinnati
Wilt Chamberlain, Philadelphia	Bill Russell, Boston
Jerry West, Los Angeles	Hal Greer, Philadelphia
Oscar Robertson, Cincinnati	Sam Jones, Boston

1967–68

First	Second
Elgin Baylor, Los Angeles	Willis Reed, New York
Jerry Lucas, Cincinnati	John Havlicek, Boston
Wilt Chamberlain, Philadelphia	Bill Russell, Boston
Dave Bing, Detroit	Hal Greer, Philadelphia
Oscar Robertson, Cincinnati	Jerry West, Los Angeles

MOST VALUABLE PLAYER

Podoloff Cup

(By vote of players)

Year	Player	Team
1955–56	Bob Pettit	St. Louis
1956–57	Bob Cousy	Boston
1957–58	Bill Russell	Boston
1958–59	Bob Pettit	St. Louis
1959–60	Wilt Chamberlain	Philadelphia
1960–61	Bill Russell	Boston
1961–62	Bill Russell	Boston
1962–63	Bill Russell	Boston
1963–64	Oscar Robertson	Cincinnati
1964–65	Bill Russell	Boston
1965–66	Wilt Chamberlain	Philadelphia
1966–67	Wilt Chamberlain	Philadelphia
1967–68	Wilt Chamberlain	Philadelphia

ROOKIE OF THE YEAR

(By vote of writers)

Year	Player	Team
1952–53	Don Meineke	Fort Wayne
1953–54	Ray Felix	Baltimore
1954–55	Bob Pettit	Milwaukee
1955–56	Maurice Stokes	Rochester
1956–57	Tom Heinsohn	Boston
1957–58	Woody Sauldsberry	Philadelphia
1958–59	Elgin Baylor	Minneapolis
1959–60	Wilt Chamberlain	Philadelphia
1960–61	Oscar Robertson	Cincinnati
1961–62	Walt Bellamy	Chicago
1962–63	Terry Dischinger	Chicago
1963–64	Jerry Lucas	Cincinnati
1964–65	Willis Reed	New York
1965–66	Rick Barry	San Francisco
1966–67	Dave Bing	Detroit
1967–68	Earl Monroe	Baltimore

10: THE GREATEST PROS

Joe Lapchick has been intimately involved with professional basketball throughout his long and productive career. He starred for the Original Celtics, the greatest professional team in basketball's early years. Later he coached the New York Knickerbockers of the NBA. During his half-century in the game, Lapchick has gained respect as one of the keenest observers of basketball talent. Here are his selections of the greatest professionals of the modern era since World War II.

Paul Arizin is en route to one of his leaping shots.

PAUL ARIZIN

It was like a Renoir or a Rembrandt. Paul Arizin's jump shot was perfection. The best description was this one in a Philadelphia newspaper: ". . . flicking the ball on the crest of his leap like a man riding an invisible surf, this is Arizin's moment of expression."

Arizin played 10 years in the National Basketball Association for the Philadelphia Warriors. During those 10 years, he averaged 22.8 points per game and won scoring championships in 1951–52 with a 25.4 average and in 1956–57 with 25.6.

There is no telling how much a two-year marine hitch hurt Arizin right after he won his first scoring championship. Certainly, it claimed what might have been two of his most productive years, but even though he missed them, he still had a remarkable career.

Arizin came to the Warriors after making All-American at Villanova University. Even in college, the jump shot was his trademark. "The truth is," Arizin said, "that it (the shot) came by accident. I was playing in the Catholic Club League in Philadelphia and our games were on a slick dance floor. When I tried to hook, my feet would go out from under me. So I jumped. The ceiling was low and I had to throw line drives. I just never changed."

It's a good thing he didn't. The 6-4, 210-pounder played forward for the Warriors and the jump shot enabled him to get the ball away despite defensive counterparts who stood 6-7 and 6-8. Theoretically, big, agile professionals should have been able to stop Arizin. But he possessed marvelous timing and an important intangible called anticipation. Of course, he had natural spring in his legs, but it was the timing and anticipation which often meant the difference between scoring and not scoring.

Arizin was the fifth man in NBA history to reach the 10,000-point mark, and his career high in a single game was 44 points. At times one wondered how Arizin even made it up and down the court because he was constantly wheezing and seemingly trying to regain his breath. Arizin laughed when people suggested he was not in shape. "That panting and coughing is a sinus condition I've always had. It doesn't hurt my endurance," he said.

And so he would run down the court, gulping for air, an unruly cowlick on the back of his head flopping up and down. He would head for the corner, take a pass, then fake and jump, hanging in the air for a split second before firing his line-drive shot. A second later the ball would nestle in the basket.

RICK BARRY

For seven straight years, Wilt Chamberlain dominated the NBA scoring statistics. Then during the 1965–66 season a rookie named Rick Barry appeared in a San Francisco uniform. That year, Wilt won the scoring championship again. It wasn't until the following season that Rick Barry stunned the basketball world by taking the title from Chamberlain.

Only in his second year, Barry was mag-

Rick Barry rose fast in the pros.

nificent, leading the Warriors into the championship finals against the Philadelphia 76ers. As a second-year man, Barry scored 2,775 points in 78 games for a 35.6 points per game average. "In his second year as a pro," said Los Angeles coach Fred Schaus, "he's ahead of Bob Pettit at the same stage. Rick's a better shooter and a little quicker than Bob."

Schaus made the comparison with Pettit because when Rick first entered the league after starring at the University of Miami (Fla.), he was a rather skinny 6-7, 200 pounds. Just like Pettit who went on to become one of the game's greats. And, like Pettit, a lot of people doubted if Barry had the physical assets to take the punishment in the NBA. They found out quickly. As a rookie, he scored 2,059 points for a 25.7 average and he grabbed 850 rebounds. For that performance he was named Rookie of the Year.

During college, Barry, a native of Roselle Park, N.J., was a controversial basketball player. He had a quick temper that often got him into trouble on the court. When he turned professional, he remained just as controversial. That first year was a tough one. Barry took much punishment. The second year wasn't quite as bad. By then, he was recognized as one of the game's superstars. His game improved, too. Not just in scoring, but playmaking also. "He and Elgin Baylor are the greatest passing forwards in the game," San Francisco coach Bill Sharman said. Center Nate Thurmond also praised Barry: "Nobody on the team got the ball into me better than Rick."

With his future ahead, Barry gambled and lost during the 1967 off-season. He had been persuaded to sign a contract with the Oakland Oaks of the newly-formed American Basketball Association. The three-year contract called for $75,000 a year, plus a 15 percent interest in the team, plus five percent of any home gate which exceeded $600,000. Barry's father-in-law (and college coach), Bruce Hale, was the general manager of the Oaks. Barry signed the contract and the Warriors contested it in court. Due to a court order, he had to miss the whole 1967–68 season, thus interrupting his sensational career.

ELGIN BAYLOR

It was during a playoff game against the Baltimore Bullets in 1965. Elgin Baylor took a nasty spill. His teammates had to help him from the floor as 16,000 fans in the Los Angeles Sports Arena looked on in stunned silence. Nobody knew it then, but Elgin Baylor had just ripped off part of his kneecap.

The next year was the toughest of Baylor's career. The old, graceful moves didn't seem to be there any more. No more of those twisting driving layups, those unbelievable jump shots. Around the league, they were saying Elgin Baylor—the greatest forward for his size—was through.

For seven years, the 6-5 Seattle graduate had been one of the leading scorers in the league and together with guard Jerry West gave the Lakers the greatest one-two scoring punch ever seen in professional basketball. Despite the pain and the problems brought on by calcium deposits in his knees, Baylor continued to work to strengthen his weak legs. And then finally on Feb. 2, 1966, he scored 29 points and grabbed 21 rebounds in a game against Cincinnati. The obituary notices were discarded.

Baylor did pretty well the next two seasons, averaging 26 points a game both years and in 1967–68 he and West steered the Lakers into the NBA finals against the Boston Celtics.

Baylor is the all-time leading scorer for the Lakers and he ranks fourth in the league overall. Two years after his injury, he was the most tireless player on the Laker squad, totaling an amazing 3,029 minutes in 77 games, almost 600 more than the number two man on the same team.

His best scoring year came in 1961–62 when he averaged 38.2 in 48 games. Baylor

Elgin Baylor does it all in the air.

Los Angeles
22

will be remembered for his sure touch with the ball. At times one wondered how he cleared opposition defenses. The answer was a combination of agility and muscle. This agility and tremendous spring and strength enabled him to outrebound forwards much bigger than he was.

When Baylor signed with the Lakers out of Seattle University, he actually saved a faltering franchise. At the time, the Lakers were still playing in Minneapolis. "If he had turned me down then," Laker President Bob Short said at the time, "I'd have been out of business. The club would have gone bankrupt."

Well, Baylor did sign and the Lakers slowly began to regain their old form. However, the team moved to Los Angeles and Baylor became one of the biggest stars in a town which had its share. His presence turned the Lakers' franchise into one of the most rewarding in sports.

He was all-pro first team on nine different occasions and played in eight consecutive All-Star games. In a game against New York in 1960 he scored 71 points. And in a game against Boston in 1959, he scored 64 points. The 71 points stood as a league record until Wilt Chamberlain broke it in 1962.

CARL BRAUN

Carl Braun came into the National Basketball Association without a glittering collegiate reputation. A "nonentity" the papers called him. When Carl Braun retired after the 1961–62 season, he left with one of the best records in professional basketball.

Braun always was a great shooter, but his greatest asset was his adaptability. His best scoring year, for example, did not come until he was in his ninth season with the New York Knickerbockers. That season he scored 1,173 points for a 16.5 average, a tribute to his ability to learn and use this knowledge on the basketball court.

Carl Braun: 13 years in the NBA.

When Braun joined the Knicks, he had no jump shot and only a standard two-hand set shot. Bud Palmer, his roommate, taught him the jump shot. Braun needed it, for at 6-5 he was meeting some stiff defensive opposition when he played forward.

Later, Braun was converted to a backcourtman. Again, he had to adapt. This time, he developed the shot that became his trademark, a two-hand, over-the-head set. The success of this unorthodox shot depended on speed, and for years Braun practiced by bouncing a ball off the wall in a gymnasium and shooting as soon as the ball reached his hands. "As you get older," he said, "you have to play more with your head."

That is exactly what kept Braun around the NBA for 13 years. During those seasons, Braun played in 789 games and scored 10,625 points for a lifetime average of 13.5. He often was the Knicks' leading scorer, their best foul shooter and twice wound up as their leading playmaker.

New York, of course, was long the showcase city of the NBA and the games in Madison Square Garden drew the largest crowds. One of the main reasons the people flocked there was to watch the smooth-operating Braun take on the "name" stars from around the country. More often than not Braun came out ahead.

Braun was not a sensational type ballplayer. He was steady and could be counted upon in tough situations. He could score, pass and rebound when he had to. Later in his career, when he became more of a playmaker than a scorer, people constantly asked him about the sudden change. Braun was simply prolonging his career. "Heck," he said. "I'm a New York City ballplayer and give-and-go is New York City ball. I always knew how to handle it." Carl Braun knew how to handle anything connected with basketball.

WILT CHAMBERLAIN

The greatest offensive player in the history of basketball. It is as simple as that. From the

Wilt Chamberlain: Highest-paid pro.

moment the 7-1 center entered the National Basketball Association for the 1959–60 season, he was an awesome, powerful figure on offense.

He will be remembered most for his scoring ability, but in the latter years of his career his game changed and as his proficiency on defense increased (and his proficiency at playmaking) so did the records of the teams he played for.

Chamberlain's best season was 1966–67 when he led the Philadelphia 76ers to a World's Championship. That ended—for a while—all the comments about Chamberlain being a great scorer, but not being very valuable when it came to helping his teams win championships. That tag went as far back as his collegiate days at the University of Kansas.

Chamberlain was one of the most publicized high school basketball players in history. He went from Philadelphia's Overbrook High School to Kansas where he played only two varsity years before dropping out to play for Abe Saperstein's Harlem Globetrotters. He joined the NBA the following season.

In his rookie season with the old Philadelphia Warriors, Chamberlain averaged 37.6 points per game. He increased that the next season to 38.4. But it was in 1961–62 that he was at his best as a scorer, finishing with 4,029 points in 80 games, an average of 50.4 points per game. On March 2, 1962, in a game against the New York Knickerbockers at Hershey, Pa., he scored an incredible 100 points on 36 field goals and 28 foul shots.

Chamberlain led the league in scoring for seven straight years until Rick Barry of San Francisco broke his string in 1966–67. He also led the league five times in rebounding, his highest figure being 2,149 in 1960–61. On Nov. 24, 1960, in a game against the Boston Celtics, Chamberlain set an NBA record with 55 rebounds.

He also won seven field goal percentage titles and was a constant leader in the minutes played department. And in the latter part of his career, he added to his all-time NBA scoring record every time he stepped on the floor.

But despite all his records and all his feats, Chamberlain also will be remembered as one of the most controversial figures in the game. A moody, introspective individual, Chamberlain often missed practice sessions, creating friction not only with his coaches, but among his teammates, too. He needed the practice, too, because he was one of the poorest foul shooters in the history of the game. His lifetime average hovered around the 50 percent mark. He set a number of records for foul shooting which he would like to forget: Most foul tries missed in one game (18); most foul tries missed in a season (528) and most foul tries missed in a playoff game (17). Opposing teams often considered it good strategy to foul Chamberlain rather than allow him to attempt a field goal.

Chamberlain, however, established some fantastic individual shooting records. At one point in the 1966–67 season he made 35 straight shots from the field. And he also finished that season with a 68.3 shooting percentage, another record.

A perennial all-league and All-Star team selection, Chamberlain was named the league's Most Valuable Player four times. His place in basketball history can not be disputed. He was considered such a valuable property that he was paid $250,000 for the 1967–68 season by the 76ers.

Before the start of the 1968–69 season, Chamberlain was traded to the Los Angeles Lakers for three players. The 76ers had been unable to reach salary terms with Chamberlain, but Jack Kent Cooke, owner of the Lakers, agreed to pay Chamberlain a reported $3,000,000 for five seasons. This contract made Chamberlain the highest-paid professional athlete in history.

BOB COUSY

It was Joe Fulks and George Mikan who first focused the public's attention on modern-day professional basketball. It was Bob Cousy, however, who made the game fun and attracted the crowds.

Boston's masterful Bob Cousy made All-NBA 10 consecutive years.

Cousy was the best ballhandler and backcourtman in the history of basketball. Writers all over the country constantly thought up new nicknames for him. "The Mobile Magician" was one; "The Houdini of the Hardwood" another. Though the nicknames may have been a little corny, they were accurate. His forte was playmaking, though he was an excellent scorer, too. Cousy's playmaking abilities were due to superb reflexes, a fine knowledge of the game and peripheral vision which enabled him to command a 180-degree angle of the action on the court.

For eight consecutive years (1953–1960), Cousy led the NBA in assists. "Cousy," said Red Auerbach, who coached him in Boston, "was one of the greatest all-around basketball players in the game, and undoubtedly he was the best backcourt player."

Put a ball in Cousy's hands and one could not anticipate the next move. It might go behind his back, between his legs, nobody knew. And frequently this led to a basket for Cousy or the Celtics. Of course, a lot of people thought Cousy was showboating, but they were wrong. "Actually," he said, "I don't use the behind-the-back pass as often as people think I do. When I use it, I have a good reason for it. When a situation develops where I can help the club with a certain maneuver, I go ahead with it."

Cousy came to the Celtics after a brilliant college career at Holy Cross. The year was 1950. Thirteen seasons later, he retired and

Cousy demonstrates his artistry to Sweetwater Clifton.

when he did, he left behind a set of statistics which serves as a standard for a backcourtman. For example, he once held the all-time league record for most minutes played (30,230) and he held the NBA record for most assists (6,949). When he retired, he was the fourth leading scorer in NBA history (16,955 points) and was second in total games played (917). He also was named to the all-league team for 10 successive seasons. And he was the only player to participate in 13 All-Star games. In 1962, a poll of sports editors of 100 major daily papers named Cousy the NBA's all-time number one player.

It is hard to pick Cousy's greatest feat. He once scored 50 points in a game, but some of his other contributions were even greater, though the amount of points was not as high. There was a game in Madison Square Garden in 1954 when the New York Knickerbockers were leading 93-89 with 30 seconds remaining. Cousy stole the ball twice within the 30 seconds and the Celtics forced an overtime. Then another. Finally they won, Cousy having scored 12 of the 20 points in overtime.

Or there was another time in New York—in 1960—when he dribbled the ball so cunningly and killed the clock for the last 23 seconds of the game. Nobody could stop him. The next day, Jimmy Cannon of the New York *Journal-American* wrote, "If Cousy never put the ball in the basket, he'd still be the most respected man in the league. At the finish, Boston had a one-point lead with 23 seconds to play. It was then that Bob proved his greatness. He held onto the ball...dribbling it among the Knicks, scampering among them in a wild solo. He ran in a lunging crouch, his body bent to protect the ball from their hands, a thrilling dwarf among the frustrated giants."

JOE FULKS

Joe Fulks was the man who focused the attention of the world on professional basketball. For when he was at his best, the game was

Joe Fulks was the first of the great scorers.

still developing and basketball was not considered a high-scoring game. But Joe Fulks changed that and he changed many other things, too. He was the link between the pre-war days and the modern era of professional basketball.

When Eddie Gottlieb, the coach and owner of the Philadelphia Warriors, signed him to a contract in 1946, he told the press: "We have a fellow by the name of Joe Fulks. You've probably never heard of him but I believe he has the potentialities of a great scorer."

Even Gottlieb did not realize how deep that potential was. In his first year, Fulks led the league in scoring with what then was considered an astounding average of 23.2 points per game (1,389 points in 60 contests). The Warriors won the World's Championship that season and the name Joe Fulks became synonymous with professional basketball.

Fulks was 24 when he started playing with the pros after serving with the Marines during World War II. He played only through the 1953–54 season, finishing his career with 8,003 points.

A graduate of Murray State College in Kentucky, Fulks was a slim 6-5, 190 pounds. His twisting pivot shots were the forerunner of the jump shot. His greatest feat came against the Indianapolis Jets at the Philadelphia Arena February 10, 1949, when he electrified the sports world by scoring a record 63 points in one game. At that time, many teams did not score 63 points in a whole game.

That night, he shot spinning one-handers, running shots with either hand and his soft, looping set shots. They all worked. Only four players in the history of the game have scored 63 points or higher in a professional basketball game: Fulks, Wilt Chamberlain, Elgin Baylor and Jerry West.

Despite his great scoring ability—when he retired, only George Mikan had scored more points—Fulks was often criticized. But even the critics had to admit his value to the Warriors. John (Honey) Russell, then coach of the Boston Celtics, once said: "Fulks is slow and he's not a great defensive player. And how can he be a great team player when he takes so many shots? But I wish I had him. I'd sure build my team around him."

Fulks viewed all the publicity and acclaim quite realistically. "They give me the ball and I shoot. That's all there is to it." That's an oversimplification, of course. Joe Fulks was a great basketball player and the game owes much of its early success to him.

NEIL JOHNSTON

Neil Johnston was another victim of the George Mikan era. And though he was a three-time scoring champion, he could never break through and win the national acceptance that Mikan had. Eddie Gottlieb, who coached Johnston in Philadelphia, said, "I doubt if Johnston will ever receive the recognition that Mikan got because Neil didn't come into the league with the fanfare and blowing of trumpets that accompanied Mikan."

Johnston was an Ohio State graduate and a 6-8 center whose hook shot was a work of art. He also was accurate with a one-hander from the outside. In eight seasons, from 1952 through 1959, he scored 10,023 points and had an average of 19.4 points per game. He won the scoring title in successive seasons. In 1951–52 he scored 1,564 points for a 22.3 average; in 1953–54 he scored 1,759 for a 24.4 average, and in 1954–55 he had 1,631 points for 22.7.

He was just as adept at shooting and rebounding, winning the shooting percentage title three times (.452, .457 and .447). He won the rebounding title in 1954–55 with 1,085. For two seasons—1952–53, 1953–54—he led the league in most minutes played.

He might have been even greater, but a knee injury cut his career short when he was only 30 years old and still had some good years left. Despite the knee trouble, he tried to play. "On one good leg," said Al Cervi, one of his coaches with the Warriors, "he's better than

Neil Johnston: Man with a hook.

6
4

some of the other men in this league. When he's out of the lineup it just kills us."

Finally, the knee no longer could stand the pain and the rigors of the rugged NBA schedule. Johnston had to end his outstanding career in 1959. He had made the NBA All-Star first team four times. When he retired, he was named coach of the Warriors just when another pretty good center, Wilt Chamberlain, was breaking in. Johnston remained as Warrior coach for two years. He was a frustrated man who had to watch from the bench instead of being out on the court playing.

ED MACAULEY

Some called him him Easy Ed because of his modest, easy-going temperament. But he really earned the nickname on the basketball court, where he made his driving layups and virtually unstoppable hook shot look as easy as pushing a button.

Actually Ed Macauley had to develop his graceful smoothness almost out of necessity. At 6-8 and only 190 pounds, he just wasn't strong enough to battle some of the beefier NBA players. So Macauley concentrated on playmaking and shooting and it paid off. In nine and a fraction seasons in the league, Macauley made the All-NBA first team three times and the second team once and established himself as one of the all-time great NBA centers.

He graduated from St. Louis University in 1949 as a two-time All-American and signed a two-year contract for a reported $30,000 with the hometown St. Louis Bombers, who were struggling to stay in business. Macauley had a good rookie year, averaging 16.1 points a game, fifth best in the league, but the Bombers folded after the season ended.

The New York Knicks thought so much of Easy Ed that they offered to buy the entire St. Louis franchise just to obtain Macauley. But the NBA vetoed the transaction and the next season Macauley wound up with the Boston Celtics. Along with Bob Cousy and Bill Sharman, Macauley helped make the pro game a success in Boston.

Macauley played in the All-Star Game seven times and always did well. He was, in fact, the outstanding player in the very first All-Star Game in 1951. Three years later, in 1954, he was the only unanimous selection for the All-Star Game.

Macauley played six seasons for the Celtics and always finished among the league leaders in scoring. Over that span, he never averaged less than 17.5 points a game. More than merely a gunner, he usually finished among the leaders in field-goal accuracy, too.

On March 6, 1953, he had the greatest scoring night of his career, riddling the Minneapolis Lakers with their great center, George Mikan, for 46 points.

For the 1956–57 season, Easy Ed moved back to St. Louis, his hometown. Ben Kerner, the owner of the St. Louis Hawks, had the draft rights to Bill Russell. But he felt that Russell, who had been a great college star at San Francisco, would probably sign with the Harlem Globetrotters after returning from the Olympic Games. So Kerner traded the rights to Russell to the Celtics in return for Macauley and Cliff Hagan.

Macauley, Bob Pettit and Hagan led the Hawks to two consecutive Western Division titles and in 1957–58 the Hawks beat Boston for the NBA championship. Early in the next season Easy Ed retired as a player and took over as coach and general manager of the Hawks. In the two seasons he coached the Hawks, they won two Western titles. But he resigned in 1962 in order to devote more time to outside business interests.

In his years in the NBA, Macauley proved that a player didn't have to be a brute to be a good NBA center. He showed that agility and coordination were at least as important as sheer strength. Macauley made the game look easy—for himself and the fans who watched him, but never for the opponents who had to stop him.

Easy Ed Macauley (22) made it look easy.

CELTICS
22

LAKERS
99
LAKERS
18

GEORGE MIKAN

When analyzing George Mikan's position in the history of basketball, you must consider only the era he played: the late 1940s and early 1950s. This was before Wilt Chamberlain and Bill Russell.

Until the emergence of Chamberlain and Russell, Mikan had been considered the greatest big man in the game's history. But it is unfair to compare him with Chamberlain and Russell because they were different types completely.

George Mikan did much to revolutionize the game. And he did a lot to make the NBA a major league attraction because he was the main reason the Minneapolis Lakers won five world's championships. Mikan was so good during his time that when every other possible defense against him, fair or foul, had been tried and found wanting, the NBA was forced to widen the lanes under the basket from six to 12 feet.

During Mikan's heyday—and that of the Lakers—he dominated the record book. The 6-10 center from DePaul University scored 44 points or more in nine different games. His best effort was 61 points against the Rochester Royals in 1952. At one point, he held the all-time seasonal scoring average of 28.4 points per game. In his six big seasons with the Lakers— from 1948 to 1954—he led the league in scoring three times, was second twice and fourth in his last and worst year. He made the league All-Star first team each of the six years.

Mikan's size (245 pounds) also made him a target for the opposition. Each of his legs was broken once. His right foot, the arch of his left foot, his right wrist, his nose and one thumb also were broken at one time or another. Three of his fingers were broken, too. His nose was ripped open by swinging elbows. He received a total of 166 stitches.

When Mikan first announced his retirement after the 1954 season, the basketball community was stunned and saddened. Of course, they realized he could not go on forever. Johnny Kundla, the Lakers' coach, was glum when he heard Mikan's plans. But later Kundla confessed to the press: "This should even up our league."

He was right. Mikan had dominated the game. Nobody was able to handle Number 99 during those years. Mikan stuck to his retirement for a year, but in the middle of the 1955–56 season he decided to try a comeback. It was not a success. He scored only 390 points in 37 games and when he retired for good at the end of the year, he left the NBA with 11,764 points and a 22.6 average.

Perhaps the greatest tribute paid Mikan was in New York at Madison Square Garden. It was not the size of the crowd nor was it a special night where he received a number of gifts. It was just a simple message on the marquee outside the Garden. All it said was:

Tonite
George Mikan
vs.
Knicks

George Mikan vs. the All-Stars.

VERN MIKKELSEN

The Minneapolis Lakers were the first team to dominate professional basketball. There were three big reasons: George Mikan, Jim Pollard and a rugged 6-7, 230-pound forward named Vern Mikkelsen.

Over the years, Mikkelsen was one of the NBA's most consistent players. His teammates thought so highly of him that he served consecutive terms as captain for six seasons. Mikkelsen joined the Lakers in 1950 after playing collegiate ball at little-known Hamline College where he excelled off the court as much as on it. At Hamline, he earned a Master of Arts degree. He played 10 years for the Lakers including the glory years when they won three championships in his first four years. Mikkel-

sen was never a sensational scorer like teammate George Mikan. Consistency was his forte. When he completed his career, he was one of the game's leading scorers with 10,063 points in 700 games, an average of 14.4 points per game.

The balding Dane was a center in college but made the transition to forward when he joined the Lakers, who had a pretty fair center in Mikan. Teaming with Mikan and Pollard in the early days at Minneapolis, Mikkelsen helped initiate a new concept of play: three big men with two little ones.

He was extremely strong under the boards and on the court his rugged features and appearance belied the placid nature underneath. Mikkelsen, extremely erudite, had been a school teacher and had been selected to make a State Department expedition to Scandinavia.

On the court, however, he often wore his opponents down. He seldom missed a game and during one six-year stretch he missed only one game. Four times he was selected to the NBA's All-Star team. He was rough on the court and has the dubious distinction of fouling out of the most NBA games (127).

But he will be remembered because he was such an integral part of one of the world's greatest teams. He never received the publicity Mikan did, or even as much as Pollard. But his contributions were just as important. He might have lasted longer as a professional, but the inception of the 24-second rule hurt. It was not tailored to the bulkier, slower giants and the type of ball control the old Lakers favored.

After the Lakers won the NBA title for the fifth time in 1954, Maurice Podoloff, commissioner of the league, paid Mikkelsen and the Lakers the ultimate tribute. "I will say it was the greatest team in the history of basketball and deserves a place not earned by any team in any other type of athletics. The Lakers have been the greatest contributing factor to the success of the NBA."

Vern Mikkelsen: A steady 10,000-point man.

Bob Pettit: 20,880 points.

BOB PETTIT

They said he was too skinny. Too light. He would not hold up as a corner man in the National Basketball Association. Bob Pettit listened politely to the evaluation. And he smiled. He had just been graduated from Louisiana State and had been drafted by the Milwaukee Hawks.

The 6-9, 215-pound Pettit reported to the Hawks in 1954 and that first year scored 1,466 points for a 20.4 average. That ended the doubt and the speculation. The following year, Bob Pettit was even more sensational. The Hawks had moved to St. Louis and Pettit made the game a success there by winning the scoring title (1,849 points) and rebounding title (1,164). He also won the Most Valuable Player Award and was selected as the MVP in the All-Star Game. You can go on and on listing Bob Pettit's records and achievements.

It would not be an overstatement to say he may have been the best frontcourtman ever to play professional basketball. He won the MVP award twice, the scoring title twice and the rebounding title once. Four times he was selected as the outstanding performer in the All-Star Game, and he was named to the All-NBA team 10 years in a row. He was a pleasure to watch: a smooth shooter with an exceedingly accurate jump shot, a deceptive rebounder who used finesse to outwit and outrebound stronger men.

Pettit ranks as the second leading scorer in the history of the NBA. He played 11 years, scoring 20,880 points in 792 games for a lifetime average of 26.4. That scoring average was the fifth best in the league's history. He also ranked second in minutes played until Chamberlain overtook him. And he was the league's third leading rebounder (12,851). He had six games in which he scored more than 50 points including a career high of 57 in 1961. Until Elgin Baylor broke the record, Pettit also was the leading scorer in playoff history.

Off the court, Pettit was all class. The same as he was in uniform. He had an inordinate amount of pride. "What it is with me, I guess," he said, "is that as you go along in life and work hard, you reach new plateaus of accomplishment. With each plateau you reach, the demands upon you become greater. And your pride increases to meet the demands. You drive yourself harder than before. You can't afford negative thinking, so you always believe you'll win. You build an image of yourself that has nothing to do with ego—but it has to be satisfied. When I fall below what I know I can do, my belly growls and growls. Anytime I'm not playing up to my very best I can count on a jolt of indigestion."

Bob Pettit had a unique barometer. But judging from the record, he could not have suffered too badly.

JIM POLLARD

In 1952, the players who had been in the National Basketball Association since its inception as the BAA voted in a poll to determine who was the best player of the period. The winner was Jim Pollard, the frontcourtman for the Minneapolis Lakers. To win the poll, Pollard finished ahead of such greats as teammate George Mikan and Joe Fulks.

It was a wonderful tribute to a player who contributed as much to the success of the Lakers as the high-scoring Mikan. Of course, Pollard never received the publicity Mikan did. Pollard was not a high scorer like Mikan. He averaged 13.1 points per game during his eight-year career and scored 6,522 points. But he was the classic team player. "You can get a lot of points in a game," he once said, "and still be dissatisfied with yourself. After all, it isn't an individual record you're after, but a victory."

Pollard's best weapon was his jump shot. Together with Vern Mikkelsen and Mikan he helped the Lakers dominate the game in those early years. Mikkelsen, Mikan and Pollard were the best one-two-three punch the game had seen.

You can get a better picture of Pollard when you listen to the comments some of his fellow pros made when the poll was taken. Said Fred Scolari of the Fort Wayne Pistons: "Pollard can do more things than anyone. He is better than most big men and decidedly better than the little men. He's been in the shade of Mikan. He is a basketball players' player all the way."

Bones McKinney, another Pollard opponent, had tremendous respect for him, too. "Pollard," McKinney said, "was the greatest corner man ever. On another club no one would touch him. He can do everything on a basketball floor and do it with finesse."

Finesse is important when you speak of Jim Pollard. He seldom made the wrong move. And he was consistent. His playoff scoring average was 13.4, three tenths of a point above

Jim Pollard: Cleanest team player.

AKERS
17

his career average.

Another interesting statistic: Pollard was considered one of the cleanest players in basketball and in one three-year stretch committed only 194 personal fouls. He was a graduate of Stanford University. Later he coached the Lakers for a brief period before becoming a college coach.

FRANK RAMSEY

Frank Ramsey started the trend. Nowadays most successful professional teams rely on the valuable "sixth starter" who can come into a game and break it open in a matter of minutes.

Ramsey was the first one. He played for the

Frank Ramsey (23) was pioneer supersub.

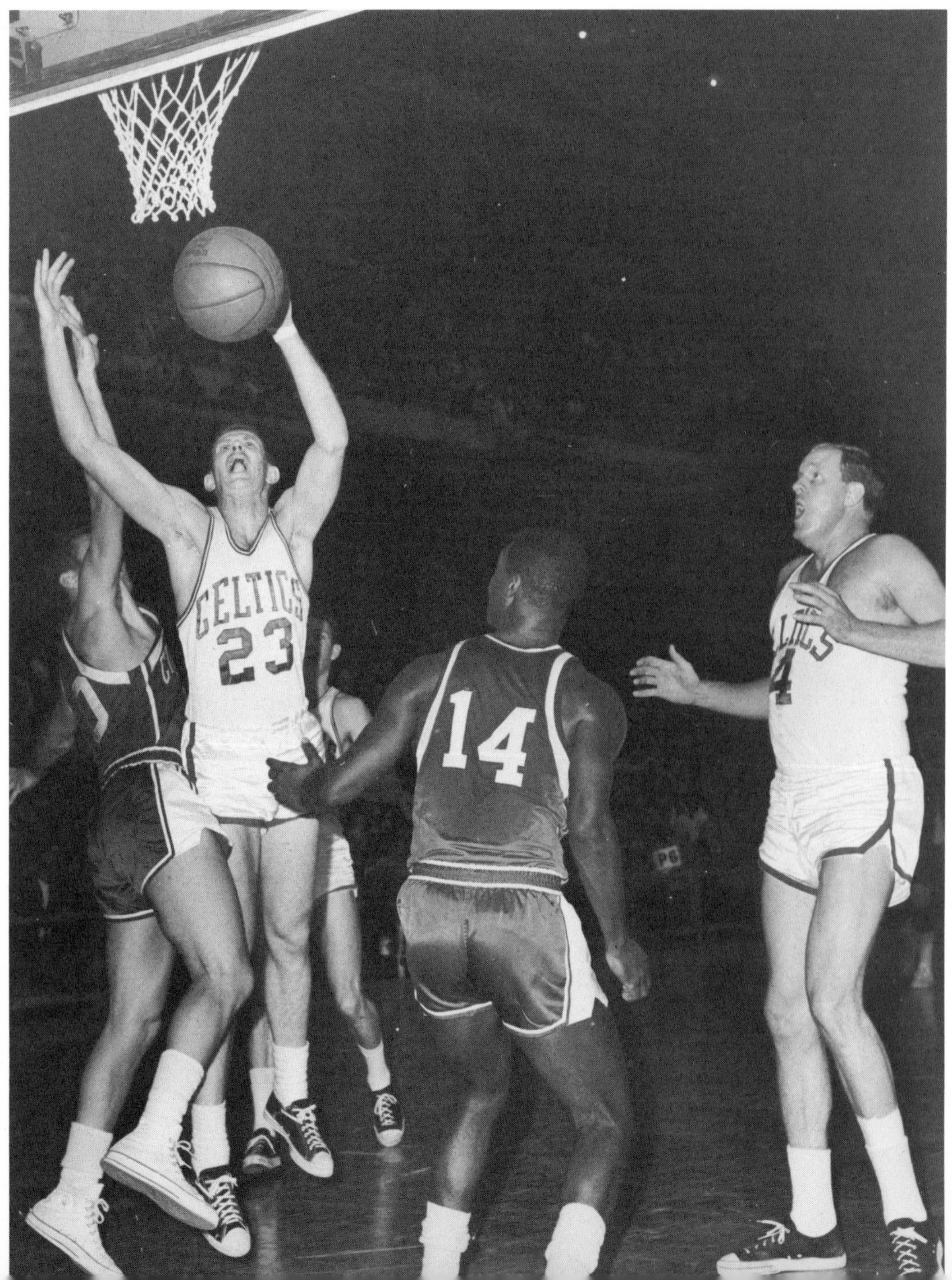

Boston Celtics in the mid-1950s and early 1960s. "He is the most versatile player in the league," his coach, Red Auerbach, said. "He can come off the bench and do the job of either a big man or little man for me and grows cooler as the game grows more tense."

In nine seasons, Ramsey scored 8,378 points for a 13.4 average. Those figures may not seem impressive but Ramsey was a substitute most of that time. "I'd rather be a sub on a great team than a regular on a losing one," he said. "Even a spare part feels sort of special when a fine mechanism like the Celtics is involved."

The Celtics would go to Ramsey when they needed a quick spark. He could, as Auerbach said, play anywhere and do the job needed. "He's the one," said teammate Bob Cousy, "who has kept us up in the standings because he's versatile and steady, a real producer."

Ramsey was a product of Adolph Rupp and the University of Kentucky. And he became as integral a part of the Celtic dynasty as any of the starters. His best season was 1957–58 when he averaged 16.5 points per game. The next four seasons he was extremely consistent, averaging 15 points per game each season. He was at his best in the playoffs and in four straight seasons (1958 through 1961) averaged the following: 18.4, 23.2, 18.1, and 17.1.

Soon other teams around the league began to learn the value of the "sixth starter." When Ramsey retired, John Havlicek assumed that role for the Celtics. Billy Cunningham was the same type of player for the Philadelphia 76ers.

Havlicek and Cunningham scored more than Ramsey, but Frank was the pathfinder. Today a specialist like Ramsey is all important. As Ramsey's teammate, Bill Russell, said, "He does the thing that has to be done to win a game." Ramsey won quite a few for the Celtics during his nine seasons in the league.

OSCAR ROBERTSON

There is a story Tom Meschery, the veteran NBA forward, enjoyed telling when asked about Oscar Robertson's myriad talents. "We

The Big O.

were playing Cincinnati and Earl Strom was one of the officials. Somehow I wound up guarding Oscar after a switch. Well, Oscar throws that ball behind his back, heads for the basket and leaves me behind. It was a fantastic move, split-second like always with him. Just as the ball goes in, Strom calls walking. Oscar gets real excited and starts screaming at him, 'How can you call that walking, you never saw that move before.' "

Oscar probably was right, but the official prevailed. Some of the moves he has made throughout his career have been unbelievable. As they say in the NBA: "Never turn your head on Oscar, there is no telling what he might show you next. His body control is even more amazing than his shooting touch."

Red Auerbach, the former Boston coach, is one of Robertson's greatest admirers. "There is nothing he can't do," Auerbach said. "No one comes close to him or has the ability to break open a game as Oscar. He's so great he scares me. He can beat you all by himself and usually does."

Robertson, 6-5 and weighing 205 pounds, was an All-American at the University of Cincinnati before joining the Cincinnati Royals in 1960–61 when he promptly showed his greatness with a 30.5 scoring average. The fifth leading scorer in NBA history, Robertson's career mark is 30 points per game.

He also is considered one of the greatest playmakers in history and holds the league record for highest assist average in a season (11.5 in 1964–65). Robertson won five assist titles in seven years, dating back to 1960. Only Guy Rodgers prevented him from going seven-for-seven. Robertson was the league's leading foul shooter twice—in 1963–64 (.853) and 1967–68 (.873).

Robertson, of course, holds virtually every Cincinnati Royals record. He was the team's leading scorer for eight consecutive seasons (1961–68), its best playmaker (1961–68). He also led in minutes played for six seasons and twice pulled the incredible feat of leading the Royals in rebounds.

He will be remembered best for his versatility. There was nothing beyond his talent—or imagination—on the basketball floor. Twice (1961 and 1964) he was named the Most Valuable Player at the NBA All-Star Game and he played in the game each year he was in the league.

In a poll of sports editors of the nation's 100 largest newspapers, the Academy of Sports selected Robertson on the all-time NBA team. He received 51 percent of the voting points, only two points behind Wilt Chamberlain.

BILL RUSSELL

If a player's value is measured by the number of championships he helps his team win, then Bill Russell must be considered the greatest player in the history of basketball.

Certainly no one will quarrel with the statement that he is the best defensive player in the game's history. In fact, he completely revolutionized professional basketball and brought back the emphasis on defense. And in doing so, he led the Boston Celtics to 11 world championships in 13 years.

Standing 6-10 and weighing 220 pounds, Russell entered the NBA during the 1956–57 season following a sensational college career at the University of San Francisco where he led his team to a pair of national championships.

He didn't change his winning habits when he turned professional. His forte was rebounding. Until Wilt Chamberlain broke it, Russell held the individual game rebounding record with 51. On two other occasions Russell gathered in 49 rebounds in a game. He led the league in rebounding four different times, and was named Most Valuable Player five times.

Russell never was a great scorer—his lifetime average being 15 points per game. Nor

Bill Russell set the standards for defense.

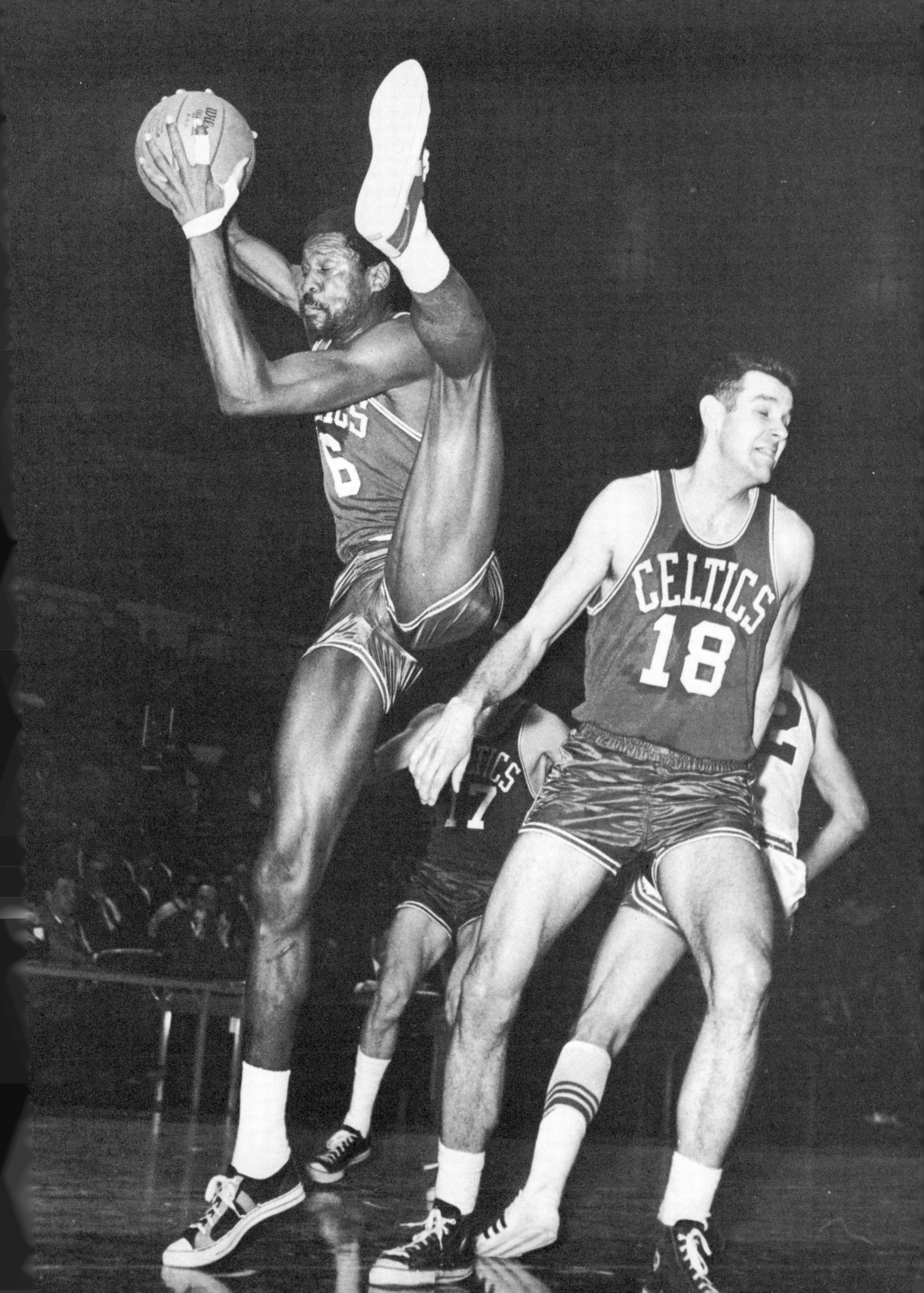
CELTICS
18

was he an outstanding shooter from the field or foul line. It was on defense where he caused the opposition so much trouble. And he was well-paid for it, reaching the $100,000 class and approaching the $200,000 class.

Too bad the NBA did not keep statistics for shots blocked or broken plays. Russell would have led in both departments. Opposing centers often could not sleep the night before they had to face Russell in the pivot. Some of Russell's greatest duels were against Chamberlain, and Chamberlain provides the final commentary on that rivalry with the statement: "I've been in seven playoffs with Boston where it came down to the final game and Boston won six."

It is also interesting to note that Russell scored at a somewhat accelerated pace (17.2) throughout his playoff career and his rebounding also was better during this period. He will be remembered as one of the game's greatest "money" players. During the 1965–66 playoffs, for example, he grabbed 428 rebounds in 17 games for an average of 25.1 rebounds per game.

The only years during his career when the Celtics did not win the World's Championship were 1957–58 and 1966–67. His finest year, however, may have been 1967–68. The Celtics finished second that year in the season's standings behind Philadelphia. In the opening round of the playoffs, they had a tough time against the Detroit Pistons. Their age, the experts claimed, was beginning to show. They were heavy underdogs when they met the 76ers for the Eastern Division championship.

Down 3 games to 1 in the best-of-seven series, Russell took command and led the Celtics to a stunning comeback. He mastered Chamberlain completely in the seventh game, holding him to a mere two shots in the second half.

In 1966, Russell took over as player-coach of the Celtics following Red Auerbach's retirement. When the Celtics failed to win the title that first year, Russell's job was considered in jeopardy. But when Boston won the next season, nobody complained.

DOLPH SCHAYES

There once was a team, a wonderful team, that night after night gave the simplest, most exciting display of pure basketball ever seen in the National Basketball Association. It wasn't a big team and it did not have a roster full of All-Americans or towering frontcourtmen. What the Syracuse Nationals did have was a distinct spirit and a forward named Dolph Schayes.

Schayes personified the spirit of the Nats. Each time he scored a goal, he would run to the opposite end of the court, fist clenched triumphantly above his head. From the start, when he made Rookie of the Year in 1949, Schayes was one of the league's class players. When he retired at the end of the 1964 season, he was the all-time leading scorer with 19,249 points (18.2). Bob Pettit and Wilt Chamberlain have passed him in the scoring tables, but it hardly matters because Schayes' place in NBA history is secure. Schayes was 6-8 and a forward but he was such a versatile performer that he was one of the last of the deadly two-hand set shooters. This helped make him great. He could score from the outside as easily as he could drive underneath for a layup.

One got a complete picture of Dolph Schayes the competitor when listening to him speak following his 29th birthday: "I feel I can still improve. Where? Defensively for one thing. And you can always become a better shot, can't you?"

Schayes was a rugged rebounder, winning the individual title in 1951 and finishing his career in fourth place on the all-time list. He was not afraid to become involved in the rough play under the boards and still holds the record for most personal fouls committed in league history (3,667). He also holds the record, however, for most foul shots made (6,979) which tells you even more about his competitive nature. He was a tireless performer, too, again ranking among the top ten in league

Dolph Schayes: Wherever the action was.

SIRAC
4

history in minutes played (29,800).

It was hard to move Schayes out of the lineup. In 1952, he broke his right wrist. A cast was applied and Schayes continued to play. "The cast," he said in a typical Schayes statement, "made me work on my lefthanded shots, which soon improved. Later, when the left wrist was cracked, my righthanded shots improved."

Though the Nats won only one world's championship during Schayes' career, they never missed the playoffs and Schayes holds the league record for most playoff series (15). During that time he played in 103 playoff games.

Schayes' hustle has become legendary when people speak of and write about NBA history. He played with broken wrists, he played with other injuries, and he played when he was sick because he had to—for all those years—carry the burden of the Syracuse offense. Watching the Nationals play was a treat. They believed in the team game and patterned, but exciting, offense. And the most exciting, most dramatic individual on that team was Dolph Schayes.

BILL SHARMAN

When listing basketball's best shooters, Bill Sharman must be included. "Sharman," said Red Auerbach, his coach with the Celtics, "is the greatest shooter from the backcourt the game has ever seen." Eddie Gottlieb, the former owner and coach of the Philadelphia Warriors, watched Sharman destroy his team on many a cold winter night. "Sharman," he said, "must be listed with the all-time greats if only for his shooting ability."

Sharman and Bob Cousy formed the most potent backcourt in the history of basketball. If the defense let up on Sharman, Cousy would explode. If the defense was tough on Cousy, Bill Sharman—with his sure, deft touch—would start pumping those one-handers which made him famous. Sharman played 11 seasons for the Celtics, joining them for the 1950–51 season and retiring at the end of the 1961 season. He ranks among the top scorers in league history with 12,665 points in 710 games, a 17.8 average.

Oddly, Sharman never was considered an exceptional "long" shooter. His best scoring range was from 20 feet. Rarely did he attempt a shot from beyond that distance. Inside it, he was a sure bet. His career field goal percentage was .423, making him the best shooting guard of his time. Writer Dick Kaplan once said: "What made Sharman's shooting remarkable was its purity. He shot with almost robot-like precision, his style so polished and precise that it seemed like an illustration for a book on how to play basketball." Appropriately, Sharman did write a book on shooting, titled "Sharman on Shooting."

Sharman and Cousy were with the Celtics when the Boston team was ripping off World's Championship after World's Championship. Though Cousy received most of the publicity, the NBA players recognized Sharman's abilities and voted him to the All-Star first team four different years. Sharman was recognized as the game's finest foul shooter and is the all-time league leader in this department. During his career, he made 3,143 of 3,557 attempts for an .883 percentage. He won the foul shooting title seven different times.

A great natural athlete from the University of Southern California, Sharman almost had a major league baseball career. He was an outfielder in the Brooklyn Dodgers' system and was with the team at the end of the 1951 season when Bobby Thomson of the New York Giants hit the celebrated home run to give the Giants the pennant.

Luckily for Auerbach and the Celtics, Sharman chose basketball. There will be few to match him. He made shooting an art and can discuss it for hours. "I aim for the back rim," he said. "Why? I've found that most shots are missed 'short' because players get tired. Their shots start bouncing off that front rim. But if you shoot for the back rim, you get three factors working for you: First, most players

Bill Sharman was sharpest-shooting Celtic.

shoot with backspin. If a backspinning ball hits the front rim, it skids away. But if it hits the back rim, the 'English' practically forces it into the basket. Second, if you overshoot and miss the back rim, you still have a chance for a cheap basket. The ball can bank in off the backboard. Third, the rim of the basket has an 18-inch diameter; the basketball about nine inches. So if you shoot for the rear rim, you have a nine-inch margin for error."

Sound like a science? It is. And Bill Sharman earned his doctorate.

JACK TWYMAN

Red Auerbach, as Boston coach, had the best description of Jack Twyman. "Show him a little daylight," Auerbach said, "and it's up and in." Twyman was one of the great shoot-

Jack Twyman (31) will be remembered for more than his playing.

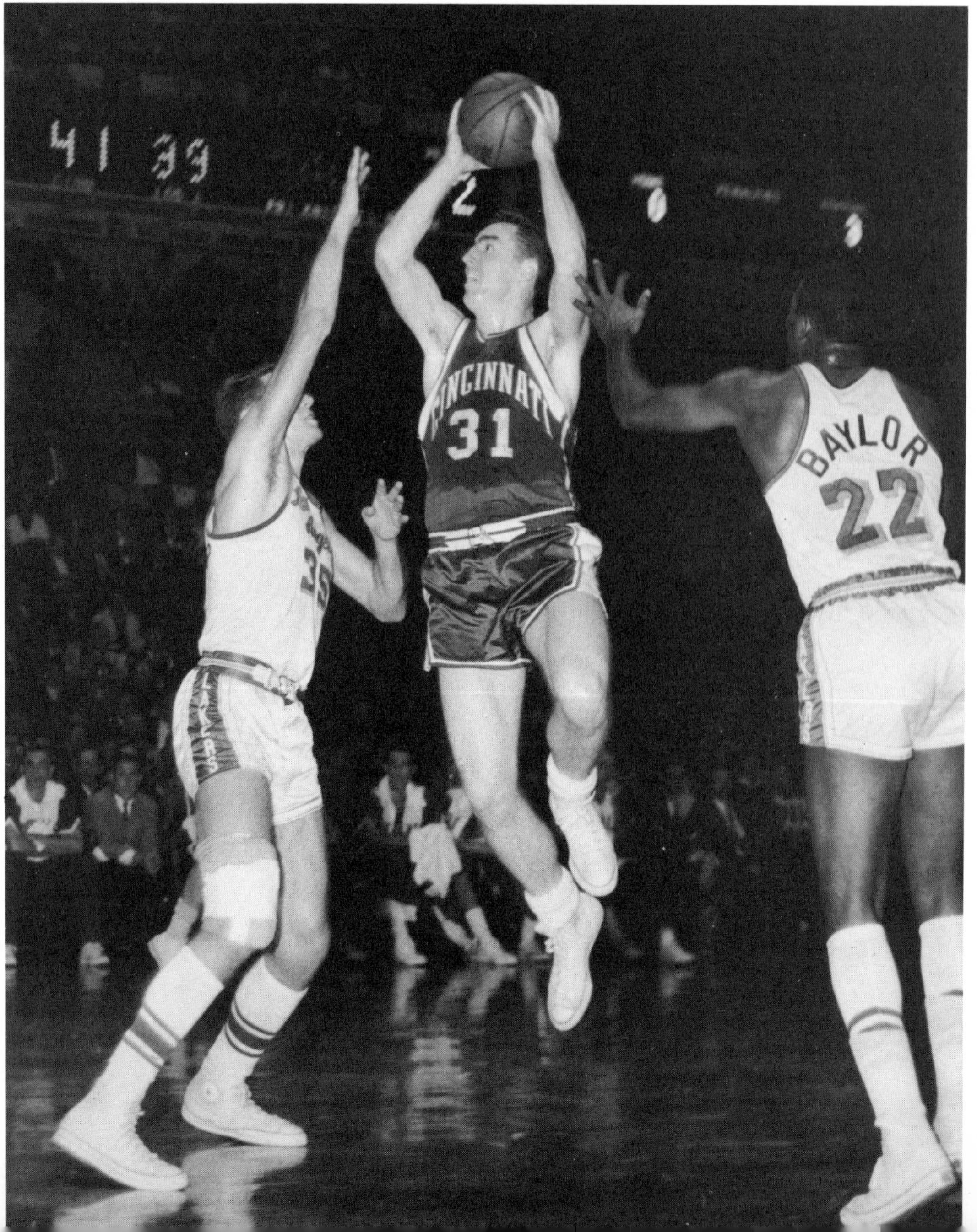

ing forwards in the NBA and ranked eighth in the all-time scoring derby with a 19.2 average and 15,840 points during an 11-year career with the Rochester Royals and then the Cincinnati Royals.

From the very start, Twyman, an All-American at the University of Cincinnati, impressed people around the NBA. Bobby Wanzer, his coach at Rochester where he broke in, claimed that "Twyman has more determination than any player I've seen. He's the kind of guy who can key himself into things."

One can understand Twyman's dedication to shooting on hearing him explain his workout routine during the off-season. "I usually work out four days a week and during every session I shoot 100 fouls, 200 jump shots and between 100 and 150 set shots." He had some fantastic scoring years for the Royals but he never won a scoring championship. In 1958–59 he finished second to Bob Pettit in the scoring race and the following season, his best as a scorer, he averaged 31.2 points and finished second to Wilt Chamberlain.

For a cornerman, Twyman had some outstanding shooting percentages. In 1960–61, he had a .488 average, in 1961–1962 it was .479 and the year after that .480. "You can feel it when you're hot," Twyman used to say. "You feel like everything you throw up there at the basket is going to drop through." In the case of Twyman, the shots fell through.

Twyman ranks in the all-time top ten in a number of categories including most games played (823), most field goals scored (6,237) and most minutes played (26,055). He won the field goal percentage title in 1957–58 with a .452 average.

But Twyman will be remembered for more than just his basketball talent. He was one of the great humanitarians—not just in sports—but in all walks of life. When his teammate Maurice Stokes was paralyzed with a brain ailment at the end of the 1958 season, Twyman became his legal guardian and raised funds for Maurice's rehabilitation. Twyman is still doing it, and Stokes' progress is slow but steady. Each year, the NBA players gather at Kutsher's Country Club in Monticello, N.Y., and play a benefit game organized by Twyman for Stokes.

JERRY WEST

Fred Schaus, who coached Jerry West at West Virginia University and later with the Los Angeles Lakers, has nothing but admiration for one of the finest guards ever to set foot on a basketball court.

Said Schaus: "If you sat down to build a 6-foot-3-inch basketball player you would come up with a Jerry West. He is the man that has everything—a fine shooting touch, speed, quickness, all the physical assets, including a tremendous dedication to the game." It was the perfect summation, and perhaps the last part of Schaus' statement was the most important. Jerry West's dedication made him great. Throughout his college career he had been compared with Oscar Robertson. Both broke into the NBA together. Oscar, however, got off to a sensational professional start, averaging 30.5 points per game as a rookie. West didn't do nearly as well, averaging 17.6. Immediately the doubters were saying "I told you so."

There was a lot of pressure, but the next season, Jerry West—through sheer determination—wound up with a 30.8 scoring average and from that point he was considered to be on the same level with Robertson. West is the seventh leading scorer in NBA history, a goal achieved despite the fact that he missed many games due to injuries.

"Jerry," said former Laker general manager Lou Mohs, "gets hurt a lot because he plays recklessly and doesn't spare himself." One of the oddities of sport is that West has suffered a broken nose eight times during his career, which says something for his gameness and willingness to mix it up under the boards despite his lack of size.

He has had some fine scoring seasons including 31.0 in 1964–65 and a career high of

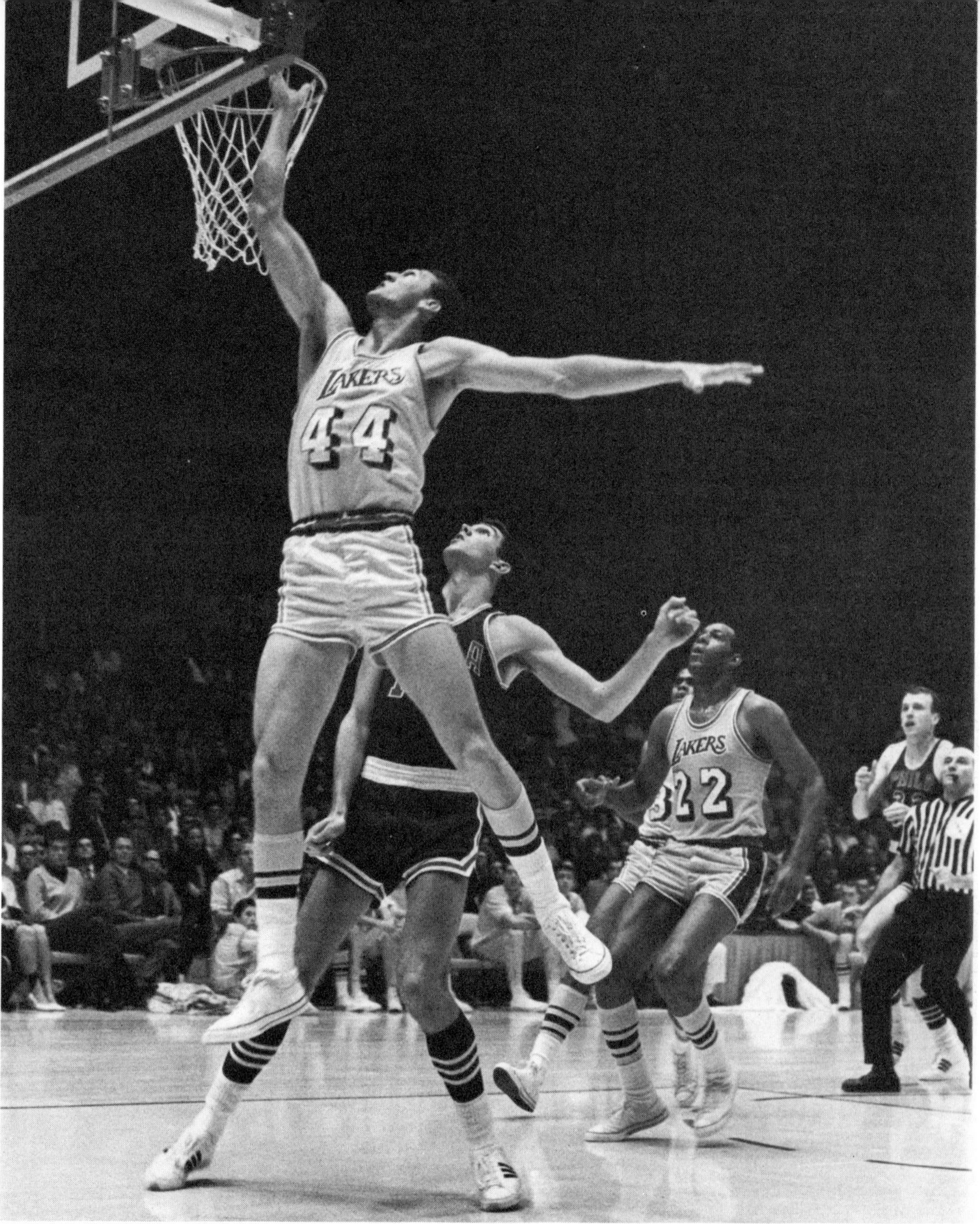

Jerry West: Greatest in the clutch.

31.4 during the 1965–66 season. He has had some fantastic playoff series including the 1964–65 season when he averaged 40.6 points for 11 games. The next season he averaged 34.2 in 14 games. Red Auerbach, the Boston Celtics coach, often became exasperated with West's performances against his teams. "You really can't stop West," Auerbach said. "You can try in a number of ways: play him close, loose, keep him away from the ball. Still he'll find a way to get his 25 to 30 points."

West's most effective weapon is a graceful jump shot from any spot on the floor. He is also an extremely good driver and an excellent playmaker. He is a perennial all-league selection and has been a yearly performer in the All-Star Game. Even after eight years in the league, West is still being compared to Robertson. This often angered Schaus. "It's unfair to both of them to make comparisons," Schaus said. "It takes something away from each. They're both great." A fitting epitaph.

11: THE TEAMS

ALL-TIME CLUB RECORDS

ANDERSON PACKERS

Season	Coach	W.	L.
1949–50	Howard Schultz (21-14)		
	Ike Duffey (1-2)		
	Doxie Moore (15-11)	37	27
	Totals	37	27

ATLANTA HAWKS

Season	Coach	W.	L.
1949–50	Roger Potter (1-6)		
	Arnold Auerbach (28-29)	29	35
1950–51	Dave McMillan (9-14)		
	John Logan (2-1)		
	Marko Todorovich (14-28)	25	43
1951–52*	Doxie Moore	17	49
1952–53	Andrew Levane	27	44
1953–54	Andrew Levane (11-35)		
	William Holzman (10-16)	21	51
1954–55	William Holzman	26	46
1955–56**	William Holzman	33	39
1956–57	William Holzman (14-19)		
	Slater Martin (5-3)		
	Alex Hannum (15-16)	34	38
1957–58	Alex Hannum	41	31
1958–59	Andy Phillip (6-4)		
	Ed Macauley (43-19)	49	23
1959–60	Ed Macauley	46	29
1960–61	Paul Seymour	51	28
1961–62	Paul Seymour (5-9)		
	Andrew Levane (20-40)		
	Bob Pettit (4-2)	29	51
1962–63	Harry Gallatin	48	32
1963–64	Harry Gallatin	46	34
1964–65	Harry Gallatin (17-16)		
	Richie Guerin (28-19)	45	35
1965–66	Richie Guerin	36	44
1966–67	Richie Guerin	39	42
1967–68***	Richie Guerin	56	26
	Totals	698	720

**Team moved from Tri-Cities to Milwaukee*
***Team moved from Milwaukee to St. Louis*
****Team moved from St. Louis to Atlanta at end of season*

BALTIMORE BULLETS

Season	Coach	W.	L.
1947–48	Buddy Jeannette	28	20
1948–49	Buddy Jeannette	29	31
1949–50	Buddy Jeannette	25	43
1950–51	Buddy Jeannette (14-23)		
	Walt Budko (10-19)	24	42
1951–52	Fred Scolari (12-27)		
	John Reiser (8-19)	20	46
1952–53	John Reiser (0-3)		
	Clair Bee (16-51)	16	54
1953–54	Clair Bee	16	56
1954–55*	Clair Bee (2-9)		
	Al Barthelme (1-2)	3	11
	Totals	161	303

**Team disbanded Nov. 27, 1954*

BALTIMORE BULLETS

Season	Coach	W.	L.
1961–62*	Jim Pollard	18	62
1962–63**	Jack McMahon (12-26)		
	Bob Leonard (13-29)	25	55
1963–64***	Bob Leonard	31	49
1964–65	Buddy Jeanette	37	43
1965–66	Paul Seymour	38	42
1966–67	Mike Farmer (1-8)		
	Buddy Jeanette (3-13)		
	Gene Shue (16-40)	20	61
1967–68	Gene Shue	36	46
	Totals	205	358

**Played in Chicago as Chicago Packers*
***Played in Chicago as Chicago Zephyrs*
****Moved to Baltimore, changed name to Bullets*

BOSTON CELTICS

Season	Coach	W.	L.
1946–47	John Russell	22	38
1947–48	John Russell	20	28
1948–49	Alvin Julian	25	35
1949–50	Alvin Julian	22	46
1950–51	Arnold Auerbach	39	30
1951–52	Arnold Auerbach	39	27
1952–53	Arnold Auerbach	46	25
1953–54	Arnold Auerbach	42	30
1954–55	Arnold Auerbach	36	36
1955–56	Arnold Auerbach	39	33
1956–57	Arnold Auerbach	44	28
1957–58	Arnold Auerbach	49	23
1958–59	Arnold Auerbach	52	20
1959–60	Arnold Auerbach	59	16
1960–61	Arnold Auerbach	57	22
1961–62	Arnold Auerbach	60	20
1962–63	Arnold Auerbach	58	22
1963–64	Arnold Auerbach	59	21
1964–65	Arnold Auerbach	62	18
1965–66	Arnold Auerbach	54	26
1966–67	Bill Russell	60	21
1967–68	Bill Russell	54	28
	Totals	998	593

CHICAGO BULLS

Season	Coach	W.	L.
1966–67	John Kerr	33	48
1967–68	John Kerr	29	53
	Totals	62	101

CHICAGO PACKERS

See Baltimore Bullets, 1961–62

CHICAGO STAGS

Season	Coach	W.	L.
1946–47	Harold Olsen	39	22
1947–48	Harold Olsen	28	20
1948–49	Harold Olsen (28-21)		
	Philip Brownstein (10-1)	38	22
1949–50	Philip Brownstein	40	28
	Totals	145	92

Season	Coach	W.	L.
	CHICAGO ZEPHYRS		
	See Baltimore Bullets, 1962–63		
	CINCINNATI ROYALS		
1948–49	Les Harrison	45	15
1949–50	Les Harrison	51	17
1950–51	Les Harrison	41	27
1951–52	Les Harrison	41	25
1952–53	Les Harrison	44	26
1953–54	Les Harrison	44	28
1954–55	Les Harrison	29	43
1955–56	Bob Wanzer	31	41
1956–57	Bob Wanzer	31	41
1957–58*	Bob Wanzer	33	39
1958–59	Bob Wanzer (3-15)		
	Tom Marshall (16-38)	19	53
1959–60	Tom Marshall	19	56
1960–61	Charles Wolf	33	46
1961–62	Charles Wolf	43	37
1962–63	Charles Wolf	42	38
1963–64	Jack McMahon	55	25
1964–65	Jack McMahon	48	32
1965–66	Jack McMahon	45	35
1966–67	Jack McMahon	39	42
1967–68	Ed Jucker	39	43
	Totals	769	709

*Team moved from Rochester to Cincinnati

Season	Coach	W.	L.
	CLEVELAND REBELS		
1946–47	Dutch Dehnert (17-20)		
	Roy Clifford (13-10)	30	30
	Totals	30	30
	DENVER NUGGETS		
1949–50	James Darden	11	51
	DETROIT FALCONS		
1946–47	Glenn Curtis (12-22)		
	Philip Sachs (8-18)	20	40
	Totals	20	40
	DETROIT PISTONS		
1948–49	Carl Bennett (0-6)		
	Paul Armstrong (22-32)	22	38
1949–50	Murray Mendenhall	40	28
1950–51	Murray Mendenhall	32	36
1951–52	Paul Birch	29	37
1952–53	Paul Birch	36	33
1953–54	Paul Birch	40	32
1954–55	Charles Eckman	43	29
1955–56	Charles Eckman	37	35
1956–57	Charles Eckman	34	38
1957–58*	Charles Eckman (9-16)		
	Ephraim Rocha (24-23)	33	39
1958–59	Ephraim Rocha	28	44
1959–60	Ephraim Rocha (13-21)		
	Dick McGuire (17-24)	30	45
1960–61	Dick McGuire	34	45
1961–62	Dick McGuire	37	43
1962–63	Dick McGuire	34	46
1963–64	Charles Wolf	23	57
1964–65	Charles Wolf (2-9)		
	Dave DeBusschere (29-40)	31	49
1965–66	Dave DeBusschere	22	58
1966–67	Dave DeBusschere (28-45)		
	Donnis Butcher (2-6)	30	51
1967–68	Donnis Butcher	40	42
	Totals	655	825

*Team moved from Fort Wayne to Detroit

Season	Coach	W.	L.
	FORT WAYNE PISTONS		
	See Detroit Pistons, 1957–58		
	INDIANAPOLIS JETS		
1948–49	Bruce Hale (4-13)		
	Burl Friddle (14-29)	18	42
	INDIANAPOLIS OLYMPIANS		
1949–50	Clifford Barker	39	25
1950–51	Clifford Barker (24-32)		
	Wallace Jones (7-5)	31	37
1951–52	Herman Schaefer	34	32
1952–53	Herman Schaefer	28	43
	Totals	132	137
	LOS ANGELES LAKERS		
1948–49	John Kundla	44	16
1949–50	John Kundla	51	17
1950–51	John Kundla	44	24
1951–52	John Kundla	46	26
1952–53	John Kundla	48	22
1953–54	John Kundla	40	26
1954–55	John Kundla	40	32
1955–56	John Kundla	33	39
1956–57	John Kundla	34	38
1957–58	George Mikan (9-30)		
	John Kundla (10-23)	19	53
1958–59	John Kundla	33	39
1959–60	John Castellani (11-25)		
	Jim Pollard (14-25)	25	50
1960–61*	Fred Schaus	36	43
1961–62	Fred Schaus	54	26
1962–63	Fred Schaus	53	27
1963–64	Fred Schaus	42	38
1964–65	Fred Schaus	49	31
1965–66	Fred Schaus	45	35
1966–67	Fred Schaus	36	45
1967–68	Bill van Breda Kolff	52	30
	Totals	824	657

*Team moved from Minneapolis to Los Angeles

Season	Coach	W.	L.
	MILWAUKEE HAWKS		
	See Atlanta Hawks, 1951–52		
	MILWAUKEE BUCKS		
1968–69	Larry Costello (first season)		
	MINNEAPOLIS LAKERS		
	See Los Angeles Lakers, 1960–61		

NEW YORK KNICKERBOCKERS

Season	Coach	W.	L.
1946-47	Neil Cohalan	33	27
1947-48	Joe Lapchick	26	22
1948-49	Joe Lapchick	32	28
1949-50	Joe Lapchick	40	28
1950-51	Joe Lapchick	36	30
1951-52	Joe Lapchick	37	29
1952-53	Joe Lapchick	47	23
1953-54	Joe Lapchick	44	28
1954-55	Joe Lapchick	34	38
1955-56	Joe Lapchick (26-25)		
	Vince Boryla (9-12)	35	37
1956-57	Vince Boryla	36	36
1957-58	Vince Boryla	35	37
1958-59	Andrew Levane	40	32
1959-60	Andrew Levane (8-19)		
	Carl Braun (19-29)	27	48
1960-61	Carl Braun	21	58
1961-62	Eddie Donovan	29	51
1962-63	Eddie Donovan	21	59
1963-64	Eddie Donovan	22	58
1964-65	Eddie Donovan (12-26)		
	Harry Gallatin (19-23)	31	49
1965-66	Harry Gallatin (6-15)		
	Dick McGuire (24-35)	30	50
1966-67	Dick McGuire	36	45
1967-68	Dick McGuire (15-22)		
	William Holzman (28-17)	43	39
	Totals	735	852

PHILADELPHIA WARRIORS

See San Francisco Warriors, 1962-63

PHILADELPHIA 76ERS

Season	Coach	W.	L.
1949-50	Al Cervi	51	13
1950-51	Al Cervi	32	34
1951-52	Al Cervi	40	26
1952-53	Al Cervi	47	24
1953-54	Al Cervi	42	30
1954-55	Al Cervi	43	29
1955-56	Al Cervi	35	37
1956-57	Al Cervi (4-8)		
	Paul Seymour (34-26)	38	34
1957-58	Paul Seymour	41	31
1958-59	Paul Seymour	35	37
1959-60	Paul Seymour	45	30
1960-61	Alex Hannum	38	41
1961-62	Alex Hannum	41	39
1962-63	Alex Hannum	48	32
1963-64*	Dolph Schayes	34	46
1964-65	Dolph Schayes	40	40
1965-66	Dolph Schayes	55	25
1966-67	Alex Hannum	68	13
1967-68	Alex Hannum	62	20
	Totals	835	581

**Team moved from Syracuse to Philadelphia, changed name to 76ers*

PHOENIX SUNS

Season	Coach	W.	L.
1968-69	John Kerr (first season)		

PITTSBURGH IRONMEN

Season	Coach	W.	L.
1946-47	Paul Birch	15	45

PROVIDENCE STEAMROLLERS

Season	Coach	W.	L.
1946-47	Robert Morris	28	32
1947-48	Albert Soar (2-17)		
	Nat Hickey (4-25)	6	42
1948-49	Ken Loeffler	12	48
	Totals	46	122

ST. LOUIS BOMBERS

Season	Coach	W.	L.
1946-47	Ken Loeffler	38	33
1947-48	Ken Loeffler	29	19
1948-49	Grady Lewis	29	31
1949-50	Grady Lewis	26	42
	Totals	122	125

ST. LOUIS HAWKS

See Atlanta Hawks, 1967-68

SAN DIEGO ROCKETS

Season	Coach	W.	L.
1967-68	Jack McMahon	15	67

SAN FRANCISCO WARRIORS

Season	Coach	W.	L.
1946-47	Edward Gottlieb	35	25
1947-48	Edward Gottlieb	27	21
1948-49	Edward Gottlieb	28	32
1949-50	Edward Gottlieb	26	42
1950-51	Edward Gottlieb	40	26
1951-52	Edward Gottlieb	33	33
1952-53	Edward Gottlieb	12	57
1953-54	Edward Gottlieb	29	43
1954-55	Edward Gottlieb	33	39
1955-56	George Senesky	45	27
1956-57	George Senesky	37	35
1957-58	George Senesky	37	35
1958-59	Al Cervi	32	40
1959-60	Neil Johnston	49	26
1960-61	Neil Johnston	46	33
1961-62	Frank McGuire	49	31
1962-63*	Bob Feerick	31	49
1963-64	Alex Hannum	48	32
1964-65	Alex Hannum	17	63
1965-66	Alex Hannum	35	45
1966-67	Bill Sharman	44	37
1967-68	Bill Sharman	43	39
	Totals	776	810

**Team moved from Philadelphia to San Francisco*

SEATTLE SUPERSONICS

Season	Coach	W.	L.
1967-68	Al Bianchi	23	59

SHEBOYGAN REDSKINS

Season	Coach	W.	L.
1949-50	Ken Suesens	22	40

Season	Coach	W.	L.
	SYRACUSE NATIONALS		
	See Phildelphia 76ers, 1963–64		
	TORONTO HUSKIES		
1946–47	Ed Sadowski (3-9) Lew Hayman (0-1) Dick Fitzgerald (2-1) Robert Rolfe (17-27)	22	38
	TRI-CITIES BLACKHAWKS		
	See Atlanta Hawks, 1951–52		

Season	Coach	W.	L.
	WASHINGTON CAPITOLS		
1946–47	Arnold Auerbach	49	11
1947–48	Arnold Auerbach	28	20
1948–49	Arnold Auerbach	38	22
1949–50	Bob Feerick	32	36
1950–51*	Horace McKinney	10	25
	Totals	157	114

**Team disbanded January 9, 1951*

Season	Coach	W.	L.
	WATERLOO HAWKS		
1949–50	Charles Shipp (8-27) Jack Smile (11-16)	19	43

ALL-ROOKIE TEAMS

1963–64

Jerry Lucas, Cincinnati
Gus Johnson, Baltimore
Nate Thurmond, San Francisco
Art Heyman, New York
Rod Thorn, Baltimore

1964–65

Willis Reed, New York
Jim Barnes, New York
Howie Komives, New York
Luke Jackson, Philadelphia
Wally Jones, Baltimore
Joe Caldwell, Detroit

1965–66

Rick Barry, San Francisco
Bill Cunningham, Philadelphia
Tom Van Arsdale, Detroit
Dick Van Arsdale, New York
Fred Hetzel, San Francisco

1966–67

Lou Hudson, St. Louis
Jack Marin, Baltimore
Erwin Mueller, Chicago
Cazzie Russell, New York
Dave Bing, Detroit

1967–68

Earl Monroe, Baltimore
Bob Rule, Seattle
Al Tucker, Seattle
Walt Frazier, New York
Phil Jackson, New York

12: NBA ALL-TIME REGISTER

The NBA All-Time Register includes the season-by-season records and lifetime summaries of every player who has appeared in the National Basketball Association (or its predecessor, the Basketball Association of America, from 1946-49). Also included are yearly records for all National Basketball League players who later performed for NBA or BAA teams.

The player's annual record lists his team, games played (G), field goals made (FG), free throws made (FT), total points (TP) and average (Avg.). In addition, the player's date of birth, height, weight and college are listed, although for some this information was unobtainable.

Yr.	Team	G	FG	FT	TP	Avg.

ABLE, FOREST

b. July 27, 1932 Ht. 6-3 Wt. 180
College—Western Kentucky

Yr.	Team	G	FG	FT	TP	Avg.
1956-57	Syracuse	1	0	0	0	0.0

ABRAMOVIC, JOHN (Brooms)

Ht. 6-3 Wt. 196
College—Salem

Yr.	Team	G	FG	FT	TP	Avg.
1946-47	Pittsburgh	47	202	123	527	11.2
1947-48	Balt.-Prov.	9	1	4	6	0.7
1947-48	Syracuse NL	35	72	42	186	5.3
	Totals	91	275	169	719	7.9

ACKERMAN, BUDDY

Ht. 6-0 Wt. 183
College—Long Island U.

Yr.	Team	G	FG	FT	TP	Avg.
1953-54	New York	28	14	15	43	1.5

ACTON, CHARLES

Ht. 6-6 Wt. 210
College—Michigan State

Yr.	Team	G	FG	FT	TP	Avg.
1967-68	San Diego	23	29	19	77	3.3

AKIN, HENRY

b. July 31, 1944 Ht. 6-10 Wt. 235
College—Morehead State

Yr.	Team	G	FG	FT	TP	Avg.
1966-67	New York	50	83	26	192	3.8
1967-68	Seattle	36	46	20	112	3.1
	Totals	86	129	46	304	3.5

ALCORN, GARY

b. Oct. 8, 1936 Ht. 6-9 Wt. 225
College—Fresno State

Yr.	Team	G	FG	FT	TP	Avg.
1960-61	Los Angeles	19	12	7	31	1.6

ANDEREGG, ROBERT

b. Aug. 24, 1937 Ht. 6-3 Wt. 200
College—Michigan State

Yr.	Team	G	FG	FT	TP	Avg.
1959-60	New York	33	55	23	133	4.0

ANDERSON, CLIFF

b. Sept. 7, 1944 Ht. 6-4 Wt. 200
College—St. Joseph's (Pa.)

Yr.	Team	G	FG	FT	TP	Avg.
1967-68	Los Angeles	18	7	12	26	1.4

ANIELAK, DON

Ht. 6-7
College—Southwest Missouri

Yr.	Team	G	FG	FT	TP	Avg.
1954-55	New York	1	0	3	3	3.0

ARCENEAUX, STACEY

b. Feb 17, 1936 Ht. 6-4 Wt. 210

Yr.	Team	G	FG	FT	TP	Avg.
1961-62	St. Louis	7	22	6	50	7.1

ARIZIN, PAUL

b. April 9, 1928 Ht. 6-4 Wt. 200
College—Villanova

Yr.	Team	G	FG	FT	TP	Avg.
1950-51	Philadelphia	65	352	417	1121	17.2
1951-52	Philadelphia	66	548	578	1674	25.4
1954-55	Philadelphia	72	529	454	1512	21.0
1955-56	Philadelphia	72	617	507	1741	24.2
1956-57	Philadelphia	71	613	591	1817	25.6
1957-58	Philadelphia	68	483	440	1406	20.7
1958-59	Philadelphia	70	632	587	1851	26.4
1959-60	Philadelphia	72	593	420	1606	22.3
1960-61	Philadelphia	79	650	532	1832	23.2
1961-62	Philadelphia	78	611	484	1706	21.9
	Totals	713	5628	5010	16266	22.8

ARMSTRONG, PAUL

Ht. 5-11
College—Indiana

Yr.	Team	G	FG	FT	TP	Avg.
1946-47	Ft. Wayne NL	44	127	134	388	8.8
1947-48	Ft. Wayne NL	53	148	139	435	8.2
1948-49	Ft. Wayne	52	131	118	380	7.3
1949-50	Ft. Wayne	63	144	170	458	7.3
1950-51	Ft. Wayne	38	72	58	202	5.3
	Totals	250	622	619	1863	7.4

ARMSTRONG, ROBERT

b. June 17, 1933 Ht. 6-8 Wt. 230
College—Michigan State

Yr.	Team	G	FG	FT	TP	Avg.
1956-57	Philadelphia	19	11	6	28	1.5

ARNELLE, JESSE

b. Dec. 30, 1933 Ht. 6-5 Wt. 220
College—Penn State

Yr.	Team	G	FG	FT	TP	Avg.
1955-56	Ft. Wayne	31	52	43	147	4.7

ARNETTE, JAY

b. Dec. 19, 1938 Ht. 6-2 Wt. 175
College—Texas

Yr.	Team	G	FG	FT	TP	Avg.
1963-64	Cincinnati	48	71	42	184	3.8
1964-65	Cincinnati	63	91	56	238	3.8
1965-66	Cincinnati	3	1	0	2	0.7
	Totals	114	163	98	424	3.7

ASMONGA, DON

Ht. 6-2 Wt. 185
College—Geneva

Yr.	Team	G	FG	FT	TP	Avg.
1953-54	Baltimore	7	2	1	5	0.7

ATHA, RICHARD

b. Sept. 21, 1931 Ht. 6-2 Wt. 195
College—Indiana State

Yr.	Team	G	FG	FT	TP	Avg.
1955-56	New York	25	36	21	93	3.7
1957-58	Detroit	18	17	10	44	2.4
	Totals	43	53	31	137	3.2

ATTLES, ALVIN

b. Nov. 7, 1936 Ht. 6-2 Wt. 175
College—North Carolina A&T

Yr.	Team	G	FG	FT	TP	Avg.
1960-61	Philadelphia	77	222	97	541	7.0
1961-62	Philadelphia	75	343	158	844	11.2
1962-63	San Francisco	71	301	133	735	10.4
1963-64	San Francisco	70	289	185	763	10.9
1964-65	San Francisco	73	254	171	679	9.3
1965-66	San Francisco	79	364	154	882	11.2
1966-67	San Francisco	70	212	88	512	7.3
1967-68	San Francisco	67	252	150	654	9.8
	Totals	582	2237	1136	5610	9.6

AUBUCHON, CHET

Ht. 5-10 Wt. 145
College—Michigan State

Yr.	Team	G	FG	FT	TP	Avg.
1946-47	Detroit	30	23	19	65	2.2

AUSTIN, JOHN

b. Aug. 31, 1944 Ht. 6-0 Wt. 175

College—Boston College

Yr.	Team	G	FC	FT	TP	Avg.
1966-67	Baltimore	4	5	13	23	5.9

BACH, JOHN

Ht. 6-2 Wt. 180

College—Fordham

Yr.	Team	G	FC	FT	TP	Avg.
1948-49	Boston	34	34	51	119	3.5

BAECHTOLD, JIM

b. Dec. 9, 1927 Ht. 6-4 Wt. 205

College—Eastern Kentucky

Yr.	Team	G	FC	FT	TP	Avg.
1952-53	Baltimore	64	242	177	661	10.3
1953-54	New York	70	170	134	474	6.8
1954-55	New York	72	362	279	1003	13.9
1955-56	New York	70	268	233	769	11.0
1956-57	New York	45	75	66	216	4.8
	Totals	321	1117	889	3123	9.7

BAKER, NORMAN

Ht. 6-0

College—McGill

Yr.	Team	G	FC	FT	TP	Avg.
1946-47	Chicago	4	0	0	0	0.0

BALTIMORE, HERSCHEL

b. June 21, 1921 Ht. 6-4 Wt. 195

College—Penn State

Yr.	Team	G	FC	FT	TP	Avg.
1946-47	St. Louis	58	53	32	138	2.4

BARBER, JOHN

b. June 27, 1927 Ht. 6-6 Wt. 210

College—Los Angeles State

Yr.	Team	G	FC	FT	TP	Avg.
1956-57	St. Louis	5	2	3	7	1.4

BARKER, CLIFF

b. Jan. 15, 1921 Ht. 6-2 Wt. 185

College—Kentucky

Yr.	Team	G	FC	FT	TP	Avg.
1949-50	Indianapolis	49	102	75	279	5.7
1950-51	Indianapolis	56	51	50	152	2.7
1951-52	Indianapolis	44	48	30	126	2.9
	Totals	149	201	155	557	3.7

BARKSDALE, DON

Ht. 6-6 Wt. 200

College—UCLA

Yr.	Team	G	FC	FT	TP	Avg.
1951-52	Baltimore	62	272	237	781	12.6
1952-53	Baltimore	65	321	257	899	13.8
1953-54	Boston	63	156	149	461	7.3
1954-55	Boston	72	267	220	754	10.5
	Totals	262	1016	863	2895	11.1

BARNES, JIM (Bad News)

b. April 13, 1941 Ht. 6-8 Wt. 240

College—Texas Western

Yr.	Team	G	FC	FT	TP	Avg.
1964-65	New York	75	454	251	1159	15.5
1965-66	N.Y.-Balt.	73	348	212	908	12.4
1966-67	Los Angeles	80	217	128	562	7.0
1967-68	L.A.-Chicago	79	221	133	575	7.3
	Totals	307	1240	724	3204	10.4

BARNETT, JIM

b. July 7, 1944 Ht. 6-4 Wt. 180

College—Oregon

Yr.	Team	G	FG	FT	TP	Avg.
1966-67	Boston	48	78	42	198	4.1
1967-68	San Diego	47	179	84	442	9.4
	Totals	95	257	126	640	6.7

BARNETT, RICHARD

b. April 5, 1936 Ht. 6-4 Wt. 190

College—Tennessee State

Yr.	Team	G	FG	FT	TP	Avg.
1959-60	Syracuse	57	289	128	706	12.4
1960-61	Syracuse	78	540	240	1320	16.9
1962-63	Los Angeles	80	547	343	1437	18.0
1963-64	Los Angeles	78	541	351	1433	18.4
1964-65	Los Angeles	74	375	270	1020	13.8
1965-66	New York	75	631	467	1729	23.1
1966-67	New York	67	454	231	1139	17.0
1967-68	New York	81	559	343	1461	18.0
	Totals	590	3936	2373	10245	17.4

BARNHILL, JOHN

b. Mar. 30, 1938 Ht. 6-1 Wt. 180

College—Tennessee State

Yr.	Team	G	FG	FT	TP	Avg.
1962-63	St. Louis	77	360	181	901	11.7
1963-64	St. Louis	74	208	70	486	6.6
1964-65	St. Louis	41	121	45	287	7.0
1965-66	St. L.-Det.	76	243	113	599	7.9
1966-67	Baltimore	53	187	66	440	8.3
1967-68	San Diego	75	295	154	744	9.9
	Totals	386	1414	629	3457	9.0

BARNHORST, LEO

b. May 17, 1924 Ht. 6-4 Wt. 195

College—Notre Dame

Yr.	Team	G	FG	FT	TP	Avg.
1949-50	Chicago	67	174	90	438	6.5
1950-51	Indianapolis	68	232	82	546	8.0
1951-52	Indianapolis	66	349	122	820	12.4
1952-53	Indianapolis	71	402	163	967	13.6
1953-54	Ft. Wayne	72	199	63	461	6.4
	Totals	344	1356	520	3232	9.4

BARR, JOHN E.

b. Aug. 18, 1918 Ht. 6-3 Wt. 205

College—Penn State

Yr.	Team	G	FG	FT	TP	Avg.
1946-47	St. Louis	58	124	47	295	5.1

BARRETT, ERNIE

Ht. 6-3 Wt. 180

College—Kansas State

Yr.	Team	G	FG	FT	TP	Avg.
1953-54	Boston	59	60	14	134	2.3
1955-56	Boston	72	207	93	507	7.0
	Totals	131	267	107	641	4.9

BARRY, RICHARD (Rick)

b. Mar. 28, 1944 Ht. 6-7 Wt. 205

College—Miami (Fla.)

Yr.	Team	G	FG	FT	TP	Avg.
1965-66	San Francisco	80	745	569	2059	25.7
1966-67	San Francisco	78	1011	753	2775	35.6
	Totals	158	1756	1322	4834	30.6

BARTELS, ED

b. Oct. 8, 1925 Ht. 6-5 Wt. 195

College—North Carolina State

Yr.	Team	G	FG	FT	TP	Avg.
1949-50	Denver	13	21	17	59	4.5
1949-50	New York	2	1	2	4	2.0
1950-51	Washington	17	24	24	72	4.2
	Totals	32	46	43	135	4.2

Yr.	Team	G	FG	FT	TP	Avg.
	BAUMHOLTZ, FRANK					
	b. Oct. 7, 1919 Ht. 5-10 Wt. 170					
	College—Ohio University					
1945-46	Youngstown NL	26	99	76	274	10.5
1946-47	Cleveland	45	255	121	631	14.0
	Totals	71	354	197	905	12.7
	BAYLOR, ELGIN					
	b. Sept. 16, 1934 Ht. 6-5 Wt. 225					
	College—Seattle					
1958-59	Minneapolis	70	605	532	1742	24.9
1959-60	Minneapolis	70	755	564	2074	29.6
1960-61	Los Angeles	73	931	676	2538	34.8
1961-62	Los Angeles	48	680	476	1836	38.2
1962-63	Los Angeles	80	1029	661	2719	34.0
1963-64	Los Angeles	78	756	471	1983	25.4
1964-65	Los Angeles	74	763	483	2009	27.1
1965-66	Los Angeles	65	415	249	1079	16.6
1966-67	Los Angeles	70	711	440	1862	26.6
1967-68	Los Angeles	77	757	488	2002	26.0
	Totals	705	7402	5040	19844	28.1
	BEACH, ED					
	b. Jan. 25, 1929 Ht. 6-3 Wt. 200					
	College—West Virginia					
1950-51	Minn.-Tri-Cit.	12	8	6	22	1.8
	BEARD, RALPH					
	b. Dec. 2, 1927 Ht. 5-10 Wt. 176					
	College—Kentucky					
1949-50	Indianapolis	60	340	215	895	14.9
1950-51	Indianapolis	66	409	293	1111	16.8
	Totals	126	749	508	2006	15.9
	BEATY, ZELMO					
	b. Oct. 25, 1939 Ht. 6-9 Wt. 235					
	College—Prairie View					
1962-63	St. Louis	80	297	220	814	10.2
1963-64	St. Louis	59	287	272	774	13.1
1964-65	St. Louis	80	505	341	1351	16.9
1965-66	St. Louis	80	616	559	1656	20.7
1966-67	St. Louis	48	328	197	853	17.8
1967-68	St. Louis	82	639	455	1733	21.1
	Totals	429	2672	1837	7181	16.7
	BECK, ERNEST					
	b. Dec. 11, 1931 Ht. 6-4 Wt. 190					
	College—Pennsylvania					
1953-54	Philadelphia	15	39	34	112	7.5
1955-56	Philadelphia	67	136	76	348	5.2
1956-57	Philadelphia	72	195	111	501	7.0
1957-58	Philadelphia	71	272	170	714	10.1
1958-59	Philadelphia	70	163	43	369	5.3
1959-60	Philadelphia	66	114	27	255	3.9
	Totals	361	919	461	2299	6.4
	BECKER, MOE					
	b. Feb. 24, 1917 Ht. 6-1 Wt. 185					
	College—Duquesne					
1945-46	Youngstown NL	30	114	40	268	8.9
1946-47	Pitt.-Bos.-Det.	43	70	22	162	3.8
	Totals	73	184	62	330	4.5

Yr.	Team	G	FG	FT	TP	Avg.
	BEENDERS, HENRY (Hank)					
	Ht. 6-6 Wt. 185					
	College—Long Island U.					
1946-47	Providence	58	266	181	713	12.3
1947-48	Prov.-Phil.	45	76	51	203	4.5
1948-49	Boston	8	6	7	19	2.4
	Totals	101	348	239	935	9.3
	BEHNKE, ELMER					
	b. Feb. 3, 1929 Ht. 6-7 Wt. 210					
	College—Bradley					
1951-52	Milwaukee	4	6	4	16	4.0
	BELL, WILLIAM H. (Whitey)					
	b. Sept. 13, 1932 Ht. 6-0 Wt. 181					
	College—North Carolina State					
1959-60	New York	31	70	28	168	5.4
1960-61	New York	5	7	1	15	3.0
	Totals	36	77	29	183	5.1
	BELLAMY, WALTER (Bells)					
	b. July 24, 1939 Ht. 6-10½ Wt. 245					
	College—Indiana					
1961-62	Chicago	79	973	549	2495	31.6
1962-63	Chicago	80	840	553	2233	27.9
1963-64	Baltimore	80	811	537	2159	27.0
1964-65	Baltimore	80	733	515	1981	24.8
1965-66	Balt.-N.Y.	80	695	430	1820	22.8
1966-67	New York	79	565	369	1499	19.0
1967-68	New York	82	511	282	1372	16.7
	Totals	560	5128	3235	13559	24.2
	BEMORAS, IRV					
	b. Nov. 18, 1930 Ht. 6-3 Wt. 187					
	College—Illinois					
1953-54	Milwaukee	69	185	139	509	7.4
1956-57	St. Louis	62	124	70	318	5.1
	Totals	131	309	209	827	6.3
	BERCE, EUGENE					
	Ht. 5-11 Wt. 175					
	College—Marquette					
1948-49	Oshkosh NL	58	120	98	338	5.8
1949-50	Tri-Cities	3	5	0	10	3.3
	Totals	61	125	98	348	5.7
	BERGEN, GARY					
	Ht. 6-8 Wt. 212					
	College—Utah					
1956-57	New York	6	3	2	8	1.3
	BIANCHI, ALFRED (Al)					
	b. Mar. 26, 1932 Ht. 6-3 Wt. 185					
	College—Bowling Green					
1956-57	Syracuse	68	199	165	563	8.3
1957-58	Syracuse	69	215	140	570	8.3
1958-59	Syracuse	72	285	149	719	10.0
1959-60	Syracuse	69	215	112	542	7.8
1960-61	Syracuse	52	118	60	296	5.7
1961-62	Syracuse	80	336	154	826	10.3
1962-63	Syracuse	61	202	120	524	8.6
1963-64	Philadelphia	78	257	109	623	8.0
1964-65	Philadelphia	60	175	54	404	6.7

Yr.	Team	G	FG	FT	TP	Avg.
1965-66	Philadelphia	78	214	66	494	6.3
	Totals	687	2216	1129	5561	8.1
	BIASETTI, HENRY					
	Ht. 5-9 Wt. 165					
	College—Assumption (Ont.)					
1946-47	Toronto	6	2	2	6	1.0
	BIELKE, DON					
	Ht. 6-8					
	College—Valparaiso					
1955-56	Ft. Wayne	7	5	4	14	2.0
	BING, DAVE					
	b. Nov. 24, 1943 Ht. 6-3 Wt. 180					
	College—Syracuse					
1966-67	Detroit	80	664	273	1601	20.0
1967-68	Detroit	79	835	472	2142	27.1
	Totals	159	1499	745	3743	23.5
	BISHOP, GALE					
	b. June 9, 1922 Ht. 6-3 Wt. 195					
	College—Washington State					
1948-49	Philadelphia	56	170	127	467	8.3
	BLACK, CHARLES					
	b. June 15, 1921 Ht. 6-5 Wt. 200					
	College—Kansas					
1947-48	Anderson NL	58	149	150	448	7.7
1948-49	Ft. W.-Ind.	58	203	161	567	9.8
1949-50	Ft. W.-Andsn.	65	226	209	661	10.2
1951-52	Milwaukee	13	6	5	17	1.3
	Totals	194	584	525	1693	8.7
	BLANEY, GEORGE					
	b. Nov. 12, 1939 Ht. 6-1 Wt. 175					
	College—Holy Cross					
1961-62	New York	36	54	9	117	3.2
	BLEVINS, LEON					
	Ht. 6-2 Wt. 160					
	College—Arizona					
1950-51	Indianapolis	3	1	0	2	0.7
	BLOCK, JOHN					
	b. April 16, 1944 Ht. 6-9 Wt. 207					
	College—Southern California					
1966-67	Los Angeles	22	20	24	64	2.9
1967-68	San Diego	52	366	316	1048	20.2
	Totals	74	386	340	1112	15.0
	BLOOM, MEYER (Mike)					
	Ht. 6-6 Wt. 190					
	College—Temple					
1947-48	Balt.-Boston	48	174	160	508	10.6
1948-49	Minn.-Chicago	45	35	56	126	2.8
	Totals	93	209	216	634	6.8
	BOBB, NELSON					
	b. Feb. 25, 1924 Ht. 6-0 Wt. 170					
	College—Temple					
1949-50	Philadelphia	57	80	82	242	4.2
1950-51	Philadelphia	53	52	44	148	2.8

Yr.	Team	G	FG	FT	TP	Avg.
1951-52	Philadelphia	62	110	167	319	5.1
1952-53	Philadelphia	55	119	105	343	6.2
	Totals	227	361	330	1052	4.7
	BOCKHORN, ARLEN					
	b. July 8, 1933 Ht. 6-4 Wt. 200					
	College—Dayton					
1958-59	Cincinnati	71	294	138	726	10.2
1959-60	Cincinnati	75	323	145	791	10.5
1960-61	Cincinnati	79	420	152	992	12.6
1961-62	Cincinnati	80	531	198	1260	15.7
1962-63	Cincinnati	80	375	183	933	11.7
1963-64	Cincinnati	70	242	96	580	8.3
1964-65	Cincinnati	19	60	39	148	7.8
	Totals	474	2245	1256	5430	11.5
	BOLGER, BILL					
	b. Aug. 21, 1931 Ht. 6-5 Wt. 205					
	College—Georgetown					
1953-54	Baltimore	20	24	8	56	2.8
	BOLSTORFF, DOUG					
	b. Oct. 29, 1931 Ht. 6-4 Wt. 195					
	College—Minnesota					
1957-58	Detroit	3	2	0	4	1.3
	BONHAM, RON					
	b. May 31, 1942 Ht. 6-5 Wt. 200					
	College—Cincinnati					
1964-65	Boston	37	91	92	274	7.4
1965-66	Boston	39	76	52	204	5.2
	Totals	76	167	144	478	6.3
	BOOZER, ROBERT					
	b. April 26, 1937 Ht. 6-8 Wt. 215					
	College—Kansas State					
1960-61	Cincinnati	79	250	166	666	8.4
1961-62	Cincinnati	79	410	263	1083	13.7
1962-63	Cincinnati	79	440	252	1132	14.3
1963-64	Cinn.-New York	81	468	272	1208	14.9
1964-65	New York	80	424	288	1136	14.2
1965-66	Los Angeles	78	365	225	955	12.2
1966-67	Chicago	80	538	360	1436	18.0
1967-68	Chicago	77	622	411	1655	21.5
	Totals	633	3517	2237	9271	14.6
	BORNHEIMER, DAVE					
	Ht. 6-5 Wt. 205					
	College—Muhlenberg					
1948-49	Philadelphia	15	34	20	88	5.9
1949-50	Philadelphia	60	88	78	254	4.2
	Totals	75	122	98	342	4.6
	BORSAVAGE, COSTIC (Ike)					
	b. July 25, 1924 Ht. 6-1 Wt. 200					
	College—Temple					
1950-51	Philadelphia	24	26	12	64	2.7
	BORYLA, VINCE					
	b. Mar. 11, 1927 Ht. 6-5 Wt. 210					
	College—Notre Dame and Denver					
1949-50	New York	59	204	204	612	10.4
1950-51	New York	66	352	332	982	14.9
1951-52	New York	42	202	96	500	11.9

Yr.	Team	G	FG	FT	TP	Avg.
1952-53	New York	66	254	165	673	10.2
1953-54	New York	52	175	70	420	8.1
	Totals	285	1187	813	3187	11.2

BOVEN, DON

b. Mar. 6, 1925 Ht. 6-4 Ht. 210
College—Western Michigan

Yr.	Team	G	FG	FT	TP	Avg.
1949-50	Waterloo	62	208	240	656	10.6
1951-52	Milwaukee	66	200	256	656	9.9
1952-53	Ft. Wayne	67	153	145	451	6.7
	Totals	195	561	641	1763	9.0

BOWMAN, NATE

b. Mar. 19, 1943 Ht. 6-10 Wt. 230
College—Wichita State

Yr.	Team	G	FG	FT	TP	Avg.
1966-67	Chicago	9	8	6	22	2.4
1967-68	New York	42	52	10	114	2.7
	Totals	51	60	16	136	2.7

BOYKOFF, HARRY

Ht. 6-10 Wt. 227
College—St. John's (N. Y.)

Yr.	Team	G	FG	FT	TP	Avg.
1947-48	Toledo NL	59	225	124	574	9.7
1948-49	Waterloo NL	61	289	189	767	12.6
1949-50	Waterloo	61	288	203	779	12.8
1950-51	Boston-Tri-Cit.	48	126	74	326	6.8
	Totals	229	928	590	2446	10.7

BRADDS, GARY

b. July 26, 1942 Ht. 6-8 Wt. 210
College—Ohio State

Yr.	Team	G	FG	FT	TP	Avg.
1964-65	Baltimore	41	46	45	137	3.3
1965-66	Baltimore	3	2	3	7	2.3
	Totals	44	48	48	144	3.1

BRADLEY, JOE

Ht. 6-3 Wt. 175
College—Oklahoma State

Yr.	Team	G	FG	FT	TP	Avg.
1949-50	Chicago	46	36	15	87	1.9

BRADLEY, BILL

b. July 28, 1943 Ht. 6-5 Wt. 205
College—Princeton

Yr.	Team	G	FG	FT	TP	Avg.
1967-68	New York	45	142	76	360	8.0

BRANNUM, ROBERT

b. May 28, 1925 Ht. 6-5 Wt. 215
College—Kentucky and Michigan State

Yr.	Team	G	FG	FT	TP	Avg.
1948-49	Sheboygan NL	64	169	169	567	7.9
1949-50	Sheboygan	59	234	245	713	12.1
1951-52	Boston	66	149	107	405	6.1
1952-53	Boston	71	188	110	486	6.8
1953-54	Boston	71	140	129	409	5.8
1954-55	Boston	71	176	99	442	6.2
	Totals	402	1056	850	2962	7.4

BRANSON, JESSE

b. Jan. 7, 1942 Ht. 6-7 Wt. 200
College—Elon

Yr.	Team	G	FG	FT	TP	Avg.
1965-66	Philadelphia	5	1	3	5	1.0

BRASCO, JIM

Ht. 6-1 Wt. 170
College—New York University

Yr.	Team	G	FG	FT	TP	Avg.
1952-53	Milwaukee	20	25	27	77	3.9
1952-53	Syracuse	10	11	11	33	3.3
	Totals	30	36	38	110	3.7

BRAUN, CARL

b. Sept. 25, 1927 Ht. 6-5 Wt. 180
College—Colgate

Yr.	Team	G	FG	FT	TP	Avg.
1947-48	New York	47	276	119	671	14.3
1948-49	New York	57	299	212	810	14.2
1949-50	New York	67	373	285	1031	15.4
1952-53	New York	70	323	331	977	14.0
1953-54	New York	71	354	354	1062	14.8
1954-55	New York	70	400	274	1074	15.1
1955-56	New York	72	396	320	1112	15.4
1956-57	New York	72	378	245	1001	13.9
1957-58	New York	71	426	321	1173	16.5
1958-59	New York	72	287	180	754	10.5
1959-60	New York	54	285	129	699	12.9
1960-61	New York	15	37	11	85	5.7
1961-62	Boston	49	78	20	176	3.6
	Totals	789	3912	2801	10625	13.5

BRENNAN, PETER

b. Sept. 23, 1936 Ht. 6-6 Wt. 205
College—North Carolina

Yr.	Team	G	FG	FT	TP	Avg.
1958-59	New York	16	13	14	40	2.5

BRENNAN, THOMAS

Ht. 6-3 Wt. 195
College—Villanova

Yr.	Team	G	FG	FT	TP	Avg.
1954-55	Philadelphia	11	5	0	10	0.9

BRIAN, FRANK

b. May 1, 1923 Ht. 6-1 Wt. 180
College—Louisiana State

Yr.	Team	G	FG	FT	TP	Avg.
1947-48	Anderson NL	59	225	158	668	11.3
1948-49	Anderson NL	64	216	201	632	9.8
1949-50	Anderson	64	368	402	1138	17.8
1950-51	Tri-Cities	68	363	418	1144	16.8
1951-52	Ft. Wayne	66	342	367	1051	15.9
1952-53	Ft. Wayne	68	245	236	726	10.7
1953-54	Ft. Wayne	64	132	137	401	6.3
1954-55	Ft. Wayne	71	237	217	691	9.7
1955-56	Ft. Wayne	37	78	72	228	6.2
	Totals	561	2206	2208	6679	11.9

BRIDGES, BILL

b. April 4, 1939 Ht. 6-6½ Wt. 228
College—Kansas

Yr.	Team	G	FG	FT	TP	Avg.
1962-63	St. Louis	27	66	51	164	6.1
1963-64	St. Louis	80	268	146	682	8.5
1964-65	St. Louis	79	362	186	910	11.5
1965-66	St. Louis	78	377	257	1011	13.0
1966-67	St. Louis	79	503	367	1373	17.4
1967-68	St. Louis	82	466	347	1279	15.6
	Totals	425	2042	1335	5419	12.8

BRIGHTMAN, ALBERT

Ht. 6-2 Wt. 195
College—Morris Harvey

Yr.	Team	G	FG	FT	TP	Avg.
1946-47	Boston	58	223	121	567	9.8

BRINDLEY, AUDLEY

Ht. 6-4 Wt. 175
College—Dartmouth

Yr.	Team	G	FG	FT	TP	Avg.
1946-47	New York	12	14	6	34	2.8

BRITT, TYRONE

Ht. 6-4 Wt. 190
College—North Carolina College

Yr.	Team	G	FG	FT	TP	Avg.
1967-68	San Diego	11	13	2	28	2.5

BROOKFIELD, PRICE

Ht. 6-4 Wt. 185
College—West Texas

Yr.	Team	G	FG	FT	TP	Avg.
1947-48	Anderson NL	48	81	27	189	3.9
1948-49	Indianapolis	54	176	90	442	8.2
1949-50	Rochester	7	11	12	34	4.9
	Totals	109	268	129	665	6.1

BROWN, BOB

Ht. 6-4 Wt. 205
College—Miami (Ohio)

Yr.	Team	G	FG	FT	TP	Avg.
1948-49	Providence	20	37	34	108	5.4
1949-50	Denver	62	276	172	724	11.7
	Totals	82	313	206	832	10.1

BROWN, DARRELL

b. March 14, 1923 Ht. 6-2 Wt. 175
College—Humboldt State

Yr.	Team	G	FG	FT	TP	Avg.
1948-49	Baltimore	3	2	0	4	1.3

BROWN, GEORGE

b. Oct. 30, 1935 Ht. 6-6 Wt. 190
College—Wayne (Mich.)

Yr.	Team	G	FG	FT	TP	Avg.
1957-58	Minneapolis	1	0	1	1	1.0

BROWN, HAROLD

Ht. 6-0 Wt. 155
College—Evansville

Yr.	Team	G	FG	FT	TP	Avg.
1946-47	Detroit	54	95	74	264	4.9

BROWN, LEON

b. Oct. 12, 1919 Ht. 6-3 Wt. 190
College—Wyoming

Yr.	Team	G	FG	FT	TP	Avg.
1946-47	Cleveland	5	3	0	6	0.8

BROWN, STANLEY

Ht. 6-3 Wt. 200

Yr.	Team	G	FG	FT	TP	Avg.
1947-48	Philadelphia	19	19	12	50	2.6
1951-52	Philadelphia	15	22	10	54	3.6
	Totals	34	41	22	104	3.1

BROWNE, JAMES

Ht. 6-0 Wt. 235

Yr.	Team	G	FG	FT	TP	Avg.
1949-50	Denver	31	17	13	47	1.5

BRYANT, EMMETTE

b. Nov. 4, 1938 Ht. 6-1 Wt. 175
College—DePaul

Yr.	Team	G	FG	FT	TP	Avg.
1964-65	New York	77	145	87	377	4.9
1965-66	New York	71	212	74	498	7.0
1966-67	New York	63	236	74	546	8.7
1967-68	New York	77	112	59	283	3.7
	Totals	288	705	294	1704	5.9

BUCKHALTER, JOSEPH

b. Aug. 1, 1937 Ht. 6-7 Wt. 210
College—Tennessee State

Yr.	Team	G	FG	FT	TP	Avg.
1961-62	Cincinnati	63	153	67	373	5.9
1962-63	Cincinnati	2	0	2	2	1.0
	Totals	65	153	69	375	5.8

BUCKNER, CLEVELAND

b. Aug. 17, 1938 Ht. 6-9 Wt. 210
College—Jackson State

Yr.	Team	G	FG	FT	TP	Avg.
1961-62	New York	62	158	83	399	6.4
1962-63	New York	6	5	2	12	2.0
	Totals	68	163	85	411	6.0

BUDD, DAVID

b. Oct. 28, 1938 Ht. 6-6 Wt. 210
College—Wake Forest

Yr.	Team	G	FG	FT	TP	Avg.
1960-61	Wake Forest	61	156	87	399	6.5
1961-62	New York	79	188	138	514	6.5
1962-63	New York	78	294	151	739	9.5
1963-64	New York	73	128	84	340	4.7
1964-65	New York	62	196	121	513	8.3
	Totals	353	962	581	2505	7.1

BUDKO, WALTER

Ht. 6-5 Wt. 220
College—Columbia

Yr.	Team	G	FG	FT	TP	Avg.
1948-49	Baltimore	60	224	244	692	11.5
1949-50	Baltimore	66	198	199	595	9.0
1950-51	Baltimore	64	165	166	496	7.8
1951-52	Philadelphia	63	97	89	254	4.0
	Totals	253	684	669	2037	8.1

BUNT, DICK

Ht. 6-0
College—New York University

Yr.	Team	G	FG	FT	TP	Avg.
1952-53	Baltimore	26	29	34	92	3.5

BUNTIN, WILLIAM

b. May 5, 1942 Ht. 6-7 Wt. 250
College—Michigan

Yr.	Team	G	FG	FT	TP	Avg.
1965-66	Detroit	42	118	88	324	7.7

BURMASTER, JACK

b. Dec. 23, 1926 Ht. 6-3 Wt. 190
College—Illinois

Yr.	Team	G	FG	FT	TP	Avg.
1948-49	Oshkosh NL	62	140	80	360	5.8
1949-50	Sheboygan	61	237	124	598	9.8
	Totals	123	377	204	958	7.8

BURNS, JIM

b. Sept. 21, 1945 Ht. 6-3 Wt. 195
College—Northwestern

Yr.	Team	G	FG	FT	TP	Avg.
1967-68	Chicago	3	2	0	4	1.3

BURRIS, ART

Ht. 6-5 Wt. 220
College—Tennessee

Yr.	Team	G	FG	FT	TP	Avg.
1950-51	Ft. Wayne	33	28	21	77	2.3
1951-52	Ft. Wayne-Milw.	41	42	26	110	2.7
	Totals	74	70	47	187	2.5

Yr.	Team	G	FG	FT	TP	Avg.

BURROW, ROBERT

b. June 29, 1934 Ht. 6-7 Wt. 230
College—Kentucky

Yr.	Team	G	FG	FT	TP	Avg.
1956-57	Rochester	67	137	130	404	6.0
1957-58	Minnesota	14	22	11	55	3.9
	Totals	81	159	141	459	5.7

BURTON, ED

b. Aug. 13, 1939 Ht. 6-6 Wt. 225
College—Michigan State

Yr.	Team	G	FG	FT	TP	Avg.
1961-62	New York	8	7	1	15	1.9
1964-65	St. Louis	7	7	4	18	2.6
	Totals	15	14	5	33	2.2

BUTCHER, DONNIS

b. Feb. 8, 1936 Ht. 6-3 Wt. 200
College—Pikeville

Yr.	Team	G	FG	FT	TP	Avg.
1961-62	New York	47	48	42	138	2.9
1962-63	New York	68	172	131	475	7.0
1963-64	N.Y.-Det.	78	202	159	563	7.2
1964-65	Detroit	71	143	126	412	5.8
1965-66	Detroit	15	45	18	108	7.2
	Totals	294	655	494	1804	6.1

BUTLER, ELBERT (Al)

b. July 9, 1938 Ht. 6-2 Wt. 175
College—Niagara

Yr.	Team	G	FG	FT	TP	Avg.
1961-62	Boston-N.Y.	59	350	131	831	14.1
1962-63	New York	74	297	144	738	10.0
1963-64	New York	76	260	138	658	8.7
1964-65	Baltimore	25	24	11	59	2.4
	Totals	234	931	424	2286	9.8

BYRNES, THOMAS

Ht. 6-3 Wt. 175
College—Seton Hall

Yr.	Team	G	FG	FT	TP	Avg.
1946-47	New York	60	175	103	453	7.6
1947-48	New York	47	117	65	299	6.4
1948-49	N.Y.-Indianap.	57	160	92	412	7.2
1949-50	Baltimore	53	197	87	327	6.2
1950-51	Balt.-Tri Cities	48	83	55	221	4.6
	Totals	265	655	402	1712	6.5

BYTZURA, MICHAEL

Ht. 6-0 Wt. 175
College—Duquesne and Long Island U.

Yr.	Team	G	FG	FT	TP	Avg.
1945-46	Cleveland NL	32	78	34	190	6.2
1946-47	Pittsburgh	60	87	36	210	3.5
	Totals	92	165	70	400	4.3

CABLE, BARNEY

b. July 29, 1935 Ht. 6-7 Wt. 200
College—Bradley

Yr.	Team	G	FG	FT	TP	Avg.
1958-59	Detroit	31	43	23	109	3.5
1959-60	Syracuse	57	109	44	262	4.6
1960-61	Syracuse	75	266	73	605	8.1
1961-62	Chicago-St. L.	67	305	118	728	10.9
1962-63	St. Louis-Chicago	62	173	62	408	6.6
1963-64	Baltimore	71	116	28	260	3.7
	Totals	363	1012	348	2372	6.5

CALABRESE, GERRY

b. Feb. 4, 1925 Ht. 6-1 Wt. 175
College—St. John's

Yr.	Team	G	FG	FT	TP	Avg.
1950-51	Syracuse	46	70	61	201	4.4
1951-52	Syracuse	58	109	73	291	5.0
	Totals	104	179	134	492	4.8

CALDWELL, JIM

b. 1943 Ht. 6-10 Wt. 240
College—Georgia Tech

Yr.	Team	G	FG	FT	TP	Avg.
1967-68	New York	2	0	0	0	0.0

CALDWELL, JOE

b. Nov. 1, 1941 Ht. 6-5 Wt. 195
College—Arizona State

Yr.	Team	G	FG	FT	TP	Avg.
1964-65	Detroit	66	290	129	709	10.7
1965-66	Det.-St. Louis	79	411	179	1001	12.7
1966-67	St. Louis	81	456	200	1116	13.8
1967-68	St. Louis	79	564	165	1293	16.4
	Totals	305	1723	673	4119	13.5

CALHOUN, WILLIAM

Ht. 6-3 Wt. 180

Yr.	Team	G	FG	FT	TP	Avg.
1947-48	Rochester NL	43	31	18	80	1.9
1948-49	Rochester	56	146	75	367	6.6
1949-50	Rochester	62	207	146	560	9.0
1950-51	Rochester	66	175	161	511	7.7
1951-52	Baltimore	55	129	125	383	7.0
1952-53	Milwaukee	62	180	211	571	9.2
1953-54	Milwaukee	72	190	214	594	8.3
1954-55	Milwaukee	69	144	166	454	6.6
	Totals	498	1202	1116	3520	7.1

CALLAHAN, THOMAS

Ht. 6-1 Wt. 180
College—Rockhurst

Yr.	Team	G	FG	FT	TP	Avg.
1946-47	Providence	13	6	5	17	1.3

CALVERLEY, ERNEST

b. Jan. 30, 1924 Ht. 5-10 Wt. 155
College—Rhode Island

Yr.	Team	G	FG	FT	TP	Avg.
1946-47	Providence	59	323	199	845	14.3
1947-48	Providence	47	226	107	559	11.9
1948-49	Providence	59	218	121	557	9.4
	Totals	165	767	427	1961	11.9

CARL, HOWARD

b. June 7, 1938 Ht. 5-9 Wt. 160
College—DePaul

Yr.	Team	G	FG	FT	TP	Avg.
1961-62	Chicago	31	67	36	170	5.5

CARLISLE, CHESTER

b. Nov. 2, 1916 Ht. 6-5 Wt. 195
College—California

Yr.	Team	G	FG	FT	TP	Avg.
1946-47	Chicago	51	100	56	256	5.0

CARLSON, DON

Ht. 6-0 Wt. 170
College—Minnesota

Yr.	Team	G	FG	FT	TP	Avg.
1946-47	Chicago	59	272	86	630	10.7
1947-48	Minneapolis NL	58	205	64	474	8.2
1948-49	Minneapolis	55	211	86	508	9.3
1949-50	Minneapolis	57	99	69	267	4.7
1950-51	Washington	9	17	8	42	4.7
	Totals	238	804	313	1921	8.1

CARNEY, BOB

b. Aug. 3, 1932 Ht. 6-3 Wt. 172

College—Bradley

Yr.	Team	G	FG	FT	TP	Avg.
1954-55	Minneapolis	19	24	21	69	3.6

CARPENTER, ROBERT

b. Nov. 6, 1917 Ht. 6-5 Wt. 200

College—East Texas

Yr.	Team	G	FG	FT	TP	Avg.
1946-47	Oshkosh NL	44	199	117	515	11.7
1947-48	Oshkosh NL	59	201	157	559	9.5
1948-49	Oshkosh NL	47	160	121	441	9.4
1949-50	Ft. Wayne	66	212	190	614	9.3
1950-51	Tri-Cities	56	109	105	323	5.8
	Totals	272	881	690	2452	9.0

CARTER, GEORGE

b. Jan. 18, 1944 Ht. 6-5 Wt. 218

College—St. Bonaventure

Yr.	Team	G	FG	FT	TP	Avg.
1967-68	Detroit	1	1	1	3	3.0

CARTER, JOHN

b. July 25, 1924 Ht. 6-5

College—East Texas

Yr.	Team	G	FG	FT	TP	Avg.
1948-49	Hammond NL	62	133	188	454	7.3
1949-50	Den.-Anderson	24	23	36	82	3.4
	Totals	86	156	224	536	6.2

CERVI, AL

b. Feb. 12, 1917 Ht. 5-11 Wt. 185

Yr.	Team	G	FG	FT	TP	Avg.
1945-46	Rochester NL	28	112	77	301	10.8
1946-47	Rochester NL	44	228	176	632	14.4
1947-48	Rochester NL	50	233	187	653	13.1
1948-49	Syracuse NL	57	204	287	695	12.2
1949-50	Syracuse	56	143	287	573	10.2
1950-51	Syracuse	53	132	194	458	8.6
1951-52	Syracuse	55	99	219	417	7.6
1952-53	Syracuse	38	31	81	143	3.8
	Totals	381	1182	1508	3872	10.2

CHAMBERLAIN, WILT

b. Aug. 21, 1936 Ht. 7-1 Wt. 275

College—Kansas

Yr.	Team	G	FG	FT	TP	Avg.
1959-60	Philadelphia	72	1065	577	2707	37.6
1960-61	Philadelphia	79	1251	531	3033	38.4
1961-62	Philadelphia	80	1597	835	4029	50.4
1962-63	San Francisco	80	1463	660	3586	44.8
1963-64	San Francisco	80	1204	540	2948	36.9
1964-65	S.F.-Philadelphia	73	1063	408	2534	34.7
1965-66	Philadelphia	79	1074	501	2649	33.5
1966-67	Philadelphia	81	785	386	1956	24.1
1967-68	Philadelphia	82	819	354	1992	24.3
	Totals	706	10321	4792	25434	36.0

CHAMBERS, JERRY

b. July 18, 1943 Ht. 6-5 Wt. 186

College—Utah

Yr.	Team	G	FG	FT	TP	Avg.
1966-67	Los Angeles	69	224	68	516	7.5

CHANEY, JOHN

b. Feb. 29, 1920 Ht. 6-3

College—Louisiana State

Yr.	Team	G	FG	FT	TP	Avg.
1946-47	Syracuse NL	42	138	86	362	8.6
1947-48	Syracuse NL	40	107	80	294	7.4
1948-49	Syracuse NL	57	79	65	223	3.9
1949-50	Tri-Cities-She.	16	25	20	70	4.4
	Totals	155	349	251	949	6.1

CHAPPELL, LEONARD

b. Jan. 31, 1941 Ht. 6-8 Wt. 240

College—Wake Forest

Yr.	Team	G	FG	FT	TP	Avg.
1962-63	Syracuse	80	281	148	710	8.9
1963-64	Philadelphia-N.Y.	79	531	288	1350	17.1
1964-65	New York	43	145	68	358	8.3
1965-66	New York	46	100	46	246	5.3
1966-67	Chicago-Cinn.	73	132	53	317	4.3
1967-68	Cinn.-Detroit	68	235	138	608	8.9
	Totals	389	1424	741	3589	9.2

CHOLLET, LEROY

Ht. 6-2 Wt. 190

College—Canisius

Yr.	Team	G	FG	FT	TP	Avg.
1949-50	Syracuse	49	61	35	157	3.2
1950-51	Syracuse	14	6	12	24	1.7
	Totals	63	67	47	181	2.9

CHRIST, FRED

Ht. 6-4 Wt. 210

College—Fordham

Yr.	Team	G	FG	FT	TP	Avg.
1954-55	New York	6	5	10	20	3.3

CHRISTENSEN, CAL

b. June 6, 1927 Ht. 6-5 Wt. 210

College—Toledo

Yr.	Team	G	FG	FT	TP	Avg.
1950-51	Tri-Cities	67	134	175	443	6.6
1951-52	Milwaukee	24	29	57	88	3.7
1952-53	Rochester	59	72	68	212	3.6
1953-54	Rochester	70	137	138	412	5.9
1954-55	Rochester	71	114	124	352	5.0
	Totals	291	486	535	1507	5.2

CLARK, ARCHIE

b. July 15, 1941 Ht. 6-2 Wt. 175

College—Minnesota

Yr.	Team	G	FG	FT	TP	Avg.
1966-67	Los Angeles	76	331	136	798	10.5
1967-68	Los Angeles	81	628	356	1612	19.9
	Totals	157	959	492	2410	15.4

CLEMENS, BARRY

b. May 1, 1942 Ht. 6-7 Wt. 210

College—Ohio Wesleyan

Yr.	Team	G	FG	FT	TP	Avg.
1965-66	New York	70	161	54	376	5.4
1966-67	Chicago	60	186	68	440	7.3
1967-68	Chicago	78	301	123	725	9.3
	Totals	208	648	245	1541	7.4

CLIFTON, NATHANIEL (Sweetwater)

b. Oct. 13, 1922 Ht. 6-7 Wt. 225

College—Xavier (La.)

Yr.	Team	G	FG	FT	TP	Avg.
1950-51	New York	65	211	140	562	8.6
1951-52	New York	62	244	170	658	10.6
1952-53	New York	70	272	200	744	10.6
1953-54	New York	72	257	174	688	9.6
1954-55	New York	72	360	224	944	13.1
1955-56	New York	64	213	135	561	8.8
1956-57	New York	71	308	146	762	10.7
1957-58	Detroit	68	217	91	525	7.7
	Totals	544	2082	1280	5444	10.0

CLOSS, WILLIAM

b. Jan 8, 1922 Ht. 6-6 Wt. 205

College—Rice

Yr.	Team	G	FG	FT	TP	Avg.
1947-48	Indianapolis NL	55	161	72	394	8.1
1949-49	Anderson NL	64	203	110	516	8.1
1949-50	Anderson	64	283	186	752	11.8
1950-51	Philadelphia	65	202	166	570	8.8
1951-52	Ft. Wayne	57	120	107	347	6.1
	Totals	305	969	641	2579	8.5

CLOYD, PAUL

Ht. 6-2 Wt. 180

College—Wisconsin

Yr.	Team	G	FG	FT	TP	Avg.
1947-48	Sheboygan NL	60	209	128	546	9.1
1948-49	Sheboygan NL	56	119	98	336	6.0
1949-50	Balt.-Waterloo	7	7	5	19	2.7
	Totals	123	335	231	901	7.3

CLUGGISH, ROBERT

Ht. 6-10 Wt. 235

College—Kentucky

Yr.	Team	G	FG	FT	TP	Avg.
1946-47	New York	54	93	52	238	6.3

COLEMAN, JACK

b. May 23, 1924 Ht. 6-7 Wt. 230

College—Louisville

Yr.	Team	G	FG	FT	TP	Avg.
1949-50	Rochester	68	250	90	590	8.7
1950-51	Rochester	67	315	134	764	11.4
1951-52	Rochester	66	308	120	736	11.2
1952-53	Rochester	70	314	135	763	10.9
1953-54	Rochester	71	289	108	686	9.7
1954-55	Rochester	72	400	124	924	12.8
1955-56	Roch.-St. Louis	75	390	177	957	12.8
1956-57	St. Louis	72	316	123	755	10.5
1957-58	St. Louis	72	231	84	546	7.6
	Totals	633	2813	1095	6721	10.6

COLONE, JOE

Ht. 6-5 Wt. 210

Yr.	Team	G	FG	FT	TP	Avg.
1948-49	New York	15	35	13	83	5.3

COMLEY, LARRY

b. Aug. 17, 1939 Ht. 6-5 Wt. 210

College—Kansas State

Yr.	Team	G	FG	FT	TP	Avg.
1963-64	Baltimore	11	8	9	25	2.3

CONLEY, GENE

b. Nov. 10, 1930 Ht. 6-8 Wt. 255

College—Washington State

Yr.	Team	G	FG	FT	TP	Avg.
1952-53	Boston	39	35	18	88	2.3
1958-59	Boston	50	86	37	209	4.2
1959-60	Boston	71	201	76	478	6.7
1960-61	Boston	75	183	106	472	6.3
1962-63	New York	70	254	122	630	9.0
1963-64	New York	46	74	44	192	4.2
	Totals	351	833	403	2069	5.9

CONLIN, EDWARD

b. Sept. 2, 1933 Ht. 6-6 Wt. 200

College—Fordham

Yr.	Team	G	FG	FT	TP	Avg.
1955-56	Syracuse	66	211	121	543	8.2
1956-57	Syracuse	71	335	283	953	13.4
1957-58	Syracuse	60	343	215	901	15.0
1958-59	Syr.-Detroit	72	329	197	855	11.9
1959-60	Detroit	70	300	181	781	11.2
1960-61	Philadelphia	76	216	104	536	7.1
1961-62	Philadelphia	70	128	66	322	4.6
	Totals	485	1862	1167	4891	10.1

CONNORS, KEVIN (Chuck)

b. April, 10, 1921 Ht. 6-7 Wt. 205

College—Seton Hall

Yr.	Team	G	FG	FT	TP	Avg.
1946-47	Boston	49	94	39	227	4.6
1947-48	Boston	4	5	2	12	3.0
	Totals	53	99	41	239	4.5

COOK, BERT

b. April 26, 1929 Ht. 6-3 Wt. 186

College—Utah State

Yr.	Team	G	FG	FT	TP	Avg.
1954-55	New York	37	42	34	118	3.2

COOK, ROBERT

Ht. 5-10 Wt. 155

College—Wisconsin

Yr.	Team	G	FG	FT	TP	Avg.
1948-49	Sheboygan NL	63	169	99	437	6.9
1949-50	Sheboygan	51	222	143	587	11.5
	Totals	114	391	242	1024	9.0

COOPER, CHARLES (Chuck)

Ht. 6-5 Wt. 215

College—Duquesne

Yr.	Team	G	FG	FT	TP	Avg.
1950-51	Boston	66	207	201	615	9.3
1951-52	Boston	66	197	149	543	8.2
1952-53	Boston	70	157	144	458	6.5
1953-54	Boston	70	78	78	234	3.3
1954-55	Milwaukee	70	193	187	573	8.2
1955-56	Ft. Wayne	67	101	100	302	4.5
	Totals	409	933	859	2725	6.7

CORLEY, KENNETH

Ht. 6-8 Wt. 220

College—Georgetown

Yr.	Team	G	FG	FT	TP	Avg.
1946-47	Cleveland	3	0	0	0	0.0

CORLEY, RAY

Ht. 6-0 Wt. 180

College—Georgetown

Yr.	Team	G	FG	FT	TP	Avg.
1949-50	Syracuse	60	117	75	309	5.2
1950-51	Tri-Cities	18	29	16	74	4.1
1952-53	Ft. Wayne	8	3	5	11	1.4
	Totals	86	149	96	394	3.4

COSTELLO, LARRY

b. July 2, 1931 Ht. 6-1 Wt. 188

College—Niagara

Yr.	Team	G	FG	FT	TP	Avg.
1954-55	Philadelphia	19	46	26	118	6.2
1956-57	Philadelphia	72	186	175	547	7.6
1957-58	Syracuse	72	378	320	1076	14.9
1958-59	Syracuse	70	414	280	1108	15.8
1959-60	Syracuse	71	372	249	993	14.0
1960-61	Syracuse	75	407	270	1084	14.5
1961-62	Syracuse	63	310	247	867	13.7
1962-63	Syracuse	78	285	288	858	11.0
1963-64	Philadelphia	45	191	147	529	11.8
1964-65	Philadelphia	64	309	243	861	13.5
1966-67	Philadelphia	49	130	120	380	7.8
1967-68	Philadelphia	28	67	67	201	7.2
	Totals	706	3095	2432	8622	12.2

COTTON, JOHN

b. Oct. 15, 1924 Ht. 6-7 Wt. 205
College—Wyoming

Yr.	Team	G	FG	FT	TP	Avg.
1948-49	Denver NL	58	71	67	209	3.6
1949-50	Denver	54	97	82	276	5.1
	Totals	112	168	149	485	4.3

COUNTS, MEL

b. Oct. 16, 1941 Ht. 7-0 Wt. 230
College—Oregon State

Yr.	Team	G	FG	FT	TP	Avg.
1964-65	Boston	55	100	58	258	4.7
1965-66	Boston	67	221	120	562	8.4
1966-67	Baltimore-L.A.	56	177	69	423	7.6
1967-68	Los Angeles	82	384	190	958	11.7
	Totals	260	882	437	2201	8.5

COURTIN, STEVE

b. Sept. 21, 1942 Ht. 6-1 Wt. 188
College—St Joseph's (Pa.)

Yr.	Team	G	FG	FT	TP	Avg.
1964-65	Philadelphia	24	42	17	101	4.2

COUSY, BOB

b. Aug. 9, 1928 Ht. 6-1 Wt. 175
College—Holy Cross

Yr.	Team	G	FG	FT	TP	Avg.
1950-51	Boston	69	401	276	1078	15.6
1951-52	Boston	66	512	409	1433	21.7
1952-53	Boston	71	464	479	1407	19.8
1953-54	Boston	72	486	411	1383	19.2
1954-55	Boston	71	522	460	1504	21.2
1955-56	Boston	72	440	476	1356	18.8
1956-57	Boston	64	478	363	1319	20.6
1957-58	Boston	65	445	277	1167	18.0
1958-59	Boston	65	484	329	1297	20.0
1959-60	Boston	75	568	319	1455	19.4
1960-61	Boston	76	513	352	1378	18.1
1961-62	Boston	75	462	251	1175	15.7
1962-63	Boston	76	392	219	1003	13.2
	Totals	917	6167	4621	16955	18.5

COX, JOHN

b. Nov. 1, 1936 Ht. 6-4 Wt. 180
College—Kentucky

Yr.	Team	G	FG	FT	TP	Avg.
1962-63	Chicago	73	239	95	573	7.8

CRAWFORD, FRED

b. Dec. 23, 1941 Ht. 6-4 Wt. 190
College—St. Bonaventure

Yr.	Team	G	FG	FT	TP	Avg.
1966-67	New York	19	44	24	112	5.9
1967-68	New York-L.A.	69	224	111	559	8.1
	Totals	88	268	135	671	7.6

CRISLER, HERBERT

Ht. 6-3 Wt. 215

Yr.	Team	G	FG	FT	TP	Avg.
1946-47	Boston	4	2	2	6	1.5

CROCKER, DILLARD

Ht. 6-4 Wt. 205
College—Western Michigan

Yr.	Team	G	FG	FT	TP	Avg.
1948-49	Anderson NL	51	101	95	297	5.8
1948-49	Ft. Wayne	2	1	4	6	3.0
1949-50	Denver	53	245	233	723	13.6
1950-51	Indap.-Milw.	38	98	97	293	7.7
1951-52	Milwaukee	61	100	130	330	5.4
	Totals	205	545	559	1649	8.0

CROSSIN, FRANCIS

b. June 4, 1924 Ht. 6-11 Wt. 165
College—Pennsylvania

Yr.	Team	G	FG	FT	TP	Avg.
1947-48	Philadelphia	39	29	13	71	1.8
1948-49	Philadelphia	44	74	26	174	3.0
1949-50	Philadelphia	64	185	79	449	7.0
	Totals	147	288	118	694	4.7

CUNNINGHAM, BILLY

b. June 3, 1943 Ht. 6-6 Wt. 220
College—North Carolina

Yr.	Team	G	FG	FT	TP	Avg.
1965-66	Philadelphia	80	431	281	1143	14.3
1966-67	Philadelphia	81	556	383	1495	18.5
1967-68	Philadelphia	74	516	368	1400	19.0
	Totals	235	1503	1032	4038	17.2

CURE, ARMAND

b. Aug. 7, 1919 Ht. 6-4 Wt. 198
College—Rhode Island

Yr.	Team	G	FG	FT	TP	Avg.
1946-47	Providence	12	4	2	10	0.8

CURRAN, FRANCIS

b. Sept. 19, 1925 Ht. 6-0 Wt. 175
College—Notre Dame

Yr.	Team	G	FG	FT	TP	Avg.
1947-48	Toledo NL	57	125	116	366	6.4
1948-49	Rochester	57	61	85	207	3.6
1949-50	Rochester	66	98	199	395	6.0
	Totals	180	284	400	968	5.4

DAHLER, ED

b. Jan. 31, 1926 Ht. 6-5 Wt. 190
College—Duquesne

Yr.	Team	G	FG	FT	TP	Avg.
1951-52	Philadelphia	14	14	7	35	2.5

DALLMAR, HOWARD

b. May 24, 1922 Ht. 6-4 Wt. 202
College—Stanford and Pennsylvania

Yr.	Team	G	FG	FT	TP	Avg.
1946-47	Philadelphia	60	199	130	528	8.8
1947-48	Philadelphia	48	215	157	587	12.2
1948-49	Philadelphia	38	105	83	293	7.7
	Totals	146	519	370	1408	9.6

DARCEY, PETER

Ht. 6-9 Wt. 217
College—Oklahoma A&M

Yr.	Team	G	FG	FT	TP	Avg.
1952-53	Milwaukee	12	3	5	11	0.9

DARDEN, JAMES

Ht. 6-1 Wt. 170
College—Denver

Yr.	Team	G	FG	FT	TP	Avg.
1948-49	Denver NL	58	197	193	587	10.1
1949-50	Denver	26	78	55	211	4.3
	Totals	84	275	248	798	9.5

DARROW, JAMES

b. Sept. 25, 1937 Ht. 5-10¾ Wt. 175
College—Bowling Green

Yr.	Team	G	FG	FT	TP	Avg.
1961-62	St. Louis	5	3	6	12	2.4

DAVIES, BOB

b. Jan. 15, 1920 Ht. 6-1 Wt. 175
College—Seton Hall

Yr.	Team	G	FG	FT	TP	Avg.
1945-46	Rochester NL	27	86	70	242	9.0
1946-47	Rochester NL	32	166	130	462	14.4

Yr.	Team	G	FG	FT	TP	Avg.
1947-48	Rochester NL	48	176	121	473	9.9
1948-49	Rochester	60	317	270	904	15.1
1949-50	Rochester	64	317	261	895	14.0
1950-51	Rochester	63	326	303	955	15.2
1951-52	Rochester	65	379	294	1052	16.2
1952-53	Rochester	66	339	351	1029	15.6
1953-54	Rochester	72	288	311	887	12.3
1954-55	Rochester	72	326	220	872	12.1
	Totals	569	2720	2331	7771	13.7

DAVIS, AUBREY

Ht. 6-2 Wt. 175

College—Oklahoma Baptist

Yr.	Team	G	FG	FT	TP	Avg.
1946-47	St. Louis	59	107	73	287	4.9
1948-49	Hammond NL	7	3	3	9	1.3
	Totals	66	110	76	296	4.5

DAVIS, JAMES

Ht. 6-7 Wt. 220

College—St. John's (N. Y.)

Yr.	Team	G	FG	FT	TP	Avg.
1955-56	Rochester	3	0	2	2	0.7

DAVIS, JIM

b. Dec. 18, 1941 Ht. 6-9½ Wt. 235

College—Colorado

Yr.	Team	G	FG	FT	TP	Avg.
1967-68	St. Louis	50	61	25	147	2.9

DAVIS, RALPH

b. Sept. 7, 1938 Ht. 6-4 Wt. 180

College—Cincinnati

Yr.	Team	G	FG	FT	TP	Avg.
1960-61	Cincinnati	73	181	34	396	5.4
1961-62	Chicago	77	364	71	799	10.4
	Totals	150	545	105	1195	8.0

DAVIS, WALTER

b. Jan. 5, 1931 Ht. 6-8 Wt. 205

College—Texas A&M

Yr.	Team	G	FG	FT	TP	Avg.
1953-54	Philadelphia	68	167	65	399	5.9
1954-55	Philadelphia	61	70	35	175	2.9
1955-56	Philadelphia	70	123	77	323	4.6
1956-57	Philadelphia	65	178	74	430	6.6
1957-58	Phila.-St. Louis	61	85	61	231	3.8
	Totals	325	623	312	1558	4.8

DAVIS, WILLIAM

b. Oct. 3, 1921 Ht. 6-3 Wt. 215

College—Notre Dame

Yr.	Team	G	FG	FT	TP	Avg.
1946-47	Chicago	47	35	14	84	1.8

DeBUSSCHERE, DAVE

b. Oct. 16, 1940 Ht. 6-6 Wt. 220

College—Detroit

Yr.	Team	G	FG	FT	TP	Avg.
1962-63	Detroit	80	406	206	1018	12.7
1963-64	Detroit	15	52	25	129	8.6
1964-65	Detroit	79	508	306	1322	16.7
1965-66	Detroit	79	524	249	1297	16.4
1966-67	Detroit	78	531	361	1423	18.2
1967-68	Detroit	80	573	289	1435	17.9
	Totals	411	2594	1436	6624	16.1

DEES, ARCHIE

b. Feb. 22, 1936 Ht. 6-8 Wt. 205

College—Indiana

Yr.	Team	G	FG	FT	TP	Avg.
1958-59	Cincinnati	68	200	159	559	8.2
1959-60	Detroit	73	271	165	707	9.7
1960-61	Detroit	28	53	39	145	5.2
1961-62	Chicago-St. Louis	21	51	35	137	6.5
	Totals	190	575	398	1548	8.1

DEHNERT, ROBERT

Ht. 6-3 Wt. 178

Yr.	Team	G	FG	FT	TP	Avg.
1946-47	Providence	10	6	2	14	1.4

DeLONG, NATE

Ht. 6-6 Wt. 220

College—River Falls

Yr.	Team	G	FG	FT	TP	Avg.
1951-52	Milwaukee	17	20	24	64	3.8

DEMPSEY, GEORGE

b. July 19, 1929 Ht. 6-3 Wt. 192

College—King's (N. Y.)

Yr.	Team	G	FG	FT	TP	Avg.
1954-55	Philadelphia	48	127	98	352	7.3
1955-56	Philadelphia	72	126	88	340	4.7
1956-57	Philadelphia	71	134	55	323	4.5
1957-58	Philadelphia	67	112	70	294	5.1
	Totals	258	499	311	1309	5.1

DENNING, BLAINE

Ht. 6-2 Wt. 175

College—Lawrence Tech

Yr.	Team	G	FG	FT	TP	Avg.
1952-53	Baltimore	1	2	1	5	5.0

DEUTSCH, DAVE

b. May 13, 1945 Ht. 6-1 Wt. 170

College—Rochester

Yr.	Team	G	FG	FT	TP	Avg.
1966-67	New York	19	6	9	21	1.1

DEVLIN, WALTER (Corky)

b. Dec. 21, 1931 Ht. 6-5 Wt. 195

College—George Washington

Yr.	Team	G	FG	FT	TP	Avg.
1955-56	Fort Wayne	69	200	146	546	7.9
1956-57	Fort Wayne	71	190	97	477	6.7
1957-58	Minneapolis	70	170	133	473	6.8
	Totals	210	560	376	1496	7.1

De ZONIE, HANK

Ht. 6-6 Wt. 215

College—Clark (Ga.)

Yr.	Team	G	FG	FT	TP	Avg.
1950-51	Tri-Cities	5	6	5	17	3.4

DICKEY, DICK

b. Oct. 26, 1926 Ht. 6-1 Wt. 175

College—North Carolina State

Yr.	Team	G	FG	FT	TP	Avg.
1951-52	Boston	45	40	47	127	2.8

DIERKING, CONNIE

b. Oct. 2, 1936 Ht. 6-10 Wt. 222

College—Cincinnati

Yr.	Team	G	FG	FT	TP	Avg.
1958-59	Syracuse	64	105	83	293	3.6
1959-60	Syracuse	71	192	108	492	6.9
1963-64	Philadelphia	76	191	114	496	6.5
1964-65	Phil.-San Fr.	68	218	100	536	7.9
1965-66	Cincinnati	57	134	50	318	5.6
1966-67	Cincinnati	77	291	134	716	9.3
1967-68	Cincinnati	81	544	237	1325	16.4
	Totals	494	1675	826	4176	8.5

DILLE, ROBERT

Ht. 6-3 Wt. 200

College—Valparaiso

Yr.	Team	G	FG	FT	TP	Avg.
1946-47	Detroit	57	111	74	296	5.2

Yr.	Team	G	FG	FT	TP	Avg.

DILLON, JOHN (Hooks)

Ht. 6-3 Wt. 180
College—Kentucky and North Carolina

Yr.	Team	G	FG	FT	TP	Avg.
1949-50	Washington	22	10	16	36	1.6

DINWIDDIE, BILL

b. 1943 Ht. 6-7 Wt. 220
College—New Mexico Highlands

Yr.	Team	G	FG	FT	TP	Avg.
1967-68	Cincinnati	67	141	62	344	5.1

DISCHINGER, TERRY

b. Nov. 21, 1940 Ht. 6-7 Wt. 189
College—Purdue

Yr.	Team	G	FG	FT	TP	Avg.
1962-63	Chicago	57	525	402	1452	25.5
1963-64	Baltimore	80	604	454	1662	20.8
1964-65	Detroit	80	568	320	1456	18.2
1967-68	Detroit	78	394	237	1025	13.1
	Totals	295	2091	1413	5595	19.0

DIUTE, FRED

Ht. 6-3 Wt. 210
College—St. Bonaventure

Yr.	Team	G	FG	FT	TP	Avg.
1954-55	Milwaukee	7	2	7	11	1.6

DODD, EARL

Ht. 6-5
College—Northeast Missouri

Yr.	Team	G	FG	FT	TP	Avg.
1949-50	Denver	9	6	3	15	1.7

DOHLON, JOE

Ht. 6-0 Wt. 175
College—New York University

Yr.	Team	G	FG	FT	TP	Avg.
1949-50	Baltimore	64	143	157	443	6.9
1950-51	Baltimore	11	15	9	39	3.5
	Totals	75	158	166	482	6.4

DOLL, ROBERT

Ht. 6-5 Wt. 195
College—Colorado

Yr.	Team	G	FG	FT	TP	Avg.
1946-47	St. Louis	60	194	134	522	8.7
1947-48	St. Louis	42	174	98	446	10.6
1948-49	Denver NL	9	16	13	45	5.0
1948-49	Boston	47	145	80	370	7.9
1949-50	Boston	47	120	75	315	6.7
	Totals	205	649	400	1698	8.3

DONHAM, BOB

b. Oct. 11, 1926 Ht. 6-2 Wt. 190
College—Ohio State

Yr.	Team	G	FG	FT	TP	Avg.
1950-51	Boston	68	151	114	416	6.1
1951-52	Boston	66	201	149	551	8.3
1952-53	Boston	71	169	113	451	6.4
1953-54	Boston	68	141	118	400	5.9
	Totals	273	662	494	1818	6.7

DONOVAN, HARRY

Ht. 6-2 Wt. 190
College—Muhlenberg

Yr.	Team	G	FG	FT	TP	Avg.
1949-50	New York	45	90	73	253	5.6

DOVE, LLOYD (Sonny)

b. Aug. 16, 1945 Ht. 6-8 Wt. 198
College—St. John's (N. Y.)

Yr.	Team	G	FG	FT	TP	Avg.
1967-68	Detroit	28	22	12	56	2.0

DOWNEY, BILL

Ht. 6-6 Wt. 210
College—Marquette

Yr.	Team	G	FG	FT	TP	Avg.
1947-48	Providence	3	0	0	0	0.0

DOYLE, DANIEL

b. Feb. 6, 1940 Ht. 6-8 Wt. 200
College—Belmont Abbey

Yr.	Team	G	FG	FT	TP	Avg.
1962-63	Detroit	4	6	4	16	4.0

DUCKETT, RICHARD

b. Mar. 25, 1933 Ht. 6-1 Wt. 185
College—St. John's (N. Y.)

Yr.	Team	G	FG	FT	TP	Avg.
1957-58	Cincinnati	34	54	24	132	3.9

DUFFY, ROBERT

Ht. 6-4 Wt. 175
College—Tulane

Yr.	Team	G	FG	FT	TP	Avg.
1946-47	Chicago-Boston	17	7	5	19	1.1

DUFFY, ROBERT

b. Sept. 26, 1940 Ht. 6-3 Wt. 185
College—Colgate

Yr.	Team	G	FG	FT	TP	Avg.
1962-63	St. Louis	42	66	22	154	3.7
1963-64	St. L.-N.Y.-Det.	48	94	44	232	4.8
1964-65	Detroit	4	4	6	14	3.5
	Totals	94	164	72	400	4.3

DUKES, WALTER

b. June 23, 1930 Ht. 7-0 Wt. 220
College—Seton Hall

Yr.	Team	G	FG	FT	TP	Avg.
1955-56	New York	60	149	167	465	7.8
1956-57	Minneapolis	71	228	264	720	10.1
1957-58	Detroit	72	278	247	803	11.2
1958-59	Detroit	72	318	297	933	13.0
1959-60	Detroit	66	314	376	1004	15.2
1960-61	Detroit	73	286	281	853	11.7
1961-62	Detroit	77	256	208	720	9.3
1962-63	Detroit	62	83	101	267	4.3
	Totals	553	1912	1941	5765	10.4

DUNCAN, ANDREW

Ht. 6-6 Wt. 195
College—William & Mary

Yr.	Team	G	FG	FT	TP	Avg.
1947-48	Rochester NL	60	200	119	519	8.7
1948-49	Rochester	55	162	83	407	7.4
1949-50	Rochester	67	125	60	310	4.6
1950-51	Boston	14	7	15	29	2.1
	Totals	196	494	277	1265	6.5

DUNN, PAT

b. Mar. 17, 1931 Ht. 6-2 Wt. 170
College—Utah State

Yr.	Team	G	FG	FT	TP	Avg.
1957-58	Philadelphia	28	28	14	70	2.5

DWAN, JACK

b. May 3, 1921 Ht. 6-4 Wt. 200
College—Loyola (Ill.)

Yr.	Team	G	FG	FT	TP	Avg.
1948-49	Minneapolis	60	121	34	276	4.6

DYKER, GENE

b. Feb. 17, 1930 Ht. 6-6 Wt. 225
College—DePaul

Yr.	Team	G	FG	FT	TP	Avg.
1953-54	Milwaukee	11	6	4	16	1.5

Yr.	Team	G	FG	FT	TP	Avg.
	EARLE, ED					
	b. April 28, 1927 Ht. 6-3 Wt. 190					
	College—Loyola (Ill.)					
1953-54	Syracuse	2	1	2	4	2.0
	EBBEN, WILLIAM					
	Ht. 6-4					
	College—Detroit					
1957-58	Detroit	8	6	3	15	1.9
	EDDLEMAN, DWIGHT					
	b. Dec. 27, 1922 Ht. 6-3 Wt. 189					
	College—Illinois					
1949-50	Tri-Cities	64	332	162	826	12.9
1950-51	Tri-Cities	68	398	244	1040	15.3
1951-52	Milw.-Ft. Wayne	65	269	202	740	11.4
1952-53	Ft. Wayne	69	241	133	615	8.9
	Totals	386	1240	741	3221	8.4
	EGAN, JOHN					
	b. Jan. 31, 1939 Ht. 6-0 Wt. 180					
	College—Providence					
1961-62	Detroit	58	128	64	320	5.5
1962-63	Detroit	46	110	53	273	5.9
1963-64	Det.-New York	66	334	193	861	13.0
1964-65	New York	74	258	162	678	9.2
1965-66	N.Y.-Balt.	76	259	173	691	9.1
1966-67	Baltimore	71	267	185	719	10.1
1967-68	Baltimore	67	163	142	468	7.0
	Totals	458	1519	972	4010	8.8
	EGGLESTON, LOU					
	Ht. 6-0 Wt. 170					
	College—Oklahoma A&M					
1948-49	St. Louis	2	1	2	4	2.0
	EHLERS, ED					
	Ht. 6-3 Wt. 198					
	College—Purdue					
1947-48	Boston	40	104	78	268	7.2
1948-49	Boston	59	182	150	514	8.7
	Totals	99	286	228	800	8.2
	EICHHORST, RICHARD					
	b. Oct. 21, 1933 Ht. 6-3 Wt. 200					
	College—Southeast Missouri					
1961-62	St. Louis	1	1	0	2	2.0
	ELIASON, ROBERT					
	Ht. 6-2					
	College—Hamline					
1946-47	Boston	1	0	0	0	0.0
	ELLEFSON, RAY					
	b. Nov. 18, 1922 Ht. 6-8					
	College—Oklahoma A&M					
1948-49	Minneapolis	3	1	0	2	0.7
1948-49	Waterloo NL	6	4	6	14	2.3
1950-51	Baltimore	3	0	4	4	1.3
	Totals	12	5	10	20	1.7
	ELLIS, ALEX (Boo)					
	b. Feb. 11, 1936 Ht. 6-5 Wt. 185					
	College—Niagara					
1958-59	Minneapolis	72	163	102	428	5.9

Yr.	Team	G	FG	FT	TP	Avg.
1959-60	Minneapolis	46	64	51	179	3.9
	Totals	118	227	153	607	5.1
	ELLIS, JOSEPH					
	b. May 3, 1944 Ht. 6-6 Wt. 175					
	College—San Francisco					
1966-67	San Francisco	41	67	19	153	3.7
1967-68	San Francisco	51	111	32	254	5.0
	Totals	92	178	51	407	4.4
	ELLIS, LEROY					
	b. Mar. 10, 1940 Ht. 6-10 Wt. 210					
	College—St. John's (N. Y.)					
1962-63	Los Angeles	80	222	133	577	7.2
1963-64	Los Angeles	78	200	112	512	6.6
1964-65	Los Angeles	80	311	198	820	10.3
1965-66	Los Angeles	80	393	186	972	12.2
1966-67	Baltimore	81	496	211	1203	14.9
1967-68	Baltimore	78	380	207	967	12.4
	Totals	477	2002	1047	5051	10.6
	EMBRY, WAYNE					
	b. Mar. 26, 1937 Ht. 6-8 Wt. 255					
	College—Miami (Ohio)					
1958-59	Cincinnati	66	272	206	750	11.4
1959-60	Cincinnati	73	303	167	773	10.6
1960-61	Cincinnati	79	458	221	1137	14.4
1961-62	Cincinnati	75	564	356	1484	19.8
1962-63	Cincinnati	76	534	343	1411	18.6
1963-64	Cincinnati	80	556	271	1383	17.3
1964-65	Cincinnati	74	352	239	943	12.7
1965-66	Cincinnati	80	232	141	605	7.6
1966-67	Boston	72	147	82	376	5.2
1967-68	Boston	78	193	109	495	6.3
	Totals	753	3611	2135	9357	12.4
	ENDRESS, NED					
	b. Mar. 2, 1918 Ht. 6-2 Wt. 200					
	College—Akron					
1946-47	Cleveland	16	3	8	14	0.9
	ENGLUND, EUGENE					
	Ht. 6-5 Wt. 205					
	College—Wisconsin					
1945-46	Oshkosh NL	33	78	65	221	6.7
1946-47	Oshkosh NL	43	178	105	461	10.7
1947-48	Oshkosh NL	58	246	244	736	12.9
1948-49	Oshkosh NL	63	284	264	832	13.2
1949-50	Boston-Tri-Cities	46	104	152	360	7.8
	Totals	243	890	830	2610	10.8
	ERIAS, BALTICO					
	Ht. 6-3					
	College—Niagara					
1957-58	Minneapolis	18	59	30	148	8.2
	ERICKSON, KEITH					
	b. April 19, 1944 Ht. 6-5 Wt. 195					
	College—UCLA					
1965-66	San Francisco	65	95	43	233	3.6
1966-67	Chicago	76	235	117	587	7.7
1967-68	Chicago	78	377	194	948	12.2
	Totals	219	707	354	1768	8.1

Yr.	Team	G	FG	FT	TP	Avg.

ESKRIDGE, JACK
b. Jan. 21, 1924 Ht. 6-5 Wt. 200
College—Kansas

Yr.	Team	G	FG	FT	TP	Avg.
1948-49	Chicago	3	0	0	0	0.0
1948-49	Indianapolis	20	25	14	64	3.2
	Totals	23	25	14	64	2.8

EVANS, BOB
b. May 31, 1925 Ht. 6-2 Wt. 175
College—Butler

Yr.	Team	G	FG	FT	TP	Avg.
1949-50	Indianapolis	47	56	30	142	3.0

EZERSKY, JOHN
Ht. 6-3 Wt. 175

Yr.	Team	G	FG	FT	TP	Avg.
1947-48	Providence	25	95	63	253	10.1
1948-49	Prov.-Bos.-Balt.	56	128	109	365	6.5
1949-50	Balt.-Boston	54	143	127	413	7.6
	Totals	135	366	299	1031	7.6

FABEL, JOSEPH
Ht. 6-1 Wt. 190
College—Pittsburgh

Yr.	Team	G	FG	FT	TP	Avg.
1946-47	Pittsburgh	30	25	13	63	2.1

FARBMAN, PHILIP
Ht. 6-2 Wt. 185
College—CCNY

Yr.	Team	G	FG	FT	TP	Avg.
1948-49	Phil.-Bos.	48	50	55	155	3.2

FAIRCHILD, JOHN
b. April 28, 1943 Ht. 6-7½ Wt. 205
College—Brigham Young

Yr.	Team	G	FG	FT	TP	Avg.
1965-66	Los Angeles	30	23	14	60	2.0

FARLEY, RICHARD
b. April 13, 1932 Ht. 6-4 Wt. 190
College—Indiana

Yr.	Team	G	FG	FT	TP	Avg.
1954-55	Syracuse	69	136	136	408	5.9
1955-56	Syracuse	72	168	143	479	6.7
	Totals	142	304	279	887	6.3

FARMER, MIKE
b. Sept. 26, 1936 Ht. 6-7 Wt. 210
College—San Francisco

Yr.	Team	G	FG	FT	TP	Avg.
1958-59	New York	72	176	83	435	6.0
1959-60	New York	67	212	70	494	7.4
1960-61	N.Y.-Cinn	59	180	69	429	7.3
1962-63	St. Louis	80	239	117	595	7.4
1963-64	St. Louis	76	178	68	424	5.6
1964-65	St. Louis	60	167	75	409	6.8
	Totals	414	1152	482	2786	6.7

FAUGHT, ROBERT
b. Sept. 2, 1921 Ht. 6-5 Wt. 185
College—Notre Dame

Yr.	Team	G	FG	FT	TP	Avg.
1946-47	Cleveland	51	141	61	343	6.7

FEDOR, DAVID
b. Dec. 10, 1940 Ht. 6-6 Wt. 192
College—Florida State

Yr.	Team	G	FG	FT	TP	Avg.
1962-63	San Francisco	7	3	0	6	0.9

FEERICK, BOB
b. Jan 2, 1920 Ht. 6-3 Wt. 190
College—Santa Clara

Yr.	Team	G	FG	FT	TP	Avg.
1945-46	Oshkosh NL	21	81	36	198	9.3
1946-47	Washington	55	364	198	926	16.8
1947-48	Washington	48	293	189	775	16.1
1948-49	Washington	58	248	256	752	13.0
1949-50	Washington	60	172	139	483	8.1
	Totals	242	1158	818	3134	13.0

FEIGENBAUM, GEORGE
b. July 2, 1929 Ht. 6-1 Wt. 185
College—Long Island U. and Kentucky

Yr.	Team	G	FG	FT	TP	Avg.
1949-50	Baltimore	12	14	8	36	3.0
1952-53	Milwaukee	5	4	8	16	3.2
	Totals	17	18	16	52	3.1

FEIREISEL, RON
b. Aug. 6, 1931 Ht. 6-3 Wt. 185
College—DePaul

Yr.	Team	G	FG	FT	TP	Avg.
1955-56	Minneapolis	10	8	14	30	3.0

FELIX, RAY
b. Dec. 10, 1930 Ht. 6-11 Wt. 220
College—Long Island U.

Yr.	Team	G	FG	FT	TP	Avg.
1953-54	Baltimore	72	410	449	1269	17.6
1954-55	New York	72	364	310	1038	14.4
1955-56	New York	72	277	331	885	12.3
1956-57	New York	72	295	277	867	12.0
1957-58	New York	72	304	271	879	12.2
1958-59	New York	72	260	229	749	10.4
1959-60	N.Y.-Minneap.	47	136	70	342	7.3
1960-61	Los Angeles	78	189	135	513	6.6
1961-62	Los Angeles	80	171	90	432	5.4
	Totals	637	2406	2162	6974	10.9

FENDLEY, JAKE
b. June 12, 1929 Ht. 6-1 Wt. 180
College—Northwestern

Yr.	Team	G	FG	FT	TP	Avg.
1951-52	Ft. Wayne	58	54	75	183	3.2
1952-53	Ft. Wayne	45	32	40	104	2.3
	Totals	103	86	115	287	2.8

FENLEY, WILLIAM
Ht. 6-3
College—Manhattan

Yr.	Team	G	FG	FT	TP	Avg.
1946-47	Boston	23	31	23	85	3.7

FERRARI, ALBERT
b. July 6, 1933 Ht. 6-4 Wt. 190
College—Michigan State

Yr.	Team	G	FG	FT	TP	Avg.
1955-56	St. Louis	68	191	164	546	8.0
1958-59	St. Louis	72	134	145	413	5.7
1959-60	St. Louis	71	216	176	608	8.6
1960-61	St. Louis	63	117	95	329	5.2
1961-62	St. Louis	79	208	175	591	7.5
1962-63	Chicago	18	12	14	38	2.1
	Totals	371	878	769	2525	6.8

FERRIN, ARNOLD
b. July 29, 1925 Ht. 6-2 Wt. 180
College—Utah

Yr.	Team	G	FG	FT	TP	Avg.
1948-49	Minneapolis	47	130	85	345	7.3
1949-50	Minneapolis	63	132	76	340	5.4

Yr.	Team	G	FG	FT	TP	Avg.
1950-51	Minneapolis	68	119	114	352	5.2
	Totals	178	381	275	1037	5.8

FERRY, ROBERT

b. May 31, 1937 Ht. 6-8 Wt. 230
College—St. Louis

Yr.	Team	G	FG	FT	TP	Avg.
1959-60	St. Louis	62	144	76	364	5.9
1960-61	Detroit	79	350	189	889	11.3
1961-62	Detroit	80	411	286	1108	13.8
1962-63	Detroit	79	426	220	1072	13.6
1963-64	Detroit	74	298	186	782	10.6
1964-65	Baltimore	77	143	122	408	5.3
1965-66	Baltimore	66	188	105	481	7.3
1966-67	Baltimore	51	132	70	334	6.5
1967-68	Baltimore	59	128	73	329	5.6
	Totals	627	2220	1327	5767	9.2

FEUTSCH, HERMAN

Ht. 6-0 Wt. 170

Yr.	Team	G	FG	FT	TP	Avg.
1945-46	Cleveland NL	28	82	61	225	8.0
1947-48	Baltimore	42	42	25	109	2.6
	Totals	70	124	86	334	4.8

FILIPEK, RON

b. Feb. 5, 1944 Ht. 6-5 Wt. 210
College—Tennessee Tech

Yr.	Team	G	FG	FT	TP	Avg.
1967-68	Philadelphia	19	18	7	43	2.3

FINKEL, HENRY

b. April 20, 1942 Ht. 7-0 Wt. 240
College—Dayton

Yr.	Team	G	FG	FT	TP	Avg.
1966-67	Los Angeles	27	17	7	41	1.5
1967-68	San Diego	53	242	131	615	11.6
	Totals	80	259	138	656	8.2

FINN, DANIEL

b. May 27, 1928 Ht. 6-1 Wt. 185
College—St. John's (N. Y.)

Yr.	Team	G	FG	FT	TP	Avg.
1952-53	Philadelphia	31	135	99	369	11.9
1953-54	Philadelphia	68	170	126	466	6.9
1954-55	Philadelphia	43	77	53	207	4.8
	Totals	142	382	278	1042	7.3

FITZGERALD, RICHARD

Ht. 6-2 Wt. 175

Yr.	Team	G	FG	FT	TP	Avg.
1946-47	Toronto	60	118	41	277	4.6
1947-48	Providence	1	0	0	0	0.0
	Totals	61	118	41	277	4.6

FLEISHMAN, JERRY

b. Feb. 14, 1922 Ht. 6-2 Wt. 190
College—New York University

Yr.	Team	G	FG	FT	TP	Avg.
1946-47	Philadelphia	59	97	69	263	4.5
1947-48	Philadelphia	46	119	95	333	7.2
1948-49	Philadelphia	59	123	177	323	5.5
1949-50	Philadelphia	65	102	93	297	4.6
1952-53	Philadelphia	33	100	96	296	9.0
	Totals	262	541	430	1512	5.8

FLEMING, EDWARD

b. July 25, 1933 Ht. 6-3 Wt. 190
College—Niagara

Yr.	Team	G	FG	FT	TP	Avg.
1955-56	Rochester	71	306	277	889	12.5
1956-57	Rochester	51	109	139	357	7.0
1957-58	Minneapolis	72	226	181	633	8.8
1958-59	Minneapolis	71	162	137	461	6.5
1959-60	Minneapolis	27	59	53	171	6.3
	Totals	292	862	787	2511	8.6

FOLEY, JACK

b. Nov. 17, 1940 Ht. 6-5 Wt. 185
College—Holy Cross

Yr.	Team	G	FG	FT	TP	Avg.
1962-63	Boston-N.Y.	11	20	13	53	4.8

FORMAN, DON

b. Jan. 17, 1926 Ht. 6-1 Wt. 175
College—New York University

Yr.	Team	G	FG	FT	TP	Avg.
1948-49	Minneapolis	44	68	43	179	4.1

FOUST, LARRY

b. June 24, 1928 Ht. 6-9 Wt. 250
College—LaSalle

Yr.	Team	G	FG	FT	TP	Avg.
1950-51	Ft. Wayne	58	327	261	915	13.5
1951-52	Ft. Wayne	66	390	267	1047	15.9
1952-53	Ft. Wayne	67	311	336	958	14.3
1953-54	Ft. Wayne	72	376	338	1090	15.1
1954-55	Ft. Wayne	70	398	393	1189	17.0
1955-56	Ft. Wayne	72	367	432	1166	16.2
1956-57	Ft. Wayne	61	243	273	759	12.4
1957-58	Minneapolis	72	391	428	1210	16.8
1958-59	Minneapolis	72	301	280	882	12.3
1959-60	Minn.-St. Louis	72	312	253	877	12.2
1960-61	St. Louis	68	194	164	552	8.1
1961-62	St. Louis	57	204	145	553	9.7
	Totals	817	3814	3570	11198	13.7

FOWLER, JERRY

Ht. 6-8 Wt. 236
College—Missouri

Yr.	Team	G	FG	FT	TP	Avg.
1951-52	Milwaukee	6	4	1	9	1.5

FOX, JIM

b. May 7, 1943 Ht. 6-10 Wt. 230
College—South Carolina

Yr.	Team	G	FG	FT	TP	Avg.
1967-68	Cinn.-Detroit	55	66	66	198	3.6

FRANKEL, NAT

Ht. 6-0 Wt. 197

Yr.	Team	G	FG	FT	TP	Avg.
1946-47	Pittsburgh	6	4	8	16	2.7

FRAZIER, WALT

b. Mar. 29, 1945 Ht. 6-4 Wt. 202
College—Southern Illinois

Yr.	Team	G	FG	FT	TP	Avg.
1967-68	New York	74	256	154	666	9.0

FRAZIER, WILBERT

b. Aug. 24, 1942 Ht. 6-7 Wt. 210
College—Grambling

Yr.	Team	G	FG	FT	TP	Avg.
1965-66	San Francisco	2	0	1	1	0.5

FREY, FRIDO

Ht. 6-2 Wt. 195
College—Long Island U.

Yr.	Team	G	FG	FT	TP	Avg.
1946-47	New York	23	28	32	88	3.8

Yr.	Team	G	FG	FT	TP	Avg.
	FRIEND, LARRY					
	b. April 14, 1935 Ht. 6-4 Wt. 186					
	College—California					
1957-58	New York	44	74	27	175	4.0
	FRITSCHE, JAMES					
	b. Dec. 10. 1931 Ht. 6-8 Wt. 210					
	College—Hamline					
1953-54	Baltimore	68	116	49	281	4.1
1954-55	Ft. Wayne	16	16	13	45	2.8
	Totals	84	132	62	326	3.9
	FUCARINO, FRANK					
	Ht. 6-2 Wt. 175					
	College—Long Island U.					
1946-47	Toronto	28	53	34	140	5.0
	FULKS, JOSEPH (Jumpin' Joe)					
	Ht. 6-5 Wt. 190					
	College—Murray State					
1946-47	Philadelphia	60	475	439	1389	23.2
1947-48	Philadelphia	43	326	297	949	22.1
1948-49	Philadelphia	60	529	502	1560	26.0
1949-50	Philadelphia	68	336	293	965	14.2
1950-51	Philadelphia	66	429	378	1236	18.7
1951-52	Philadelphia	61	336	250	922	15.1
1952-53	Philadelphia	70	332	168	832	11.9
1953-54	Philadelphia	61	61	28	150	2.5
	Totals	489	2824	2355	8003	16.4
	GABOR, WILLIAM					
	b. May 13, 1922 Ht. 5-11 Wt. 170					
	College—Syracuse					
1948-49	Syracuse NL	55	113	124	350	6.4
1949-50	Syracuse	56	226	157	609	10.9
1950-51	Syracuse	61	255	179	689	11.3
1951-52	Syracuse	57	173	142	488	8.6
1952-53	Syracuse	69	215	217	647	9.4
1953-54	Syracuse	61	204	194	547	9.0
1954-55	Syracuse	3	7	3	17	5.7
	Totals	362	1193	961	3347	9.2
	GAINER, ELMER					
	Ht. 6-6 Wt. 195					
1947-48	Baltimore	5	1	3	5	1.0
1948-49	Waterloo NL	34	34	27	95	2.2
1949-50	Waterloo	15	9	6	24	4.6
	Totals	54	44	36	124	2.3
	GALLATIN, HARRY (The Horse)					
	b. April 26, 1928 Ht. 6-6 Wt. 215					
	College—Northeast Missouri					
1948-49	New York	52	157	120	434	8.3
1949-50	New York	68	263	277	803	11.8
1950-51	New York	66	293	259	845	12.8
1951-52	New York	66	233	275	741	11.2
1952-53	New York	70	282	301	865	12.4
1953-54	New York	72	258	433	949	13.2
1954-55	New York	72	330	393	1053	14.6
1955-56	New York	72	322	358	1002	13.9
1956-57	New York	72	332	415	1079	15.0
1957-58	Detroit	72	340	392	1072	14.9
	Totals	682	2810	3223	8843	13.0

Yr.	Team	G	FG	FT	TP	Avg.
	GAMBEE, DAVE					
	b. April 16, 1937 Ht. 6-6 Wt. 215					
	College—Oregon State					
1958-59	St. Louis	2	1	0	2	1.0
1959-60	St. L.-Cincinnati	61	117	69	303	5.0
1960-61	Syracuse	79	397	291	1085	13.7
1961-62	Syracuse	80	477	384	1338	16.7
1962-63	Syracuse	60	239	199	669	11.2
1963-64	Philadelphia	41	149	151	449	11.0
1964-65	Philadelphia	80	356	299	1011	12.6
1965-66	Philadelphia	72	168	159	495	6.9
1966-67	Philadelphia	63	150	107	407	6.5
1967-68	San Diego	80	375	321	1071	13.4
	Totals	618	2425	1980	6830	11.1
	GANTT, ROBERT					
	Ht. 6-4 Wt. 205					
	College—Duke					
1946-47	Washington	23	29	13	71	3.1
	GARDNER, EARL					
	Ht. 6-3 Wt. 200					
	College—DePaul					
1948-49	Minneapolis	50	38	13	89	1.8
	GARDNER, VERN					
	b. May 14, 1925 Ht. 6-5 Wt. 200					
	College—Utah					
1949-50	Philadelphia	63	313	227	853	13.5
1950-51	Philadelphia	61	129	69	327	5.4
1951-52	Philadelphia	27	72	15	159	5.9
	Totals	151	514	311	1339	8.9
	GARFINKEL, JACK (Dutch)					
	Ht. 6-0 Wt. 190					
	College—St. John's (N. Y.)					
1946-47	Boston	40	81	17	179	4.5
1947-48	Boston	43	114	35	263	6.1
1948-49	Boston	9	12	10	34	3.8
	Totals	92	207	62	476	5.2
	GARMAKER, DICK					
	b. Oct. 29, 1932 Ht. 6-3½ Wt. 206					
	College—Minnesota					
1955-56	Minneapolis	68	138	112	388	5.7
1956-57	Minneapolis	72	406	365	1177	16.3
1957-58	Minneapolis	68	390	314	1094	16.1
1958-59	Minneapolis	72	350	284	984	13.7
1959-60	Minn.-N.Y.	70	323	203	849	12.1
1960-61	New York	71	415	275	1105	15.6
	Totals	421	2022	1553	5597	13.3
	GATES, FRANK					
	b. April 12, 1920 Ht. 6-0 Wt. 167					
	College—Sam Houston State					
1948-49	Anderson NL	64	150	78	378	5.9
1949-50	Anderson	64	113	61	287	4.5
	Totals	129	263	139	665	5.2
	GAYDA, EDWARD					
	b. May 11, 1927 Ht. 6-4 Wt. 210					
	College—Washington State					
1950-51	Tri-Cities	14	18	18	54	3.9

GEORGE, JACK

b. Nov. 13, 1928 Ht. 6-3 Wt. 190
College—LaSalle

Yr.	Team	G	FG	FT	TP	Avg.
1953-54	Philadelphia	71	259	157	675	9.5
1954-55	Philadelphia	68	291	192	774	11.4
1955-56	Philadelphia	72	352	296	1000	13.9
1956-57	Philadelphia	67	253	200	706	10.5
1957-58	Philadelphia	72	232	178	642	8.9
1958-59	Phil.-N.Y.	71	233	153	619	8.7
1959-60	New York	69	250	155	655	9.5
1960-61	New York	16	31	20	82	5.1
	Totals	506	1901	1351	5153	10.2

GETCHELL, GORHAM

b. Aug. 14, 1920 Ht. 6-6 Wt. 215
College—Temple

Yr.	Team	G	FG	FT	TP	Avg.
1946-47	Pittsburgh	16	0	5	5	0.3

GIBSON, DEE

Ht. 6-5 Wt. 200

Yr.	Team	G	FG	FT	TP	Avg.
1948-49	Tri-Cities NL	62	93	113	299	4.8
1949-50	Tri-Cities	44	77	127	281	6.4
	Totals	106	170	240	580	5.5

GIBSON, MEL

b. Dec. 30, 1940 Ht. 6-3 Wt. 180
College—Western California

Yr.	Team	G	FG	FT	TP	Avg.
1963-64	Los Angeles	9	6	1	13	1.4

GIBSON, WARD

b. Dec. 6, 1921 Ht. 6-5 Wt. 198
College—Creighton

Yr.	Team	G	FG	FT	TP	Avg.
1948-49	Tri-Cities NL	63	293	223	809	12.8
1949-50	Waterloo	32	67	42	176	5.5
	Totals	95	360	265	985	10.4

GILLETTE, GENE

Ht. 6-2 Wt. 205
College—St. Mary's (Calif.)

Yr.	Team	G	FG	FT	TP	Avg.
1946-47	Washington	14	1	6	8	0.6

GILMUR, CHARLES

b. Aug. 13, 1922 Ht. 6-4 Wt. 225
College—Washington

Yr.	Team	G	FG	FT	TP	Avg.
1946-47	Chicago	51	76	26	178	3.5
1947-48	Chicago	48	181	97	459	9.6
1948-49	Chicago	56	110	66	286	5.1
1949-50	Chic.-Wash.	68	127	164	418	6.1
1950-51	Washington	16	17	17	51	3.2
	Totals	239	511	370	1392	5.8

GLAMACK, GEORGE

b. June 17, 1919 Ht. 6-6 Wt. 225
College—North Carolina

Yr.	Team	G	FG	FT	TP	Avg.
1948-49	Indianapolis	11	30	42	102	9.3

GLICK, NORMIE

b. Nov. 10, 1927 Ht. 6-7 Wt. 190
College—Loyola (Calif.)

Yr.	Team	G	FG	FT	TP	Avg.
1949-50	Minneapolis	1	1	0	2	2.0

GOLA, TOM

b. Jan. 13, 1933 Ht. 6-6 Wt. 205
College—LaSalle

Yr.	Team	G	FG	FT	TP	Avg.
1955-56	Philadelphia	68	244	244	732	10.8
1957-58	Philadelphia	59	295	223	813	13.8
1958-59	Philadelphia	64	310	281	901	14.1
1959-60	Philadelphia	75	426	270	1122	15.0
1960-61	Philadelphia	74	420	210	1050	14.2
1961-62	Philadelphia	60	322	176	820	13.7
1962-63	S.F.-N.Y.	73	363	170	896	12.3
1963-64	New York	74	258	174	670	9.1
1964-65	New York	77	204	133	541	7.0
1965-66	New York	74	122	82	326	4.4
	Totals	698	2964	1943	7871	11.3

GOLDFADEN, BEN

Ht. 6-1 Wt. 185
College—George Washington

Yr.	Team	G	FG	FT	TP	Avg.
1946-47	Washington	2	0	2	2	1.0

GOODRICH, GAIL

b. April 23, 1943 Ht. 6-1 Wt. 170
College—UCLA

Yr.	Team	G	FG	FT	TP	Avg.
1965-66	Los Angeles	65	203	103	509	7.8
1966-67	Los Angeles	77	352	253	957	12.4
1967-68	Los Angeles	79	395	302	1092	13.8
	Totals	221	950	658	2558	11.6

GOODWIN, WILFRED

Ht. 6-2 Wt. 203

Yr.	Team	G	FG	FT	TP	Avg.
1946-47	Providence	55	98	60	256	4.7
1947-48	Providence	24	36	19	91	3.8
	Totals	79	134	79	347	4.4

GORDON, PAUL

b. April 8, 1927 Ht. 6-3
College—Notre Dame

Yr.	Team	G	FG	FT	TP	Avg.
1949-50	Baltimore	4	0	3	3	0.8

GOTTLIEB, LEO

Ht. 5-11 Wt. 180

Yr.	Team	G	FG	FT	TP	Avg.
1946-47	New York	57	149	36	334	5.9
1947-48	New York	27	59	13	131	4.9
	Totals	84	208	49	465	5.3

GOVEDARICA, BATO

Ht. 5-11 Wt. 185
College—DePaul

Yr.	Team	G	FG	FT	TP	Avg.
1953-54	Syracuse	23	25	25	75	3.3

GRABOWSKI, JOE

b. Jan. 15, 1930 Ht. 6-8 Wt. 230

Yr.	Team	G	FG	FT	TP	Avg.
1948-49	Chicago	45	54	17	125	2.8
1949-50	Chicago	57	75	53	203	3.6
1951-52	Indianapolis	66	320	264	904	13.7
1952-53	Indianapolis	69	272	350	894	13.0
1953-54	Philadelphia	71	354	236	944	13.3
1954-55	Philadelphia	70	373	208	954	13.6
1955-56	Philadelphia	72	397	240	1034	14.4
1956-57	Philadelphia	72	390	252	1032	14.3
1957-58	Philadelphia	72	341	227	909	12.6
1958-59	Philadelphia	72	394	210	1058	14.7
1959-60	Philadelphia	73	217	131	565	7.7
1960-61	Philadelphia	68	169	127	465	6.8
1961-62	St. L.-Chi.-Syr.	38	77	39	193	5.1
	Totals	845	3433	2414	9280	11.0

Yr.	Team	G	FG	FT	TP	Avg.
	GRAHAM, MAL					
	b. Feb. 23, 1945 Ht. 6-1 Wt. 185					
	College—New York University					
1967-68	Boston	48	117	56	290	6.0
	GRANT, BUD					
	Ht. 6-3 Wt. 193					
	College—Michigan					
1949-50	Minneapolis	35	42	7	91	2.6
1959-51	Minneapolis	61	53	52	158	2.6
	Totals	96	95	59	249	2.6
	GRATE, DON					
	b. Aug. 27, 1922 Ht. 6-2					
	College—Ohio State					
1949-50	Sheboygan	2	1	2	4	2.0
	GRAY, GARY					
	b. 1945 Ht. 6-1 Wt. 185					
	College—Oklahoma City					
1967-68	Cincinnati	44	49	7	105	2.4
	GRAY, WYNDOL					
	b. Mar. 20, 1922 Ht. 6-1 Wt. 175					
	College—Harvard and Bowling Green					
1946-47	Boston	55	139	72	350	6.4
1947-48	Prov.-St. Louis	12	6	1	13	1.1
	Totals	67	145	73	363	5.4
	GREEN, JOHN					
	b. Dec. 8, 1933 Ht. 6-5 Wt. 200					
	College—Michigan State					
1959-60	New York	69	209	63	481	7.0
1960-61	New York	78	326	145	797	10.2
1961-62	New York	80	514	257	1285	16.1
1962-63	New York	80	582	280	1444	18.1
1963-64	New York	80	482	195	1159	14.5
1964-65	New York	78	346	165	857	11.0
1965-66	N.Y.-Balt.	79	358	202	918	11.6
1966-67	Baltimore	61	203	96	502	8.2
1967-68	San Diego-Phila.	77	310	139	759	10.0
	Totals	682	3330	1542	8202	12.0
	GREEN, SIHUGO					
	b. Aug. 20, 1934 Ht. 6-2 Wt. 185					
	College—Duquesne					
1956-57	Rochester	13	50	49	149	11.5
1958-59	Cinn.-St. Louis	46	146	104	396	8.6
1959-60	St. Louis	70	159	111	429	6.1
1960-61	St. Louis	76	263	174	700	9.2
1961-62	St.L.-Chicago	71	341	218	900	12.7
1962-63	Chicago	73	322	209	853	11.7
1963-64	Baltimore	75	287	198	772	10.3
1964-65	Baltimore	70	152	101	405	5.8
1965-66	Boston	10	12	8	32	3.2
	Totals	504	1732	1172	4636	9.2
	GREENSPAN, JERRY					
	b. Nov. 22, 1941 Ht. 6-5 Wt. 195					
	College—Maryland					
1963-64	Philadelphia	20	32	34	98	4.9
1964-65	Philadelphia	5	8	8	24	4.8
	Totals	25	40	42	122	4.9

Yr.	Team	G	FG	FT	TP	Avg.
	GREER, HAL					
	b. June 26, 1936 Ht. 6-2 Wt. 176					
	College—Marshall					
1958-59	Syracuse	68	308	137	753	11.1
1959-60	Syracuse	70	388	148	924	13.2
1960-61	Syracuse	79	623	305	1551	19.6
1961-62	Syracuse	71	644	331	1619	22.8
1962-63	Syracuse	80	600	359	1559	19.5
1963-64	Philadelphia	80	715	435	1865	23.3
1964-65	Philadelphia	70	539	335	1413	20.2
1965-66	Philadelphia	80	703	413	1819	22.7
1966-67	Philadelphia	80	699	367	1765	22.1
1967-68	Philadelphia	82	777	422	1976	24.1
	Totals	760	5996	3252	15244	20.1
	GREKIN, NORMAN					
	b. June 22, 1930 Ht. 6-5 Wt. 180					
	College—LaSalle					
1953-54	Philadelphia	1	0	0	0	0.0
	GRIGSBY, CHUCK					
	Ht. 6-5 Wt. 190					
	College—Dayton					
1954-55	New York	7	7	2	16	2.3
	GRIMSHAW, GEORGE					
	b. Sept. 24, 1919 Ht. 6-1 Wt. 185					
	College—Brown					
1946-47	Providence	21	20	21	61	2.9
	GROAT, DICK					
	b. Nov. 4, 1930 Ht. 6-1 Wt. 185					
	College—Duke					
1952-53	Ft. Wayne	26	100	109	309	11.9
	GROTE, JERRY					
	b. Dec. 28, 1940 Ht. 6-4 Wt. 216					
	College—Loyola (Calif.)					
1964-65	Los Angeles	11	6	2	14	1.3
	GROZA, ALEX					
	b. Oct. 7, 1926 Ht. 6-7 Wt. 218					
	College—Kentucky					
1949-50	Indianapolis	64	521	454	1496	23.4
1950-51	Indianapolis	56	492	445	1429	21.7
	Totals	130	1013	899	2925	22.5
	GUARILIA, GENE					
	b. Sept. 13, 1937 Ht. 6-5 Wt. 220					
	College—George Washington					
1959-60	Boston	48	58	29	145	3.0
1960-61	Boston	25	38	3	79	3.2
1961-62	Boston	46	61	41	163	3.5
1962-63	Boston	11	11	4	26	2.4
	Totals	130	168	77	413	3.2
	GUERIN, RICHIE					
	b. May 29, 1932 Ht. 6-4 Wt. 210					
	College—Iona					
1956-57	New York	72	257	181	695	9.7
1957-58	New York	63	344	353	1041	16.5
1958-59	New York	71	443	405	1291	18.2
1959-60	New York	74	579	457	1615	21.8
1960-61	New York	79	612	496	1720	21.8
1961-62	New York	78	839	625	2303	29.5

Yr.	Team	G	FG	FT	TP	Avg.
1962-63	New York	79	596	509	1701	21.5
1963-64	N.Y.-St. L.	80	351	347	1049	13.1
1964-65	St. Louis	57	295	231	821	14.4
1965-66	St. Louis	80	414	362	1190	14.9
1966-67	St. Louis	79	394	304	1092	13.8
	Totals	812	5124	4270	14518	17.9

GUNTHER, COULBY

b. Feb. 5, 1924 Ht. 6-4 Wt. 190
College—Brown

Yr.	Team	G	FG	FT	TP	Avg.
1946-47	Pittsburgh	52	254	226	734	14.1
1948-49	St. Louis	32	57	45	154	5.0
	Totals	84	311	271	893	10.6

GUNTHER, DAVID

b. July 22, 1937 Ht. 6-7 Wt. 220
College—Iowa

Yr.	Team	G	FG	FT	TP	Avg.
1962-63	San Francisco	1	1	0	2	2.0

GUOKAS, ALBERT

b. Aug. 7, 1925 Ht. 6-5 Wt. 200
College—St. Joseph's (Pa.)

Yr.	Team	G	FG	FT	TP	Avg.
1948-49	Denver NL	62	146	81	373	6.0
1949-50	Den.-Phil.	57	93	28	214	3.8
	Totals	119	239	109	587	4.9

GUOKAS, SR., MATT

b. Nov. 11, 1915 Ht. 6-3 Wt. 195
College—St. Joseph's (Pa.)

Yr.	Team	G	FG	FT	TP	Avg.
1946-47	Philadelphia	47	28	26	82	1.7

GUOKAS, JR., MATT

b. Feb. 25, 1944 Ht. 6-5 Wt. 175
College—St. Joseph's (Pa.)

Yr.	Team	G	FG	FT	TP	Avg.
1966-67	Philadelphia	69	79	49	207	3.0
1967-68	Philadelphia	82	190	118	498	6.1
	Totals	151	269	167	705	4.7

HAGAN, CLIFF

b. Dec. 9, 1931 Ht. 6-4 Wt. 215
College—Kentucky

Yr.	Team	G	FG	FT	TP	Avg.
1956-57	St. Louis	67	134	100	368	5.5
1957-58	St. Louis	70	503	385	1391	19.9
1958-59	St. Louis	72	646	415	1707	23.7
1959-60	St. Louis	75	719	421	1859	24.8
1960-61	St. Louis	78	661	383	1705	21.9
1961-62	St. Louis	77	701	362	1764	22.9
1962-63	St. Louis	79	491	244	1226	15.5
1963-64	St. Louis	77	572	269	1413	18.4
1964-65	St. Louis	77	393	214	1000	13.0
1965-66	St. Louis	74	419	176	1014	13.7
	Totals	746	5239	2969	13447	18.0

HAHN, BOB

b. Aug. 25, 1925 Ht. 6-10 Wt. 240
College—North Carolina State

Yr.	Team	G	FG	FT	TP	Avg.
1949-50	Chicago	10	4	2	10	1.0

HAIRSTON, HAROLD (Happy)

b. May 31, 1942 Ht. 6-7 Wt. 225
College—New York University

Yr.	Team	G	FG	FT	TP	Avg.
1964-65	Cincinnati	61	131	110	372	6.1
1965-66	Cincinnati	72	398	220	1016	14.1
1966-67	Cincinnati	79	461	252	1174	14.9
1967-68	Cinn.-Detroit	74	481	365	1327	17.9
	Totals	286	1471	947	3889	13.6

HALBERT, CHARLES

b. Feb. 27, 1919 Ht. 6-9 Wt. 225
College—West Texas

Yr.	Team	G	FG	FT	TP	Avg.
1946-47	Chicago	61	280	213	773	12.7
1947-48	Chi.-Phila.	46	156	140	452	9.8
1948-49	Bos.-Prov.	60	202	214	618	10.3
1950-51	Wash.-Balt.	68	164	172	500	7.4
	Totals	235	802	739	2343	9.9

HALBROOK, WADE (Swede)

b. Jan 30, 1933 Ht. 7-3 Wt. 235
College—Oregon State

Yr.	Team	G	FG	FT	TP	Avg.
1960-61	Syracuse	79	155	76	386	4.9
1961-62	Syracuse	64	152	96	400	6.2
	Totals	143	307	172	786	5.5

HALE, BRUCE

b. Aug. 31, 1918 Ht. 6-1 Wt. 170
College—Santa Clara

Yr.	Team	G	FG	FT	TP	Avg.
1946-47	Chicago NL	41	156	141	428	10.4
1947-48	Indianapolis NL	48	190	162	560	11.7
1948-49	Ft.W.-Ind.	52	187	172	546	10.5
1949-50	Indianapolis	64	217	223	657	10.3
1950-51	Indianapolis	26	40	14	94	3.6
	Totals	231	799	687	2285	9.9

HAMILTON, DALE

b. Aug. 16, 1919 Ht. 6-0 Wt. 198
College—Franklin

Yr.	Team	G	FG	FT	TP	Avg.
1947-48	Toledo NL	52	88	62	238	4.6
1948-49	Waterloo NL	61	77	93	247	4.0
1949-50	Waterloo	14	8	9	25	1.8
	Totals	127	173	164	510	4.0

HAMILTON, DENNIS

b. May 8, 1944 Ht. 6-8 Wt. 210
College—Arizona State

Yr.	Team	G	FG	FT	TP	Avg.
1967-68	Los Angeles	44	54	13	121	2.8

HAMILTON, RALPH

b. June 10, 1921 Ht. 6-1 Wt. 188
College—Indiana

Yr.	Team	G	FG	FT	TP	Avg.
1947-48	Ft. Wayne NL	49	143	101	387	7.9
1948-49	Ft. W.-Ind.	48	114	61	289	3.9
	Totals	97	257	162	676	7.0

HAMILTON, STEVE

b. Nov. 30, 1934 Ht. 6-7 Wt. 190
College—Morehead State

Yr.	Team	G	FG	FT	TP	Avg.
1958-59	Minneapolis	67	294	74	292	4.4
1959-60	Minneapolis	15	77	18	76	5.1
	Totals	82	138	92	368	4.5

HANKINS, CECIL

b. Jan. 6, 1922 Ht. 6-1 Wt. 175
College—Oklahoma A&M

Yr.	Team	G	FG	FT	TP	Avg.
1946-47	St. Louis	55	117	90	324	5.9
1947-48	Boston	25	23	24	70	2.8
	Totals	80	140	114	394	4.9

Yr.	Team	G	FG	FT	TP	Avg.
	HANNUM, ALEX					
	b. July 19, 1923 Ht. 6-7 Wt. 225					
	College—Southern California					
1948-49	Oshkosh NL	62	126	113	365	5.9
1949-50	Syracuse	64	177	128	482	7.5
1950-51	Syracuse	63	182	107	471	7.5
1951-52	Balt.-Rochester	66	170	98	438	6.6
1952-53	Rochester	68	129	88	346	5.1
1953-54	Rochester	72	175	102	452	6.3
1954-55	Milwaukee	53	126	61	313	5.9
1955-56	St. Louis	71	146	93	385	5.4
1956-57	Ft. W.-St. Louis	59	77	37	191	3.2
	Totals	578	1308	827	3443	6.0
	HANRAHAN, DON					
	b. Feb. 6, 1929 Ht. 6-7 Wt. 200					
	College—Loyola (Ill.)					
1952-53	Indianapolis	18	11	11	33	1.8
	HANS, ROLLEN					
	Ht. 6-2 Wt. 210					
	College—Long Island U.					
1953-54	Baltimore	67	191	101	483	7.2
1954-55	Baltimore	13	30	13	73	5.6
	Totals	80	221	114	556	7.0
	HARDING, REGGIE					
	b. May 4, 1942 Ht. 7-0 Wt. 255					
1963-64	Detroit	39	184	61	429	11.0
1964-65	Detroit	78	405	128	938	12.0
1966-67	Detroit	74	172	63	407	5.5
1967-68	Chicago	14	24	17	65	4.6
	Totals	205	785	269	1839	9.0
	HARDNETT, CHARLES					
	b. Sept. 13, 1938 Ht. 6-8 Wt. 225					
	College—Grambling					
1962-63	Chicago	78	301	225	827	10.6
1963-64	Baltimore	67	107	84	298	4.4
1964-65	Baltimore	20	25	23	73	3.7
	Totals	165	433	332	1198	7.3
	HARGIS, JOHN					
	b. Aug. 20, 1920 Ht. 6-0 Wt. 180					
	College—Texas					
1947-48	Anderson NL	59	232	172	636	10.8
1948-49	Anderson NL	57	169	106	444	7.8
1949-50	Anderson	60	223	197	643	10.7
1950-51	Tri-Cities-Ft. Wayne	14	25	17	67	4.8
	Totals	190	649	402	1790	9.4
	HARKNESS, JERRY					
	b. May 7, 1940 Ht. 6-2 Wt. 175					
	College—Loyola (Ill.)					
1963-64	New York	5	13	3	29	5.8
	HARRIS, BOB					
	b. Mar. 16, 1927 Ht. 6-7 Wt. 195					
	College—Oklahoma State					
1949-50	Ft. Wayne	62	168	140	476	7.7
1950-51	Ft. W.-Boston	56	98	86	282	5.0
1951-52	Boston	66	190	134	514	7.8
1952-53	Boston	70	192	133	517	7.4
1953-54	Boston	71	156	108	421	5.9
	Totals	325	804	601	2209	6.8
	HARRIS, CHRIS					
	Ht. 6-3 Wt. 190					
	College—Dayton					
1955-56	St. Louis-Roch.	41	37	27	101	2.5
	HARRISON, BOB					
	b. Aug. 12, 1927 Ht. 6-1 Wt. 190					
	College—Minneapolis					
1949-50	Minneapolis	66	125	50	300	4.6
1950-51	Minneapolis	68	150	101	401	5.9
1951-52	Minneapolis	65	156	89	401	6.2
1952-53	Minneapolis	70	195	107	497	7.1
1953-54	Milwaukee	64	144	94	382	6.0
1954-55	Milwaukee	72	299	126	724	10.1
1955-56	St. Louis	72	260	97	617	8.6
1956-57	Syracuse	66	243	93	579	8.8
1957-58	Syracuse	72	210	97	517	7.2
	Totals	615	1782	854	4418	7.2
	HASKINS, CLEM					
	b. Aug. 11, 1944 Ht. 6-2 Wt. 195					
	College—Western Kentucky					
1967-68	Chicago	76	273	133	679	8.9
	HASSETT, WILLIAM					
	b. Oct. 21, 1921 Ht. 6-1 Wt. 180					
	College—Notre Dame					
1947-48	Tri-Cities NL	57	203	196	602	10.6
1948-49	Tri-Cities NL	63	119	106	344	5.6
1949-50	Tri-Cities-Minn.	60	84	104	272	4.5
1950-51	Baltimore	30	45	40	130	4.3
	Totals	210	451	446	1348	6.4
	HATTON, VERNON					
	b. Jan. 13, 1936 Ht. 6-3 Wt. 195					
	College—Kentucky					
1958-59	Cincinnati-Phila.	64	149	77	375	5.9
1959-60	Philadelphia	67	127	53	307	4.6
1960-61	Philadelphia	54	97	46	240	4.4
1961-62	Chicago-St. Louis	40	112	98	322	8.0
	Totals	225	485	274	1244	5.5
	HAVLICEK, JOHN (Hondo)					
	b. April 8, 1940 Ht. 6-5 Wt. 205					
	College—Ohio State					
1962-63	Boston	80	483	174	1140	14.3
1963-64	Boston	80	640	315	1595	19.9
1964-65	Boston	75	570	235	1375	18.3
1965-66	Boston	71	530	274	1334	18.8
1966-67	Boston	81	684	365	1733	21.4
1967-68	Boston	82	666	368	1700	20.7
	Totals	469	3573	1731	8877	19.0
	HAWKINS, MARSHALL					
	b. Aug. 3, 1924 Ht. 6-3					
	College—Tennessee					
1949-50	Indianapolis	39	55	42	152	3.9
	HAWKINS, THOMAS					
	b. Dec. 22, 1936 Ht. 6-5 Wt. 210					
	College—Notre Dame					
1959-60	Minneapolis	69	220	106	546	7.9

Yr.	Team	G	FG	FT	TP	Avg.
1960-61	Los Angeles	78	310	140	760	9.7
1961-62	Los Angeles	79	289	143	721	9.1
1962-63	Cincinnati	79	299	147	745	9.4
1963-64	Cincinnati	73	256	113	625	8.6
1964-65	Cincinnati	79	220	116	556	7.0
1965-66	Cincinnati	79	273	116	662	8.4
1966-67	Los Angeles	76	275	82	632	8.3
1967-68	Los Angeles	78	389	125	903	11.6
	Totals	690	2531	1088	6150	9.0

HAZEN, JOHN

Ht. 6-2 Wt. 172
College—Indiana State

Yr.	Team	G	FG	FT	TP	Avg.
1948-49	Boston	6	6	6	18	3.0

HAZZARD, WALT

b. April 15, 1942 Ht. 6-2 Wt. 190
College—UCLA

Yr.	Team	G	FG	FT	TP	Avg.
1964-65	Los Angeles	66	117	46	280	4.2
1965-66	Los Angeles	80	458	182	1098	13.7
1966-67	Los Angeles	79	301	129	731	9.3
1967-68	Seattle	79	733	428	1894	23.9
	Totals	304	1609	785	4003	13.2

HEDDRICK, HERMAN

b. 1930 Ht. 6-5 Wt. 170
College—Canisius

Yr.	Team	G	FG	FT	TP	Avg.
1954-55	New York	5	2	0	4	0.8

HEINSOHN, TOM

b. Aug. 26, 1934 Ht. 6-7 Wt. 218
College—Holy Cross

Yr.	Team	G	FG	FT	TP	Avg.
1956-57	Boston	72	446	271	1163	16.2
1957-58	Boston	69	468	294	1230	17.8
1958-59	Boston	66	465	312	1242	18.8
1959-60	Boston	75	673	283	1629	21.7
1960-61	Boston	74	627	325	1579	21.3
1961-62	Boston	78	692	358	1742	22.3
1962-63	Boston	77	550	340	1440	18.7
1963-64	Boston	76	487	283	1257	16.5
1964-65	Boston	67	365	182	912	13.6
	Totals	654	4773	2648	12194	18.6

HEMRIC, DIXON (Dick)

b. Aug. 29, 1933 Ht. 6-6 Wt. 220
College—Wake Forest

Yr.	Team	G	FG	FT	TP	Avg.
1955-56	Boston	71	161	177	499	7.0
1956-57	Boston	67	109	146	364	5.4
	Totals	138	270	323	863	6.3

HENNESSEY, LAWRENCE

b. May 20, 1929 Ht. 6-3 Wt. 185
College—Villanova

Yr.	Team	G	FG	FT	TP	Avg.
1955-56	Philadelphia	53	85	26	196	3.7
1956-57	Syracuse	21	56	23	135	6.4
	Totals	74	141	49	331	4.5

HENDRICKSEN, DON

b. Oct. 10, 1929 Ht. 6-7 Wt. 225
College—California

Yr.	Team	G	FG	FT	TP	Avg.
1952-53	Baltimore	68	199	176	574	8.4
1954-55	Rochester	70	139	137	415	5.9
	Totals	138	338	313	989	7.2

HENRY, WILLIAM

b. Dec. 27, 1924 Ht. 6-9 Wt. 215
College—Rice

Yr.	Team	G	FG	FT	TP	Avg.
1948-49	Ft. Wayne	32	96	125	317	9.9
1949-50	Ft. W.-Tri-Cities	63	89	118	296	4.7
	Totals	95	185	243	613	6.4

HERMAN, BILL

b. May 17, 1924 Ht. 6-3 Wt. 170
College—Mt. Union

Yr.	Team	G	FG	FT	TP	Avg.
1949-50	Denver	13	25	6	56	4.3

HERMSEN, CLARENCE

b. Mar. 12, 1923 Ht. 6-9 Wt. 235
College—Minnesota

Yr.	Team	G	FG	FT	TP	Avg.
1946-47	Cleve.-Tor.	32	113	71	297	9.3
1947-48	Baltimore	48	212	151	575	12.0
1948-49	Washington	60	248	212	708	11.8
1949-50	Chicago	67	196	153	545	8.1
1950-51	Tri-Cities-Boston	71	189	155	533	7.5
1952-53	Bos.-Ind.	10	4	3	11	1.1
	Totals	288	962	745	2669	9.3

HERTZBERG, SIDNEY (Sonny)

b. July 29, 1922 Ht. 6-0 Wt. 195
College—CCNY

Yr.	Team	G	FG	FT	TP	Avg.
1946-47	New York	59	201	113	515	8.7
1947-48	N.Y.-Wash.	41	110	58	278	6.8
1948-49	Washington	60	154	134	442	7.4
1949-50	Boston	68	275	191	693	10.2
1950-51	Boston	65	206	223	635	9.8
	Totals	293	946	671	2563	8.7

HETZEL, FRED

b. July 21, 1942 Ht. 6-8 Wt. 230
College—Davidson

Yr.	Team	G	FG	FT	TP	Avg.
1965-66	San Francisco	56	160	63	383	6.8
1966-67	San Francisco	77	373	192	938	12.2
1967-68	San Francisco	77	533	395	1461	19.0
	Totals	210	1066	650	2782	13.2

HEWSON, JACK

b. Sept. 7, 1924 Ht. 6-6 Wt. 195
College—Temple

Yr.	Team	G	FG	FT	TP	Avg.
1947-48	Boston	24	22	21	65	2.7

HEYMAN, ARTHUR

b. June 24, 1941 Ht. 6-5 Wt. 205
College—Duke

Yr.	Team	G	FG	FT	TP	Avg.
1963-64	New York	75	432	289	1153	15.4
1964-65	New York	55	114	88	316	5.7
1965-66	Cinn.-Phila.	17	18	14	50	2.9
	Totals	147	564	391	1519	10.3

HICKEY, NAT

Ht. 5-11 Wt. 190

Yr.	Team	G	FG	FT	TP	Avg.
1947-48	Providence	1	0	0	0	0.0

HIGHTOWER, WAYNE

b. Jan. 14, 1940 Ht. 6-8½ Wt. 192
College—Kansas

Yr.	Team	G	FG	FT	TP	Avg.
1962-63	San Francisco	66	192	105	489	7.4
1963-64	San Francisco	79	393	260	1046	13.2
1964-65	San Fran.-Balt.	75	196	195	587	7.8

Yr.	Team	G	FG	FT	TP	Avg.
1965-66	Baltimore	24	63	57	183	7.6
1966-67	Balt.-Detroit	72	195	153	543	7.5
	Totals	316	1039	770	2848	9.0

HILL, CLEO

b. May 24, 1938 Ht. 6-1 Wt. 185
College—Winston-Salem State

1961-62	St. Louis	58	110	106	326	5.6

HILL, GARY

b. Oct. 7, 1941 Ht. 6-4 Wt. 185
College—Oklahoma City

1963-64	San Francisco	66	145	51	341	5.2
1964-65	San Fran.-Balt.	12	10	7	27	2.3
	Totals	78	155	58	368	4.7

HILLHOUSE, ARTHUR

Ht. 6-7 Wt. 220
College—Long Island U.

1946-47	Philadelphia	60	120	120	360	6.0
1947-48	Philadelphia	11	14	30	58	5.3
	Totals	71	134	150	418	5.9

HIRSCH, MEL

b. July 31, 1921 Ht. 5-8 Wt. 165
College—Brooklyn College

1946-47	Boston	13	9	1	19	1.5

HITCH, LEW

b. July 16, 1929 Ht. 6-8 Wt. 200
College—Kansas State

1951-52	Minneapolis	61	77	63	217	3.6
1952-53	Minneapolis	70	89	83	261	3.7
1953-54	Milwaukee	72	221	133	575	8.0
1954-55	Milwaukee	74	167	115	449	6.1
1955-56	Milw.-Minn.	69	94	100	288	4.2
1956-57	Minn.-Phila.	68	111	63	285	4.2
	Totals	414	759	557	2075	5.0

HOEFER, CHARLES (Dutch)

Ht. 5-9 Wt. 158
College—Hofstra

1946-47	Toronto	58	139	91	351	6.1
1947-48	Boston	7	3	4	10	1.4
	Totals	65	142	95	361	5.6

HOFFMAN, PAUL

b. April 12, 1922 Ht. 6-2 Wt. 205
College—Purdue

1947-48	Baltimore	37	142	104	388	10.5
1949-50	Baltimore	60	312	242	866	14.4
1950-51	Baltimore	41	127	105	359	8.8
1952-53	Baltimore	69	240	224	704	10.2
1953-54	Baltimore	72	253	217	723	10.0
1954-55	Phila.-N.Y.	38	65	64	194	5.1
	Totals	317	1139	956	3234	10.2

HOGGSETT, BOB

b. Jan. 29, 1941 Ht. 6-7 Wt. 230
College—Tennessee

1966-67	Detroit	7	5	6	16	2.3

HOGUE, PAUL

b. April 28, 1940 Ht. 6-9 Wt. 240
College—Cincinnati

Yr.	Team	G	FG	FT	TP	Avg.
1962-63	New York	50	152	79	383	7.7
1963-64	N.Y.-Balt.	15	12	2	26	1.7
	Totals	65	164	81	409	6.3

HOLCOMB, DOUGLAS

Ht. 6-4 Wt. 200
College—Wisconsin

1948-49	Baltimore	3	3	9	15	5.0

HOLLAND, JOE

b. Sept. 26, 1925 Ht. 6-4 Wt. 185
College—Kentucky

1949-50	Indianapolis	64	145	98	388	6.1
1950-51	Indianapolis	67	196	78	470	7.0
1951-52	Indianapolis	55	93	40	226	4.1
	Totals	186	434	216	1084	5.8

HOLSTEIN, JIM

b. Sept. 24, 1930 Ht. 6-3 Wt. 180
College—Cincinnati

1952-53	Minneapolis	66	98	70	266	4.0
1953-54	Minneapolis	70	88	64	240	3.4
1954-55	Minneapolis	62	107	67	281	4.5
1955-56	Ft. Wayne	27	24	24	72	2.7
	Totals	225	317	225	859	3.3

HOLUB, RICHARD

Ht. 6-6 Wt. 205
College—Long Island U.

1947-48	New York	48	195	114	504	10.5

HOLUP, JOSEPH

b. Feb. 26, 1934 Ht. 6-6 Wt. 215
College—George Washington

1956-57	Syracuse	71	160	204	524	7.4
1957-58	Syr.-Det.	59	91	71	258	4.8
	Totals	124	251	275	777	6.3

HOLZMAN, WILLIAM (Red)

b. Aug. 10, 1920 Ht. 5-10 Wt. 175
College—CCNY

1945-46	Rochester NL	34	144	77	365	10.7
1946-47	Rochester NL	44	227	74	528	12.0
1947-48	Rochester NL	60	246	117	609	10.2
1948-49	Rochester	60	225	96	546	9.1
1949-50	Rochester	68	206	144	556	8.2
1950-51	Rochester	68	183	130	496	7.3
1951-52	Rochester	65	104	61	269	4.1
1952-53	Rochester	46	38	27	103	2.2
1953-54	Rochester	51	74	48	196	3.8
	Totals	496	1447	774	3668	7.4

HOOVER, THOMAS

b. Jan. 23, 1941 Ht. 6-10 Wt. 240
College—Villanova

1963-64	New York	59	102	81	285	4.8
1964-65	New York	24	13	8	34	1.4
1966-67	St. Louis	17	13	5	31	1.8
	Totals	100	128	94	350	3.5

HOPKINS, ROBERT

b. Nov. 3, 1934 Ht. 6-8 Wt. 205
College—Grambling

1956-57	Syracuse	62	130	94	354	5.7

Yr.	Team	G	FG	FT	TP	Avg.
1957-58	Syracuse	69	221	123	565	8.2
1958-59	Syracuse	67	246	176	668	10.0
1959-60	Syracuse	75	257	136	650	8.7
	Totals	273	854	529	2237	8.2

HORAN, JOHN

b. Nov. 24, 1932 Ht. 6-8 Wt. 190
College—Dayton

Yr.	Team	G	FG	FT	TP	Avg.
1955-56	Minneapolis	19	12	10	34	1.8

HORN, RON

b. May 24, 1938 Ht. 6-7 Wt. 225
College—Indiana

Yr.	Team	G	FG	FT	TP	Avg.
1961-62	St. Louis	3	1	1	3	1.0
1962-63	Los Angeles	28	27	20	74	2.6
	Totals	31	28	21	77	2.5

HOUBREGS, BOB

b. Mar. 12, 1932 Ht. 6-8 Wt. 225
College—Washington

Yr.	Team	G	FG	FT	TP	Avg.
1953-54	Baltimore	70	209	190	608	8.7
1954-55	Balt.-Bos.-Ft. W.	64	148	129	425	6.6
1955-56	Ft. Wayne	70	247	283	777	11.1
1956-57	Ft. Wayne	60	253	167	673	11.2
1957-58	Detroit	17	49	30	128	7.5
	Totals	281	906	799	2611	9.3

HOWELL, BAILEY

b. Jan. 20, 1937 Ht. 6-7 Wt. 220
College—Mississippi State

Yr.	Team	G	FG	FT	TP	Avg.
1959-60	Detroit	75	510	312	1332	17.8
1960-61	Detroit	77	607	601	1815	23.4
1961-62	Detroit	79	553	470	1576	19.9
1962-63	Detroit	79	637	519	1793	22.7
1963-64	Detroit	77	598	470	1666	21.6
1964-65	Baltimore	80	515	504	1534	19.2
1965-66	Baltimore	79	481	402	1364	17.3
1966-67	Boston	81	636	349	1621	20.0
1967-68	Boston	82	643	335	1621	19.8
	Totals	709	5180	3962	14322	20.2

HUBBARD, ROBERT

Ht. 6-6 Wt. 215

Yr.	Team	G	FG	FT	TP	Avg.
1947-48	Providence	28	58	36	152	5.4
1948-49	Providence	34	25	22	72	2.1
	Totals	62	83	58	224	3.6

HUDSON, LOU

b. July 11, 1944 Ht. 6-5 Wt. 220
College—Minnesota

Yr.	Team	G	FG	FT	TP	Avg.
1966-67	St. Louis	80	620	231	1471	18.4
1967-68	St. Louis	46	227	120	574	12.5
	Totals	126	847	351	2045	16.2

HUNDLEY, RODNEY (Hot Rod)

b. Oct. 26, 1934 Ht. 6-4 Wt. 185
College—West Virginia

Yr.	Team	G	FG	FT	TP	Avg.
1957-58	Minneapolis	65	174	104	452	7.0
1958-59	Minneapolis	71	259	164	682	9.6
1959-60	Minneapolis	73	365	203	933	12.8
1960-61	Los Angeles	79	323	223	869	11.0
1961-62	Los Angeles	79	173	83	429	5.4
1962-63	Los Angeles	65	88	84	260	4.0
	Totals	432	1382	861	3625	8.4

HUNTER, LESLIE

b. Aug 16, 1942 Ht. 6-7 Wt. 212
College—Loyola (Ill.)

Yr.	Team	G	FG	FT	TP	Avg.
1964-65	Baltimore	24	18	6	42	1.8

HURLEY, ROY

Ht. 6-2 Wt. 170
College—Murray State

Yr.	Team	G	FG	FT	TP	Avg.
1946-47	Toronto	46	100	39	239	5.2

HUSTON, PAUL

b. June 2, 1925 Ht. 6-3 Wt. 175
College—Ohio State

Yr.	Team	G	FG	FT	TP	Avg.
1947-48	Chicago	46	51	62	164	3.6

HUTCHINS, MEL

b. Nov. 22, 1928 Ht. 6-6 Wt. 205
College—Brigham Young

Yr.	Team	G	FG	FT	TP	Avg.
1951-52	Milwaukee	66	231	145	607	9.2
1952-53	Milwaukee	71	319	193	831	11.7
1953-54	Ft. Wayne	72	295	151	741	10.3
1954-55	Ft. Wayne	72	341	182	864	12.0
1955-56	Ft. Wayne	66	325	142	792	12.0
1956-57	Ft. Wayne	72	369	152	890	12.4
1957-58	New York	18	51	24	126	7.0
	Totals	437	1931	989	4851	11.1

HUTTON, JOE

b. Oct. 6, 1928 Ht. 6-1 Wt. 170
College—Hamline

Yr.	Team	G	FG	FT	TP	Avg.
1950-51	Minneapolis	60	59	29	147	2.5
1951-52	Minneapolis	60	53	49	155	2.6
	Totals	120	112	78	302	2.5

IMHOFF, DARRALL

b. Oct. 11, 1938 Ht. 6-10 Wt. 220
College—California

Yr.	Team	G	FG	FT	TP	Avg.
1960-61	New York	62	122	49	293	4.7
1961-62	New York	76	186	80	452	5.9
1962-63	Detroit	45	48	24	120	2.7
1963-64	Detroit	58	104	69	277	4.8
1964-65	Los Angeles	76	145	88	378	4.8
1965-66	Los Angeles	77	151	77	379	4.9
1966-67	Los Angeles	81	370	127	867	10.7
1967-68	Los Angeles	82	293	177	763	9.3
	Totals	557	1419	699	3529	6.3

INGRAM, McCOY

b. Aug. 31, 1931 Ht. 6-0 Wt. 210
College—Jackson State

Yr.	Team	G	FG	FT	TP	Avg.
1957-58	Minneapolis	24	27	13	67	2.8

JACOBS, FRED

b. Dec. 2, 1922 Ht. 6-3 Wt. 175
College—Denver

Yr.	Team	G	FG	FT	TP	Avg.
1946-47	St. Louis	18	19	12	50	2.8

JACKSON, AL

b. July 29, 1943 Ht. 6-1½ Wt. 185
College—Wilberforce

Yr.	Team	G	FG	FT	TP	Avg.
1967-68	Cincinnati	2	0	0	0	0.0

JACKSON, LUCIOUS (Luke)

b. Oct. 31, 1941 Ht. 6-9 Wt. 240
College—Pan American

Yr.	Team	G	FG	FT	TP	Avg.
1964-65	Philadelphia	76	419	288	1126	14.8

Yr.	Team	G	FG	FT	TP	Avg.
1965-66	Philadelphia	79	246	158	650	8.2
1966-67	Philadelphia	81	386	198	970	12.0
1967-68	Philadelphia	82	401	166	968	11.8
	Totals	318	1452	810	3714	11.7

JACKSON, PHIL

b. Sept. 17, 1945 Ht. 6-8 Wt. 220
College—North Dakota

Yr.	Team	G	FG	FT	TP	Avg.
1967-68	New York	75	182	99	463	6.2

JAMES, GENE

b. Feb. 15, 1925 Ht. 6-4 Wt. 180
College—Marshall

Yr.	Team	G	FG	FT	TP	Avg.
1948-49	New York	11	18	6	42	3.8
1949-50	New York	29	19	14	52	1.8
1950-51	N.Y.-Baltimore	48	79	44	202	4.2
	Totals	88	116	64	296	3.1

JANISCH, JOHN

b. Mar. 15, 1920 Ht. 6-3 Wt. 200
College—Valparaiso

Yr.	Team	G	FG	FT	TP	Avg.
1946-47	Detroit	60	283	131	697	11.6
1947-48	Boston-Prov.	10	14	9	37	3.7
1947-48	Flint NL	35	36	22	94	2.7
	Totals	105	333	162	828	7.9

JANOTTA, TONY

Ht. 6-3
College—Seton Hall

Yr.	Team	G	FG	FT	TP	Avg.
1949-50	Baltimore	9	9	13	31	3.4

JAROS, ANTHONY

b. Feb. 22, 1920 Ht. 6-3 Wt. 185
College—Minnesota

Yr.	Team	G	FG	FT	TP	Avg.
1946-47	Chicago	59	177	128	482	8.2
1947-48	Minneapolis NL	57	89	82	260	4.6
1948-49	Minneapolis	59	132	79	343	5.8
1949-50	Minneapolis	61	84	72	240	3.9
1950-51	Minneapolis	63	88	65	241	3.8
	Totals	299	570	426	1586	5.2

JEANNETTE, HARRY (Buddy)

b. Sept. 15, 1917 Ht. 5-11 Wt. 175
College—Washington and Jefferson

Yr.	Team	G	FG	FT	TP	Avg.
1945-46	Fort Wayne NL	34	99	97	299	5.2
1947-48	Baltimore	46	150	191	491	10.7
1948-49	Baltimore	56	73	167	313	5.6
1949-50	Baltimore	37	42	109	193	5.2
	Totals	173	364	572	1300	7.5

JOHNSON, ANDY

b. Nov. 3, 1931 Ht. 6-5 Wt. 215
College—Portland

Yr.	Team	G	FG	FT	TP	Avg.
1958-59	Philadelphia	67	174	115	463	6.9
1959-60	Philadelphia	75	245	125	615	8.2
1960-61	Philadelphia	79	299	157	755	9.6
1961-62	Chicago	71	365	284	1014	14.3
	Totals	292	1083	681	2847	9.8

JOHNSON, ARNITZ

b. May 17, 1920 Ht. 6-5 Wt. 240
College—Bemidji State

Yr.	Team	G	FG	FT	TP	Avg.
1947-48	Rochester NL	57	101	97	299	5.2
1948-49	Rochester	60	156	199	511	8.5
1949-50	Rochester	68	149	200	498	7.3
1950-51	Rochester	68	185	269	639	9.4
1951-52	Rochester	66	178	301	657	10.0
1952-53	Rochester	70	140	303	583	8.3
	Totals	389	909	1369	3187	8.2

JOHNSON, GUS

b. Dec. 13, 1938 Ht. 6-6 Wt. 235
College—Idaho

Yr.	Team	G	FG	FT	TP	Avg.
1963-64	Baltimore	78	571	210	1352	17.3
1964-65	Baltimore	76	577	261	1415	18.6
1965-66	Baltimore	42	273	131	677	16.1
1966-67	Baltimore	73	620	271	1511	20.7
1967-68	Baltimore	60	482	180	1144	19.0
	Totals	329	2523	1053	6099	18.5

JOHNSON, HAROLD

b. Jan. 30, 1920 Ht. 6-6 Wt. 240
College—Indiana State

Yr.	Team	G	FG	FT	TP	Avg.
1946-47	Detroit	27	4	7	15	0.6

JOHNSON, NEIL

b. April 14, 1943 Ht. 6-7 Wt. 220
College—Creighton

Yr.	Team	G	FG	FT	TP	Avg.
1966-67	New York	51	59	57	175	3.4
1967-68	New York	43	44	23	111	2.6
	Totals	94	103	80	286	3.0

JOHNSON, RALPH

b. Dec. 6, 1921 Ht. 5-11 Wt. 170
College—Huntington

Yr.	Team	G	FG	FT	TP	Avg.
1948-49	Anderson NL	64	218	85	521	8.1
1949-50	Anderson-Ft. W.	67	243	104	590	8.8
1950-51	Ft. Wayne	68	235	114	584	8.6
1951-52	Ft. Wayne	66	211	101	523	7.9
1952-53	Ft. Wayne	3	3	2	8	2.7
	Totals	268	910	406	2226	8.3

JOHNSON, RONALD

b. July 20, 1938 Ht. 6-8 Wt. 215
College—Minnesota

Yr.	Team	G	FG	FT	TP	Avg.
1960-61	Detroit-L.A.	14	13	11	37	2.6

JOHNSTON, NEIL

b. Feb. 4, 1929 Ht. 6-8 Wt. 215
College—Ohio State

Yr.	Team	G	FG	FT	TP	Avg.
1951-52	Philadelphia	64	141	100	382	6.0
1952-53	Philadelphia	70	504	556	1564	22.3
1953-54	Philadelphia	72	591	577	1759	24.4
1954-55	Philadelphia	72	521	589	1631	22.7
1955-56	Philadelphia	70	499	549	1547	22.1
1956-57	Philadelphia	69	520	535	1575	22.8
1957-58	Philadelphia	71	473	442	1388	19.5
1958-59	Philadelphia	28	54	69	177	6.3
	Totals	516	3303	3417	10023	19.4

JOLLIFF, HOWARD

b. July 20, 1938 Ht. 6-7 Wt. 218
College—Ohio University

Yr.	Team	G	FG	FT	TP	Avg.
1960-61	Los Angeles	46	46	11	103	2.2
1961-62	Los Angeles	64	104	41	249	3.9
1962-63	Los Angeles	28	15	6	36	1.3
	Totals	138	165	58	388	2.8

JONES, JOHN

b. Mar. 12, 1943 Ht. 6-7 Wt. 205
College—Los Angeles State

Yr.	Team	G	FG	FT	TP	Avg.
1967-68	Boston	51	86	42	214	4.2

JONES, K. C.

b. May 25, 1932 Ht. 6-1 Wt. 202
College—San Francisco

Yr.	Team	G	FG	FT	TP	Avg.
1958-59	Boston	49	65	41	171	3.5
1959-60	Boston	74	169	128	466	6.3
1960-61	Boston	78	203	186	592	7.6
1961-62	Boston	79	289	145	723	9.1
1962-63	Boston	79	230	112	572	7.2
1963-64	Boston	80	283	88	654	8.2
1964-65	Boston	78	253	143	649	8.3
1965-66	Boston	80	240	209	689	8.6
1966-67	Bsoton	78	182	110	483	6.2
	Totals	675	1914	1171	4999	7.4

JONES, NICK

b. Mar. 28, 1945 Ht. 6-2 Wt. 191
College—Oregon

Yr.	Team	G	FG	FT	TP	Avg.
1967-68	San Diego	42	86	55	227	5.4

JONES, SAM

b. June 24, 1933 Ht. 6-4 Wt. 205
College—North Carolina College

Yr.	Team	G	FG	FT	TP	Avg.
1957-58	Boston	56	100	60	260	4.6
1958-59	Boston	71	305	151	761	10.7
1959-60	Boston	74	355	168	878	11.9
1960-61	Boston	78	474	210	1158	14.8
1961-62	Boston	78	589	239	1417	18.2
1962-63	Boston	76	621	257	1499	19.7
1963-64	Boston	76	612	249	1473	19.4
1964-65	Boston	80	821	428	2070	25.9
1965-66	Boston	68	626	325	1577	23.2
1966-67	Boston	72	638	318	1594	22.1
1967-68	Boston	73	621	311	1553	21.3
	Totals	802	5762	2716	14240	17.8

JONES, WALLACE (Wah Wah)

b. July 14, 1926 Ht. 6-4 Wt. 225
College—Kentucky

Yr.	Team	G	FG	FT	TP	Avg.
1949-50	Indianapolis	60	264	223	751	12.5
1950-51	Indianapolis	22	93	61	247	11.2
1951-52	Indianapolis	58	164	102	430	7.4
	Totals	140	521	386	1428	10.2

JONES, WALLY

b. Feb. 14, 1942 Ht. 6-2 Wt. 180
College—Villanova

Yr.	Team	G	FG	FT	TP	Avg.
1964-65	Baltimore	77	154	99	407	5.3
1965-66	Philadelphia	80	296	128	720	9.0
1966-67	Philadelphia	81	423	223	1069	13.2
1967-68	Philadelphia	77	413	159	985	12.8
	Totals	315	1286	609	3181	10.1

JONES, WALTER (Larry)

b. Sept. 22, 1941 Ht. 6-2 Wt. 180
College—Toledo

Yr.	Team	G	FG	FT	TP	Avg.
1964-65	Philadelphia	23	47	37	131	5.7

JONES, WILLIE

b. June 29, 1936 Ht. 6-3 Wt. 185
College—Northwestern

Yr.	Team	G	FG	FT	TP	Avg.
1960-61	Detroit	35	78	40	196	5.6
1961-62	Detroit	69	177	64	418	6.0
1962-63	Detroit	79	305	118	728	9.2
1963-64	Detroit	77	265	100	630	8.2
1964-65	Detroit	12	21	2	44	3.7
	Totals	272	846	324	2016	7.4

JORDON, PHIL

b. Sept. 12, 1933 Ht. 6-10 Wt. 205
College—Whitworth

Yr.	Team	G	FG	FT	TP	Avg.
1956-57	New York	9	18	8	44	4.9
1957-58	N.Y.-Detroit	58	193	64	450	7.8
1958-59	Detroit	72	399	231	1029	14.3
1959-60	Cincinnati	75	381	242	1004	13.4
1960-61	Cin.-N.Y.	79	360	208	928	11.7
1961-62	New York	76	403	96	902	11.9
1962-63	St. Louis	73	211	56	478	6.5
	Totals	442	1965	905	4835	10.9

JORGENSEN, JOHN

b. Dec. 28, 1921 Ht. 6-2 Wt. 185
College—DePaul

Yr.	Team	G	FG	FT	TP	Avg.
1947-48	Chicago-Balt.	3	4	1	9	3.0
1947-48	Minneapolis NL	32	33	24	90	2.8
1948-49	Minneapolis	48	41	24	106	2.2
	Totals	83	78	49	205	2.5

JORGENSEN, NOBLE

b. May 18, 1925 Ht. 6-9 Wt. 230
College—Iowa and Westminster (Pa.)

Yr.	Team	G	FG	FT	TP	Avg.
1946-47	Pittsburgh	15	25	16	66	4.4
1948-49	Sheboygan NL	64	218	194	630	9.6
1949-50	Sheboygan NL	54	218	268	704	13.0
1950-51	Tri-Cities-Syr.	63	223	182	628	10.0
1951-52	Syracuse	66	190	149	529	8.0
1952-53	Syracuse	70	145	146	436	6.2
	Totals	332	1019	955	2993	9.0

JORGENSEN, ROGER

b. Sept. 2, 1920 Ht. 6-5 Wt. 200
College—Ohio State

Yr.	Team	G	FG	FT	TP	Avg.
1946-47	Pittsburgh	28	14	13	41	1.5

KACHAN, ED

b. Sept. 15, 1925 Ht. 6-2 Wt. 175
College—DePaul

Yr.	Team	G	FG	FT	TP	Avg.
1948-49	Chicago	33	22	21	65	2.0
1948-49	Minneapolis	19	16	15	47	2.5
	Totals	52	38	36	112	2.2

KAFTAN, GEORGE

b. Feb. 22, 1928 Ht. 6-3 Wt. 190
College—Holy Cross

Yr.	Team	G	FG	FT	TP	Avg.
1948-49	Boston	21	116	72	304	14.5
1949-50	Boston	55	199	136	534	9.7
1950-51	New York	61	111	78	300	4.9
1951-52	New York	52	115	92	322	6.2
1952-53	Baltimore	23	45	44	134	5.8
	Totals	212	586	422	1594	7.5

KALAFAT, ED

b. Oct. 13, 1932 Ht. 6-6 Wt. 245
College—Minnesota

Yr.	Team	G	FG	FT	TP	Avg.
1954-55	Minneapolis	72	118	111	347	4.8

Yr.	Team	G	FG	FT	TP	Avg.
1955-56	Minneapolis	72	194	186	574	8.0
1956-57	Minneapolis	65	178	197	553	8.5
	Totals	209	490	494	1474	7.1

KAPLOWITZ, RALPH

Ht. 6-2 Wt. 170
College—New York University

Yr.	Team	G	FG	FT	TP	Avg.
1946-47	New York-Phila.	57	146	111	403	7.1
1947-48	Philadelphia	48	71	47	189	3.9
	Totals	105	217	158	592	5.6

KAPPEN, ANTHONY

Ht. 5-10

Yr.	Team	G	FG	FT	TP	Avg.
1946-47	Pitt.-Boston	59	128	128	384	6.5

KASID, EDWARD

b. Aug. 13, 1923 Ht. 5-11 Wt. 185

Yr.	Team	G	FG	FT	TP	Avg.
1946-47	Toronto	8	6	0	12	1.5

KATKAVECH, LEO

b. April 17, 1923 Ht. 6-0 Wt. 185
College—North Carolina State

Yr.	Team	G	FG	FT	TP	Avg.
1948-49	Washington	53	84	53	221	4.2
1949-50	Washington	54	101	34	236	4.4
	Totals	107	185	87	457	4.3

KAUTZ, WILBERT

Ht. 6-0 Wt. 180
College—Loyola (Ill.)

Yr.	Team	G	FG	FT	TP	Avg.
1946-47	Chicago	50	107	39	253	5.1

KEARNS, MICHAEL

Ht. 6-2 Wt. 178
College—Princeton

Yr.	Team	G	FG	FT	TP	Avg.
1954-55	Philadelphia	6	0	1	1	0.2

KELLER. KENNETH

Ht. 6-1 Wt. 180
College—St. John's (N. Y.)

Yr.	Team	G	FG	FT	TP	Avg.
1946-47	Wash.-Prov.	28	10	2	22	0.8

KELLEY, GERARD

Ht. 6-2 Wt. 172
College—Marshall

Yr.	Team	G	FG	FT	TP	Avg.
1946-47	Boston	43	91	74	256	6.0
1947-48	Providence	3	3	0	6	2.0
	Totals	46	94	74	262	5.7

KELLY, TOM

b. Mar. 5, 1924 Ht. 6-2 Wt. 172
College—New York University

Yr.	Team	G	FG	FT	TP	Avg.
1948-49	Boston	27	73	45	191	7.1

KENNEDY, WILLIAM (Pickles)

b. May 17, 1938 Ht. 5-11 Wt. 180
College—Temple

Yr.	Team	G	FG	FT	TP	Avg.
1960-61	Philadelphia	7	4	4	12	1.7

KENVILLE, BILL

b. Dec. 1, 1930 Ht. 6-2 Wt. 190
College—St. Bonaventure

Yr.	Team	G	FG	FT	TP	Avg.
1953-54	Syracuse	72	149	136	434	6.0
1954-55	Syracuse	70	172	154	498	7.1
1955-56	Syracuse	72	170	195	535	7.4
1956-57	Ft. Wayne	71	204	174	582	8.2
1957-58	Detroit	35	106	46	258	7.4

Yr.	Team	G	FG	FT	TP	Avg.
1959-60	Detroit	25	47	33	127	5.1
	Totals	345	848	738	2434	7.1

KERR, JOHN (Red)

b. Aug. 17, 1932 Ht. 6-9 Wt. 230
College—Illinois

Yr.	Team	G	FG	FT	TP	Avg.
1954-55	Syracuse	72	301	152	754	10.5
1955-56	Syracuse	72	377	207	961	13.3
1956-57	Syracuse	72	333	225	891	12.4
1957-58	Syracuse	72	407	280	1094	15.2
1958-59	Syracuse	72	502	281	1285	17.8
1959-60	Syracuse	75	436	233	1105	14.7
1960-61	Syracuse	79	419	218	1056	13.4
1961-62	Syracuse	80	541	222	1304	16.3
1962-63	Syracuse	80	507	241	1255	15.7
1963-64	Philadelphia	80	536	268	1340	16.8
1964-65	Philadelphia	80	264	126	654	8.2
1965-66	Baltimore	71	286	209	781	11.0
	Totals	905	4909	2682	12480	13.8

KERRIS, JACK

b. Jan. 30, 1925 Ht. 6-6 Wt. 215
College—Loyola (Ill.)

Yr.	Team	G	FG	FT	TP	Avg.
1949-50	Tri-Cities-Ft. W.	68	157	169	483	7.1
1950-51	Ft. Wayne	68	255	201	711	10.5
1951-52	Ft. Wayne	66	186	217	589	8.9
1952-53	Baltimore	69	93	88	274	4.0
	Totals	271	691	675	2057	7.6

KILEY, JACK

Ht. 6-1 Wt. 170
College—Syracuse

Yr.	Team	G	FG	FT	TP	Avg.
1951-52	Ft. Wayne	47	44	30	118	2.5
1951-52	Ft. Wayne	6	2	2	6	1.0
	Totals	53	46	32	124	2.3

KIMBALL, TOBY

b. Sept. 23, 1942 Ht. 6-8 Wt. 220
College—Connecticut

Yr.	Team	G	FG	FT	TP	Avg.
1966-67	Boston	38	36	27	97	2.6
1967-68	San Diego	81	354	181	889	11.0
	Totals	119	390	208	986	8.3

KING, DANIEL

b. Jan. 7, 1931 Ht. 6-6 Wt. 220
College—Western Kentucky

Yr.	Team	G	FG	FT	TP	Avg.
1954-55	Baltimore	12	7	5	19	1.6

KING, GEORGE

b. Aug. 16, 1928 Ht. 6-0 Wt. 185
College—Morris Harvey

Yr.	Team	G	FG	FT	TP	Avg.
1951-52	Syracuse	66	235	188	658	10.0
1952-53	Syracuse	71	255	284	794	11.2
1953-54	Syracuse	72	280	257	807	11.3
1954-55	Syracuse	67	228	140	596	8.9
1955-56	Syracuse	72	284	176	744	10.3
1957-58	Cincinnati	63	235	140	610	9.7
	Totals	411	1517	1185	4219	10.4

KING, JAMES

b. Feb. 7, 1941 Ht. 6-2 Wt. 175
College—Tulsa

Yr.	Team	G	FG	FT	TP	Avg.
1963-64	Los Angeles	60	84	66	234	3.9

Yr.	Team	G	FG	FT	TP	Avg.
1964-65	Los Angeles	77	184	118	486	6.3
1965-66	Los Angeles	76	238	94	570	7.5
1966-67	San Francisco	67	286	174	746	11.1
1967-68	San Francisco	54	340	217	897	16.6
	Totals	334	1132	669	2933	8.8

KING, MAURICE

b. Mar. 12, 1935 Ht. 6-3 Wt. 195
College—Kansas

Yr.	Team	G	FG	FT	TP	Avg.
1959-60	Boston	1	5	0	10	10.0
1962-63	Chicago	37	94	28	216	5.8
	Totals	38	99	28	226	5.9

KING, THOMAS

b. Jan. 23, 1926 Ht. 6-11 Wt. 165
College—Michigan

Yr.	Team	G	FG	FT	TP	Avg.
1946-47	Detroit	58	97	101	295	5.1

KINNEY, ROBERT

b. Sept. 16, 1920 Ht. 6-6 Wt. 215
College—Rice

Yr.	Team	G	FG	FT	TP	Avg.
1948-49	Ft. W.-Boston	58	161	136	458	7.9
1949-50	Boston	60	233	201	667	11.1
	Totals	118	394	337	1125	9.5

KIRK, WALTON

Ht. 6-3 Wt. 173
College—Illinois

Yr.	Team	G	FG	FT	TP	Avg.
1948-49	Ft. Wayne-Ind.	49	140	167	447	9.1
1949-50	And.-Tri-Cities	58	97	155	349	6.0
1951-52	Milwaukee	11	28	55	111	10.1
	Totals	118	265	377	907	7.7

KISTLER, DOUGLAS

b Mar. 21, 1938 Ht. 6-9 Wt. 210
College—Duke

Yr.	Team	G	FG	FT	TP	Avg.
1961-62	New York	5	3	2	8	1.5

KLIER, LEO (Crystal)

b. May 21, 1923 Ht. 6-2 Wt. 170
College—Notre Dame

Yr.	Team	G	FG	FT	TP	Avg.
1946-47	Indianapolis NL	44	162	93	417	9.5
1947-48	Indianapolis NL	56	228	156	612	10.9
1948-49	Ft. Wayne	47	125	97	347	7.4
1949-50	Ft. Wayne	66	157	141	455	6.9
	Totals	213	672	487	1831	8.5

KLOTZ, HERMAN (Red)

b. Oct. 21, 1921 Ht. 5-7 Wt. 150
College—Villanova

Yr.	Team	G	FG	FT	TP	Avg.
1947-48	Baltimore	11	7	1	15	1.4

KLUEH, DUANE

b. Jan 6, 1926 Ht. 6-3 Wt. 175
College—Indiana State

Yr.	Team	G	FG	FT	TP	Avg.
1949-50	Denver-Ft. W.	52	159	157	475	8.6
1950-51	Ft. Wayne	61	157	135	449	7.4
	Totals	113	316	292	924	7.9

KNIGHT, BOB

Ht. 6-2

Yr.	Team	G	FG	FT	TP	Avg.
1954-55	New York	2	3	1	7	3.5

KNOREK, LEE

b. July 15, 1921 Ht. 6-7 Wt. 215
College—Detroit

Yr.	Team	G	FG	FT	TP	Avg.
1946-47	New York	22	62	47	171	7.8
1947-48	New York	48	99	61	259	5.4
1948-49	New York	60	156	131	443	7.4
1949-50	Baltimore	1	0	0	0	0.0
	Totals	131	317	239	873	6.6

KNOSTMAN, RICHARD

b. Aug. 9, 1931 Ht. 6-6 Wt. 215
College—Kansas State

Yr.	Team	G	FG	FT	TP	Avg.
1953-54	Syracuse	5	3	7	13	2.6

KOJIS, DON

b. Jan. 15, 1939 Ht. 6-3 Wt. 215
College—Marquette

Yr.	Team	G	FG	FT	TP	Avg.
1963-64	Baltimore	78	203	82	488	6.3
1964-65	Detroit	65	180	62	422	6.5
1965-66	Detroit	60	182	76	440	7.3
1966-67	Chicago	78	329	134	792	10.2
1967-68	San Diego	69	530	300	1360	19.7
	Totals	350	1424	654	3502	10.0

KOMENICH, MILO

b. June 23, 1920 Ht. 6-7 Wt. 212
College—Wyoming

Yr.	Team	G	FG	FT	TP	Avg.
1947-48	Anderson NL	51	127	46	300	5.9
1948-49	Anderson NL	64	243	124	610	9.5
1949-50	Anderson	64	244	146	634	9.9
	Totals	179	614	316	1544	8.0

KOMIVES, HOWARD (Butch)

b. May 9, 1941 Ht. 6-1 Wt. 185
College—Bowling Green

Yr.	Team	G	FG	FT	TP	Avg.
1964-65	New York	80	381	212	974	12.2
1965-66	New York	80	436	241	1113	13.9
1966-67	New York	65	402	217	1021	15.7
1967-68	New York	78	233	132	598	7.7
	Totals	303	1452	807	2740	9.0

KOPER, HERBERT (Bud)

b. Aug. 9, 1942 Ht. 6-6 Wt. 210
College—Oklahoma City

Yr.	Team	G	FG	FT	TP	Avg.
1964-65	San Francisco	56	106	35	247	4.4

KOSTECKA, ANDY

b. Feb. 10, 1921 Ht. 6-3 Wt. 203
College—Georgetown

Yr.	Team	G	FG	FT	TP	Avg.
1948-49	Indianapolis	21	46	43	135	6.4

KOTTMAN, HAROLD

b. Aug. 22, 1922 Ht. 6-8 Wt. 220
College—Culver-Stockton

Yr.	Team	G	FG	FT	TP	Avg.
1946-47	Boston	53	59	47	165	3.1

KRAMER, BARRY

b. Nov. 10, 1942 Ht. 6-4 Wt. 200
College—New York University

Yr.	Team	G	FG	FT	TP	Avg.
1964-65	San Fran.-N.Y.	52	63	60	186	3.6

KRAUS, DANIEL

Ht. 6-0 Wt. 195
College—Georgetown

Yr.	Team	G	FG	FT	TP	Avg.
1948-49	Baltimore	13	5	11	21	1.6

Yr.	Team	G	FG	FT	TP	Avg.
	KRAUTBLATT, HERB					
	b. Nov. 19, 1926 Ht. 6-1 Wt. 190					
	College—Rider					
1948-49	Baltimore	10	4	5	13	1.3
	KREBS, JAMES					
	b. Sept. 8, 1935 Ht. 6-8 Wt. 230					
	College—Southern Methodist					
1957-58	Minneapolis	68	199	135	533	7.8
1958-59	Minneapolis	72	271	92	634	8.8
1959-60	Minneapolis	75	237	98	572	7.6
1960-61	Los Angeles	75	275	79	629	8.4
1961-62	Los Angeles	78	312	156	780	10.0
1962-63	Los Angeles	79	272	115	659	8.3
1963-64	Los Angeles	68	134	65	333	4.9
	Totals	515	1700	740	4140	8.0
	KRON, TOMMY					
	b. Feb. 28, 1943 Ht. 6-5 Wt. 200					
	College—Kentucky					
1966-67	St. Louis	33	27	13	67	2.0
1967-68	Seattle	76	277	184	738	9.7
	Totals	109	304	197	805	7.4
	KUBIAK, LEO					
	b. Dec. 25, 1927 Ht. 5-11 Wt. 160					
	College—Bowling Green					
1948-49	Waterloo NL	61	173	106	452	7.4
1949-50	Waterloo	62	259	192	710	11.5
	Totals	123	432	298	1162	9.4
	KUDELKA, FRANK					
	Ht. 6-2 Wt. 193					
	College—St. Mary's (Calif.)					
1949-50	Chicago	65	172	80	433	6.7
1950-51	Wash.-Baltimore	62	179	83	441	7.1
1951-52	Baltimore	65	204	198	606	9.3
1952-53	Balt.-Phila.	36	59	44	162	4.5
	Totals	228	614	414	1642	7.2
	KUKA, RAY					
	b. Feb. 17, 1922 Ht. 6-3 Wt. 200					
	College—Notre Dame					
1947-48	New York	44	89	50	228	5.2
1948-49	New York	8	10	5	25	3.0
	Totals	52	99	55	253	4.9
	LaCOUR, FRED					
	b. Feb. 7, 1938 Ht. 6-5 Wt. 210					
	College—San Francisco					
1960-61	St. Louis	55	123	63	309	5.6
1961-62	St. Louis	73	230	106	566	7.7
1963-64	San Francisco	16	28	9	65	4.1
	Totals	144	381	178	940	6.5
	LARESE, YORK					
	b. July 18, 1938 Ht. 6-4 Wt. 183					
	College—North Carolina					
1961-62	Chicago-Phila.	59	122	58	302	5.1
	LaRUSSO, RUDY					
	b. Nov. 11, 1937 Ht. 6-8 Wt. 220					
	College—Dartmouth					
1959-60	Minneapolis	71	355	265	975	13.7

Yr.	Team	G	FG	FT	TP	Avg.
1960-61	Los Angeles	79	416	323	1155	14.6
1961-62	Los Angeles	80	516	342	1374	17.1
1962-63	Los Angeles	74	321	282	924	12.5
1963-64	Los Angeles	79	337	298	972	12.3
1964-65	Los Angeles	78	381	415	1083	13.9
1965-66	Los Angeles	77	410	350	1170	15.2
1966-67	Los Angeles	45	211	156	578	12.8
1967-68	San Francisco	79	602	522	1726	21.8
	Totals	662	3549	2859	9957	15.0
	LALICH, PETER					
	Ht. 6-2 Wt. 190					
	College—Ohio University					
1946-47	Cleveland	1	0	0	0	0.0
	LATTIN, DAVID					
	b. Dec. 23, 1943 Ht. 6-7 Wt. 230					
	College—Texas Western					
1967-68	San Francisco	44	37	23	97	2.2
	LAUTENBACH, WALTER					
	Ht. 6-2 Wt. 190					
	College—Wisconsin					
1947-48	Oshkosh NL	60	159	38	356	5.9
1948-49	Oshkosh NL	56	93	26	212	3.8
1949-50	Sheboygan	55	100	38	238	4.3
	Totals	171	352	102	806	4.7
	LAVELLI, TONY					
	b. July 11, 1926 Ht. 6-3 Wt. 185					
	College—Yale					
1949-50	Boston	56	162	168	492	8.8
1950-51	New York	30	32	35	99	3.3
	Totals	86	194	203	591	6.9
	LAVOY, BOB					
	b. June 29, 1926 Ht. 6-7 Wt. 185					
	College—Western Kentucky					
1950-51	Indianapolis	63	221	84	526	8.3
1951-52	Indianapolis	63	240	168	648	10.3
1952-53	Indianapolis	70	225	168	618	8.8
1953-54	Syracuse	68	135	94	364	5.4
	Totals	264	821	514	2156	8.2
	LEAR, HAL					
	b. Jan. 31, 1935 Ht. 6-0 Wt. 163					
	College—Temple					
1956-57	Philadelphia	3	2	0	4	1.3
	LEE, CLYDE					
	b. Mar. 14, 1944 Ht. 6-10 Wt. 205					
	College—Vanderbilt					
1966-67	San Francisco	74	205	105	515	7.0
1967-68	San Francisco	82	373	229	975	11.9
	Totals	156	578	334	1490	9.6
	LEE, GEORGE					
	b. Nov. 23, 1936 Ht. 6-4 Wt. 200					
	College—Michigan					
1960-61	Detroit	74	310	276	896	12.1
1961-62	Detroit	75	179	213	571	7.6
1962-63	San Francisco	64	149	152	450	7.0
1963-64	San Francisco	54	64	47	175	3.2
1964-65	San Francisco	19	27	38	92	4.8
1966-67	San Francisco	1	3	6	12	12.0

Yr.	Team	G	FG	FT	TP	Avg.
1967-68	San Francisco	10	8	17	33	3.3
	Totals	297	740	749	2229	7.5

LEEDE, ED

b. July 17, 1927 Ht. 6-3 Wt. 185
College—Dartmouth

Yr.	Team	G	FG	FT	TP	Avg.
1949-50	Boston	64	174	223	571	8.9
1950-51	Boston	57	119	140	378	6.6
	Totals	121	293	363	949	7.8

LEFKOWITZ, HENRY

Ht. 6-2 Wt. 190
College—Western Reserve

Yr.	Team	G	FG	FT	TP	Avg.
1946-47	Cleveland	24	22	7	51	2.1

LEHMAN, GEORGE

b. May 1, 1942 Ht. 6-3 Wt. 190
College—Campbell

Yr.	Team	G	FG	FT	TP	Avg.
1967-68	St. Louis	55	59	35	153	2.8

LEONARD, ROBERT

b. July 17, 1932 Ht. 6-3 Wt. 185
College—Indiana

Yr.	Team	G	FG	FT	TP	Avg.
1956-57	Minneapolis	72	303	186	792	11.0
1957-58	Minneapolis	66	266	205	737	11.2
1958-59	Minneapolis	58	206	120	737	9.2
1959-60	Minneapolis	73	231	136	598	8.2
1960-61	Los Angeles	55	61	71	193	3.5
1961-62	Chicago	70	423	279	1125	16.1
1962-63	Chicago	32	84	59	227	7.1
	Totals	426	1574	1056	4204	9.9

LEVANE, ANDREW (Fuzzy)

b. April 11, 1920 Ht. 6-2 Wt. 190
College—St. John's (N. Y.)

Yr.	Team	G	FG	FT	TP	Avg.
1945-46	Rochester NL	22	50	11	111	5.0
1947-48	Rochester NL	59	148	45	339	6.3
1948-49	Rochester	36	55	13	123	3.4
1949-50	Syracuse	60	139	54	332	5.5
1952-53	Milwaukee	7	3	2	8	1.1
	Totals	184	394	125	913	5.0

LEWIS, BOB

b. Mar. 20, 1945 Ht. 6-3 Wt. 185
College—North Carolina

Yr.	Team	G	FG	FT	TP	Avg.
1967-68	San Francisco	41	59	61	179	4.4

LEWIS, FRED

b. Jan. 6, 1921 Ht. 6-2 Wt. 195
College—Eastern Kentucky

Yr.	Team	G	FG	FT	TP	Avg.
1946-47	Sheboygan NL	44	230	125	585	13.3
1947-48	Sheboygan NL	44	166	99	431	9.8
1948-49	Ind.-Baltimore	61	272	138	682	11.2
1949-50	Balt.-Phila.	34	46	25	117	3.4
	Totals	183	714	387	1815	9.9

LEWIS, FRED

b. Jan. 7, 1943 Ht. 6-0 Wt. 180
College—Arizona State

Yr.	Team	G	FG	FT	TP	Avg.
1966-67	Cincinnati	32	60	29	149	4.7

LEWIS, GRADY

b. Mar. 25, 1917 Ht. 6-7 Wt. 215
College—Oklahoma

Yr.	Team	G	FG	FT	TP	Avg.
1946-47	Detroit	60	106	75	287	4.8
1947-48	Balt.-St. Louis	45	114	87	315	7.0
1948-49	St. Louis	34	53	42	148	4.4
	Totals	139	273	204	750	5.4

LIVINGSTONE, RONALD

b. Oct. 9, 1925 Ht. 6-10 Wt. 220
College—Wyoming

Yr.	Team	G	FG	FT	TP	Avg.
1949-50	Balt.-Phila.	54	163	122	448	8.3
1950-51	Philadelphia	63	104	76	284	4.5
	Totals	117	267	198	732	6.2

LLOYD, EARL

b April 3, 1928 Ht. 6-6 Wt. 220
College—West Virginia State

Yr.	Team	G	FG	FT	TP	Avg.
1950-51	Washington	7	16	11	43	6.1
1952-53	Syracuse	64	156	160	472	7.4
1953-54	Syracuse	72	249	156	654	9.1
1954-55	Syracuse	72	286	159	731	10.2
1955-56	Syracuse	72	213	186	612	8.5
1956-57	Syracuse	72	256	134	646	9.0
1957-58	Syracuse	61	119	79	317	5.2
1958-59	Detroit	72	234	137	605	8.4
1959-60	Detroit	68	237	128	602	8.8
	Totals	560	1766	1150	4682	8.4

LOCHMUELLER, ROBERT

Ht. 6-5 Wt. 185
College—Louisville

Yr.	Team	G	FG	FT	TP	Avg.
1952-53	Syracuse	62	79	74	232	3.7

LOFGRAN, DON

Ht. 6-6 Wt. 200
College—San Francisco

Yr.	Team	G	FG	FT	TP	Avg.
1950-51	Syracuse-Ind.	61	79	79	237	3.9
1951-52	Indianapolis	63	149	156	454	7.2
1952-53	Philadelphia	64	173	126	472	7.4
1953-54	Milwaukee	21	35	32	102	4.9
	Totals	209	436	393	1265	6.1

LOGAN, JOHN

b. Jan. 1, 1921 Ht. 6-2 Wt. 175
College—Indiana

Yr.	Team	G	FG	FT	TP	Avg.
1946-47	St. Louis	61	290	190	770	12.6
1947-48	St. Louis	48	221	202	644	13.4
1948-49	St. Louis	57	282	239	803	14.1
1949-50	St. Louis	62	251	253	755	12.2
1950-51	Tri-Cities	29	81	62	224	7.7
	Totals	257	1125	946	3196	12.4

LONG, PAUL

b. Feb. 8, 1944 Ht. 6-2 Wt. 180
College—Wake Forest

Yr.	Team	G	FG	FT	TP	Avg.
1967-68	Detroit	16	23	11	57	3.6

LOSCUTOFF, JAMES (Jungle Jim)

b. Feb. 4, 1930 Ht. 6-5 Wt. 230
College—Oregon

Yr.	Team	G	FG	FT	TP	Avg.
1955-56	Boston	71	226	139	591	8.3
1956-57	Boston	70	306	132	744	10.6
1957-58	Boston	5	11	1	23	4.6
1958-59	Boston	66	242	62	546	8.3
1959-60	Boston	28	66	22	154	5.5
1960-61	Boston	76	154	50	358	4.7
1961-62	Boston	79	188	45	421	5.3

Yr.	Team	G	FG	FT	TP	Avg.
1962-63	Boston	64	94	22	210	3.3
1963-64	Boston	53	56	18	130	2.5
	Totals	512	1343	491	3177	6.2

LOTT, PLUMMER

b. Dec. 11, 1945 Ht. 6-5 Wt. 210
College—Seattle

Yr.	Team	G	FG	FT	TP	Avg.
1967-68	Seattle	44	46	19	111	2.5

LOUGHERY, KEVIN

b. Mar. 28, 1940 Ht. 6-3 Wt. 190
College—St. John's (N. Y.)

Yr.	Team	G	FG	FT	TP	Avg.
1962-63	Detroit	57	146	71	363	6.4
1963-64	Det.-Baltimore	66	236	126	598	9.1
1964-65	Baltimore	80	406	212	1024	12.8
1965-66	Baltimore	74	526	297	1349	18.2
1966-67	Baltimore	76	520	340	1380	18.2
1967-68	Baltimore	77	458	305	1221	15.9
	Totals	430	2292	1351	5935	13.8

LOVE, BOB

b. Dec. 8, 1942 Ht. 6-8 Wt. 215
College—Southern University

Yr.	Team	G	FG	FT	TP	Avg.
1966-67	Cincinnati	66	173	93	439	6.7
1967-68	Cincinnati	72	193	78	464	6.4
	Totals	138	366	171	903	6.5

LOVELLETTE, CLYDE

b. Sept. 7, 1929 Ht. 6-9 Wt. 235
College—Kansas

Yr.	Team	G	FG	FT	TP	Avg.
1953-54	Minneapolis	72	237	114	588	8.2
1954-55	Minneapolis	70	519	273	1311	18.7
1955-56	Minneapolis	71	594	338	1526	21.5
1956-57	Minneapolis	69	574	286	1434	20.8
1957-58	Cincinnati	71	679	301	1659	23.4
1958-59	St. Louis	70	402	205	1009	14.4
1959-60	St. Louis	68	550	316	1416	20.8
1960-61	St. Louis	67	599	273	1471	22.0
1961-62	St. Louis	40	341	155	837	20.9
1962-63	Boston	61	161	73	395	6.5
1963-64	Boston	45	128	45	301	6.7
	Totals	704	4784	2379	11947	17.0

LUCAS, AL

Ht. 6-3 Wt. 195
College—Fordham

Yr.	Team	G	FG	FT	TP	Avg.
1945-46	Sheboygan NL	32	75	24	174	5.4
1947-48	Sheboygan NL	58	100	42	242	4.2
1948-49	Boston	2	1	0	2	1.0
	Totals	92	176	66	418	4.5

LUCAS, JERRY

b. Mar. 30, 1940 Ht. 6-8 Wt. 230
College—Ohio State

Yr.	Team	G	FG	FT	TP	Avg.
1963-64	Cincinnati	79	545	310	1400	17.7
1964-65	Cincinnati	66	558	298	1414	21.4
1965-66	Cincinnati	79	690	317	1697	21.5
1966-67	Cincinnati	81	577	284	1438	17.8
1967-68	Cincinnati	82	707	346	1760	21.4
	Totals	387	3077	1555	7709	19.9

LUISI, JAMES

Ht. 6-2 Wt. 180
College—St. Francis (N. Y.)

Yr.	Team	G	FG	FT	TP	Avg.
1953-54	Baltimore	31	31	27	89	2.9

LUJACK, AL

b. Oct. 5, 1921
College—Georgetown

Yr.	Team	G	FG	FT	TP	Avg.
1946-47	Washington	5	1	2	4	0.8

LUMPP, RAY

Ht. 6-1 Wt. 178
College—New York University

Yr.	Team	G	FG	FT	TP	Avg.
1948-49	Indap.-N.Y.	61	279	219	777	12.7
1949-50	New York	58	91	86	268	4.6
1950-51	New York	64	153	124	430	6.7
1951-52	New York	62	184	90	458	7.4
1952-53	Baltimore	55	188	153	529	9.6
	Totals	300	895	672	2462	8.2

MACAULEY, EDWARD (Easy Ed)

b. Mar. 22, 1928 Ht. 6-8 Wt. 190
College—St. Louis

Yr.	Team	G	FG	FT	TP	Avg.
1949-50	St. Louis	67	351	379	1081	16.1
1950-51	Boston	68	459	466	1384	20.4
1951-52	Boston	66	384	496	1264	19.2
1952-53	Boston	69	451	500	1402	20.3
1953-54	Boston	71	462	420	1344	18.9
1954-55	Boston	71	403	442	1248	17.6
1955-56	Boston	71	420	400	1240	17.5
1956-57	St. Louis	72	414	359	1187	16.5
1957-58	St. Louis	72	376	267	1019	14.2
1958-59	St. Louis	14	22	21	65	4.6
	Totals	641	3742	3750	11234	17.5

MacGILVRAY, RONNIE

b. July 20, 1930 Ht. 6-2 Wt. 185
College—St. John's (N. Y.)

Yr.	Team	G	FG	FT	TP	Avg.
1954-55	Milwaukee	6	2	4	8	1.3

MacKENZIE, STAN

b. Oct. 6, 1944 Ht. 6-5 Wt. 210
College—New York University

Yr.	Team	G	FG	FT	TP	Avg.
1967-68	Baltimore	50	73	58	204	4.1

MACKNOWSKI, JOHN

Ht. 6-0 Wt. 185
College—Seton Hall

Yr.	Team	G	FG	FT	TP	Avg.
1948-49	Syracuse NL	61	146	128	420	6.0
1949-50	Syracuse	59	154	131	439	7.4
1950-51	Syracuse	58	131	122	384	6.6
	Totals	178	431	381	1243	7.0

MADDOX, JACK

College—West Texas

Yr.	Team	G	FG	FT	TP	Avg.
1947-48	Oshkosh NL	60	146	59	351	5.9
1948-49	Ham. NL	17	39	18	96	5.4
1950-51	Indianapolis	1	0	0	0	0.0
	Totals	78	185	77	447	5.7

MAGER, NORM

Ht. 6-5 Wt. 185
College—CCNY

Yr.	Team	G	FG	FT	TP	Avg.
1950-51	Baltimore	22	32	37	101	4.6

MAHNKEN, JOHN

b. June 16, 1922 Ht. 6-8 Wt. 220
College—Georgetown

Yr.	Team	G	FG	FT	TP	Avg.
1945-46	Rochester NL	16	50	23	123	7.7
1946-47	Washington	60	223	111	557	9.3

Yr.	Team	G	FG	FT	TP	Avg.
1947-48	Washington	48	131	54	316	6.6
1948-49	Balt.-Ft. W.-Indap.	57	215	104	534	9.4
1949-50	Ft. W.-Tri-Cit.-Bos.	62	132	77	341	5.5
1950-51	Bos.-Indap.	58	111	45	267	4.6
1951-52	Boston	60	78	26	182	3.0
1952-53	Boston	69	76	39	191	2.8
	Totals	430	1016	479	2511	5.8

MAHONEY, FRANCIS (Mo)

b. Nov. 20, 1927 Ht. 6-0 Wt. 205
College—Brown

Yr.	Team	G	FG	FT	TP	Avg.
1952-53	Boston	6	4	4	12	2.0
1953-54	Baltimore	2	0	0	0	0.0
	Totals	8	4	4	12	1.5

MALAMED, LIONEL

b. Nov. 15, 1924 Ht. 5-9 Wt. 150
College—CCNY

Yr.	Team	G	FG	FT	TP	Avg.
1948-49	Ind.-Rochester	44	97	64	258	5.9

MANDIC, JOHN

b. Oct. 3, 1919 Ht. 6-4 Wt. 205
College—Oregon State

Yr.	Team	G	FG	FT	TP	Avg.
1947-48	Rochester NL	34	32	13	77	2.3
1948-49	Indianapolis	56	97	75	269	4.8
1949-50	Wash.-Bos.	25	22	22	66	2.6
	Totals	115	151	110	412	3.6

MANGIAPANE, FRANK

b. Aug. 25, 1925 Ht. 5-10 Wt. 195
College—New York University

Yr.	Team	G	FG	FT	TP	Avg.
1946-47	New York	6	2	1	5	0.8

MANNING, ED

b. Jan. 2, 1944 Ht. 6-7½ Wt. 215
College—Jackson State

Yr.	Team	G	FG	FT	TP	Avg.
1967-68	Baltimore	71	112	60	284	4.0

MANTIS, NICHOLAS

b. Dec. 7, 1935 Ht. 6-3 Wt. 190
College—Northwestern

Yr.	Team	G	FG	FT	TP	Avg.
1959-60	Minneapolis	10	10	1	21	2.1
1962-63	St. Louis-Chic.	42	94	27	215	5.1
	Totals	52	104	28	236	4.5

MARAVICH, PRESS

Ht. 6-0 Wt. 185
College—Davis and Elkins

Yr.	Team	G	FG	FT	TP	Avg.
1945-46	Youngstown NL	31	70	34	174	5.6
1946-47	Pittsburgh	51	102	30	234	4.6
	Totals	82	172	64	408	5.0

MARIASCHIN, SAUL

b. Sept. 1, 1924 Ht. 5-11 Wt. 165
College—Harvard

Yr.	Team	G	FG	FT	TP	Avg.
1947-48	Boston	43	125	83	333	7.7

MARIN, JACK

b. Oct. 12, 1944 Ht. 6-6½ Wt. 200
College—Duke

Yr.	Team	G	FG	FT	TP	Avg.
1966-67	Baltimore	74	283	145	711	9.6
1967-68	Baltimore	82	429	250	1108	13.5
	Totals	156	612	395	1819	11.7

MARSHALL, THOMAS

b. Jan. 6, 1931 Ht. 6-4 Wt. 215
College—Western Kentucky

Yr.	Team	G	FG	FT	TP	Avg.
1956-57	Rochester	40	56	47	159	4.0
1957-58	Cinn.-Det.-Cinn.	38	52	48	152	4.0
	Totals	78	108	95	311	4.0

MARTIN, DONALD

Ht. 6-8 Wt. 220
College—Georgetown

Yr.	Team	G	FG	FT	TP	Avg.
1946-47	Providence	60	311	111	733	12.3
1947-48	Providence	32	46	9	101	3.2
	Totals	92	357	120	834	9.1

MARTIN, JAMES D.

b. May 25, 1920 Ht. 5-8 Wt. 160
College—Central Missouri

Yr.	Team	G	FG	FT	TP	Avg.
1946-47	St. Louis	54	89	13	191	3.5
1947-48	St. Louis	39	35	15	85	2.2
1948-49	St. Louis-Balt.	44	52	30	134	3.0
	Totals	137	176	58	410	3.0

MARTIN, PHIL

Ht. 6-3 Wt. 190
College—Toledo

Yr.	Team	G	FG	FT	TP	Avg.
1954-55	Milwaukee	7	5	2	12	1.7

MARTIN, RONALD (Whitey)

b. Apr. 11, 1939 Ht. 6-2 Wt. 185
College—St. Bonaventure

Yr.	Team	G	FG	FT	TP	Avg.
1961-62	New York	66	95	37	227	3.4

MARTIN, SLATER

b. Oct. 22, 1925 Ht. 5-10 Wt. 170
College—Texas

Yr.	Team	G	FG	FT	TP	Avg.
1949-50	Minneapolis	67	106	59	271	4.0
1950-51	Minneapolis	68	227	121	575	8.5
1951-52	Minneapolis	66	237	142	616	9.3
1952-53	Minneapolis	70	260	224	744	10.6
1953-54	Minneapolis	69	254	176	684	9.9
1954-55	Minneapolis	72	350	276	976	13.6
1955-56	Minneapolis	72	309	329	947	13.2
1956-57	N.Y.-St. L.	66	244	230	718	10.9
1957-58	St. Louis	60	258	206	722	12.0
1958-59	St. Louis	71	245	197	687	9.4
	Totals	681	2490	1960	6940	10.2

MAUGHAN, ARIEL

b. April 23, 1923 Ht. 6-4 Wt. 190
College—Utah State

Yr.	Team	G	FG	FT	TP	Avg.
1946-47	Detroit	59	224	84	532	9.0
1947-48	Prov.-St. Louis	42	76	32	184	4.4
1948-49	St. Louis	55	206	184	596	10.8
1949-50	St. Louis	68	160	157	477	7.0
1950-51	Washington	35	78	101	257	7.3
	Totals	259	744	558	2046	7.9

MASINO, AL

Ht. 5-11 Wt. 174
College—Canisius

Yr.	Team	G	FG	FT	TP	Avg.
1952-53	Milwaukee	72	134	128	396	5.5
1953-54	Syracuse	27	26	30	82	3.0
	Totals	99	160	158	478	4.8

Yr.	Team	G	FG	FT	TP	Avg.

MAZZA, MATT
b. Sept. 23, 1923 Ht. 6-3 Wt. 210
College—Michigan State

1949-50	Sheboygan	26	33	32	98	3.8

McBRIDE, KEN
Ht. 6-3 Wt. 190
College—Maryland State

1954-55	Milwaukee	12	48	21	117	9.8

McCANN, BRENDAN
b. July 5, 1935 Ht. 6-2 Wt. 178
College—St. Bonaventure

1957-58	New York	36	22	25	69	1.9
1958-59	New York	1	0	0	0	0.0
1959-60	New York	4	1	4	6	1.5
	Totals	41	23	29	75	1.8

McCARRON, MICHAEL
Ht. 5-11 Wt. 180
College—Seton Hall

1946-47	Toronto	60	236	177	649	10.8
1949-50	Balt.-St. Louis	8	3	3	9	1.1
	Totals	68	239	180	658	9.7

McCARTHY, HOWARD
Ht. 6-2 Wt. 190

1946-47	Detroit	19	10	1	21	1.1

McCARTHY, JOHN
b. April 25, 1934 Ht. 6-7 Wt. 185
College—Canisius

1956-57	Rochester	72	173	130	476	6.6
1958-59	Cincinnati	47	245	116	606	12.9
1959-60	St. Louis	75	240	149	629	8.4
1960-61	St. Louis	79	266	122	654	8.3
1961-62	St. Louis	15	18	12	48	3.2
1963-64	Boston	28	16	5	37	1.3
	Totals	316	958	534	2450	7.8

McCLOSKEY, JACK
Ht. 6-2 Wt. 192
College—Pennsylvania

1952-53	Philadelphia	1	3	0	6	6.0

McCONATHY, JOHN
Ht. 6-5 Wt. 195
College—Northwest Louisiana

1951-52	Milwaukee	11	4	6	14	1.3

McCONNELL, BUCKY
Ht. 5-10 Wt. 170
College—Marshall

1952-53	Milwaukee	14	27	14	68	4.9

McGAHA, MEL
b. Sept. 26, 1926 Ht. 6-1 Wt. 190
College—Arkansas

1948-49	New York	51	62	52	176	3.5

McGILL, BILL (The Hill)
b. Sept. 16, 1939 Ht. 6-9 Wt. 225
College—Utah

Yr.	Team	G	FG	FT	TP	Avg.
1962-63	Chicago	61	181	80	442	7.2
1963-64	Balt.-New York	74	456	204	1116	15.1
1964-65	St. Louis-L.A.	24	21	13	55	2.3
	Totals	159	658	297	1613	10.1

McGLOCKLIN, JON
b. June 10, 1943 Ht. 6-5 Wt. 205
College—Indiana

1965-66	Cincinnati	72	153	62	368	5.1
1966-67	Cincinnati	60	217	74	508	8.5
1967-68	San Diego	65	316	156	788	12.1
	Totals	197	686	292	1664	8.4

McGUIRE, AL
b. Sept. 7, 1928 Ht. 6-2 Wt. 180
College—St. John's (N. Y.)

1951-52	New York	59	72	64	208	3.5
1952-53	New York	58	112	128	352	6.1
1953-54	New York	64	58	58	174	2.7
1954-55	Baltimore	10	9	5	23	2.3
	Totals	191	251	255	757	3.9

McGUIRE, RICHARD (Tricky Dick)
b. Jan. 25, 1926 Ht. 6-0 Wt. 180
College—St. John's (N. Y.)

1949-50	New York	68	190	204	584	8.6
1950-51	New York	64	179	179	537	8.4
1951-52	New York	64	204	183	591	9.2
1952-53	New York	61	142	153	437	7.2
1953-54	New York	68	201	220	622	9.1
1954-55	New York	71	226	195	647	9.1
1955-56	New York	62	152	121	425	6.9
1956-57	New York	72	140	105	385	5.3
1957-58	Detroit	69	203	150	556	8.1
1958-59	Detroit	71	232	191	655	9.2
1959-60	Detroit	68	179	124	482	7.1
	Totals	738	2048	1825	5921	8.0

McKINNEY, HORACE (Bones)
b. Jan. 1, 1919 Ht. 6-6 Wt. 187
College—North Carolina

1946-47	Washington	58	275	145	695	12.0
1947-48	Washington	43	182	121	485	11.3
1948-49	Washington	57	263	197	723	12.7
1949-50	Washington	53	187	118	492	9.3
1950-51	Wash.-Boston	44	102	58	262	6.0
1951-52	Boston	63	136	65	337	5.3
	Totals	318	1145	704	2994	9.4

McLEMORE, McCOY
b. Apr. 3, 1942 Ht. 6-7 Wt. 230
College—Drake

1964-65	San Francisco	78	244	157	645	8.3
1965-66	San Francisco	80	225	142	592	7.4
1966-67	Chicago	79	258	210	726	9.2
1967-68	Chicago	76	374	216	963	12.7
	Totals	313	1101	725	2926	9.3

McLEOD, GEORGE
Ht. 6-5
College—Texas Christian

1952-53	Baltimore	10	2	8	12	1.2

Yr.	Team	G	FG	FT	TP	Avg.

McMAHON, JACK

b. Dec. 3, 1928 Ht. 6-1 Wt. 185
College—St. John's (N. Y.)

Yr.	Team	G	FG	FT	TP	Avg.
1952-53	Rochester	70	176	155	507	7.2
1953-54	Rochester	71	250	211	711	10.0
1954-55	Rochester	72	251	143	645	9.0
1955-56	Roch.-St. Louis	70	202	110	514	7.3
1956-57	St. Louis	72	239	142	620	8.6
1957-58	St. Louis	72	216	134	566	7.9
1958-59	St. Louis	72	248	96	592	8.2
	Totals	499	1582	991	4155	8.3

McMILLON, SHELLIE

b. Mar. 11, 1936 Ht. 6-5 Wt. 205
College—Bradley

Yr.	Team	G	FG	FT	TP	Avg.
1958-59	Detroit	48	127	55	309	6.4
1959-60	Detroit	75	267	132	666	8.9
1960-61	Detroit	78	322	140	784	10.1
1961-62	Det.-St. Louis	62	265	108	638	10.3
	Totals	263	981	435	2397	9.1

McMULLAN, MALCOLM

b. Aug. 23, 1927 Ht. 6-5 Wt. 210
College—Xavier (Ohio)

Yr.	Team	G	FG	FT	TP	Avg.
1949-50	Indianapolis	58	123	77	323	5.6
1950-51	Indianapolis	51	78	48	204	4.0
	Totals	109	201	125	527	4.8

McNABB, CHESTER

Ht. 6-2
College—West Texas

Yr.	Team	G	FG	FT	TP	Avg.
1947-48	Baltimore	2	0	0	0	0.0

McNAMEE, JOE

Ht. 6-6 Wt. 210
College—San Francisco

Yr.	Team	G	FG	FT	TP	Avg.
1950-51	Rochester	60	48	27	123	2.1
1951-52	Roch.-Balt.	58	68	30	166	2.9
	Totals	118	116	57	289	2.5

McNEILL, ROBERT

b. Oct. 22, 1938 Ht. 6-1 Wt. 180
College—St. Joseph's (Pa.)

Yr.	Team	G	FG	FT	TP	Avg.
1960-61	New York	75	166	105	437	5.8
1961-62	Phila.-L.A.	50	56	26	138	2.8
	Totals	125	222	131	575	4.6

McNULTY, CARL

b. Feb. 14, 1930 Ht. 6-3 Wt. 185
College—Purdue

Yr.	Team	G	FG	FT	TP	Avg.
1954-55	Milwaukee	1	1	0	2	2.0

McREYNOLDS, THALES

b. June 8, 1943 Ht. 6-3 Wt. 185
College—Miles

Yr.	Team	G	FG	FT	TP	Avg.
1965-66	Baltimore	5	1	1	3	0.6

MEARNS, GEORGE

Ht. 6-3 Wt. 175
College—Rhode Island

Yr.	Team	G	FG	FT	TP	Avg.
1946-47	Providence	57	128	126	382	6.7
1947-48	Providence	24	23	15	61	2.5
	Totals	81	151	141	443	5.5

MEHEN, RICHARD

b. May 20, 1922 Ht. 6-6 Wt. 195
College—Tennessee

Yr.	Team	G	FG	FT	TP	Avg.
1947-48	Toledo NL	57	151	85	387	6.8
1948-49	Waterloo NL	61	306	208	820	13.4
1949-50	Waterloo	62	347	198	892	14.4
1950-51	Balt.-Bos.-Ft. W.	66	192	90	474	7.2
1951-52	Milwaukee	65	293	117	703	10.8
	Totals	311	1289	698	3276	10.5

MEINEKE, DON (Monk)

Ht. 6-7 Wt. 210
College—Dayton

Yr.	Team	G	FG	FT	TP	Avg.
1952-53	Ft. Wayne	68	240	245	725	10.7
1953-54	Ft. Wayne	71	135	136	406	5.7
1954-55	Ft. Wayne	68	136	119	391	5.8
1955-56	Rochester	69	154	181	489	7.1
1957-58	Cincinnati	67	125	77	327	4.9
	Totals	343	790	758	2338	6.8

MEINHOLD, CARL

Ht. 6-2 Wt. 185
College—Long Island U.

Yr.	Team	G	FG	FT	TP	Avg.
1947-48	Baltimore	48	108	37	253	5.3
1948-49	Chicago-Prov.	50	101	61	263	5.2
	Totals	98	209	98	516	5.2

MELCHIONNI, BILL

b. Oct. 19, 1944 Ht. 6-1 Wt. 165
College—Villanova

Yr.	Team	G	FG	FT	TP	Avg.
1966-67	Philadelphia	71	138	39	315	4.4
1967-68	Philadelphia	71	146	33	325	4.6
	Totals	142	284	72	640	4.5

MELVIN, EDWARD

b. Feb. 13, 1916 Ht. 5-9 Wt. 170
College—Duquesne

Yr.	Team	G	FG	FT	TP	Avg.
1946-47	Pittsburgh	57	99	83	281	4.9

MENCEL, CHUCK

b. Apr. 21, 1933 Ht. 6-0 Wt. 168
College—Minnesota

Yr.	Team	G	FG	FT	TP	Avg.
1955-56	Minneapolis	69	120	78	318	4.6
1956-57	Minneapolis	72	243	179	665	9.2
	Totals	141	363	257	983	7.0

MENKE, KEN

Ht. 6-0 Wt. 168
College—Illinois

Yr.	Team	G	FG	FT	TP	Avg.
1949-50	Waterloo	6	6	3	15	2.5

MERIWETHER, PORTER

b. Mar. 16, 1940 Ht. 6-2 Wt. 180
College—Tennessee State

Yr.	Team	G	FG	FT	TP	Avg.
1962-63	Syracuse	31	48	23	119	3.8

MESCHERY, TOM

b. Oct. 26, 1938 Ht. 6-6 Wt. 215
College—St. Mary's (Calif.)

Yr.	Team	G	FG	FT	TP	Avg.
1961-62	Philadelphia	80	375	216	966	12.1
1962-63	San Francisco	64	397	228	1022	16.0
1963-64	San Francisco	80	436	207	1079	13.5
1964-65	San Francisco	79	361	278	1000	12.2
1965-66	San Francisco	80	401	224	1026	12.8

Yr.	Team	G	FG	FT	TP	Avg.
1966-67	San Francisco	72	293	175	761	10.6
1967-68	Seattle	82	473	244	1190	14.5
	Totals	537	2736	1572	7044	13.1

MIASEK, STAN

Ht. 6-5 Wt. 210

Yr.	Team	G	FG	FT	TP	Avg.
1946-47	Detroit	60	331	233	895	14.9
1947-48	Chicago	48	263	190	716	14.9
1948-49	Chicago	58	169	113	451	7.8
1949-50	Chicago	68	176	146	498	7.3
1951-52	Baltimore	66	258	263	779	11.8
1952-53	Milwaukee	65	178	156	512	7.9
	Totals	365	1375	1101	3851	10.5

MIHALIK, ZIGMUND (Red)

Ht. 6-0 Wt. 180

Yr.	Team	G	FG	FT	TP	Avg.
1946-47	Pittsburgh	7	3	0	6	0.9

MIKAN, EDWARD

b. Oct. 20, 1925 Ht. 6-8 Wt. 230
College—DePaul

Yr.	Team	G	FG	FT	TP	Avg.
1948-49	Chicago	60	229	136	594	9.9
1949-50	Chi.-Rochester	65	89	92	270	4.2
1950-51	Roch.-Wash.-Phila.	61	193	137	523	8.6
1951-52	Philadelphia	66	202	116	520	7.9
1952-53	Indianapolis	62	78	79	235	3.8
1953-54	Boston	9	8	5	21	2.3
	Totals	323	799	565	2163	6.7

MIKAN, GEORGE

b. June 18, 1924 Ht. 6-10 Wt. 245
College—DePaul

Yr.	Team	G	FG	FT	TP	Avg.
1946-47	Chicago NL	25	147	119	413	16.5
1947-48	Minneapolis NL	56	406	383	1195	21.3
1948-49	Minneapolis	60	583	532	1698	28.3
1949-50	Minneapolis	68	649	567	1865	27.4
1950-51	Minneapolis	68	678	576	1932	28.4
1951-52	Minneapolis	64	545	433	1523	23.8
1952-53	Minneapolis	70	500	442	1442	20.6
1953-54	Minneapolis	72	441	424	1306	18.1
1955-56	Minneapolis	37	148	94	390	10.5
	Totals	520	4097	3570	11764	22.6

MIKKELSEN, VERN

b. Oct. 21, 1928 Ht. 6-7 Wt. 230
College—Hamline

Yr.	Team	G	FG	FT	TP	Avg.
1949-50	Minneapolis	68	288	215	791	11.6
1950-51	Minneapolis	64	359	186	904	14.1
1951-52	Minneapolis	66	363	283	1009	15.3
1952-53	Minneapolis	70	378	291	1047	15.0
1953-54	Minneapolis	72	288	221	797	11.1
1954-55	Minneapolis	71	440	447	1327	18.7
1955-56	Minneapolis	72	317	328	962	13.4
1956-57	Minneapolis	72	322	342	986	13.7
1957-58	Minneapolis	72	439	370	1248	17.3
1958-59	Minneapolis	72	353	286	992	13.8
	Totals	699	3547	2969	10063	14.4

MIKSIS, AL

b. Feb. 2, 1928 Ht. 6-7 Wt. 210
College—Eastern Illinois

Yr.	Team	G	FG	FT	TP	Avg.
1949-50	Waterloo	8	5	17	27	3.4

MILES, EDDIE

b. July 5, 1940 Ht. 6-4 Wt. 196
College—Seattle

Yr.	Team	G	FG	FT	TP	Avg.
1963-64	Detroit	60	131	62	324	5.4
1964-65	Detroit	76	439	166	1044	13.7
1965-66	Detroit	80	634	298	1566	19.6
1966-67	Detroit	81	582	261	1425	17.6
1967-68	Detroit	76	561	282	1404	18.5
	Totals	373	2347	1069	5763	15.5

MILITZOK, NAT

Ht. 6-3 Wt. 195
College—CCNY, Hofstra and Cornell

Yr.	Team	G	FG	FT	TP	Avg.
1946-47	N.Y.-Toronto	56	90	64	244	4.4

MILLER, EDWARD

Ht. 6-8 Wt. 225
College—Syracuse

Yr.	Team	G	FG	FT	TP	Avg.
1952-53	Baltimore	70	273	187	733	10.5
1953-54	Baltimore	72	244	231	719	10.0
	Totals	144	517	418	1452	10.1

MILLER, HARRY

Ht. 6-4 Wt. 230
College—North Carolina

Yr.	Team	G	FG	FT	TP	Avg.
1946-47	Toronto	53	58	36	152	2.9

MILLER, JAY

b. July 19, 1943 Ht. 6-5 Wt. 210
College—Notre Dame

Yr.	Team	G	FG	FT	TP	Avg.
1967-68	St. Louis	8	8	4	20	2.5

MILLER, WALTER

b. July 30, 1915 Ht. 6-2 Wt. 191
College—Duquesne

Yr.	Team	G	FG	FT	TP	Avg.
1946-47	Pittsburgh	12	7	9	23	1.9

MILLER, WILLIAM

b. Nov. 23, 1924 Ht. 6-3 Wt. 190
College—North Carolina

Yr.	Team	G	FG	FT	TP	Avg.
1948-49	Chi.-St. Louis	28	21	11	53	1.9

MILLS, JOHN

b. Sept. 7, 1919 Ht. 6-8 Wt. 210
College—Western Kentucky

Yr.	Team	G	FG	FT	TP	Avg.
1946-47	Pittsburgh	47	55	71	181	3.9

MINOR, DAVAGE (Dave)

Ht. 6-2 Wt. 185
College—Toledo and UCLA

Yr.	Team	G	FG	FT	TP	Avg.
1951-52	Baltimore	57	185	101	471	8.3
1952-53	Milwaukee	59	154	98	406	6.9
	Totals	116	339	199	877	7.6

MISAKA, WAT

b. Dec. 21, 1923 Ht. 5-7 Wt. 150
College—Utah

Yr.	Team	G	FG	FT	TP	Avg.
1947-48	New York	3	3	1	7	2.3

MITCHELL, MURRAY

b. Mar. 19, 1923 Ht. 6-6
College—Sam Houston

Yr.	Team	G	FG	FT	TP	Avg.
1949-50	Anderson	2	1	0	2	1.0

MLKVY, BILL

b. Jan. 19, 1931 Ht. 6-4 Wt. 190
College—Temple

Yr.	Team	G	FG	FT	TP	Avg.
1952-53	Philadelphia	31	75	31	181	5.8

Yr.	Team	G	FG	FT	TP	Avg.

MOGUS, LEO

b. Apr. 13, 1921 Ht. 6-4 Wt. 205
College—Youngstown

Yr.	Team	G	FG	FT	TP	Avg.
1945-46	Youngstown NL	16	61	68	190	11.9
1946-47	Cleve.-Toronto	58	259	235	753	13.0
1948-49	Balt.-Ft. W.-Ind.	52	172	177	521	10.0
1949-50	Philadelphia	64	172	218	562	8.8
1950-51	Philadelphia	57	43	53	139	2.4
	Totals	247	707	751	2165	8.8

MOLINAS, JACK

Ht. 6-6 Wt. 200
College—Columbia

Yr.	Team	G	FG	FT	TP	Avg.
1953-54	Ft. Wayne	29	168	134	350	12.1

MOLIS, WAYNE

b. Apr. 17, 1943 Ht. 6-8 Wt. 230
College—Lewis

Yr.	Team	G	FG	FT	TP	Avg.
1966-67	New York	13	19	7	45	3.5

MONROE, EARL (The Pearl)

b. Nov. 21, 1944 Ht. 6-3 Wt. 180
College—Winston-Salem State

Yr.	Team	G	FG	FT	TP	Avg.
1967-68	Baltimore	82	742	507	1991	24.3

MONTGOMERY, HOWARD

b. Aug. 22, 1940 Ht. 6-6 Wt. 220
College—Pan-American

Yr.	Team	G	FG	FT	TP	Avg.
1962-63	San Francisco	20	65	14	144	7.2

MOONEY, JAMES

Ht. 6-5 Wt. 215
College—Villanova

Yr.	Team	G	FG	FT	TP	Avg.
1952-53	Philadelphia	18	54	27	135	7.5

MOORE, JACKIE

b. Sept. 24, 1932 Ht. 6-5 Wt. 182
College—LaSalle

Yr.	Team	G	FG	FT	TP	Avg.
1954-55	Philadelphia	23	44	22	110	4.8
1955-56	Philadelphia	54	50	32	132	2.4
1956-57	Philadelphia	51	43	37	123	2.2
	Totals	134	137	91	365	2.7

MORELAND, JACK

b. Mar. 11, 1938 Ht. 6-7 Wt. 215
College—Louisiana Tech

Yr.	Team	G	FG	FT	TP	Avg.
1960-61	Detroit	64	191	86	468	7.3
1961-62	Detroit	74	205	139	549	7.4
1962-63	Detroit	78	271	145	687	8.8
1963-64	Detroit	78	272	164	708	9.1
1964-65	Detroit	54	103	66	272	5.0
	Totals	348	1042	600	2684	7.7

MORGENTHALER, ELMORE

Ht. 6-9 Wt. 230
College—Boston College

Yr.	Team	G	FG	FT	TP	Avg.
1946-47	Providence	11	4	7	15	1.4
1948-49	Philadelphia	20	15	12	42	2.1
	Totals	31	19	19	57	1.8

MORRIS, MAX

b. Mar. 14, 1925 Ht. 6-2 Wt. 195
College—Northwestern

Yr.	Team	G	FG	FT	TP	Avg.
1947-48	Sheboygan NL	39	135	131	401	10.3
1948-49	Sheboygan NL	40	70	68	208	5.2
1956-57	Philadelphia	57	43	37	123	2.2
	Totals	141	457	476	1390	9.9

MORRISON, DWIGHT

Ht. 6-8 Wt. 225
College—Idaho

Yr.	Team	G	FG	FT	TP	Avg.
1954-55	Boston	71	120	72	312	4.4
1955-56	Boston	71	89	44	222	3.1
1957-58	St. Louis	13	9	3	21	1.6
	Totals	155	218	119	555	3.6

MRAZOVICH, CHARLES

b. Feb. 26, 1924 Ht. 6-5 Wt. 185
College—Eastern Kentucky

Yr.	Team	G	FG	FT	TP	Avg.
1950-51	Indianapolis	23	24	28	76	3.3

MUELLER, ERWIN

b. Mar. 12, 1944 Ht. 6-8 Wt. 230
College—San Francisco

Yr.	Team	G	FG	FT	TP	Avg.
1966-67	Chicago	80	422	171	1015	12.7
1967-68	Chic.-L.A.	74	223	109	555	7.5
	Totals	154	645	280	1570	10.2

MULLANEY, JOE

Ht. 6-0 Wt. 165
College—Holy Cross

Yr.	Team	G	FG	FT	TP	Avg.
1949-50	Boston	37	9	12	30	0.8

MULLEN, ROBERT

Ht. 6-1 Wt. 175
College—Fordham

Yr.	Team	G	FG	FT	TP	Avg.
1946-47	N.Y.-Toronto	54	125	64	314	5.8

MULLINS, JEFF

b. Mar. 18, 1942 Ht. 6-4 Wt. 190
College—Duke

Yr.	Team	G	FG	FT	TP	Avg.
1964-65	St. Louis	44	87	41	215	4.9
1965-66	St. Louis	44	113	29	255	5.8
1966-67	San Francisco	77	421	150	992	12.9
1967-68	San Francisco	79	610	273	1493	18.9
	Totals	244	1231	493	2955	12.1

MUNROE, GEORGE

b. Jan. 5, 1922 Ht. 5-11 Wt. 180
College—Dartmouth

Yr.	Team	G	FG	FT	TP	Avg.
1946-47	St. Louis	59	164	86	414	7.0
1947-48	Boston	21	27	17	71	3.4
	Totals	80	191	103	485	6.1

MURPHY, JOHN

Ht. 6-2 Wt. 175

Yr.	Team	G	FG	FT	TP	Avg.
1946-47	N.Y.-Phila.	20	11	10	32	1.6

MURPHY, RICHARD

Ht. 6-1 Wt. 180
College—Manhattan

Yr.	Team	G	FG	FT	TP	Avg.
1946-47	N.Y.-Boston	31	15	4	34	1.1

MURRAY, KEN

b. Apr. 20, 1928 Ht. 6-2 Wt. 195
College—St. Bonaventure

Yr.	Team	G	FG	FT	TP	Avg.
1950-51	Balt.-Ft. Wayne	66	301	248	850	12.9
1953-54	Ft. Wayne	49	53	43	149	3.0
1954-55	Philadelphia	66	187	98	472	7.2
	Totals	181	541	389	1471	8.1

Yr.	Team	G	FG	FT	TP	Avg.

MURREY, DORRIE

b. Sept. 7, 1943 Ht. 6-8 Wt. 215
College—Detroit

Yr.	Team	G	FG	FT	TP	Avg.
1966-67	Detroit	35	33	32	98	2.8
1967-68	Seattle	81	211	168	590	7.3
	Totals	116	244	200	688	5.9

MUSI, ANGELO

b. July 25, 1918 Ht. 5-9 Wt. 145
College—Temple

Yr.	Team	G	FG	FT	TP	Avg.
1946-47	Philadelphia	60	230	102	562	9.4
1947-48	Philadelphia	43	134	51	319	7.4
1948-49	Philadelphia	58	194	90	478	8.2
	Totals	161	558	243	1359	8.4

NABER, ROBERT

b. Sept. 3, 1929 Ht. 6-3 Wt. 185
College—Louisville

Yr.	Team	G	FG	FT	TP	Avg.
1952-53	Indianapolis	4	0	1	1	0.3

NACHAMKIN, BORIS

Ht. 6-6 Wt. 210
College—New York University

Yr.	Team	G	FG	FT	TP	Avg.
1954-55	Rochester	6	6	8	20	3.3

NAGEL, JERRY

b. May 18, 1928 Ht. 6-0
College—Loyola (Ill.)

Yr.	Team	G	FG	FT	TP	Avg.
1949-50	Ft. Wayne	14	6	1	13	0.9

NAGY, FRITZ

b. Jan. 3, 1924 Ht. 6-2 Wt. 185
College—Akron

Yr.	Team	G	FG	FT	TP	Avg.
1947-48	Indianapolis NL	39	42	42	126	3.2
1948-49	Indianapolis	50	94	65	253	5.1
	Totals	89	136	107	379	4.2

NAPOLITANO, PAUL

Ht. 6-2 Wt. 185
College—San Francisco

Yr.	Team	G	FG	FT	TP	Avg.
1947-48	Minneapolis NL	52	72	11	155	3.0
1948-49	Indianapolis	1	0	0	0	0.0
	Totals	53	72	11	155	2.9

NASH, CHARLES (Cotton)

b. July 24, 1942 Ht. 6-5 Wt. 225
College—Kentucky

Yr.	Team	G	FG	FT	TP	Avg.
1964-65	L.A.-San Fran.	45	47	43	137	3.0

NAULLS, WILLIE

b. Oct. 7, 1934 Ht. 6-6 Wt. 225
College—UCLA

Yr.	Team	G	FG	FT	TP	Avg.
1956-57	St. L.-New York	71	293	132	718	10.1
1957-58	New York	68	472	284	1228	18.1
1958-59	New York	68	405	258	1068	15.7
1959-60	New York	65	559	286	1388	21.3
1960-61	New York	79	737	372	1846	23.4
1961-62	New York	75	747	383	1877	25.0
1962-63	N.Y.-San Fran.	70	370	166	906	12.7
1963-64	Boston	78	769	125	767	9.8
1964-65	Boston	71	302	143	747	10.5
1965-66	Boston	71	328	104	760	10.7
	Totals	716	4526	2253	11305	15.8

NEIL, EBBERLE (Jim)

Ht. 6-11 Wt. 235

Yr.	Team	G	FG	FT	TP	Avg.
1953-54	Syracuse	67	117	78	312	4.7
1954-55	Baltimore	13	12	15	39	3.3
	Totals	80	129	93	351	4.4

NEGRATTI, ALBERT

Ht. 6-3 Wt. 200
College—Seton Hall

Yr.	Team	G	FG	FT	TP	Avg.
1946-47	Washington	11	13	5	31	2.8

NELSON, DON

b. May 15, 1940 Ht. 6-6 Wt. 210
College—Iowa

Yr.	Team	G	FG	FT	TP	Avg.
1962-63	Chicago	63	129	161	419	6.7
1963-64	Los Angeles	80	135	149	419	5.2
1964-65	Los Angeles	39	36	20	92	2.4
1965-66	Boston	75	271	223	765	10.2
1966-67	Boston	79	227	141	595	7.5
1967-68	Boston	82	312	195	819	10.0
	Totals	418	1110	889	3109	7.4

NEUMANN, PAUL

b. Jan. 30, 1938 Ht. 6-1 Wt. 175
College—Stanford

Yr.	Team	G	FG	FT	TP	Avg.
1961-62	Syracuse	79	172	133	477	6.0
1962-63	Syracuse	80	237	181	655	8.2
1963-64	Philadelphia	74	324	210	858	11.6
1964-65	Phila.-San Fran.	76	365	234	964	12.7
1965-66	San Francisco	66	343	265	951	14.4
1966-67	San Francisco	78	386	312	1084	13.9
	Totals	453	1827	1335	4989	11.0

NICHOLS, JACK

b. April 9, 1926 Ht. 6-7 Wt. 230
College—Washington

Yr.	Team	G	FG	FT	TP	Avg.
1948-49	Washington	34	153	92	398	11.7
1949-50	Wash.-Tri-Cities	67	310	259	789	13.1
1950-51	Tri-Cities	48	18	10	46	9.2
1952-53	Milwaukee	69	425	240	1090	15.8
1953-54	Mil.-Boston	75	163	113	439	5.9
1954-55	Boston	64	249	138	636	9.9
1955-56	Boston	60	330	200	860	14.3
1956-57	Boston	61	195	108	498	8.2
1957-58	Boston	69	170	59	399	5.8
	Totals	504	2013	1219	5245	10.4

NIEMIERA, RICHARD

b. May 26, 1926 Ht. 6-1 Wt. 165
College—Notre Dame

Yr.	Team	G	FG	FT	TP	Avg.
1947-48	Ft. Wayne NL	59	118	97	333	5.6
1948-49	Ft. Wayne	55	115	132	362	6.6
1949-50	Ft. W.-Anderson	60	110	104	324	5.4
	Totals	174	343	334	1019	5.8

NOBLE, CHUCK

b. July 24, 1931 Ht. 6-4 Wt. 195
College—Louisville

Yr.	Team	G	FG	FT	TP	Avg.
1955-56	Ft. Wayne	72	270	146	686	9.5
1956-57	Ft. Wayne	54	200	76	476	8.8
1957-58	Detroit	61	199	56	454	7.4
1958-59	Detroit	65	189	83	461	7.1
1959-60	Detroit	58	276	102	653	11.3
1960-61	Detroit	75	196	82	474	6.3

Yr.	Team	G	FG	FT	TP	Avg.
1961-62	Detroit	26	32	8	72	2.8
	Totals	411	1362	552	3276	8.0

NOEL, PAUL

Ht. 6-4 Wt. 185
College—Kentucky

Yr.	Team	G	FG	FT	TP	Avg.
1947-48	New York	29	40	19	99	3.4
1948-49	New York	47	70	37	177	3.8
1949-50	New York	65	98	53	249	3.8
1950-51	Rochester	52	49	32	130	2.5
1951-52	Rochester	8	2	2	6	0.8
	Totals	201	259	143	661	3.3

NOLAN, JIM

Ht. 6-8 Wt. 210
College—Georgia Tech

Yr.	Team	G	FG	FT	TP	Avg.
1949-50	Philadelphia	5	4	0	8	1.6

NOLEN, PAUL

b. June 9, 1927 Ht. 6-10 Wt. 215
College—Texas Tech

Yr.	Team	G	FG	FT	TP	Avg.
1953-54	Baltimore	1	0	0	0	0.0

NORDMANN, ROBERT (Bevo)

b. Dec. 11, 1939 Ht. 6-10 Wt. 225
College—St. Louis

Yr.	Team	G	FG	FT	TP	Avg.
1961-62	Cincinnati	58	51	29	131	2.2
1962-63	St. L.-N.Y.	53	156	59	371	7.0
1963-64	N.Y.-St. L.	19	27	9	63	3.3
1964-65	Boston	3	3	0	6	2.2
	Totals	133	237	97	571	4.3

NORLANDER, JOHN

b. March 5, 1921 Ht. 6-3 Wt. 180
College—Hamline

Yr.	Team	G	FG	FT	TP	Avg.
1946-47	Washington	60	232	180	626	10.4
1947-48	Washington	48	167	135	469	9.8
1948-49	Washington	60	164	116	444	7.4
1949-50	Washington	40	99	53	251	6.3
1950-51	Washington	9	6	9	21	2.3
	Totals	217	659	493	1811	8.3

NOSTRAND, GEORGE

b. April 5, 1924 Ht. 6-8 Wt. 197
College—Wyoming

Yr.	Team	G	FG	FT	TP	Avg.
1946-47	Cleve.-Toronto	61	192	98	482	7.9
1947-48	Providence	45	196	129	251	11.6
1948-49	Prov.-Boston	60	212	165	598	9.8
1949-50	Bost.-T.-C.-Chic.	55	78	56	212	3.9
	Totals	221	678	448	1804	8.2

NOSZKA, STANLEY

b. Sept. 19, 1920 Ht. 6-1 Wt. 185
College—Duquesne

Yr.	Team	G	FG	FT	TP	Avg.
1946-47	Pittsburgh	48	199	109	507	8.6
1947-48	Boston	22	27	24	78	3.5
1948-49	Boston	30	30	15	75	2.5
	Totals	110	256	148	660	6.0

NOVAK, MICHAEL

Ht. 6-9 Wt. 220
College—Loyola (Ill.)

Yr.	Team	G	FG	FT	TP	Avg.
1945-46	Sheboygan NL	34	111	89	311	9.1
1946-47	Syracuse NL	36	153	73	379	9.1
1947-48	Syracuse NL	60	212	124	548	9.1
1948-49	Rochester	60	124	72	320	5.3
1949-50	Roch.-Phila.	60	37	25	99	1.7
1953-54	Syracuse	5	0	1	1	0.2
	Totals	255	637	384	1558	6.5

NOWELL, MEL

b. Dec. 27, 1939 Ht. 6-2 Wt. 174
College—Ohio State

Yr.	Team	G	FG	FT	TP	Avg.
1962-63	Chicago	39	92	48	232	5.9

O'BOYLE, JOHN

b. March 7, 1928 Ht. 6-2 Wt. 186
College—Colorado State

Yr.	Team	G	FG	FT	TP	Avg.
1952-53	Milwaukee	5	8	5	21	4.2

O'BRIEN, RALPH

b. April 28, 1928 Ht. 5-9 Wt. 160
College—Butler

Yr.	Team	G	FG	FT	TP	Avg.
1951-52	Indianapolis	64	228	122	578	9.0
1952-53	Baltimore	55	96	78	270	4.9
	Totals	119	324	200	848	7.1

O'BRIEN, ROBERT

b. Jan. 26, 1927 Ht. 6-4 Wt. 190
College—Pepperdine

Yr.	Team	G	FG	FT	TP	Avg.
1947-48	Philadelphia	22	17	15	49	2.2
1948-49	Phila.-St. Louis	24	10	12	32	1.3
	Totals	46	27	27	81	1.8

O'CONNELL, DERMOTT

b. April 13, 1928 Ht. 6-0 Wt. 174
College—Holy Cross

Yr.	Team	G	FG	FT	TP	Avg.
1948-49	Boston	21	87	30	204	9.7
1949-50	Bos.-St. Louis	61	111	47	269	4.4
	Totals	82	198	77	473	5.8

O'DONNELL, ANDY

b. March 10, 1925 Ht. 6-1 Wt. 180
College—Loyola (Md.)

Yr.	Team	G	FG	FT	TP	Avg.
1949-50	Baltimore	25	38	14	90	3.6

O'GRADY, FRANCIS

b. Jan. 19, 1920 Ht. 5-11 Wt. 160
College—Georgetown

Yr.	Team	G	FG	FT	TP	Avg.
1946-47	Washington	55	55	38	148	2.7
1947-48	Washington	44	67	36	170	3.9
1948-49	St. L.-Prov.	47	85	49	219	4.7
	Totals	146	207	123	537	3.7

OHL, DON

b. April 18, 1936 Ht. 6-3 Wt. 190
College—Illinois

Yr.	Team	G	FG	FT	TP	Avg.
1960-61	Detroit	79	427	200	1054	13.1
1961-62	Detroit	77	555	201	1311	17.0
1962-63	Detroit	80	636	275	1547	19.3
1963-64	Detroit	71	500	225	1225	17.3
1964-65	Baltimore	77	568	284	1420	18.4
1965-66	Baltimore	73	593	316	1502	20.6
1966-67	Baltimore	58	452	276	1180	20.3
1967-68	Balt.-St. Louis	70	393	197	983	14.0
	Totals	585	4124	1974	10222	17.5

Yr.	Team	G	FG	FT	TP	Avg.
	O'KEEFE, RICHARD					
	b. Sept. 29, 1923 Ht. 6-2 Wt. 185					
	College—Santa Clara					
1947-48	Washington	37	63	30	156	4.2
1948-49	Washington	50	70	51	191	3.8
1949-50	Washington	68	162	150	474	7.0
1950-51	Washington	17	21	25	67	3.9
	Totals	172	316	256	888	5.2
	O'KEEFE, THOMAS					
	b. July 16, 1926 Ht. 6-2 Wt. 185					
	College—Georgetown					
1950-51	Balt.-Wash.	6	10	3	23	3.8
	OLDHAM, JOHN					
	b. June 22, 1923 Ht. 6-3 Wt. 175					
	College—Western Kentucky					
1949-50	Ft. Wayne	59	127	103	357	6.1
1950-51	Ft. Wayne	68	199	171	569	8.4
	Totals	127	326	274	926	7.3
	OLLRICH, GENE					
	Ht. 5-11 Wt. 160					
	College—Drake					
1949-50	Waterloo	14	17	10	44	3.1
	OLSEN, ENOCH (Bud)					
	b. July 25, 1940 Ht. 6-8 Wt. 220					
	College—Louisville					
1962-63	Cincinnati	52	43	27	113	2.2
1963-64	Cincinnati	49	85	32	202	4.1
1964-65	Cincinnati	79	224	144	592	7.5
1965-66	Cinn.-San. Fran.	59	81	39	201	3.4
1966-67	San Francisco	40	75	23	173	4.3
1967-68	Seattle	73	130	17	277	3.8
	Totals	352	638	282	1558	4.4
	O'NEIL, MIKE					
	Ht. 6-3 Wt. 210					
1952-53	Milwaukee	4	4	4	12	3.0
	ORR, JOHN					
	Ht. 6-3					
	College—Beloit					
1949-50	St. L.-Waterloo	34	40	12	92	2.7
	OSBORNE, CHARLES					
	b. Jan. 21, 1939 Ht. 6-6 Wt. 210					
	College—Western Kentucky					
1961-62	Syracuse	4	1	3	5	2.1
	O'SHEA, KEVIN					
	Ht. 6-2 Wt. 175					
	College—Notre Dame					
1950-51	Minneapolis	63	87	97	271	4.3
1951-52	Milw.-Balt.	65	153	144	450	6.9
1952-53	Baltimore	46	71	48	190	4.1
	Totals	174	311	289	911	5.2
	O'SHIELDS, GARLAND					
	b. May 23, 1921 Ht. 6-1 Wt. 195					
	College—Tennessee					
1946-47	Chicago	9	2	0	4	0.4

Yr.	Team	G	FG	FT	TP	Avg.
	OSTERKORN, WALLY					
	Ht. 6-5 Wt. 215					
	College—Illinois					
1951-52	Syracuse	66	145	199	489	7.4
1952-53	Syracuse	49	85	106	276	5.6
1953-54	Syracuse	70	203	209	615	8.8
1954-55	Syracuse	19	20	16	56	2.9
	Totals	204	453	530	1436	7.0
	OTTEN, DON					
	b. Apr. 18, 1921 Ht. 6-9 Wt. 245					
	College—Bowling Green					
1946-47	Tri-Cities NL	44	196	169	561	12.8
1947-48	Tri-Cities NL	60	282	260	824	13.7
1948-49	Tri-Cities NL	63	290	292	872	13.8
1949-50	Tri-Cities-Wash.	64	242	341	825	12.9
1950-51	Wash.-Balt.-Ft. W.	67	162	246	570	8.5
1951-52	Ft. W.-Milw.	64	222	323	767	12.0
1952-53	Milwaukee	24	34	64	132	5.5
	Totals	386	1428	1695	4551	11.8
	OTTEN, MAC					
	b. Dec. 16, 1925 Ht. 6-7 Wt. 220					
	College—Bowling Green					
1949-50	Tri-Cities-St. L.	59	51	40	142	2.4
	OVERTON, CLAUDE					
	b. Dec. 16, 1927 Ht. 6-2 Wt. 195					
	College—East Central Oklahoma					
1952-53	Philadelphia	15	19	20	58	3.9
	OWENS, JAMES					
	b. Sept. 2, 1925 Ht. 6-3 Wt. 185					
	College—Baylor					
1949-50	Tri-Cities-And.	61	86	68	240	3.9
1951-52	Balt.-Milwaukee	29	83	64	230	7.9
	Totals	90	169	132	470	5.2
	PAINE, FRED					
	b. Dec. 7, 1925 Ht. 6-5 Wt. 210					
	College—Westminster (Pa.)					
1948-49	Providence	3	3	1	7	2.3
	PALAZZI, TOGO					
	b. Aug. 8, 1932 Ht. 6-4 Wt. 205					
	College—Holy Cross					
1954-55	Boston	53	101	45	247	4.7
1955-56	Boston	63	145	85	375	6.0
1956-57	Bos.-Syracuse	63	210	136	556	8.8
1957-58	Syracuse	67	228	123	579	8.6
1958-59	Syracuse	71	240	115	595	8.4
1959-60	Syracuse	7	13	4	30	4.3
	Totals	324	937	508	2382	7.4
	PALMER, JAMES					
	b. June 8, 1933 Ht. 6-8 Wt. 224					
	College—Dayton					
1958-59	Cincinnati	67	256	178	690	10.3
1959-60	Cin.-New York	74	246	119	611	8.3
1960-61	New York	56	125	44	294	5.3
	Totals	197	627	341	1595	8.1

Yr.	Team	G	FG	FT	TP	Avg.
	PALMER, JOHN (Bud)					
	b. Sept. 14, 1921 Ht. 6-4 Wt. 180					
	College—Princeton					
1946-47	New York	42	160	81	401	9.5
1947-48	New York	48	224	174	622	13.0
1948-49	New York	58	240	234	714	12.3
	Totals	148	624	489	1737	11.7
	PARHAM, EASY					
	b. Dec. 27, 1921 Ht. 6-3 Wt. 200					
	College—Texas Wesleyan					
1948-49	St. Louis	60	124	96	344	5.7
1949-50	St. Louis	66	137	88	362	5.5
1950-51	Philadelphia	7	3	4	10	1.4
	Totals	133	264	188	716	5.4
	PARK, MEDFORD (Med)					
	b. Apr. 11, 1933 Ht. 6-2 Wt. 205					
	College—Missouri					
1955-56	St. Louis	40	53	44	150	3.8
1956-57	St. Louis	66	118	108	344	5.2
1957-58	St. Louis	71	133	118	384	5.4
1958-59	St. L.-Cincinnati	62	145	115	405	6.5
1959-60	Cincinnati	74	226	189	641	8.7
	Totals	313	675	574	1924	6.1
	PARKINSON, JACK					
	Ht. 6-0 Wt. 174					
	College—Kentucky					
1949-50	Indianapolis	4	1	1	3	0.8
	PARR, JACK					
	b. Mar. 13, 1936 Ht. 6-9 Wt. 222					
	College—Kansas State					
1958-59	Cincinnati	66	109	44	262	4.0
	PARRACK, DOYLE					
	b. Dec. 6, 1921 Ht. 6-0 Wt. 165					
	College—Oklahoma A&M					
1946-47	Chicago	58	110	52	272	4.7
	PARSLEY, CHARLES					
	Ht. 6-2 Wt. 175					
	College—Western Kentucky					
1948-49	Philadelphia	9	8	6	22	2.4
	PASSAGLIA, MARTIN					
	Ht. 6-1 Wt. 195					
	College—Santa Clara					
1946-47	Washington	43	51	18	120	2.8
1948-49	Indianapolis	19	14	3	31	1.6
	Totals	62	65	21	151	2.4
	PASTUSHOK, GEORGE					
	Ht. 6-1 Wt. 195					
	College—St. John's (N. Y.)					
1946-47	Providence	39	48	25	121	3.1
	PATRICK, STANLEY					
	Ht. 6-3 Wt. 215					
	College—Illinois					
1959-60	Wat.-Sheboygan	53	116	89	321	6.1
	PATTERSON, GEORGE					
	b. Nov. 26, 1939 Ht. 6-8 Wt. 240					
	College—Toledo					
1967-68	Detroit	59	44	32	120	2.0

Yr.	Team	G	FG	FT	TP	Avg.
	PATTERSON, WORTHY					
	Ht. 6-2 Wt. 175					
	College—Connecticut					
1957-58	St. Louis	4	3	1	7	1.8
	PAULSON, GERALD					
	Ht. 6-2 Wt. 187					
	College—Manhattan					
1957-58	Cincinnati	6	8	4	20	3.3
	PAXSON, JAMES					
	b. Dec. 19, 1932 Ht. 6-6 Wt. 200					
	College—Dayton					
1956-57	Minneapolis	71	138	170	446	6.3
1957-58	Cincinnati	67	225	209	659	9.8
	Totals	138	363	379	1105	7.9
	PAYAK, JOHN					
	b. Nov. 20, 1926 Ht. 6-4 Wt. 174					
	College—Bowling Green					
1949-50	Phila.-Waterloo	52	98	121	317	6.1
1952-53	Milwaukee	68	128	180	436	6.4
	Totals	120	226	301	753	6.3
	PAYTON, MEL					
	Ht. 6-4 Wt. 185					
	College—Tulane					
1951-52	Philadelphia	45	54	21	129	2.9
1952-53	Indianapolis	66	173	120	466	7.1
	Totals	111	227	141	595	5.4
	PEARCY, GEORGE					
	Ht. 6-1 Wt. 165					
	College—Indiana State					
1946-47	Detroit	37	31	32	94	2.5
	PEARCY, HENRY					
	Ht. 6-1 Wt. 170					
	College—Indiana State					
1946-47	Detroit	29	24	25	73	2.5
	PELKINGTON, JOHN					
	Ht. 6-6 Wt. 220					
	College—Manhattan					
1945-46	Ft. Wayne NL	33	92	76	260	8.0
1946-47	Ft. Wayne NL	42	129	125	383	9.1
1947-48	Ft. Wayne NL	54	174	157	505	9.4
1948-49	Ft. W.-Baltimore	54	193	211	597	11.1
	Totals	183	588	569	1745	9.5
	PERKINS, WARREN					
	b. Feb. 2, 1924 Ht. 6-3 Wt. 190					
	College—Tulane					
1949-50	Tri-Cities	60	128	115	371	6.2
1950-51	Tri-Cities	66	135	126	396	6.0
	Totals	126	263	241	767	6.1
	PETERSON, EDWARD					
	Ht. 6-9 Wt. 230					
	College—Cornell					
1948-49	Syracuse NL	62	159	100	418	6.8
1949-50	Syracuse	62	167	111	445	7.2
1950-51	Syr.-Tri-Cities	53	130	99	359	6.8
	Totals	177	456	310	1222	6.9

Yr.	Team	G	FG	FT	TP	Avg.
	PETERSON, MEL					
	b. Mar. 23, 1938 Ht. 6-4 Wt. 185					
	College—Wheaton					
1963-64	Baltimore	2	1	0	2	1.0
	PETERSON, ROBERT					
	Ht. 6-5 Wt. 210					
	College—Oregon					
1953-54	Milwaukee	8	3	9	15	1.9
1954-55	New York	37	62	30	154	4.2
1955-56	New York	58	121	68	310	5.3
	Totals	103	186	107	479	4.6
	PETTIT, BOB					
	b. Dec. 12, 1932 Ht. 6-9 Wt. 215					
	College—Louisiana State					
1954-55	Milwaukee	72	520	426	1466	20.4
1955-56	St. Louis	72	646	557	1849	25.7
1956-57	St. Louis	71	613	529	1755	24.7
1957-58	St. Louis	70	581	557	1719	24.6
1958-59	St. Louis	72	719	667	2105	29.2
1959-60	St. Louis	72	669	544	1882	26.1
1960-61	St. Louis	76	769	582	2120	27.9
1961-62	St. Louis	78	867	695	2429	31.1
1962-63	St. Louis	79	778	685	2241	28.4
1963-64	St. Louis	80	791	608	2190	27.4
1964-65	St. Louis	50	396	332	1124	22.5
	Totals	792	7349	6182	20880	26.4
	PHELAN, JACK					
	Ht. 6-5					
	College—DePaul					
1949-50	Wat.-Sheboygan	55	87	52	226	4.1
	PHELAN, JIM					
	Ht. 6-1 Wt. 175					
	College—LaSalle					
1953-54	Philadelphia	4	0	3	3	0.8
	PHILLIP, ANDY					
	b. Mar. 7, 1922 Ht. 6-2 Wt. 195					
	College—Illinois					
1947-48	Chicago	32	143	60	346	10.8
1948-49	Chicago	60	285	148	718	12.0
1949-50	Chicago	65	284	190	758	11.2
1950-51	Philadelphia	66	275	190	740	11.2
1951-52	Philadelphia	66	279	232	790	12.0
1952-53	Ft. Wayne	70	250	222	722	10.3
1953-54	Ft. Wayne	71	255	241	751	10.6
1954-55	Ft. Wayne	64	202	213	617	9.6
1955-56	Ft. Wayne	70	148	112	408	5.8
1956-57	Boston	67	105	88	298	4.4
1957-58	Boston	70	97	42	236	3.4
	Totals	701	2323	1738	6384	9.1
	PHILLIPS, GARY					
	b. Dec. 7, 1939 Ht. 6-3 Wt. 189					
	College—Houston					
1961-62	Boston	72	110	50	270	3.7
1962-63	San Francisco	75	256	97	609	8.1
1963-64	San Francisco	75	256	146	658	10.0
1964-65	San Francisco	73	198	120	516	7.1
1965-66	San Francisco	67	106	54	266	4.0
	Totals	353	926	467	2319	6.6

Yr.	Team	G	FG	FT	TP	Avg.
	PILCH, JOHN					
	Ht. 6-3 Wt. 185					
	College—Wyoming					
1951-52	Minneapolis	9	1	3	6	5.5
	PIONTEK, DAVID					
	b. Aug. 27, 1934 Ht. 6-6 Wt. 230					
	College—Xavier (Ohio)					
1956-57	Rochester	71	257	122	636	9.0
1957-58	Cincinnati	71	150	95	395	5.6
1958-59	Cincinnati	72	305	156	766	10.6
1959-60	Cinn.-St. Louis	77	292	129	713	9.3
1960-61	St. Louis	29	47	16	110	3.8
1961-62	Chicago	45	83	39	205	4.5
1962-63	Cincinnati	48	60	10	130	2.6
	Totals	413	1193	567	2955	7.1
	POLLARD, JIM					
	Ht. 6-3 Wt. 190					
	College—Stanford					
1947-48	Minneapolis NL	59	310	140	760	12.9
1948-49	Minneapolis	53	314	156	784	14.8
1949-50	Minneapolis	66	394	185	973	14.7
1950-51	Minneapolis	54	256	117	629	11.6
1951-52	Minneapolis	65	411	183	1005	15.5
1952-53	Minneapolis	66	333	193	859	13.0
1953-54	Minneapolis	71	326	179	831	11.7
1954-55	Minneapolis	63	265	151	681	10.8
	Totals	497	2609	1304	6522	13.1
	POLSON, RALPH					
	Ht. 6-7 Wt. 205					
	College—Whitworth					
1952-53	N.Y.-Phila.	49	65	61	191	3.9
	PRIDDY, ROBERT					
	Ht. 6-3 Wt. 190					
	College—New Mexico A&M					
1952-53	Baltimore	16	14	8	36	2.3
	PRITCHARD, JOHN					
	Ht. 6-9 Wt. 220					
	College—Drake					
1949-50	Waterloo	7	9	4	22	3.1
	PUGH, LESLIE					
	b. Sept. 18, 1923 Ht. 6-8 Wt. 190					
	College—Ohio State					
1948-49	Providence	60	168	125	461	7.7
1949-50	Baltimore	56	68	115	251	4.5
	Totals	116	236	240	712	6.1
	PUGH, ROY					
	Ht. 6-6 Wt. 210					
	College—Southern Methodist					
1948-49	Ft. W.-Ind.-Phila.	23	13	6	32	1.4
	PUTNAM, DONALD					
	Ht. 6-1 Wt. 170					
	College—Colorado					
1946-47	St. Louis	58	156	68	380	6.6
1947-48	St. Louis	42	105	57	367	6.4
1948-49	St. Louis	59	98	52	248	4.2
1949-50	St. Louis	57	51	33	135	2.4
	Totals	216	410	210	1030	4.8

Yr.	Team	G	FG	FT	TP	Avg.

RADER, HOWARD

Ht. 6-1 Wt. 190
College—Long Island U.

Yr.	Team	G	FG	FT	TP	Avg.
1948-49	Baltimore	13	7	3	17	1.3

RADOVICH, FRANK

b. Mar. 3, 1938 Ht. 6-8 Wt. 235
College—Indiana

Yr.	Team	G	FG	FT	TP	Avg.
1961-62	Philadelphia	37	37	13	87	2.3

RADOVICH, MOE

Ht. 6-0 Wt. 160
College—Wyoming

Yr.	Team	G	FG	FT	TP	Avg.
1952-53	Philadelphia	4	5	4	14	3.5

RADZISZEWSKI, RAY

b. Mar. 1, 1935 Ht. 6-5 Wt. 210
College—St. Joseph's (Pa.)

Yr.	Team	G	FG	FT	TP	Avg.
1957-58	Philadelphia	1	0	0	0	0.0

RAGELIS, RAY

Ht. 6-4 Wt. 205
College—Northwestern

Yr.	Team	G	FG	FT	TP	Avg.
1951-52	Rochester	51	25	18	68	1.3

RAIKEN, SHERWIN

Ht. 6-2 Wt. 185
College—Villanova

Yr.	Team	G	FG	FT	TP	Avg.
1952-53	New York	6	3	3	9	1.5

RAMSEY, CAL

b. July 13, 1937 Ht. 6-4 Wt. 200
College—New York University

Yr.	Team	G	FG	FT	TP	Avg.
1959-60	St. L.-New York	11	39	19	97	8.8
1960-61	Syracuse	2	2	2	6	3.0
	Totals	13	41	21	103	7.9

RAMSEY, FRANK

b. July 13, 1931 Ht. 6-3 Wt. 190
College—Kentucky

Yr.	Team	G	FG	FT	TP	Avg.
1954-55	Boston	64	236	243	715	11.2
1956-57	Boston	35	137	144	418	11.9
1957-58	Boston	69	377	383	1137	16.5
1958-59	Boston	72	383	341	1107	15.4
1959-60	Boston	73	422	273	1117	15.3
1960-61	Boston	79	448	295	1191	15.1
1961-62	Boston	79	436	334	1206	15.3
1962-63	Boston	77	284	271	839	10.9
1963-64	Boston	75	226	196	648	8.6
	Totals	623	2949	2480	8378	13.4

RAMSEY, RAY

Ht. 6-2 Wt. 166
College—Bradley

Yr.	Team	G	FG	FT	TP	Avg.
1948-49	Baltimore	2	0	2	2	1.0

RANZINO, SAM

Ht. 6-1 Wt. 185
College—North Carolina State

Yr.	Team	G	FG	FT	TP	Avg.
1951-52	Rochester	39	30	26	86	2.2

RATKOVICZ, GEORGE

Ht. 6-7 Wt. 225

Yr.	Team	G	FG	FT	TP	Avg.
1945-46	Chicago NL	32	80	66	226	7.1
1947-48	Rochester NL	51	76	75	227	4.2
1948-49	Tri-Cities NL	63	108	106	322	5.1
1949-50	Syracuse	62	162	211	535	8.6
1950-51	Syracuse	66	264	321	849	12.9
1951-52	Syracuse	66	165	163	493	7.5
1952-53	Milwaukee	71	208	262	678	9.5
1953-54	Milwaukee	69	197	176	570	8.3
1954-55	Milwaukee	9	3	10	16	1.8
	Totals	489	1263	1390	3916	8.0

RAY, DON

Ht. 6-6
College—Western Kentucky

Yr.	Team	G	FG	FT	TP	Avg.
1948-49	Tri-Cities	45	123	78	324	7.2
1949-50	Tri-Cities	61	130	104	364	6.0
	Totals	106	253	182	688	6.5

RAY, JAMES

b. Jan. 12, 1934 Ht. 6-1 Wt. 180
College—Toledo

Yr.	Team	G	FG	FT	TP	Avg.
1956-57	Syracuse	4	2	3	7	1.8
1959-60	Syracuse	4	1	0	2	0.5
	Totals	8	3	3	9	1.1

REA, CONNIE

Ht. 6-3 Wt. 175
College—Centenary

Yr.	Team	G	FG	FT	TP	Avg.
1953-54	Baltimore	20	9	5	23	1.2

REDDOUT, FRANK

Ht. 6-5 Wt. 195
College—Syracuse

Yr.	Team	G	FG	FT	TP	Avg.
1953-54	Rochester	7	5	3	13	1.9

REED, HUBERT (Hub)

b. Oct. 4, 1936 Ht. 6-9 Wt. 220
College—Oklahoma City

Yr.	Team	G	FG	FT	TP	Avg.
1958-59	St. Louis	65	136	53	125	5.0
1959-60	St. L.-Cincinnati	71	270	134	674	9.5
1960-61	Cincinnati	75	156	85	397	5.3
1961-62	Cincinnati	80	203	60	466	5.8
1962-63	Cincinnati	80	199	74	472	5.9
1963-64	Los Angeles	46	33	10	76	1.7
1964-65	Detroit	62	84	40	208	3.4
	Totals	479	1081	456	2618	5.5

REED, RON

b. Nov. 2, 1942 Ht. 6-5 Wt. 205
College—Notre Dame

Yr.	Team	G	FG	FT	TP	Avg.
1965-66	Detroit	57	186	54	426	7.5
1966-67	Detroit	62	223	79	525	8.5
	Totals	119	409	133	951	8.0

REED, WILLIS

b. June 25, 1942 Ht. 6-10 Wt. 235
College—Grambling

Yr.	Team	G	FG	FT	TP	Avg.
1964-65	New York	80	629	302	1560	19.5
1965-66	New York	76	438	302	1178	15.5
1966-67	New York	78	635	358	1628	20.9
1967-68	New York	81	659	367	1685	20.8
	Totals	315	2361	1329	6051	19.2

REGAN, RICHIE

b. Nov. 30, 1930 Ht. 6-2 Wt. 180
College—Seton Hall

Yr.	Team	G	FG	FT	TP	Avg.
1955-56	Rochester	72	240	85	565	7.8

Yr.	Team	G	FG	FT	TP	Avg.
1956-57	Rochester	71	257	182	696	9.8
1957-58	Cincinnati	72	202	120	524	7.3
	Totals	215	699	387	1785	8.6
	REHFELDT, DON					
	Ht. 6-6 Wt. 210					
	College—Wisconsin					
1950-51	Baltimore	59	164	103	431	8.6
1951-52	Balt.-Milwaukee	39	99	63	261	6.7
	Totals	98	263	166	692	7.1
	REID, JIM					
	b. Aug. 3, 1945 Ht. 6-6 Wt. 210					
	College—Winston-Salem State					
1967-68	Philadelphia	6	10	1	21	3.5
	REISER, JOHN (Chick)					
	Ht. 5-11 Wt. 165					
	College—New York University					
1945-46	Ft. Wayne NL	34	90	53	233	6.8
1946-47	Ft. Wayne NL	44	154	104	412	9.4
1947-48	Baltimore	47	202	137	541	11.5
1948-49	Baltimore	57	218	188	626	11.0
1949-50	Washington	67	197	212	606	9.0
	Totals	249	862	694	2418	9.7
	RENNICKE, JOHN					
	Ht. 6-2 Wt. 185					
	College—Drake					
1951-52	Milwaukee	6	4	3	11	1.8
	RENSBERGER, ROBERT					
	Ht. 6-2 Wt. 170					
	College—Notre Dame					
1946-47	Chicago	3	0	0	0	0.0
	RHODES, GENE					
	Ht. 6-1 Wt. 170					
	College—Western Kentucky					
1952-53	Indianapolis	65	109	119	337	5.2
	RICHTER, JOHN					
	b. Mar. 12, 1937 Ht. 6-9 Wt. 225					
	College—North Carolina State					
1959-60	Boston	66	113	59	285	4.3
	RICKETTS, DICK					
	b. Dec. 4, 1933 Ht. 6-7 Wt. 220					
	College—Duquesne					
1955-56	St. L.-Rochester	68	235	138	608	8.9
1956-57	Rochester	72	299	206	804	11.2
1957-58	Cincinnati	72	215	132	562	7.8
	Totals	212	749	476	1974	9.6
	RIEBE, MEL					
	Ht. 6-11 Wt. 180					
1943-44	Cleveland NL	18	113	98	324	18.0
1944-45	Cleveland NL	30	224	158	606	20.2
1946-47	Cleveland	55	276	111	663	12.1
1947-48	Boston	48	202	85	489	10.2
1948-49	Bos.-Providence	43	172	79	423	9.8
	Totals	194	987	531	2505	12.9
	RIFFEY, JAMES					
	Ht. 6-4 Wt. 200					
	College—Tulane					

Yr.	Team	G	FG	FT	TP	Avg.
1949-50	Ft. Wayne	35	65	20	150	4.3
	RILEY, PAT					
	b. Mar. 20, 1945 Ht. 6-4 Wt. 208					
	College—Kentucky					
1967-68	San Diego	80	250	128	628	7.9
	RISEN, ARNOLD					
	b. Oct. 9, 1924 Ht. 6-9 Wt. 200					
	College—Ohio State					
1945-46	Indianapolis NL	18	77	65	219	12.2
1946-47	Indianapolis NL	44	204	174	582	13.2
1947-48	Rochester NL	59	275	237	787	13.3
1948-49	Rochester	60	345	305	995	16.6
1949-50	Rochester	62	206	213	625	10.1
1950-51	Rochester	66	377	323	1077	16.3
1951-52	Rochester	66	365	302	1032	15.6
1952-53	Rochester	68	295	294	884	13.0
1953-54	Rochester	72	321	307	949	11.6
1954-55	Rochester	69	259	279	797	11.6
1955-56	Boston	68	189	170	548	8.1
1956-57	Boston	43	119	106	344	8.0
1957-58	Boston	63	134	114	382	6.1
	Totals	758	3166	2889	9221	12.2
	RITTER, GOEBEL (Tex)					
	Ht. 6-2 Wt. 185					
	College—Eastern Kentucky					
1948-49	New York	55	123	91	337	6.1
1949-50	New York	62	100	125	325	5.2
1950-51	New York	34	39	71	127	3.7
	Totals	151	262	265	789	5.2
	ROBBINS, LEE					
	Ht. 6-3 Wt. 175					
	College—Colorado					
1947-48	Providence	31	72	51	195	6.3
1948-49	Providence	16	9	11	29	1.8
	Totals	47	81	62	224	4.8
	ROBERTS, JOSEPH					
	b. May 18, 1936 Ht. 6-6 Wt. 214					
	College—Ohio State					
1960-61	Syracuse	68	130	62	322	4.7
1961-62	Syracuse	80	243	129	615	7.7
1962-63	Syracuse	33	73	35	181	5.5
	Totals	181	446	226	1118	6.2
	ROBERTS, WILLIAM					
	Ht. 6-9 Wt. 210					
	College—Wyoming					
1948-49	Chic.-Bos.-St. L.	50	89	44	222	4.4
1949-50	St. Louis	67	77	28	182	2.7
	Totals	117	166	72	404	3.5
	ROBERTSON, OSCAR (The Big O)					
	b. Nov. 24, 1938 Ht. 6-5 Wt. 205					
	College—Cincinnati					
1960-61	Cincinnati	71	756	653	2165	30.5
1961-62	Cincinnati	79	866	700	2432	30.8
1962-63	Cincinnati	80	825	614	2264	28.3
1963-64	Cincinnati	79	840	800	2480	31.4
1964-65	Cincinnati	75	807	665	2279	30.4
1965-66	Cincinnati	76	818	742	2378	31.3
1966-67	Cincinnati	79	838	736	2412	30.5

Yr.	Team	G	FG	FT	TP	Avg.
1967-68	Cincinnati	65	660	576	1896	29.2
	Totals	604	6410	5486	18306	30.3

ROBINSON, FLYNN

b. Apr. 28, 1941 Ht. 6-1 Wt. 190
College—Wyoming

Yr.	Team	G	FG	FT	TP	Avg.
1966-67	Cincinnati	76	274	120	668	8.8
1967-68	Cinn.-Chicago	75	444	288	1176	15.7
	Totals	151	718	408	1844	12.2

ROCHA, EPHRAIM (Red)

Ht. 6-9 Wt. 185
College—Oregon State

Yr.	Team	G	FG	FT	TP	Avg.
1947-48	St. Louis	48	232	147	611	12.8
1948-49	St. Louis	58	223	162	608	10.5
1949-50	St. Louis	65	275	220	770	11.8
1950-51	Baltimore	64	297	242	836	13.1
1951-52	Syracuse	66	300	254	854	12.9
1952-53	Syracuse	69	268	234	770	11.2
1954-55	Syracuse	72	295	222	812	11.3
1955-56	Syracuse	72	250	220	720	10.0
1956-57	Ft. Wayne	72	136	109	381	5.3
	Totals	586	2276	1810	6362	10.9

ROCK, GENE

Ht. 5-9 Wt. 155
College—Southern California

Yr.	Team	G	FG	FT	TP	Avg.
1947-48	Chicago	11	4	2	10	0.9

ROCKER, JACK

Ht. 6-5 Wt. 286
College—California

Yr.	Team	G	FG	FT	TP	Avg.
1947-48	Philadelphia	9	8	1	17	1.9

RODGERS, GUY

b. Sept. 1, 1935 Ht. 6-0 Wt. 185
College—Temple

Yr.	Team	G	FG	FT	TP	Avg.
1958-59	Philadelphia	45	211	61	483	10.7
1959-60	Philadelphia	68	338	111	787	11.6
1960-61	Philadelphia	78	397	206	1000	12.8
1961-62	Philadelphia	80	267	121	655	8.2
1962-63	San Francisco	78	445	208	1098	14.1
1963-64	San Francisco	79	337	198	872	11.0
1964-65	San Francisco	79	465	223	1153	14.6
1965-66	San Francisco	79	586	296	1468	18.6
1966-67	Chicago	81	538	383	1459	18.0
1967-68	Chic.-Cincinnati	78	148	107	403	5.2
	Totals	745	3732	1914	9378	12.6

ROGES, ALBERT

Ht. 6-4 Wt. 200
College—Long Island U.

Yr.	Team	G	FG	FT	TP	Avg.
1953-54	Baltimore	67	220	130	570	8.5
1954-55	Ft. Wayne	17	23	15	61	3.6
	Totals	84	243	145	631	7.5

ROHLOFF, KEN

b. Apr. 18, 1939 Ht. 6-0 Wt. 195
College—North Carolina State

Yr.	Team	G	FG	FT	TP	Avg.
1963-64	St. Louis	2	0	0	0	0.0

ROLLINS, KEN

b. Sept. 14, 1923 Ht. 6-0 Wt. 168
College—Kentucky

Yr.	Team	G	FG	FT	TP	Avg.
1948-49	Chicago	59	144	77	365	6.2
1949-50	Chicago	66	144	66	354	5.4
1952-53	Boston	23	38	22	98	2.2
	Totals	168	326	165	817	4.9

ROLLINS, PHILIP

b. Jan. 19, 1934 Ht. 6-2 Wt. 190
College—Louisville

Yr.	Team	G	FG	FT	TP	Avg.
1958-59	Phila.-Cin.	44	83	63	229	5.2
1959-60	Cincinnati	72	158	77	393	5.5
1960-61	Cin.-St. L.-N.Y.	61	105	56	266	4.4
	Totals	177	346	196	888	5.0

ROSENBERG, ALEXANDER (Petey)

Ht. 5-10 Wt. 165
College—St. Joseph's (Pa.)

Yr.	Team	G	FG	FT	TP	Avg.
1946-47	Philadelphia	51	60	30	150	2.9

ROSENBLUTH, LEONARD

b. Jan. 22, 1933 Ht. 6-5 Wt. 200
College—North Carolina

Yr.	Team	G	FG	FT	TP	Avg.
1957-58	Philadelphia	53	91	53	235	4.4
1958-59	Philadelphia	29	43	21	107	3.7
	Totals	82	134	74	342	4.2

ROSENSTEIN, HENRY

Ht. 6-4
College—CCNY

Yr.	Team	G	FG	FT	TP	Avg.
1946-47	New York	31	38	57	133	4.3
1947-48	Providence	29	81	87	249	8.6
	Totals	60	119	144	382	6.4

ROSENTHAL, RICHARD

Ht. 6-5 Wt. 205
College—Notre Dame

Yr.	Team	G	FG	FT	TP	Avg.
1954-55	Ft. Wayne	67	197	130	524	7.8
1956-57	Ft. Wayne	18	21	9	51	2.8
	Totals	85	218	139	575	6.8

ROTHENBERG, IRVING

Ht. 6-5 Wt. 215
College—Long Island U.

Yr.	Team	G	FG	FT	TP	Avg.
1946-47	Cleveland	29	36	30	102	3.5
1947-48	Balt.-St. L.-Wash.	49	103	87	293	6.0
1948-49	New York	53	101	112	314	5.9
	Totals	131	240	229	609	4.6

ROTTMAN, MARVIN

Ht. 5-10 Wt. 185
College—Loyola (Ill.)

Yr.	Team	G	FG	FT	TP	Avg.
1946-47	Chicago	56	190	43	423	7.6
1947-48	Chicago	44	53	11	117	2.7
	Totals	100	243	54	540	5.4

ROUX, GIFFORD

Ht. 6-5 Wt. 195

Yr.	Team	G	FG	FT	TP	Avg.
1946-47	St. Louis	60	142	70	354	5.9
1947-48	St. Louis	46	68	40	176	3.8
1948-49	St. L.-Prov.	45	29	29	87	1.9
	Totals	151	239	139	617	4.1

ROYER, BOB

Ht. 5-10 Wt. 155
College—Indiana State

Yr.	Team	G	FG	FT	TP	Avg.
1949-50	Denver	42	78	41	197	4.7

Yr.	Team	G	FG	FT	TP	Avg.
	RUDOMETKIN, JOHN					
	b. June 6, 1940 Ht. 6-6 Wt. 205					
	College—Southern California					
1962-63	New York	56	108	73	289	5.2
1963-64	New York	52	154	87	395	7.6
1964-65	N.Y.-San Fran.	23	52	34	138	6.0
	Totals	131	314	194	822	6.3
	RUKLICK, JOSEPH					
	b. Aug. 3, 1938 Ht. 6-9 Wt. 220					
	College—Northwestern					
1959-60	Philadelphia	39	85	26	196	5.0
1960-61	Philadelphia	29	43	8	94	3.2
1961-62	Philadelphia	46	48	12	108	1.8
	Totals	114	176	46	398	3.5
	RULE, BOB					
	b. June 29, 1944 Ht. 6-9 Wt. 220					
	College—Colorado St. U.					
1967-68	Seattle	82	568	348	1484	18.1
	RULLO, JERRY					
	Ht. 5-10 Wt. 165					
	College—Temple					
1946-47	Philadelphia	50	52	23	127	2.5
1947-48	Baltimore	2	0	0	0	0.0
1948-49	Philadelphia	39	53	31	137	3.5
1949-50	Philadelphia	4	3	1	7	1.8
	Totals	95	108	55	271	2.9
	RUSSELL, CAZZIE					
	b. June 7, 1944 Ht. 6-5½ Wt. 218					
	College—Michigan					
1966-67	New York	77	344	179	867	11.3
1967-68	New York	82	551	282	1384	16.9
	Totals	159	895	461	2251	14.2
	RUSSELL, BILL					
	b. Feb. 12, 1934 Ht. 6-10 Wt. 220					
	College—San Francisco					
1956-57	Boston	48	277	152	706	14.7
1957-58	Boston	69	456	230	1142	16.6
1958-59	Boston	70	456	256	1168	16.7
1959-60	Boston	74	555	240	1350	18.2
1960-61	Boston	78	532	258	1322	16.9
1961-62	Boston	76	575	286	1436	18.9
1962-63	Boston	78	511	287	1309	16.8
1963-64	Boston	78	466	236	1168	15.0
1964-65	Boston	78	429	244	1102	14.1
1965-66	Boston	78	391	223	1005	12.9
1966-67	Boston	81	395	285	1075	13.4
1967-68	Boston	78	365	247	977	12.5
	Totals	886	5408	2944	13760	15.5
	SADOWSKI, EDWARD					
	b. July 11, 1917 Ht. 6-5 Wt. 240					
	College—Seton Hall					
1945-46	Ft. Wayne NL	34	122	82	326	9.6
1946-47	Tor.-Cleveland	53	329	219	877	16.5
1947-48	Boston	47	308	294	910	19.4
1948-49	Philadelphia	60	340	240	920	15.3
1949-50	Phila.-Balt.	69	299	274	872	12.6
	Totals	263	1398	1109	3905	14.8

Yr.	Team	G	FG	FT	TP	Avg.
	SAILORS, KEN					
	b. Jan. 14, 1922 Ht. 5-10 Wt. 176					
	College—Wyoming					
1946-47	Cleveland	58	229	119	577	9.9
1947-48	Chic.-Phila.-Prov.	44	207	110	524	12.2
1948-49	Providence	57	309	281	899	15.8
1949-50	Denver	57	329	329	987	17.3
1950-51	Bos.-Baltimore	60	181	131	493	8.2
	Totals	276	1255	970	3480	12.6
	SANDERS, THOMAS (Satch)					
	b. Nov. 8, 1938 Ht. 6-6 Wt. 210					
	College—New York University					
1960-61	Boston	68	148	67	363	5.3
1961-62	Boston	80	350	197	897	11.2
1962-63	Boston	80	339	186	864	10.8
1963-64	Boston	80	349	213	911	11.4
1964-65	Boston	80	374	193	941	11.8
1965-66	Boston	72	349	211	909	12.6
1966-67	Boston	81	323	178	824	10.2
1967-68	Boston	78	296	200	792	10.2
	Totals	619	2528	1445	6501	10.5
	SANTINI, ROBERT					
	Ht. 6-5					
	College—Iona					
1955-56	New York	4	5	1	11	2.8
	SAUL, FRANK (Pep)					
	Ht. 6-2 Wt. 185					
	College—Seton Hall					
1949-50	Rochester	49	74	34	182	3.7
1950-51	Rochester	65	105	72	282	4.3
1951-52	Balt.-Minneap.	64	157	119	433	6.8
1952-53	Minneapolis	70	187	142	516	7.4
1953-54	Minneapolis	71	162	128	452	6.4
1954-55	Milwaukee	65	96	95	287	4.4
	Totals	384	781	590	2152	5.6
	SAULDSBERRY, WOODY					
	b. July 11, 1934 Ht. 6-7 Wt. 220					
	College—Texas Southern					
1957-58	Philadelphia	71	389	134	912	12.8
1958-59	Philadelphia	72	501	110	1112	15.4
1959-60	Philadelphia	71	325	55	705	9.9
1960-61	St. Louis	68	230	56	516	7.6
1961-62	St. L.-Chicago	63	298	79	675	10.7
1962-63	Chi.-St. Louis	77	366	107	839	10.9
1965-66	Boston	39	80	11	171	4.4
	Totals	461	2189	552	4930	10.7
	SAVAGE, DON					
	b. Apr. 9, 1929 Ht. 6-3 Wt. 205					
	College—LeMoyne (N. Y.)					
1951-52	Syracuse	12	9	18	36	3.0
1956-57	Syracuse	5	6	6	18	3.6
	Totals	17	15	24	54	3.2
	SAWYER, ALAN					
	Ht. 6-5 Wt. 195					
	College—UCLA					
1950-51	Washington	33	87	43	217	6.6

Yr.	Team	G	FG	FT	TP	Avg.

SCHADLER, BEN
Ht. 6-2
College—Northwestern

Yr.	Team	G	FG	FT	TP	Avg.
1947-48	Chicago	37	23	10	56	1.5
1948-49	Waterloo NL	54	145	58	348	6.5
	Totals	91	168	68	404	4.4

SCHAEFFER, CARL
Ht. 6-0 Wt. 175
College—Indiana

Yr.	Team	G	FG	FT	TP	Avg.
1948-49	Minneapolis	58	214	174	602	10.4
1949-50	Minneapolis	65	122	86	330	5.1
	Totals	123	336	260	932	7.6

SCHAEFFER, CARL
Ht. 6-3 Wt. 185
College—Alabama

Yr.	Team	G	FG	FT	TP	Avg.
1949-50	Indianapolis	43	59	32	150	3.5
1950-51	Indianapolis	10	6	3	15	1.5
	Totals	53	65	35	165	3.1

SCHAFER, ROBERT
Ht. 6-3 Wt. 195
College—Villanova

Yr.	Team	G	FG	FT	TP	Avg.
1955-56	Phila.-St. Louis	54	81	62	224	4.1
1956-57	Syracuse	11	19	11	49	4.5
	Totals	65	100	73	273	4.2

SCHARNES, BEN
Ht. 6-2 Wt. 173
College—Seton Hall

Yr.	Team	G	FG	FT	TP	Avg.
1946-47	Cleveland	51	33	37	103	2.0
1948-49	Providence	1	0	0	0	0.0
	Totals	52	33	37	103	2.0

SCHATZMAN, MARVIN
Ht. 6-5 Wt. 200
College—St. Louis

Yr.	Team	G	FG	FT	TP	Avg.
1949-50	Baltimore	34	43	29	115	3.4

SCHAUS, FRED
b. June 30, 1925 Ht. 6-5 Wt. 210
College—West Virginia

Yr.	Team	G	FG	FT	TP	Avg.
1949-50	Ft. Wayne	68	351	270	972	14.3
1950-51	Ft. Wayne	68	312	404	1028	15.1
1951-52	Ft. Wayne	62	281	310	872	14.1
1952-53	Ft. Wayne	69	240	243	723	10.5
1953-54	New York	67	161	153	475	7.1
	Totals	334	1345	1380	4070	12.2

SCHAYES, DOLPH
b. May 19, 1928 Ht. 6-8 Wt. 220
College—New York University

Yr.	Team	G	FG	FT	TP	Avg.
1948-49	Syracuse NL	63	272	267	811	12.8
1949-50	Syracuse	64	348	376	1072	16.8
1950-51	Syracuse	66	332	457	1121	17.0
1951-52	Syracuse	63	263	342	868	13.8
1952-53	Syracuse	71	375	512	1262	17.8
1953-54	Syracuse	72	370	488	1228	17.1
1954-55	Syracuse	72	422	489	1333	18.5
1955-56	Syracuse	72	465	542	1472	20.4
1956-57	Syracuse	72	496	625	1617	22.5
1957-58	Syracuse	72	581	629	1791	24.9
1958-59	Syracuse	72	504	526	1534	21.3
1959-60	Syracuse	75	578	533	1689	22.5
1960-61	Syracuse	79	594	680	1868	23.6
1961-62	Syracuse	56	268	286	822	14.7
1962-63	Syracuse	66	223	181	627	9.5
1963-64	Philadelphia	24	44	46	134	5.6
	Totals	1059	6135	6979	19249	18.2

SCHECTMAN, OSCAR (Ossie)
Ht. 6-0 Wt. 175
College—Long Island U.

Yr.	Team	G	FG	FT	TP	Avg.
1946-47	New York	54	162	111	435	8.1

SCHELLHASE, DAVE
b. Oct. 14, 1944 Ht. 6-3½ Wt. 205
College—Purdue

Yr.	Team	G	FG	FT	TP	Avg.
1966-67	Chicago	31	40	14	94	3.0
1967-68	Chicago	42	47	20	114	2.7
	Totals	73	87	34	208	2.9

SCHERER, HERB
Ht. 6-9
College—Long Island U.

Yr.	Team	G	FG	FT	TP	Avg.
1950-51	Tri-Cities	20	24	20	68	3.4
1951-52	New York	12	19	9	47	3.9
	Totals	32	43	29	115	3.6

SCHNELLBACHER, OTTO
b. Apr. 15, 1923 Ht. 6-5 Wt. 185
College—Kansas

Yr.	Team	G	FG	FT	TP	Avg.
1948-49	Prov.-St. Louis	43	93	89	275	6.4

SCHNITTKER, RICHARD
b. May 27, 1928 Ht. 6-5 Wt. 205
College—Ohio State

Yr.	Team	G	FG	FT	TP	Avg.
1950-51	Washington	29	85	123	293	10.1
1953-54	Minneapolis	71	122	86	330	4.6
1954-55	Minneapolis	72	226	298	750	10.4
1955-56	Minneapolis	72	254	304	812	11.3
1956-57	Minneapolis	70	113	160	386	5.5
1957-58	Minneapolis	50	128	201	457	9.1
	Totals	364	928	1172	3028	8.3

SCHOON, MILTON
Ht. 6-9 Wt. 230
College—Valparaiso

Yr.	Team	G	FG	FT	TP	Avg.
1946-47	Detroit	41	43	34	120	2.9
1947-48	Flint NL	54	113	119	345	6.4
1948-49	Sheboygan NL	56	81	109	271	4.8
1949-50	Sheboygan	62	150	196	496	8.0
	Totals	213	387	458	1232	5.8

SCHULTZ, HOWARD
Ht. 6-8 Wt. 220
College—Hamline

Yr.	Team	G	FG	FT	TP	Avg.
1946-47	Anderson NL	41	155	147	457	11.1
1947-48	Anderson NL	60	214	180	608	10.1
1948-49	Anderson NL	63	172	183	527	8.5
1949-50	And.-Ft. Wayne	67	179	196	554	8.3
1951-52	Minneapolis	66	89	90	268	4.1
1952-53	Minneapolis	40	24	43	91	2.3
	Totals	337	833	839	2505	7.4

Yr.	Team	G	FG	FT	TP	Avg.

SCHULZ, RICHARD

b. July 3, 1922 Ht. 6-2 Wt. 192
College—Wisconsin

Yr.	Team	G	FG	FT	TP	Avg.
1945-46	Anderson NL	41	155	147	457	11.1
1946-47	Cleve.-Toronto	57	130	94	354	6.2
1947-48	Baltimore	48	133	117	383	8.0
1948-49	Washington	50	65	65	195	3.9
1949-50	Wash.-Tri-Cities	50	63	83	209	4.2
	Totals	234	446	425	1317	5.9

SCOLARI, FRED

b. Mar. 1, 1922 Ht. 5-10 Wt. 180
College—San Francisco

Yr.	Team	G	FG	FT	TP	Avg.
1946-47	Washington	58	291	146	728	12.6
1947-48	Washington	47	292	131	589	12.5
1948-49	Washington	48	196	146	538	11.2
1949-50	Washington	66	312	236	860	13.0
1950-51	Wash.-Syracuse	66	302	279	883	13.4
1951-52	Baltimore	64	290	353	933	14.6
1952-53	Ft. Wayne	62	277	276	830	13.4
1953-54	Ft. Wayne	64	159	144	462	7.2
1954-55	Boston	59	76	39	191	3.2
	Totals	534	2132	1750	6014	11.3

SCOTT, RAY

b. July 12, 1938 Ht. 6-9 Wt. 215
College—Portland

Yr.	Team	G	FG	FT	TP	Avg.
1961-62	Detroit	75	370	255	995	13.3
1962-63	Detroit	76	460	308	1228	16.2
1963-64	Detroit	80	539	328	1406	17.6
1964-65	Detroit	66	402	220	1024	15.5
1965-66	Detroit	79	544	323	1411	17.9
1966-67	Det.-Baltimore	72	458	256	1172	16.3
1967-68	Baltimore	81	490	348	1328	16.4
	Totals	529	3263	2038	8564	16.2

SEARS, KEN

b. Aug. 17, 1933 Ht. 6-9 Wt. 195
College—Santa Clara

Yr.	Team	G	FG	FT	TP	Avg.
1955-56	New York	70	319	258	896	12.8
1956-57	New York	72	343	383	1069	14.8
1957-58	New York	72	445	452	1342	18.6
1958-59	New York	71	491	506	1488	21.0
1959-60	New York	71	412	363	1187	18.5
1960-61	New York	52	241	268	750	14.4
1962-63	N.Y.-San Fran.	77	161	131	453	5.9
1963-64	San Francisco	51	53	64	170	3.3
	Totals	529	2465	2425	7355	13.9

SEE, WAYNE

Ht. 6-3
College—Arizona State U.

Yr.	Team	G	FG	FT	TP	Avg.
1949-50	Waterloo	61	113	94	320	5.2

SELBO, GLEN

Ht. 6-3 Wt. 195
College—Wisconsin

Yr.	Team	G	FG	FT	TP	Avg.
1947-48	Oshkosh NL	59	157	62	376	6.5
1948-49	Oshkosh NL	60	119	77	315	5.2
1949-50	Sheboygan	13	10	22	42	3.2
	Totals	132	286	161	733	5.6

SELTZ, ROLLIE

Ht. 5-10 Wt. 170
College—Hamline

Yr.	Team	G	FG	FT	TP	Avg.
1947-48	Anderson NL	59	118	89	325	5.5
1948-49	Waterloo NL	61	189	127	505	8.4
1949-50	Anderson	34	93	80	266	7.8
	Totals	154	400	296	1096	7.1

SELVY, FRANK

b. Nov. 9, 1932 Ht. 6-2 Wt. 180
College—Furman

Yr.	Team	G	FG	FT	TP	Avg.
1954-55	Balt.-Milwaukee	71	452	444	1348	19.0
1955-56	St. Louis	17	67	53	187	11.0
1957-58	St. L.-Minneap.	38	44	47	135	3.6
1958-59	New York	68	233	201	667	9.8
1959-60	Syracuse-Minn.	62	205	153	563	9.1
1960-61	Los Angeles	77	311	210	832	10.8
1961-62	Los Angeles	79	433	298	1164	14.7
1962-63	Los Angeles	80	317	192	826	10.3
1963-64	Los Angeles	73	160	78	398	5.5
	Totals	565	2222	1676	6120	10.8

SEMINOFF, JAMES

Ht. 6-2 Wt. 200
College—Southern California

Yr.	Team	G	FG	FT	TP	Avg.
1946-47	Chicago	60	184	71	439	7.3
1947-48	Chicago	48	113	73	299	6.3
1948-49	Boston	58	153	151	457	7.9
1949-50	Boston	65	85	142	315	4.8
	Totals	231	535	437	1507	6.5

SENESKY, GEORGE

b. Apr. 4, 1922 Ht. 6-2 Wt. 180
College—St. Joseph's (Pa.)

Yr.	Team	G	FG	FT	TP	Avg.
1946-47	Philadelphia	58	142	82	336	6.3
1947-48	Philadelphia	47	158	98	414	8.8
1948-49	Philadelphia	60	138	111	387	6.4
1949-50	Philadelphia	68	227	157	611	9.0
1950-51	Philadelphia	65	249	181	679	10.4
1951-52	Philadelphia	57	164	146	474	8.3
1952-53	Philadelphia	69	160	93	413	6.0
1953-54	Philadelphia	58	41	29	111	1.9
	Totals	482	1279	897	3455	7.1

SEYMOUR, PAUL

b. Jan. 30, 1928 Ht. 6-2 Wt. 180
College—Toledo

Yr.	Team	G	FG	FT	TP	Avg.
1947-48	Baltimore	22	27	22	76	3.5
1947-48	Syracuse NL	29	78	46	202	6.9
1948-49	Syracuse NL	61	114	80	308	5.0
1949-50	Syracuse	62	175	126	476	7.7
1950-51	Syracuse	51	125	117	367	7.2
1951-52	Syracuse	66	206	186	598	9.1
1952-53	Syracuse	67	306	340	952	14.2
1953-54	Syracuse	71	316	299	931	13.1
1954-55	Syracuse	72	375	300	1050	14.6
1955-56	Syracuse	57	227	188	642	11.3
1956-57	Syracuse	65	143	101	387	6.0
1957-58	Syracuse	64	107	53	267	4.2
1958-59	Syracuse	21	32	26	90	4.3
1959-60	Syracuse	4	1	0	2	0.5
	Totals	712	2232	1884	6348	8.9

SHABACK, NICHOLAS

Ht. 5-11 Wt. 182

Yr.	Team	G	FG	FT	TP	Avg.
1946-47	Cleveland	53	102	38	242	4.6

SHAFFER, LEE

b. Feb. 23, 1939 Ht. 6-7 Wt. 220
College—North Carolina

Yr.	Team	G	FG	FT	TP	Avg.
1961-62	Syracuse	75	514	239	1267	16.9
1962-63	Syracuse	80	597	294	1488	18.6
1963-64	Philadelphia	41	217	102	536	13.1
	Totals	196	1328	635	3291	16.8

SHANNON, EARL

Ht. 5-11 Wt. 170
College—Rhode Island

Yr.	Team	G	FG	FT	TP	Avg.
1946-47	Providence	57	245	197	687	12.0
1947-48	Providence	45	123	116	362	8.0
1948-49	Prov.-Boston	32	34	39	107	3.3
	Totals	134	402	352	1156	8.6

SHANNON, HOWARD

Ht. 6-3 Wt. 175
College—Kansas

Yr.	Team	G	FG	FT	TP	Avg.
1948-49	Providence	55	292	152	736	13.1
1949-50	Boston	67	222	143	587	8.8
	Totals	122	514	295	1323	10.8

SHARE, CHARLIE

b. Mar. 14, 1927 Ht. 6-11 Wt. 235
College—Bowling Green

Yr.	Team	G	FG	FT	TP	Avg.
1951-52	Ft. Wayne	63	76	96	249	3.9
1952-53	Ft. Wayne	67	91	172	354	5.3
1953-54	Ft. Wayne	68	188	188	564	8.3
1954-55	Milwaukee	69	235	351	821	11.9
1955-56	St. Louis	72	315	346	976	13.6
1956-57	St. Louis	72	235	269	739	10.3
1957-58	St. Louis	72	216	190	622	8.6
1958-59	St. Louis	72	147	139	433	6.6
	Totals	555	1503	1751	4757	8.6

SHARMAN, BILL

b. May 25, 1926 Ht. 6-1 Wt. 190
College—Southern California

Yr.	Team	G	FG	FT	TP	Avg.
1950-51	Washington	31	141	96	378	12.2
1951-52	Boston	63	244	183	671	10.7
1952-53	Boston	71	403	341	1147	16.2
1953-54	Boston	72	412	331	1155	16.0
1954-55	Boston	68	453	347	1253	18.4
1955-56	Boston	72	538	358	1434	19.9
1956-57	Boston	67	516	381	1413	21.1
1957-58	Boston	63	550	302	1402	22.3
1958-59	Boston	72	562	342	1466	20.4
1959-60	Boston	71	599	252	1370	19.3
1960-61	Boston	60	383	210	976	16.3
	Totals	710	4761	3143	12665	17.8

SHAVLIK, RON

b. D c. 4, 1933 Ht. 6-8 Wt. 200
College—North Carolina State

Yr.	Team	G	FG	FT	TP	Avg.
1956-57	New York	7	4	2	10	1.4
1957-58	New York	1	0	0	0	0.0
	Totals	8	4	2	10	1.3

SHEA, ROBERT

Ht. 6-2 Wt. 194
College—Rhode Island

Yr.	Team	G	FG	FT	TP	Avg.
1946-47	Providence	43	37	19	93	2.2

SHEFFIELD, FRED

Ht. 6-2 Wt. 165
College—Utah

Yr.	Team	G	FG	FT	TP	Avg.
1946-47	Philadelphia	22	29	16	74	3.4

SHIPP, CHARLES

Ht. 6-1 Wt. 205

Yr.	Team	G	FG	FT	TP	Avg.
1947-48	Anderson NL	54	103	63	269	5.0
1948-49	Waterloo NL	55	100	57	257	4.7
1949-50	Waterloo	23	35	37	107	4.7
	Totals	132	238	157	633	4.8

SHRIDER, DICK

Ht. 6-2 Wt. 190
College—Ohio University

Yr.	Team	G	FG	FT	TP	Avg.
1948-49	New York	4	0	1	1	0.3

SHUE, GENE

b. Dec. 18, 1931 Ht. 6-2 Wt. 175
College—Maryland

Yr.	Team	G	FG	FT	TP	Avg.
1954-55	Phila.-New York	62	100	59	259	4.2
1955-56	New York	72	240	181	661	9.2
1956-57	Ft. Wayne	72	273	241	787	10.9
1957-58	Detroit	63	353	276	982	15.6
1958-59	Detroit	72	464	338	1266	17.6
1959-60	Detroit	75	620	472	1712	22.8
1960-61	Detroit	78	650	465	1765	22.6
1961-62	Detroit	80	580	362	1522	19.0
1962-63	New York	78	354	208	916	11.7
1963-64	Baltimore	48	81	36	198	4.1
	Totals	700	3715	2638	10068	14.4

SIEGFRIED, LARRY

b. May 22, 1939 Ht. 6-4 Wt. 192
College—Ohio State

Yr.	Team	G	FG	FT	TP	Avg.
1963-64	Boston	31	35	31	101	3.3
1964-65	Boston	72	173	109	455	6.3
1965-66	Boston	71	349	274	972	13.7
1966-67	Boston	73	368	294	1030	14.1
1967-68	Boston	62	261	236	758	12.2
	Totals	309	1186	944	3316	10.7

SIEWERT, RALPH

Ht. 7-1 Wt. 230
College—North Dakota State

Yr.	Team	G	FG	FT	TP	Avg.
1946-47	St. Louis	7	1	2	4	0.6
1947-48	Toronto	14	5	6	16	1.1
	Totals	21	6	8	20	1.0

SILAS, PAUL

b. July 12, 1943 Ht. 6-7 Wt. 235
College—Creighton

Yr.	Team	G	FG	FT	TP	Avg.
1964-65	St. Louis	79	140	83	363	4.6
1965-66	St. Louis	46	70	35	175	3.8
1966-67	St. Louis	76	207	113	527	6.9
1967-68	St. Louis	82	399	299	1097	13.4
	Totals	283	816	530	2162	7.6

SIMMONS, CONNIE

b. Mar. 15, 1925 Ht. 6-8 Wt. 225

Yr.	Team	G	FG	FT	TP	Avg.
1946-47	Boston	60	246	128	620	10.3
1947-48	Bos.-Baltimore	45	162	62	386	8.6
1948-49	Baltimore	60	299	181	779	13.0
1949-50	New York	60	241	198	680	11.3
1950-51	New York	66	229	146	604	9.2
1951-52	New York	66	227	175	629	9.5
1952-53	New York	65	240	249	729	11.2
1953-54	New York	72	255	210	720	10.0
1954-55	Syracuse	36	137	72	346	9.6
1955-56	Rochester	68	144	78	366	5.4
	Totals	598	2200	1499	5859	9.8

SIMMONS, JOHN

Ht. 6-1 Wt. 184
College—New York University

Yr.	Team	G	FG	FT	TP	Avg.
1946-47	Boston	60	120	78	318	5.3

SIMS, ROBERT

b. Oct. 9, 1938 Ht. 6-5 Wt. 220
College—Pepperdine

Yr.	Team	G	FG	FT	TP	Avg.
1961-62	L.A.-St. Louis	65	193	123	509	7.8

SINICOLA, EMILIO (Zeke)

Ht. 5-10 Wt. 165
College—Niagara

Yr.	Team	G	FG	FT	TP	Avg.
1951-52	Ft. Wayne	3	1	0	2	0.7
1953-54	Ft. Wayne	9	4	3	11	1.2
	Totals	12	5	3	13	1.1

SKOOG, MEYER (Whitey)

b. Nov. 2, 1926 Ht. 5-11 Wt. 180
College—Minnesota

Yr.	Team	G	FG	FT	TP	Avg.
1951-52	Minneapolis	35	102	30	234	6.7
1952-53	Minneapolis	68	102	46	250	3.7
1953-54	Minneapolis	71	212	72	496	7.0
1954-55	Minneapolis	72	330	125	785	10.9
1955-56	Minneapolis	72	340	155	835	11.0
1956-57	Minneapolis	23	78	44	200	8.7
	Totals	341	1164	472	2800	8.2

SLADE, JEFFREY

b. Mar. 1, 1941 Ht. 6-6 Wt. 220
College—Kenyon

Yr.	Team	G	FG	FT	TP	Avg.
1962-63	Chicago	3	2	0	4	1.3

SLAUGHTER, JIM

Ht. 6-11 Wt. 212
College—South Carolina

Yr.	Team	G	FG	FT	TP	Avg.
1951-52	Baltimore	28	53	41	147	5.3

SLOAN, JERRY

b. Mar. 28, 1942 Ht. 6-6 Wt. 195
College—Evansville

Yr.	Team	G	FG	FT	TP	Avg.
1965-66	Baltimore	59	120	98	338	5.7
1966-67	Chicago	80	525	340	1390	17.4
1967-68	Chicago	77	369	289	1027	13.3
	Totals	216	1014	629	2755	12.8

SMAWLEY, BELUS

Ht. 6-1 Wt. 195
College—Appalachian State

Yr.	Team	G	FG	FT	TP	Avg.
1946-47	St. Louis	22	113	36	262	11.9
1947-48	St. Louis	48	212	111	535	11.2
1948-49	St. Louis	59	352	210	914	15.9
1949-50	St. Louis	61	287	260	834	13.7
1950-51	Syracuse-Balt.	60	252	227	731	12.2
	Totals	250	1216	844	3276	13.1

SMILEY, JACK

Ht. 6-3 Wt. 190
College—Illinois

Yr.	Team	G	FG	FT	TP	Avg.
1947-48	Ft. Wayne NL	60	104	89	297	5.0
1948-49	Ft. Wayne	59	141	112	394	6.7
1949-50	And.-Waterloo	59	98	136	332	5.6
	Totals	178	343	337	1023	5.7

SMITH, ADRIAN (Odie)

b. Oct. 5, 1936 Ht. 6-1 Wt. 180
College—Kentucky

Yr.	Team	G	FG	FT	TP	Avg.
1961-62	Cincinnati	80	202	172	576	7.2
1962-63	Cincinnati	79	241	223	705	8.9
1963-64	Cincinnati	66	234	154	622	9.4
1964-65	Cincinnati	80	463	284	1210	15.1
1965-66	Cincinnati	80	531	408	1470	18.4
1966-67	Cincinnati	81	502	343	1347	16.6
1967-68	Cincinnati	82	480	320	1280	15.6
	Totals	549	2653	1904	7210	13.1

SMITH, DEB

Ht. 6-3 Wt. 180
College—Utah

Yr.	Team	G	FG	FT	TP	Avg.
1946-47	St. Louis	48	32	9	73	1.5

SMITH, DON

Ht. 6-2 Wt. 190
College—Minnesota

Yr.	Team	G	FG	FT	TP	Avg.
1948-49	Minneapolis	8	2	2	6	0.8

SMITH, EDWARD

b. July 5, 1929 Ht. 6-6 Wt. 180

Yr.	Team	G	FG	FT	TP	Avg.
1953-54	New York	11	11	6	28	2.5

SMITH, ROBERT

b. Aug. 20, 1937 Ht. 6-4 Wt. 190
College—West Virginia

Yr.	Team	G	FG	FT	TP	Avg.
1959-60	Minneapolis	10	13	11	37	3.7
1961-62	Los Angeles	3	0	0	0	0.0
	Totals	13	13	11	37	2.8

SMITH, THOMAS

Ht. 6-1 Wt. 165
College—St. Peter's

Yr.	Team	G	FG	FT	TP	Avg.
1951-52	New York	1	0	4	4	4.0

SMITH, WILLIAM

b. Apr. 26, 1939 Ht. 6-5 Wt. 190
College—St. Peter's

Yr.	Team	G	FG	FT	TP	Avg.
1961-62	New York	9	8	7	23	2.5

SMYTH, JOSEPH

Ht. 6-3 Wt. 215
College—Niagara

Yr.	Team	G	FG	FT	TP	Avg.
1953-54	Baltimore	40	48	35	131	3.3

SNYDER, DICK

b. Feb. 1, 1944 Ht. 6-5 Wt. 210
College—Davidson

Yr.	Team	G	FG	FT	TP	Avg.
1966-67	St. Louis	54	144	46	334	6.2

Yr.	Team	G	FG	FT	TP	Avg.
1967-68	St. Louis	75	257	129	643	8.6
	Totals	129	401	175	977	7.6

SOBEK, GEORGE

Ht. 6-0 Wt. 180

College—Notre Dame

Yr.	Team	G	FG	FT	TP	Avg.
1947-48	Toledo NL	42	186	179	551	13.1
1948-49	Hamline NL	57	143	232	518	9.0
1949-50	Sheboygan	60	95	156	346	5.8
	Totals	159	424	567	1415	8.9

SOBIESZCZYK, RON (Sobie)

b. Sept. 21, 1934 Ht. 6-3 Wt. 195

College—DePaul

Yr.	Team	G	FG	FT	TP	Avg.
1956-57	New York	71	166	152	484	6.8
1957-58	New York	55	217	196	630	11.5
1958-59	New York	50	144	112	400	8.0
1959-60	N.Y.-Minneap.	16	37	31	105	6.6
	Totals	192	564	491	1619	8.4

SOMERSET, WILLIE

b. Mar. 17, 1942 Ht. 5-10 Wt. 190

College—Duquesne

Yr.	Team	G	FG	FT	TP	Avg.
1965-66	Baltimore	8	18	9	45	5.6

SOVRAN, GINO

Ht. 6-2 Wt. 175

College—Assumption (Ont.)

Yr.	Team	G	FG	FT	TP	Avg.
1946-47	Toronto	6	5	1	11	1.8

SPARROW, GUY

b. Nov. 2, 1932 Ht. 6-6 Wt. 218

College—Detroit

Yr.	Team	G	FG	FT	TP	Avg.
1957-58	New York	72	318	165	801	11.1
1958-59	N.Y.-Phila.	67	129	78	336	5.0
1959-60	Philadelphia	11	14	2	30	2.7
	Totals	150	461	245	1167	7.8

SPEARS, MARION (Odie)

b. June 26, 1925 Ht. 6-5 Wt. 205

College—Western Kentucky

Yr.	Team	G	FG	FT	TP	Avg.
1948-49	Chicago	57	200	131	531	9.3
1949-50	Chicago	57	227	158	712	10.5
1951-52	Rochester	66	225	116	566	8.6
1952-53	Rochester	62	198	199	595	9.6
1953-54	Rochester	72	184	183	551	7.7
1954-55	Rochester	71	226	220	672	9.5
1955-56	Ft. Wayne	72	166	159	491	6.8
1956-57	Ft. W.-St. Louis	11	12	19	43	3.9
	Totals	479	1488	1185	4161	8.8

SPECTOR, ARTHUR

b. Oct. 17, 1920 Ht. 6-4 Wt. 200

College—Villanova

Yr.	Team	G	FG	FT	TP	Avg.
1946-47	Boston	55	123	83	329	6.0
1947-48	Boston	48	67	60	194	4.0
1948-49	Boston	59	130	64	324	5.5
1949-50	Boston	7	2	1	5	0.7
	Totals	169	322	208	852	5.0

SPICER, LOU

Ht. 6-2 Wt. 195

College—Syracuse

Yr.	Team	G	FG	FT	TP	Avg.
1946-47	Providence	4	2	1	1	0.3

SPITZER, CRAIG

Ht. 7-0 Wt. 220

College—Tulane

Yr.	Team	G	FG	FT	TP	Avg.
1967-68	Chicago	10	8	2	18	1.8

SPOELSTRA, ART

b. Sept. 11, 1932 Ht. 6-9 Wt. 220

College—Western Kentucky

Yr.	Team	G	FG	FT	TP	Avg.
1954-55	Rochester	70	159	108	426	6.1
1955-56	Rochester	72	226	163	615	8.5
1956-57	Rochester	69	217	88	522	7.6
1957-58	Minn.-N.Y.	67	161	127	449	6.7
	Totals	278	763	486	2012	7.2

SPRINGER, JIM

Ht. 6-9 Wt. 235

College—Canterbury

Yr.	Team	G	FG	FT	TP	Avg.
1948-49	Indianapolis	2	0	1	1	0.5

SPRUILL, JIM

Ht. 6-2

College—Rice

Yr.	Team	G	FG	FT	TP	Avg.
1948-49	Indianapolis	1	1	0	2	2.0

STALLWORTH, DAVID

b. Dec. 20, 1941 Ht. 6-7 Wt. 200

College—Wichita State

Yr.	Team	G	FG	FT	TP	Avg.
1965-66	New York	80	373	258	1004	12.6
1966-67	New York	76	380	229	989	13.0
	Totals	156	753	487	1993	12.8

STANCZAK, EDWARD

Ht. 6-1 Wt. 185

Yr.	Team	G	FG	FT	TP	Avg.
1946-47	Anderson NL	44	142	118	402	9.1
1947-48	Anderson NL	56	77	62	216	3.9
1948-49	Anderson NL	64	191	202	584	9.1
1949-50	Anderson	57	159	203	521	9.1
1950-51	Boston	17	11	34	57	3.4
	Totals	238	580	620	1780	7.5

STAVERMAN, LARRY

b. Oct. 11, 1936 Ht. 6-7 Wt. 205

College—Villa Madonna

Yr.	Team	G	FG	FT	TP	Avg.
1958-59	Cincinnati	57	101	45	247	4.3
1959-60	Cincinnati	49	70	47	187	3.8
1960-61	Cincinnati	66	111	79	301	4.6
1962-63	Chicago	33	94	49	237	7.2
1963-64	Balt.-Det.-Cinn.	60	98	69	265	4.4
	Totals	265	474	289	1237	4.7

STEPHENS, JACK

b. May 18, 1933 Ht. 6-3 Wt. 185

College—Notre Dame

Yr.	Team	G	FG	FT	TP	Avg.
1955-56	St. Louis	72	248	247	743	10.3

STEVENS, WAYNE

b. June 19, 1936 Ht. 6-3½ Wt. 185

College—Cincinnati

Yr.	Team	G	FG	FT	TP	Avg.
1959-60	Cincinnati	8	3	7	13	1.6

STEWART, NORMAN

Ht. 6-5 Wt. 205

College—Missouri

Yr.	Team	G	FG	FT	TP	Avg.
1956-57	St. Louis	5	4	2	10	2.0

Yr.	Team	G	FG	FT	TP	Avg.
	STITH, SAM					
	b. July 22, 1937 Ht. 6-2 Wt. 185					
	College—St. Bonaventure					
1961-62	New York	32	59	23	141	4.4
	STITH, THOMAS					
	b. Jan. 21, 1939 Ht. 6-5 Wt. 210					
	College—St. Bonaventure					
1962-63	New York	25	37	3	77	3.1
	STOKES, MAURICE (Mo)					
	b. June 17, 1933 Ht. 6-7 Wt. 235					
	College—St. Francis (Pa.)					
1955-56	Rochester	67	403	319	1125	16.8
1956-57	Rochester	72	434	256	1124	15.6
1957-58	Cincinnati	63	414	238	1066	16.9
	Totals	202	1251	813	3315	16.4
	STOLKEY, ARTHUR					
	Ht. 6-1 Wt. 180					
	College—Detroit					
1946-47	Detroit	23	36	30	102	4.4
	STRAWDER, JOSEPH					
	b. Sept. 21, 1940 Ht. 6-10 Wt. 235					
	College—Bradley					
1965-66	Detroit	79	250	176	676	8.6
1966-67	Detroit	79	281	188	750	9.4
1967-68	Detroit	73	206	139	551	7.5
	Totals	231	737	503	1977	8.6
	STRICKLAND, ROGER					
	b. Sept. 4, 1940 Ht. 6-5 Wt. 200					
	College—Jacksonville					
1963-64	Baltimore	1	1	0	2	2.0
	STUMP, EUGENE					
	b. Nov. 13, 1923 Ht. 6-2 Wt. 185					
	College—DePaul					
1947-48	Boston	43	59	24	142	3.3
1948-49	Boston	56	193	92	478	8.5
1949-50	Minn.-Waterloo	49	63	37	163	3.3
	Totals	148	315	153	783	5.3
	STUTZ, STAN					
	b. Apr. 14, 1920 Ht. 5-11 Wt. 175					
	College—Rhode Island					
1946-47	New York	66	172	133	477	8.0
1947-48	New York	47	109	113	331	7.0
1948-49	Baltimore	59	121	131	373	6.3
	Totals	166	402	377	1181	7.1
	SUNDERLAGE, DON					
	Ht. 6-1 Wt. 180					
	College—Illinois					
1953-54	Milwaukee	68	254	252	760	11.2
1954-55	Minneapolis	45	33	48	114	2.5
	Totals	113	287	300	874	7.7
	SURHOFF, RICHARD					
	Ht. 6-4					
	College—Long Island					
1952-53	New York	26	13	19	45	1.7
1953-54	Milwaukee	32	43	47	133	4.2
	Totals	58	56	66	172	3.1
	SWAIN, BENNIE					
	b. Dec. 16, 1933 Ht. 6-8 Wt. 222					
	College—Texas Southern					
1958-59	Boston	58	99	67	265	4.6
	SWANSON, NORMAN					
	Ht. 6-6 Wt. 212					
	College—Detroit					
1953-54	Rochester	63	31	38	100	1.6
	SWARTZ, DAN					
	b. Dec. 23, 1934 Ht. 6-4 Wt. 215					
	College—Morehead State					
1962-63	Boston	39	57	61	175	4.5
	SYDNOR, WALLACE					
	b. Sept. 19, 1921 Ht. 5-10 Wt. 175					
	College—Western Kentucky					
1946-47	Chicago	15	5	5	15	1.0
	TANNENBAUM, SIDNEY					
	Ht. 6-0 Wt. 160					
	College—New York University					
1947-48	New York	24	90	62	242	10.1
1948-49	N.Y.-Baltimore	46	146	99	391	8.5
	Totals	70	236	161	633	9.0
	THACKER, TOM					
	b. Nov. 2, 1939 Ht. 6-2 Wt. 170					
	College—Cincinnati					
1963-64	Cincinnati	48	53	26	132	2.8
1964-65	Cincinnati	55	56	23	135	2.5
1965-66	Cincinnati	50	84	15	183	3.7
1967-68	Boston	65	114	43	271	4.2
	Totals	218	307	107	721	3.3
	THIEBEN, WILLIAM					
	Ht. 6-7 Wt. 215					
	College—Hofstra					
1956-57	Ft. Wayne	58	90	57	237	4.1
1957-58	Ft. Wayne	27	42	16	100	3.7
	Totals	85	132	73	337	4.0
	THOMPSON, JOHN					
	b. Sept 2, 1941 Ht. 6-10 Wt. 230					
	College—Providence					
1964-65	Boston	64	84	62	230	3.6
1965-66	Boston	10	14	4	32	3.2
	Totals	74	98	66	262	3.5
	THORN, ROD					
	b. May 23, 1941 Ht. 6-4 Wt. 195					
	College—West Virginia					
1963-64	Baltimore	75	411	258	1080	14.4
1964-65	Detroit	74	320	176	816	11.0
1965-66	Det.-St. Louis	73	306	168	780	10.7
1966-67	St. Louis	67	233	125	591	8.8
1967-68	Seattle	66	377	252	1006	15.2
	Totals	355	1647	979	4273	12.0
	THURMOND, NATE					
	b. July 25, 1941 Ht. 6-11 Wt. 225					
	College—Bowling Green					
1963-64	San Francisco	76	219	95	533	7.0
1964-65	San Francisco	77	519	235	1273	16.5

Yr.	Team	G	FG	FT	TP	Avg.
1965-66	San Francisco	73	454	280	1188	16.3
1966-67	San Francisco	65	467	280	1214	18.7
1967-68	San Francisco	51	382	282	1046	20.5
	Totals	342	2041	1172	5254	15.4

THURSTON, MEL

Ht. 6-0 Wt. 175

College—Canisius

Yr.	Team	G	FG	FT	TP	Avg.
1947-48	Providence	14	32	14	78	5.6

TIDRICK, HAROLD

Ht. 6-1 Wt. 190

College—Washington & Jefferson

Yr.	Team	G	FG	FT	TP	Avg.
1946-47	Toledo NL	44	232	115	579	13.1
1947-48	Toledo NL	59	267	189	723	13.7
1948-49	Balt.-Indianapolis	61	194	164	552	9.0
	Totals	164	693	468	1854	11.3

TIEMAN, DANIEL

b. Nov. 30, 1940 Ht. 6-0 Wt. 185

College—Villa Madonna

Yr.	Team	G	FG	FT	TP	Avg.
1962-63	Cincinnati	29	15	4	34	1.2

TINGLE, JACK

Ht. 6-4 Wt. 205

College—Kentucky

Yr.	Team	G	FG	FT	TP	Avg.
1947-48	Washington	37	36	17	89	2.4
1948-49	Minneapolis	2	1	0	2	1.0
	Totals	39	37	17	91	2.3

TODOROVICH, MARKO

b. June 11, 1923 Ht. 6-5 Wt. 229

College—Wyoming

Yr.	Team	G	FG	FT	TP	Avg.
1947-48	Sheboygan NL	60	227	225	779	13.0
1948-49	Sheboygan NL	60	239	170	648	10.8
1949-50	St. L.-Tri-Cities	65	263	266	792	12.2
1950-51	Tri-Cities	66	221	211	653	9.9
	Totals	251	1000	872	2872	11.4

TONKOVICH, ANDY

Ht. 6-1 Wt. 185

College—Marshall

Yr.	Team	G	FG	FT	TP	Avg.
1948-49	Providence	17	19	6	44	2.6

TOOMEY, JOHN

Ht. 6-6 Wt. 215

College—College of Pacific

Yr.	Team	G	FG	FT	TP	Avg.
1947-48	Chicago-Prov.	23	61	60	182	7.9
1948-49	Balt.-Wash.	36	32	36	100	2.8
1949-50	Denver	62	204	186	594	9.6
	Totals	121	297	282	876	7.2

TORGOFF, IRVING

Ht. 6-2 Wt. 192

College—Long Island U.

Yr.	Team	G	FG	FT	TP	Avg.
1946-47	Washington	58	187	116	490	8.4
1947-48	Washington	47	111	117	339	7.2
1948-49	Balt.-Phila.	42	59	50	168	4.0
	Totals	147	357	283	997	6.7

TORMOHLEN, EUGENE

b. May 12, 1937 Ht. 6-9 Wt. 245

College—Tennessee

Yr.	Team	G	FG	FT	TP	Avg.
1962-63	St. Louis	7	5	2	12	1.7
1963-64	St. Louis	49	95	22	210	4.3
1965-66	St. Louis	71	144	54	342	4.8
1966-67	St. Louis	63	172	50	394	6.3
1967-68	St. Louis	77	98	33	229	3.0
	Totals	267	513	161	1187	4.4

TOSHEFF, BILL

Ht. 6-1 Wt. 175

College—Indiana

Yr.	Team	G	FG	FT	TP	Avg.
1951-52	Indianapolis	65	213	182	608	9.4
1952-53	Indianapolis	67	253	253	759	11.3
1953-54	Milwaukee	71	168	156	492	6.9
	Totals	203	634	591	1859	9.2

TOUGH, ROBERT

Ht. 6-0 Wt. 185

College—St. John's (N. Y.)

Yr.	Team	G	FG	FT	TP	Avg.
1947-48	Ft. Wayne NL	60	131	42	304	5.1
1948-49	Ft. Wayne	53	183	100	466	8.8
1949-50	Balt.-Waterloo	20	43	37	123	4.2
	Totals	142	357	179	893	6.3

TOWERY, CARLISLE

b. June 20, 1940 Ht. 6-4 Wt. 210

College—Western Kentucky

Yr.	Team	G	FG	FT	TP	Avg.
1947-48	Ft. Wayne NL	60	136	134	406	6.8
1948-49	Ft. W.-Ind.	60	203	195	601	10.0
1949-50	Baltimore	68	222	153	597	8.8
	Totals	188	561	482	1604	8.5

TRESVANT, JOHN

b. Nov. 6, 1939 Ht. 6-7 Wt. 215

College—Seattle

Yr.	Team	G	FG	FT	TP	Avg.
1964-65	St. Louis	4	4	6	14	3.5
1965-66	St. L.-Detroit	61	171	142	484	7.9
1966-67	Detroit	68	256	164	676	9.9
1967-68	Det.-Cincinnati	85	396	250	1042	12.3
	Totals	218	827	562	2216	10.2

TRIPTOW, RICHARD

b. Nov. 3, 1922 Ht. 6-0 Wt. 170

College—DePaul

Yr.	Team	G	FG	FT	TP	Avg.
1945-46	Chicago NL	34	68	86	222	6.5
1948-49	Ft. Wayne	55	116	102	334	6.1
1949-50	Baltimore	4	0	2	2	0.5
	Totals	93	184	190	558	6.0

TSIOROPOULOS, LOUIS

b. Aug. 31, 1930 Ht. 6-5 Wt. 195

College—Kentucky

Yr.	Team	G	FG	FT	TP	Avg.
1956-57	Boston	52	79	69	227	4.4
1957-58	Boston	70	198	142	538	7.7
1958-59	Boston	35	60	25	145	4.1
	Totals	157	337	236	910	5.8

TUCKER, AL

b. Feb. 24, 1943 Ht. 6-8 Wt. 190

College—Oklahoma Baptist

Yr.	Team	G	FG	FT	TP	Avg.
1967-68	Seattle	81	437	186	1060	13.1

TUCKER, JAMES

Ht. 6-7 Wt. 185

College—Duquesne

Yr.	Team	G	FG	FT	TP	Avg.
1954-55	Syracuse	20	39	27	105	5.3
1955-56	Syracuse	70	101	66	268	3.8

Yr.	Team	G	FG	FT	TP	Avg.
1956-57	Syracuse	9	17	0	34	3.8
	Totals	99	157	93	407	4.1

TURNER, JACK

b. June 29, 1930 Ht. 6-4 Wt. 170
College—Western Kentucky

Yr.	Team	G	FG	FT	TP	Avg.
1954-55	New York	65	111	60	282	4.3

TURNER, JOHN

b. June 5, 1939 Ht. 6-5 Wt. 200
College—Louisville

Yr.	Team	G	FG	FT	TP	Avg.
1961-62	Chicago	42	84	32	200	4.8

TURNER, WILLIAM

b. Feb. 18, 1944 Ht. 6-7 Wt. 220

Yr.	Team	G	FG	FT	TP	Avg.
1967-68	San Francisco	42	68	36	172	4.1

TWYMAN, JACK

b. May 11, 1934 Ht. 6-6 Wt. 210
College—Cincinnati

Yr.	Team	G	FG	FT	TP	Avg.
1955-56	Rochester	72	417	204	1038	14.4
1956-57	Rochester	72	449	276	1174	16.3
1957-58	Cincinnati	72	465	307	1237	17.2
1958-59	Cincinnati	72	710	437	1857	25.8
1959-60	Cincinnati	75	870	598	2338	31.2
1960-61	Cincinnati	79	796	405	1997	25.3
1961-62	Cincinnati	80	739	353	1831	22.9
1962-63	Cincinnati	80	641	204	1586	19.8
1963-64	Cincinnati	68	447	189	1083	19.9
1964-65	Cincinnati	80	479	198	1156	14.5
1965-66	Cincinnati	73	224	95	543	7.4
	Totals	823	6237	3366	15840	19.2

TYRA, CHARLES

b. Aug. 16, 1935 Ht. 6-8 Wt. 235
College—Louisville

Yr.	Team	G	FG	FT	TP	Avg.
1957-58	New York	68	175	150	500	7.4
1958-59	New York	69	240	129	609	8.8
1959-60	New York	74	406	133	945	12.8
1960-61	New York	59	199	120	518	8.8
1961-62	Chicago	78	193	133	519	6.6
	Totals	348	1213	665	3091	8.9

UPLINGER, HAL

Ht. 6-4 Wt. 185
College—Long Island U.

Yr.	Team	G	FG	FT	TP	Avg.
1953-54	Baltimore	23	33	20	86	3.7

VAN ARSDALE, RICHARD

b. Feb. 22, 1943 Ht. 6-4 Wt. 210
College—Indiana

Yr.	Team	G	FG	FT	TP	Avg.
1965-66	New York	79	359	251	969	12.3
1966-67	New York	79	410	371	1191	15.1
1967-68	New York	78	316	227	859	11.0
	Totals	236	1085	849	3019	12.8

VAN ARSDALE, THOMAS

b. Feb. 22, 1943 Ht. 6-5 Wt. 215
College—Indiana

Yr.	Team	G	FG	FT	TP	Avg.
1965-66	Detroit	79	312	209	833	10.5
1966-67	Detroit	79	347	272	966	12.2
1967-68	Det.-Cin.	77	211	188	610	7.9
	Totals	235	870	669	2409	10.3

VAN BREDA KOLFF, WILLIAM (Butch)

Ht. 6-3 Wt. 185
College—Princeton and New York University

Yr.	Team	G	FG	FT	TP	Avg.
1946-47	New York	16	7	11	25	1.6
1947-48	New York	44	53	74	180	4.1
1948-49	New York	59	127	161	415	7.0
1949-50	New York	56	55	96	206	3.7
	Totals	175	242	342	826	4.7

VANCE, ELLIS (Gene)

Ht. 6-3 Wt. 196
College—Illinois

Yr.	Team	G	FG	FT	TP	Avg.
1947-48	Chicago	48	163	76	402	8.4
1948-49	Chicago	56	222	131	575	10.3
1949-50	Tri-Cities	35	110	86	306	8.7
1950-51	Tri-Cities	28	44	43	131	4.7
1951-52	Milwaukee	7	7	9	23	3.3
	Totals	174	546	345	1437	8.3

VANDEWEGHE, ERNIE

Ht. 6-3 Wt. 195
College—Colgate

Yr.	Team	G	FG	FT	TP	Avg.
1949-50	New York	42	164	93	421	10.0
1950-51	New York	44	135	68	338	7.7
1951-52	New York	57	200	124	524	9.2
1952-53	New York	61	272	187	731	12.0
1953-54	New York	15	37	25	99	6.6
1955-56	New York	5	10	2	22	4.4
	Totals	224	818	499	2135	9.5

VAUGHN, CHARLES (Chico)

b. Feb. 19, 1940 Ht. 6-3 Wt. 215
College—Southern Illinois

Yr.	Team	G	FG	FT	TP	Avg.
1962-63	St. Louis	77	295	188	778	10.1
1963-64	St. Louis	68	238	107	583	8.6
1964-65	St. Louis	75	344	182	870	11.6
1965-66	St. L.-Det.	56	182	106	470	8.4
1966-67	Detroit	51	85	50	220	4.3
	Totals	327	1144	633	2921	8.9

VAUGHN, VIRGIL

Ht. 6-4 Wt. 205
College—Kentucky Wesleyan

Yr.	Team	G	FG	FT	TP	Avg.
1946-47	Boston	17	15	15	45	2.6

VOLKER, FLOYD

Ht. 6-4
College—Wyoming

Yr.	Team	G	FG	FT	TP	Avg.
1947-48	Oshkosh NL	57	102	31	235	3.9
1948-49	Oshkosh NL	64	165	88	418	6.5
1949-50	Ind.-Denver	54	163	71	397	7.4
	Totals	175	430	190	1050	6.0

VON NIEDA, STANLEY

Ht. 6-1 Wt. 175
College—Penn State

Yr.	Team	G	FG	FT	TP	Avg.
1947-48	Tri-Cities NL	60	276	174	726	12.1
1948-49	Tri-Cities NL	63	240	143	623	9.9
1949-50	Tri-Cities-Balt.	59	120	73	313	5.3
	Totals	182	636	390	1662	9.1

Yr.	Team	G	FG	FT	TP	Avg.
	WAGER, CLINT					
	Ht. 6-6 Wt. 230					
	College—St. Mary's (Minn.)					
1945-46	Oshkosh NL	34	68	32	168	4.9
1947-48	Oshkosh NL	59	90	93	232	3.9
1948-49	Hamline NL	61	125	82	332	5.4
1949-50	Ft. Wayne	63	57	29	143	2.3
	Totals	217	340	195	875	4.0
	WAGNER, DON					
	Ht. 6-0					
	College—Texas					
1947-48	Flint NL	49	95	57	247	5.0
1948-49	Sheboygan NL	62	111	109	331	5.3
1949-50	Sheboygan	11	19	31	69	6.3
	Totals	122	225	197	647	5.3
	WALKER, BRADY					
	Ht. 6-6 Wt. 205					
	College—Brigham Young					
1948-49	Providence	59	202	87	491	8.3
1949-50	Boston	68	218	72	508	7.5
1950-51	Bost.-Baltimore	66	164	72	400	6.1
1951-52	Baltimore	35	89	26	204	5.8
	Totals	228	673	257	1603	7.0
	WALKER, CHESTER (Chet)					
	b. Feb. 22, 1940 Ht. 6-6 Wt. 200					
	College—Bradley					
1962-63	Syracuse	78	352	253	957	12.3
1963-64	Philadelphia	76	492	330	1314	17.3
1964-65	Philadelphia	79	377	288	1042	13.2
1965-66	Philadelphia	80	443	335	1221	15.3
1966-67	Philadelphia	81	561	445	1567	19.3
1967-68	Philadelphia	82	539	387	1465	17.9
	Totals	476	2764	2038	7566	15.9
	WALKER, HORACE					
	b. Apr. 17, 1938 Ht. 6-3 Wt. 210					
	College—Michigan State					
1961-62	Chicago	64	147	139	433	6.8
	WALKER, JIM					
	b. Apr. 8, 1944 Ht. 6-3 Wt. 205					
	College—Providence					
1967-68	Detroit	81	289	134	712	8.8
	WALLACE, MICHAEL					
	Ht. 6-1 Wt. 185					
	College—Scranton					
1946-47	Bos.-Toronto	61	225	106	556	9.1
	WALSH, JAMES					
	b. Aug. 29, 1931 Ht. 6-4 Wt. 195					
	College—Stanford					
1957-58	Philadelphia	10	5	10	20	2.0
	WALTHER, PAUL					
	Ht. 6-2 Wt. 160					
	College—Tennessee					
1949-50	Minn.-Ind.	53	114	63	291	5.5
1950-51	Indianapolis	63	213	145	571	9.1
1951-52	Indianapolis	55	220	231	671	12.2
1952-53	Indianapolis	67	227	264	718	10.7
1953-54	Philadelphia	64	138	145	421	6.6
1954-55	Ft. Wayne	68	56	54	166	2.4
	Totals	370	968	902	2838	7.7
	WALTHOUR, ISAAC (Rabbit)					
	Ht. 5-11 Wt. 163					
1953-54	Milwaukee	4	1	0	2	0.5
	WANZER, ROBERT (Bobby)					
	Ht. 6-0 Wt. 172					
	College—Seton Hall					
1947-48	Rochester NL	39	55	56	160	4.3
1948-49	Rochester	60	202	209	613	10.2
1949-50	Rochester	67	254	283	791	11.8
1950-51	Rochester	68	252	232	736	10.8
1951-52	Rochester	66	328	377	1033	15.7
1952-53	Rochester	70	318	384	1020	14.6
1953-54	Rochester	72	322	428	958	13.3
1954-55	Rochester	72	324	294	942	13.1
1955-56	Rochester	72	245	259	749	10.4
1956-57	Rochester	21	23	36	82	3.9
	Totals	607	2323	2444	7090	11.7
	WARD, GERRY					
	b. Sept. 6, 1941 Ht. 6-4 Wt. 200					
	College—Boston College					
1963-64	St. Louis	24	16	11	43	1.8
1964-65	Boston	3	2	1	5	1.7
1965-66	Philadelphia	66	67	39	173	2.6
1966-67	Chicago	76	117	87	321	4.2
	Totals	169	202	138	542	3.2
	WARE, JIM					
	b. May 2, 1944 Ht. 6-7 Wt. 210					
	College—Oklahoma City					
1966-67	Cincinnati	33	30	10	70	2.1
1967-68	San Diego	30	25	23	73	2.4
	Totals	63	55	33	143	2.2
	WARLEY, BEN					
	b. Sept. 4, 1936 Ht. 6-5 Wt. 200					
	College—Tennessee State					
1962-63	Syracuse	26	50	25	125	4.8
1963-64	Philadelphia	79	215	220	650	8.2
1964-65	Philadelphia	65	94	124	312	4.8
1965-66	Phila.-Balt.	57	116	64	296	5.2
1966-67	Baltimore	62	125	134	384	6.2
	Totals	289	600	567	1767	6.1
	WARLICK, ROBERT					
	b. Mar. 20, 1941 Ht. 6-5 Wt. 205					
	College—Pepperdine					
1965-66	Detroit	10	11	2	24	2.4
1966-67	San Francisco	12	15	6	36	3.0
1967-68	San Francisco	69	257	97	611	8.9
	Totals	91	283	105	671	7.4
	WASHINGTON, JAMES					
	b. July 1, 1943 Ht. 6-7 Wt. 215					
	College—Villanova					
1965-66	St. Louis	65	158	68	384	5.9
1966-67	Chicago	77	252	88	592	7.7
1967-68	Chicago	82	418	187	1023	12.5
	Totals	224	828	343	1999	8.9

Yr.	Team	G	FG	FT	TP	Avg.
	WATSON, BOB					
	b. Mar. 22, 1930 Ht. 6-10 Wt. 162					
	College—Kentucky					
1954-55	Milwaukee	63	72	31	175	2.8
	WATTS, RONALD					
	b. May 21, 1943 Ht. 6-6 Wt. 210					
	College—Wake Forest					
1965-66	Boston	1	1	0	2	2.0
1966-67	Boston	27	11	16	38	1.4
	Totals	28	12	16	40	1.4
	WEBER, FORREST					
	Ht. 6-6 Wt. 225					
	College—Purdue					
1946-47	N.Y.-Prov.	50	59	55	173	3.5
	WEHR, DICK					
	Ht. 6-4 Wt. 180					
	College—Rice					
1948-49	Indianapolis	9	5	2	12	1.3
	WEISS, ROBERT					
	b. May 7, 1942 Ht. 6-2 Wt. 180					
	College—Penn State					
1965-66	Philadelphia	7	3	0	6	0.9
1966-67	Philadelphia	6	5	2	12	2.0
1967-68	Seattle	82	295	213	803	9.8
	Totals	95	303	215	821	8.6
	WEITZMAN, RICK					
	b. Apr. 30, 1946 Ht. 6-2 Wt. 185					
	College—Northeastern					
1967-68	Boston	25	12	9	33	1.3
	WELLS, RALPH					
	b. Sept. 3, 1940 Ht. 6-1 Wt. 180					
	College—Northwestern					
1962-63	Chicago	3	1	0	2	0.7
	WERTIS, RAY					
	Ht. 5-11 Wt. 175					
	College—St. John's (N. Y.)					
1946-47	Cleve.-Toronto	61	79	56	214	3.5
1947-48	Providence	7	13	6	32	4.6
	Totals	68	92	62	243	3.7
	WESLEY, WALT					
	b. Apr. 25, 1945 Ht. 6-11 Wt. 230					
	College—Kansas					
1966-67	Cincinnati	64	131	52	314	4.9
1967-68	Cincinnati	66	188	76	452	6.8
	Totals	130	319	128	766	5.9
	WEST, JERRY					
	b. May 28, 1938 Ht. 6-3 Wt. 175					
	College—West Virginia					
1960-61	Los Angeles	79	529	331	1389	17.6
1961-62	Los Angeles	75	799	712	2310	30.8
1962-63	Los Angeles	56	559	371	1489	26.6
1963-64	Los Angeles	72	740	584	2064	28.7
1964-65	Los Angeles	74	822	648	2292	31.0
1965-66	Los Angeles	79	818	840	2476	31.4
1966-67	Los Angeles	66	645	602	1892	28.7
1967-68	Los Angeles	51	476	391	1343	26.3
	Totals	552	5388	4479	15255	27.6

Yr.	Team	GG	F	FT	TP	Avg.
	WEST, ROLAND					
	Ht. 6-4 Wt. 178					
	College—Cincinnati					
1967-68	Baltimore	4	2	0	4	1.0
	WHITE, HUBIE					
	b. Jan. 26, 1940 Ht. 6-4 Wt. 205					
	College—Villanova					
1962-63	San Francisco	29	40	12	92	3.2
1963-64	Philadelphia	23	31	17	79	3.4
	Totals	52	71	29	171	3.3
	WHITTAKER, LUCIAN (Skippy)					
	Ht. 6-1 Wt. 185					
	College—Kentucky					
1954-55	Boston	3	1	0	2	0.7
	WEIR, MURRAY					
	Ht. 5-9 Wt. 155					
	College—Iowa					
1948-49	Tri-Cities NL	59	79	79	237	4.0
1949-50	Tri-Cities	56	157	115	429	7.7
	Totals	115	236	194	666	5.8
	WETZEL, JOHN					
	b. Oct. 22, 1944 Ht. 6-5 Wt. 185					
	College—VPI					
1967-68	Los Angeles	38	52	35	139	3.7
	WIESENHAHN, ROBERT					
	b. Dec. 22, 1938 Ht. 6-4 Wt. 215					
	College—Cincinnati					
1961-62	Cincinnati	60	51	17	119	2.0
	WILBURN, KEN					
	b. June 8, 1944 Ht. 6-6 Wt. 195					
	College—Central State (Ohio)					
1967-68	Chicago	3	5	1	11	3.3
	WILCUTT, D. C.					
	Ht. 6-2 Wt. 165					
	College—St. Louis					
1948-49	St. Louis	22	18	15	51	2.3
1949-50	St. Louis	37	24	29	77	2.1
	Totals	59	42	44	128	2.2
	WILEY, EUGENE					
	b. Nov. 12, 1937 Ht. 6-10 Wt. 210					
	College—Wichita					
1962-63	Los Angeles	75	109	23	241	3.2
1963-64	Los Angeles	77	144	45	333	4.3
1964-65	Los Angeles	80	175	56	406	5.1
1965-66	Los Angeles	67	123	43	289	4.3
	Totals	299	551	167	1269	4.2
	WILFONG, WIN					
	b. Mar. 18, 1932 Ht. 6-2 Wt. 185					
	Memphis State					
1957-58	St. Louis	71	196	163	555	7.8
1958-59	St. Louis	63	99	62	260	4.1
1959-60	Cincinnati	72	283	161	727	10.1
1960-61	Cincinnati	62	109	75	293	4.7
	Totals	268	687	461	1835	6.8

Yr.	Team	G	FG	FT	TP	Avg.
WILKENS, LEN						
b. Oct. 28, 1937	Ht. 6-1	Wt. 185				
College—Providence						
1960-61	St. Louis	75	335	220	890	11.9
1961-62	St. Louis	20	140	84	364	18.2
1962-63	St. Louis	75	333	222	888	11.8
1963-64	St. Louis	78	334	270	938	12.0
1964-65	St. Louis	78	434	416	1284	16.5
1965-66	St. Louis	69	411	422	1244	18.0
1966-67	St. Louis	78	448	459	1355	17.4
1967-68	St. Louis	82	546	546	1638	20.0
	Totals	555	2981	2639	8601	15.5
WILLIAMS, ART (Hambone)						
b. Sept. 29, 1939	Ht. 6-2	Wt. 180				
College—California Poly						
1967-68	San Diego	79	265	113	643	8.1
WILLIAMS, ROBERT						
b. May 12, 1931	Ht. 6-6	Wt. 230				
College—Florida A&M						
1955-56	Minneapolis	20	21	24	66	3.3
1956-57	Minneapolis	4	1	2	4	1.0
	Totals	24	22	26	70	2.9
WILLIAMS, WARD						
	Ht. 6-4	Wt. 195				
College—Indiana						
1948-49	Ft. Wayne	53	61	93	215	4.1
WILSON, BOB						
	Ht. 6-4	Wt. 185				
College—West Virginia State						
1951-52	Milwaukee	63	79	78	236	3.7
WILSON, GEORGE						
b. May 9, 1942	Ht. 6-8	Wt. 225				
College—Cincinnati						
1964-65	Cincinnati	39	41	9	91	2.3
1965-66	Cincinnati	47	54	27	135	2.9
1966-67	Cin.-Chicago	55	85	58	228	4.1
1967-68	Seattle	77	179	109	467	6.1
	Totals	218	359	203	921	4.2
WINDSOR, JOHN						
b. Apr. 3, 1940	Ht. 6-8	Wt. 215				
College—Stanford						
1963-64	San Francisco	10	9	7	25	2.5
WOOD, BOB						
	Ht. 5-10					
College—Illinois						
1949-50	Sheboygan	6	3	1	7	1.2
WORKMAN, MARK						
	Ht. 6-9	Wt. 217				
College—West Virginia						
1952-53	Philadelphia	65	130	70	330	5.1
1953-54	Baltimore	14	25	6	56	4.0
	Totals	69	155	76	386	5.6

Yr.	Team	G	FG	FT	TP	Avg.
WORKMAN, TOM						
b. Nov. 14, 1944	Ht. 6-7	Wt. 230				
College—Seattle						
1967-68	St. Louis-Balt.	20	19	18	56	2.8
YATES, WAYNE						
b. Nov. 7, 1937	Ht. 6-8	Wt. 235				
College—Memphis State						
1961-62	Los Angeles	37	31	10	72	1.9
YARDLEY, GEORGE						
b. Nov. 3, 1928	Ht. 6-5	Wt. 195				
College—Stanford						
1953-54	Ft. Wayne	63	209	146	564	9.0
1954-55	Ft. Wayne	60	363	310	1036	17.3
1955-56	Ft. Wayne	71	434	365	1233	17.4
1956-57	Ft. Wayne	72	522	503	1547	21.5
1957-58	Detroit	72	673	655	2001	27.8
1958-59	Det.-Syracuse	61	446	317	1209	19.8
	Totals	399	2647	2296	7590	19.0
ZASLOFSKY, MAX						
b. Dec. 7, 1925	Ht. 6-2	Wt. 170				
College—St. John's (N.Y.)						
1946-47	Chicago	61	336	205	877	14.4
1947-48	Chicago	48	373	261	1007	21.0
1948-49	Chicago	58	425	347	1197	20.6
1949-50	Chicago	68	397	321	1115	16.4
1950-51	New York	66	302	231	835	12.7
1951-52	New York	66	322	287	931	14.1
1952-53	New York	20	123	98	344	11.9
1953-54	Balt.-Milw.-Ft. W.	65	278	255	811	12.5
1954-55	Ft. Wayne	70	269	247	785	11.2
1955-56	Ft. Wayne	9	29	30	88	9.8
	Totals	540	2854	2282	7990	14.8
ZAWOLUK, ROBERT (Zeke)						
	Ht. 6-7	Wt. 215				
College—St. John's (N.Y.)						
1952-53	Indianapolis	41	55	77	187	4.6
1953-54	Philadelphia	71	203	186	592	8.3
1954-55	Philadelphia	67	138	155	431	6.4
	Totals	179	396	418	1210	6.8
ZELLER, DAVID						
b. June 8, 1939	Ht. 6-1½	Wt. 175				
College—Miami (Ohio)						
1961-62	Cincinnati	61	36	18	90	1.5
ZELLER, HARRY						
	Ht. 6-4	Wt. 210				
College—Pittsburgh						
1946-47	Pittsburgh	48	120	122	362	7.5
ZUNIC, MATT						
b. Sept. 12, 1919	Ht. 6-7	Wt. 195				
College—George Washington						
1947-48	Flint NL	57	123	85	331	5.8
1948-49	Washington	56	98	77	273	4.9
	Totals	113	221	162	504	4.5

OAKS
24

13: THE OTHER PROS

AMERICAN BASKETBALL ASSOCIATION

The American Basketball Association, a professional league with teams in eleven cities, began play in the 1967–68 season. George Mikan, the former great center with the Minneapolis Lakers of the NBA, was appointed the ABA's commissioner.

The Pittsburgh Pipers, coached by Vince Cazzetta, won the Eastern Division championship and the New Orleans Buccaneers, under Babe McCarthy, took Western Division honors. In the final playoff series for the first league championship, Pittsburgh defeated New Orleans, four games to three.

Connie Hawkins of Pittsburgh led the league in scoring with a 26.8 average and was also voted the ABA's Most Valuable Player. Mel Daniels of Minnesota was the league's top rebounder with a 15.6 average.

The ABA's Oakland Oaks had scored a significant victory for the league by signing Rick Barry, who had been one of the NBA's brightest stars with the San Francisco Warriors. The Oaks, owned by singer Pat Boone and coached by Bruce Hale, Barry's old college coach and also his father-in-law, signed him to a long-term contract. The NBA Warriors, however, insisted that Barry was still legally obligated to play for them and brought legal action to keep him from switching leagues. The court action forced Barry to sit out the ABA's first campaign.

Four of the ABA franchises shifted to new cities before the start of the second season of play. Minnesota moved to Miami, Pittsburgh to Minnesota, Anaheim to Los Angeles and New Jersey to New York (Long Island).

FINAL 1967-68 STANDINGS

Eastern Division

	W.	L.	Pct.
Pittsburgh	54	24	.692
Minnesota	50	28	.641
Indiana	38	40	.487
Kentucky	36	42	.462
New Jersey	36	42	.462

Western Division

	W.	L.	Pct.
New Orleans	48	30	.615
Dallas	46	32	.590
Denver	45	33	.577
Houston	29	49	.372
Anaheim	25	53	.321
Oakland	22	56	.282

Rick Barry quit the NBA to play with Oakland in the ABA.

AMERICAN BASKETBALL LEAGUE

The American Basketball League, planned as a rival to the NBA, began play in the 1961-62 season and collapsed midway through the following campaign. Abe Saperstein, the owner of the Harlem Globetrotters, organized the ABL and served as its commissioner.

The league opened play with Cleveland, Pittsburgh, Chicago and Washington in the Eastern Division and Kansas City, Los Angeles, San Francisco and Hawaii in the West. Before the end of the season, Washington moved to New York (Long Island) and Los Angeles disbanded.

The ABL season was divided into halves, with Kansas City winning both halves of the Western title. Cleveland won the first-half Eastern title and tied Chicago in the second half of the schedule. Cleveland defeated Kansas City for the ABL championship.

Connie Hawkins of Pittsburgh won the scoring title with a 27.5 average. Several NBA players, the most prominent of whom were Dick Barnett, Ken Sears and Mike Farmer, jumped to the ABL.

On December 31, 1963, the ABL folded, with losses to the owners estimated at $2,000,000. In its brief history the ABL introduced one interesting feature, awarding three points for field goals scored from 25 or more feet from the basket.

EASTERN LEAGUE

The Eastern Professional Basketball League has served since 1947 as a training ground for basketball players and officials. As professional basketball's most prominent minor league, the circuit has served as a farm for the NBA and other major leagues as they have appeared on the scene. In addition, a number of NBA officials began their pro careers in the Eastern League.

The EPBL was organized on April 23, 1946 in Hazleton, Pennsylvania, with William Morgan, a local newspaperman, as the first president. The six charter members included Binghamton, (N.Y.) and Hazleton, Reading, Wilkes-Barre, Lancaster and Allentown, all Pennsylvania. Harry Rudolph, a former basketball, football and baseball official, has been the league's president since 1954.

The North American Basketball League, another pro minor league, though of more recent vintage, operates in the Midwest. It was organized as the Midwest League.

EASTERN LEAGUE CHAMPIONS

Year	Pennant Winner	Playoff Winner
1946-47	Wilkes-Barre Barons	Wilkes-Barre Barons
1947-48	Pottsville Packers	Reading Keys
1948-49	Williamsport Billies	Pottsville Packers
1949-50	Williamsport Billies	Williamsport Billies
1950-51	Sunbury Mercuries	Sunbury Mercuries
1951-52	Pottsville Packers	Pottsville Packers
1952-53	Sunbury Mercuries	Williamsport Billies
1953-54	Sunbury Mercuries	Williamsport Billies
1954-55	Williamsport Billies	Wilkes-Barre Barons
1955-56	Williamsport Billies	Wilkes-Barre Barons
1956-57	Scranton Miners	Scranton Miners
1957-58	Wilkes-Barre Barons	Wilkes-Barre Barons
1958-59	Scranton Miners	Wilkes-Barre Barons
1959-60	Easton Madisons	Easton Madisons
1960-61	Allentown Jets	Baltimore Bullets
1961-62	Allentown Jets	Allentown Jets

1962–63	Allentown Jets	Allentown Jets
1963–64	Allentown Jets	Camden Bullets
1964–65	Camden Bullets	Allentown Jets
1965–66	Wilmington Blue Bombers (East. Div.) Wilkes-Barre Barons (West. Div.)	Wilmington Blue Bombers
1966–67	Wilmington Blue Bombers (East. Div.) Scranton Miners (West. Div.)	Wilmington Blue Bombers
1967–68	Allentown Jets	Allentown Jets

THE WRITERS

The United States Basketball Writers Association, founded in Chicago on September 14, 1956, has grown since then to an organization with nearly 1,000 members. The members are all professional writers who cover basketball on a level above high-school competition. The USBWA came into existence after a year of organizing efforts by Bob Russell, then of the Chicago *Daily News*, and Ed Schneider of Chicago's *American*. Russell became the group's first president, and Schneider secretary-treasurer.

In recent years the USBWA has directed its efforts toward securing improved press box services and facilities and standardizing procedures in the compiling of basketball statistics.

The group also makes a number of annual awards to outstanding players and coaches on both the collegiate and professional levels.

A list of these awards follows:

COLLEGIATE COACH OF THE YEAR

1959—Ed Hickey, Marquette
1960—Pete Newell, California
1961—Fred Taylor, Ohio State
1962—Fred Taylor, Ohio State
1963—Ed Jucker, Cincinnati
1964—John Wooden, UCLA
1965—Bill van Breda Kolff, Princeton
1966—Adolph Rupp, Kentucky
1967—John Wooden, UCLA
1968—Guy Lewis, Houston

COLLEGIATE PLAYER OF THE YEAR

1959—Oscar Robertson, Cincinnati
1960—Oscar Robertson, Cincinnati
1961—Jerry Lucas, Ohio State
1962—Jerry Lucas, Ohio State
1963—Art Heyman, Duke
1964—Walt Hazzard, UCLA
1965—Bill Bradley, Princeton
1966—Cazzie Russell, Michigan
1967—Lew Alcindor, UCLA
1968—Elvin Hayes, Houston

NATIONAL BASKETBALL ASSOCIATION MOST VALUABLE PLAYER

1959—Bob Pettit, St. Louis
1960—Wilt Chamberlain, Philadelphia Warriors
1961—Bill Russell, Boston Celtics
1962—Bill Russell, Boston Celtics
1963—Bill Russell, Boston Celtics
1964—Wilt Chamberlain, San Francisco Warriors
1965—Bill Russell, Boston Celtics
1966—Wilt Chamberlain, Philadelphia 76ers
1967—Wilt Chamberlain, Philadelphia 76ers
1968—Wilt Chamberlain, Philadelphia 76ers

AMERICAN BASKETBALL ASSOCIATION MOST VALUABLE PLAYER

1968—Connie Hawkins, Pittsburgh Pipers

NAIA COACH OF THE YEAR

1962—Charles (Buzz) Ridl, Westminster
1963—Fred Hodby, Grambling
1964—Sam Williams, Pan American
1965—Dick Campbell, Carson-Newman
1966—Ted Kjolhede, Central Michigan
1967—Bob Bass, Oklahoma Baptist
1968—Jack Dobbins, Northeastern Oklahoma State

NCAA COLLEGE DIVISION TOURNAMENT MOST VALUABLE PLAYER

1960—Ed Smallwood, Evansville
1961—Don Jacobson, South Dakota State
1962—Bill Rohrer, Sacramento State
1963—Wayne Rasmussen, South Dakota State
1964—Jerry Sloan, Evansville
1965—Jerry Sloan, Evansville
1966—Sam Smith, Kentucky Wesleyan
1967—Earl Monroe, Winston-Salem
1968—Jerry Newsom, Indiana State

Founder Abe Saperstein made the Globetrotters a familiar sight around the world.

14: THE GLOBETROTTERS

Basketball fans around the world will attest that the Harlem Globetrotters are the game's greatest show. Their hilarious blend of comedy and outstanding basketball talent has captivated millions of fans in more than 90 countries. They've played before kings, princes and Popes and have drawn the biggest crowds in basketball's history, including 75,000 in Berlin's Olympic Stadium in 1951.

Everywhere the Trotters go, their show is the same. Numerous television appearances have made their routines familiar to all, but the exposure has never hurt the Trotters' drawing power. From their opening warm-up drill—always performed to the musical accompaniment of "Sweet Georgia Brown"—to their last trick shot, the Trotters provoke a torrent of laughter no matter where they appear.

Today the Globetrotters are strictly a show; they make little effort to play serious basketball. Both the opponents and the officials are part of the act and they fully realize that the fans are more interested in seeing the Trotters' antics than in watching an authentic game. The final score is really an incidental matter and Red Klotz, the perennial coach of the touring opposition team, can't remember when he last beat the Trotters.

But it wasn't always this way. When Abe Saperstein founded the team in 1926, the Trotters were strictly a serious barnstorming team. The humorous side of their play didn't appear immediately. Saperstein had organized a team that played in Chicago's Savoy Ballroom. When the dance hall failed and was turned into a skating rink, Saperstein's team was left without a place to play.

Saperstein saw no alternative but to take the team on the road. Since he reached that decision, the Globetrotters have never had a home court. Basketball at that time had not caught on generally and an unknown team from Chicago didn't seem like much of an attraction, the players were all Negro, as they still are today. Although none were from New York, Saperstein decided to call the team the Harlem Globetrotters. "'Harlem' because I wanted people to know the team was Negro and 'Globetrotters' because I wanted them to know we'd been around," Saperstein said.

The Trotters traveled around the country, playing any team anywhere they could schedule a game. The early years, especially during the Depression, were bleak, but Saperstein hung on. He found the best Negro players he could and the team soon became so good that nobody wanted to play them. To stimulate interest, Saperstein began to add the clowning routines that were to become the team's trademark. Fans liked the act but real success didn't come until the Globetrotters won the world professional tournament in Chicago in 1940.

Although it has been the style of play rather than the individual players that has made the team famous, several outstanding stars have emerged. Among the most famous have been Reece "Goose" Tatum, Marques Haynes and Meadowlark Lemon. Tatum, probably the team's greatest clown, was an amazing physical specimen. Although only 6-3, he had a reach of 84 inches, which the Trotters billed as the longest in pro sports. A lanky, loose-jointed man, the Goose drew laughs with his antics. When he chose to, though, he could also play extraordinary basketball. He had an amazingly accurate hook shot, which he would casually launch seemingly without paying any attention to the location of the basket. Tatum eventually left the Trotters to form a touring team of his own.

Haynes excelled as a dribbler and ranks as one of the best ball-handlers in the history of the game. He could dribble from every conceivable position—sitting down, lying on his back, his stomach, or on his knees, in addition to the conventional running style. He would frequently dribble around his opponents for minutes at a time, faking them off their feet. Like Tatum, Haynes left to tour with his own team.

Lemon filled Tatum's role as the premier comedian and to many fans around the world he has become the clown prince of basketball. Meadowlark plays the pivot and masterminds the Trotters' offense, which is just as likely to kick the ball into the basket as shoot it.

To call the Globetrotters a team is inaccurate, since they are in fact several teams. Saperstein divided his players into several units because he couldn't possibly meet all the requests for bookings with just one team. Today the various Globetrotter units will frequently appear simultaneously in different parts of the United States and overseas.

Regardless of which team plays, the show never varies much. Tricky ball-handling has always been the Globetrotters' hallmark and all the players are adept at this. One of their favorite maneuvers is a weave pattern around the foul circle. The Trotters spread themselves out and pass the ball back and forth at lightning speed, behind the back, between their legs, up one arm down the other. They'll frequently take time out to spin the ball on a fingertip or hide it in someone's jersey. The overall effect is of the entire team moving at breakneck speed in an intricate pattern. Because the team has to be fresh enough to play nearly every night, the key to all their routines is to keep the ball moving quickly while the players remain relatively stationary and have a chance to rest.

Through the years the Globetrotters have signed several famous college players to tour with them. The most prominent of these was Wilt Chamberlain, who appeared with the Trotters for a season. A few other Globetrotters, notably Nat "Sweetwater" Clifton, have gone on to play in the National Basketball Association. Today virtually all of the good Negro collegians choose to play in the professional leagues, but the Trotters still manage to come up with enough new talent to keep the show going.

Saperstein died in 1966, and his heirs sold the team for more than $3,000,000. The new owners decided not to tamper with success, and the Trotters continued to operate as they had under their founder.

The great clown of the Globetrotters: "Goose" Tatum.

ORIGINAL
ARLEM

Lew Alcindor was a High School All-American at New York's Power Memorial Academy.

15: THE HIGH SCHOOLS

The success of the nation's interscholastic athletic programs can be attributed to the efficient and powerful direction provided by the National Federation of State High School Athletic Associations.

Organized in 1920 by administrators from Illinois, Iowa, Michigan and Wisconsin, the Federation quickly became national in scope and now includes 50 member state high school associations as well as affiliated associations in six Canadian provinces.

The growth in size and influence of the state associations as well as the National Federation insures some degree of teamwork on the part of the 20,100 member high schools—each of which fields a varsity basketball team.

The Federation, based in Chicago, was organized primarily to secure adherence to the eligibility rules of the various state associations in interstate contests. Other Federation rules cover sanctioned interstate contests, including distance to be traveled, sponsor, amount of school time involved and the extent to which such interstate events interfere with smaller (local) meets which insure greater participation.

Basketball has been the subject of much of the Federation's legislation. The 1934 rule banning the sanctioning of national championship contests was passed to curb the rash of national tournaments run by various promoters. But this did not close the book on basketball's problems. According to the Federation's Handbook, some promoters attempted to circumvent the rules and the Federation's National Council voted to refuse to sanction any new interstate basketball tournament except where geographic or topographic conditions make such play practical.

The Federation, whose Executive Secretary is Clifford B. Fagan, also formulates national policy on high school bowl and charity games, all-star and out-of-season contests, NCAA all-star regulations (summer games for college-bound seniors), specialized camps, etc. The Federation also is represented on the basketball rules committee.

With more than 687,000 basketball players at the more than 20,000 member schools, basketball is one of the Federation's major activities. Of the member and affiliated state and provincial associations, all but California, Delaware, Massachusetts, New York and Ontario conduct post-season state-championship tournaments.

The following lists of state high school basketball champions since 1938 were furnished by the National Federation and the state associations.

STATE HIGH SCHOOL CHAMPIONS

1938–39

STATE	CLASS	CHAMPION	STATE	CLASS	CHAMPION
ALABAMA		Scottsboro	NEW HAMPSHIRE	A	Portsmouth
ARIZONA		Duncan	NEW JERSEY		New Brunswick
CONNECTICUT	A	Manchester	NEW MEXICO		House
FLORIDA	A	Jacksonville (Jackson)	NORTH CAROLINA	A	Durham
GEORGIA	A	Macon (Lanier)	NORTH DAKOTA	A	Fargo
IDAHO	A	Boise	OHIO		Newark
ILLINOIS		Dundee	OKLAHOMA	A	Ponca City
INDIANA		South Side	OREGON		Baker
IOWA		Diagonal	RHODE ISLAND	A	Pawtucket
KANSAS	A	Kansas City (Ward)	SOUTH DAKOTA	A	Aberdeen
KENTUCKY		Sharpe	TEXAS		Dallas (Wilson)
MAINE		Winslow	UTAH		Granite
MICHIGAN	A	Kalamazoo (Central)	VERMONT	A	Barre (Spaulding)
MINNESOTA		Thief River Falls	WASHINGTON		Vancouver
MISSOURI		Houston	WEST VIRGINIA		Wheeling
MONTANA	A	Great Falls	WISCONSIN	A	Wausau
NEBRASKA	A	Lincoln	WYOMING		Rock Springs
NEVADA		Carson			

1939–40

STATE	CLASS	CHAMPION	STATE	CLASS	CHAMPION
ALABAMA		Clanton (Chilton)	NEW HAMPSHIRE		Portsmouth
ARIZONA		Duncan	NEW JERSEY		West New York
ARKANSAS	A	Ash Flat	NEW MEXICO		Lordsburg
COLORADO	A	Denver (Manual)	NORTH CAROLINA	A	Jamestown
CONNECTICUT	A	Bridgeport (Central)	OHIO	A	Akron (North)
FLORIDA	A	Daytona Beach	OKLAHOMA	A	Tulsa (Central)
IDAHO	A	Blackfoot	OREGON		Salem
ILLINOIS		Rockford	RHODE ISLAND	A	Providence (Hope)
INDIANA		Frankfort	SOUTH CAROLINA	A	Charleston
IOWA		Creston	SOUTH DAKOTA	A	Flandreau Indian
KANSAS	A	Winfield	TENNESSEE		Knoxville (City)
KENTUCKY		Brooksville	TEXAS		Livingston
LOUISIANA	A	New Orleans (Jesuit)	UTAH		Vernal (Uintah)
MAINE		Winslow	VERMONT	A	Burlington (Cathedral)
MICHIGAN	A	Flint (Northern)	VIRGINIA	A	Hampton
MINNESOTA		Mountain Lake	WASHINGTON		Hoquiam
MISSISSIPPI		Mossville	WEST VIRGINIA		Fairmont (West)
MISSOURI	A	Joplin	WISCONSIN	A	Rhinelander
MONTANA	A	Park County	WYOMING		Casper
NEBRASKA	A	Falls City			
NEVADA		Panaca (Lincoln)			

1940–41

STATE	CLASS	CHAMPION	STATE	CLASS	CHAMPION
ALABAMA		Guin (Marion)	ARKANSAS	A	Jonesboro
ARIZONA		Duncan	COLORADO	A	Pueblo (Centennial)

STATE	CLASS	CHAMPION	STATE	CLASS	CHAMPION
CONNECTICUT	A	Bridgeport (Bassick)	NEW MEXICO		Sante Fe (St. Michael)
FLORIDA	A	Jacksonville (R.E. Lee)	NORTH CAROLINA	A	Durham
GEORGIA	A	Marion (Lanier)	OHIO	A	New Philadelphia
IDAHO	A	Emmett	OKLAHOMA	A	Ada
ILLINOIS		Granite City	OREGON		Salem
INDIANA		Hammond (Technical)	PENNSYLVANIA		Lebanon
IOWA		Mason City	RHODE ISLAND		Pawtucket
KANSAS	A	Winfield	SOUTH CAROLINA	A	Greenville
KENTUCKY		Hazel Green	TENNESSEE		Bradley
LOUISIANA		Shreveport (Byrd)	TEXAS		San Marcos
MAINE		Portland (Cheverus)	UTAH		Ogden
MICHIGAN	A	Flint (Northern)	VERMONT	A	Burlington (Cathedral)
MINNESOTA		Breckenridge	VIRGINIA	A	Lynchburg (E.C. Glass)
MISSISSIPPI		Runnelstown	WASHINGTON		Everett
MISSOURI	A	St. Louis (McBride)	WEST VIRGINIA		Wheeling
MONTANA	A	Havre	WISCONSIN		Shawano
NEBRASKA	A	Omaha (Creighton)	WYOMING	A	Casper
NEVADA		Sparks			
NEW HAMPSHIRE	A	Berlin			
NEW JERSEY		East Orange			

1941–42

STATE	CLASS	CHAMPION	STATE	CLASS	CHAMPION
ALABAMA		Clanton (Chilton)	NEVADA		White Pine
ARIZONA		Miami	NEW JERSEY		Asbury Park
ARKANSAS		Beebe	NEW MEXICO		Las Cruces
COLORADO	A	Fort Collins	NORTH CAROLINA	A	Durham
CONNECTICUT	A	Willimantic (Windham)	NORTH DAKOTA	A	Wahpeton
FLORIDA	A	Tampa (H.B. Plant)	OHIO	A	Martin's Ferry
GEORGIA	A	Savannah	OKLAHOMA	A	Tulsa (Will Rogers)
IDAHO	A	Burley	OREGON		Astoria
ILLINOIS		Cicero (Morton)	PENNSYLVANIA		Lower Merion
INDIANA		Washington	SOUTH DAKOTA	A	Sioux Falls (Washington)
KANSAS	AA	Wyandotte	UTAH		Provo
KENTUCKY		Inez	VIRGINIA	A	Roanoke (Jefferson)
MICHIGAN	A	Benton Harbor	WASHINGTON		Bremerton
MINNESOTA		Buhl	WEST VIRGINIA	A	Clarksburg (Victory)
MONTANA	A	Butte	WISCONSIN		Two Rivers
NEBRASKA	A	Scotts Bluff	WYOMING	A	Rock Springs

1942–43

STATE	CLASS	CHAMPION	STATE	CLASS	CHAMPION
ALABAMA		Birmingham (Woodlawn)	GEORGIA	A	Columbus (Jordan)
ARKANSAS	A	No. Little Rock	ILLINOIS		Paris
COLORADO	A	Denver (East)	INDIANA		Fort Wayne (Central)
CONNECTICUT	A	Bridgeport (Harding)	IOWA		Mason City
FLORIDA	A	Ft. Lauderdale (Central)	KANSAS	AA	Shawnee Mission
			KENTUCKY		Hindman

STATE	CLASS	CHAMPION
LOUISIANA	A	New Orleans (Holy Cross)
MINNESOTA		St. Paul (Washington)
MISSISSIPPI		Belmont
MISSOURI		St. Louis (Beaumont)
NEBRASKA	A	Lincoln
NEW MEXICO		Capitan
NORTH DAKOTA	A	Fargo
OHIO	A	Newark
OKLAHOMA	A	Enid
OREGON	A	Klamath Falls

STATE	CLASS	CHAMPION
PENNSYLVANIA		Ardmore
RHODE ISLAND		Pawtucket (St. Raphael)
SOUTH DAKOTA	A	Sioux Falls
TENNESSEE		Chattanooga (Central)
TEXAS		Houston (Jefferson Davis)
WEST VIRGINIA		Wheeling
WISCONSIN		Racine (Washington)
WYOMING	A	Cheyenne

1943–44

STATE	CLASS	CHAMPION
ALABAMA		Scottsboro
ARIZONA		Phoenix
ARKANSAS		Little Rock
COLORADO	A	Fort Collins
CONNECTICUT	A	Torrington
FLORIDA	A	Miami (Senior)
GEORGIA	A	Columbus
ILLINOIS		Taylorville
INDIANA		Evansville (Bosse)
IOWA		Waverly
KANSAS	AA	Shawnee Mission
KENTUCKY		Harlan
LOUISIANA	A	New Orleans (Jesuit)
MICHIGAN	A	Saginaw
MINNESOTA		Minneapolis (Patrick Henry)
MISSISSIPPI		Macedonia
MISSOURI		Bismarck
MONTANA		Great Falls
NEBRASKA	A	Omaha (South)
NEW HAMPSHIRE		Portsmouth

STATE	CLASS	CHAMPION
NEW JERSEY	IV	New Brunswick
NEW MEXICO		Virden
NORTH DAKOTA	A	Wahpeton
OHIO	A	Middletown
OKLAHOMA	A	Oklahoma City (Cap. Hill)
OREGON		Ashland
PENNSYLVANIA		Duquesne
RHODE ISLAND		Newport (De LaSalle)
SOUTH CAROLINA	B	Mullins
SOUTH DAKOTA		Pierre
TENNESSEE		Nashville (West)
TEXAS	AA	Dallas (Sunset)
UTAH	A	Provo
VERMONT		Montpelier
WASHINGTON		Spokane (Lewis & Clark)
WEST VIRGINIA		Huntington (Central)
WISCONSIN		Waukesha
WYOMING		Cheyenne

1944–45

STATE	CLASS	CHAMPION
ALABAMA		Selma (Parish)
ARIZONA		Tucson
ARKANSAS	A	Little Rock
COLORADO	A	Fort Collins
GEORGIA	A	Macon (Lanier)
ILLINOIS		Decatur
INDIANA		Evansville (Bosse)
IOWA		Ames
KANSAS	AA	Salina
KENTUCKY		Louisville (Male)
LOUISIANA	A	New Orleans (Holy Cross)
MAINE		Waterville
MASSACHUSETTS	W	South Hadley

STATE	CLASS	CHAMPION
MICHIGAN	A	Lansing (Sexton)
MINNESOTA		Minneapolis (Henry)
MISSISSIPPI		New Site
MISSOURI		Conway
MONTANA	A	Helena
NEBRASKA	A	Omaha (Creighton)
NEVADA	A	Las Vegas
NEW HAMPSHIRE		Manchester (Central)
NEW JERSEY	IV	Camden
NEW MEXICO		Las Cruces
NORTH CAROLINA	A	Greensboro
NORTH DAKOTA	A	Valley City
OHIO	A	Bellevue
OKLAHOMA	A	Norman

STATE	CLASS	CHAMPION
OREGON	A	Portland (Washington)
PENNSYLVANIA		Allentown
RHODE ISLAND		East Providence
SOUTH CAROLINA	A	Greenville
SOUTH DAKOTA	A	Huron
TENNESSEE		Chattanooga (Central)
TEXAS	AA	Fort Worth (Paschal)
UTAH	A	Provo
VIRGINIA		Alexandria (Washington)
WASHINGTON		Seattle (Lincoln)
WEST VIRGINIA		Normantown
WISCONSIN		Madison (West)
WYOMING		Cheyenne

1945–46

STATE	CLASS	CHAMPION
ALABAMA		Selma
ARIZONA		Mesa
ARKANSAS	A	Little Rock
COLORADO	A	Boulder
CONNECTICUT	A	New Haven (Hillhouse)
FLORIDA	A	Miami Beach
GEORGIA	A	Savannah
IDAHO	A	Preston
ILLINOIS		Champagne
INDIANA		Anderson
IOWA		Iowa City
KANSAS	AA	Newton
KENTUCKY		Morehead (Breckinridge)
LOUISIANA	AA	New Orleans (Jesuit)
MAINE	A	Auburn (Little)
MASSACHUSETTS	A	New Bedford
MICHIGAN	A	Holland
MINNESOTA		Austin
MISSISSIPPI		New Site
MISSOURI		St. Louis (University)
MONTANA	A	Missoula
NEBRASKA	A	Lincoln
NEVADA		Boulder City
NEW HAMPSHIRE	A	Nashua
NEW JERSEY	IV	Elizabeth (Jefferson)
NEW MEXICO		Albuquerque
NORTH CAROLINA		Durham
NORTH DAKOTA	A	Grand Forks
OHIO	A	Middletown
OKLAHOMA	A	El Reno
OREGON	A	Eugene
PENNSYLVANIA	A	Allentown
RHODE ISLAND		Pawtucket (East)
SOUTH DAKOTA	A	Brookings
TENNESSEE		Nashville (West)
TEXAS	AA	Dallas (Crozier)
UTAH	A	North Cache
VERMONT	A	Springfield
VIRGINIA		Richmond (Jefferson)
WASHINGTON	A	Seattle (Roosevelt)
WEST VIRGINIA		Beckley (Wilson)
WISCONSIN		Reedsville
WYOMING	A	Casper (Natroua)

1946–47

STATE	CLASS	CHAMPION
ALABAMA		Campbell
ARIZONA		Florence
ARKANSAS	A	Little Rock
COLORADO	AA	Denver (South)
CONNECTICUT	A	New Haven
FLORIDA	A	Tampa (Hillsborough)
GEORGIA	A	Havana
IDAHO	A	Boise
ILLINOIS		Paris
INDIANA		Shelbyville
IOWA		Davenport
KANSAS	AA	Wellington
KENTUCKY		Maysville
LOUISIANA	AA	New Orleans (St. Aloysius)
MAINE		Bangor
MASSACHUSETTS		Worcester (South)
MICHIGAN	A	Fall River (Durfee)
MINNESOTA		Duluth (Denfield)
MISSISSIPPI		Belmont
MISSOURI		St. Louis (Beaumont)
MONTANA	A	Missoula
NEBRASKA	A	Grand Island
NEW HAMPSHIRE		Portsmouth
NEW JERSEY	IV	Newark (Central)

STATE	CLASS	CHAMPION
NEW MEXICO		Carlsbad
NEVADA		Henderson (Basie)
NORTH DAKOTA	A	Grand Forks
OHIO	A	Middletown
OKLAHOMA	A	Muskogee
OREGON		Marshfield
PENNSYLVANIA	A	Allentown
RHODE ISLAND		Westerly
SOUTH CAROLINA		Olympia (Boys')
SOUTH DAKOTA	A	Sturgis
TENNESSEE		Soddy
TEXAS	AA	El Paso
UTAH	A	Granite
VERMONT		Rutland
VIRGINIA	I	Norfolk (Granby)
WASHINGTON		Pasco
WEST VIRGINIA		Huntington (East)
WISCONSIN		Beloit
WYOMING	A	Cheyenne

1947–48

STATE	CLASS	CHAMPION
ALABAMA	A	Attalla (Etowah)
ARIZONA		Tucson
ARKANSAS	A	Fayetteville
COLORADO	AA	Denver (Manual)
CONNECTICUT	A	New Haven (Hillhouse)
FLORIDA	A	Miami
GEORGIA	A	Macon (Lanier)
IDAHO	A	Lewiston
ILLINOIS		Pinckneyville (Comm.)
INDIANA		Lafayette (Jefferson)
IOWA		Manning
KANSAS	AA	Liberty
KENTUCKY		Brewers
LOUISIANA	AA	New Orleans (Jesuit)
MAINE	A	Cheverus
MASSACHUSETTS		Fall River
MICHIGAN	A	Jackson
MINNESOTA		Bemidji
MISSOURI		St. Louis (Beaumont)
MISSISSIPPI		Baldwyn
MONTANA	A	Anaconda
NEBRASKA	A	Grand Island
NEVADA	A	Elko County
NEW HAMPSHIRE	A	Concord
NEW JERSEY	IV	Orange
NEW MEXICO		Portales
NORTH CAROLINA	AA	High Point
NORTH DAKOTA	A	Williston
OHIO	A	Findlay
OKLAHOMA	A	Oklahoma City Classen
OREGON	A	Corvallis
PENNSYLVANIA	A	Norristown
RHODE ISLAND		Westerly
SOUTH CAROLINA	A	North Charleston
SOUTH DAKOTA	A	Mitchell
TENNESSEE		Nashville (West End)
TEXAS	AA	Dallas (Crozier)
UTAH		Ogden (Weber)
VERMONT	A	Burlington
VIRGINIA	I	Richmond (Marshall)
WASHINGTON	A	Spokane (No. Central)
WEST VIRGINIA		Princeton
WISCONSIN		Wauwatosa
WYOMING	A	Cheyenne

1948–49

STATE	CLASS	CHAMPION
ALABAMA	A	Lanier
ARIZONA	A	Tucson
ARKANSAS		No. Little Rock
COLORADO	AA	La Junta
CONNECTICUT	A	New Britain
FLORIDA	A	Miami
GEORGIA	A	Roosevelt
IDAHO	A	Coeur d'Alene
ILLINOIS		Mount Vernon
INDIANA		Jasper
IOWA	A	Ottumwa
KANSAS	AA	Newton
KENTUCKY		Owensboro
LOUISIANÁ	AA	New Orleans (St. Aloysius)
MAINE	L	Many
MARYLAND	A	Cumberland (Fort Hill)
MASSACHUSETTS	A	Somerville
MICHIGAN	A	Kalamazoo
MINNESOTA		St. Paul (Humboldt)
MISSISSIPPI		Booneville
MISSOURI		Buffalo
MONTANA	A	Missoula

STATE	CLASS	CHAMPION
NEBRASKA	A	Seward
NEVADA	A	Las Vegas
NEW HAMPSHIRE	A	Nashua
NEW JERSEY	IV	West Orange
NEW MEXICO		Lovington
NORTH CAROLINA	AA	Reynolds
NORTH DAKOTA	A	Minot
OHIO	A	Hamilton
OKLAHOMA	A	El Paso
OREGON	A	Roosevelt
PENNSYLVANIA	A	Aliquippa
RHODE ISLAND		Pawtucket

STATE	CLASS	CHAMPION
SOUTH CAROLINA	A	Gaffney
SOUTH DAKOTA	A	Aberdeen
TENNESSEE		Humboldt
TEXAS	AA	Texas City
UTAH	A	Davis
VERMONT		Montpelier
VIRGINIA	II	Radford
WASHINGTON	A	Spokane (Lewis & Clark)
WEST VIRGINIA	A	Fairmont (West)
WISCONSIN		Hurley
WYOMING	A	Casper

1949–50

STATE	CLASS	CHAMPION
ALABAMA	AA	Birmingham (Ensley)
ARIZONA	A	Mesa
ARKANSAS		Van Buren
COLORADO	AA	Denver (Manual Arts)
CONNECTICUT	L	New Britain
FLORIDA	A	Tampa (Jesuit)
GEORGIA	AA	Macon (Lanier)
IDAHO	A	Nampa
ILLINOIS		Mount Vernon
INDIANA		Madison
IOWA		Davenport
KANSAS	AA	Salina
KENTUCKY		Lexington (Lafayette)
LOUISIANA	AA	Baton Rouge
MAINE	L	Portland
MARYLAND	A	Cleveland (Alleghany)
MICHIGAN	A	Kalamazoo (Central)
MINNESOTA		Duluth (Central)
MISSISSIPPI	A	Booneville
MISSOURI	A	Joplin
MONTANA	A	Butte (Central Catholic)
NEBRASKA	A	Lincoln (Northeast)

STATE	CLASS	CHAMPION
NEVADA	A	Reno
NEW HAMPSHIRE	A	Portsmouth
NEW JERSEY	IV	Union City (Emerson)
NEW MEXICO		Tucumcari
NORTH CAROLINA	AA	High Point
NORTH DAKOTA	A	Minot
OHIO	A	Springfield
OKLAHOMA	A	Oklahoma City (Classen)
OREGON		Salem
PENNSYLVANIA	A	Homestead
SOUTH CAROLINA	A	Lancaster
SOUTH DAKOTA	A	Mitchell
TENNESSEE		Happy Valley
TEXAS	AA	Corpus Christi
UTAH	A	Salt Lake City (South)
VIRGINIA		Norfolk (Granby)
WASHINGTON		South Kitsap
WEST VIRGINIA	A	Wheeling
WISCONSIN		St. Croix Falls
WYOMING		Rock Springs

1950–51

STATE	CLASS	CHAMPION
ALABAMA		Florence (Coffey)
ARIZONA	A	Mesa
ARKANSAS	A	Fort Smith
COLORADO	AA	Denver (East)
CONNECTICUT	L	New London (Bulkeley)
FLORIDA	AA	Jacksonville (Jackson)
GEORGIA	AA	Macon (Lanier)
IDAHO	A	Idaho Falls

STATE	CLASS	CHAMPION
ILLINOIS		Freeport
INDIANA		Muncie (Central)
IOWA		Davenport
KANSAS	AA	Wichita (East)
KENTUCKY		Clark County
LOUISIANA	AA	New Orleans (St. Aloysius)
MAINE	L	Westbrook
MARYLAND	A	Hagerstown

STATE	CLASS	CHAMPION
MASSACHUSETTS	A	Quincy
MICHIGAN	A	Kalamazoo (Central)
MINNESOTA		Gilbert
MISSISSIPPI	A	Fulton
MISSOURI	A	Normandy
MONTANA		Kalispell (Flathead County)
NEBRASKA	A	Fremont
NEVADA	A	Ely (White Pine)
NEW HAMPSHIRE	A	Portsmouth
NEW JERSEY	IV	Bayonne
NEW MEXICO		Clovis
NORTH CAROLINA	AAA	Wilmington
NORTH DAKOTA	A	Bismarck (St. Mary's)
OHIO		Columbus (East)
OKLAHOMA	A	Shawnee
OREGON		Portland (Jefferson)
PENNSYLVANIA	A	Allentown
RHODE ISLAND		Westerly
SOUTH CAROLINA	A	Wellford
SOUTH DAKOTA	A	Sturgis
TENNESSEE		Knoxville
TEXAS	AA	Houston (Lamar)
UTAH	A	Jordan
VERMONT		Barre (Spaulding)
VIRGINIA	I	Newport News
WASHINGTON	A	Highline
WEST VIRGINIA	A	Beckley (Wilson)
WISCONSIN		Wisconsin Rapids
WYOMING	A	Cheyenne

1951–52

STATE	CLASS	CHAMPION
ALABAMA	AA	Winfield
ARIZONA	A	Phoenix (West)
ARKANSAS	A	Pine Bluff
COLORADO	AA	Denver (East)
CONNECTICUT	L	New Haven (Hillhouse)
FLORIDA	AA	Pensacola
GEORGIA	AA	Atlanta (Brown)
IDAHO	A	Idaho Falls
ILLINOIS		Hebron
INDIANA		Muncie
IOWA		Davenport
KANSAS		Newton
KENTUCKY		Cuba
LOUISIANA	AA	New Orleans (St. Aloysius)
MAINE	L	Old Town
MARYLAND	A	Silver Spring (Blair)
MASSACHUSETTS		Fall River (Durfee)
MICHIGAN	A	Highland Park
MINNESOTA		Hopkins
MISSISSIPPI	A	Kossuth
MISSOURI	A	St. Louis (University)
MONTANA	A	Kalispell (Flathead County)
NEBRASKA	A	Scottsbluff
NEVADA	A	White Pine
NEW HAMPSHIRE	A	Portsmouth
NEW JERSEY	IV	Elizabeth (Jefferson)
NEW MEXICO		Roswell
NORTH CAROLINA	AAA	Hendersonville
NORTH DAKOTA	A	Grand Forks (Central)
OHIO	A	Middletown
OKLAHOMA	A	Enid
OREGON	A	Portland (Lincoln)
PENNSYLVANIA	A	Farrell
RHODE ISLAND		Newport (Rogers)
SOUTH CAROLINA	A	Walhalla
SOUTH DAKOTA	A	Brookings
TENNESSEE		Selmer
TEXAS	I	San Antonio (Alamo)
UTAH	A	Salt Lake City (South)
VERMONT	A	Rutland
VIRGINIA	I	Newport News
WASHINGTON	A	Walla Walla
WEST VIRGINIA	A	Beckley (Wilson)
WISCONSIN		Milwaukee (South)
WYOMING	AA	Cheyenne

1952–53

STATE	CLASS	CHAMPION
ALABAMA	AA	Eufula
ARIZONA	A	Phoenix (Technical)
ARKANSAS		Clinton
COLORADO	AA	Denver (South)
CONNECTICUT	L	Waterbury (Wilby)
FLORIDA	AA	Fort Lauderdale
GEORGIA	AA	Atlanta (No. Fulton)
IDAHO	A	Idaho Falls

STATE	CLASS	CHAMPION	STATE	CLASS	CHAMPION
ILLINOIS		LaGrange (Lyons)	NORTH DAKOTA	A	Bismarck
INDIANA		South Bend (Central)	OHIO	A	Middletown
IOWA		Clinton (St. Mary's)	OKLAHOMA	AA	El Reno
KANSAS	AA	Merriam (Shawnee Mission)	OREGON	A	Coos Bay (Marshfield)
KENTUCKY		Lexington (Lafayette)	PENNSYLVANIA	A	Yeadon
LOUISIANA	AA	New Orleans (St. Aloysius)	RHODE ISLAND		Newport (De LaSalle Academy)
MAINE	L	Jonesboro (Hodge)	SOUTH CAROLINA	A	Columbia (Olympia)
MARYLAND	A	Ellsworth	SOUTH DAKOTA	A	Aberdeen
MASSACHUSETTS	A	Boston (Mission)	TENNESSEE		Old Hickory (DuPont)
MICHIGAN	A	Dearborn (Fordson)	TEXAS	AAAA	Pampa
MINNESOTA		Hopkins	UTAH	A	Jordan
MISSISSIPPI		Hickory	VERMONT	A	Burlington
MISSOURI		St. Louis (Cleveland)	VIRGINIA	I	Lynchburg (E.C. Glass)
MONTANA	A	Helena	WASHINGTON	A	Renton
NEBRASKA	A	Boys Town	WEST VIRGINIA	A	Beckely (Wilson)
NEVADA	A	Las Vegas	WISCONSIN		Menasha
NEW HAMPSHIRE	A	Portsmouth	WYOMING	AA	Cheyenne
NEW JERSEY	IV	Bloomfield			
NEW MEXICO		Clovis			
NORTH CAROLINA	AAA	Raleigh			

1953–54

STATE	CLASS	CHAMPION	STATE	CLASS	CHAMPION
ALABAMA	AA	Dothan	NEW HAMPSHIRE	A	Nashua
ARIZONA	A	Phoenix (West)	NEW JERSEY	IV	Elizabeth (Jefferson)
ARKANSAS	A	Jonesboro	NEW MEXICO	A	Carlsbad
COLORADO	A	Brighton	NORTH CAROLINA	AAA	Raleigh
CONNECTICUT	L	Hartford (Weaver)	NORTH DAKOTA	A	Wahpeton
FLORIDA	AA	Miami (Senior)	OHIO	A	Hamilton
GEORGIA	AA	Columbus (Baker)	OKLAHOMA	AA	Capitol Hill
IDAHO	A	Rexburg (Madison)	OREGON		Milwaukie
ILLINOIS		Mt. Vernon	PENNSYLVANIA	A	Farrell
INDIANA		Milan	RHODE ISLAND		East Providence (Senior)
IOWA		Muscatine	SOUTH CAROLINA	A	Orangeburg
KANSAS	AA	Wichita (North)	SOUTH DAKOTA	A	Deadwood
KENTUCKY		Inez	TENNESSEE		Nashville (West End)
LOUISIANA	AA	Baton Rouge	TEXAS	AAAA	Pampa
MAINE		Ellsworth	UTAH	A	Jordan
MARYLAND	A	Allegany	VERMONT		Rutland (Mt. St. Joseph)
MASSACHUSETTS		Cathedral	VIRGINIA	I	Richmond (Marshall)
MICHIGAN	A	Muskegon Heights	WASHINGTON	A	Seattle (Franklin)
MINNESOTA		Brainerd	WEST VIRGINIA	A	Beckley (Wilson)
MISSISSIPPI		Walnut	WISCONSIN		Stevens Point
MISSOURI	A	Cape Giradeau (Central)	WYOMING	A	Thermopolis
MONTANA	A	Helena			
NEBRASKA	A	Hastings			
NEVADA	A	Reno			

1954–55

STATE	CLASS	CHAMPION	STATE	CLASS	CHAMPION
ALABAMA	AA	Tuscaloosa	ARIZONA	AA	Phoenix (Union)

STATE	CLASS	CHAMPION
ARKANSAS	A	Fort Smith
COLORADO	AA	Denver (Man.)
CONNECTICUT	L	New Haven (Hillhouse)
FLORIDA	AA	Miami (Senior)
GEORGIA	AA	East Point (Russell)
IDAHO	A	Kellogg
ILLINOIS		Rockford (West)
INDIANA		Indianapolis (Crispus Attucks)
IOWA		Ames
KANSAS		Kansas City (Wyandotte)
KENTUCKY		Hazard
LOUISIANA	AAA	Lake Charles
MAINE		Bangor
MARYLAND	A	Montgomery (Blair)
MASSACHUSETTS	A	Sommerville
MICHIGAN	A	Jackson
MINNESOTA		Minneapolis (Washburn)
MISSISSIPPI		Wheeler
MISSOURI	A	Joplin
MONTANA	A	Helena
NEBRASKA	AA	Scottsbluff

STATE	CLASS	CHAMPION
NEVADA	A	Reno
NEW HAMPSHIRE	A	Manchester (Central)
NEW JERSEY	IV	Union City (Union Hill)
NEW MEXICO	A	Carlsbad
NORTH CAROLINA	AAA	Asheville
NORTH DAKOTA	A	Minot
OHIO	A	Zanesville
OKLAHOMA	AA	Norman
OREGON	A	Eugene
PENNSYLVANIA	A	McKeesport
RHODE ISLAND		Westerly
SOUTH CAROLINA	AA	Spartanburg
SOUTH DAKOTA	A	Sioux Falls (Washington)
TENNESSEE		Linden
TEXAS	AAAA	Dallas (Crozier)
UTAH	A	Jordan
VERMONT	A	Burlington
VIRGINIA	I	Roanoke (Jefferson)
WASHINGTON	A	Seattle (Garfield)
WEST VIRGINIA	A	Mullens
WISCONSIN		Eau Claire
WYOMING	A	Casper

1955–56

STATE	CLASS	CHAMPION
ALABAMA	AA	Murphy
ARIZONA	AA	Phoenix (Union)
ARKANSAS	A	Jonesboro
COLORADO	AA	Greeley
CONNECTICUT		Hartford (Weaver)
FLORIDA	AA	Miami (Senior)
GEORGIA	AA	Columbus (Baker)
IDAHO	A	Kellogg
ILLINOIS		Rockford (West Sr.)
INDIANA		Indianapolis (Crispus Attucks)
IOWA	A	Marshalltown
KANSAS	AA	Newton
KENTUCKY		Carr Creek
LOUISIANA	AAA	New Orleans (Fortier)
MAINE	L	Bath (Morse)
MARYLAND	A	Northwestern
MASSACHUSETTS		West Worcester (Commerce)
MICHIGAN	A	Muskegon Heights
MINNESOTA		Minneapolis (Roosevelt)
MISSISSIPPI		Nantachee
MISSOURI	L	St. Louis (Beaumont)

STATE	CLASS	CHAMPION
MONTANA	A	Butte (Central)
NEBRASKA		Boys Town
NEVADA	A	Henderson (Basic)
NEW HAMPSHIRE	A	Concord
NEW JERSEY	IV	Union City (Union Hill)
NEW MEXICO	A	Hobbs
NORTH CAROLINA	AAA	Wilmington
NORTH DAKOTA	A	Grand Forks
OHIO	A	Middletown
OKLAHOMA	AA	Tulsa (Will Rogers)
OREGON	AI	Portland (Franklin)
PENNSYLVANIA	A	Farrell
RHODE ISLAND		Westerly
SOUTH CAROLINA	AA	Columbia (Dreher)
SOUTH DAKOTA	A	Sioux Falls (Washington)
TENNESSEE		Linden
UTAH	A	Provo
VERMONT		Springfield
VIRGINIA	I	Newport News
WASHINGTON	A	Seattle (Lincoln)
WEST VIRGINIA	A	East Bank
WISCONSIN		Shawano
WYOMING	A	Cheyenne

1956–57

STATE	CLASS	CHAMPION	STATE	CLASS	CHAMPION
ALABAMA	AA	Woodlawn	NEBRASKA	AA	Boys Town
ALASKA		Anchorage	NEVADA	A	Fallon
ARKANSAS	A	Rogers	NEW HAMPSHIRE	L	Manchester (Central)
COLORADO	AA	Greeley	NEW JERSEY	IV	Bloomfield
CONNECTICUT	L	Hartford (Weaver)	NEW MEXICO	A	Hobbs
FLORIDA	AA	Lakeland	NORTH CAROLINA	AAA	Wilmington
GEORGIA	AAA	Decatur	NORTH DAKOTA	A	Bismarck
IDAHO	A	Pocatello	OHIO	AA	Middletown
ILLINOIS		Herrin	OKLAHOMA	AA	Enid
INDIANA		South Bend (Central)	OREGON	A1	Lincoln
IOWA	A	Des Moines (Dowling)	PENNSYLVANIA	A	Sharon
			RHODE ISLAND	A	Providence
KANSAS	AA	Kansas City (Wyandotte)	SOUTH CAROLINA	AA	Columbia (Dreher)
KENTUCKY		Lafayette	SOUTH DAKOTA	A	Belle Fourche
LOUISIANA	AAA	New Orleans (DeLaSalle)	TENNESSEE		Linden
			TEXAS	AAAA	Port Arthur (Thom. Jefferson)
MAINE	L	Old Town			
MARYLAND	A	Frederick	UTAH	A	Salt Lake City (South)
MASSACHUSETTS		Worcester (West)			
MICHIGAN	A	Muskegon Heights	VERMONT	A	Springfield
MINNESOTA		Minneapolis (Roosevelt)	VIRGINIA	I	Newport News
			WASHINGTON	A	Seattle (Lincoln)
MISSISSIPPI		Coffeville	WEST VIRGINIA	A	Beckley (Wilson)
MISSOURI	L	St. Charles	WISCONSIN		Shawano
MONTANA	AA	Butte	WYOMING	A	Cody

1957–58

STATE	CLASS	CHAMPION	STATE	CLASS	CHAMPION
ALABAMA	AA	Fayette (County)	MICHIGAN	A	Detroit (Austin Cath.)
ALASKA		Juneau	MINNESOTA		Austin
ARIZONA		Phoenix (Union)	MISSISSIPPI		Philadelphia
ARKANSAS	AA	Fort Smith	MISSOURI	A	St. Louis (University)
COLORADO	AA	Upper Denver	MONTANA	AA	Butte
CONNECTICUT	L	New Haven (Wilbur Cross)	NEBRASKA	A	Lincoln
			NEVADA	A	Las Vegas
DISTRICT OF COLUMBIA		Cardozo	NEW HAMPSHIRE	L	Manchester (Bradley)
FLORIDA	AA	Atlanta (Murphy)			
GEORGIA	AAA	Darien	NEW JERSEY	IV	Bloomfield
IDAHO	AAA	Moreland (Snake River)	NEW MEXICO	A	Hobbs
			NORTH CAROLINA	AAA	Wilmington (New Hanover)
ILLINOIS		Chicago (Marshall)			
INDIANA		Fort Wayne (South Side)	NORTH DAKOTA	A	Bismarck
			OHIO	AA	Cleveland (East Tech.)
IOWA	A	Davenport			
KANSAS	AA	Kansas City (Wyandotte)	OKLAHOMA	AA	Tulsa (Will Rogers)
			OREGON	A1	Klamath Falls
KENTUCKY		Louisville (St. Xavier)	PENNSYLVANIA	A	Haverford
LOUISIANA	AAA	New Orleans (DeLaSalle)	RHODE ISLAND		Westerly
			S. CAROLINA	AAA	Spartanburg
MAINE	A	South Portland	SOUTH DAKOTA	A	Huron
MARYLAND	A	Cumberland (Fort Hill)	TENNESSEE		Lenoir City
MASSACHUSETTS		Somerville (East)	TEXAS	AAAA	Pampa

STATE	CLASS	CHAMPION
UTAH	A	Springville
VERMONT	L	Rutland
VIRGINIA	III	Stuart
WASHINGTON	AA	Richland
WEST VIRGINIA	A	Parkersburg
WISCONSIN		Madison (East)
WYOMING	A	Gillette

1958–59

STATE	CLASS	CHAMPION
ALABAMA	AA	Pisgah
ALASKA		Fairbanks
ARIZONA		Phoenix (Union)
ARKANSAS	AA	Fort Smith
COLORADO	AAA	Greeley
DISTRICT OF COLUMBIA		Cardozo
GEORGIA	AAA	Atlanta (Brown)
HAWAII		Farrington
IDAHO	AAA	Kellogg
ILLINOIS		Springfield
INDIANA		Indianapolis (Crispus Attucks)
IOWA	A	Sioux Center
KANSAS	AA	Kansas City (Wyandotte)
KENTUCKY		Calvert City (N. Marshall)
LOUISIANA	AAA	New Orleans (DeLaSalle)
MAINE		Bangor
MARYLAND	A	Bethesda (Chevy Chase)
MICHIGAN	A	Lansing (Sexton)
MINNESOTA		Wayzata
MISSISSIPPI		Wheeler
MISSOURI		St. Louis (Christian Bros.)
MONTANA	AA	Missoula
NEBRASKA	AA	Lincoln
NEVADA	AA	Basic
NEW HAMPSHIRE	L	Nashua
NEW JERSEY	IV	Camden
NEW MEXICO	A	Las Cruces
NORTH CAROLINA	AAA	Greensboro
NORTH DAKOTA	A	Bismarck
OHIO	AA	Cleveland (East Tech.)
OKLAHOMA	AA	Norman
OREGON	A-1	Portland (Franklin)
PENNSYLVANIA	A	Farrell
RHODE ISLAND		Providence (Hope)
SOUTH CAROLINA	AAA	Greenville (Parker)
SOUTH DAKOTA	A	Watertown
TENNESSEE		Alcoa
UTAH	A	Bear River
VERMONT	L	St. Albans (Bellows Free)
VIRGINIA	I	Lynchburg (E. C. Glass)
WASHINGTON	AA	Tacoma (Stadium)
WEST VIRGINIA	AAA	South Charleston
WISCONSIN		Milwaukee (Lincoln)
WYOMING	A	Sheridan

1959–60

STATE	CLASS	CHAMPION
ALABAMA	AA	Tuscaloosa
ALASKA		Juneau
ARIZONA	AA	Phoenix (Union)
ARKANSAS	AAA	Leachville
COLORADO	AAA	Greeley
CONNECTICUT	L	New Haven (Wilbur Cross)
FLORIDA	AA	North Miami
GEORGIA	AAA	Atlanta (Sylvan)
HAWAII		Honolulu (Farrington)
IDAHO	AAA	Idaho Falls
ILLINOIS		Chicago (Marshall)
INDIANA		East Chicago (Washington)
IOWA	A	Marshalltown
KANSAS	AA	Kansas City (Wyandotte)
KENTUCKY		Flaget
LOUISIANA	AAA	Bossier
MAINE		Lewiston
MARYLAND	A	Bladensburg
MICHIGAN	A	Lansing (Sexton)
MINNESOTA		Edgerton
MISSISSIPPI		Pass Christian (N. Central)
MISSOURI		St. Louis (Christian Bros.)
MONTANA	AA	Billings
NEBRASKA	A	Omaha (South)

STATE	CLASS	CHAMPION
NEVADA	AA	Las Vegas
NEW HAMPSHIRE	L	Nashua
NEW JERSEY	A	Camden
NEW MEXICO	A	Las Cruces
NORTH CAROLINA		Wilmington
NORTH DAKOTA	A	Valley City
OHIO		Dayton (Roosevelt)
OKLAHOMA	AA	Enid
OREGON		Medford
PENNSYLVANIA	A	Farrell
RHODE ISLAND		Westerly
SOUTH CAROLINA	AAA	Anderson (Boys')
SOUTH DAKOTA	A	Rapid City
TENNESSEE		Hampton
TEXAS	AAAA	Beaumont (S. Park.)
UTAH	A	Bingham
VIRGINIA	I	Highland Springs
WASHINGTON	AA	Renton
WEST VIRGINIA	AAA	Parkersburg
WISCONSIN		Wausau
WYOMING	A	Rock Springs

1960–61

STATE	CLASS	CHAMPION
ALABAMA	AA	Tuscaloosa
ALASKA		Juneau (Douglas)
ARIZONA	AA	Phoenix (Union)
ARKANSAS	AA	Helena
COLORADO	AAA	Denver (Washington)
CONNECTICUT	L	New Haven (Wilbur Cross)
DISTRICT OF COLUMBIA		Spingarn
FLORIDA	AA	St. Petersburg (D. Hollins)
GEORGIA	AAA	Atlanta (Sylvan)
IDAHO	AAA	Idaho Falls
ILLINOIS		Collinsville
INDIANA		Kokomo
IOWA		Marshalltown
KANSAS	AA	Kansas City (Wyandotte)
KENTUCKY		Ashland
LOUISIANA	AAA	Baton Rouge
MAINE	L	Portland (Cheverus)
MICHIGAN	A	Detroit (Cath. Central)
MINNESOTA		Duluth (Central)
MISSISSIPPI		Potts Camp
MISSOURI	A	St. Louis (University)
MONTANA	AA	Missoula (County)
NEBRASKA	A	Fremont
NEVADA	AA	Rancho
NEW HAMPSHIRE	L	Portsmouth
NEW JERSEY	IV	Trenton
NEW MEXICO	A	Las Cruces
NORTH CAROLINA	AAAA	Wilmington
NORTH DAKOTA	A	Minot
OHIO	AA	Portsmouth
OKLAHOMA	AA	Norman
OREGON	AI	Klamath Falls
PENNSYLVANIA	A	Nanticoke
RHODE ISLAND		Providence (Hope)
SOUTH CAROLINA	AAA	Columbia (Dreher)
SOUTH DAKOTA	A	Aberdeen (Central)
TENNESSEE		Oak Ridge
TEXAS	AAAA	Houston (Austin)
UTAH	A	Davis
VERMONT	L	Barre (Spaulding)
VIRGINIA	IA	Arlington (Wakefield)
WASHINGTON	AA	Seattle (Garfield)
WEST VIRGINIA	AAA	Huntington
WISCONSIN		Milwaukee (Lincoln)
WYOMING	A	Cheyenne (Central)

1961–62

STATE	CLASS	CHAMPION
ALABAMA	AA	Montgomery (Lanier)
ALASKA	A	Ketchikan
ARIZONA	AA	Tucson
ARKANSAS	AAA	Jonesboro
COLORADO	AAA	Greeley
CONNECTICUT	L	Hartford
DISTRICT OF COLUMBIA		Eastern
FLORIDA	AA	St. Petersburg (Hollins)
GEORGIA	AAA	Columbus
HAWAII		Kamehameha
IDAHO	AAA	Pocatello
ILLINOIS		Decatur
INDIANA		Evansville (Bosee)
IOWA		Ceder Rapids (Regis)
KANSAS	AA	Wichita (East)
KENTUCKY		Louisville (St. Xavier)
LOUISIANA	AAA	New Orleans (DeLaSalle)

STATE	CLASS	CHAMPION
MAINE	LL	Bath (Morse)
MARYLAND	AA	Montgomery (Blair)
MICHIGAN	A	Saginaw
MINNESOTA		St. Louis Park
MISSISSIPPI		McComb
MISSOURI	L	Columbia (Hickman)
MONTANA	AA	Great Falls
NEBRASKA	A	Lincoln (Northeast)
NEVADA	AA	Western
NEW HAMPSHIRE	L	Concord
NEW JERSEY	IV	Newark (Weequahic)
NEW MEXICO	A	Albuquerque (Sandia)
NORTH CAROLINA	AAAA	Wilmington (New Hanover)
NORTH DAKOTA	A	Rugby
OHIO	AA	Hamilton (Taft)
OKLAHOMA	AA	Lawton
OREGON	A-1	Grants Press
PENNSYLVANIA	A	Uniontown
RHODE ISLAND		East Providence
SOUTH CAROLINA	AAA	Greenville
SOUTH DAKOTA	A	Broolings
TENNESSEE		Cleveland
TEXAS	AAAA	Dallas (Jefferson)
UTAH	A	Jordan
VERMONT	L	Barre (Spaulding)
VIRGINIA	L-A	Arlington (Wash.-Lee)
WASHINGTON	AA	Seattle (Garfield)
WEST VIRGINIA		Beckley (Wilson)
WISCONSIN	A	Milwaukee (Lincoln)
WYOMING		Cheyenne

1962–63

STATE	CLASS	CHAMPION
ALABAMA	AA	Montgomery (Lanier)
ALASKA	A	Juneau (Douglas)
ARIZONA	AA	Tucson (Catalina)
ARKANSAS	AAA	Paragould
COLORADO	AAA	Wheat Ridge
CONNECTICUT	L	New Haven (Hillhouse)
DISTRICT OF COLUMBIA		Eastern
FLORIDA	AA	Pompano
GEORGIA	AAA	LaGrange
HAWAII		Kamehameha
IDAHO	AAA	Couer d'Alene
ILLINOIS		Chicago (Carver)
INDIANA		Muncie (Central)
IOWA		Newton
KANSAS	AA	Salina
KENTUCKY		Louisville (Seneca)
LOUISIANA	AAA	Fair Park
MAINE	LL	Bath (Morse)
MARYLAND	AA	Towson
MICHIGAN	A	Ferndale
MINNESOTA		Marshall
MISSISSIPPI		Bonneville
MISSOURI		St. Louis (Christian Bros.)
MONTANA	AA	Billings (West)
NEBRASKA	A	Omaha Technical
NEVADA	AA	Reno
NEW HAMPSHIRE	L	Manchester (Bradley)
NEW JERSEY	IV	Newark Catholic
NEW MEXICO	A	Roswell
NEW YORK	AA	Oneonta
NORTH CAROLINA	AAAA	Rocky Mount
NORTH DAKOTA	A	Williston
OHIO	AA	Columbus (East)
OKLAHOMA	A	Norman
OREGON	A-1	North Eugene
PENNSYLVANIA	A	Plymouth Meet. (Whitemarsh)
RHODE ISLAND		Newport (Rogers)
SOUTH CAROLINA	AAA	Columbia (Dreher)
SOUTH DAKOTA	A	Sisserton
TENNESSEE		Oak Ridge
TEXAS	AAAA	San Angelo (Central)
VERMONT	L	Barre (Spaulding)
VIRGINIA	IA	Arlington (Wash.-Lee)
WASHINGTON	AA	Seattle (Blanchet)
WEST VIRGINIA	AAA	Weirton
WISCONSIN		Manitowoc
WYOMING	AA	Cheyenne (Central)

1963–64

STATE	CLASS	CHAMPION
ALABAMA	AAAA	Tuscaloosa
ALASKA		Fairbanks (Lathrop)
ARIZONA	AA	Phoenix (Camelback)
ARKANSAS	AA	N. Little Rock

STATE	CLASS	CHAMPION
COLORADO	AAA	Denver (East)
CONNECTICUT	L	New Haven (Hillhouse)
DISTRICT OF COLUMBIA		Cardozo
FLORIDA	AA	Pensacola
GEORGIA	AAA	Marietta (Osborne)
HAWAII		Hilo
IDAHO	A-l	Kellogg
ILLINOIS		Pekin
INDIANA		Lafayette (Jefferson)
IOWA		Newton
KANSAS	AA	Kansas City (Wyandotte)
KENTUCKY		Louisville (Seneca)
LOUISIANA	AAA	New Orleans (Jesuit)
MAINE	A	Millinocket (Stearns)
MARYLAND	AA	Allegany
MICHIGAN	A	Benton Harbor
MINNESOTA		Luverne
MISSISSIPPI		Baldwin
MISSOURI	L	St. Louis (Bishop Dubourg)
MONTANA	A	Missoula
NEBRASKA	A	Omaha (Creighton)
NEVADA	AA	Western
NEW HAMPSHIRE	L	Manchester (Bradley)
NEW JERSEY	IV	Newark (Central)
NEW MEXICO	AA	Roswell
NORTH CAROLINA	AAAA	Grimsley
NORTH DAKOTA	A	Grafton
OHIO	AA	Dayton (Belmont)
OKLAHOMA	AA	Oklahoma City (Classen)
OREGON		Portland (Parkrose)
PENNSYLVANIA		Uniontown
RHODE ISLAND		Pawtucket (Tolman)
SOUTH CAROLINA	AAA	Greenville
SOUTH DAKOTA	A	Mitchell
TENNESSEE		Donelson
TEXAS	AAAA	Houston (Austin)
UTAH	A	East
VERMONT	L	Barre (Spaulding)
VIRGINIA	l-A	Newport News
WASHINGTON	AA	Vancouver (Hudson's Bay)
WEST VIRGINIA	AAA	Logan
WISCONSIN		Dodgeville
WYOMING	AA	Laramie

1964–65

STATE	CLASS	CHAMPION
ALABAMA	AAAA	Montgomery (Lanier)
ALASKA		Ketchikan
ARIZONA	AA	Tucson (Rincon)
ARKANSAS	AAA	Fort Smith
COLORADO	AAA	Denver (East)
CONNECTICUT	L	New Haven (Hillhouse)
DISTRICT OF COLUMBIA		Cardozo
FLORIDA	AA	Jacksonville (Paxon)
GEORGIA	AAA	LaGrange
HAWAII	A	Kamehameha
IDAHO	A-1	Boise (Borah)
ILLINOIS		Collinsville
INDIANA		Indianapolis (Washington)
IOWA		Des Moines (Roosevelt)
KANSAS	AA	Kansas City (Wyandotte)
KENTUCKY		Breckinridge
LOUISIANA	AAA	Jesuit
MAINE	A	Millinocket (Strarns)
MARYLAND	AA	Surrattsville
MASSACHUSETTS		West Roxbury (Cath. Memorial)
MICHIGAN	A	Benton Harbor
MINNESOTA		Minnetonka
MISSISSIPPI	AA	Tupelo
MISSOURI	L	Springfield (Parkview)
MONTANA	A	Great Falls
NEBRASKA	A	Boys Town
NEVADA	AA	Las Vegas
NEW HAMPSHIRE	L	Portsmouth
NEW JERSEY	IV	Bridgewater-Raritan
NEW MEXICO	AA	Albuquerque (Valley)
NORTH CAROLINA	AAAA	Fayetteville
NORTH DAKOTA	A	Minot
OHIO	AA	Columbus (South)
OKLAHOMA	AA	Oklahoma City (Northwest)
OREGON	A-1	Klamath Falls
PENNSYLVANIA	A	Midland
RHODE ISLAND		South Kingston
SOUTH CAROLINA	AAA	Greenville
SOUTH DAKOTA	A	Sioux Falls (Washington)

STATE	CLASS	CHAMPION	STATE	CLASS	CHAMPION
TENNESSEE		Murfreesboro (Central)	VIRGINIA	I-A	Portsmouth (Wilson)
			WASHINGTON	AA	Yakima (Davis)
TEXAS	AAAA	Houston (Jones)	WEST VIRGINIA	AAA	Beckley (Wilson)
UTAH	A	Highland	WISCONSIN		Monroe
VERMONT	L	Bennington Catholic	WYOMING	AA	Laramie

1965–66

STATE	CLASS	CHAMPION	STATE	CLASS	CHAMPION
ALABAMA	AAAA	Huntsville (Butler)	MISSOURI	L	Kansas City (Central)
ALASKA		Ketchikan	MONTANA	A	Libby
ARIZONA	AA	Phoenix (Camelback)	NEBRASKA	A	Boys Town
ARKANSAS	AAA	Little Rock (Central)	NEVADA	AAA	Las Vegas
COLORADO	AAA	Denver (Manual)	NEW HAMPSHIRE	L	Winnacunnet
CONNECTICUT	LL	New Haven (Wilbur Cross)	NEW JERSEY	IV	Newark (Weequahic)
			NEW MEXICO	AA	Hobbs
DISTRICT OF COLUMBIA		McKinley	NORTH CAROLINA	AAAA	Fayetteville
			NORTH DAKOTA	A	Mandan
FLORIDA	AA	Pensacola	OHIO	AA	Dayton (Chaminade)
GEORGIA	AAA	Augusta (Butler)	OKLAHOMA	AA	Tulsa (Webster)
HAWAII	A	St. Louis	OREGON	A-1	Eugene (North)
IDAHO	A-1	Boise (Borah)	PENNSYLVANIA	A	Pittsburgh (Schenley)
ILLINOIS		Harvey (Thornton Twp.)	RHODE ISLAND		South Kingston
INDIANA		Michigan City (Elston)	SOUTH CAROLINA	AAA	Anderson
			SOUTH DAKOTA	A	Webster
IOWA		Marshalltown	TENNESSEE		Nashville (Pearl)
KANSAS	AA	Garden City	TEXAS	AAAA	Houston (Memorial)
KENTUCKY		Shelby County	UTAH	A	Highland
LOUISIANA	AA	North Caddo	VERMONT	L	Bennington Catholic
MAINE		Augusta (Cony)	VIRGINIA	IA	Arlington (Washington-Lee)
MARYLAND	AA	Richard Montgomery			
MASSACHUSETTS		Fall River	WASHINGTON	AA	Renton
MICHIGAN	A	Ferndale	WEST VIRGINIA	AAA	Dunbar
MINNESOTA		Edina	WISCONSIN		Milwaukee (Lincoln)
MISSISSIPPI		Tupelo	WYOMING	AA	Powell

1966–67

STATE	CLASS	CHAMPION	STATE	CLASS	CHAMPION
ALABAMA	AAAA	Sidney Lanier	GEORGIA	AAA	Savannah (Beach)
ALASKA	A	Ketchikan	HAWAII		St. Louis
ARIZONA	AA	Phoenix (Union)	IDAHO	A-1	Caldwell
ARKANSAS	AAA	N. Little Rock	ILLINOIS		Pekin
COLORADO	AAA	Denver (Jefferson)	INDIANA		Evansville (North)
CONNECTICUT	LL	New Haven (Wilbur Cross)	IOWA	AA	Cedar Rapids (Jefferson)
DELAWARE		Mt. Pleasant	KANSAS	AA	Kansas City (Wyandotte)
DISTRICT OF COLUMBIA		Cardozo	KENTUCKY		Earlington
FLORIDA	AA	St. Petersburg (Gibbs)	LOUISIANA	AAA	LaGrange
			MAINE		Old Town

STATE	CLASS	CHAMPION
MARYLAND	AA	Northwestern
MASSACHUSETTS		Melrose
MICHIGAN	A	Detroit (Pershing)
MINNESOTA		Edina
MISSISSIPPI		Forest Hill
MISSOURI	L	Joplin
MONTANA	A	Billings
NEBRASKA	A	Lincoln (Northeast)
NEVADA	AAA	Las Vegas
NEW HAMPSHIRE	L	Manchester (Central)
NEW JERSEY	IV	Newark (Weequahic)
NEW MEXICO	AA	Albuquerque (Sandia)
NORTH CAROLINA	AAAA	Gastonia (Ashley)
NORTH DAKOTA	A	Mandan
OHIO	AA	Columbus (McKinley)

STATE	CLASS	CHAMPION
OKLAHOMA	AAA	Bartlesville (College)
OREGON	A-l	David Douglas
PENNSYLVANIA	A	Ambridge
RHODE ISLAND	A	South Kingston
SOUTH CAROLINA	AAA	Hanna
SOUTH DAKOTA	A	Milbank
TENNESSEE		Alcoa
UTAH	A	Clearfield
VERMONT	L	Rutland
VIRGINIA	l-A	Lynchburg (Glass)
WASHINGTON	AA	Renton
WEST VIRGINIA	AAA	Beckley (Wilson)
WISCONSIN		Milwaukee (Lincoln)
WYOMING	AA	Cheyenne (Central)

1967–68

STATE	CLASS	CHAMPION
ALABAMA	AAAA	Lee
ALASKA		Ketchikan
ARIZONA	AA	Phoenix (Union)
ARKANSAS	AAA	Fort Smith (Northside)
COLORADO	AAA	Wheat Ridge
CONNECTICUT	LL	New Haven (Wilbur Cross)
DELAWARE		Wilmington (P. S. DuPont)
DISTRICT OF COLUMBIA		McKinley
FLORIDA	AA	Key West
GEORGIA	AAA	Savannah (Johnson)
HAWAII		St. Louis
IDAHO	A-1	Boise (Capital)
ILLINOIS		Evanston Twp.
INDIANA		Gary (Roosevelt)
IOWA	AA	Storm Lake
KANSAS	AA	Kansas City (Wyandotte)
KENTUCKY		Glasgow
LOUISIANA	AAA	Baton Rouge
MAINE	LL	Millinockett (Stearns)
MARYLAND	AA	Northwestern
MASSACHUSETTS		Boston (English)
MICHIGAN	A	Grand Rapids (Ottawa Hills)
MINNESOTA		Edina
MISSISSIPPI		Tupelo
MISSOURI	L	St. Louis (O'Fallon)

STATE	CLASS	CHAMPION
MONTANA	A	Wolf Point
NEBRASKA	A	Lincoln (Northeast)
NEVADA	AA	Clark
NEW HAMPSHIRE	L	Dover
NEW JERSEY	IV	Perth Amboy
NEW MEXICO	AA	Hobbs
NORTH CAROLINA	AAAA	New Hanover
NORTH DAKOTA	A	Williston
OHIO	AA	Columbus (East)
OKLAHOMA	AAA	Oklahoma City (Northwest)
OREGON	A-1	McNary
PENNSYLVANIA	A	Laurel Highlands
RHODE ISLAND	A	Sacred Heart Academy
SOUTH CAROLINA	AAA	Spartanburg
SOUTH DAKOTA	A	Brookings
TENNESSEE		Chattanooga (Riverside)
TEXAS	AAAA	Houston (Wheatley)
UTAH	A	Hillcrest
VERMONT	L	Rice Memorial
VIRGINIA	L-A	Salem (Andrew Lewis)
WASHINGTON	AA	Spokane (Central Valley)
WEST VIRGINIA	AAA	Charleston
WISCONSIN		Manitowoc
WYOMING	AA	Lander (Fremont Vocational)

Selection to a bona-fide All-American team is the ultimate individual achievement of every high school basketball player. Most of the greatest basketball names first became known to the public when they appeared on an All-American list.

One of the most reliable A-A lists is annually prepared by *Scholastic Magazines'* All-American selection board under the direction of Bob Lapidus. Over the last 13 years Scholastic's squad has included such names as Jerry Lucas (three times), Lew Alcindor (three times), Jerry West, Cazzie Russell, Dick and Tom Van Arsdale, Bill Bradley, Calvin Murphy, and many others.

ALL-AMERICAN HIGH SCHOOL SQUAD

1955–56

Name and School	Ht.
Al Attar (Durfee) Fall River, Mass.	6-2
Dennis Boone (Manual) Denver, Colo.	5-11
George Burkel (Cleveland) St. Louis, Mo.	6-7
Kelly Coleman (Wayland) Ky.	6-3
Albert Ellison (Linden) Tenn.	6-4
Nolden Gentry (West Rockford) Ill.	6-7
Earl Irvine (Lincoln) Seattle, Wash.	6-4
Tony Jackson (Jefferson) Brooklyn, N.Y.	6-3½
Bjarne Jensen (Franklin) Portland, Ore.	6-9
Ron Johnson (New Prague) Minn.	6-7
Fred LaCour (St. Ignatius) San Francisco	6-4½
Art Lambiotte (Warwick) Hilton Village, Va.	6-4
Jerry Lucas (Middletown) O.	6-7
Walt Mangham (New Castle) Pa.	6-3
Douglas Moe (Erasmus) Brooklyn, N.Y.	6-4
Lance Olson (Green Bay West) Wis.	6-3
Mel Peterson (Stephenson) Mich.	6-5
Jerry Pimm (Montebello) Cal.	5-11
Jack Pirrie (Maplewood) Mo.	6-6
George Ramming (Union Hill) Union City, N.J.	6-5
Oscar Robertson (Attucks) Indianapolis, Ind.	6-4
Barry Shetrone (Southern) Baltimore, Md.	6-3
Tom Stith (St. Francis) Brooklyn, N.Y.	6-5
Larry Swift (Keokuk) Iowa	6-6
Mike Tipton (Natrona County) Casper, Wyo.	6-2
Horace Walker (Chester) Pa.	6-3
Jerry West (East Bank) W. Va.	6-3
Max Williams (Avoca) Tex.	5-10
Rollie Williams (Kellogg) Ida.	6-6
Corky Withrow (Central City) Ky.	6-4

1956–57

Name and School	Ht.
Jim Altenhofen (Cent. Cath.) Portland, Ore.	6-5
Terry Bethel (Collinsville) Ill.	6-7
Norris Brown (Richland) Wash.	6-0
Ed Burton (Muskegon Heights) Mich.	6-6
Al Butler (East) Rochester, N.Y.	6-2
Jerry Cobb (Sunset) Dallas, Tex.	6-3
Julie Cohen (Erasmus) Brooklyn, N.Y.	5-11
Larry Conley (Wyandotte) Kansas City, Kan.	6-5
Ray Cronk (Bemidji) Minn.	6-4
Dick Cullers (High Point) N.C.	5-11
Howard Dardeen (Gersimeyer) Terre Haute, Ind.	6-4
John Egan (Weaver) Hartford, Conn.	5-11
Edmond Gary (Forest Hill) Miss.	6-3
Jerry Graves (Lexington) Tenn.	6-5
Bob Heffner (Allentown) Pa.	6-4
Dave Jackson (Central) Pueblo, Colo.	6-3
Tony Jackson (Jefferson) Brooklyn, N.Y.	6-4
Bill Kilmer (Citrus) Azusa, Calif.	6-0
Billy Ray Lickert (Lafayette) Lexington, Ky.	6-3
Jerry Lucas (Middletown) Ohio	6-8
Billy McGill (Jefferson) Los Angeles, Calif.	6-11
Bob McLeod (Markel) Tex.	6-4
Tom Meschery (Lowell) San Francisco, Calif.	6-4½
Bob Mlkvy (Polmerton) Pa.	6-4½
George Ramming (Union Hill) Union City, N.J.	6-6
Wayne Richards (Richmond Acad.) Augusta, Ga.	6-7
Lee Sager (East Orange) N.J.	6-5
Tom Smith (St. Francis) Brooklyn, N.Y.	6-5
Loren Wolf (Shawano) Wis.	6-4½
Dave Woolery (Rosedale) Kansas City, Kan.	5-11

1957–58

Name and School	Ht.
Ernie Cage (DeMatha) Hyattsville, Md.	6-3
Ernie Davis (Elmira Free Academy) N.Y.	6-2
Dave DeBusschere (Austin) Detroit, Mich.	6-5½
Jack Foley (Assumption) Worcester, Mass.	6-5
Norman Grow (Foley) Minn.	6-5
Willie Hall (Malloy) Queens, N.Y.	6-4
Phil Hart (El Cerrito) Calif.	6-3
Wayne Hightower (Overbrook) Phila., Pa.	6-8
Herman Keller (Newport News) Va.	6-4
Gene Kunz (Ogden) Utah	6-3
Jerry Lucas (Middletown) O.	6-9½
Mike McCoy (South Side) Fort Wayne, Ind.	7-0

Name and School	Ht.
Bill McGill (Jefferson) Los Angeles, Calif.	6-11
Sandy Pomerantz (University City) Mo.	6-5½
John Rudometkin (Santa Maria) Calif.	6-5½
Rod Thorn (Princeton) W. Va.	6-4
Harry Todd (Earlington) Ky.	6-8
Charles Vaughn (Alexander) Tamms, Ill.	6-2
Charles Warren (South) Eugene, Ore.	6-4
Gary White (Midwest City) Okla.	6-5

1958–59

Name and School	Ht.
Tom Hoover (Carroll) Washington, D.C.	6-9
Tom McGrann (Watertown) S.D.	6-8
Al Santio (Hope) Providence, R.I.	6-7
Ken Glenn (East Tech) Cleveland, O.	6-6
Tommy Boyer (Fort Smith) Ark.	6-6
Pat Richter (Madison East) Wis.	6-6
Dave Downey (Canton) Ill.	6-5
Bill Galantai (James Madison) Brooklyn, N.Y.	6-5
Rod Thorn (Princeton) W. Va.	6-5
Steve Gray (Washington) San Francisco, Calif.	6-4½
Tom Bolyard (South Side) Fort Wayne, Ind.	6-4
Bob Cozby (Olympus) Holladay, Utah	6-4
Art Heyman (Oceanside) N.Y.	6-4
Rich Porter (Kellogg) Ida.	6-4
Jim Smith (Santa Cruz) Calif.	6-4
Bill Raftery (St. Cecilia's) Kearny, N.J.	6-3½
Steve Pauly (Beaverton) Ore.	6-3½
Ralph Heyward (Overbrook) Philadelphia, Pa.	6-3
Tom Kezar (Austin) Minn.	6-3
Darrell Sutherland (Glendale) Calif.	6-3
Ed Thomas (McClymonds) Oakland, Calif.	6-3
Pat Doyle (North Marshall County) Ky.	6-2
Nolan Ellison (Wyandotte) Kansas City, Kan.	6-2
Bill Small (West Aurora) Ill.	6-2
Dom Perno (Wilbur Cross) New Haven, Conn.	6-1
Jim Rayl (Kokomo) Ind.	6-1
Granny Lash (Chester) Pa.	6-½
Donnie Burks (Molloy) Queens, N.Y.	5-11
Ernie Moore (Sumner) Kansas City, Kan.	5-10
Vinnie Ernst (St. Aloysius) Jersey City, N.J.	5-8

1959–60

Name and School	Ht.
John Thompson (Carroll) Washington, D.C.	6-11
Jay Buckley (Bladensburg) Md.	6-10
Mel Counts (Marshfield) Coos Bay, Ore.	6-10
James Barnes (Stillwater) Okla.	6-8
Gene Lane (East Tech) Cleveland, O.	6-8
Bill Vincent (South) Omaha, Neb.	6-8
George Wilson (Marshall) Chicago, Ill.	6-8
Tom Dose (Glendale) Calif.	6-7
Garry Garrison (Christian Bros.) Clayton, Mo.	6-7
Bernie Mills (Dunbar) Chicago, Ill.	6-7
Paul Silas (McClymonds) Oakland, Calif.	6-6½
Ray Brown (Roosevelt) Dayton, O.	6-6
Connie Hawkins (Boys) Brooklyn, N.Y.	6-6
Bill Bradley (Crystal City) Mo.	6-5
Roger Brown (Wingate) Brooklyn, N.Y.	6-5
Dennis Dairman (North Phoenix) Ariz.	6-5
Dave Hicks (Wilbur Cross) New Haven Conn.	6-5
Barry Kramer (Linton) Schenectady, N.Y.	6-5
Charles Nash (Lake Charles) La.	6-5
Ron Bonham (Central) Muncie, Ind.	6-4
Joe Caldwell (Fremont) Los Angeles, Calif.	6-4
Don Frye (Monticello) Ky.	6-4
Bill Maphis (Romney) W. Va.	6-4
Walt Hazzard (Overbrook) Philadelphia, Pa.	6-3
Jeff Mullins (Lafayette) Lexington, Ky.	6-3
Jim McKay (Greeley) Colo.	6-2
Ron Smith (Camden) N.J.	6-1
Donnie Kessinger (Forrest City) Ark.	6-0
George Leftwich (Carroll) Washington, D.C.	6-0
Doug Hutton (Clinton) Miss.	5-10½

1960–61

Name and School	Ht.
Reggie Harding (Eastern) Detroit, Mich.	6-11
Haskell Tison (Geneva) Ill.	6-11
Ron Krick (West Reading) Pa.	6-9
Gary Cook (Idaho Falls) Ida.	6-8
Fred Hetzel (Landon) Bethesda, Md.	6-8
A. W. Davis (Rutledge) Tenn.	6-7
Bogie Redmon (Collinsville) Ill.	6-7
Bill Bradley (Crystal City) Mo.	6-5
Carlos Gripado (Pawhuska) Okla.	6-6
Marty Lentz (Mount Vernon) Va.	6-6
Harry Hammonds (Tuscaloosa) Ala.	6-5
Dave Hicks (W. Cross) West Haven, Conn.	6-5
Don Nelson (Marshalltown) Ia.	6-5
Jerry Rook (Nettletown) Ark.	6-5
Bill Cunningham (Erasmus) Brooklyn, N.Y.	6-4½
Emerson Baynard (Chester) Pa.	6-4
George Lee (Central) Trenton, N.J.	6-4
Dick VanArsdale (Manual) Indianapolis	6-4
Tom VanArsdale (Manual) Indianapolis	6-4
Keith Allred (Pleasant Grove) Utah	6-3½
Fred Goss (Compton) Calif.	6-1½
Luther Harper (Phoenix Union) Ariz.	6-1½
Roy Birk (Waukesha) Wis.	6-1
Lloyd Hinchey (Norwich) Conn.	6-1
Ken Cunningham (East Liverpool) O.	6-0
Jim Jarvis (Roseburg) Ore.	6-0
Gail Goodrich (Poly) Los Angeles	5-11
Bill Lawrence (Molloy) Queens, N.Y.	5-11
Ricky Ray (Huntington) W. Va.	5-11
Randy Embry (Owensboro) Ky.	5-10½

1961–62

Name and School	Ht.
Ray Kosanke (Tucson) Ariz.	6-9

Name and School	Ht.
Gary Keller (Hollins) St. Petersburg, Fla.	6-9
Bob Bedell (Bell Gardens) Cal.	6-7
Jim Ligon (Kokomo) Ind.	6-7
Henry Burlong (Roosevelt) Dayton, Ohio	6-6
David Lattin (Worthing) Houston, Tex.	6-6
Ed Bastian (Washington) Cedar Rapids, Ia.	6-6
Barrie Haynie (Ringgold) Ga.	6-5
Mike Silliman (St. Xavier) Louisville, Ky.	6-5
Bob McIntyre (Holy Cross) Queens, N.Y.	6-5
Cazzie Russell (Carver) Chicago, Ill.	6-5
Paul Presthus (Rugby) N. D.	6-5
Dick Sherman (Central) Cheyenne, Wyo.	6-4
Rich Calmus (Webster) Tulsa, Okla.	6-4
Albie Grant (Columbus) Bronx, N.Y.	6-4
Larry Humes (Madison) Ind.	6-4
Louis Hudson (Dudley) Greensboro, N.C.	6-4
Dave Fearheller (Hickman) Columbia, Mo.	6-4
Larry Conley (Ashland) Ky.	6-4
Ernie Thompson (Saginaw) Mich.	6-3
David Bing (Spingarn) Washington, D.C.	6-2
Don Yates (Uniontown) Pa.	6-2
Tony Horton (University) Los Angeles, Cal.	6-2
Ron Paradis (Washburn) Bethel, Kan.	6-2
Bob Bruggers (Danube) Minn.	6-2
Max Walker (Lincoln) Milwaukee, Wis.	6-1
Lon Wright (Southside) Newark, N.J.	6-1
John Austin (DeMatha) Hyattsville, Md.	6-0
Ed Griffin (Hartford) Conn.	5-11
Dan Homan (Ingraham) Seattle, Wash.	5-10

1962–63

Name and School	Ht.
Lewis Alcindor (Power) New York City	7-¼
Nick Pino (St. Michael's) Santa Fe, N.M.	7-0
Frank Hollendoner (St. Patrick) Chicago, Ill.	6-11
Craig Dill (Arthur Hill) Saginaw, Mich.	6-10
Rich Mason (Washington) E. Chicago, Ind.	6-8
Lloyd Dove (St. Francis) Brooklyn, N.Y.	6-7
Jim Gardner (Harding) Warren, Ohio.	6-7
Edgar Lacey (Jefferson) Los Angeles, Cal.	6-7
David Lattin (Worthing) Houston, Tex.	6-7
Randy Mahaffey (LaGrange) Ga.	6-7
Ed Hummer (Washington-Lee) Arlington, Va.	6-6
Henry Watkins (Pearl) Nashville, Tenn.	6-5½
Dick Harrington (Morse) Bath, Me.	6-5
Bob Krulish (El Camino) Sacramento, Cal.	6-5
Paul Presthus (Rugby) N.D.	6-5
Tom Workman (Blanchet) Seattle, Wash.	6-5
Terry Campbell (Pocatello) Ida.	6-4
James Cummins (Regis) Cedar Rapids, Ia.	6-4
Clem Haskins (Taylor) Campbellsville, Ky.	6-4
Doug Hice (Cathedral) Trenton, N. J.	6-4
Don Kaull (Rogers) Newport, R.I.	6-4
Larry Miller (Catasauqua) Pa.	6-4
Pat Riley (Linton) Schenectady, N.Y.	6-4
Gary Hill (Gunnison) Utah	6-3
Bob Lewis (St. John's) Washington, D.C.	6-3
Cliff Williams (Southwestern) Detroit, Mich.	6-3
Mike Redd (Seneca) Louisville, Ky.	6-2½
Jay Cole (South) Knoxville, Tenn.	6-2
Ian Morrison (St. Petersburg) Fla.	6-2
Ron Williams (Weirton) W.Va.	6-2
Fred Hare (Omaha Tech) Neb.	6-1
Pat Frink (Wheat Ridge) Colo.	6-1
Steve Sarantopoulos (Brockton) Mass.	6-1
Ron Coleman (Jefferson City) Mo.	6-0
Rick Jones (Central) Muncie, Ind.	5-11

1963–64

Name and School	Ht.
Lewis Alcindor (Power) New York, N.Y.	7-¼
David Newmark (Lincoln) Brooklyn, N. Y.	6-11
Rich Nieman (DuBourg) St. Louis, Mo.	6-10
Ron Teixeira (Cath. Memorial) Roxbury, Mass.	6-8
Westley Unseld (Seneca) Louisville, Ky.	6-8
Wally Anderzunas (Creighton) Omaha, Neb.	6-7
Richard Jones (Lester) Memphis, Tenn	6-7
Mike Lewis (Missoula) Mont.	6-7
John Pinkstaff (South Eugene) Ore.	6-7
Steve Vandenberg (Allegany) Cumberl'd, Md.	6-7
Bill Hosket (Belmont) Dayton, Ohio	6-6
Jerry Newsom (Columbus) Ind.	6-6
Mike Weaver (Huntington) Ind.	6-6
Richard Baldwin (North Little Rock) Ark.	6-5
Willie Betts (River Rouge) Mich.	6-5
Rodger Bohnenstiehl (Collinsville) Ill.	6-5
Tim Kolodziej (Amsterdam) N.Y.	6-5
Don Chaney (McKinley) Baton Rouge, La.	6-4
Chris Ellis (Newport News) Va.	6-4
Richard Hanson (Blaine) Wash.	6-4
Bobby Lane (Newman) New Orleans, La.	6-4
Larry Miller (Catasauqua) Pa.	6-4
Mike Butler (Kingsbury) Memphis, Tenn.	6-3
Bryan Grohnke (Edina-Morningside) Minn.	6-3
James McBride (Dunbar) Washington, D.C.	6-3
Alan Robinson (Emporia) Kan.	6-3
Doug Timmer (Hanford) Calif.	6-3
Warren Armstrong (Central) Kansas City, Mo.	6-2
Dennis Brady (Jefferson) Lafayette, Ind.	6-2
Jim Davidson (Logan) W. Va.	6-2
David Lawyer (Oxnard) Calif.	6-2
Jerry Sharman (Charter Oak) Covina, Calif.	6-2
Walter Simon (Roosevelt) Los Angeles, Calif.	6-2
Ron Williams (Weirton) W Va.	6-2
Bill Schutsky (Hillside) N.J.	6-1
Eldridge Webb (Boys) Brooklyn, N.Y.	6-0
Doug Wardlaw (W. Cross) New Haven, Conn.	5-11
Willie Worsley (DeWitt Clinton) Bronx, N.Y.	5-9

1964–65

Name and School	Ht.
Lewis Alcindor (Power) New York, N.Y.	7-1
Rusty Clark (Fayetteville) N.C.	6-11

Name and School	Ht.
Chris Thomforde (Lutheran) Brookville, N.Y.	6-10
Mike Davis (Hinkley) Aurora, Colo.	6-9
Joe Bergman (St. Mary's) Clinton, Ia.	6-9
Ron Teixeira (Memorial) Roxbury, Mass.	6-8½
Ted Wierman (Davis) Yakima, Wash.	6-8¼
Mike Grosso (Bridgewater-Raritan) N.J.	6-8
Bob Bundy (Manchester) Richmond, Va.	6-8
Don Ross (East) Waterloo, Ia.	6-8
Howard Arndt (Republic) Mo.	6-8
Fred Lind (Highland Park) Ill.	6-7
Isiah King (St. Augustine) New Orleans	6-7
Melvin Bell (Clinton) Okla.	6-7
Sam Robinson (Jefferson) Los Angeles, Cal.	6-7
Steve Vandenberg (Allegany) C'berland, Md.	6-7
Sim Hill (Midland) Pa.	6-6
Andy Owens (Hillsborough) Tampa, Fla.	6-6
Dick Haucke (LaSalle) Cincinnati, O.	6-6
Roger Leitner (McCook) Neb.	6-6
Bob Portman (St. Ignatius) San Francisco	6-5
Lee Lafayette (South) Grand Rapids, Mich.	6-5
Bob Smith (Melrose) Memphis, Tenn.	6-5
Walt Esdaille (Hillhouse) New Haven, Conn.	6-5
Larry Cannon (Lincoln) Philadelphia, Pa.	6-4
L. C. Bowen (Benton Harbor) Mich.	6-4
Bob Sullivan (Manitowoc) Wis.	6-4
Lynn Parsons (South Sevier) Monroe, Utah	6-4
Lynn Shackelford (Burroughs) Burbank, Cal.	6-4
Rick Mount (Lebanon) Ind.	6-3
Bernard Williams (DeMatha) Hyattsville, Md.	6-3
Al Beard (Breckenridge) Hardinsburg, Ky.	6-3
Dave Golden (Pekin) Ill.	6-2½
Lucius Allen (Wyandotte) Kansas City, Kan.	6-2
Jon MacDonald (Stearns) Millinocket, Me.	6-1
Larry Hisle (Portsmouth) O.	6-0

1965–66

Name and School	Ht.
Chuck Bavis (Garrett) Ind.	7-0
Bob Lienhard (Rice) New York, N.Y.	6-11
Dan Issel (Batavia) Ill.	6-9
Gary Freeman (Borah) Boise, Idaho	6-9
Dennis Awtrey (Blackford) San Jose, Cal.	6-9
Mike Mardy (Memorial) West New York, N.J.	6-8½
Greg Douglas (Keokuk) Iowa	6-8
John Hummer (Wash.-Lee) Arlington, Va.	6-7
Elvin Ivory (C. W. Hayes) Birmingham, Ala.	6-7
Rudy Tomjanovich (Hamtramck) Mich.	6-7
Sam Robinson (Jefferson) Los Angeles, Cal.	6-7
Ken Durrett (Schenley) Pittsburgh, Pa.	6-6
Dave Sorenson (Findlay) Ohio	6-6
Doug Cook (Ridgewood) N.J.	6-6
Jim McMillian (Jefferson) Brooklyn, N.Y.	6-5
Perry Wallace (Pearl) Nashville, Tenn.	6-5
Doug Jackson (West) Shawnee Mission, Kan.	6-5

Name and School	Ht.
Ralph Ogden (Lincoln) San Jose, Cal.	6-5
Mike Casey (Shelby Co.) Shelbyville, Ky.	6-4½
Jeff Petrie (Springfield) Delaware Co., Pa.	6-4
Charlie Scott (Laurinberg Institute) N.C.	6-4
Rick Tannenberger (Little Rock Central) Ark.	6-4
Fabien Mang (Jesuit) New Orleans, La.	6-4
Jerry Kroll (Memorial) Spring Branch, Texas	6-4
Chuck Moore (Polytechnic) Long Beach, Cal.	6-4
Ron White (Boys Town) Neb.	6-3½
Bob Dukiet (Livingston) N.J.	6-3½
Marshall Lewis (Technical) Boston, Mass.	6-3
Roosevelt Philips (Troy) N.Y.	6-3
Rick Mount (Lebanon) Ind.	6-3
Rich Bradshaw (Marshall) Chicago, Ill.	6-3
Bob Hummell (Moundsville) W. Va.	6-2
Jerry Francis (West) Columbus, Ohio.	6-2
Frank Price (River Rouge) Mich.	6-1
Tom Little (Mackin) Washington, D.C.	6-0
Dean Meminger (Rice) New York, N.Y.	6-0
Trent Gaines (Polytechnic) Long Beach, Cal.	6-0
Don Crosby (Cony) Augusta, Maine.	5-11
Calvin Murphy (Norwalk) Conn.	5-10
Billy Nickleberry (Jefferson) Portland, Ore.	5-8

1966–67

Name and School	Ht.
Artis Gilmore (Carver) Dothan, Ala.	7-2
Jim McDaniels (Allen Cty.) Scottsville, Ky.	7-½
Greg Northington (Wood) Indianapolis, Ind.	6-11½
Steve Niles (Lee) San Antonio, Texas	6-11
Dana Lewis (Weequahic) Newark, N.J.	6-10
Randy Denton (Enloe) Raleigh, N.C.	6-10
Dave Robisch (Springfield) Ill.	6-9
Tom Masterson (Walnut Grove) Minn.	6-9
Harold Porter (Booker) Sarasota, Fla.	6-8
Levi Wyatt (Liddell) Fayette, Miss.	6-8
Spencer Haywood (Pershing) Detroit, Mich.	6-8
Oscar Foster (San Diego) Calif.	6-7
Dean Kratovil (West) Billings, Mont.	6-7
Willie Long (South Side) Fort Wayne, Ind.	6-7
Rich Yunkus (Benton) Ill.	6-7
Thorpe Weber (Joplin) Mo.	6-7
Ken Durrett (Schenley) Pittsburgh, Pa.	6-6
Curtis Rowe (Fremont) Los Angeles, Calif.	6-6
Ernie Fleming (Durfee) Fall River, Mass.	6-5
Mike Garman (Caldwell) Idaho	6-4
Ray Russell (Northeast) Oklahoma City, Okla.	6-4
James Mayberry (Thompson) Natchez, Miss.	6-4
Art Roberts (Washington) Montgomery, Ala.	6-4
Rudy Benjamin (Roosevelt) Dayton, Ohio	6-3
Austin Carr (Mackin) Washington, D.C.	6-3
Jim Rose (Hazard) Ky.	6-3
Curry Todd (Treadwell) Memphis, Tenn.	6-3
Pierre Russell (Wyandotte) Kansas City, Kan.	6-3
Jack Ridgle (Martin) Altheimer, Ark.	6-3
Greg Starrick (Marion) Ill.	6-3
James Welch (LaGrange) Lake Charles, La.	6-2

Name and School	Ht.
Dana Pagett (El Segundo) Calif.	6-1
Charlie Davis (Bklyn. Tech) Brooklyn N.Y.	6-1
Dean Meminger (Rice) New York, N.Y.	6-0
Lanny Taylor (Hana) Anderson, S.C.	6-0
Jim Harris (Adm. King) Lorain, Ohio	5-11½
Mel Knight (Seton Hall) South Orange, N.J.	5-11
Chas. Johnson (Sequoia) Redwood City, Cal.	5-11
Dwight Tolliver (Public) Hartford Conn.	5-10
Dick DeVenzio (Ambridge) Pa.	5-10

1967–68

Name and School	Ht.
Steve Turner (Bartlett) Memphis, Tenn.	7-2
Charles Jura (Schuyler) Neb.	6-10
Ansley Truitt (Wilson) San Francisco, Calif.	6-9½
Tom Riker (St. Dominic's) Oyster Bay, N.Y.	6-9
Cyril Baptiste (Curley) Miami, Fla.	6-8
Ken Grabinski (Clear Lake) Iowa.	6-7
Randy Noll (Catholic) Covington, Ky.	6-7
Joby Wright (Johnson) Savannah, Ga.	6-7
Dennis Wuycik (Ambridge) Pa.	6-7
Bob Ford (North) Evansville, Ind.	6-7
Bob Zender (Edina) Minn.	6-7
Clyde Baker (Bonneville) Utah	6-7
Roland Garrett (Rogers) Canton, Miss.	6-7
Steve Berg (Shorewood) Wis.	6-6
Al Sanders (Baton Rouge) La.	6-6
Tom Parker (Collinsville) Ill.	6-6

Name and School	Ht.
William Franklin (B. T. Washington) Norfolk, Va.	6-6
Bill Chamberlain (Lutheran) Brookville, N.Y.	6-6
Greg Davis (Schlarman) Danville, Ill.	6-5
John Fraley (Middletown) Ohio	6-5
Joe Mackey (Coronado) Scottsdale, Ariz.	6-5
Russell Lee (Hyde Park) Mass.	6-5
Jeff Hickman (Central) Lockport, Ill.	6-5
Kent Hollenbeck (Bearden) Knoxville, Tenn.	6-4
Chris Ford (Holy Spirit) Absecon, N. J.	6-4
Ralph Simpson (Pershing) Detroit, Mich.	6-4
Pat Taylor (Leavenworth) Kan.	6-4
Jerry Bonney (Wheatley) Houston, Tex.	6-3
Henry Bacon (Male) Louisville, Ky.	6-3
Alex Scott (Wilbur Cross) New Haven, Conn.	6-2
Aubrey Nash (DeMatha) Hyattsville, Md.	6-2
Wilbert Robinson (Highlands) Uniontown, Pa.	6-2
Henry Harris (Greene Co. Boligee, Ala.	6-2
Phil Westphal (Aviation) Redondo Beach, Calif.	6-2
Henry Bibby (Person-Albion) Franklinton, N.C.	6-2
Harold Fox (Northwestern) Hyattsville, Md.	6-1
Almer Lee (Northside) Ft. Smith, Ark.	6-0
Ron Johnson (Van Buren) Queens, New York	5-11
John Somogyi (St. Peter's) New Brunswick, N.J.	5-11
Billy Shepherd (Carmel) Ind.	5-10

16: THE AMATEURS

OLYMPICS

The history of Olympic basketball is an unbroken record of United States victories. Since the sport was introduced to the Olympics in 1936, the U.S. teams have won not only every gold medal but every game they have played.

U.S. teams played exhibition games in the 1904, 1924 and 1928 Olympics, but these games were officially classified as demonstrations and no medals were awarded.

But by 1936 basketball had become sufficiently popular around the world to be included on the Olympic program. The U.S. set the pattern for its future appearances that year, winning all five of its games in Berlin by lopsided scores. In the final, the U.S. crushed Canada, 19-8, in a game played outdoors in a driving rain.

When Olympic competition resumed in 1948 after a twelve-year break forced by World War II, the United States picked up in London right where it had left off in Berlin. Led by collegiate stars Alex Groza of Kentucky and 7-1 Bob Kurland of Oklahoma A&M, the U.S. swept through seven opponents to win its second gold medal. France finished second and Brazil third.

Four years later in Helsinki, with Clyde Lovellette and Kurland leading the way, the U.S. won again. The United States played the Soviet Union for the first time ever in the final game and overcame the Russians' stalling, ball-control tactics to score a 36-25 triumph.

At the Melbourne Olympics in 1956, the U.S. again completely outclassed its opponents, winning all eight of its games by at least 30 points. Bill Russell and K.C. Jones, who had led the University of San Francisco to two consecutive national championships, starred as the U.S. crushed the USSR, 89-55, in the final. Uruguay won its second consecutive bronze medal.

The 1960 U.S. team is generally considered to have been the strongest ever to represent this country in the Olympics. It boasted such collegiate stars as Jerry Lucas, Oscar Robertson, Jerry West, Walt Bellamy and Terry Dischinger, all of whom went on to star in professional basketball. With this pool of talent, the U.S. had no trouble with any of its eight opponents, winning four of the games by more than 40-point margins.

In the 1964 Olympics at Tokyo, the U.S. again swept through all eight foes on the way to its sixth basketball gold medal. The play-making talents of Princeton's Bill Bradley kept the team together. The squad also included Luke Jackson, Walt Hazzard and 7-0 Mel Counts. In the final, the U.S. again trounced the USSR, 73-59.

The 1968 team continued the nation's unbeaten streak through nine more games and another gold medal. For the first time, though, the U.S. entered Olympic competition as an underdog. Many of the nation's top collegiate players, including Lew Alcindor, Elvin Hayes and Westley Unseld, had passed up the Olympic trials, leaving the squad without big-name stars.

Coach Henry Iba, though, stressing defense and team play, molded his players into a powerful, cohesive unit that crushed Yugoslavia, 65-50, in the championship game. The outstanding players included Spencer Haywood, a 6-8, 19-year-old center with amazing defensive talents, and Jo Jo White, a sharp-shooting guard.

OLYMPIC BASKETBALL RESULTS

1936—Berlin

United States 2, Spain 0 (forfeit)
United States 52, Estonia 28
United States 56, Philippines 23
United States 25, Mexico 10
United States 19, Canada 8 (final)

1948—London

United States 86, Switzerland 21
United States 53, Czechoslovakia 28
United States 59, Argentina 57
United States 66, Egypt 28
United States 61, Peru 33
United States 63, Uruguay 28
United States 71, Mexico 40
United States 65, France 21 (final)

1952—Helsinki

United States 66, Hungary 48
United States 72, Czechoslovakia 47
United States 57, Uruguay 44
United States 86, USSR 58
United States 103, Chile 55
United States 57, Brazil 53
United States 85, Argentina 76
United States 36, USSR 25 (final)

1956—Melbourne

United States 98, Japan 40
United States 101, Thailand 29
United States 121, Philippines 53
United States 85, USSR 55
United States 113, Brazil 51
United States 101, Uruguay 38
United States 89, USSR 55 (final)

1960—Rome

United States 88, Italy 54
United States 125, Japan 66
United States 107, Hungary 63
United States 104, Yugoslavia 42
United States 108, Uruguay 50
United States 81, USSR 57
United States 112, Italy 81
United States 90, Brazil 63 (final)

1964—Tokyo

United States 78, Australia 45
United States 77, Finland 51
United States 60, Peru 45
United States 83, Uruguay 28
United States 69, Yugoslavia 61
United States 86, Brazil 53
United States 116, Korea 50
United States 62, Puerto Rico 42
United States 73, USSR 59 (final)

1968—Mexico City

United States 81, Spain 46
United States 93, Senegal 36
United States 96, Philippines 75
United States 95, Panama 60
United States 100, Italy 61
United States 73, Yugoslavia 58
United States 61, Puerto Rico 56
United States 75, Brazil 63
United States 65, Yugoslavia 50 (final)

Russia's I. Krouminch congratulates USA's Bill Russell at 1956 Olympic Games.

AMATEUR ATHLETIC UNION

The Amateur Athletic Union conducts the oldest basketball championship in the United States, dating back to 1897. That year the first "national" championship, little more than a sectional series of games, was held in New York City under the auspices of the Metropolitan Association of the AAU. The winner was New York's 23rd St. YMCA.

Two of the early champions were the Ravenswood YMCA of Chicago, 1901, and the Buffalo Germans, 1904 (no national championships were held in 1902 or '03). The Germans' victory came in a tournament that was held in conjunction with the Olympic Games in St. Louis. It was the first AAU tourney that was truly national in scope. In addition to Buffalo, there were the Xavier AA of New York, Chicago Central YMCA, the Turner Tigers of Los Angeles and the Missouri AA.

From 1905 through 1912 no AAU championships were held, paving the way for many unofficial claims to the crown. The first came in 1905 when the Kansas City AC, whose player-manager, Forrest (Phog) Allen, was later to become a famous college coach at Kansas, whipped the Buffalo Germans. Allen's club was "dethroned" the following year by the Wachter brothers' Company E team from Schenectady, N.Y. They subsequently were declared professionals. This development caused many member clubs to defect from the AAU and to form the Protective Basketball Association. The PBA lasted only a couple of years.

The AAU tournament bounced around a number of cities after its New York debut, and included Buffalo, St. Louis, Kansas City, Chicago, San Francisco, Los Angeles and Atlanta before it was housed in Kansas City's Convention Hall in 1921 for 14 years. The tourney was moved to Denver in 1935 and has remained there but for one year, 1949, when Oklahoma City was host.

The 1920 staging at Atlanta was hailed as the move that triggered a basketball boom throughout the South. The final was all-collegiate, with New York University beating Rutgers. A forward on NYU was Howard Cann, who was to coach at his alma mater for many years.

The NYU triumph was one of only four fashioned by the colleges over the years. The others were by Utah, 1916, Butler, 1924, and Washburn, 1925.

The most successful of all teams in the AAU festival has been the Phillips 66ers. They won their first crown in 1940 and 10 more have followed (including six in a row, 1943–48).

The tournament is replete with great names, many of whom went on to play in professional basketball. They include Bob Boozer, Don Ohl, Hank Luisetti, Bob Doll, Kenny Sailors, Andy Phillip, Bob Kurland, Vince Boryla, Don Barksdale, George Yardley, Cazzie Russell, Ken Sears and Richie Guerin.

The list of AAU champions, runners-up and scores of the final game for all years in which an official tournament was held:

1897—New York 23rd Street YMCA (Round Robin)
1899—New York Knickerbocker YMCA (Round Robin)
1900—New York Knickerbocker YMCA (Round Robin)
1901—Chicago Ravenswood YMCA 16, Fond du Lac, Wis. 15
1904—Buffalo Germans (Round Robin)
1910—Company F, Portage, Wis. 36, Premiere Lodge 14.
1913—Chicago Cornell-Armour (Round Robin)
1914—Chicago Cornell-Armour 83, Young Men's Fellowship 26
1915—San Francisco Olympic Club 29, Whittier College 16
1916—Utah University 28, Illinois Athletic Club 27
1917—Illinois Athletic Club 27, Brigham Young 14

Phillips' 66er Bob Kurland scores in 1947 AAU game at Bartlesville, Okla.

1919—Los Angeles Athletic Club 23, San Francisco Olympic Club 22
1920—New York University 49, Rutgers University 24
1921—Kansas City Athletic Club 42, SW Kansas College 36
1922—Kansas City Lowe-Campbell 42, Kansas City Athletic Club 28
1923—Kansas City Athletic Club 31, Kansas City Hillyards, 18
1924—Butler University 30, Kansas City Athletic Club 26
1925—Washburn College 42, Kansas City Hillyards 30
1926—Kansas City Hillyards 25, Kansas City Athletic Club 20
1927—Kansas City Hillyards 29, Ke-Nash-A 10
1928—Kansas City Cooks 25, Kansas City Athletic Club 23
1929—Kansas City Cooks 51, Wichita Henrys 35
1930—Wichita Henrys 29, San Francisco Olympic Club 16
1931—Wichita Henrys 38, Kansas City Athletic Club 14
1932—Wichita Henrys 15, NW Missouri State College 14
1933—Tulsa Diamond Oilers 25, Chicago Rosenberg-Arveys 23
1934—Tulsa Diamond Oilers 29, Wyoming University 19
1935—Kansas City Stage Lines 45, McPherson Globe Refiners 26
1937—Denver Safeways 43, Phillips 66ers 38
1938—Kansas City Healeys 40, Denver Safeways 38
1939—Denver Nuggets 25, Phillips 66ers 22
1940—Phillips 66ers 39, Denver Nuggets 36
1941—20th Century-Fox 47, San Francisco Olympic Club 34
1942—Denver Legion 45, Phillips 66ers 32
1943—Phillips 66ers 57, Denver Legion 40
1944—Phillips 66ers 50, Denver Legion 43
1945—Phillips 66ers 47, Denver Ambrose 46
1946—Phillips 66ers 45, San Diego Dons 34
1947—Phillips 66ers 62, Oakland Bittners 41
1948—Phillips 66ers 62, Denver Nuggets 48
1949—Oakland Bittners 55, Phillips 66ers 51
1950—Phillips 66ers 65, Oakland Blue-Gold Nuggets 42
1951—San Francisco Stewarts 76, Poudre Valley Creamery 55
1952—Peoria Cats 66, Phillips 66ers 53
1953—Peoria Cats 73, Los Alamitos Navy 62
1954—Peoria Cats 63, San Diego Grihalva Buicks 55
1955—Phillips 66ers 66, Boulder Luckett-Nix Clippers 64
1956—Seattle Buchan Bakers 59, Phillips 66ers 57
1957—Air Force All-Stars 87, San Francisco Olympic Club 74
1958—Peoria Cats 74, Denver D-C Truckers 71 (4 overtimes)
1959—Wichita Vickers 105, Phillips 66ers 83
1960—Peoria Cats 87, Akron Goodyear Wingfoots 73
1961—Cleveland Pipers 107, Denver D-C Truckers 96
1962—Phillips 66ers 70, Denver D-C Truckers 59
1963—Phillips 66ers 100, Denver D-C Truckers 70
1964—Akron Goodyears 86, Phillips 66ers 78
1965—Armed Forces All-Stars 77, Denver Capitol Federal 75
1966—Ford Mustangs 71, Phillips 66ers 67
1967—Akron Goodyear Tires 77, Phillips 66ers 62
1968—Armed Forces All-Stars 73, Spokane Vaughn Realty 69

THE WOMEN

The first National AAU championship for women, in 1926, was staged at Pasadena, California. Champion of the six-team field, which played under men's rules, was the Pasadena Athletic and Country Club. Today the women play under their own rules, which call for six players on a team. As with the men's AAU, the girls' tournament tried many locations before it found a permanent home. After 11 years at Wichita, Kansas, the tourney was moved to St. Joseph, Missouri, in 1940, to Dallas in 1951, returned to Wichita for the next two years and then on once again to St. Joseph, where it has stayed.

The greatest name ever to grace AAU Women's Basketball was that of Mildred "Babe" Didrikson. Although she went on to her biggest fame in track and field and in golf, she was outstanding enough on the court to lead her Dallas Golden Cyclones to the crown in Dallas in 1931. Babe scored 106 points in five tournament games. She was named captain of the All-American team. The phenomenal Texan, voted by the nation's sports writers in 1950 the greatest female athlete of the first half of the 20th century, died of cancer in 1956. She was 42.

The AAU women's champions:

1926—Pasadena A. and C.C., Pasadena, California
1929—Schepps Aces, Dallas, Texas
1930—Sunoco Oilers, Dallas, Texas
1931—Golden Cyclones, Dallas, Texas
1932—Durant Cardinals, Oklahoma
1933—Durant Cardinals, Oklahoma
1934—Tulsa Business College, Oklahoma
1935—Tulsa Business College, Oklahoma
1936—Tulsa Business College, Oklahoma
1937—Little Rock Flyers, Arkansas
1938—Galveston, Texas, Anicos
1939—Galveston, Texas, Anicos
1940—Lewis-Norwood Flyers, Little Rock, Arkansas
1941—Lewis-Norwood Flyers, Little Rock, Arkansas
1942—A.I.C., Davenport, Iowa
1943—A.I.C., Davenport, Iowa
1944—Vultee Aircraft, Nashville, Tennessee
1945—Vultee Aircraft, Nashville, Tennessee
1946—Nashville Goldblumes, Tennessee
1947—Atlanta, Georgia, Sports Arenas
1948—Nashville Goldblumes, Tennessee
1949—Nashville Goldblumes, Tennessee
1950—Nashville Business College, Tennessee
1951—Hanes Hosiery Mills, Winston-Salem, North Carolina
1952—Hanes Hosiery Mills, Winston-Salem, North Carolina
1953—Hanes Hosiery Mills, Winston-Salem, North Carolina
1954—Wayland College, Plainview, Texas
1955—Wayland College, Plainview, Texas
1956—Wayland College, Plainview, Texas
1957—Wayland College, Plainview, Texas
1958—Nashville Business College, Tennessee
1959—Wayland College, Plainview, Texas

1960—Nashville Business College, Tennessee
1961—Wayland College, Plainview, Texas
1962—Nashville Business College, Tennessee
1963—Nashville Business College, Tennessee
1964—Nashville Business College, Tennessee
1965—Nashville Business College, Tennessee
1966—Nashville Business College, Tennessee
1967—Nashville Business College, Tennessee
1968—Nashville Business College, Tennessee

BIDDY BASKETBALL

Biddy Basketball was originated in 1951 by Jay Archer, a physical education instructor from Scranton, Pennsylvania. It was designed to give boys and girls no taller than 5-6 a game which they could consider their own. Unlike Midget Basketball, played by smaller persons with equipment normally used by adults, Biddy Basketball is scaled down proportionately to the size and physical ability of the youngsters.

This has been achieved by 1) reducing the diameter of the ball from 30 to 28 inches; 2) lowering the height of the basket from 10 to 8½ feet; 3) shortening the foul line from 15 to 12 feet; 4) shortening the length of the court by the use of snap-on units in front of the regulation backboards.

The game, played by boys up to 12 and girls up to 13, is divided into four periods of six minutes each. A player is allowed six fouls.

The U.S. State Department Education Exchange Program has promoted the international recognition of Biddy Basketball through its sponsorship of Biddy clinics in South America, the Far East, Southeast Asia and Spain. The clinics have proved particularly popular in these countries because of the small stature of the children.

Mr. Archer, national commissioner for the sport, staged the first World Biddy Basketball championship in Scranton in February, 1967. Participating were Peru, Spain, Trinidad, Puerto Rico, Canada, Mexico, Ecuador, El Salvador, the Virgin Islands and the United States. The United States, represented by New Orleans, La., was the winner.

The first national tournament was held for the 1951–52 season and nationals have been held ever since. List of champions:

Year	Champion	Year	Champion	Year	Champion
1951–52	Jersey City, N.J.	1957–58	Bridgeport, Conn.	1963–64	Chester, Pa.
1952–53	Peoria, Ill.	1958–59	Bridgeport, Conn.	1964–65	New York, N.Y.
1953–54	Jersey City, N.J.	1959–60	Gary, Ind.	1965–66	New Orleans, La.
1954–55	Jersey City, N.J.	1960–61	Jefferson Parish, La.	1966–67	Wichita, Kan.
1955–56	Atlantic City, N.J.	1961–62	Wichita, Kan.	1967–68	Augusta, Ga.
1956–57	New Orleans, La.	1962–63	New Orleans, La.		

USA (white shirts) plays Ecuador in first World Biddy Championship in 1967.

8
13
31
23

17: THE OFFICIALS

A basketball official has never appeared on any list of 10 Most Admired Men. It was so from the beginning of basketball in 1891. It is so today.

Regardless of his degree of popularity, the official has always played a vital role in the game. Dr. James Naismith, inventor of basketball, described the function of officials in his original 13 rules:

"RULE 10: The umpire shall be judge of the men and shall note the fouls and notify the referee when three consecutive fouls have been made. He shall have power to disqualify men . . . .

"RULE 11: The referee shall be judge of the ball and shall decide when the ball is in play, in bounds, to which side it belongs and shall keep the time. He shall decide when a goal has been made, and keep account of the goals, with any other duties that are usually performed by a referee."

Two major rules changes affecting officials occurred in 1895. The referee was given authority to call fouls. Also, timers and scorers were instituted, relieving the referee of that duty. The use of just one official on the playing floor was commonplace, and remained so until 1929 when the double floor official system became standard. Today, the distinction between a referee and an umpire is slight. The referee is usually the senior official, in age and experience. Also, he has the job of tossing up the ball.

The game was devised by Dr. Naismith to be an entertaining, noncontact form of wintertime physical recreation. However, games often resembled tribal warfare. Walls and pillars in the small gyms would form part of the boundaries, and tactics called for balls and opponents to be bounced off the woodwork. The official had the thankless job of arbiter. One early official told Dr. Naismith that he always checked to see which window in his dressing room was unlocked, in case a hasty exit was imperative. Fans and players alike treated him with deep derision. It was in these early years that the Philadelphia YMCA dropped basketball because of the "rowdy element" it attracted. At one point the Trenton YMCA discontinued play because it was "unfit for Christians." In 1908 Charles W. Eliot, Harvard president, called the game "more brutal than football." Two years later many college athletic administrators felt the game was getting uncontrollable and some began using two floor officials.

George Hepbron, the first to author a book on basketball, *How to Play Basketball*, in

1904, was also the first outstanding referee in the game's history. He approached officiating with a seriousness and dedication that was uncommon. George Hoyt, another widely respected official of the early years, founded in 1920 the Eastern Massachusetts officials board, the first officiating organization. Hepbron and Hoyt were instrumental in elevating the standards of their profession.

"Distinctive attire" for officials was recommended by college basketball boards in 1917. Before that an official would wear anything that pleased him. Adolph Rupp, University of Kentucky coach, refereed games in those early years. "I'd just grab an old pair of pants and a shirt, usually white or blue," said Rupp. "Sometimes my shirt was the same color as a team's jersey. And I'd be ducking a lot of passes."

A basic requirement of a good official is to have complete knowledge of the rules. This criterion presented a problem in the early years. There were as many as five sets of rules, with many variations designed to fit local conditions.

Not until 1934 were basketball rules standardized. Disparities, however, did not disappear overnight. Rupp recalled when sectional difference of rules emphasis cost his team a game. In January, 1935, at Madison Square Garden, Kentucky lost to New York University in the last six seconds of play. Kentucky had the ball and a foul was called on the Wildcats on a "pickoff" play. "NYU sank the free throw," said Rupp, "and we lost 23-22. This created quite a furor because that kind of foul was never called in our area. Now it is established throughout the country."

Though interpretation has grown more uniform, differences still exist. The Big 10, for example, with its "no harm, no foul" concept, permits more contact than most college conferences. UCLA coach John Wooden noted that East and Midwest refs give an advantage to the offense. "In those areas," said Wooden, "the man with the ball often can do no harm. It's similar to the pros. In the West, charging and other offensive infractions are called much closer by officials."

No two officials see the same game in precisely the same way. A division is made by basketball people between the "book" referee and the "loose" referee. The "loose" referee is preferred by the majority. He allows the game to flow easily, though exercising his authority in a respectable manner. He is, as one coach termed it, "inconspicuous but always there." He is not a "too loose" referee, one that allows the game to get out of hand. The "book" referee has a stringent grasp on the rules. He often inhibits play, and does not enjoy the good rapport with players and coaches that a "loose" ref has. A West Coast coach described the difference this way: "If a foul shooter has his foot a 32nd of an inch over the line, and makes the shot, the 'book' ref will call it no shot. A 'loose' ref gives more leeway. He believes the infraction was too slight to bother with."

Another difference marks officials with a "quick whistle" and those with a "slow whistle." One of the officiating arts is to decide in a split second whether there is an infraction. A "quick whistle" referee often is heavily criticized because it appears his call was hasty. On the other hand, a whistle that is too slow may demonstrate an official's indecisiveness.

The first requirement for a prospective official of organized basketball competition is membership in the International Association of Approved Basketball Officials (IAABO). This membership must be gained by passing a written examination and floor test. The IAABO is a nonprofit group dedicated to the advancement of basketball officiating.

The College Basketball Officials Association (CBOA), begun in 1948, is the largest college officials' organization in the world. It encompasses over 650 members in 12 Eastern states and the District of Columbia. The members work Eastern College Basketball Conference (ECBC) games. There are over 250 schools in the ECBC. Officials are rated after each game by the respective coaches. They also are scrutinized by the supervisor of officials, John Nucatola. The ratings take into account the following factors: physical condition, personal appearance, personal conduct (businesslike, but not officious), mechanics (ability and technique), knowledge and enforcement of the rules, mental alertness, poise, judgement and intestinal fortitude ("guts—ability to withstand pressure"). The rating scale is determined thus: 10 and 9 points—superior; 8 and 7—good; 6 and 5—average; 4 and 3—unsatisfactory; 2 and 1—inferior.

The CBOA, like other major college officials' groups, has a graduating advancement scheme. The prospective official must of course be a member of the IAABO. Then he has to get recommendations from respected officials or other basketball-connected persons. Once approved, he receives assignments in freshman and junior varsity games. He is rated by coaches and supervisors. The officials with the highest ratings over a season rise to varsity competition. At first, "rookie" officials are assigned by the organization's office to varsity games of lesser importance. With experience and good ratings, they move into tougher contests. The age limit for a CBOA referee is 55. College pay scales range from \$30 to \$60 per game and expenses in the ECBC to \$110 per game and expenses in the Big 10. Top referees may make as much as \$1,500 a season.

Season ratings are compiled by this 100-point system: Game marks by colleges (30 per cent of total), ratings from fellow varsity officials (30 per cent), ratings from ECBC based on availability and general value (30 per cent), attendance at annual clinic (5 per cent) and the annual written examination (5 per cent). Varsity officials with very low ratings are demoted to freshman and junior varsity contests.

The written test of 100 questions changes each year. Questions on a recent exam included: (1) A-1's hand, while still in contact with the ball, is slapped by B-1 on a missed shot at the basket. The official is correct in awarding A-1 two free throws. (Answer is false.) (2) A-1 has left his feet on a try for goal when B-1 steps into his path. Contact ensues as A-1 returns to the floor. Official awards A-1 two free throws for intentional foul. (Answer is true.)

Professional referees are not required to undergo written examinations. However, they must also be members of the IAABO. Surprisingly, few NBA referees gained experience in collegiate circles. (Mendy Rudolph, the NBA's senior official, is a notable exception. He officiated big-time college basketball for two years.) Most NBA officials were scouted by league administrators while working club and other amateur and semi-pro and professional (like the Eastern League) games. Prospective officials work preseason games and a process of elimination is conducted. Adolph Schayes is the supervisor of NBA officials.

Beginning with the 1967–68 season, NBA referees were given contracts for the first time. Before that, they were paid on a game-to-game basis. "We felt that our officials deserved security," said NBA president Walter Kennedy. Top veteran pro officials make \$200 a game and up to \$15,000 a year, including playoff work.

Basketball officiating is not the sole means of income of most referees. In the pros, for example, Rudolph is Eastern sales manager for WGN-TV in Chicago; Earl Strom is a steel company executive; Norm Drucker is a recreation director in the New York City educational system. The same is true in college circles. Jim Enright, for example, is a Chicago sports writer. Many of them also officiate in other sports. Two of the best-known referees in the 1920s and '30s, Bill Grieve and Ernie Quigley, were also major-league baseball umpires.

Joe Lapchick explained why an outstanding college official may not be successful in the pros: "The abuse of officials by players, coaches and fans is much greater than in college basketball. It takes a different breed of cat to make it in pro ball. I'll never forget the undoing of a rookie pro referee who had a distinguished college career. The game was at Syracuse, which was one of the roughest towns on the pro circuit. Syracuse was losing by three points with only seconds left. Dolph Schayes, the Syracuse star, had the ball and went head-hunting. That is, he drove for the hoop and tried to make contact while making the basket. He was trying for a three-point play to tie the game. But this rookie referee called Schayes for charging. Well, all hell broke loose. The ref was so unhappy with this degradation of a person that he soon left the pro ranks."

Rudolph, an NBA referee since 1953, is philosophical about such vilifying. "I don't let it bother me," he said. "That comes only with experience, but eventually you learn to shut out criticism during a game. You hear it, but you ignore it. Rabbit ears in this business can be fatal for an official."

A pro official will work several games involving one team over a season. The players and coaches come to learn his characteristics. "There are some officials," said one NBA player, "who we know we can get to if we crab enough. In close situations, he might give us the edge on a call. So the complaining sometimes pays off."

The good officials, of course, are not intimidated or swayed. The classic example of a fearless official was Chuck Solodare. He won respect by his solid work, but he was also a fine showman. In a game at Fort Wayne (Ind.) in the early years of the NBA, Solodare was under a barrage of jeers by the fans. Late in the game he suddenly stopped play. He opened his shirt, withdrew a steak and flung it into the stands. "Here, you wolves," he shouted. "Chew on that." Pat Kennedy was another official known for his skill and dramatic style. He was described as "sometimes appearing on the verge of apoplexy, so fervently does he throw himself into his job." Besides working top college and pro games (he was supervisor of NBA officials from 1946 to 1950), Kennedy became widely known through his tours with the Harlem Globetrotters.

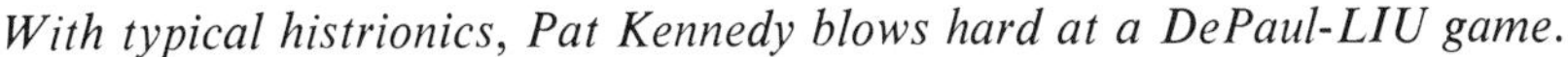

With typical histrionics, Pat Kennedy blows hard at a DePaul-LIU game.

Why do men become basketball officials? Rudolph quipped: "Don't ask me. Just ask a psychiatrist." Sid Borgia, former NBA official, said officiating presents a great challenge, "Especially when refereeing under pressure," he said. "It either brings out the best in a man, or the worst. But it is satisfying to know that you are part of a spectacle that interests all those people in the stands. And that you contribute to keeping the game moving. Most important, I think, is that you just plain love the game." There are no physical requirements to be a referee, other than good general health to withstand the swift pace. Officials have been reluctant to wear glasses, but some do. Use of contact lenses, though, has increased sharply. Physical deformity has not been a deterrent, either. John Catalano has one hand. Joe Burns has an arm shrivelled by polio. Dominic Cuccinello works, amazingly, with an artificial leg. It is a curious fact that most officials are relatively short. Various reasons are given. One is that smaller men have greater maneuverability; they can get into good position easier. Another is that smaller men are more temperamentally suited to control a game. It is, ventured a prominent basketball executive, the Napoleon complex of the small man coming out.

Good physical condition is also a factor in maneuverability. Referees often go through rigorous training programs to prepare for the season. Borgia, for example, said that even during the early part of a season he would run two miles after some games. "When I could run two miles without getting tired," he said, "then I knew I was in condition." A Midwest coach qualified the need for an official to be in top shape. "A referee can run all over the place, but never be in the right place. Jim Enright is one of the finest referees, yet he is overweight. But he has the knack for getting good position."

Some referees are known as "homers." That is, they have a reputation for giving the advantage to the local team. In basketball's early years this was expected of an official. The athletic director or coach hired the official, often his friend. The official knew that if he wanted to work a game for that team again, he must meet certain expectations. "Homers" still exist, but to a much lesser extent. Officials' organizations, like the CBOA, have elevated the profession by achieving pay increases and insisting on probity and good work.

Basketball experts agree that most modern-day officials are superior to those in years past. For one thing, officials have had to keep up with the fantastic improvements in the game. The players, now, are bigger, faster and better, thus demanding more from an official. Changes in the game, like the elimination of center jump, and the introduction of the three-second and ten-second rules, also have necessitated a more alert and competent official.

Another factor in improving the work of officials has been the construction of newer and better basketball facilities. Officials are less troubled by rabid fans. Once it was common for spectators to sit alongside the court, sometimes even tripping the official. It is rarer now for officials to have to fight their way out of gymnasiums. But precautions are still being employed. In the Southeastern Conference, for example, highway patrolmen or local policemen often escort officials to the game, on and off the court, and away from the gymnasium.

It is apparent that despite the growth of the game, officials are as beloved now as they were in 1891. They just have more protection today.

18: THE HALL OF FAME

The opening of the Naismith Memorial Basketball Hall of Fame in February, 1968, climaxed more than 30 years of planning, fund-raising, and many setbacks. The Hall of Fame, named after the founder of basketball, and located on the Springfield College campus where Dr. James Naismith invented the game in 1891, honors the sport's outstanding individuals and teams.

Dr. Naismith himself first suggested in 1936 that a Hall of Fame be built. After his death in 1939, Springfield College alumni began a fund-raising campaign that came to a standstill during World War II. In 1946, Ed Hickox retired as Springfield College coach, and as the first Executive Secretary he began working toward the establishment of the Hall of Fame. In 1948 the National Association of Basketball Coaches (NABC) set up a Hall of Fame Committee, headed by John Bunn, a former student of Dr. Naismith's and later the coach at Stanford and Springfield.

Since then the NABC spearheaded the building drive. It paid the operating costs of the Hall of Fame, thus allowing every dollar contributed by outsiders to be used for construction of the building itself.

Among the features of the Hall of Fame facility are a museum with souvenirs and mementos from basketball's earliest days, a library and an Honors Court.

Election is in the hands of a 13-member Honors Committee. The members represent every level of the game: college, professional, high school, the Amateur Athletic Union and news media. Players must be retired for at least 10 years and officials for five years before they can be considered for election.

The first group of fifteen individuals and two teams was elected in 1959. Since then elections have been held every year and a total of 66 individuals and four teams have been enshrined. Individuals gain election in one of four categories: Contributions to the game, College Player, Pro Player, Coach.

Lee Williams, former basketball coach and director of athletics at Colby College, has been Executive Director of the Hall of Fame since 1964. He succeeded Clifford Wells.

Colored reproductions of each of the Hall of Fame members appear on glass in the Honors Court. The names of the members with the inscriptions as they appear in the Hall of Fame are as follows:

JAMES NAISMITH, M.D. 1861–1939
ELECTED 1959—CONTRIBUTOR
Graduated from McGill (1887), Presbyterian (1890), and Springfield (1893). Minister, Doctor, Teacher, Leader of Men. Founded Game of Basketball in December 1891.

OSWALD TOWER 1883–1968
ELECTED 1959—CONTRIBUTOR

Graduated from Drury (Mass.) H.S. '01 and Williams '07. Player, Official 35 years. Member Rules Committee, 49 years. Editor and Rules Interpreter, 44 years.

RALPH MORGAN 1884–1965
ELECTED 1959—CONTRIBUTOR

Graduated from Friends (Pa.) School '02 and Pennsylvania '06. Founder of Collegiate Rules Committee 1905, now National B.B. Rules Committee; Member 26 years. Organized Eastern Intercollegiate Basketball League in 1910, now Ivy League.

JOHN J. SCHOMMER 1884–1960
ELECTED 1959—COLLEGE PLAYER

Graduated from Chicago '09. First "C" man to win 12 letters. Led Big Ten scorers 1907–08–09. Captain 1909 National Champions. Recognized as first great Western player. Taught at Illinois Tech 47 years. Leading football and basketball official.

FORREST C. ALLEN 1885–
ELECTED 1959—CONTRIBUTOR

Graduated from Independence (Mo.) H.S. 1905 and Kansas, 1909. Great Player. UK Athletic Director 19 years. Basketball coach 39 years. NCAA Champion 1952. Founded Coaches Association 1927; President 1927 and 1928. Helped organize basketball in Olympics 1936 and NCAA Tournament 1939. Teams won 771 games and 31 championships.

H. CLIFFORD CARLSON, M.D. 1894–1964
ELECTED 1959—COACH

Graduated from Bellefonte (Pa.) Academy '14 and Pittsburgh '18. M.D. Degree '20 from Pitt. Coached Pitt teams 31 years, won National Championships 1928 and 1930. Invented "Figure 8" offense. President, Coaches Association 1937. Practiced medicine since 1921 at Carnegie Steel and Pitt.

DR. LUTHER H. GULICK 1865–1918
ELECTED 1959—CONTRIBUTOR

Graduated from Oberlin (O.) Prep '85 and M.D. Degree from NYU '89. Leading authority on Physical Training. Originated the Triangle of the YMCA. Organized the Public School League of N.Y.C., the Playground Assoc., the National Recreation Assoc., the Camp Fire Girls and assisted with the Boy Scouts. Asked James Naismith to create "an indoor game" while Physical Training Chairman at Springfield College.

EDWARD J. HICKOX 1878–1966
ELECTED 1959—CONTRIBUTOR

Edward J. Hickox, Coach for forty years, was elected in 1959 and was our first Executive Secretary. His honors included Presidency of NABC 1944–46, membership of the Rules Committee 18 years and Historian 20 years. He received a purple heart in WWI. In 1961 he was awarded a Doctorate in Humanics by Springfield College.

CHARLES D. HYATT 1908–
ELECTED 1959—COLLEGE PLAYER

Graduated from Uniontown (Pa.) H.S. '26 and Pittsburgh '30. All-State 1925, 26-H.S. All-American 1926. All-American 1928–29–30. Nation's leading scorer 1930. Led Pitt to Nat'l. Championship 1928 and 1930. Teams won 60 lost 7 in 3 years. A.A.U. All-American 9 years. Known as "Chuck."

MATTHEW P. KENNEDY 1908–1957
ELECTED 1959—REFEREE

Graduated from Hoboken (N.J.) Demarest H.S. '26 and Montclair (N.J.) State '28. Began refereeing at age 20 to become nation's best known official. Many of the great games demonstrated his dramatic manner. After legendary college career he became supervisor of NBA officials 4 years before working as a truly great attraction with Harlem Globetrotters 7 years. Known as "Pat."

ANGELO LUISETTI 1916–
ELECTED 1959—COLLEGE PLAYER

Graduated from San Francisco (Calif.) Galileo H.S. 1934 and Stanford 1938. All-City 3 years, All-American 1937 and 1938. Led team to 3 Conference Titles, All-time All Pacific Coast. First player to score 50 points in a regular game, scored 1,596 in 4 years. Nearly 3,000 in career. Began one-hand shot. Known as "Hank."

WALTER E. MEANWELL, M.D. 1884–1953
ELECTED 1959—COACH

Graduated from Rochester (N.Y.) H.S. and Maryland 1909. Born in England, never played basketball, yet coached Wisconsin 20 years, and Missouri 2 years to 290 wins. Won 2 titles at Missouri and 4 Big Ten Titles and 4 ties at Wisconsin. Writer, member Rules Committee, charter member Coaches Association, Athletic Director and Doctor. Developed criss-cross system of offense. Known as "Little Doctor."

GEORGE L. MIKAN 1924–
ELECTED 1959—COLLEGE PLAYER

Graduated from Chicago (Ill.) Quigley Prep 1941 and DePaul 1946. All-American 1944–45–46, scored 1,870 points including high of 53 at Madison Square Garden. Player of Year 1945 and 1946. Led Minneapolis Lakers to 5 titles, All-League 9 years with 11,764 points scored. Voted top player of First-Half Century.

HAROLD G. OLSEN 1895–1953
ELECTED 1959—CONTRIBUTOR

Graduated from Rice Lake (Wis.) H.S. 1913 and Wisconsin 1917. Three-sport H.S. player, 2 years All-Conference for Wisconsin Big Ten

Champions. Coached Ripon, Ohio State, Northwestern, and Chicago Stags. Won 5 titles at O.S.U. Helped found NCAA Tournament; Committee Chairman 8 years. President of Coaches Association 1933. Chairman NCAA Rules Committee, member 1948 Olympic Committee. Helped initiate 10-second rule.

AMOS ALONZO STAGG 1862–1965
ELECTED 1959—CONTRIBUTOR

Graduated from Exeter (Mass.) Academy 1884, Yale 1890, and Springfield 1892. Star pitcher and All-American End at Yale. Played in first public basketball game March 11, 1892. Became athletic head at Chicago, coached 7 basketball champions and football 40 years. He awarded first varsity letter for basketball 1908. Organized Big Ten Conference, conducted National High School Tournament 1917–1930 which did much to standardize rules. Member football Hall of Fame.

JOHN R. WOODEN 1910–
ELECTED 1959—COLLEGE PLAYER

Graduated from Martinsville (Ind.) H.S. 1928 and Purdue 1932. High School All-State 1926–27–28. All-Big Ten 1930–31–32. All-American 1930–31–32. Captain 1931, 1932; set Conference scoring record 1932. Led Nat'l. Champions 1932. Star in semi-pro basketball. Made 138 consecutive free throws in competition. Member All-time All-American Team. Became outstanding high school and university coach.

ERNEST A. BLOOD 1872–1955
ELECTED 1960—COACH

First played game in 1892, began coaching in 1897. Never lost to high school opponent, at Potsdam (N.Y.) H.S., 1906–1915. Won 200, lost 1, including 159 straight wins at Passaic (N.J.) H.S., 1915–1924. Won 421 at St. Benedict's Prep (Newark) 1925–1949. Won 56, lost 7 at West Point and Clarkson. "Prof" won 5 State Prep titles at St. Benedict's and 7 State H.S. titles with the immortal Passaic "Wonder Team."

VICTOR A. HANSON 1903–
ELECTED 1960—COLLEGE PLAYER

Graduated from Syracuse, N.Y. (Central H.S.) 1922, Manlius Acad. 1923 and Syracuse U. 1927. Four-sport H.S. star, led Central to N.Y. State title 1921. At Syracuse "Vic" was a nine-letter man, three-sport captain 1926–27, Basketball All-American 1925–26–27. Led 1926 team to Nat'l. title, teams won 48, lost 7 in 3 years. Player of Year 1927, named All-time All-American in 1952. New York State's greatest amateur player. Great pro with Cleveland Rosenblums, played baseball with N.Y. Yankees, coached football at Syracuse 1930–36.

GEORGE T. HEPBRON 1863–1946
ELECTED 1960—REFEREE

As friend of Naismith and Gulick was a pioneer authority on Basketball. As YMCA Director, saw need to curb roughness in game. First official referee at Brooklyn YMCA. Refereed first AAU Tournament at Bay Ridge A.C. Helped with first Guide in 1896. Secretary Olympic Basketball Committee 1903. Secretary AAU Committee 1896–1915, Sec'y Joint Rules Committee 1915–1936. (Made Life Member 1936.) Conducted First Nat'l. Rules Questionnaire. Served on many committees which organized early basketball.

FRANK W. KEANEY 1886–1967
ELECTED 1960—COACH

Graduated from Boston, Mass. (Cambridge Latin) 1906 and Bates 1911. Four-sport college star with flair for speed. Stole 38 bases in 1910, college record. Coached Putnam, Conn., Woonsocket, R.I. & Everett, Mass. 1911–1920. Coached all sports Rhode Island, Basketball 28 yrs and A.D. 36 yrs. Changed slow-break pattern basketball to fast-break, high scoring "Point a Minute." Won 401, lost 124, took "Little Rhody" 4 times to NIT. Awarded NABC Metropolitan Award 1957.

WARD L. LAMBERT 1888–1958
ELECTED 1960—COACH

Graduated from Crawfordsville, Ind. H.S. and Wabash College 1911. Trained in chemistry, "Piggy" played and coached basketball through all its rules changes from groups to 5-man game. Led Lebanon, Ind. H.S. to great records 1912–1916. Coached Purdue to 11 Big Ten titles, 371 victories and several all-American players in 29 years. Pioneered fast-break style of offense. Wrote "Practical Basketball." Honored as nation's outstanding coach in 1945. Awarded NABC Metropolitan Award in 1954.

EDWARD C. MACAULEY 1928–
ELECTED 1960—COLLEGE PLAYER

Graduated from St. Louis, Mo. (University) H.S. 1945 and St. Louis U. 1949. After 6.8 points average in 81 high school games, "Easy Ed" became one of Billikens' great players. During yrs. 1946–49, was named to every All-American team selected. Was All-Conference 4 years, was MVP in NIT Tournament in 1948, and AP. Player-of-the-Year 1949. Led nation with .524 shooting in 1947. Was All-NBA 1950 through 1954, played in 8 NBA All-Star Games. Scored over 11,000 points in 9 NBA seasons.

BRANCH McCRACKEN 1908–
ELECTED 1960—COLLEGE PLAYER

Graduated from Monrovia, Ind. H.S. 1926 and Indiana U. 1930. Led his H.S. team to Tri-State titles 1925 and 1926, was MVP both years. Led college team in scoring 3 years, was All Big Ten 3 years. Was Conference MVP 1928. Set Big Ten scoring record in senior year when he was named on every All-American team elected. In playing career scored 32% of all points scored by his team and twice won Indiana Balfour Award. Became great coach at Indiana to win 4 Conference titles and 2 NCAA Championships in 1940 and 1953.

CHARLES C. MURPHY 1907–
ELECTED 1960—COLLEGE PLAYER

Graduated from Marion, Ind. H.S. 1926 and Purdue 1930. All-State in 1926 as team won Indiana State title. "Stretch" was one of first great "Big Men" in game. Big Ten's foremost offensive threat. Led team to Co-Championship in 1928. Set Big Ten scoring record in 1929, was captain in 1930 as undefeated team won Conference title. Named All-American 1929 and 1930. Named to All-time All-American team.

HENRY V. PORTER 1891–
ELECTED 1960—CONTRIBUTOR

Graduated from Illinois State Normal 1918 and M.A., U. of Illinois 1925. After winning a letter in baseball and coaching basketball at Mt. Zion, Keithsburg, Delavan, and Athens, Ill. 1913–28, "H.V." turned to administration. As State Assoc. Executive and Executive Director of Nat'l. Federation he pioneered the invention of the "Molded" Basketball, the fan-shaped backboard and 29½″ ball. With Mr. Tower he codified the Basketball Rules and started nationwide system of rules analysis. Was first high school representative on Rules Committee, a member 30 years and Secretary 18 years. Wrote basketball handbook and developed use of films.

FORREST S. DeBERNARDI 1899–
ELECTED 1961—A.A.U. PLAYER

Graduated from Iola, Kan. and Kansas City (North East) H.S. 1919 and Westminster Coll. 1923. After selection as Kansas All-State and All Kansas City, "De" was 2 years All Conference. Considered one of greatest players in Mid-West. He was an A.A.U. All-American 1921–22–23. Led Hillyards to A.A.U. title in 1926 and 1927 and Cook Painters in 1928 and 1929. In 11 A.A.U. Tournaments, "De" was All Tournament 7 times and All-American in 3 positions. Elected All-time All-American in 1938.

GEORGE H. HOYT 1883–1962
ELECTED 1961—REFEREE

An early pioneer of the game concerned with Sportsmanship and Fair Play, he traveled throughout New England to help players and officials. Living in South Boston, Mass., he organized first Officials' Board in Eastern Mass. and was admitted to the Collegiate Officials Directory in 1911. Coached many teams and for 34 years was associated with Eastern Mass. H.S. Tournament as an official and Honorary Chief Official. Considered "Mr. Basketball" in New England.

GEORGE E. KEOGAN 1890–1943
ELECTED 1961—COACH

Graduated from Detroit Lakes, Minn. H.S. 1909. Began great coaching career in high schools at Lockport and Riverside, Ill. and Superior State, St. Louis U., St. Thomas, Allegheny and Valparaiso before reaching Notre Dame in 1923. Led "Fighting Irish" to 327 wins in 20 years to win 77% of games played. During 1925–28 teams won 56, lost 5 while the 1935–36 and 1936–37 teams won 42, lost 5 for a strong claim to national title. Created "shifting man-to-man" defense and coached many All-Americans in career suddenly shortened by death during 1943 season.

ROBERT A. KURLAND 1924–
ELECTED 1961—COLLEGE PLAYER

Graduated from St. Louis, Mo. (Jennings) H.S. 1942 and Oklahoma State 1946. The first of the truly great "7 Footers," Bob wrote basketball history of his time. Four years a college regular, he led his team to NCAA titles in 1945 and 1946 when he was the nat'l. scoring leader and in 1945–46 the NCAA-MVP winner. Elected to every All-American team, he joined AAU Phillips "Oilers" to become selected All League and All AAU for 6 years. Was a member of U.S. Olympic Teams in 1948 and 1952. Selected by Grantland Rice on All-time All-American Team.

ERNEST C. QUIGLEY 1880–1960
ELECTED 1961—REFEREE

Graduated from Concordia, Kansas, H.S. 1900 and Kansas U. 1904. An outstanding four-sport star at Kansas, "Quig" had thoughts of Law, but coached St. Mary's (Kansas) from 1903–12. Turned to officiating football and baseball in spare time to become National League umpire in 1913. Became one of greatest year-round officials as he handled all top games in football and basketball and 5 World's Series. Traveled 100,000 miles a year before retiring in 1944 to become Athletic Director at Kansas. One of basketball's most colorful and respected officials, relying on his shrill voice rather than the whistle.

JOHN S. ROOSMA 1900–
ELECTED 1961—COLLEGE PLAYER

Graduated from Passaic, N.J. H.S. 1921 and U.S. Military Academy 1926. All-State 1918–1921 and State Tournament high scorer all 3 years. Johnny was a key part of the "Wonder Team" as his team won 41 straight games in the string of 159. Coach Blood called him Passaic's Greatest. A 10-letter winner at West Point, he led his team to 73 wins and 13 losses, scoring 44% of his team's points, 354 in one season and over 1,100 overall. Won coveted Army Athletic Sabre as outstanding athlete as he scored game high of 28 points several times while starring as a defensive player. Served in Army 1926–56, retiring as Colonel.

LEONARD D. SACHS 1897–1942
ELECTED 1961—COACH

Graduated from Chicago, Ill. (Carl Schurz H.S.) in 1914, Am. College of Phys. Educ. 1923, and Loyola (Chicago) 1935. Won 11 H.S. letters and became star of Illinois A.C. which won AAU title in 1918. Coached at Wendell Phillips and Marshall H.S. before taking over Loyola in 1924. Lennie's great 2-2-1 zone defense with goal tender created great new interest in "big" man and new rule in basketball, prohibiting goal tending. In 1927–29 teams won 32 straight and 20 straight in 1938–39 before losing NIT title to undefeated LIU. With 3 City titles, won great recognition with use of meager material to win 224 games in 19 years.

ARTHUR A. SCHABINGER 1889–

ELECTED 1961—CONTRIBUTOR

Graduated from Emporia, Kansas, H.S. 1908, Coll. of Emporia 1913 and Springfield Coll. 1915. Four-letter man in H.S. and college, "Schabie" had an 80% winning mark in 20 years of coaching at Ottawa U., Emporia State, and Creighton U., where he won 9 Conference titles. Pioneered Intersectional games, conducted clinics, and helped organize NABC. Held many offices and was President 1932. Directed Olympic Basketball Tournament 1936, member Rules Committee, helped research molded ball, founder and director of Offical Sports Film Service 1946–56, a great aid to uniform rules interpretation. Awarded NABC Metropolitan Award in 1955.

CHRISTIAN STEINMETZ 1882–1963

ELECTED 1961—COLLEGE PLAYER

Graduated from Milwaukee, Wis. (South Division) H.S. 1902 and Wisconsin 1905. Great two-sport captain in H.S. "Chris" organized first team at Alma Mater. The "Father of Wisconsin Basketball" scored 462 points in 1905—50 points, 20 field goals in one game and with 238 free-throws averaged 25.7 points per game, all long-standing records. As captain in 1905, he was elected All-Western Conference as he became first player ever to score over 1,000 points in college career. For 19 years selected the All-Western Conference Teams as he gained fame as one of his State's All-time Athletic Greats.

DAVID TOBEY 1898–

ELECTED 1961—REFEREE

Graduated from New York City (DeWitt Clinton H.S.), Savage School 1918, and New York U. 1935 and 1940. In a life devoted entirely to Youth and Physical Training, Dave enjoyed every outlet. He played on many great pro teams with and against all great players of his time. Enjoyed great coaching success in H.S. with 367 wins and in colleges with 348 wins including 35 straight wins at Savage School 1924–27. From 1918 to 1925 he refereed all important pro games and in 1926 was assigned vital West Point-Syracuse game (Hanson vs. Roosma). Until 1946 he was leading E.I.A. official working most important Eastern games. Wrote first officiating book, "Basketball Officiating" in 1943.

ARTHUR L. TRESTER 1878–1944

ELECTED 1961—CONTRIBUTOR

Graduated from Plainfield, Ind. Academy 1897 and Earlham Coll. 1904, Columbia U. 1913. First a teacher then a coach, a H.S. Principal and Superintendent, "A.L." became Secretary of the struggling Indiana H.S. Athletic Assoc. in 1913. He led its growth to more than 800 schools and in 1922 became Commissioner of the now financially sound, politically devoid organization which became the model for many states. His administrative ability, unquestioned integrity, and warm good humor enabled Indiana's Basketball Tournament to be universally recognized as a model of efficiency.

EDWARD A. WACHTER 1883–1966

ELECTED 1961—PRO PLAYER

Began basketball in 1895 and in '96–97 joined Troy YMCA team to begin a career that was to include perhaps 1,800 games and over 20 years of coaching. Nearly all towns and leagues in the East enjoyed Ed's talent which saw him chosen All-League regularly and which was culminated when he led Schenectady, N.Y. Co. "E" to the World's title win over Kansas City Blue Diamonds in 1905. In 1922 called "the greatest Center Man in Basketball." He led scoring in every league he played. Selected All-time Center in 1928. Worked for common rules and conditions, as he led discussion at first Officials' meeting in Boston. A Basketball Legend who played on more championship teams than anyone in his generation.

DAVID H. WALSH 1889–

ELECTED 1961—REFEREE

Graduated from Hoboken, N.J. H.S. 1907 and Montclair State 1911. Began teaching and coaching at Hoboken 1911 and combined basketball officiating in Pro, H.S. and College. About 1914 concentrated on college game to become one of East's leading referees while he enjoyed great coaching success. Appointed Assoc. Director Collegiate Officials Bureau 1941–1956, conducting clinics, supervising and assigning officials. Since 1922 very active with group forerunner of I.A.A.B.O. and in 1948 elected Secretary of I.A.A.B.O. Did much for rules uniformity and improving officials. Considered one of six best Eastern officials of his era.

BERNHARD BORGMANN 1899–

ELECTED 1961—PRO PLAYER

Graduated from Clifton, N.J. H.S. 1917. As a brillant H.S. scorer and continuing through 2,500 Pro games, Benny was recognized as an All-time All-pro playing in the American, National, Metropolitan, Eastern, New York State, and Western Mass. Leagues. He was always one of the highest scorers, frequently scoring 10 or more points when the team scored 20. At 5′8″, he was a brilliant offensive performer. He was in demand by many teams and cities wherever pro ball was played.

Upon his retirement as a great performer, he enjoyed a successful coaching career with 7 years with pro teams and 6 years at St. Michael's and Muhlenberg Colleges.

JOHN J. O'BRIEN 1888–1967

ELECTED 1961—CONTRIBUTOR

Graduated from Brooklyn, N.Y. (Commercial H.S.) 1907. Played three sports in H.S. and continued basketball activity by playing YMCA and pro ball 1908–19 and refereeing 1910–30. From 1920–30 "Jack" was a senior Intercollegiate Basketball League official. Administration was his real hobby as he helped organize the Interstate Pro League 1914 and served as President 1915–16–17. He organized the Metropolitan Basketball League in 1921 as well as the Brooklyn Arcadians who were to defeat the Celtics. Served as President and Treasurer of the League 1922–28 before reorganizing the American Basketball League as its President until 1953. New dignity and integrity were brought to owners, players, officials, and the game under his leadership.

ANDY PHILLIP 1922–

ELECTED 1961—COLLEGE PLAYER

Graduated from Granite City, Ill. H.S. 1940 and Illinois U. 1947. First team All State 1940 while his team won coveted State Title, Andy became one of nation's greatest players as vital member of the Illini "Whiz Kids." Set Big Ten scoring records in 1941–42 and 1942–43 as his team won 2 Conference titles. He led them to 14 straight wins and 25 of 27 in Soph. and Jr. years. Scored 40 pts and 16 goals for Conference record in 1943. MVP of team as a Soph., Conference MVP, and member of every All-American team as Jr. He was elected captain of 1944 before serving 3 years in Marines. Regained outstanding class in delayed senior year to again become All-American before embarking on very successful NBA career.

JACK McCRACKEN 1911–1958

ELECTED 1962—A.A.U. PLAYER

Graduated from Oklahoma City, Okla. (Classen) H.S. 1929, and Northwest Missouri State, 1933. All-State 1928, 1929; All-American, 1929. College All-American, 1931, 1932, as one of nation's great all-round players. A.A.U.-All American 7 times, with Denver Pigs and Denver Nuggets. Considered an All-Time Great of his time.

FRANK MORGENWECK 1875–1941

ELECTED 1962—CONTRIBUTOR

A great veteran of Pro Basketball, "Pop" wielded much influence among players, coaches, and owners. Starting 1901–02 as a Manager in the National League, "Morgie" was a successful leader of basketball through 1931. Introducing many young players destined for greatness, he led teams to various championships from 1912 to 1931. His 30 years' contribution served to raise the standards of the game and players.

HARLAN O. PAGE 1887–1965

ELECTED 1962—COLLEGE PLAYER

Graduated from Chicago (Lewis Institute), 1906, and U. Chicago, 1910. Led high school to a midwest Championship. Was a great three-sport star at the University. A stellar defensive player, his team won Western Conference titles 1907, 1909, and 1910; the A.A.U. Title, 1907. They defeated Penn. for National Title in 1908 and were undefeated 1909. "Pat" was Player-of-Year, 1910, before embarking on successful coaching career at Chicago, Butler, College of Idaho, and Indiana.

BARNEY SEDRAN 1891–

ELECTED 1962—PRO PLAYER

Graduated from DeWitt Clinton (NYC) H.S. 1907, and C.C.N.Y., 1911. At 5′4″, adjudged too small for H.S. team, played independent ball before starring for C.C.N.Y. Leading scorer for 3 years, Captain 1910. Selected on many All-Star teams. Beginning in 1911 in 15 years played on 10 Championship teams. In 1913 scored 17 goals from 25–30 feet on court with no backboards. Played with all major Eastern pro teams including Carbondale when team won 35 straight, 1914–15. Led great Ft. Wayne "K of C" in 1923–24 and finished playing with Cleveland Rosenblums 1924–26. Later coached Pro Basketball for 20 years.

LYNN W. ST. JOHN 1876–1950

ELECTED 1962—CONTRIBUTOR

Graduated from Monroe, Ohio, H.S. 1896, Ohio State, 1900, College of Wooster, 1906. Played 4 sports in high school and football in college. Successful basketball coach at College of Wooster and Ohio Wesleyan before Ohio State, 1912–19. OSU Athletic Director, 1915–1947. Member NCAA Rules Committee, 25 years; Chairman, 18 years. Chairman, Joint Committee, 5 years. Instrumental in formation of National Basketball Committee of U.S. and Canada. Chairman, 1933–37. Member Olympic Basketball Committee, 1936.

JOHN A. THOMPSON 1906–

ELECTED 1962—COLLEGE PLAYER

Graduated from St. George, Utah (Dixie) H.S. 1926, and Montana State, 1930. Led H.S. to Utah State Title and consolation Championship at National Tournament in Chicago in 1925. At Montana State, led Golden Bobcats to their greatest record. Team won 72, lost 4 in 1928 and 1929. Were selected Helms National Champions in 1929 when "Cat" was Player-of-Year. Captain in 1930, All-Rocky Mountain Conference, 1928, 29, 30. He scored 1,539 points in 3 years of play. Played one year AAU before a 14-year coaching career.

ROBERT F. GRUENIG 1913–1958

ELECTED 1963—A.A.U. PLAYER

Graduated from Chicago, Ill. (Crane Tech.) H.S. 1931. All-City 3 years, All-State 3 years, led his team to a State Championship. All 3 years he was League High Scorer, with a single game high of 35 points. An A.A.U. Immortal, the 6′8″ Center was first team All-Tournament 10 times from 1937 through 1948 and led the Denver Safeways, in 1937, and Denver Legion, in 1942, to A.A.U. Championships. Awarded the Los Angeles Sports Award Medallion as nation's greatest player, 1943. "Ace" became a high school coach after retiring as a great player.

WILLIAM A. REID 1893–1955
ELECTED 1963—CONTRIBUTOR

Graduated from Adrian, Mich. H.S. 1912 and Colgate, 1918. Captain and All-State Center of 1912, Michigan State Champions. Led Colgate teams to three-year, won 40 lost 12, record and A.E.F. Tours Team to service title, 1919. Coached Colgate to 151 wins in 10 years. Graduate Manager and Athletic Director at Colgate, 36 years. President, E.C.A.C., 1944–45. Vice President, N.C.A.A., 1942–46. Honorary LL.D., Colgate, 1946, as distinguished Coach and Administrator.

JOHN W. BUNN 1898–
ELECTED 1964—CONTRIBUTOR

Graduated from Humboldt, Kan. H.S. 1916, and Kansas 1921 (B.S.) and 1936 (M.S.). A 12-letter man in high school, became the first U-K athlete to earn 10 varsity letters. Assisted his coach "Phog" Allen 9 years at U-K before 25 successful years as head coach at Stanford, Springfield, and Colorado State (Greeley) for 321 wins and 3 Pacific Coast Titles, 1936–37–38. Wrote 6 textbooks on Basketball. Chairman Basketball Hall of Fame Committee, 1949–64; Editor of Basketball Guide and Official Rules Interpreter, 1959–67. Became first Executive Director of Basketball Federation, 1965. NABC President, 1949–50. NABC Metropolitan Award winner 1961.

HAROLD E. FOSTER 1906–
ELECTED 1964—COLLEGE PLAYER

Graduated from Mason City, Iowa, H.S. 1924, and Wisconsin, 1930. Led the high school to a third in State Tournament in 1924 and Mason City Jr. College to 21 wins in 1925. "Bud" was a 3-year star at Wisconsin in 1928–29–30. Team was Western Conference Champion in 1929 as he was named to several All-Conference and All-Western Teams in 1929 and 1930. All-American, 1930. Played pro ball with Oshkosh, Chicago, and Milwaukee before coaching 25 years at Wisconsin, winning 3 Big Ten Titles in 1935, 1941, and 1947, with NCAA Championship in 1941. NABC President, 1955–56. NABC Metropolitan Award winner, 1964.

NAT HOLMAN 1896–
ELECTED 1964—PRO PLAYER

Graduated from New York City (Commerce) H.S. 1916 and attended Savage School and N.Y.U. Played 4 sports in high school. In 1916, as a "young kid" was picked to play for Hoboken, N.J., and scored 23 of team's 28 to 25 win. Until 1920 starred for Bridgeport, Scranton, Germantown, and N.Y. Whirlwinds. In 1920–28 he led fabulous Original Celtics era as a great shooter, fine team player, and exceptional ball handler and passer. Team never lost a series. Later starred for Syracuse and Chicago. Retired from playing in 1933 to concentrate on 41-year coaching career at C.C.N.Y. which saw his team win NIT and NCAA Titles in 1950, a feat never before accomplished. NABC President, 1940–41. NABC Metropolitan Award winner, 1941.

EDWARD S. IRISH 1905–
ELECTED 1964—CONTRIBUTOR

Graduated from New York City (Erasmus Hall) H.S., and Penn., 1928. While in high school launched an extensive newspaper career and throughout college covered sports for three NYC and Philadelphia papers. Returned to NYC upon graduation, to continue newspaper work. In 1934 became Basketball Director of Madison Square Garden and immediately began Collegiate double-header programs. Basketball enjoyed instant popularity, as great crowds could attend the games. When "Ned" began intersectional play, the game became truly national; helped standardize rules and coaching; helped to build larger facilities and became Number One in fan interest. He helped organize the NBA and formed the N.Y. Knickerbockers in 1946. Received NABC Metropolitan Award in 1942.

R. WILLIAM JONES 1906–
ELECTED 1964—CONTRIBUTOR

British born in Rome, Italy. Graduated from high school in Rome, 1923, and Springfield College, 1928. Attended colleges in Denmark, Germany, and Switzerland, 1929–32. Introduced basketball in Switzerland, 1929. Co-founder International Amateur Basketball Federation (FIBA) 1932. In June 1932 became Secretary General of FIBA which controls all international competition, including the Olympics, which he supervised each 4 years since 1936. Through this, helped spread basketball to 130 nations. Director, UNESCO Youth Institute, 1956, and appointed Secretary-General International Council of Sport and Physical Education, 1958. Honorary Doctor of Humanics, Springfield 1963.

KENNETH D. LOEFFLER 1902–
ELECTED 1964—COACH

Graduated from Beaver Falls, Pa., H.S. 1920, and Penn. State, 1924, plus Law degree from Pitt. Starred in 3 sports in high school. Played 3 years at Penn State, 1921–24. Captain, 1924. Played pro ball, 1924–29, before a coaching career of 22 years in colleges and 3 years in NBA. At Geneva, Yale , LaSalle, and Texas A&M, he won 310 games. At LaSalle he won the NIT Title in 1952 and was runner-up, 1953; also won the

NCAA Title in 1954 and was second in 1955. His St. Louis Bombers won NBA Division Title in 1948. Coached East All-Stars in 1955.

JOHN D. RUSSELL 1903–

ELECTED 1964—PRO PLAYER

Graduated from Brooklyn, N.Y. (Alexander Hamilton) H.S. 1919; Seton Hall, B.S., and NYU, M.A. In high school "Honey" began a pro career that in 28 years saw him playing in every major Pro League and gaining acclaim as the top Defensive Player of his era. In over 3,200 games, he played the game's great individual opponents and led many teams to championships, including 5 straight titles, 1925–29, with Cleveland Rosenblums. As Player-Coach for 20 years, "Honey" was selected All-League, 1926–27–28–29. He coached Seton Hall to 294 wins, including 44 straight, and the NIT Title. Was the first coach of the NBA Boston Celtics, 1947.

WALTER A. BROWN 1905–1964

ELECTED 1965—CONTRIBUTOR

Graduated from Hopkinton, Mass. H.S. 1922, Boston Latin, 1923, and Exeter, N.H., Academy, 1926. Served apprenticeship in Sports Promotion under his father, George, General Manager of Boston Arena. Succeeded in 1937 as President of Boston Garden Arena Corp. Made Boston the Sports Center of New England. In 1946 was the driving force to organize the NBA and the Boston Celtics were his great basketball gift. Walter brought College Doubleheaders and the State and New England H.S. Tournaments to the Garden. Tireless worker for many charities and athletic projects. Was an Olympic official. Was Chairman of the Board of Trustees of the Basketball Hall of Fame, 1961–64. He helped all sports, all groups, and persons.

PAUL D. HINKLE 1899–

ELECTED 1965—CONTRIBUTOR

Graduated from Chicago, Ill., (Calumet) H.S. 1916, and Chicago, 1921. A 3-sport star in H.S. and College. One of only two to win 3 letters at Chicago. All-Conference 2 years, Captain 2 years, and All-American in 1920. Arriving at Butler in 1921, "Tony" took his only job as he coached three sports and was Athletic Director continuously to become Dean of Indiana coaches. At one time had 55 proteges coaching in Indiana. Led his teams to over 500 wins with a National Title in 1929. Coached Great Lakes N.T.S. to 98 wins, 1942–44, and National Service Title, 1942–43. Member of National Basketball Rules Committee, 1937–38, '42–48; Chairman, 1948–50 "Tony" was NABC President, 1954–55, and received the NABC Metropolitan Award, 1962.

HOWARD A. HOBSON 1903–

ELECTED 1965—COACH

Graduated from Portland, Ore. (Franklin) H.S. 1922, Oregon (B.A.) 1926 and Columbia (M.A. and EDD) 1929 and 1947. Won 12 letters and was All-State in H.S. Brilliant two-sport record at Oregon; two years Captain of Baseball and Basketball. Three-sport coaching career of about 1,100 games in 28 years with 725 wins. In basketball won 495 games at Southern Oregon, U. of Oregon, and Yale. At Oregon he won the first NCAA Title in 1939 along with 3 Conference Titles in 1937–38–39. His teams pioneered intersectional play. At Yale won or tied 5 Big Three crowns. He was the first coach to win major titles on both coasts. "Hobby" was a member of the Olympic Committee 12 years; Rules Committee 4 years. Contributed much to basketball through his extensive studies and writings. NABC President, 1947–48.

WILLIAM G. MOKRAY 1907–

ELECTED 1965—CONTRIBUTOR

Graduated from Passaic, N.J., H.S. 1925, and Rhode Island, 1929. Seeing most of the 159 straight wins of the Passaic "Wonder Teams" gave Bill early ideas on basketball and statistics. Helping URI exploit its "2 points-a-minute" Rams led to his prolific contributions as basketball Director at Boston Garden. Since 1946 has provided statistics for Converse Yearbook. He was editor of the NBA Guide. Wrote history of the game for *Encyclopaedia Britannica* in 1957. Helped organize several basketball tournaments. Bill is an honorary Life Member of NABC and the IAABO. He was first Chairman of Hall of Fame Honors Committee, 1959–64.

EVERETT S. DEAN 1898–

ELECTED 1966—COACH

Graduated from Salem, Ind., H.S. 1917, and Indiana 1921 (A.B.) and 1936 (M.A.). Four-year star in H.S., three-year regular at Indiana U. In 1921 Everett was All-Conference Center, All-American, and won the Western Conference Medal for Proficiency in Scholarship and Athletics. After winning 48 of 52 games at Carleton College, 1921–24, he returned to Indiana to coach 14 years to win 163 games and tie for Big Ten Titles in 1926–28–36. In 1938 he joined Stanford to lead them to an NCAA crown in 1942. In 1955 completed 34 years of coaching with the universal recognition of being one of finest gentlemen in the game. He wrote two important books, was a member of the All-American Selection Committee, 1949, and a member of the National Sports Committee, 1948.

JOE LAPCHICK 1900–

ELECTED 1966—PRO PLAYER

As immigrant parents needed his support, Joe began playing at 17 without a H.S. education. Attracted by his agility and 6′5″ frame, great teams sought him and for 19 years, 1917–36, he was the best Center of his time. Holyoke (Western Mass. League), Brooklyn Visitations (Metropolitan League), Troy (N.Y. State League), 1919–23. He became the Center for the immortal Original Celtics, 1923–27. They never lost a series and were broken up, with Joe going to Cleveland Rosenblums. In 1927–30 they won 2 world titles. Reorganized the Celtics for a tour, 1930–36, before becoming one of America's great coaches in 20 years at St. John's U. and 9 years with the N.Y. Knickerbockers in NBA. Won NABC Metropolitan Award, 1965.

CLAIR F. BEE 1900–

ELECTED 1967—CONTRIBUTOR

Graduated from Grafton, West Virginia, H.S. 1917, B.A. from Waynesburg College 1925, and M.A. from Rutgers 1932. Coach 29 years. Lost 7 games in 5 years at Rider; won 95% of games at Long Island University 1931–1952, including 43 straight. Undefeated teams 1936 and 1939. NIT Champions in 1939 and 1941. Baltimore "Bullets" 1952–54. Member All-American Selection Board. Traveled and lectured extensively abroad. Rules Innovator including "3 Second" and "24 Second" Rules. Prolific writer including 5 "Clair Bee" books in 1935 and many books and articles that remain valuable references. Received many coaching awards around the world.

HOWARD G. CANN 1895–

ELECTED 1967—COACH

Graduated from New York (Commerce) H.S. 1913 and New York University 1920. Great three sport athlete in high school and college. Member 1920 Olympic team. Led N.Y.U. to National AAU Title 1920 as its "Greatest All-Around Athlete." Coached at N.Y.U. 35 years. Teams won 409, lost 232. Coach of Year 1947. East Coach 1948. Received N.Y. Writers Distinguished Service Award. NABC Merit Award 1967. Coached many great players in outstanding coaching career.

AMORY T. GILL 1901–1966

ELECTED 1967—COACH

Graduated from Salem, Oregon, H.S. 1920 and Oregon State University 1924. Captain and twice All-State 1919 and 1920. All Conference and All American 1924. Coached 2 years at Oakland, California, H.S.; 36 years at Oregon State where he won 599 games. Won Pacific Coast Title 5 years, Far West Classic 8 years. Fourth in NCAA Tourney 1949 and 1963. Olympic Trials Coach 1964. NABC West Coach 1964. "Slats" was NABC President, 1957–58.

ALVIN F. JULIAN 1901–1967

ELECTED 1967—COACH

Graduated from Reading, Pennsylvania, H.S. 1919 and Bucknell University 1923. Won 12 letters in high school and 10 in college. After playing pro football and baseball, began 41 years' coaching 3 sports at various times. In basketball won 381 games at Albright, Muhlenberg, Holy Cross, Dartmouth, and the Boston Celtics. Teams were in 5 NCAA Tourneys and 2 NIT Tourneys, won NCAA Title for Holy Cross in 1947. Won 3 Ivy Titles at Dartmouth 1956, 1958, 1959. Boston Writers Coach of Year, 1947; Philadelphia Writers Award, 1966. Coach NABC West Team, 1965. NABC Merit Award 1967. "Doggie" was NABC President, 1966–67. NABC Metropolitan Award 1967.

ARNOLD J. AUERBACH 1917–

ELECTED 1968—COACH

Graduated Eastern District H.S. (Brooklyn) 1935; George Washington U. 1940. Captain and 3-year regular in H.S. and College. Coach at St. Albans Prep and Roosevelt H.S., (D.C.) 1940–43. Joined newly formed NBA in 1946. Led Washington Caps and Tri-Cities to 143 wins. "Red" took over Boston Celtics in 1950 to lead them to 9 Division Championships and 8 straight World Titles. Coached 11 straight NBA East Teams; won 99 Play-off games. NBA Coach of the Year 1965 en route to 1,037 pro victories. Only coach to win over 1,000 games, leading Boston Celtics to World Professional dominance 1956–66. Washington, D.C. Touchdown Club, Coach of Decade. Wrote outstanding book; traveled internationally for clinics and game promotion. Recipient of several civic awards in career which developed many great players and led Pro Basketball to its greatest recognition and acclaim.

HENRY G. DEHNERT 1898–

ELECTED 1968—PLAYER

Without high school or collegiate training, "Dutch" began memorable basketball career playing in Eastern, Penn. State, New York State, and New England Leagues before joining immortal Original Celtics in 1920. While dominating Eastern Basketball for 8 years and to make an easy game interesting, "Dutch" went to foul line to receive passes from famous Celtic teammates. The Pivot Play was born. He became famous for its execution and success. Played with Cleveland Rosenblums for American League titles 1928, 1929, 1930, and New York Celtics for 1900 Wins until 1939. As Coach, led Detroit Eagles to World Titles 1940 and 1941; Sheboygan, Wisconsin, Indians to Western Titles 1945 and 1946. Though he discovered the Pivot Play by chance, he played and coached it so well that the 3-Second Rule was adopted.

HENRY P. IBA 1904–

ELECTED 1968—COACH

Graduated from Easton, Missouri, H.S. 1923; Westminster and Maryville, Missouri, 1929. Played 4 years H.S.; 2 years All-Conference at Westminster; AAU Sterling Milk (Oklahoma City) and Hillyards. Coached Classen (Oklahoma City) H.S. to 51 wins in 3 years; moved to Maryville for 61 wins. After 1 year at U-Colorado joined Oklahoma State U. in 1934. Memorable coaching career of nearly 800 wins included a National AAU Runner-up, 1932 (Maryville); 14 Missouri Valley Titles, and 1965 Big 8 Championship at OSU. Won consecutive NCAA Titles 1945 and 1946 which won him two Coach of

Year Awards. NCAA Runner-up 1949. Led Championship USA Team in 1964 Olympics at Tokyo. Chosen unprecendented 2nd time, 1968, and led USA to Championship in Olympics at Mexico City. N.A.B.C. President 1968. N.A.B.C. Metropolitan Award 1947.

ADOLPH F. RUPP 1901–

ELECTED 1968—COACH

Graduated from Halstead, Kansas, H.S. 1919; U-Kansas 1923. Member 1923 Kansas National Champions, coached by Forrest C. Allen who won 771 games. Coach Allen saw his protege win over 800 games to become the winningest college coach. Coached 5 years at Marshalltown, Iowa, and Freeport, Illinois, H.S. and since 1930 at U-Kentucky. Adolph has won 24 Southeast Conference Titles; 4 NCAA Titles in 1948, 1949, 1951, 1958; NIT Title in 1946; NCAA Runner-up, 1966. Was Co-Coach of 1948 USA Olympic Team at London. Won every important award including Coach of the Year, 4 times and Columbus, Ohio, Touchdown Club Coach of the Century, 1967. Coached 24 All-Americans, 7 Olympic Team players, and 26 Professional Players. Has taken 11 overseas clinic trips. Won many civic awards. Member Basketball Rules Committee, 1964–68. N.A.B.C. Metropolitan Award 1966.

CHARLES H. TAYLOR 1901–

ELECTED 1968—CONTRIBUTOR

Graduated from Columbus, Indiana, H.S. 1918. Two years All-State in outstanding 4 years of high school play. Played 11 years of pro ball. In 1921 "Chuck" became interested in developing a shoe designed for the growing game. What began as a business promotion developed into a career of selling Basketball. In 1922 at North Carolina State he did a public demonstration which became first "Basketball Clinic." A lifetime of building players, coaches and spectator interest through clinics and demonstrations took him to every major American city as well as Puerto Rico, Hawaii, Canada, Mexico, South America, Africa, and Europe. Began Converse Yearbook of Basketball in 1922; designed "Chuck" Taylor Basketball shoe in 1931; selected All-American Teams since 1932. Coached Air Force Basketball Team in World War II, won award for outstanding services in Air Force as he conducted clinics at many bases in USA and Overseas. Truly an an Ambassador of Basketball.

TEAMS

Teams in the Hall of Fame and year of election:

THE FIRST TEAM, 1959

ORIGINAL CELTICS, 1959

BUFFALO GERMANS, 1961

THE RENAISSANCE (THE RENS), 1963

APPENDICES

APPENDIX A

THE RULES

Out of the confusing and often contradictory sets of rules that governed basketball in its early years, a basic uniformity has been established. One set of rules adopted by the National Basketball Committee of the United States and Canada regulates all amateur basketball played in the U.S. and Canada.

Thus the only real differences in rules occur between the basic set and the professional and international rules.

For example, the National Basketball Association (the pros) allows six personal fouls, rather than the five of college or high school play before a player is disqualified. The professional game is 48 minutes long, divided into four 12-minute quarters, rather than the 40 minutes of a college game or 32 minutes of a high school contest.

Professional basketball rules include the 24-second regulation, under which a team must attempt a shot within 24 seconds of gaining possession of the ball. Professional rules also outlaw any variety of zone defense.

The American Basketball Association, a professional league that began play in the 1967–68 season, revived the three-point field goal which was first introduced by the defunct American Basketball League in 1961–62. A field goal from 25 feet or more from the basket counts for three points.

The rules adopted by the International Amateur Basketball Federation (FIBA) govern international and Olympic play. The FIBA rules include a 30-second limit for attempting a shot. No free throws are awarded for personal fouls unless the fouled player is in the act of shooting. During the last five minutes of play, however, free throws are awarded for all personal fouls. A player fouls out on his fifth personal foul.

OFFICIAL RULES

(Reprinted by permission of the National Association of State High School Athletic Associations)

As adopted by the National Basketball Committee of the United States and Canada representing the National Collegiate Athletic Association, the National Federation of State High School Athletic Associations, the National Junior College Athletic Association, the Young Men's Christian Association, the Canadian Intercollegiate Athletic Union and the Canadian Amateur Basketball Association.

BASKETBALL COURT DIAGRAM

IF COURT IS LESS THAN 74 FEET LONG IT SHOULD BE DIVIDED BY TWO LINES, EACH PARALLEL TO AND 40 FEET FROM THE FARTHER END LINE.

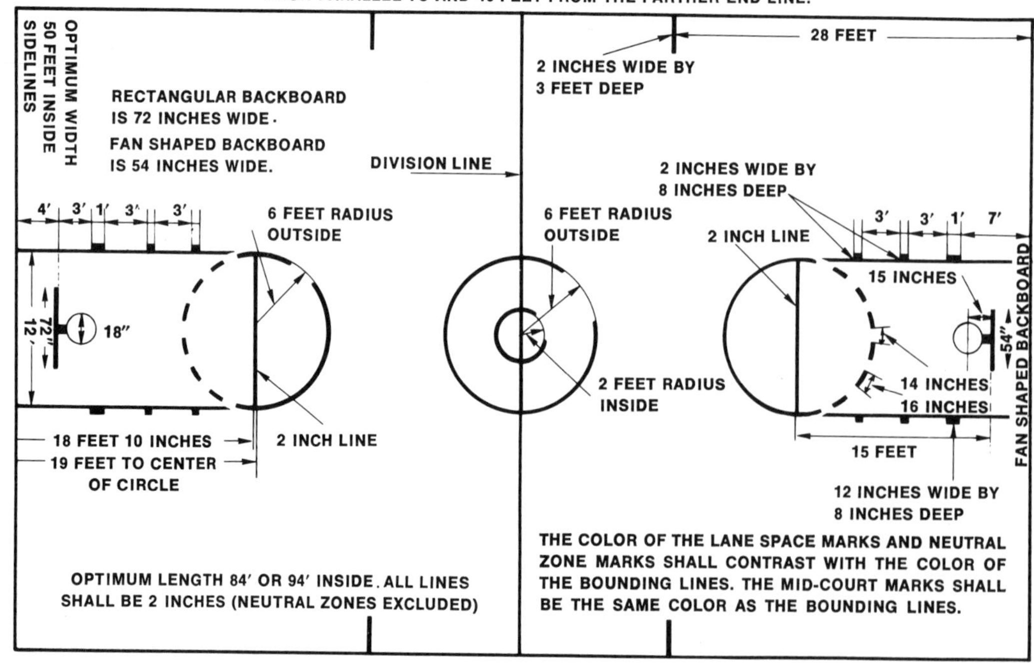

Left end shows large backboard for college games

MINIMUM OF 3 FEET
Preferably 10 feet of unobstructed space outside. If impossible to provide 3 feet, a narrow broken 1″ line should be marked inside the court parallel with and 3 feet inside the boundary.

SEMICIRCLE BROKEN LINES
For the broken line semicircle in the free throw lane, it is recommended there be 8 marks 16 inches long and 7 spaces 14 inches long.

Right end shows small backboard for high school and Y.M.C.A. games.

THE GAME Basketball is played by two teams of five players each. The purpose of each team is to throw the ball into its own basket and to prevent the other team from scoring. The ball may be thrown, batted, rolled or dribbled in any direction, subject to restrictions laid down in the following rules.

RULE 1

EQUIPMENT

SECTION 1. **The playing court** shall be a rectangular surface free from obstructions and with dimensions not greater than 94 feet in length by 50 feet in width.

IDEAL MEASUREMENTS ARE:
High School Age............................50 by 84 feet
College Age................................50 by 94 feet
These are the dimensions for the playing court only.

SECTION 2. **The playing court** shall be marked with **sidelines, end lines** and other lines as shown on the appended court diagram. There shall be at least 3 feet (and preferably 10 feet) of unobstructed space outside. If, on an unofficial court, there are less than 3 feet of unobstructed space outside any sideline or end line, a narrow broken line shall be marked in the court parallel with and 3 feet inside that boundary. This **restraining line** becomes the boundary line during a throw-in as in 7-6, on that side or end. It continues to be the boundary until the ball crosses the line.

SECTION 3. **The center circle** is a circle 2 inches in width and having a radius of 2 feet measured to the inside. A 2-inch wide circle concentric with the center circle shall be drawn with a radius of 6 feet measured to the outside.

SECTION 4. A division line 2 inches wide dividing the court into two parts shall be formed by extending the center circle diameter in both directions until it intersects the sidelines. If the court is less than 74 feet long, it should be divided by two lines, each parallel to and 40 feet from the farther end line.

SECTION 5. A free throw lane, 12 feet wide measured to the outside of each lane boundary and the semicircle with the free throw line as a diameter, shall be marked at each end of the court with dimensions and markings as shown on the court diagram. All boundary lines, but not lane space marks and neutral zone marks, are part of the lane. The color of the lane space marks and neutral zone marks shall contrast with the color of the boundary lines. The lane space marks (2 inches by 8 inches) and neutral zone marks (12 inches by 8 inches) identify areas which extend from the outer edge of the lane lines 36 inches toward the sidelines.

SECTION 6. A free throw line, two inches wide, shall be drawn across each of the circles which have an outside radius of 6 feet as shown on the court diagram. It shall be parallel to the end line and shall have its farther edge 15 feet from the plane of the face of the backboard.

SECTION 7. Each of the two backboards shall be of any rigid material. The front surface shall be flat and, unless it is transparent, it shall be white. The backboard shall be either of two types: (1) a rectangle 6 feet horizontally and 4 feet vertically, or (2) a fan-shaped backboard, 54 inches wide and with dimensions as shown on the diagram.

If the backboard is transparent, it shall be marked as follows: A rectangle shall be centered behind the ring and marked by a 2-inch white line. The rectangle shall have outside dimensions of 24 inches horizontally and 18 inches vertically. For the rectangular backboard, the top edge of the baseline shall be level with the ring. For the fan-shaped backboard, the baseline shall be omitted and the two vertical lines shall be extended to the bottom of the backboard.

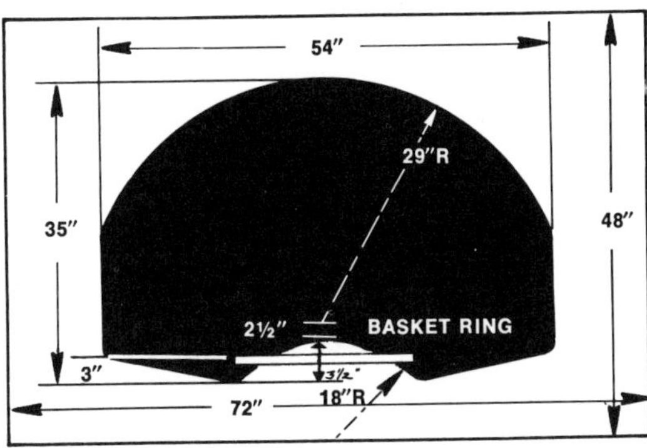

NOTE—Any backboard support, all of which is not directly behind the backboard, should be at least 6 inches behind it if the support extends above the top and at least 2 feet behind it if the support extends beyond the side. Attachment of ring to backboard shall be as prescribed in standards adopted by the Committee and available on request. For the fan-shaped backboard in transparent material, the recurved cut-out at the bottom may be filled in and the ring attached to the front of the backboard.

(The rectangular target in a bright orange color may be used on a non-transparent backboard.) The border of the backboard shall be marked with a white line. The border shall be 3 inches in width for the rectangular backboard and 3 inches or less in width for the fan-shaped backboard.

For college games, the transparent rectangular backboard shall be used. For other games, either type backboard in either transparent or non-transparent material is legal, but when new equipment is being installed for high school or Y.M.C.A. games, the fan-shaped backboard shall be used.

SECTION 8. Each backboard shall be midway between the sidelines, with the plane of its front face perpendicular to the floor, parallel to the end line and 4 feet from it. The upper edge of the backboard shall be: 13 feet above the floor for the rectangular and 12 feet 8 inches for the fan-shaped backboard.

NOTE—The Committee urges that the bottom and each side of the rectangular backboard be padded in accordance with adopted specifications.

It has been customary for a Committee recommendation to become a provision of the rules following a transitional period.

SECTION 9. The backboards shall be protected from spectators to a distance of at least 3 feet at each end.

SECTION 10. Each basket shall consist of a metal ring, 18 inches in inside diameter, its flange and braces, and a white cord 12-mesh net, 15 to 18 inches in length, suspended from beneath the ring. Each ring shall be not more than ⅝ of an inch in diameter, with the possible addition of small-gauge loops on the under-edge for attaching a 12-mesh net. The ring and its attaching flange and braces shall be bright orange in color. The cord of the net shall be not less than 120-thread nor more than 144-thread seine twine, and shall be so constructed as to check the ball momentarily as it passes through.

SECTION 11. Each basket ring shall be securely attached to the backboard. It shall have its upper edge 10 feet above and parallel to the floor and shall be equidistant from the vertical edges of the backboard. The nearest point of the inside edge of the ring shall be 6 inches from the plane of the face of the backboard.

SECTION 12. The ball shall be spherical. Its color shall be the approved orange shade or natural tan. For college games, it shall have a leather cover unless the teams agree to use a ball with a composition cover. For high school or Y.M.C.A. games, it shall have a leather or composition cover. It shall be of the molded type. If the panels are leather, they shall be cemented to the spherically molded fabric which surrounds an air-tight rubber lining. Its circumference shall be within a maximum of 30 inches and a minimum of 29½ inches for adults and within a maximum of 29½ inches and a minimum of 29 inches for players below senior high school age. Its weight shall be not less than 20 nor more than 22 ounces. It shall be inflated to an air pressure such that when it is dropped to a solid wood floor from a height of six feet, measured to the bottom of the ball, it will rebound to a height, measured to the top of the ball, of not less than 49 inches when it strikes on its least resilient spot nor more than 54 inches when it strikes on its most resilient spot.

NOTE—To be legal, a ball must be tested for resilience at the factory and the air pressure which will give the required reaction must be stamped on it. The pressure for game use must be such as to make the ball bounce legally.

SECTION 13. The home team shall provide a ball which meets the specifications of section 12. If the ball is not legal, the referee may select for use a ball provided by the visiting team.

SECTION 14. The benches for players of both teams shall be placed along that side of the court on which the scorers' and timers' table is located.

RULE 2

OFFICIALS AND THEIR DUTIES

SECTION 1. The officials shall be a referee and an umpire, who shall be assisted by two timers and by two scorers. A single timer and a single scorer may be used if they are trained men acceptable to the referee. The scorers and timers shall be located at the scorers' and timers' table on the side of the court.

NOTE—The officials should wear uniforms distinct from those of either team.

SECTION 2. The referee shall inspect and approve all equipment, including court, baskets, ball, backboards, timers' and scorers' signals. Prior to the scheduled starting time of the game, he shall designate the official timepiece, its operator, the official scorebook and official scorer. He shall be responsible for notifying each captain 3 minutes before each half is to begin.

The referee shall not permit any player to wear equipment which, in his judgment, is dangerous to other players. Elbow, hand, finger, wrist or arm guard, cast or brace made of sole leather, plaster, metal or any other hard substance, even though covered with soft padding, shall always be declared illegal.

Any equipment, which is unnatural and designed to increase a player's height or reach or to gain an advantage, shall not be used.

SECTION 3. The referee shall toss the ball at center to start the game. He shall decide whether a goal shall count if the officials disagree. He shall have power to forfeit a game when conditions warrant. He shall decide matters upon which the timers and the scorers disagree. At the end of each half he shall check and approve the score. His approval at the end of the game terminates the jurisdiction of the officials.

SECTION 4. The referee shall have power to make decisions on any points not specifically covered in the rules.

SECTION 5. The officials shall conduct the game in accordance with the rules. This includes: notifying the captains when play is about to begin at the start of the game, following an intermission or charged time-out, or after any unusual delay in putting the ball in play; putting the ball in play; determining when the ball becomes dead; prohibiting practice during a dead ball, except between halves; administering penalties; ordering time-out; beckoning substitutes to enter the court; warning a team for lack of sufficient action; signaling the point value of a goal by raising one or two fingers to face level and silently counting seconds to administer rules 4-13, 7-6, 8-4, 9-1, 9-7, 9-8, and 10-1-(c).

SECTION 6. The officials shall penalize unsportsmanlike conduct by any player, coach, substitute, team attendant or follower. If there is flagrant misconduct, the officials shall penalize by removing any offending player from the game and banishing any offending coach, substitute, team attendant or follower from the vicinity of the court. A player who commits his fifth personal foul shall also be removed from the game.

Ques.—Who is responsible for behavior of spectators? **Ans.**—The home management or game committee, insofar as they can reasonably be expected to control the spectators. The officials may call fouls on either team if its supporters act in such a way as to interfere with the proper conduct of the game. Discretion must be used in calling such fouls, however, lest a team be unjustly penalized.

SECTION 7. Neither official shall have authority to set aside or question decisions made by the other within the limits of his respective outlined duties.

Ques. (1)—Does referee's decision take precedence over umpire's in calling a foul? **Ans.**—No.

Ques. (2)—A violation, as outlined in Rule 9-2 to 10, and personal contact occur at about the same time. Both are observed by the same official or the violation is observed by one official and the contact by the other. What is the proper procedure? **Ans.**—The officials should decide which occurred first. If the violation was first, it caused the ball to become dead, hence, the contact which followed was not a foul unless unsportsmanlike. If the contact occurred first, it caused the ball to become dead and no violation occurred.

SECTION 8. The officials shall have power to make decisions for infractions of rules committed either within or outside the boundary lines; also at any moment from 10 minutes before the scheduled starting time of the game to the referee's approval of the final score. This includes the periods when the game may be momentarily stopped for any reason.

SECTION 9. (a) When a foul occurs, an official shall signal the timer to stop his watch and he shall designate the offender to the scorers and indicate with his fingers the number of free throws. The offending player shall raise his hand at arm's length above his head.

(b) When a team is entitled to a throw-in, an official shall clearly signal the act which caused the ball to become dead, the throw-in spot unless it follows a successful goal or an awarded goal, and the player or team entitled to the throw-in. The official shall hand (not toss) the ball to the thrower-in for a throw-in unless the throw-in is from outside an endline following a successful goal.

SECTION 10. Officials may correct an error if a rule is inadvertently set aside and results in: (a) failure to award a merited free throw; or (b) awarding an unmerited free throw; or (c) permitting a wrong player to attempt a free throw; or (d) attempting a free throw at the wrong basket; or (e) erroneously counting or canceling a score. If such error is made while the clock is stopped, it must be recognized before the clock is next started. If the error is made while the clock is running, it must be recognized before the second live ball after the error.

If the error is a free throw by the wrong player, or at the wrong basket or the awarding of an unmerited free throw, the free throw and the activity during it, other than unsportsmanlike conduct, shall be canceled. However, other points scored, consumed time and additional activity, which may occur prior to the recognition of a mistake, shall not be nullified. Errors because of free throw attempts by the wrong player or at the wrong basket shall be corrected by applying rule 8-1 and 2.

If an error, which occurs while the clock is running, is corrected, play shall be resumed from the point at which it was interrupted to rectify the error.

NOTE—Having more than five squad members participating simultaneously, or participating after having been disqualified, or a player participating after changing his number, without reporting it to the scorers and an official, are infractions which shall also be penalized if discovered during the time a provision is being violated. (See penalty following Rule 10, Sec. 7.)

SECTION 11. The scorers shall record the field goals made, the free throws made and missed, and shall keep a running summary of the points scored. They shall record the personal and technical fouls called on each player and shall notify the referee immediately when the fifth personal foul is called on any player. They shall record the time-outs charged to each team, and shall notify a team and its coach through an official whenever that team takes a fifth charged time-out. They shall signal the nearer official each time a team is granted a charged time-out in excess of the legal number and when a player commits a common foul after his team has been charged with its 4th or 6th personal foul during the half. The score-book of the home team shall be the official book, unless the referee rules otherwise. The scorers shall compare their records after each goal, each foul and each charged time-out, notifying the referee at once of any discrepancy. If the error cannot be found, the referee shall accept the record of the official book, unless he has knowledge which permits him to decide otherwise. If the discrepancy is in the score and the error is not resolved, the referee shall accept the progressive team totals of the official scorebook.

The scorers shall keep a record of the names and number of players who are to start the game and of all substitutes who enter the game. When there is an infraction of the rules pertaining to submission of the roster, substitutions or numbers of players, they shall notify the nearer official.

The scorers shall use a horn or other device unlike that used by the officials or timers to signal the officials. This may be used immediately if (or as soon as) the ball is dead, or is in control of the offending team.

NOTE—The **Rules Committee** strongly recommends that the official scorer wear a **black and white striped garment** and that his location be clearly marked.

Ques. (1)—What is the procedure if a player who has committed his 5th personal foul continues to play because the scorers have failed to notify the official? **Ans.**—As soon as scorers discover the irregularity, they should sound the horn after (or as soon as) the ball is in control of the offending team or is dead. The disqualified player must be removed immediately. Any points which may have been scored while such player was illegally in the game are counted. **If other aspects of the error are corrected, the procedure to be followed is included among the duties of the officials (2-10).**

Ques. (2)—Should scorers notify a player when he has committed his 4th personal foul? **Ans.**—No; but a captain may request an official to obtain this information when it can be done without delaying the game.

Ques. (3)—What should be done if the scorer's horn sounds while the ball is alive? **Ans.**—Players should ignore the horn since it does not make the ball dead. The scorers should not signal while the ball is in play except in certain cases such as are noted in the first question above. The officials must use their judgment in blowing the ball dead to consult the scorers.

Ques. (4)—If the scorers fail to notify a team or its coach when it takes its fifth charged time-out, should the team be penalized if it takes a sixth time-out? **Ans.**—Yes.

SECTION 12. The timers shall note when each half is to start and shall notify the referee more than three minutes before this time so that he may notify the teams, or cause them to be notified, at least three minutes before the half is to start. They shall signal the scorers three minutes before starting time. They shall record playing time and time of stoppages as provided in the rules.

The timers shall be provided with at least one stop-watch which shall be the game watch and which shall be operated by one of the timers, but so placed that both may see it.

The game watch shall be started as prescribed in rule 5-10.

Fifteen seconds before the expiration of an intermission, a charged time-out or a time-out for replacing a disqualified player, the timer shall sound a warning signal immediately after which the players shall be ready to resume play.

The game watch shall be stopped: at the expiration of time for each period, and when an official signals time-out as in 5-8. For a charged time-out, the timers shall start a time-out watch and shall direct the scorers to signal the referee when it is time to resume play.

Expiration of playing time in each quarter, half or extra period shall be indicated by the timer's signal. This signal terminates player activity. If the timer's signal fails to sound, or is not heard, the timers shall go on the court or use other means to notify the referee immediately. If, in the meantime, a goal has been made or a foul has occurred, the referee shall consult the timers. If the timers agree that time expired before the ball was in flight, the goal shall not count. If they agree that the period ended (as in 5-6 (b)) before the foul occurred, the foul shall be disregarded unless it was unsportsmanlike. If the timers disagree, the goal shall count or the foul shall be penalized unless the referee has knowledge which alters such ruling.

If an obvious error by the timer has occurred because of the failure to start or stop the clock at the proper moment, the referee may correct the error only when he has definite information relative to the time involved.

NOTE—The use of an electric timing device is hereby authorized, together with such modifications in the foregoing as are essential to its operation. If two watches are used, one timer should operate the game watch and signal, and the other should serve as checker of the game watch and operator of the time-out watch.

Ques.—Should timers tell players or coaches how much time remains? **Ans.**—On request of a captain, an official should give this information to both teams when the ball is dead and time is out.

RULE 3

PLAYERS AND SUBSTITUTES

SECTION 1. Each team consists of 5 players, one of whom is the captain.

Ques.—May a team play with less than 5 players? **Ans.**—A team must begin with 5 players, but if it has no substitutes to replace disqualified players, it must continue with less than 5.

SECTION 2. The captain is the representative of his team and may address an official on matters of interpretation or to obtain essential information, if it is done in a courteous manner. Any player may address an official to request a time-out (5-8-Item 3) or permission to leave the court.

At least 10 minutes before scheduled starting time each team shall supply the scorers with name and number of each squad member who may participate.

At least 3 minutes before scheduled starting time each team shall designate to the scorers its 5 starting players.

Failure to comply with either one of these provisions is a technical foul, unless the referee considers the failure unavoidable.

SECTION 3. A substitute who desires to enter shall report to the scorers, giving his number and the number of the player who is being replaced. If entry is at any time other than between halves, and a substitute, who is entitled and ready to enter, reports to the scorers before change of status of the ball is about to occur, the scorers shall sound the horn if (or as soon as) the ball is dead and time is out. The substitute shall remain outside the boundary until an official beckons him, whereupon he shall enter immediately. If the ball is about to become alive, the beckoning signal should be withheld. The entering player shall not replace a free thrower or a jumper except as stated in 6-3-c, d and e and 8-2 and 3. If he enters to replace a player who must jump or attempt a free throw, he shall withdraw until the next opportunity to substitute.

A player who has been withdrawn may not reenter before the next opportunity to substitute after the clock has started following his replacement.

Ques. (1)—When does a substitute become a player? **Ans.**—When he legally enters the court.

Ques. (2)—Following substitutions, should the official line up players to aid them in locating opponents? **Ans.**—This shall be done at the request of a captain only when three or more substitutes for the same team enter during an opportunity to substitute.

SECTION 4. Each player shall be numbered on the front and back of his shirt with plain numbers of solid color contrasting with the color of his shirt, and made of material not less than ¾ inch wide. The number on the back shall be at least 6 inches high and that on the front at least 4 inches high. Neither of the single digit numbers (1) or (2) nor any digit greater than 5 shall be used, nor shall members of the same squad wear identical numbers.

Ques. (1)—If contesting teams have suits of the same color, what shall be done? **Ans.**—If possible, each team should have two sets of suits, one of light color and the other dark. The light color is for home games. The team which violates this policy should change. If there is doubt, the officials should request the home team to change; on a neutral floor the officials decide.

Ques. (2)—What is the penalty for wearing an illegal number? **Ans.**—The penalty is a technical foul if the player enters the game, and the infraction is discovered before the clock starts.

Ques. (3)—May the numbers on the shirt have a border? **Ans.**—Yes, but only when the border is no wider than ¼ inch.

RULE 4

DEFINITIONS

SECTION 1. A basket is the 18-inch ring, its flange and braces and appended net through which players attempt to throw the ball. A team's own basket is the one into which its players try to throw the ball. The visiting team shall have the irrevocable choice of baskets at which it may practice before the game and this basket shall be its choice for the 1st half. The teams shall change baskets for the 2nd half.

SECTION 2. Blocking is personal contact which impedes the progress of an opponent who does not have the ball.

SECTION 3. A bonus free throw is a second free throw which is awarded for each common foul (except a player control foul) committed by a player of a team after that team has committed 6 personal fouls in a half of a game played in halves, or 4 personal fouls in a half of a game played in quarters, provided the first free throw for the foul is successful.

SECTION 4. Change of status is the time at which a dead ball becomes alive or a live ball becomes dead. Change of status is about to occur when:

a. A player has started to make a throw-in; or
b. 80% of the time limit count has expired; or
c. An official is ready to make the toss for a jump; or
d. An official starts to place the ball at the disposal of a free thrower.

SECTION 5. A player is in control when he is holding a live ball or dribbling it.

A team is in control when a player of the team is in control and also while a live ball is being passed between teammates. Team control continues until: the ball is in flight after a try for goal; or an opponent secures control; or the ball becomes dead. There is no team control: during a jump ball; a throw-in; during the tapping of a rebound; or after the ball is in flight following a try for goal. In these situations, team control is reestablished when a player secures control.

SECTION 6. A disqualified player is one who is barred from further participation in the game because of committing his fifth personal foul, or a flagrant foul, or for infraction of Rule 10-4 (a) or (b).

SECTION 7. A dribble is ball movement caused by a player in control who throws, bats or taps the ball in the air and/or throws, bats or pushes the ball to the floor and then catches it or touches it once or several times before catching it. The dribble ends when: (a) the dribbler catches the ball with one or both hands; or (b) the dribbler touches the ball with both hands simultaneously; or (c) the dribbler is unable to immediately catch or continue to dribble the ball; or (d) an opponent bats the ball; or (e) the ball becomes dead.

An air dribble is that part of a dribble during which the dribbler throws or taps the ball in the air and then touches it before it touches the floor or is caught.

Ques. (1)—Is a player dribbling while tapping the ball during a jump, or when a pass rebounds from his hand, or when he fumbles, or when he taps a rebound or a pass away from other players who are attempting to get it? **Ans.**—No. The player is not in control under these conditions.

Ques. (2)—Is it a dribble when a player stands still and: (a) bounces the ball; or (b) holds the ball and touches it to the floor once or more? **Ans.**—(a) Yes. (b) No.

Ques. (3)—May a dribbler alternate hands? **Ans.**—Yes.

SECTION 8. Extra period is the extension of playing time necessary to break a tie score.

SECTION 9. a. A foul is an infraction of the rules, the penalty for which is one or more free throws unless it is a double foul, or is a player control foul, in which case the free throw provision is cancelled. For convenience, a personal foul, which is neither flagrant nor intentional nor committed against a player trying for field goal, nor a part of a double or multiple foul, is termed a **common foul.**

b. A double foul is a situation in which two opponents commit personal fouls against each other at approximately the same time. **A false double foul** is a situation in which there are fouls by both teams, the second of which occurs before the clock is started following the first, but such that at least one of the attributes of a double foul is absent.

c. A flagrant foul is an unsportsmanlike act and may be a personal or technical foul of a violent or savage nature, or a technical noncontact foul, which displays vulgar or abusive conduct. It may or may not be intentional.

d. An intentional foul is a personal foul, which in the judgment of the official appears to be designed or premeditated. It is not based on the severity of the act.

e. A multiple foul is a situation in which two or more teammates commit personal fouls against the same opponent at approximately the same time. **A false multiple foul** is a situation in which there are two or more fouls by the same team and such that the last foul is committed before the clock is started following the first, and such that at least one of the attributes of a multiple foul is absent.

f. A personal foul (10-8) is a player foul which involves contact with an opponent while the ball is alive or after the ball is in possession of a player for a throw-in.

g. A player control foul is a common foul committed by a player while he or a teammate is in control.

h. A technical foul (10-1 to 7) is: a foul by a non-player, or a player foul which does not involve contact with an opponent, or a player foul which involves unsportsmanlike contact with an opponent while the ball is dead, except as indicated in last clause of (d) above.

i. An unsportsmanlike foul is a technical foul which consists of unfair, unethical or dishonorable conduct.

SECTION 10. A fumble is the accidental loss of player control by unintentionally dropping the ball or permitting it to slip from one's grasp.

SECTION 11. A free throw is the privilege given a player to score one point by an unhindered try for goal from within the free throw circle and behind the free throw line. A free throw starts when the ball is given to the free thrower at the free throw line or is placed on the line. It ends when: the attempt is successful; or it is certain the attempts will not be successful; or when the ball following the try touches the floor or any player; or when the ball becomes dead.

SECTION 12. (a) A team's front court consists of that part of the court between its end line and the nearer edge of the division line and including its basket and the inbounds part of its backboard. **A team's back court** consists of the rest of the court including its opponents' basket and inbounds part of the backboard and the entire division line.

(b) A live ball is in the front or back court of the team in control as follows: (1) **A ball which is in contact** with a player or with the court is in the back court if either the ball or the player (either player if the ball is touching more than one) is touching the back court. It is in the front court if neither the ball nor the player is touching the back court. **(2) A ball which is not in contact** with a player or the court retains the same status as when it was last in contact with a player or the court.

Ques.—From the front court, A passes the ball across the division line. It touches a teammate who is in the air after leaping from the back court or it touches an official in the back court? Is the ball in the back court? Ans.—Yes. See 4-17.

SECTION 13. Held ball occurs when:

a. Opponents have hands so firmly on the ball that control cannot be obtained without undue roughness; or

b. A closely guarded player anywhere in his front court holds the ball for 5 seconds; or

c. A team, in its front court, controls the ball for 5 seconds in an area enclosed by screening teammates; or

d. A closely guarded player within a few feet of a front court boundary intersection dribbles, or combines dribbling and holding the ball for 5 seconds; or

e. A closely guarded player, in his mid-court area, dribbles, or combines dribbling and holding the ball for 5 seconds.

The player in control is closely guarded when his opponent is in a guarding stance at a distance not exceeding 6 feet from him.

Ques.—Is it a held ball merely because the player holding the ball is lying or sitting on the floor? **Ans.**—No.

SECTION 14. Holding is personal contact with an opponent which interferes with his freedom of movement.

SECTION 15. A jump ball is a method of putting the ball into play by tossing it up between two opponents in one of the three circles. It begins when the ball leaves the official's hand, and ends as outlined in rule 6-4.

SECTION 16. Lack of sufficient action is the failure of the responsible team to force play as required.

SECTION 17. The location of a player (or non-player) is determined by where he is touching the floor as far as being inbounds or out of bounds or being in the front court or back court is concerned. When he is in the air from a leap, his status with reference to these two factors is the same as at the time he was in contact with the floor or an extension of the floor such as a bleacher. When the ball touches an official, it is the same as touching the floor at the official's location.

SECTION 18. The mid-court area of a team is that part of its front court between the division line and a parallel imaginary line 28 feet from the inside edge of the end line to the nearer edge of the mid-court area marker. This imaginary line is located by two 3 feet lines 2 inches wide measured from the inside edge of each sideline and drawn at right angles to it.

SECTION 19. A multiple throw is a succession of free throws attempted by the same team.

SECTION 20. A pass is movement of the ball caused by a player, who throws, bats or rolls the ball to another player.

SECTION 21. A penalty for a foul is the charging of the offender with the foul and awarding one or more free throws, or awarding the ball to the opponents for a throw-in. The penalty for a violation is the awarding of the ball to the opponents for a throw in or one or more points or a substitute free throw.

SECTION 22. A pivot takes place when a player who is holding the ball steps once or more than once in any direction with the same foot, the other foot, called the pivot foot, being kept at its point of contact with the floor.

SECTION 23. A rule is one of the groups of laws which govern the game. A game law (commonly called a rule) sometimes states or implies the ball is dead or a foul or violation is involved. If it does not, it is assumed the ball is alive and no foul or violation has occurred to affect the given situation. A single infraction is not complicated by a second infraction unless so stated or implied.

SECTION 24. Running with the ball (traveling) is moving a foot or the feet in any direction in excess of prescribed limits while holding the ball. The limits follow:

Item 1. A player who receives the ball while standing still may pivot, using either foot as the pivot foot.

Item 2. A player, who receives the ball while his feet are moving or who is dribbling, may stop as follows:

(a) If he catches the ball while **both feet** are off the floor and:
  (1) **He alights with both feet** touching the floor simultaneously, he may pivot using either foot as the pivot foot; or
  (2) **He alights with first one foot** touching the floor followed by the other, he may pivot using the first foot to touch the floor as the pivot foot; or
  (3) **He alights on one foot, he** may jump off that foot and alight with both feet simultaneously but he may not pivot before releasing the ball.

(b) If he catches the ball while only **one foot** is off the floor:
  (1) **He may step** with the foot which is off the floor and may then pivot using the other foot as the pivot foot; or
  (2) **He may jump** with the foot which is on the floor and alight with both feet simultaneously, but he may not pivot before releasing the ball.

Item 3. After a player has come to a stop, he may pass or throw for goal under the following conditions:

(a) In Items 1, 2a(1), 2a(2) and 2b(1), he may **lift either foot,** but if he lifts his pivot foot or jumps before he passes or throws for goal, the ball must leave his hand before the pivot foot again touches the floor; or if he has jumped before either foot touches the floor.

(b) In Items 2a(3) and 2b(2), he may **lift either foot or jump** before he passes or throws for goal. However, the ball must leave his hand before a foot which has left the floor retouches it.

Item 4. A player who receives the ball as in Item 1 or a player, who comes to a stop after he receives the ball while he is moving his feet, may start a dribble under the following conditions:

(a) In Items 1, 2a(1), 2a(2) and 2b(1), the ball must leave his hand **before the pivot foot leaves the floor.**

(b) In Items 2a(3) and 2b(2), the ball must leave his hand **before either foot leaves the floor.**

Ques. (1)—Is it traveling, if a player falls to the floor while holding the ball? **Ans.**—No, unless he makes progress by sliding.

Ques. (2)—A1 jumps to throw the ball. B1 prevents the throw by placing one or both hands firmly on the ball so that: (a) A1; or (b) A1 and B1 both return to the floor holding it. **Ans.**—Held ball. However, if A1 voluntarily drops the ball before he returns to the floor and he then touches the ball before it is touched by another player, A1 has committed a traveling violation.

SECTION 25. A screen is legal action by a player who, without causing contact, delays or prevents an opponent from reaching a desired position.

SECTION 26. A throw-in is a method of putting the ball in play from out of bounds in accordance with Rule 7. The throw-in begins when the ball is at the disposal of the player or team entitled to it and ends when the passed ball touches or is touched by an inbounds player other than the thrower-in, or when a violation occurs.

SECTION 27. A try for field goal is an attempt by a player to score 2 points by throwing the ball into his basket. The try starts when the player begins the motion which habitually precedes the release of the ball. The try ends when the ball is clearly in flight.

SECTION 28. A violation is a rule infraction of the type listed in Rule 9.

RULE 5

SCORING AND TIMING REGULATIONS

SECTION 1. A goal is made when a live ball enters the basket from above and remains in or passes through.

Ques.—If the ball enters the basket from below, goes through and drops back into the basket, is a goal scored? **Ans.**—No, it is a violation.

SECTION 2. A goal from the field counts 2 points for the team into whose basket the ball is thrown. A goal from a free throw is credited to the thrower and counts 1 point for his team.

NOTE—A field goal in A's basket after being last touched by B is not credited to any player but is mentioned in a footnote and two points are added to A's total.

Ques.—A player throws a field goal in his opponents' basket. Who gets credit for the goal? **Ans.**—It is not credited to a player. It is added to the opponents' score and mentioned in a footnote.

SECTION 3. The winning team is the one which has accumulated the greater number of points when the game ends.

SECTION 4. The referee shall forfeit the game if a team refuses to play after being instructed to do so by either official. If the team to which the game is forfeited is ahead, the score at the time of forfeiture shall stand. If this team is not ahead the score shall be recorded as 2-0 in its favor.

Ques.—When the game is forfeited, are the points made by each player credited to him? **Ans.**—The league officers should decide. It is customary to include such points in the scoring records.

SECTION 5. Playing time shall be: (a) for teams of college age, two halves of 20 minutes each with an intermission of 15 minutes between halves; (b) for teams of high school age, four quarters of 8 minutes each with intermissions of one minute after the 1st and 3rd quarters and 10 minutes between halves; (c) for teams younger than in (b), four quarters of 6 minutes each with intermissions the same as for (b).

SECTION 6. Each period begins when the ball first becomes alive. **It ends** when time expires except that: (a) if the ball is in flight after a try for field goal, the period ends when the ball goes through the basket; or it is certain the ball will not go through the basket; or when the ball, in flight as the result of a try, touches the floor or any player; or when the ball becomes dead; or (b) if a held ball occurs so near the expiration of time that the clock is not stopped before time expires, the period ends with the held ball; or (c) if a foul occurs so near the expiration of time that the timer cannot get the clock stopped before time expires or if the foul occurs after time expires but while the ball is in flight after a try for field goal, the period ends when the free throw or throws and all related activity have been completed.

SECTION 7. If the score is tied at the end of the second half, play shall continue without change of baskets for one or more extra periods with a one-minute intermission before each extra period. The game ends if, at the end of any extra period, the score is not tied.

In games played in halves, the length of each extra period shall be 5 minutes. **In games played in quarters,** the length of each extra period shall be 3 minutes. As many such periods as are necessary to break the tie shall be played. Extra periods are an extension of the 2nd half.

Ques.—With the score tied, a foul is committed near the expiration of time in the second half. If the free throw is successful, should an extra period be played? **Ans.**—If the foul occurs before the ball becomes dead and the period is ended as outlined in 5-6, no extra period is played. But if the foul occurs after the period has clearly ended, the extra period is played.

SECTION 8. Time-out occurs and the game watch, if running, shall be stopped when an official:

Item 1. Signals: (a) a foul; (b) held ball; or (c) a violation.

Item 2. Stops play: (a) because of an injury; (b) to confer with scorers or timers; (c) because of unusual delay in getting a dead ball alive; or (d) for any emergency.

Item 3. Grants a player's request for a time-out, such request being granted only when the ball is dead or in control of a player of his team and when no change of status of the ball is about to occur.

Item 4. Responds to the scorer's signal to grant a coach's request that a correctable error be prevented or rectified. Such a request shall be presented while the ball is dead and the clock is stopped. The appeal to the official shall be presented at the scorer's table when a coach of each team may be present.

NOTE—When a player is injured as in Item 2(a), the official may suspend play when the ball is dead or is in control of the injured player's team or when the opponents complete a play. A play is completed when a team loses control (including throwing for goal), or withholds the ball from play by ceasing to attempt to score or advance the ball to a scoring position. When necessary to protect an injured player, the official may suspend play immediately.

SECTION 9. A time-out shall be charged to a team for each minute or fraction of a minute consumed under Items 2(a), 3 and 4 of Section 8.

EXCEPTIONS: No time-out is charged:

(a) If in Item 2(a) an injured player is ready to play immediately or is replaced within 1½ minutes; or

(b) If in Item 3 the player's request results from displaced eyeglasses or lens; or

(c) If in Item 4 a correctable error is prevented or rectified; or

(d) If a disqualified player is replaced within 1 minute.

SECTION 10. After time has been out, the game watch shall be started when the official signals time-in. If official neglects to signal, the timer is authorized to start the watch unless an official specifically signals continued time-out.

a. **If play is resumed by a jump,** the watch shall be started when the tossed ball is legally tapped.

b. **If a free throw is not successful** and ball is to remain alive, the watch shall be started when the ball is touched or touches a player on the court.

c. **If play is resumed by a throw-in,** the watch shall be started when the ball touches or is touched by a player on the court.

Ques.—During a free throw which is not successful, a violation occurs. Should the clock be started when the ball is touched or touches a player on the court? **Ans.**—No, and official should avoid using the time-in chopping motion, if the ball is not to remain alive.

SECTION 11. Five charged time-outs may be granted each team during an untied game. During each extra period, each team is always entitled to at least one time-out. Unused time-outs accumulate and may be used at any time. Time-outs in excess of the allotted number may be granted at the expense of a technical foul for each.

RULE 6

LIVE BALL AND DEAD BALL

SECTION 1. The game shall be started by a jump ball in the center circle. After any subsequent dead ball, play shall be resumed by a jump ball or by a throw-in or by placing it at the disposal of a free thrower. The ball becomes alive when: (a) on a jump ball, the ball leaves the official's hand; or (b) on a throw-in, the ball touches or is touched by a player who is inbounds; or (c) on a free throw, the ball is placed at the disposal of the free thrower.

SECTION 2. The ball shall be put in play in the center circle by a jump between two opponents: (a) at the beginning of each quarter and extra period; or (b) after a double foul; or (c) after the last free throw following a false double foul.

Ques.—Does a quarter, half or extra period start with a jump ball if a foul occurs before the ball becomes alive? **Ans.**—No. Any rules statement is made on the assumption that no infraction is involved unless mentioned or implied. If such infraction occurs, the rule governing it is followed in accordance with Rule 4-23.

SECTION 3. The ball shall be put in play by a jump ball at the center of the restraining circle which is nearest the spot where: (a) a held ball occurs; or (b) the ball goes out of bounds as in 7-3; or (c) a double free throw violation occurs; or (d) the ball lodges on a basket support; or (e) the ball becomes dead when neither team is in control and no goal or infraction or end of a period is involved. In (a) and (b), the jump shall be between the two involved players unless injury or disqualification requires substitution for a jumper, in which case his substitute shall jump. In (c), (d), and (e), the jump shall be between any two opponents.

SECTION 4. For any jump ball, each jumper shall have one or both feet on or inside that half of the jumping circle (imaginary if in a free throw restraining circle) which is farther from his own basket. An official shall then toss the ball upward between the jumpers in a plane at right angles to the sidelines, to a height greater than either of them can jump and so that it will drop between them. The ball must be tapped by one or both of the jumpers after it reaches its highest point. If it touches the floor without being tapped by at least one of the jumpers, the official shall toss the ball again.

Neither jumper shall: tap the tossed ball before it reaches its highest point; nor leave the jumping circle until the ball has been tapped; nor catch the jump ball; nor touch it more than twice. The jump ball and these restrictions end when the tapped ball touches one of the eight non-jumpers, the floor, the basket or the backboard.

None of the 8 non-jumpers shall have either foot in the restraining circle cylinder until the ball has been tapped. Teammates may not occupy adjacent positions around the restraining circle if an opponent indicates his desire for one of these positions before the official is ready to toss the ball.

Ques.—During jump ball, is a jumper required to: (a) face his own basket; and (b) jump and attempt to tap the tossed ball? **Ans.**—(a) No specific facing is required. However, a jumper must be in the proper half of the jumping circle. (b) No. But if neither jumper taps the ball, it should be tossed again with both jumpers being ordered to jump.

SECTION 5. The ball shall be put in play by a throw-in under circumstances as outlined in Rules 7, 8-5 and 9-1 to 11.

SECTION 6. The ball shall be put in play by placing it at the disposal of a free thrower before each free throw.

SECTION 7. The ball becomes dead or remains dead when:

- **a. Any goal** is made as in 5-1;
- **b. It is apparent** the free throw will not be successful: on a free throw for a technical foul or a false double foul, or a free throw which is to be followed by another throw;
- **c. Held ball** occurs or ball lodges on the basket support;
- **d. Official's whistle** is blown;
- **e. Time expires** for a quarter, half or extra period;
- **f. A foul occurs:** or
- **g. Any floor violation** (9-2 to 10) occurs, or there is basket interference (9-11), or there is a free throw violation by the thrower's team (9-1).

EXCEPTION: The ball does not become dead when: (1) d, e or f occurs after a try for a field goal is in flight; or (2) d or f occurs after a try for a free throw is in flight; or (3) a foul is committed by an opponent of a player who has started a try for goal before the foul occurred provided time did not expire before the ball was in flight. The trying motion must be continuous and begins after the ball comes to rest in the player's hand or hands and is completed when the ball is clearly in flight. The trying motion may include arm, foot, or body movements used by the player when throwing the ball at his basket.

Ques.—If the ball is in flight after A's try for field goal when time for the period expires, and if the ball is subsequently touched, does the goal count if made? **Ans.**—No. The ball becomes dead when touched while in flight after the try. If it is basket interference (9-11) by B, 2 points are awarded to A.

RULE 7

OUT OF BOUNDS AND THE THROW-IN

SECTION 1. A player is out of bounds when he touches the floor or any object on or outside a boundary. For location of a player in the air, see 4-17.

The ball is out of bounds when it touches: a player who is out of bounds; or any other person, the floor, or any object on or outside a boundary; or the supports or back of the backboard; or ceiling, overhead equipment or supports.

NOTE—When the rectangular backboard is used, the ball is out of bounds if it passes over the backboard.

Ques. (1)—Ball rebounds from the edge of the backboard and across boundary line, but before it touches the floor or any obstruction out of bounds, it is caught by a player who is inbounds. Is the ball inbounds or out of bounds? **Ans.**—Inbounds.

Ques. (2)—The ball touches or rolls along the edge of the backboard without touching the supports. Is the ball dead? **Ans.**—No, unless ground rules to the contrary have been mutually agreed upon before the game.

SECTION 2. The ball is caused to go out of bounds by the last player to touch or to be touched by it before it goes out, provided it is out of bounds because of touching something other than a player.

If the ball is out of bounds because of touching or being touched by a player who is on or outside a boundary, such player causes it to go out.

Ques. (1)—Live ball is held by A. (a) The ball held by or passed by A touches B when B is on or outside the boundary; or (b) the ball is batted to out of bounds by B who is inbounds. **Ans.**—Ball awarded to A for a throw-in.

Ques. (2)—Ball passed by A touches an official and goes out of bounds. Whose ball? **Ans.**—B's ball.

SECTION 3. If the ball goes out of bounds and was last touched simultaneously by two opponents, both of whom are inbounds or out of bounds, or if the official is in doubt as to who last touched the ball, or if the officials disagree, play shall be resumed by a jump ball between the two involved players in the nearest restraining circle.

SECTION 4. The ball is awarded out of bounds after: (a) a violation as in Rule 9; or (b) a free throw for a technical foul as in Rule 8-5-b; or (c) a field goal or a successful free throw for personal foul as in 8-5-a or an awarded goal as in 9-11; or (d) the ball becomes dead while a team is in control provided no infraction or the end of a period is involved; or (e) a player control foul.

SECTION 5. a. When the ball is out of bounds after any violation as outlined in sections 2 through 11 in Rule 9, the official shall designate a nearby opponent of the player who committed the violation, and he shall hand the ball to this player or his substitute for a throw-in from the designated spot nearest the violation, except as indicated in the penalties which follow Rule 9-10 and 11.

b. After a dead ball, as listed in section 4 (d), any player of the team in control shall make the throw-in from the designated out of bounds spot nearest to the ball when it became dead.

c. After a player control foul, any player of the offended team shall make the throw-in from the designated spot nearest the foul, except that, if the ball has passed through the basket during the dead ball period immediately following the foul, no point can be scored and the ball is awarded to any player of the offended team out of bounds at either end of that free throw line extended which is nearer the goal through which the ball was thrown.

d. If in items a, b or c, the throw-in spot is behind a backboard, the throw-in shall be made from the nearer free throw lane line extended.

e. After a goal as listed in section 4 (c), the team not credited with the score shall make the throw-in from the end of the court where the goal was made and from any point outside the end line. Any player of the team may make a direct throw-in or he may pass the ball along the end line to a teammate behind the line.

f. After a technical foul, any player of the team to whom the free throw has been awarded shall make the throw-in from out of bounds at mid-court on either side.

g. After a free throw violation by the throwing team as listed in section 1 of rule 9, any opponent of the throwing team shall make the throw-in from out of bounds at either end of the free throw line extended.

SECTION 6. The throw-in starts when the ball is at the disposal of a player entitled to the throw-in and he shall pass the ball directly into the court, except as provided in 7-5(e), so that, after it crosses the boundary line and before going out of bounds, it touches or is touched by another player on the court within 5 seconds from the time the throw-in starts. Until the passed ball has crossed the plane of the boundary: (a) the thrower shall not leave the designated throw-in spot; (b) no player shall have any part of his person over the boundary line; and (c) teammates shall not occupy adjacent positions near the boundary if an opponent desires one of the positions. The 3-foot restraining line is sometimes the temporary boundary as in rule 1-2.

Ques.—B has the ball out of bounds. His throw-in: (a) enters a basket before touching anyone; or (b) strikes ring or backboard and rebounds; or (c) touches another player and then enters basket. **Ans.**—(a) Violation by B. A's ball at either end of the nearer free throw line extended. No goal because ball is dead. (b) Ball becomes alive when touched. (c)—Legal goal for team in whose basket the ball remains or through which it passes.

RULE 8

FREE THROW

SECTION 1. When a free throw is awarded, an official shall take the ball to the free throw line of offended team. After allowing reasonable time for players to take their positions, he shall put the ball in play by placing it at the disposal of the free thrower. The same procedure shall be followed for each free throw of a multiple throw. During a free throw for personal foul, each of the lane spaces adjacent to the end line shall be occupied by one opponent of the free thrower. A teammate of the free thrower is entitled to the next adjacent lane space on each side and to each other alternate position along each lane line. Not more than one player may occupy any part of the first, second or third lane spaces. If the ball is to become dead when the last free throw for a specific penalty is not successful, players shall not take positions along the free throw lane.

NOTE—To avoid disconcerting the free thrower, neither official should stand in the free throw lane or the lane extended.

SECTION 2. The free throw or throws awarded because of a personal foul shall be attempted by the offended player. If such player must withdraw because of an injury or disqualification, his substitute shall attempt the throw or throws unless no substitute is available, in which event any teammate may attempt the throw or throws. See ques. (1) under 2-11.

SECTION 3. The free throw awarded because of a technical foul may be attempted by any player, including an entering substitute, of the offended team.

SECTION 4. The try for goal shall be made within 10 seconds after the ball has been placed at the disposal of the free thrower at the free throw line. This shall apply to each free throw.

SECTION 5. After a free throw which is not followed by another free throw, the ball shall be put in play by a throw-in: (a) as after a field goal (7-5) if the try is for a personal foul and is successful; or (b) by any player of the free thrower's team from out of bounds at mid-court if the free throw is for a technical foul.

SECTION 6. If a free throw for a personal foul is unsuccessful, or if there is a multiple throw for a personal foul (or fouls) and the last free throw is unsuccessful, the ball remains alive.

If there is a multiple throw and both a personal and technical foul are involved, the tries shall be attempted in the order in which the related fouls were called and if the last try is for a technical foul the ball shall be put in play as after any technical foul.

SECTION 7. After the last free throw following a false double foul (4-9(b)), the ball shall be put in play by a jump at center between any two opponents.

Ques.—Two free throws are awarded to A and, before time is in, one free throw is awarded to B. What is the correct procedure? **Ans.**—Jump ball at center after the third free throw.

RULE 9

VIOLATIONS AND PENALTIES

A player shall not—

SECTION 1. Violate the free throw provisions: (a) The try shall be attempted from within the free throw circle and behind the free throw line. (b) After the ball is placed at the disposal of a free thrower: (1) he shall throw within 10 seconds and in such a way that the ball enters the basket or touches the ring before the free throw ends; (2) no opponent may disconcert the free thrower; and (3) the free thrower shall not have either foot beyond the vertical plane of that edge of the free throw line which is farther from the basket; and no other player of either team shall have either foot beyond the vertical plane or cylinder of the outside edge of any lane boundary, nor beyond the vertical plane of any edge of the space (2 inches by 36 inches) designated by a lane space mark or the space (12 inches by 36 inches) designated by a neutral zone mark, nor enter nor leave the lane space which is nearest the end line. The restrictions in (3) apply until the ball touches the ring or backboard or until the free throw ends. (c) An opponent of the free thrower shall occupy each lane space adjacent to the end line during the try, and no teammate of the free thrower may occupy either of these lane spaces.

PENALTY—(1) If violation is by the free thrower or his teammate only, no point can be scored by that throw. Ball becomes dead when violation occurs. Ball is awarded out of bounds on the sideline to the free thrower's team opposite center circle after a technical foul, and to any opponent out of bounds at either end of the free throw line extended after a personal foul. (2) If violation is by the free thrower's opponent only: if the try is successful, the goal counts and violation is disregarded; if it is not successful, a substitute throw shall be attempted by the same thrower under conditions the same as for the throw for which it is substituted. In these cases, ball becomes dead when the free throw ends. (3) If there is a violation by each team, ball becomes dead when violation by the free thrower's team occurs, no point can be scored, and play shall be resumed by a jump between any two opponents in the nearest circle. The out of bounds provision in penalty item (1) and the jump ball provision in penalty item (3) do not apply if the free throw is to be followed by another free throw, or if there are free throws by both teams. In penalty item (3), if an opponent of the thrower touches the free throw before it has touched the ring, the violation for failure to touch the ring is ignored.

Ques.—During a free throw by A1, B1 pushes A2 and also B1 or B2 is in the lane too soon. **Ans.**—If the free throw is not successful, award a substitute free throw and also penalize the foul.

SECTION 2. Cause the ball to go out of bounds.

Ques.—Dribbler in control steps on or outside a boundary, but does not touch the ball while he is out of bounds. Is this a violation? **Ans.**—Yes.

SECTION 3. Violate provisions governing the throw-in. The thrower-in shall not: (a) leave the designated throw-in spot; (b) fail to pass the ball directly into the court so that after it crosses the boundary line it touches or is touched by another player on the court before going out of bounds; (c) consume more than 5 seconds from the time the throw-in starts until it touches or is touched by a player on the court; (d) carry the ball onto the court; (e) touch it in the court before it has touched another player; nor (f) throw the ball so that it enters a basket before touching anyone.

No player shall: (g) have any part of his person over the boundary line before the ball has been passed across the line; (h) become the thrower-in after an official has designated another player.

Ques.—On throw-in, A steps on the line or reaches through its plane while holding the ball. **Ans.**—Violation. Allowance should be made if space is limited.

SECTION 4. Run with the ball, kick it, strike it with the fist or cause it to enter and pass through the basket from below.

NOTE—Kicking the ball is a violation only when it is a positive act; accidentally striking the ball with the foot or leg is not a violation.

Ques.—What is kicking the ball? **Ans.**—Kicking the ball is striking it intentionally with the knee or any part of the leg or foot below the knee. It is a fundamental of basketball that the ball must be played with the hands.

SECTION 5. Dribble a second time after his first dribble has ended, unless it is after he has lost control because of: (a) a try for field goal after the ball is in flight; or (b) a bat by an opponent; or (c) a pass or fumble which has then touched or been touched by another player. He shall not make more than one air dribble during a dribble.

SECTION 6. Violate any provision of 6-4. If both teams simultaneously commit violations during the jump ball, or if the official makes a bad toss, the toss should be repeated.

SECTION 7. Remain for more than 3 seconds in that part of his free throw lane between the end line and the farther edge of the free throw line while the ball is in control of his team. Allowance shall be made for a player who, having been in the restricted area for less than 3 seconds, dribbles in to try for goal.

Ques.—Does the 3-second restriction apply: (a) to a player who has only one foot touching the lane boundary; or (b) while the ball is dead or is in flight on a try? **Ans.**—(a) Yes, the line is part of the lane. (b) No, the team is not in control.

SECTION 8. Be (and his team shall not be) **in continuous control of** a ball which is in his back court for more than 10 consecutive seconds.

SECTION 9. Be the first to touch a ball which he or a teammate caused to go from front court to back court by being the last to touch the ball while it was in control of his team and before it went to the back court. **EXCEPTION:** This restriction does not apply if, after a jump ball in the center circle, the player who first secures control of the tapped ball is in his front court at the time he secures such control and he causes the ball to go to his back court not later than the first loss of player control by him and provided it is the first time the ball is in his back court following the jump ball.

Ques.—A receives pass in his front court and throws ball to his back court where ball (a) is touched by a teammate; or (b) goes directly out of bounds; or (c) lies or bounces with all players hesitating to touch it. **Ans.**—Violation when touched in (a). In (b) it is a violation for going out of bounds. In (c) ball is alive so that B may secure control. If A touches the ball first, it is a violation. The ball continues to be in team control of A and if A does not touch it the 10-second count starts when the ball arrives in the back court.

SECTION 10. Excessively swing his arms or elbows, even though there is no contact with an opponent.

PENALTY (Sections 2 to 10): Ball becomes dead or remains dead when violation occurs. Ball is awarded to a nearby opponent for a throw-in at the out of bounds spot nearest the violation. If the ball passes through a basket during the dead ball period immediately following a violation, no point can be scored and the ball is awarded to an opponent out of bounds at either end of that free throw line extended nearer the goal through which the ball was thrown.

SECTION 11. (a) Touch the ball or basket when the ball is on or within either basket; or (b) touch the ball when it is touching the cylinder having the ring as its lower base; or (c) touch the ball following a field goal try but while it is in its downward flight entirely above the basket ring level and has the possibility of entering the basket in flight. If the ball has touched or been touched by a player before it began its downward flight or if the ball has touched the ring, the restrictions in (c) do not apply.

PENALTY If violation is at the opponents' basket, offended team is awarded one point if during a free throw and two points in any other case. The crediting of the score and subsequent procedure is the same as if the awarded score had resulted from the ball having gone through the basket, except that the official shall hand the ball to a player of the team entitled to the throw-in.

If the violation is at a team's own basket, no points can be scored and the ball is awarded to the offended team at the out of bounds spot on the side at either end of the free throw line extended.

If there is a violation by both teams, play shall be resumed by a jump ball between any two opponents in the nearest circle.

Ques.—While the ball is in flight on a try for field goal by A, a teammate of A pushes an opponent. After this personal foul, the ball is on the ring when B bats it away. Which infraction should be penalized? **Ans.**—Both. Award 2 points to A. Then penalize for personal foul.

RULE 10

FOULS AND PENALTIES

A. TECHNICAL FOUL . . .

A team shall not—

SECTION 1. Delay the game by preventing ball from being promptly made alive, or by allowing the game to develop into an actionless contest.

This includes the following and similar acts:

(a) When clock is not running—consuming a full minute through not being ready when it is time to start either half; or

(b) Failure to supply scorers with data as outlined in rule 3-2; or

(c) When behind in the score or while on defense with the score tied and after a warning by an official, failing to be reasonably active in attempts to secure the ball if on defense or to advance the ball beyond the mid-court area if on offense and there is no opposing action in the mid-court area.

SECTION 2. **Be charged with an excess time-out (5-11).**

SECTION 3. **Have more than five** squad members participating simultaneously.

A player shall not

SECTION 4. **(a) Participate after changing his number** without reporting it to the scorers and an official;

(b) **Participate after having been disqualified:**

(c) **Attempt to gain an advantage:** by interfering with ball after a goal or by failing to immediately pass ball to nearer official if in control when a violation is called, or by repeated infractions of 9-3g and h;

(d) **Wear an illegal number;**

(e) **Grasp either basket;**

(f) **Cause the opponents' backboard to** vibrate while the ball is in flight after a try or is touching the backboard or is on or in the basket or in the cylinder above the basket;

(g) **Leave the court** for an unauthorized reason; or

(h) **Purposely delay his return** to the court after being legally out of bounds.

Ques. (1)—If two or more squad members are wearing identical numbers, what is the penalty? **Ans.**—Technical foul for each infraction. The penalty shall be imposed whenever the infraction is discovered. When there is duplication, only one of the squad will be permitted to wear a given number. All others must change to a number not already in use before they may participate.

Ques. (2)—A player steps out of bounds to avoid contact. **Ans.**—This is not a foul unless he leaves to conceal himself or to deceive in some other way. If he is a dribbler, ball is out of bounds.

SECTION 5. **Use unsportsmanlike tactics,** such as: (a) disrespectfully addressing or contacting an official, or failing to raise his hand at arm's length above his head after being charged with a foul or raising it in such a way as to indicate resentment; (b) using profanity; (c) baiting an opponent or obstructing his vision by waving hands near his eyes; (d) climbing on a teammate to secure greater height to handle ball; (e) knowingly attempting a free throw to which he was not entitled; or (f) causing unsportsmanlike contact as in 4-9 (h).

NOTE—Contact after the ball has become dead is ignored unless it is unsportsmanlike or is during a throw-in.

A substitute shall not—

SECTION 6. **Enter the court:** (a) without reporting to scorers; or (b) without his name appearing on the pregame squad list; or (c) (unless between halves) without being beckoned by an official.

A coach, substitute, team attendant or follower shall not

SECTION 7. **Disrespectfully address** an official nor attempt to influence his decisions; nor disrespectfully address or bait an opponent; nor indicate his objection to an official's decision by rising from the bench or using gestures; nor do anything to incite undesirable crowd reactions; nor shall he enter the court unless by permission of an official to attend an injured player. Coaches shall remain seated on the bench except, while the clock is stopped, they may leave the bench to direct or encourage players who are on the court. Coaches may, at any time, leave the bench to confer with substitutes, to signal players to request a time-out, or to perform other necessary coaching responsibilities. During an intermission or a time-out charged to a team, the coach and/or team attendants may confer with their players at or near their bench.

PENALTY **(Sections 1 to 7):** Offended team is awarded one free throw and its captain shall designate the thrower. A second free throw shall be awarded if the foul is flagrant.

For sections 3 and 4 (a) or (b), an infraction shall be penalized if it is discovered during the time the rule is being violated or an error for failure to penalize may be corrected by applying rule 2-10.

For sections 4(a) and (b), or for flagrant or persistent infraction of any section, the offender shall be disqualified. If the offender is a coach, substitute, team attendant or follower, he shall be banished from the vicinity of the court. For failure to comply, referee may forfeit the game.

B. PERSONAL FOUL . . .

SECTION 8. **A player shall not:** hold, push, charge, trip; nor impede the progress of an opponent by extended arm, shoulder, hip or knee, or by bending the body into other than a normal position; nor use any rough tactics. He shall not contact an opponent with his hand unless such contact is only with the opponent's hand while it is on the ball and is incidental to an attempt to play the ball. Contact caused by a defensive player approaching the ball holder from behind is a form of pushing and that caused by the momentum of a player who has thrown for goal is a form of charging.

A dribbler shall not charge into nor contact an opponent in his path nor attempt to dribble between two opponents or between an opponent and a boundary, unless the space is such as to provide a reasonable chance for him to go through without contact. If a dribbler, without contact, passes an opponent sufficiently to have head and shoulders in advance of him, the greater responsibility for subsequent contact is on the opponent. If a dribbler in his progress has established a straight line path, he may not be crowded out of the path but, if an opponent is able legally to establish a defensive position in that path, the dribbler must avoid contact by changing direction or ending his dribble.

A player who screens shall not: (a) when he is behind a stationary opponent, take a position closer than a normal step from him; (b) when he assumes a position at the side or in front of a stationary opponent, make contact with him; (c) take a position so close to a moving opponent that this opponent cannot avoid contact by stopping or changing direction. In (c), the speed of the player to be screened will determine where the screener may take his stationary position. This position will vary and may be one to two normal steps or strides from his opponent. (d) Move after assuming his screening position, except in the same direction and path of his opponent.

If the screener violates any of these provisions and contact results, he has committed a personal foul.

PENALTY Offender is charged with one foul and if it is his fifth personal foul, or if it is flagrant, he is disqualified. The offended player is awarded free throws as follows:

1. One free throw for:
   a. each common foul (except a player control foul) before the bonus rule is in effect; or
   b. a foul against a field goal thrower whose try is successful; or
   c. each foul which is a part of a multiple foul.
2. Two free throws for:
   a. a foul against a field goal thrower whose try is unsuccessful; or
   b. an intentional foul; or
   c. any single flagrant foul.
3. Bonus free throw for:
   a. each common foul (except player control) after a team is charged with six personal fouls during the half in a game played in halves; or
   b. each common foul (except player control) after a team is charged with its fourth personal foul during the half in a game played in quarters, provided the first attempt in either (a) or (b) is successful.
4. No free throws for:
   a. a double foul; or
   b. a player control foul; or
   c. a double foul, one or both fouls of which are flagrant.
5. In case of a false double or false multiple foul, each foul carries its own penalty.

The specified number of free throws is awarded for each foul which is a part of a false double or a false multiple foul.

NOTE—If there is any doubt as to whether there is player control during the time he or a teammate commits a common foul, the interpretation shall be that the ball was in player control.

Ques. (1)—A guard moves into the path of a dribbler and contact occurs. Who is responsible? **Ans.**—Either may be responsible but the greater responsibility is that of the dribbler if the guard conforms to the following principles which officials use in reaching a decision. The guard is assumed to have established a guarding position if he is in the dribbler's path facing him. No specific stance or distance is specified. It is assumed the guard may shift to maintain his position in the path of the dribbler provided he does not charge into the dribbler nor otherwise cause contact as outlined in the 2nd paragraph of 10-8. However, if he jumps into position, both feet must return to the floor after the jump, before he has established guarding position.

The responsibility of the dribbler for contact is not shifted merely because the guard turns or ducks to absorb shock when contact caused by the dribbler is imminent. The guard may not cause contact by moving under or in front of a passer or thrower after he is in the air with feet off the floor.

Ques. (2)—One or both fouls of either a multiple foul or of a double foul is flagrant. What is the procedure? **Ans.**—For a multiple foul, one free throw is awarded for each foul. For a double foul no free throws are awarded. In either case, any player who commits a flagrant foul is disqualified.

Ques. (3)—Does goal count if ball goes in the basket after a foul? **Ans.**—Yes, unless ball becomes dead (as in rule 6-7) before it enters the basket.

OFFICIAL BASKETBALL SIGNALS

APPENDIX B

FURTHER READING

(*Source: BOOKS IN PRINT,* R. R. *Bowker Co.*)

American Association for Health, Physical Education, and Recreation: *Basketball, Boys.* (*Sports Skills Test Manuals, Vol. I*). 75¢. NEA.

Anderson, Forrest, and Micoleau, T.: *Basketball Techniques Illustrated.* $3.50. Ronald Press (1952).

Antonacci, Robert, and Barr, J.: *Basketball for Young Champions.* $3.95. McGraw-Hill (1960).

Bee, Clair, and Norton, Ken: *Bee-Norton Basketball Series.* Four Volumes. $3.50 each. McGraw-Hill (1959).

Bee, Clair: *Make the Team in Basketball.* $2.95. Grosset-Dunlap.

Bee, Clair: *Winning Basketball Plays.* $5.50. Ronald (1963).

Bevington, Raymond H.: *Basketball Record Book.* $2.95. Interstate (1953).

Brown, Lyle: *Offensive and Defensive Drills for Winning Basketball.* $6.95. Prentice-Hall (1965).

Bunn, John: *Basketball Techniques and Team Play.* $6.95. Prentice-Hall (1964).

Caudle, Edwin C.: *Collegiate Basketball.* $6.95. Blair (1960).

Cousy, Bob, and Hirschberg, Al: *Basketball Is My Life.* $4.95. Prentice-Hall (1958).

Cousy, Bob: *Last Loud Roar.* $5.95. Prentice-Hall (1964).

Dobbs, Wayne, and Pinholster, Garland: *Basketball's Stunting Defenses.* $5.95. Prentice-Hall (1964).

Dwyer, Robert I.: *How to Coach and Attack the Zone Defenses.* $5.95. Prentice-Hall (1963).

Eaves, Joel: *Basketball's Shuffle Offense.* $5.95. Prentice-Hall (1964).

Gill, Amory (Slats): *Basic Basketball.* $3.50. Ronald (1962).

Haarlow, Bill: *Basketball Officiating.* $4.00. Ronald (1960).

Healy, William A.: *Basketball's Rotation Offense.* $5.95. Interstate (1960).

Hirschberg, Al: *Basketball's Greatest Stars.* Putnam (1963).

Hobson, Howard: *Basketball Illustrated.* $3.50. Ronald (1948).

Jacobs, G.: *Basketball Rules in Pictures.* Grossett-Dunlap.

Jucker, Ed: *Cincinnati Power Basketball.* $7.25. Prentice-Hall (1962).

Koppett, Leonard: *24 Seconds to Shoot.* $5.95. The Macmillan Company (1968).

Lindburg, F.: *How to Play and Teach Basketball.* $5.95. Association Press (1962).

McLane, Hardin (editor): *Championship Basketball by 12 Great Coaches.* $6.95. Prentice-Hall (1966).

McLendon, John: *Fast Break Basketball.* $6.95. Prentice-Hall (1965).

Mokray, William: *Encyclopedia of Basketball* (2nd edition). $15.00. Ronald (1965).

Pinholster, Garland: *Coach's Guide to Modern Basketball Defense.* $5.95. Prentice-Hall (1962).

Pinholster, Garland: *Encyclopedia of Basketball Drills.* $6.50. Prentice-Hall (1958).

Pinholster, Garland: *Pinholster's Wheel Offense in Basketball.* $6.95. Prentice-Hall (1966).

Ridl, Charles: *How to Develop a Deliberate Basketball Offense.* $6.95. Prentice-Hall (1966).

Rosenburg, John: *Basic Basketball.* $2.95. Oceana (1962).

Rubin, Roy: *Attacking Basketball's Pressure Defenses.* $6.95. Prentice-Hall (1966).

Rupp, Adolph: *Adolph Rupp's Basketball Guidebook.* $1.95. McGraw-Hill (1967).

Rupp, Adolph: *Rupp's Championship Basketball.* $6.95. Prentice-Hall (1957).

Samarras, Robert: *Blitz Basketball.* $6.95. Prentice-Hall (1966).

Santos, Harry G.: *How to Attack and Defeat Zone Defenses in Basketball.* $6.95. Prentice-Hall (1966).

Scholastic Coach Magazine: *Best of Basketball* edited by Herman L. Masin. $5.95. Prentice-Hall (1962).

Sharman, Bill: *Sharman on Basketball Shooting.* $6.95. Prentice-Hall (1965).

Sports Illustrated: *Book of Basketball.* $2.95. Lippincott (1962).

Strack, Dave: *Basketball.* $5.95. Prentice-Hall (1966).

Toomasian, John: *Developing a Winning Offense for High School Basketball.* $5.95. Prentice-Hall (1964).

Van Ryswyk, Ron: *Complete System for Winning Basketball.* $6.95. Prentice-Hall (1967).

Ward, Charles R.: *Basketball's Match-Up Defense.* $5.95. Prentice-Hall (1964).

Wilkes, Glenn: *Winning Basketball Strategy.* $5.95. Prentice-Hall (1955).

Winter, Morrice: *Triple-Post Offense.* $6.95. Prentice-Hall (1962).

JUVENILE LITERATURE

Parentheses indicate grades

Cella, George: *Young Sportsman's Guide to Basketball* (5–9). $2.75. Nelson (1962).

Cooke, David: *Better Basketball for Boys* (4–6). $3.00. Dodd, Mead (1960).

Hirschberg, Al: *Basketball's Greatest Teams.* $3.49. Putnam (1965).

Hutton, Joe, and Hoffman, Vern: *Basketball.* (4–8). $5.95. Creative Education (1962).

Masin, Herman L.: *How to Star in Basketball* (5–10). $2.50. Four Winds Press (1966).

Schiffer, Donald: *First Book of Basketball* (3–5). $2.65. Watts (1959).

COACHING TEXTS

Anderson, Forrest, and Albeck, Stan: *Coaching Better Basketball.* $6.00. Ronald (1964).

Baisi, Neal: *Coaching the Zone and Man-to-Man Pressing Defenses.* $5.95. Prentice-Hall (1961).

Bunn, John: *Basketball Coach: Guides to Success.* $6.25. Prentice-Hall (1961).

Coaching Clinic Magazine: *Best of Basketball.* $6.95. Prentice-Hall (1966).

Esposito, Mike: *Successful Team Techniques in Basketball.* $6.95. Prentice-Hall (1966).

Harrell, Bill D.: *Championship-Tested Offensive and Defensive Basketball Strategy.* Prentice-Hall (1968).

LaGrand, Louis: *Coach's Complete Guide to Winning Basketball.* $6.95. Prentice-Hall (1967).

McGuire, Frank: *Team Basketball: Offense and Defense.* $6.50. Prentice-Hall (1966).

Meyer, Ray: *Basketball as Coached by Ray Meyer.* $6.95. Prentice-Hall (1967).

Newell, Pete, and Benington, John: *Basketball Methods.* $6.00. Ronald (1962).

Newsom, Herbert: *Basketball for the High School Coach and Physical Education Teacher.* $3.75. W.C. Brown.

Pinholster, Garland: *Illustrated Basketball Coaching Techniques.* $5.95. Prentice-Hall (1960).

Ramsay, Jack: *Pressure Basketball.* $5.95. Prentice-Hall (1963).

Richards, Jack: *The Scramble Attack for Winning Basketball.* Prentice-Hall (1968).

Tarleton, Tom: *Tips and Ideas for Winning Basketball.* $6.95. Prentice-Hall (1965).

Van Ryswyk, Ron: *Ball Control Offense and Disciplined Defense.* $6.95. Prentice-Hall (1967).

Verderame, Sal: *Organization for Championship High School Basketball.* $5.95. Prentice-Hall (1963).

Wilkes, Glenn: *Basketball Coach's Complete Handbook.* $6.95. Prentice-Hall (1962).

Wolfe, Herman: *From Tryouts to Championships.* $5.95. Prentice-Hall (1964).

Wooden, John R.: *Practical Modern Basketball.* $6.50. Ronald (1966).

INDEX

INDEX

Tabular material which is listed in the Table of Contents, such as the All-Time NBA Register, has not been indexed, nor have the box scores and team and individual standings in the collegiate and professional yearly roundups. To clarify double references, such as Cincinnati the university team and Cincinnati the professional team, (U) or (C) [for college] follows the team name. Professional teams are listed by name of city, with use of nicknames (Denver Nuggets) limited to early non-league teams. Boldface numerals denote page references to photo captions.

A

Adair, Jerry, 72
Adams, Johnny, 25
Adcock, Joe, **41,** 42
Air Force Academy, 75, 82
Akers, Willie, 74
Akron, 51, 219
Akron (U), 201
Alabama, 20, 22, 44, 66
Alcindor, Lew, 94, 95, **95**, 96, 97, **100**, **103**, 103–05, **384,** 402, 409
All-American high school squad, 402–406
All-Star Games (NBA), 233, 235, 237, 239, 241, 242, 243, 246, 248, 250, 253, 255, 258, 260, 263, 265, 268, 272, 275, 288, 290, 292, 296, **298**, 299, 301, 302, 306, 310, 314
Allen, Forrest C. ("Phog"), 10, 120, 126, 138, **138**, 410, 423
Allen, Joe, 93, 98
Allen, Lucius, 95, 97
Allentown, 378
Amateur Athletic Union (AAU), 9, 203, 410, **411,** 421
AAU champions (men), 410, 412
AAU champions (women), 413–14
American Basketball Association (ABA), 105, 106, 274, 286, **376,** 377, 435
American Basketball League, 143, 211, 217, 218, 219, 378, 435
Amherst, 9
Anaheim, 377
Anderson, 219, 228, 229, 231
Anderson, Cliff, 91
Anderson, Harold, 144
Andres, Ernie, 18
Anet, Bob, 19, **19**
Archer, Jay, 414
Arizin, Paul, 46, **48**, 49, 234, 235, 241, 242, 243, 246, 250, 258, **284,** 284–85
Arizona, 22, 30, 37, 42, 44, 47, 49, 55, 144
Arizona State, 74, 80, 82, 85, 86
Arkansas, 18, 25, 26, 31, 47, 72
Arkansas State, 72
Armstrong, Warren, 93, 98
Army (West Point), 32, 36, 87, 93, 98, 145
Arnelle, Jesse, 62
Arnett, Jay, 78
Arnzen, Bob, 98
Artis, Orsten, 91
Ashland, 204
Atlanta, Ga., 410
Aubrey, Lloyd, 67
Auburn, 75, 78
Auerbach, Arnold ("Red"), 114, 222, 227, 233, **266,** 269, 291, 305, 306, 308, 310, 312, 314, 430

Austin, John, 90, 93
Azary, John, 54

B

Baker, Terry, 84
Baltimore, 224, 226, 237, 239, 241, 261, 265, 266, 286
Banks, Davey, **212**, 216, **216**
Baric, Rudy, 26
Barksdale, Don, 40, 410
Barnes, Jim ("Bad News"), 87
Barnett, Dick, 143, 203, 378
Barnett, Jim, 93
Barnhill, John, 143, 203
Barrett, Ernie, 54
Barry, John ("Pete"), 213, **215**, 218, **218**
Barry, Rick, 85, 86, 89, **267**, 268, 269, 271, 272, 274, **285**, 285–86, 290, **376**, 377
Bart, John, 25
Basketball Association of America (BAA), 219, 220, 222, 223, 224, 226, 227, 228, 229, 234, 243, 320
Baumholtz, Frank, 25, **25**
Baylor, 37, 43, 47, 49, 91
Baylor, Elgin, 70, 71, 248, 250, 251, 253, 254, 255, 257, 258, **259**, 260, 263, 265, 266, 272, 274, 286, **287**, 288, 294, 302
Beard, Butch, 96
Beard, Ralph, 37, 40, 43, 45, **46**, 116, 118, 233
Beasley, John, 87
Beaty, Zelmo, 203, **203**
Beck, Ernie, 57
Beck, Lou, 40
Beckel, Bob, 75
Becker, Art, 85
Becker, Moe, 25
Beckman, Johnny, 213
Bee, Clair, 53, 138, **138**, 140, 430
Beenders, Hank, **24**
Begovich, Matty, 10, **10**
Beisser, Ed, 30
Bell, Alva, 118
Bell, Corky, 93
Bellamy, Walt, 78, 80, 123, 257, 258, 268, 407
Bemoras, Irv, 57
Berce, Gene, 44
Bianchi, Al, 60
Biddy Basketball, 414, **415**
Biddy overseas clinics, 414
Biddy team (Ecuador), **415**
Biddy team (U.S.), **415**
Bing, Dave, 87, 90, 91, **271**, 272, 274, 275
Binghamton, 378
Birch, Paul, **212**
Bishop, Gale, 31
Black, C.B., 30, 39, 133
Black, Howie, 20
Blackburn, Tom, 144
Block, Jon, 93
Blood, Ernest A., 424
Bloom, Meyer, 18
Bockhorn, Arlen, 256
Boerwinkle, Tom, 98
Bohnenstiehl, Roger, 97
Bonham, Ron, 84, 86
Bonsalle, George, 70
Boone, Pat, 377
Boozer, Bob, 72, 74, 410
Borgia, Sid (official), 420
Borgmann, Bernhard, 426–27
Born, Bertram H., 58, 61
Boryla, Vince, 47, **105**, 105–06, 134, **234**, 243, 410
Boston, 108, 116, 121, 135, 220, 223, 229, 231, 233, **234**, 237, 238, 242, 244, 247, 250, 251, **252**, 253, 254, **254**, 255, **256**, 257, 258, 260, 261, 264, **264**, 265, 266, 269, **269**, 271, 272, 286, 288, 290, 291–93, 296, 305, 306, 308, 310, 314
Boston (C), 57, 90, 93, 96, 98, 136, 261
Boston, Mass., 134–35
Boudreau, Lou, 18
Boushka, Dick, 65
Bowling Green, 31, 32, 33, 34, 37, **38**, 43, 44, 47, 74, 78, 82, 85, 98, 144
Boykoff, Harry, 30, 42, 106-08, **107**, 119
Boyle, Ed, 17–18
Bradds, Gary, 85, 86
Bradley, 17, 20, 25, 43, 46, 48, 49, 50, 52, 55, 61, 65, 70, 74, 76, 80, 81, 86
Bradley, Bill, 61, 85, 86, 88, 89, **89**, 108–10, **109**, 131, 275, **276**, 402, 408
Bradley, Hal, 113
Brandeis, 116
Brannum, Bob, 31
Bratton, Albert, 6
Braun, Carl, 114, 224, 226, 228, 253, **288**, 288–89
Breda Kolff, Butch van, 110, 145
Brennan, Johnny, 42
Brennan, Pete, 72
Brian, Frank, 228
Bridges, Bill, 78, 80
Brigham Young, 44, 49, 54, 70, 90, 91, 96, 145
Brightman, Al, 144
Brindley, Aud, 32
Broberg, Gus, 20, 25
Brody, Tal, 90
Brookfield, Price, 27
Brooklyn College, 51
Brooklyn Jewels, 10
Brooklyn, N.Y., 107
Broussard, Carroll, 80
Brown, Charlie ("Sweet Charlie"), 75
Brown, Gene, 66, 70
Brown, Jimmy, 70
Brown, Walter, 220, 265, 429
Bubas, Vic, 46, 54, 144
Buckley, Jay, 86
Budd, Dave, 78
Budko, Walt, 42
Buffalo Germans, **210**, 211, 410, 431
Buffalo, N.Y., 410
Bunche, Ralph, 104
Bunn, John, 138, **139**, 421, 428
Bunte, Art, 65, 67
Buntin, Bill, 85, 86, 89
Burness, Don, 26
Burns, Joe (official), 420
Burrow, Bob, 67
Butcher, Donnis, 271

Butler, 42, 139–40, 410
Butler, Al, 78
Butler, Bill, 98
Byrd, Leland, 42
Byrd, Leo, 71, 75

C

Cable, Barney, 70
Cager, Willie, 91, **93**
Cain, Carl, 62, 66
Caldwell, Joe, 85
California, 10, 19, 32, 37, 39, 42, 43, 70, 73, 76, 121, 145
Calverley, Ernie, 33, 37, **38**, 223
Canisius, 65, 66
Cann, Howard, 144, 410, 430
Cannon, Jimmy, 293
Capua, Joe, 67
Carl, Howie, 80
Carlson, Dr. H. Clifford, 79, **137**, 139, **139**, 423
Carnegie Tech, 20
Carnesecca, Lou, 53
Carnevale, Ben, 144
Carrier, Darel, 82
Carver (Chicago) H.S., 129
Casares, Rick, 57
Case, Ev, 144
Catalano, John (official), 420
Catholic University, 33
Cazzetta, Vince, 377
CCNY, 9, 13, 23, 25, 27, 43, 45, 48, **49**, 50, 51, 52, 53, 140
Celtics, **212**, 213, 216–18, 219 (*See also* Original Celtics)
Central League, 211
Central Missouri State, 204
Central State (Ohio), 205
Cervi, Al, 223, 226, 228, 294–95
Chamberlain, Wilt, 68, **69**, 70, 71, 72, 121, 129, 251, **252**, 253, 254, 255, 257, 258, 260, 263, 264, 265, 266, 268, 269, **269**, 271, 272, **273**, 274, 275, 285, 288, **289**, 289–90, 294, 296, 299, 302, 306, 308, 313, 382
Chambers, Jerry, 91
Chanute Field, 124
Chapman, 201
Chappell, Len, 78, 79, 82
Charlton, Ken, 85
Chicago, 219, 220, 222, 223, 224, 226, **230**, 231, 257, 260, 261, 271, 378
Chicago (early pro team), 129
Chicago, Ill., 410
Chicago (U), 6
Chmielewski, Bill, 82, **82**
Chollet, Hillary, 46
Chuckovitz, Chuck, 18
Cincinnati, 121, 123, 126, 129, 247, 250, 254, **254**, **256**, 257, 261, 264, 286, 306, 313
Cincinnati (U), 42, 44, 47, 49, 55, 65, 71, 74, 76, 79, 80, **80**, 81, 82, 83, 84, **84**, 86, 93, 123, 126, 129, 145, 254, 306, 313
Clark, Archie, 90
Clemson, 20
Cleveland, 220, 223, 224, 378
Cleveland Pipers, 143
Cleveland Rosenblums, 218, **218**
Cleveland State, 142
Clifton, Nat ("Sweetwater"), 231, **232**, **292**, 382
Closs, Bill, 30
Clune, John, 62
Cohen, Jeff, 80
Cohen, Vince, 70
Coleman, Jim, 93
Colgate, 39, 43, 47, 133–34
College Basketball Officials Association (CBOA), 417, 418, 420
Colorado, 17, **17**, 18, 20, 21, 26, 43, 65, 82, 85
Colorado A&M, 61
Colorado State, 44, 47, 57, 79, 82, 90, 138
Columbia, 9, 13, 42, 44, 54, 64, 70, 98
Columbus (O.) North H.S., 121
Combs, Glen, 96
Conley, Fred, 25
Conley, Larry, 91
Conlin, Ed, 60, 61, 65
Connecticut, 25, 42, 44, 47, 53, 55, 57, 58, 65, 70 72, 74, 78, 85, 87, 90, 93, 96
Cook, Bob, 40, 44
Cooke, Jack Kent, 290
Cooper, Charlie, 49, 231
Cooper, Charles ("Tarzan"), 219, **219**
Cooper, Fred, 6, 211
Cornell, 9, 61
Costello, Larry, **59**, 60, 62, 260, 265
Counts, Mel, 84, 87, 408
Courtin, Steve, 87
Cousy, Bob, 43, **43**, 47, 49, 104, 116, 136, 231, 235, **236**, 237, 238, 239, 241, 243, 244, 246, 247, 248, 250, 253, 254, 255, **256**, 257, 258, 261, 290–93, **291**, **292**, 296, 305, 310
Cox, Johnny, 74
Crandall, Cliff, 40
Crawford, Fred, 85, 87
Creighton, 25, 27, 30, 70, 82, 145
Crispus Attucks (Indianapolis) H.S., 126
Critchfield, Russ, 96
Crystal City, Mo., 108
Cuccinello, Dominic (official), 420
Cunningham, Billy, 85, 87, 90, 305

D

Dallas Golden Cyclones, 413
Dallas, Tex., 413
Dallmar, Howard, 26, 36, **225**, 226
Dambrot, Irwin, 48, 49
Dampier, Louis, 91
Dana, Jack, 26
Daniels, Mel, 90, 96, 377
D'Antoni, Danny, 98
Darden, Oliver, 91
Darling, Chuck, 57
Darling, Lonnie, 219
Darrow, Jim, 78
Dartmouth, 9, 18, 20, 22, 25, 26, 30, 31, 32, 37, 66, 72, 74, 145
Davidson, 87, 90, 93, 98, 144

Davies, Bob, 23, 27, 110–12, **111,** 223, 227, 228, 230, 233, 235, 237, 241
Davies, Chick, 144
Davis, A.W., 90
Davis, Deacon, 64
Davis, Walter, 55
Dayton, 228
Dayton (U), 54, 57, 64, 66, 71, 80, 82, 90, 93, 95 96, 97, 131, 144
Dean, Everett, 144, 429
DeBernardi, Forrest S., 425
DeBusschere, Dave, 78, 80, **264,** 265, 271
Dees, Archie, 72
Dehner, Lew, 20
Dehnert, Henry ("Dutch"), 141, **212,** 213, **214,** 217, **218,** 430
DeMatha H.S., 104
DeNike, Tommy, 124
Denver, 219, 228, 229, 231
Denver, Colo., 203, 410
Denver Central Bankers, 106
Denver Nuggets, 106
Denver Rockets, 106
Denver (U), 47, 75, 106
DePaul, 20, 22, 25, 31, 32, 34, **34,** 37, 39, 43, 57, 60, 67, 78, 93, 145, 299, **419**
Detroit, 136, 219, 220, 223, 224, 226, 247, 253, **264,** 265, 271, 308
Detroit (U), 67, 78, 88, 90
Devlin, Corky, 65
Dick, John, 19
Dickerson, Ray, **218**
Dickey, Dick, 43, 46, 49
Diddle, Ed, 139, **139**
Didrikson, Mildred ("Babe"), 413
Dierking, Connie, 71, 264
Dixie Classic, 126
Dillon, John, 37
Dischinger, Terry, 78, 80, 82, 123, 260, 407
Dolan, Joe, **41**
Doll, Bob, 21, 22, 26, 410
Donohue, John, 104
Dose, Tom, 85
Douglas, Bob, 218, **219**
Dove, Sonny, 93, 96
Downey, Dave, 85
Drake, 20, 72, 80, 86
Driesell, Lefty, 144
Driscoll, Terry, 96, 98
Drucker, Norm (official), 418
Duffey, Ike W., 220
Duke, 22, 27, 30, 32, 37, 42, 57, 65, 72, 78, 82, 84, 86, 90, 91, 95, 98, 113–15, 144
Dukes, Walter, 55, 58, **59**
Duquesne, 20, 22, 23, 25, 27, 42, 47, 49, 60, 61, 64, 67, 82, 90, 124, 144, 145, 231
Durden, Don, 31
Dyer, Rich, 91

E

East Central Oklahoma, 204
East Chicago, Ind., 106
East Tennessee, 60, 98
East Texas State, 205
Eastern College Basketball Conference (ECBC), 417, 418
Eastern Kentucky, 49, 58, 65, 74, 80, 90
Eastern League, 211, 378–79
Eastern Massachusetts officials board, 417
Ebben, Bill, 67
Ebert, Paul 62
Eddleman, Dwight, 46
Egan, John (Loyola, Ill.), 83
Egan, Johnny, 79, 136
Eliot, Charles W., 416
Elliott, Pete, 43
Ellis, Alex ("Boo"), 70, 71
Ellis, Dick, 90
Ellis, Leroy, 82
Embry, Wayne, 70, 72
Engleman, Howard, 25
Englund, Gene, 23, 228
Enke, Fred, 144
Enright, Jim (official), 418, 420
Erickson, Bill, 46
Erickson, Keith, 89
Ernst, Vinnie, 79, 136
Estes, Wayne, 85, 87, 89
Evans, Ray, 31
Evansville, 145, 201

F

Fagan, Clifford B., 385
Fairchild, John, 90
Fairmont, 205
Faris, Bob, 20
Farley, Dick, 61
Farmer, Mike, 70, 72, 378
Faught, Bob, 27
Feerick, Bob, 223, 226
Felix, Ray, 239
Ferrari, Al, 60
Ferrin, Arnie, 31, 32, **32,** 36, 40, 229
Ferry, Bob, 74
Finkel, Henry, 90, 93
Fleishman, Jerry, 31
Fletcher, Rod, 57
Fliegel, Bernard, 18
Flint, 219, 228
Flora, Dom, 72
Florida, 96
Floyd, Darrell, 65, 66
Foley, Jack ("The Shot"), 78, 79
Follmer, Clive, 57
Fordham, 13, 21, 31, 60, 61, 65
Forman, Don, 43
Fort Wayne, 217, 219, 227, 229, 233, 235, **240,** 241, 242, 244, 246, 247, 419
Forte, Chet, 70
Foster, Fred, 98
Foster, Harold ("Bud"), 144, 428
Foust, Larry, 43, 235, 241, 253
Francis, Clarence ("Bevo"), 204, **204**
Frank, Wally, 78
Franklin, Joe, 98
Frazier, Walt, 95

Frederick, Rex, 75
Freeman, Don, 93
Freeman, James ("Buck"), 10
Freeman, Robin, 66
Friel, Jack, 144
Friendlich, Duck, 123
Fulks, Joe, 222, 223, 226, 227, 228, 235, 251, 290, 293–94, **293,** 302
Furey, Jim, 213, 216
Furey, Tom, 213
Furman, 60, 61, 65, 66

G

Gabor, Bill, 37
Gainer, Elmer, 25
Gale, Laddie, 19
Galileo (San Francisco) H.S., 124
Gallagher, Taps, 144
Gallatin, Harry ("The Horse"), 239, 247, 258
Gambee, Dave, 72
Gardner, Jack, 144
Gardner, Vern, 40, 106
Garmaker, Dick, 64, 248
Gayda, Ed, 50
Gayles, Zip, 144
Gerson, Rip, 10, **10**
Gill, Slats, 145
Gebert, Kirk, 23
Gensich, Hal, 31
Gent, Pete, 82
George Washington, 20, 30, 42, 51, 62, 65, 67, 79, 115
Georgetown, 20, 21, 28, 42, 145
Georgetown (Ky.), 205
Georgia, 98
Georgia Southern, 205
Georgia Tech, 18, 64, 78
Gerber, Bob, 25, 26
Gettysburg, 112
Gibbon, Joe, 70
Giermak, Chet, 46, 49
Gibson, Bob, 70
Gill, Amory T., 430
Glamack, George, 22, 25
Glaser, Ron, 85
Gola, Tom, 57, 58, 61, 64, 112–13, **113,** 115, 126, 268
Goldsmith, Jack, 39
Goldstein, Don, 75
Goldstein, "Little" Lou, **34**
Gonzaga, 42, 43, 93
Goodrich, Gail, 86, **87,** 89
Gotkin, Hy, **33,** 36
Gottlieb, Eddie, 219, 223, 258, 294, 310
Goukas, Matt, 18, 90, 91
Graf, Irwin ("Ike"), 20
Graham, Bonnie, 18
Graham, Mal, 91, 96
Graham, Otto, **30,** 31
Grambling, 145, 205
Granite City, Ill., 124
Grate, Don, 32
Gray, Wyndol, 34, 37
Great Lakes Naval Training Station, 112
Green, Bill, 82
Green, Cornell, 78
Green, Johnny, 68, 82
Green, Sihugo, 61, 64, **64,** 67
Greer, Hal, 71, 250, 266, 268, 275
Grekin, Norm, 57, 112
Grieve, Bill (official), 418
Grimstead, Swede, 213
Groat, Dick, 54, 57, 113–15, **114**
Groza, Alex, 40, 43, 45, **46,** 116, 118, 134, 230, 233, 248, 407
Gruenig, Robert F., 427–28
Guerin, Richie, 260, 265, 410
Gulick, Dr. Luther H., 3, 423

H

Hadnot, Jim, 79
Hagan, Cliff, 54, **54,** 57, 61, 248, **257,** 260, 296
Haggerty, Horace ("Horse"), 216
Hairston, Harold ("Happy"), 82, 85, 86
Halbrook, Wade, 61, 64
Hale, Bruce, 25, 145, 274, 286, 377
Halimon, Shaler, 98
Hall of Fame, 138, 139, 140, 141, 142, 144, 219, 421–31
Hamilton, Ralph, 42
Hamilton, Scotty, 26
Hamilton, Steve, 70
Hamline, 6, 9, 204, 205, 299
Hammond, 219, 228
Hampton Institute, 142
Hangar, Chuck, 43
Hankin, Cecil, 34
Hankins, Norm, 44
Hannum, Alex, 44, 261, 269
Hansen, Victor A., 424
Hardin-Simmons, 58, 60
Harge, Ira ("Large"), 86
Hargis, John, 28
Harkness, Jerry, 82, 83
Harlan (Ky.) H.S., 118
Harlem Globetrotters, 57, 129, 133, 228, 230, 231, 251, 290, 296, 381–82, **384,** 419
Harmon, Richard, 50
Harper, Jerry, 67
Harris, Bob, 46
Harrisburg, Pa., 110
Harrison, Bob, 43
Hartman, Jack, 145
Harvard, 9, 32, 37
Harvey, Jack, 21
Haskins, Clem, 91, 96
Hassett, Bill, 36, 37
Hatton, Vern, 71
Haverford, 9
Havlicek, John, 46, 76, 79, **80,** 82, 265, 272, 275, **275,** 305
Hawaii, 378
Hawkins, Connie, 377, 378
Hawkins, Larry, 129
Hawkins, Tom, 72

Hayes, Elvin, 96, 97, **98, 100,** 104, 409
Haynes, Marques, 382
Haywood, Spencer, 409
Hazleton, Pa., 378
Hazzard, Walt, 85, 86, 408
Head, Carl, 96
Heathington, Don, 43
Heinsohn, Tom, 61, 65, 67, 257, 260, 266
Hemric, Dickie, 57, 58, 65
Hennessey, Larry, 55, 60
Hennon, Don, 72
Hepbron, George (official), 416, 424
Herkimer, N.Y., 211
Herlihy, Pat, **212**
Herrerias, Rene, 45
Hetzel, Fred, 85, 87, 90
Heyman, Art, 82, 84
Hickey, Ed, 145
Hickey, Nat, **212,** 216
Hickman, Peck, 96, 145
Hickox, Ed, 421, 423
Hickox, Dick, 75
Hicks, Roger, 26
Hightower, Wayne, 78, 80
Hill, Bobby Joe, 91
Hinkle, Paul ("Tony"), 81, 139–40, **140,** 429
Hitch, Lew, 54
Hobdy, Fred, 145
Hobson, Howard, 145, 429
Hodesblatt, Mac, 108
Hoffman, Paul, 39
Hogan, Frank, 52
Hogue, Paul, 79, **80,** 82
Holiday Festival (Madison Square Garden), 129, 136
Hollines, Harry, 98
Holman, Nat, **49,** 51, 110, 140, **140, 214,** 216, 217, 218, 428
Holt, John ("Casey"), 219, **219**
Holub, Dick, **225**
Holup, Joe, 67
Holy Cross, 9, 40, **40,** 43, **43,** 47, 55, 57, 61, 65, 67, 78, 82, 145, 291
Holzman, Bill ("Red"), 27, 226, 275
Homer, James, 42
Hopkins, Farrell, 104
Hornack, Bob, 85
Horvath, Paul, 54
Houbregs, Bob, 57, 58
Houston, 66, 91, 96, 97, **98, 100,** 104, 145
How to Play Basketball, 416
Howard, Frank, 70
Howell, Bailey, 70, 72, 268, 272
Hoyt, George (official), 417, 425
Hudgens, Harold, 82
Hudson, Lou, 90, 93
Hudson River League, 211, 213
Huffman, Marv, 21
Hull, James, 19
Hundley, Rod ("Hot Rod"), 65, 67, 70
Hunter, Les, 83, **84**
Husta, Carl ("Sox"), **218**
Huston, Paul, 39
Hutchins, Mel, 54, 134, 235
Hyatt, Charles D., 423

I

Iba, Henry, **37,** 118–19, 140–41, **140,** 409, 430–31
Iba, Moe, 141
Idaho, 37
Idaho State, 60, 62, 65, 70, 72, 74, 78
Illinois, 20, 26, **28,** 30, 34, 45, 46, **46,** 54, 56, 57, 62, 70, 72, 85, 124–25
Imhoff, Darrall, 73, 76, 121
Indiana, 21, 23, 57, 58, 61, 72, 78, 96, 142, 144
Indiana State, 201, 204
Indianapolis, 118, 227, 228, 229, 230, 233, 238, 294
International Amateur Basketball Federation (FIBA), 435
International Association of Approved Basketball Officials (IAABO), 417, 418
Inter-State League, 211
Iowa, 34, 62, 64, 66, **67,** 98
Iowa State, 25, 32, 36, 70
Ireland, George, 145
Irish, Ned, **12,** 13, 16, 53, 428
Irvin, Roy, 61
Irwin, George ("Dink"), **218**
Isaac, Warren, 90
Ives, Dick, 34

J

Jackson, Lucious ("Luke"), 203, **203,** 408
Jackson, Merv, 98
Jackson, Tony, 74, 78, 80
Jaros, Tony, 39
Jarvis, Jim, 90
Jaworski, Chet, 20
Jeanette, Buddy, 226
Jenkins, Clarence ("Fat"), 218, **219**
Joeckel, Ralph, 49
Johansen, Wally, 19
Johnson, Don, 57
Johnson, Gus, 85, 265
Johnson, Ollie, 85, 87
Johnson, Rafer, 70
Johnson, Robert, 18
Johnston, Neil, 237, 238, **238,** 239, 241, 242, 243, 246, 250, 294–95, **295**
Jones, K. C., 66, 115–16, **116,** 144, **254,** 407
Jones, Nick, 93
Jones, R. William, 428
Jones, Sam, 135, 143, 257, 268, 272
Jones, Wallace ("Wah Wah"), 43, 45, **46,** 116–18, **117**
Jones, Wally, 87
Jordan, Jim, 36, 37
Jucker, Ed, 145
Judson, Paul, 67
Julian, Alvin ("Doggy"), 145, 430

K

Kaftan, George, 40, **40,** 43
Kaiser, Roger, 78, 80

Kansas, 10, 18, 21, 25, 27, 30, 37, 49, 56, 58, 61, 68, **69,** 72, 78, 90, 93, 96, 97, 120–21, 138, 250, 290
Kansas City, 378
Kansas City AC, 410
Kansas City, Mo., 202–03, 410
Kansas State, 43, 49, 54, 66, 70, 72, 74, 78, 80, 85, 87, 98, 120, 145
Kaplan, Bruce, 91
Kaplan, Dick, 310
Kautz, Wilbert, 20
Keaney, Frank, 10, 145, 424
Keller, Gary, 90
Kellogg, Junius, 51–52
Kennedy, Pat (official), 419, **419,** 423
Kennedy, Walter J., 261, **261,** 418
Kenny, Art, 104
Kentucky, 18, 20, 22, 25, 27, 32, 36, 37, 40, 42, 43, 45, 49, 50, 52, 53, 54, **54,** 56, 57, 61, 64, 70, 71, 74, 78, 79, 82, 87, 91, **93,** 95, 98, 116, 118, 124, 138, 143, 230, 305, 407, 417
Kentucky State, 142
Kentucky Wesleyan, 201
Keogan, George, 141, **141,** 425
Kerr, Dave, **218**
Kerr, Johnny, 57, 62, **261,** 268, 271
Kerris, Jack, 42
Kerner, Ben, 296
Kimball, Toby, 90
King, Bob, 145
King, George, 241
King, Jim, 90
Kinney, Bob, 25, 26
Kinsbrunner, Mac, 10, **10**
Kirkpatrick, Hubert, 18
Klier, Leo, 37
Klotz, Red, 381
Knostman, Dick, 60
Koffenberger, Ed, 37
Kojis, Don, 75, 80
Kok, George, 39, 44
Komenich, Milo, 28
Komives, Howie, 82, 86
Kondla, Tom, 96
Koper, Bud, 85, 87
Kotsores, Bill, 31, 32, **33,** 36
Kotz, Johnny, 23, 27, 31
Kraft, Jack, 145
Kramer, Barry, 82, 85
Kramer, Ron, 70
Kramer, Steve, 91
Krebs, Jim, 65, 70
Krouminch, I., **408**
Kundla, Johnny, 299
Kurland, Bob, 34, **35,** 36, 37, **37,** 118–19, **119,** 133, 141, 407, 410, **411,** 425

L

Lacy, Jim, 46
Lafayette, 37
Lambert, Ward L. ("Piggy"), 141, **141,** 424
Lancaster, 378
Langston, 144–45
Lanier, Bob, 98
Lapchick, Joe, 53, 87, 88, 89, 106, 115, 126, 134, 136, 142, **142,** 144, **212,** 216, 217, 218, **218,** 243, 283, 418, 429–30
Lapidus, Bob, 42
Larese, York, 78
LaRusso, Rudy, 72, 74
LaSalle, 42, 43, 47, 49, 55, 57, 60, 61, 64, 112, 115, 133, 145
LaSalle (Philadelphia) H.S., 112
Lattin, Dave, 91, 96
Laurinberg (N.C.) Prep, 135
Lavelli, Tony, 37, 44, 46, 134
Lavoy, Bob, 49
Lawrence Tech, 44, 55
Leaks, Manny, 98
Lear, Hal, 66
Lee, Clyde, 90, 93
Lehman, Lou, **44**
Leinhard, Bob, 98
Lemon, Meadowlark, 382
Leonard, Bob, 58, 61
Leonard, Chris, **215,** 216
Levane, Andrew ("Fuzzy"), 30
Lewis, Bob (North Carolina), 95
Lewis, Bob (NYU), 20
Lewis, Fred, 223
Lewis, Guy, 145
Lewis, Mike, 98
Lindeman, Paul, 25
Liston, Emil S., 203
Littleton, Cleo, 62
Litwack, Harry, 129, 145
Lloyd, Bill, 20, **20**
Lloyd, Bob, 93, 95, 96
Lobsinger, John, 20
Loeffler, Ken, 112, 145, 428–29
Lofgran, Don, 45
Logan, Bill, 66
Lonberg, Dutch, 145
Long Island, 377, 378
Long Island University (LIU), 16, 17, 20, 21, 23, 24, 25, 26, 27, 34, 42, 43, 49, 52, 123, 138, **419**
Lord, Joe, 42
Los Angeles, 253, 255, 257, 260, 265, 266, 272, 274, 286, 288, 290, 313, 377, 378
Los Angeles, Cal., 410
Loudermilk, Jan, 82
Louisiana State University (LSU), 30, 37, **41,** 42, 58, 61, 301
Louisville, 36, 55, 57, 60, 65, 66, 70, 75, 80, 96, 98, 145, 204
Lovelette, Clyde, 49, 56, 57, 120–21, **120,** 407
Lowry AFB, 106
Lowther, Robert, 37
Loyola (Cal.), 78, 80
Loyola (Ill.), 18, 20, 42, 43, 45, 52, 82, 83, **84,** 87, 93, 145
Loyola (La.), 33, 36, 204
Lucas, Jerry, 76, **77,** 79, **80,** 82, 121–23, **122,** 261, **262,** 263, 265, 268, 275, 402, 407
Lucas, Mrs. Treva Geib, 121
Luisetti, Hank, 16, 17, **18,** 25, 27, 110, 123–24, **123,** 138, 410, 423
Lynn, W. St. John, 427

M

Macauley, Ed, 40, 43, **44,** 46, 134, 230, 233, **234,** 235, 237, 238, 239, 296, **297,** 424
MacGilvary, Ron, 57
MacKenzie, Stan, 93, 94
MacKinnon, Bob, 50
Mahnken, John, 28
Maloy, Mike, 98
Mandic, John, 27
Manhattan College, 13, 31, 45, 51, 52, 60, 65, 70, 93, 129
Mankato State, 204
Maravich, Pete, 97
Marin, Jack, 90, 91
Marquette, 18, 20, 25, 31, 57, 65, 75, 80, 85, 95, 96, 98, 124, 145
Marshall, 62, 65, 66, 71, 75, 95, 97, 98, 204
Marshall, George Preston, 217
Marshall, Tom, 61
Martin, Slater, 47, 229
Maryland, 62, 65
Mason, Bobby Joe, 74, 76
Massachusetts, 82, 98
Mathisen, Art, **28,** 30, 124
Matson, Randy, 91
Mattick, Bob, 60, 61
May, Don, 96, 97
McArthur, Gale, 55
McCann, Brendan, 70
McCarthy, Babe, 377
McCarthy, John, 65, 66
McClintock, Bill, 74, 76
McCloud, Leason, 26
McCormack, Frank, 213
McCoy, Julius, 67
McCoy, Mike, 85
McCracken, Branch, 142, **142,** 424–25
McCracken, Jack, 427
McCutchan, Arad, 145
McDermott, Bobby, 223
McFadden, Banks, 20
McGill, Billy ("The Hill"), 78, 79, 82
McGuire, Al, 55
McGuire, Dick, 31, 230, **249,** 275
McGuire, Frank, 121, 145
McHenry, Clarence, 93
McIntyre, Ken, 89
McKinney, Bones, **222,** 223, 302
McLaughlin, Walter, 131
McLemore, McCoy, 86
McLendon, John, 142–43, **143**
McMahon, Jack, 57
McMillian, Jim, 98
McMillon, Shelly, 70
McNamee, Joe, 45
McNatt, James, 20
McNeese State, 205
Meanwell, Walter E., 423
Mears, Ray, 145
Mehen, Bernie, 27
Mehen, Dick, 27, 228
Meineke, Don, 54, 57
Melchionni, Bill, 91
Melchiorre, Gene ("Squeaky"), 49
Memphis State, 57, 65, 78, 82, 141
Mencel, Chuck, 64
Menke, Ken, **28,** 30, 124, 125
Meschery, Tom, 74, 80, 305
Metropolitan AAU Association (N.Y.), 410
Metropolitan Basketball League, 211
Meyer, Ray, 145
Miami, 377
Miami (Fla.), 47, 75, 85, 89, 145, 268, 286
Miami (O.), 57, 58, 65, 70, 72, 74, 90, 93
Miasek, Stan, 223
Michigan, 43, 70, 86, 89, 91, **92,** 96, 104, 108, 129, 131
Michigan State, 68, 74
Middletown (O.) H.S., 121
Miculi, Franklin, 264
Mikan, Ed, 43
Mikan, George, 31, 32, 34, **34,** 36, 37, 119, 124, 220, **221,** 222, 223, 226, 227, **227,** 228, 229, 230, 233, 234, 235, 237, 238, 239, 241, 247, 251, 290, 294, 296, **298,** 299, 301, 302, 377, 423
Mikklesen, Vern, 229, 234, 250, 299, **300,** 301, 302
Miles, Eddie, 80, 82, 85
Miller, Larry, 95, 97
Miller, Ron, 83
Millikin (Illinois), 205
Mills, Dave, 93
Mills, Doug, 124, 125
Milwaukee, 105, 129, 134, 235, 241, 243, 276, 301
Minneapolis, 121, 124, 219, 220, 226, 227, **227,** 228, 229, 233, 234, 235, 237, 238, **240,** 241, 242, 244, 246, 248, 250, 288, 296, 299, 301, 302
Minnesota, 377
Minnesota School of Agriculture, 6, 9
Minnesota (U), 47, 64, 90
Minor, Davage, 30, 40
Minson, Roland ("The Cat"), 54
Misaka, Wat, 40
Mississippi, 70
Mississippi Southern, 57, 60
Mississippi State, 70, 72, 74, 79, 82, 85
Missouri, 20, 21, 33, 72
Missouri AA, 410
Mlkvy, Bill, 54
Modzelewski, Stan ("Stutz"), 22, 25, 27, **27**
Moe, Doug, 78
Moers, Bobby, 20
Mohs, Lou, 313
Moir, John, 18
Mokray, William G., 429
Molodet, Vic, 66
Monroe, Earl ("The Pearl"), **274,** 275
Montana, 43, 57
Montana State, 42, 49, 55, 57, 87
Montreal, 133
Moore, Dudy, 145
Moran, Mike, 75
Morehead State, 66, 70, 80
Morgan, Ralph, 423
Morgan, William, 378
Morgenweck, Frank, 427
Morningside (Iowa), 204
Morris, Max, 39
Morris, William, 30

Mount, Rick, 98
Mounts, Del Ray, 79
Moschetti, Al, **29**
Mount St. Mary's, 201
Mueller, Erwin, 87
Muhlenberg, 36, 49
Mullaney, Joe, 136, 145
Mullen, Robert, 31
Mullins, Jeff, 85, 86
Munroe, George, 26
Murphy, Calvin, 97, 402
Murphy, Charles S., 425
Murray, Dorrie, 90, 93
Murray State, 55, 87, 98, 204, 205, 294
Murrell, Phil, 72
Murrell, Willie, 85, 87

N

Naismith, Dr. James, **2,** 3–4, 6, 9, 21, 52, 138, 203, 211, 416, 421, 422
Naismith, Mrs. James, (*See* Sherman, Maude)
Nash, Cotton, 82, 85, 87
National Association of Basketball Coaches (NABC), 421
National Association of Intercollegiate Athletics (NAIA), 202–07
National Association of Intercollegiate Basketball (NAIB), 203
National Basketball Association (NBA), 105, 112, 116, 121, 123, 129, 131, 133, 143, 220, 229, 230, **230,** 231, **232,** 233, 234, 235, 237, 243, 244, 247, 250, 253, 255, 261, 265, 271, 272, 275, 276, 284, 292, 296, 299, 302, 308, 320, **376,** 377, 378, 418, 419, 435
NBA Players Association, 276
National Basketball Committee, 435
National Basketball League (NBL), 211, 219, 220, 222, 226, 227, 228, 229, 234, 235, 243, 320
National Collegiate Athletic Association (NCAA), 9, 19, 20, 21, 23, 26, 27, 28, 30, 31, 33, 34, 36, 37, 39, 40, 42, 43, 45, 47, 48, 49, 50, 51, 53, 54, 55, 57, 58, 60, 61, 62, 63, 64, 65, 66, 67, 68, 70, 71, 73, 74, 75, 76, 78, 79, 81, 82, 83, 85, 86, 87, 88, 89, 90, 91, 94, 95, 96, 97, 98, 99, 103, 104, 105, 110, 115, 116, 118, 119, 120, 121, 123, 124, 126, 129, 131, 138, 140, 141, 143, 144, 146, 201–02, 385
National Federation of State H.S. Athletic Associations, 385
National Invitation Tournament (NIT), 16, 17, 18, 20, 21, 23, 25, 26, 27, 28, 30, 31, 32, 33, 34, 36, 37, 39, 40, 42, 43, 45, 47, 48, 49, 50, 51, 54, 55, 57, 58, 60, 61, 64, 65, 66, 67, 68, 70, 71, 73, 74, 75, 76, 78, 79, 81, 82, 83, 85, 86, 88, 89, 90, 91, 94, 95, 96, 97, 99, 108, 112, 116, 118, 129, 131, 140, 142, 146
Naulls, Willie, 65, 67, 265, 268
Navy (Annapolis), 37, 42, 61, 62, 144
Nebraska, 47, 49, 95, 120
Nelson, Don, 80, 82
Nelson, Ron, 98
Nemelka, Dick, 91
Neu, Bob, 20
Neuman, Paul, 264
New Jersey, 377
New Mexico, 36, 57, 86, 90, 98, 145
New Mexico A&M, 20, 22, 57
New Mexico State, 74, 78, 80, 96
New Orleans, 377
New Orleans, La., 414
New York, 53, 106, 110, 113, 131, 134, 220, 223, 224, **225,** 227, 229, 230, **230,** 231, 233, **234,** 235, 237, 238, 241, 243, 250, 254, 255, 268, **270,** 272, 275, **276,** 283, 288–89, 290, 292–93, 296, 299
New York Athletic Club, 134
New York Celtics, 213
New York Jewels, 10, 219
New York *Journal-American*, 293
New York State League, 211
New York Whirlwinds, 213, 216
Newberry, 61
Newell, Pete, 123, 145
Newmark, Dave, 98
Newsome, Manny, 86
Niagara, 47, 49, **59,** 60, 62, 65, 70, 71, 78, 144
NIBC, 203
Nicholas, Ab, 57
Nicholls, Jack, 43
Nixon, Dick, 85
Noel, Paul, **230**
Noon, Pete, 114
Norman, Jay, 71
North American Basketball League, 378
North Carolina, 22, 25, 32, 36, 37, 42, 65, 68, **69,** 72, 74, 78, 79, 91, 95, 97, 115, 121, 145
North Carolina (C), 142
North Carolina State, 42, 43, 44, 46, 49, 54, 57, 58, 61, 62, 66, 74, 144
North Texas State, 126
Northway, Mel, 87
Northwest Missouri State, 204
Northwestern, 39, 75, 145
Notre Dame, 13, **14–15, 16,** 18, 20, 25, 27, 31, 36, 37, 39, 42, 43, 47, 49, 60, 62, 65, 67, 72, 78, 98, 106, 141
Novak, Mike, 18, 20
Nowak, Paul, 18
Nowell, Mel, 76, 82
Nucatola, John, 418
NYU, 9, 13, **14–15, 16,** 17, 20, 21, 31, 34, 37, 43, 45, 52, 74, 78, 82, 85, 91, 104, 144, 410, 417

O

Oakes, Billy, 91
Oakland, 274, 286, **376,** 377
O'Brien, Eddie, 55
O'Brien, John (Columbia), 18
O'Brien, Johnny, 55, **56,** 57, 60, 427
Oceanside, N.Y., 133
O'Connor, Ed, 65
Ohio State, 19–20, **19,** 32, 37, 39, 49, 62, 66, 70, 76, 79, **80,** 81, 82, 85, 86, 98, 121, 123, 294
Ohio University, 23, 25, 78, 80, 87, 90

Ohl, Don, 72, 410
Oklahoma, 20, 21, 27, 28, 32, 40, 44, 47, 61
Oklahoma A&M, 17, 18, 20, 22, 27, 32, 33, 34, **35,** 36, 37, 42, 44, 45, 46, 49, 55, 58, 60, 61, 67, 118, 119, 407
Oklahoma Baptist, 205
Oklahoma City, Okla., 410
Oklahoma City (U), 57, 62, 65, 70, 96, 98, 140–41
Oklahoma State, 72, 90, 118
Olsen, Harold G., 423–24
Olympic Games, 106, 110, 115, 119, 123, 131, 138, 141, 244, 260, 407–09, **408,** 410
Berlin, 407
Helsinki, 407
London, 407
Melbourne, 407
Mexico City, 409
Rome, 407
Tokyo, 408
O'Neal, Richard, 65
Opper, Bernie, 20
Oregon, 19, **19,** 36, 145
Oregon State, 17, 40, 43, 47, 61, 64, 72, 84, 87, 90, 93, 145
Original Celtics, 140, 141, 142, 213, 283, 431, (*See also* Celtics)
O'Shea, Kevin, 42, 43, 49
Oshkosh, 219, 228
Otten, Don, 33, 37, 133, 228

P

Pacific Lutheran, 205
Page, Harlan O., 427
Paine, Alva, 32
Palazzi, Togo, 60, 61
Palmer, Bud, 289
Pan American, 205
Parkinson, Jack, 37
Parr, Jack, 70
Pasadena Athletic and Country Club, 413
Pasadena, Cal., 413
Passaic (N.J.) High School, **9,** 10
Patrone, Lee, 79
Patterson, Bob, 65
Peeples, George, 93
Pelkington, Bob, 86
Penn, 9, 36, 40, 64, 93
Penn State, 27, 57, 61, 62, 65
Pennsylvania State League, 211
Pepperdine, 55, 57, 82, 204
Pete, Kelly, 90
Peterson, Loy, 93
Peterson, Vadal, 145
Pettit, Bob, 57, 58, 61, 241, 242, **242,** 243, 244, 246, 247, 248, 250, 253, 255, 258, 260, 261, 263, 265, 266, 286, 296, 301–02, **301,** 308, 313
Philadelphia, 113, 129, 220, 222, 223, 224, **225,** 226, 227, 228, 229, 233, 234, 237, 241, 242, 248, 251, **252,** 255, 257, 258, 263, 264, 265, 266, 269, **269,** 271, 272, 284–85, 286, 290, 294, 296, 305, 308, 310
Philadelphia League, 211
Philadelphia, Pa., 112, 128
Philadelphia Sphas, 219
Phillip, Andy, 26, **28,** 30, 42, **123,** 124–26, **230,** 233, 410, 427
Phillips, Gary, 80
Phillips 66ers, 119, 410
Phoenix, 276
Piatkowski, Walt, 96
Pilch, John, 50
Pitt, 21, 25, 72, 114, 139
Pittsburgh, 220, 223, 224, 377, 378
Podoloff, Maurice, 220, 261, 301
Poliskin, Jack, **10**
Pollard, Jim, 26, 124, 226, 228, 229, 230, 234, 239, **240,** 299, 301, 302–03, **303**
Porter, Henry V., 425
Portland, 55
Posnack, Max, 10, **10**
Power Memorial Academy (N.Y.), 104, **384**
Prairie View A&M, 205
Pralle, Fred, 18
Price, Nibs, 145
Princeton, 9, 26, 49, 57, 64, 74, 78, 80, 85, 87, 89, 96, 98, 108, 110, 129, 145, 275, 408
Protective Basketball Association, 410
Providence 220, 223, 226
Providence (C), 76, 79, 82, 87, 90, 93, 96, 135–36
Purdue, 18, 21, 78, 98, 141

Q

Quabius, Dave, 20
Quiggle, Jack, 68
Quigley, Ernie, (official), 418, 425
Quinn, Fred, 39

R

Ramsay, Jack, 145
Ramsey, Cal, 74
Ramsey, Frank, 54, 57, 61, 244, 304–05, **304**
Rand, Terry, 65
Ranzino, Sam, 46, 49, 54
Rascoe, Bobby, 82
Ray, James, 67
Rayl, Jimmy, 82, 85
Raymond, Craig, 91
Reading, 378
Reaser, Dave, 96
Reed, Hub, 70
Reed, Willis, 203, **203,** 265
Regan, Richie, 58
Regis (Colorado), 204
Rehfeldt, Don, 50
Reich, Ernie, 213
Reid, William A., 428
Renaissance Big Five (Rens), 218–19, **219,** 431
Renick, Jesse, 22
Rensselaer, 36
Rhode Island, 23, 27, 30, 33, 34, 36, 37, **38,** 42, 44, 49, 80, 87, 93, 98, 112, 145
Rhode Island State, 10, 20, 22, 25, 223

Rice, 22, 26, 30, 31, 36, 47, 61, 91
Rickard, Tex, 216
Ricketts, Dick, 60, 61, 64
Ricks, James ("Pappy"), 218, **219**
Ridley, Bill, 67
Riley, Pat, 91
Rio Grande (Ohio), 204
Ripley, Elmer, 145
Risen, Arnie, 32, 227, 233
Roanoke, 20, **20,** 204
Robbins, Jack, 18
Roberts, Joe, 76
Robertson, Oscar, 71, **72,** 74, **75,** 76, 97, 103, 123, 126–28, **127,** 129, 136, 254, **254,** 255, 257, 258, 260, 261, 263, 264, 265, 268, 269, 272, 275, 276, 305–06, **305,** 313, 314, 407
Robinson, Flynn, 90
Robinson, Jack, (Baylor), 39, 43
Robinson, Jackie, 21, **22,** 25, 104
Rocha, Ephraim ("Red"), 40
Rochester, 112, 133, 222, 223, 226, 227, 229, 230, 233, 234, 235, 238, 241, 243, 244, 247, 299, 313
Rockhurst, 205
Rodgers, Guy, 70, 71, 128–29, **128,** 260, 271, 306
Roggenburk, Gary, 80
Rolek, Martin, 18
Roosma, John S., 425
Rosenbluth, Len, 67, 68, **69**
Rosenthal, Dick, 62
Rossini, Lou, 54
Rouse, Vic, 83
Rubinstein, Willie, 16
Rudolph, Harry, 378
Rudolph, Mendy, (official), 418, 419, 420
Rudometkin, John, 79
Ruklick, Joe, 75
Rupp, Adolph, 45, 52, 116, 118, 138, 143, **143,** 305, 417, 431
Russell, Bill, 64, 66, 115, 116, 144, 244, **245,** 246, 247, 248, 250, 251, **252,** 255, 257, 258, 260, 261, 263, **264,** 265, **266,** 268, 269, **269,** 272, 275, 296, 299, 306, **307,** 308, 407, **408**
Russell, Bob, 379
Russell, Cazzie, 86, 89, 91, **92,** 108, 129–31, **130, 270,** 402, 410
Russell, John, ("Honey"), **10,** 110, 112, 145, 294, 429
Rutgers, 95, 410

S

Sachs, Leonard D., 425–26
Sacramento State, 201
Sadowski, Ed, 226
Sailors, Ken, 28, **29,** 39, 133, 410
St. Benedict's (Kansas), 205
St. Bonaventure, 55, 70, 72, 76, 79, 87, 98
St. Francis (Brooklyn), **41,** 42, 66, 108
St. Francis (Loretto, Pa.), 62, 64, 131, 244
St. John's, 10, **10,** 13, 20, **20,** 21, 27, 28, **29,** 30, 31, 32, **32,** 36, 37, 42, 45, 49, 53, **54,** 55, 56, 57, 58, 72, 74, 78, 80, 82, 87, 88, 89, 93, 96, 104, 106, 108, 142, 145, 219
St. Joseph, Mo., 413
St. Joseph's, 53, 66, 74, 78, 79, 82, 85, 90, 91, 108, 145
St. Jude's School, 104
St. Louis, 121, 220, 223, 224, 229, 230, 231, 242, 243, 244, 246, 247, 248, 250, 253, 255, 257, **257,** 260, 261, 265, 271, 273, 274, 296, 301
St. Louis, Mo., 410
St. Louis (U), 37, 40, 43, **44,** 45, 46, 55, 65, 70, 74, 79, 80, 119, 121, 145, 230, 296
St. Mary's, 74
St. Mary's Pre-Flight School, 124
St. Michael's, 201
St. Peter's (Jersey City), 95, 97
Saitch, Eyre ("Bruiser"), 218, **219**
San Diego, 275
San Diego State, 204
San Francisco, 258, 261, 264, 271, 274, 275, 285–86, 377, 378
San Francisco, Cal., 410
San Francisco (U), 45, 49, 50, 60, 63, 64, 66, **67,** 70, 72, 85, 87, 90, 115, 144, 244, 296, 306, 407
San Jose State, 44, 47, 55
Sanders, Tom, 78
Santa Clara, 42, 56, 60, 61, 65, 78, 98
Saperstein, Abe, 290, 378, **380,** 381–82
Sauldsberry, Woody, 248
Schabinger, Arthur A., 426
Schaus, Freddie, 43, **259,** 286, 313, 314
Schayes, Dolph, **44,** 233, 235, 237, 239, 241, 246, 247, 248, 250, 251, 253, 257, **257,** 258, 260, 263, 308, **309,** 310, 418, 419
Schectman, Oscar, 25
Schellhase, Dave, 90, 91
Schlundt, Don, 58, 61
Schneider, Ed, 379
Schnittker, Dick, 49
Scholastic Magazines, 402
Schommer, John J., 423
Schuckman, Allie, 10, **10**
Schultz, Dan, 87
Schutsky, Bill, 98
Scolari, Fred, 302
Scott, Charlie, 97
Sears, Kenny, 57, 65, 250, 253, 378, 410
Seattle, 275
Seattle (U), 52, 53, 55, 57, 62, 65, 67, 70, 71, 75, 80, 82, 85, 96, 144, 286, 288
Sedran, Barney, 216, 427
Seiden, Al, 72, 74
Selvy, Frank, 60, 61, **62,** 104, 241
Senesky, George, 31
Seton Hall, 23, **24,** 25, 27, 43, 53, 55, 57, 58, **59,** 65, 110, 112, 126, 145
Severance, Al, 131
Shackleford, Lynn, 97
Shaffer, Lee, 78, 264
Share, Charlie, 43
Sharman, Bill, 50, 237, 239, 241, 243, 244, 246, 247, 248, **249,** 250, 253, 254, 286, 296, 310, **311,** 312
Sharman on Shooting, 310
Sharrar, Lloyd, 71
Shavlik, Ronnie, 66

Sheboygan, 223, 226, 229, 231
Shed, Neville, 91
Sheffield, Fred, 36
Sherman, Maude, 6, **8**
Shields, Don, 18
Short, Arnie, 60, 62
Short, Bob, 288
Shue, Gene, 60, 62, 253
Shugart, Ken, 42
Shultz, Earl, 76
Siebert, Sonny, 72
Siegfried, Larry, 76, 79, 268
Siena, 47, 60
Silas, Paul, 82, 85, 86
Silliman, Mike, 87, 93
Simmons, Connie, 243
Skaug, Stan, 30
Skoog, Meyer ("Whitey"), 47
Skurnick, Red, **218**
Slack, Charlie, 60, 65
Slott, George, **10**
Smart, Doug, 75
Smiley, Jack, **28,** 30, 42, 124, 125
Smith, Adrian, 71, 268, 271
Smith College, 6
Smith, Dean, 145
Smith, Glenn, 57
Smith, Wee Willie, 219, **219**
Smolick, Mike, 213
Snyder, Dick, 90, 93
Sobek, George, 25
Sobieszczyk, Ron, 67
Solodare, Chuck (official), 419
Somerset, Willie, 82, 90
South Carolina, 70, 145
South Dakota, 201
South Dakota State, 201
Southeast Missouri, 201
Southeast Missouri State, 204
Southeastern Conference, 420
Southeastern Oklahoma, 204, 205
Southern California, 21, 30, 61, 79, 94, 310
Southern Illinois, 95, 145, 201, 204
Southern Methodist, 65, 66, 70, 72, 82, 90, 91, 96
Southwest Missouri, 201
Southwest Missouri State, 205
Southwest Texas State, 205
Southwestern (Kansas), 204
Spivey, Bill, 54
Spoelstra, Art, 57
Springfield College, 3, 6, 138, 421
Springfield, Mass., 3, 6, 23
Sprowl, Forest, 27
Stagg, Amos Alonzo, 6, **7,** 424
Stallworth, Dave, 85, 86, 90
Stanford, 16, 17, 25, 26, 85, 123–24, 138, 144, 304
Stannich, George, 50
Stauffer, Bill, 57
Stein, Hank, 71
Steinmetz, Christian, 426
Stephenson, Art, 96
Stevens, Jack, 65
Stewart, Norm, 67
Stith, Tom, 72, 76, 79
Stokes, Maurice, 64, 131–33, **132,** 244, 246, 248, 313
Stone, George, 95, 98
Strawder, Joe, 86
Streit, Judge Saul B., 53
Strom, Earl, 306, 418
Stroud, W.D., 82, 85
Studebaker, Gene, **20**
Sullivan Award, 110
Sunderlage, Don, 54
Sutphin, Al, 220
Swagerty, Keith, 93
Swissvale, Pa., 114
Syracuse, 219, 228, 229, 233, 235, 237, 238, 241, 244, 247, 251, 255, **257,** 260, 308, 310, 418–19
Syracuse (U), 27, 37, 49, 70, 87, 91

T

Tannenbaum, Sid, 34, 37, 42
Tarkio, 204
Tart, Levern, 86
Tatum, Reece ("Goose"), 382, **383**
Taylor, Charles H., 431
Tebell, Gus, 114
Temple, 9, 17, **17,** 20, **35,** 51, 66, 70, 71, 87, 96, 128–29, 145
Tennessee, 25, 27, 30, 36, 75, 96, 98, 118, 145
Tennessee State, 142, 205
Tennessee Tech, 72, 83
Terre Haute, Ind., 120
Terrell, Lee, 57
Texas, 20, 28, 30, 40, 47, 55, 61, 78, 85, 90
Texas A&M, 55, 87, 91
Texas Christian, 55, 57, 58, 65, 74, 98
Texas Southern, 205
Texas Tech, 61, 65, 66, 79, 82, 90
Texas Wesleyan, 91
Texas Western, 70, 74, 87, 91, **93,** 96
Thacker, Tom, 84
Thomas Jefferson H.S., 108
Thomas, Steve, 86
Thomforde, Chris, 96
Thompson, Gary, 70
Thompson, George ("Brute Force"), 95, 98
Thompson, John, 87
Thompson, John A., 427
Thoren, Skip, 90
Thorn, Rod, 79, 85
Thurmond, Nate, 82, 85, 271, 286
Ticco, Milton, 31
Tison, Hack, 86
Tobey, David, 426
Todorovich, Marko, 226
Toledo, 219, 228
Toledo (U), 25, 26, 30, 42, 49, 52, 55, 62, 96, 144
Torgoff, Irving, 20
Tormohlen, Gene, 75
Toronto, 220, 223, 224
Torrence, Walt, 75
Tower, Oswald, 423
Townsend, John, 18
Townsend, Vic, 25
Travis, Rich, 98
Trenton, N.J., 211

Trester, Arthur L., 426
Tresvant, John, 82, 87
Tri-Cities, 219, 228, 229, 235, 243
Trinity, 9
Trippe, Joe, 213
Tsiropoulos, Lou, 61
Troy Trojans, 211, 213
Tucker, Al, 203
Tucker, Gerry, 28, 40
Tucker, Jim, 60, 61
Tucker, Temple, 67
Tulane, 32
Tulsa, 65
Turner, John, 80
Turner Tigers, 410
Twyman, Jack, 65, 133, 244, 247, **251,** 253, 263, 265, 268, 312–13, **312**
Tyra, Charles, 66, 70

U

UCLA, 21, 36, 40, 49, 57, 63, 65, 66, 70, 75, 82, 85, 86, **87,** 89, 94, 95, **95,** 97, **100,** 103–05, 115
Udall, Stewart, 38, **39**
Uhl, Bill, 66
U.S. Basketball Writers Association, 379
University of the Pacific, 93, 96
Unruh, Paul, 43, 45, 49
Unseld, Westley, 93, 96, 98, 409
Utah, 18, 21, 31, 32, **32,** 36, 40, 45, 47, 65, 66, 78, 79, 82, 91, 145, 410
Utah State, 144
Utica (N.Y.), 211

V

Vacendak, Steven, 91
Valparaiso, 36
Van Arsdale, Dick, 90, 402
Van Arsdale, Tom, 90, 402
Vance, Gene, **28,** 30, 124, 125
Vanderbilt, 6, 53, 90, 93, 96
Vandeweghe, Ernie, 39, 43, 47, **74,** 133–34, **134**
Vandeweghe, Mrs. Colleen Hutchins, 134
Vassar, 6
Vaughn, Ralph, 21
Verga, Bobby, 90, 91, 96
Vermont, 42
Villanova, 20, 31, 45, 46, 49, 55, 65, 78, 82, 87, 89, 131, 145, 284
Virginia, 23, 65
Virginia Military, 87
Virginia Tech, 78, 96
Volpe, Nat, 18
Voss, Ed, 26

W

Wabash, 9
Wachter, Ed, 211, 213, 410, 426
Wagnon, Dave, 91
Wake Forest, 58, 65, 78, 79, 82
Walk, Neal, 98
Walker, Chet, 76, 80, 81, 266
Walker, Jimmy, 90, 93, 96, 134–36, **135**
Walker, Mayor James J., 13
Wallace, Grady, 70
Walowac, Walt, 60, 62
Walsh, David H., 426
Walthall, Joe, 31
Walther, Paul, 240
Wanzer, Bob, 233, 313
Warley, Ben, 143, 203
Warner, Ed, 48
Warren, Mike, 95, 97
Washburn, 410
Washington, 220, 222, 223, 224, 226, 227, 229, 233, 378
Washington & Lee, 72
Washington, Jim, 89
Washington, Kenny, 86
Washington Palace Five, 217–18
Washington, Stan, 93
Washington State, 23, 25, 42, 49, 144
Washington (U), 30, 32, 43, 55, 57, 58, 75
Waterloo, 219, 228, 229, 231
Waterloo Hawks, 108
Watson, Leon, 44
Watson, Lou, 50
Watts, Stan, 145
Weber State, 90, 93
Webster, Elnardo, 97
Weir, Murray, 44
Wells, Clifford, 421
Werkman, Nick, 85, 86
Wesley, Walt, 90, 93
West, Jerry, 71, 74, **74,** 78, 123, 253, 257, 258, **259,** 260, 263, 264, 265, 266, 268, 272, 286, 294, 313–14, **314,** 402, 407
West Texas State, 26, 30, 57, 65
West Virginia, 26, 36, 37, 42, 43, 47, 55, 57, 65, 66, 70, 71, 73, 78, 79, 82, 85, 96, 313
Westbrook, Dexter, 93
Western Carolina, 205
Western Illinois, 205
Western Kentucky, 26, 45, 47, 49, 57, 61, 65, 78, 80, 82, 91, 96, 139
Western Michigan, 42, 57
Western Pennsylvania League, 211
Westminster, 13, 23
Wetzel, John, 93
Wheaton, 201
White, Eddie, 213
White, Hubie, 82
White, Jo Jo, 93, 97, 409
White, Sherm, 49
White, Whizzer, **17,** 18
Whitemore, Bob, 98
Whitty, John, 213, 217
Wichita, 62, 80, 110
Wichita, Kans., 413
Wichita State, 86, 89, 90
Widby, Ron, 96
Widowitz, Paul, 22
Wiesenhahn, Bob, 79
Wilcutt, D.C., 43

Wilfong, Win, 70
Wilkens, Lenny, 76, 136
Wilkes-Barre, 378
Wilkinson, Dave, 34
Wilkinson, Herb, 31, 39
Wilkinson, Richard ("Buzz"), 65
Williams College, 9
Williams, Lee, 421
Williams, Ron, 96, 98
Wilson, George, 84, **84**
Windis, Tony, 75
Winston-Salem State, 201
Winter, Tex, 145
Wintermute, Urgel ("Slim"), 19
Wisconsin, 23, 40, 144
Wittenberg, 201
Wolfe, Andy, 39, 43
Wolfe, Bob, 95
Wooden, John, 104, 143–44, **144,** 417, 424
Woolpert, Phil, 115, 144, **144**
Workman, Mark, 55, 57
Worsley, Willie, 91
Wright, Lonnie, 90
Wynne, Clayton, 31
Wyoming, 25, 28, **29,** 37, 42, 47, 57, 58, 75, 96

X

Xavier AA (N.Y.), 410
Xavier (O.), 43, 71

Y

Yale, 9, 32, 37, 40, 46, 70, 82, 145
Yancey, Bill, 219, **219**
Yardley, George, 50, 247, **247,** 248, 410
Yates, Don, 90
Yates, Tony, 84
YMCA, International, 9
YMCA teams
    Armory Hill, 6
    Brooklyn Central, 6
    Chicago Central, 410
    Chicago West Side, 6
    East District (N.Y.), 6
    Minneapolis, 6
    Nashville, 6
    Philadelphia, 416
    Ravenswood (Chicago), 410
    Springfield (Mass.) Central, 6
    Trenton, N.J., 6, 416
    23rd Street (N.Y.), 410
YMCA Training School, 3, 6
Young, Jewell, 18
Youngstown, 219

Z

Zaslofsky, Max, 223, 226, 228, 230, 243
Zawoluk, Robert ("Zeke"), 49, 55, 57
Zimmer, Andy, 27
Zuber, Dallas, 42